Second Edition

New Media Technology
Cultural and Commercial Perspectives

John V. Pavlik
Columbia University

Foreword by
Everette E. Dennis
Fordham University

Allyn and Bacon
Boston • London • Toronto • Sydney • Tokyo • Singapore

Vice President, Editor in Chief: Paul Smith
Series Editor: Karon Bowers
Editorial Assistant: Leila Scott
Marketing Manager: Kris Farnsworth
Editorial Production Service: Chestnut Hill Enterprises, Inc.
Manufacturing Buyer: Megan Cochran
Cover Administrator: Jennifer Hart

Library of Congress Cataloging-in-Publication Data
Pavlik, John Vernon.
   New media technology : cultural and commercial perspectives / by
John V. Pavlik. -- 2nd [rev.] ed.
     p. cm.
   Rev. ed. of: New media technology and the information
superhighway.   1996.
   Includes bibliographical references (p.) and index.
   ISBN 0-205-27093-X
   1. Mass media--Technological innovations.   2. Mass media--Social
aspects.   3. Mass media--Economic aspects.   4. Mass media--United
States.   I. Pavlik, John Vernon. New media technology and the
information superhighway.   II. Title.
P96.T42P38   1997
302.23--dc21   97-37599
                                                       CIP

Printed in the United States of Amerca

10 9 8 7 6 5 4 3 2 1   02 01 00 99 98 97

Contents

Foreword

Efforts to understand, explain, and analyze the new media are demanding and endlessly complex. For that reason few experts in industry or the academy have done so in a fashion that blends timeless concerns with those that are fresh and current. To do so is to tune in on and monitor three simultaneous bargaining games as the forces of technology grapple with politics and economics. And within that framework are some big ideas, towering figures, starts and stops, winner and losers.

What John Pavlik has done in *New Media Technology: Cultural and Commercial Perspectives* is impressive and unique. Now in its second edition, *New Media Technology* connects commercial imperatives in the largely commercial system in which new media function with social and cultural understandings that are rarely the direct concern of the marketplace. Few books do both, and for that reason this is a particularly important and useful entry into the various efforts—many of them failed—to sort out and navigate the always dynamic world of new media.

In doing so, Dr. Pavlik, who heads Columbia University's Center for New Media, has drawn a detailed map that covers the territory admirably and in broad relief, but also focuses close up on the specific industries in the new media field and their various products. The book is an exhilarating journey behind the scenes in some of the largest media companies and technology labs in the United States to see what they have been doing, how it is coming along, and to what end. Richly informed by history and connections to the tension between government policy and commercial interests, this is a massive inventory of new media developments (and their predecessors) while at the same time a sense-making effort to examine long-term trends and new inventions, some still in development. For the reader uninformed about the new machines and software making waves in the information society, this is one-stop shopping, since the book is comprehensive across different media industries and specific technologies as well as their interface with consumers and citizens. Blessedly, the new media are also subjected to considerable scrutiny as to their consequences for individuals, institutions, and society.

This is neither a technophile nor technophobe treatment, but a book that enthuses about possibilities and new developments, while soberly assessing their prospects in an often harsh consumer environment. We learn how and why new developments only rarely appear dramatically, but most often blend into our lives in incremental fashion, so we hardly notice them at all.

With an emphasis both on the future and on historical developments, John Pavlik takes the reader through concepts and applications whose mastery is vital to understanding new media venues (or platforms) as well as the content and services delivered. The book takes its readers into the minds of inventive and entrepreneurial individuals, the organizations they have formed to create new products and services, and the competitive new media market or environment. All of this is interesting enough—and sometimes requires a technical mastery—but such material would ring hollow without a variety of social and cultural contexts against which the author charts new media developments.

Continuous observation, study, and analysis is required to produce a book like this one and to recast it in light of inevitable change. This is what John Pavlik has done here, something that is typical of his dedication to new knowledge and professional applications, which I have observed at close range for more than two decades. While I had known Dr. Pavlik from his graduate student days forward, as an author and young faculty member, I am especially grateful for the work he did in developing and articulating a distinctive and important research and technology program at the Freedom Forum Media Studies Center at Columbia University of which I was then the director. The book is, in fact, a substantial extension of the many ideas, concepts, and practical examples of new media he worked with then. After leaving the Center for an administrative post in San Diego, it was Columbia's good fortune to lure him back to guide the Center for New Media. The payoff for Columbia and for the field of journalism and media studies is large indeed as this book clearly attests.

Being part of the launch of this important book is a special privilege and one I cherish because Dr. Pavlik has given students of new media of whatever age or sophistication a very real gift.

Everette E. Dennis
Arlington, Virginia, and New York City

Preface

> *"All modes of communication we humans*
> *have devised since the beginnings of*
> *humanity are coming together into a single*
> *electronic system, driven by computers."*
> —*JOHN WICKLEIN, ELECTRONIC NIGHTMARE, 1981*

From a remote encampment in northwest Tanzania, a team of young, new media journalists transmits a series of digital dispatches via satellite phone. These dispatches instantly reach a global audience, as they are posted directly to the Project Candide site on the World Wide Web.[1] Visitors to the site experience an interactive, multimedia tour of East Africa. They read about a Chuini spice farm in Zanzibar founded in 1886 by Omani Emperor Sultan Seyyid Said, view digital photographs of pink Tanzanite mined by hand from 300 meter depths, and listen via "streaming" audio to four Masai warriors singing a traditional Masai ballad. Visitors to the site can even post their own electronic mail messages to the journalists trekking from Arusha to Zanzibar.

In less than a decade, such cyberspace correspondents have gone from the realm of virtual reality to the main stream of today's international new media business. From Wall Street to the White House, new media technology is increasingly seen and employed as central to twenty-first century commerce and culture. Gerald M. Levin, chairman and Chief Executive Officer of Time Warner, one of the world's largest media companies, has declared that successful corporations must use new media technologies to "think locally, but act globally."[2] In other words: use the Internet to tell local stories to the world. Even President William J. Clinton has set a lofty new media goal for the United States.

> *In our schools, every classroom in America must be connected to the information superhighway. We are working with the telecommunications industry, educators and parents to connect 20 percent of California's classrooms this spring, and every classroom and every library in the entire United States by the year 2000.*
> **President Bill Clinton's 1996 State of the Union Address[3]**

Meanwhile, many scholarly voices caution against creating an electronic nightmare in which individual privacy is lost and only a few global conglomerates control access to information technology. Ohio University's John Wicklein warns that the convergence of all communications in a digital world may create nothing less than an electronic nightmare for those living in it.[4] There is little doubt the social cost of new media technologies will be high. Despite the falling price of computer technology, social inequities will increase as low-income families and individuals struggle to keep pace in the fast-paced, high-priced world of new media.

Important questions about the future of new media technologies include:

- How much will it cost to access the global information infrastructure?
- What will happen to those who can't afford the price?
- Who will control access to information in an increasingly electronic, pay-as-you-go media system?
- What will be the future of civil liberties in cyberspace?
- What content will fill the digital airwaves and wires?

THE SHAPE OF THINGS TO COME: DIGITAL

Regardless of the view one subscribes to, one thing is certain: the onrush of new media technologies is inevitable. They are, in fact, already here. Publishers distribute best-selling books on CD-ROM and Digital Video Discs (DVD). Author Michael Crichton's novel "Jurassic Park" was published in 1991 as a Macintosh HyperCard™ stack, complete with squawking velociraptors, long before moviegoers saw a single frame of Steven Speilberg's film adaptation. Writers are even venturing into a new form of non-linear text known as hyperfiction, in which notions of beginning, middle and end have little meaning and the reader enters the realm of story creator.

Interactive television is being offered in a number of markets throughout North America bringing an abrupt end to the legacy of the couch potato. Families in test communities in California are playing *Jeopardy!* via computer in simultaneous competition with the competitors seen on television each evening. Viewers in Montreal, Canada, are selecting stories of their own choice each evening on nightly newscasts and playing armchair director during telecasts of Montreal Canadian hockey games, choosing camera angles and instant replays as they desire. Despite all the tests and research, one question no one has adequately answered about this new technology is How much interactivity do people really want? After nearly a half century of passive entertainment, will TV viewers suddenly want to become active participants in the communication process? "The consumer doesn't want to work to be entertained," observes Francine Sommer, a securities analyst and expert on new technologies.[5]

Many people around the globe have already demonstrated an interest in accessing an electronic superhighway, however. For example, more than 15 million people in more than 40 countries already send and receive electronic messages around the world on the Internet, a network of computers. Use of the Internet is growing by as much as 15 percent a month, with little end in sight. Everything from an electronic evangelical network to direct electronic access to the White House exist on the Internet. The Internet even offers a 24-hour radio station, RTFM, offering gavel-to-gavel audio broadcasts from the House and Senate floors.[6]

Some new media products are available only via the new electronic technologies. Horror novelist Stephen King's short story, "Umney's Last Case," for example, was published on Sunday, September 19, 1993, by Viking Press only on the Internet. Science fiction writer William Gibson, who coined the term cyberspace in his classic 1984 novel *Neuromancer*, wrote an entire novel available only on computer disc. In *Mission Impossible* style, however, the novel can be read only once, since each disc is programmed to erase its contents after being opened.

THE PURPOSE OF THIS BOOK

New Media Technology is devoted to a systematic exploration of the commercial and cultural implications of the rapidly evolving new media landscape. In the eleven chapters that follow, the discussion systematically and critically reviews not only the technologies themselves, but the ways they are affecting how people live, work, and communicate. Chapter 1 outlines the broad contours and parameters of the new media landscape and communication industry. Chapter 2 examines the Internet, what has emerged in the 1990s as the prototype for a global information superhighway. Chapter 3 places new media technology into an historical context. Chapter 4 examines the emerging technologies themselves, the infrastructure of the information age. Chapter 5 reviews the fundamental concepts and applications driving the development of new media technology. Chapter 6 identifies the principal players on the new media landscape, the emerging new media barons. Chapter 7 outlines key considerations in publishing in the new media environment, while Chapter 8 reviews marketing considerations. Chapter 9 discusses legal and regulatory concerns, while Chapter 10 examines the social and cultural consequences of new media technology. Chapter 11 provides a summary and gazes into the hazy future of new media technology. A glossary provides a road map to key terms in the field of new media technology. A complete index and bibliography of references cited in this book is also included.

Scope of This Book

The boundaries of the new media landscape are in a constant state of flux, and are extremely difficult to pin down. Readers are invited to visit the Web site of The Center for New Media at www.cnm.columbia.edu for periodic updates on new media technology developments. As the traditional distinctions between print and broadcast media technologies rapidly vanish, we are witnessing the emergence of "a united state of media," concludes Everette E. Dennis, Distinguished Professor of Communications at the Fordham University Graduate School of Business.[7] In agreement is Walter Wriston, former chairman and chief executive officer of Citicorp and author of *Twilight of Sovereignty: How the Information Revolution is Transforming Our World*, who states, "The law of technology is the law of convergence."[8] Journalist and technology seer George Gilder refers to this convergence as the "telecosm," a process in which telecommunications and computing blend into one seamless state.[9]

Thus, included within the scope of this book are electronic media technologies which, driven by computers, are rapidly merging into a single digital communication environment. Most prominent on today's new media commercial landscape are the Internet and the World Wide Web. But other new media technologies, from the digital watermark to omnidirectional cameras, are just emerging from experimental laboratories, and are also included in this book. Moreover, included in this book are communication technologies whose nature and impact are largely unsettled, primarily because they are still developing both in their form and function. Some technologies, although decades old, have undergone significant changes in recent years and are included here because of their unsettled nature and influence in global commerce and culture.

ACKNOWLEDGMENTS

Many people have contributed greatly to this book. I am especially thankful to Everette E. Dennis, Distinguished Professor of Communications at the Fordham University Graduate School of Business and former Senior Vice President of The Freedom Forum, who was my mentor, colleague, and boss during my six years as associate director for Research and Technology Studies at The Freedom Forum Media Studies Center, where Ev served as founding executive director. Several other current and former Center staff also deserve thanks, including Shirley Gazsi, Mark A. Thalhimer (now Project Director, News in the Next Century Project, the Radio Television News Directors Foundation), Debbie Rogers, Wendy Boyd, Judy Annozine, and Marcella Steingart, as well as my former research assistants, Sujoya Roy, Bruce Cronin, David Lawrence, and Rosemary Culver.

I am grateful to veteran news executive Adam Clayton Powell, III, now Vice President of Technology and Programs for The Freedom Forum, and telecommunications consultant John Carey, director of Greystone Communications, for their frank and useful comments on the book. Thanks also to all the scholars, journalists, and colleagues whose groundbreaking work on new media technology precedes this writing and is cited extensively within these chapters. Special thanks go to series editor Albert N. Greco, Associate Professor, Fordham University Graduate School of Business Administration, for inviting me to write this book, Joseph Terry, editor responsible for this book at Allyn and Bacon, Steven P. Hull, former senior editor at Allyn and Bacon, with whom I originally worked on this book, and Joe Opiela, Vice President and Editor in Chief, Humanities, at Allyn and Bacon.

Finally, my sincerest thanks go to my friendliest critic, best friend, and wife, Jackie Dina Oregel Pavlik, who gave me the time to work on both editions of this book, while caring for our two lovely daughters, Tristan Mariana, born May 15, 1993, and Orianna Magdalena, born June 13, 1994.

NOTES

[1]Utopia Web site, http://candide.utopia.com/

[2]Levin, Gerald. Keynote speech delivered on January 20, 1996, at Global Information Infrastructures, a conference sponsored by the Japan–U.S. Telecommunications Research Institute and the Japan Society, New York, NY.

[3]http://www.whitehouse.gov/WH/EOP/OP/edtech/

[4]Wicklein, John. *Electronic Nightmare*. New York: Viking Press, 1981.

[5]Sommer, Francine, Panelist, "Media Mania," Columbia Business School Alumni Day, November 13, 1993.

[6]Lewis, Peter H. "Radio Internet to Broadcast around Clock," *The New York Times*, Sept. 19, 1994: A10.

[7]Dennis, Everette E. *Of Media and People*. Newbury Park, CA: Sage Publications, 1992.

[8]Wriston, Walter. *Twilight of Sovereignty: How the Information Revolution Is Transforming Our World*, New York: Scribners, 1992. Wriston, Walter. "Public Opinion: 'Mistress of the World.'" Inaugural address in The Freedom Forum Media Studies Center Technology Lecture Series, October 25, 1993.

[10]Gilder, George. "Telecosm: Digital Darkhorse—Newspapers," *Forbes ASAP*, Oct. 25, 1993: 138–149.

1

New Media Technology:
An Industry Overview

"'Tis true, There's magic in the web of it."
—WILLIAM SHAKESPEARE, OTHELLO[1]

CONTOURS OF THE NEW MEDIA LANDSCAPE

From virtual reality to the World Wide Web, the new media technology landscape is as diverse as it is fast changing. These new technologies are radically transforming almost every aspect of how we communicate and with whom, as well as just about any other dimension of our lives, from dating to making money to health care. Each year the pace of technological change seems to accelerate, as bold new technological advances are announced nearly every day. Likewise, regulatory changes have opened new technology vistas and the world has moved startlingly closer to realizing Marshall McLuhan's global village.[2] Although nearly 200 years elapsed between Gutenberg's invention of movable type in 1450 and the arrival of the printing press in America in 1639, the past century alone has seen the invention of the telephone, radio and television, satellite communications, the computer, Internet, and countless other technologies, each one revolutionizing some aspect of human communication.

A CONCEPTUAL ROAD MAP
TO NEW MEDIA TECHNOLOGIES

A conceptual framework is useful to help organize and make sense of the dimensions, qualities, and consequences of these new media technologies. One way to map these new technologies is by their primary technical function: production, distribution, display, and storage.

Although this approach is limited by the convergence of media technologies, and the blurring of lines between different media functions, it still has usefulness in charting the most distinctive or distinguishing contours of the landscape of new media technologies. Its value is articulated by Oxford University's Anthony Smith, who writes,

> The impact of electronics upon our ways of creating, storing and disseminating text goes through our whole culture, since the composition and use of text permeates everything we are as a civilization. The electronic transformation of text does not, however, displace our values or identity so much as superimpose itself on what has gone before; it is useful to remind ourselves what the traditional method of printing itself offered our culture when it arrived some centuries ago.[3]

Today, however, the world of multimedia communication extends well beyond text-based communication, and the impact of digital technology is truly transforming all forms of human communication.

Production

Production technologies refer to those used in gathering and processing information. These technologies include computers, electronic photography, optical scanners, and remote sensing technologies. Electronic production technologies have not only created new ways to collect and interpret information, but they have enabled us to gather new kinds of information, solve new problems, and solve old problems more rapidly and efficiently. Conversely, these same technologies have sometimes replaced human workers, posed a serious threat to individual privacy, oftentimes greatly increased the cost of information, and raised thorny questions about the ownership of information. Moreover, they have invariably outpaced human ability to cope with the new possibilities created by these technologies. Use of computer technologies in the workplace has also been linked to an increase in the occurrence of repetitive stress injury (RSI), such as carpal tunnel syndrome among persons spending long, uninterrupted periods typing on a computer keyboard.

Distribution

Distribution technologies refer to those involved in the transmission or movement of electronic information. Included are six primary technology systems:

1. Over-the-air broadcasting
2. Land-based telecommunications, including twisted pair, optical fiber (e.g., Asynchronous Transfer Mode, or ATM), the switched telephone network, the advanced intelligent network (AIN), integrated services digital network (ISDN), asymmetrical digital subscriber line (ADSL)
3. Coaxial cable (i.e., cable TV)
4. Satellite communications, including direct broadcast satellite (DBS)
5. Wireless transmission, including personal communication services (PCS)
6. Electrical power lines

These technologies have both positive and negative cultural and commercial consequences. They have made information globally available at the speed of light. They have made video on demand a practical reality. They have brought target marketing and audience specialization to unprecedented levels. Moreover, they have made telecommuting more practical than ever before. Research shows that more than 10 percent of Americans conduct at least some of their work from home offices made possible by these technologies. One percent now telecommute full time.

Meanwhile, these distribution technologies have contributed to a number of social ills, making, for instance, the piracy of electronic information a multibillion dollar industry worldwide. Some argue that they have contributed to growing social fragmentation, the division between society's information rich and information poor, and the formation of an information underclass.

Display

Display devices refer to a variety of technologies for presenting information to the end user, audience member, or consumer of information. They include devices for presenting electronic information in a variety of formats, such as video, audio, text, data, or any combination of these. Some even present information in three-dimensional, tactile, or touch-sensitive format. Many of these technologies are dependent on or interconnected to the technologies of distribution, production, or storage, and are separated here only conceptually. Examples include various multimedia computer displays, such as personal digital appliances (PDAs) or flat panel screens, a new generation of display telephones, emerging forms of interactive television, high definition television (HDTV), and virtual reality technologies of the dataglove and the bodysuit. The cultural and commercial consequences of these technologies are not yet clear, and often interact with other factors, such as the nature of the content as well as the characteristics of the user. Collectively, however, these technologies make it increasingly easy to access vast amounts of information while on the move. Flat panel display technologies, already commonly used by overnight delivery carriers, hold the promise of bringing about a "mediamorphosis," or the electronic transformation of the newspaper. Many of these multimedia display devices act as enabling technologies, facilitating communication between and among persons with or without disabilities.

Conversely, these same technologies may also pose an array of potential negative consequences. Video display terminals (VDTs), for instance, present potential public health risks by exposing users to large doses of electromagnetic radiation, sometimes linked to cancer, miscarriage, and stress. Many are alarmed by the potential mental health risks posed by heavy exposure to violent or sexist computer games. Some are concerned that an increasingly heavy reliance on electronic media has contributed to a steady erosion in America's literacy rate.

Storage

Storage technologies refer to those media used in housing information in electronic format. These media are evolving from largely magnetic to optical in format. While the standard computer storage devices have been the floppy magnetic diskette and the magnetic hard drive, the compact disk emerged in the mid-1990s as the storage medium of choice for storing large amounts of information, such as data, text, audio, video, and combined multimedia information. The compact disc-read only memory (CD-ROM) is the most common CD format, although the interactive format (CD-I) is growing in use. Laserdiscs have also been used primarily for storing video information and for distributing movies. The digital video disk (DVD) is now developing as the first global standard for digital video storage, with a single DVD capable of storing an entire two-hour feature-length video in digital form. The lasercard is a likely candidate for storing information for use in PDAs, such as the Apple Newton or the Casio/Tandy Zoomer. Video servers are an increasingly important storage technology for the development of interactive television and video on demand. Video servers, a class of powerful minicomputers, are the engines that will drive not only the availability of large libraries of video but also the emergence of tapeless television stations and TV networks, which today largely rely on analog videotape file servers. By 2000, most stations and networks will use digital video servers to play back previously recorded programming and advertising content and permit remote access to video on demand.

MAPPING THE CONSEQUENCES OF NEW MEDIA TECHNOLOGIES

The rapid pace of technological change and convergence has made it increasingly difficult to develop a coherent framework for understanding the nature and shape of new media technologies. This analysis poses four fundamental questions:

- How does technological change affect the way communication professionals do their work?

TABLE 1-1   Mapping the Consequences of Technological Change

	Communication Worker	Product	Structure	Society
Intended Consequence	Efficiency, Lower Cost, Greater Speed,	Interactivity User Control Multimedia Freedom Flexibility	Decentralization Virtual Newsroom Telecommuting Content	Economic Benefit
Unintended/ Unexpected Consequence	Health Effects Fewer Jobs	Information More Costly, Intellectual Property Rights Hard to Define	Redefined Roles Organization	Privacy Lost, Pace of Tech Change Faster Than Society's Ability to Cope

- How does new technology influence the nature of the communication product or content?
- How does changing technology affect the structure of communication industries?
- How do new media technologies affect the nature of the media audience and society at large?

Table 1-1 presents a conceptual framework for mapping these four types of consequences of new media technologies. The dimensions are the nature of the consequences, intended or unintended, and the level of impact, on the communication worker, the communication product, the media structure, and on society, the ultimate media audience. Intended consequences of new media technologies for the communication worker include greater efficiency and flexibility. Unintended social consequences of new technologies include, by contrast, an increasing loss of privacy and an inability for social institutions to keep pace with technological change. Table 1-1 includes selected examples of these consequences, and is not a comprehensive listing of all of the effects of technological change. It is offered as an analytical framework for mapping the consequences of new media technologies.

The Technological Transformation of How Communication Professionals Do Their Work

Journalists, public relations practitioners, and advertisers all use new technology to do their work more effectively. They use new technologies to increase their work efficiency and speed, as well as to reduce cost. Moreover, new technologies can enable communication professionals to do things in new and creative ways, or even do entirely new things.

There are seemingly endless examples of how the work of journalists has been irretrievably transformed by a variety of technologies, from desktop publishing technologies that have spawned a new era in information graphics to speech recognition and synthesis technologies for persons with disabilities. One noteworthy example comes from the annals of television coverage of the 1988 presidential campaign. ABC News developed a new anchor information system for its 1988 election coverage by creating a hypertext computer database on all the candidates, their voting records, speeches, and positions on the issues. MAGNA (ABC News's Macintosh General News Almanac created by then executive producer David Bohrman and Apple Computer's Larry Wood) also included a complete database on the Republican and Democratic Party Conventions.[4] MAGNA was created using HyperCard®, a hypertext software authoring system for the Macintosh computer. MAGNA replaced an old card file system that ABC News had previously used on the candidates, as had the other television networks. Unlike previous campaigns, MAGNA enabled ABC *World News Tonight* anchor Peter Jennings to come equipped to the debates and other news events with an exhaustive database at his fingertips in fully electronic, instantly searchable form on a laptop computer. While in years past it was impossible to verify statements by the candidates the moment they made them while in the field, MAGNA changed all that. What's more, MAGNA eventually lead to the creation of an entirely new unit at ABC. Called ABC Interactive, the new unit spun off the hypertext framework developed for MAGNA and linked it to the full motion video archives of *ABC News*. The unit's first product was *The '88 Vote,* which included both the MAGNA software and nearly an hour of audio and video on the 1988 presidential campaign. Since then, the unit has produced interactive laser disks on the Middle East, called "The Holy Land," Martin Luther King, and several of other subjects. ABC Interactive functions as an educational service arm of *ABC News,* primarily targeting high schools and universities as the consumers of its product line. A major user has been the state of Florida public school system, which has widely tested and adopted the innovative multimedia products. As a result of the educational focus, ABC Interactive has generated only modest revenues to date.

Surveying the Newsroom Consequences

To systematically assess the impact of new technology in the newsroom, The Freedom Forum's Media Studies Center surveyed a panel of executives from dozens of news organizations represented at Technology Studies seminars hosted by the Center between 1991 and 1993.[5] The survey suggests that technological convergence is driving today's newsroom. Most of those responding to the survey report that the following technologies have transformed their newsrooms: personal computers (80 percent); photography (70 percent); online databases, as in libraries (70 percent); and cell phones and faxes (60 percent).

Those surveyed also mention a number of telecommunications advances, from cellular telephones to fax communications to advanced radio communications, as well as computer-based technologies for investigative reporting, electronic image scanning and processing, video capture technology, and electronic mail. Survey respondents point to the benefits of technology convergence in the newsroom, such as improved efficiency and speed, greater access to information, and new abilities.

Technology convergence also presents a variety of challenges to newsroom management, from new staffing requirements to maintaining compatibility between alternative platforms. Some newspaper editors foresee the need for new editorial and design skills and probably for increased editorial staffing. Pagination, for example, shifts the page-makeup function from back shop to newsroom, and may require more editors who are "technically coordinated."

Pagination refers to computerized page design and layout technologies. It is the newspaper analog to desktop publishing. The 1980s saw pagination systems widely adopted in the newspaper industry, though not without problems. Typically, electronic pagination was introduced to streamline production and reduce costs. In the process, however, many newspapers did not anticipate the unexpected consequence of moving back-room production and layout processes into the newsroom, where editors suddenly found themselves learning a new technical system, as well as having responsibility for the design of the daily newspaper. This meant spending less time editing text for content and style. In the 1980s, one newspaper company in Westchester County, New York, experimented with applying artificial intelligence to its pagination technology in an effort to automate the page design process fully. Although admirable in its philosophy, the experiment was ahead of its time and failed after a few years' trial.

News executives are also concerned about the ethical questions raised by technological convergence and digitization. Although computerization may provide greater access to information, it must be weighed against each citizen's right to privacy. Electronic image processing also poses important ethical questions in today's newsroom. Synthetic images or manipulated pictures are easier to create and are virtually undetectable in the electronic darkrooms now prevalent in the newsroom. It is inevitable that distorted news photos will appear in newspapers and television news reports. One recent case involved a manipulated Pulitzer prize-winning photo. As more and more readers and viewers become aware of the use of digital image processing, what will be the effect on the credibility of visual news?

News executives foresee a number of profound technologically driven changes looming on the newsroom horizon.[6] These changes include:

- A possible redefinition of news based on the development of real-time news information
- A new definition of what it means to be a journalist, whereby editors may soon have to function as compositor, production quality control supervisor and, to an extent, production manager

- A reconceptualization of the audience in terms of specialized interests
- The advent of personalized news on demand and delivered through the information highway or the Internet

The results of this survey demonstrate how the communication product has been indelibly altered by new technology. We have seen the emergence of new communication products that are more and more computer-based, nonlinear (i.e., hypertext), multimedia (incorporating text, data, video, and audio) and user controlled (both in terms of form, function, and time). Moreover, more communication products are reaching the end user in real-time via online and satellite technology. It is perhaps this final quality that will prove the most important in transforming human communication. As more information is received the moment it is transmitted, whether by electronic mail, satellite communications, or cellular transmission, decisions will be instantly made based on that real-time information. We will return to this theme later in the book. An interesting historical precedent suggests that large news organizations may be poised to once again redefine news, driven in part by the availability of relatively costly news services to a small, but important, minority of the organization's customers. The major commercial networks, ABC, NBC, and CBS, cut back on coverage of some events in 1980 and 1981 because of coverage available on then fledgling CNN. At the time, CNN reached only a small minority of U.S. television households, but it was an elite minority made up of higher income, well-educated audience members. Even today, CNN is seen on a regular basis by only a small portion of TV households, but around the world the CNN audience includes many opinion leaders, decision makers, and relatively affluent audience members.

Technological Transformations of the Media Product

Case Studies in Technological Change
in the Media Industry

Oftentimes the effects of technologies have been hidden and long-term, while on other occasions the effects have been more direct, intended, and dramatic. Two commercially successful examples of direct, intended, and dramatic technology applications in the news industry include *USA Today* and Bloomberg Business News. Founded more than a decade ago, *USA Today* capitalized on satellite technologies to make possible the first truly national newspaper in the United States. Bloomberg Business News, founded a decade ago, has capitalized on the convergence of computing and telecommunications technology to make possible a successful real-time multimedia information service. A more recent example comes from the world of magazine publishing, and reflects the role of new technology in developing new communication products as well as transforming the way the communication professionals do their work. For five weeks in the fall of 1996, a team of five journalists trekked throughout China on a modern project Candide, reporting on the cultural and commercial transformation of the world's most populated country. With funding from Simon & Schuster's Curriculum Corporation and the Boston-based Utopia (an Internet consulting company), the intrepid team reported their online magazine to a global audience in real-time via the World Wide Web directly from China using a variety of cutting-edge technologies, including RealAudio, Shockwave, QuickTime VR, and CU-SeeMe.

While many of the consequences of new media have been intentional, others have been unexpected. Veteran network news executive Adam Clayton Powell III has studied the unexpected consequences of technological change in the television newsroom.

Powell has found that as new technology gains ground in television newsrooms, it often becomes largely invisible to its users. He says it is analogous to learning to ride a bicycle: "you do not need to think about the process while you are pedaling." As a result, the extent of the changes brought about by new technology has often come as a surprise to many network producers and executives. Powell states:

> As recently as 1976, television news teams covered the world on film. During the Vietnam war, for example, film was usually shipped by air to the United States, where it was developed, edited and fed into the final broadcast. This process consumed at least a day, often two. Viewers saw yesterday's news today, and then only if the networks moved quickly.
>
> Things have changed: Film has been replaced by videotape and live satellite feeds, and yesterday's pictures are now overset. Interestingly, many network news producers and executives questioned about the demise of film maintained that nothing else had changed: Good pictures are good pictures, they said, and good journalism is still good journalism.[7]

Powell's study of network news coverage suggests that the demise of film in broadcast news actually exerted a profound although subtle effect. Looking at a 1976 network newscast, Powell found that the graphics were flat and the editing almost leisurely—"some pictures are allowed to run for several seconds, a rarity today" since the introduction of videotape and satellite technologies.

An important question, Powell asks, is whether flashy graphics and fast-paced editing are synonymous with better journalism. The answer, he says, can be found in a summer 1986 article in *Niemen Report*.[8] In the article, Burton Benjamin, executive producer of the *CBS Evening News* during the 1970s asked, "Are we in danger of emulating MTV with NTV—News TV? What does it profit you when no shot is longer than three seconds and the total is zero?"

Looking to the future, Powell contends that one of the major changes looming on the television news horizon is the complete digitization of moving images. While there have been celebrated cases of the digital manipulation of still images, such as the *National Geographic* case in which editors manipulated a digitized image of the great pyramids to get an improved aspect ratio on the magazine's cover, few viewers or even news executives realize the same thing can be done seamlessly with moving pictures in today's digital darkrooms.

"Totally synthetic news events are now within reach," Powell wrote in 1993.[9] Using composite video, editors can make synthetic news events look absolutely real. Digital darkrooms, he concludes, symbolize nothing less than the end of truth in video photography. The implications for the credibility of television news are alarming. Don E. Tomlinson, an associate professor of journalism at Texas A&M University, agrees.[10] He contends that the digital revolution will directly lead to the manipulation of images and sounds and with dire consequences.

Soon, then, the capability will be such that the recorded, digitized, sampled voice of, say, the president of the United States, could be made to sound perfectly as if he had said something he in fact had not said. All it would require, once a representative sample of his voice's binary codes has been fed into the computer, is their rearrangement.

Powell's 1993 prediction became all too real during the 1996 senatorial campaign in Virginia. In that campaign, it was revealed that the advertising consultant, Greg Stevens of Alexandria, Virginia, hired by Senator John W. Warner (R-Virginia) created and aired on television a negative political advertisement showing Warner's Republican rival, Mark R. Warner, shaking hands at a political rally with former Governor L. Douglas Wilder and President Clinton smiling between them. The handshake never occurred. Stevens had digitally manufactured a completely seamless and synthetic video by electronically placing Mark Warner's head onto the body of Senator Charles S. Robb, a Virginia Democrat.[11]

Digital image processing, of course, has transformed far more than just the news. Anyone who has seen a Hollywood movie, a television commercial, or a music video in the 1990s has almost certainly seen hundreds, perhaps thousands, of images that have been digitally altered or rearranged in some way. Almost routinely now, movie and television special effects are created digitally by computer. Everything from Arnold Schwartzenegger's *Terminator II* to Michael Jackson's latest video owe much of their video magic to the digital darkroom. In a 1994 political campaign spot run on TV by Sam Cravotta, a Republican house candidate in West Virginia, an image of his opponent, Representative Bob Wise, is transformed digitally into one of President Clinton. Technological advances now make the digital imaging process virtually seamless, with no significant degradation of the original image and invisible to even a well-trained eye. If you're not convinced, just watch *Jurassic Park* and see if you can find a dinosaur or any other digital effect that looks anything less than real.

Although many would say these technological advances have led to ever better communication products, some have pointed out the possible downside. Technology critics argue that the growth of electronic communication signals the death of literacy, or at least verbal literacy. Interactive, multimedia hold the potential for a reduced role of linear narrative, one in which storytelling may become a nostalgic relic of the past. When immersed in a sea of data, a reader may see no beginning, middle, or end. Important questions include:

- What will be the grammar of interactive media?
- What will become the storytelling conventions of virtual reality?
- Will literacy as we know it be as irrelevant to the post-Gutenberg era as the art of illumination?

Benjamin M. Compaine, Bell Atlantic Professor of Telecommunications at Temple University, suggests that we need to think in terms of new media literacy, a literacy based on fluency with all media, especially those based on images and sound.[12] Posing both a potential commercial bonanza as well as a cultural threat is the development of a new digital editor that can superimpose ads in real time over action video. The primary use of the technology to date is inserting commercial banners in the scenes at sporting events. For example, imagine you're watching a basketball game and a billboard for Coke appears behind the basket. In the next play, the billboard might be advertising Canon cameras. None of these messages actually appear at the sporting event. They are all superimposed electronically, either by a central network location, or by any local station. The digital editor can provide the ultimate in custom tailoring of commercial messages in real time. It also means a further erosion of the reality of the television image.

Even the advent of the electronic newspaper has alarmed some, who are concerned that one of the greatest social benefits of the newspaper, at least since the days of the penny press, its low cost and widespread availability, will be forever lost in an electronic world where expensive electronic devices will be needed to read the morning newspaper. Arthur Ochs Sulzberger, publisher of The New York Times Co., says his company has had mixed results with high-tech information delivery and is a "long way from saying good-bye to our newsprint suppliers."[13] Although electronic news delivery will have an important place in the future, Sulzberger says computerized news-on-demand services will never entirely replace newspapers. In agreement is Charles Brumback, chair and CEO of The Tribune Co. "People won't abandon newspapers in our lifetime," Brumback said.[14] "But advertising will flow to other distribution channels."

Restructuring Media Organizations

Technology has also affected the structure of communication industries. The convergence of computers and telecommunications has created an era of wired and nonwired network computing. This distributed computing environment has enabled media organizations from newsrooms to advertising agencies to rethink the structure of their offices. Decentralization is the primary shift in the structure of these media organizations. No longer need all employees work at the same location, in the same city, or even in the same country. With satellite communications, fiber optics, and powerful desktop computers, communication workers can work together, sharing files, sending messages and creating new communication products simultaneously from all parts of the world.

Virtual Spaces

During Operation Desert Storm, each of the network news divisions created "virtual newsrooms" linking offices in New York City with correspondents on assignment in the Persian Gulf.

> *Through the use of advanced communication technologies—laptop computers, modems, cellular phones and beepers—journalists now can hook into an electronic "virtual newsroom" wherever they go, keeping in touch with editors and sources, searching databases and researching, writing and filing stories on the road from their newsrooms without walls.*[15]

Similarly, such virtual structures are being adopted in other media organizations. One major advertising agency has already gone virtual. Chiat/Day's Venice, California headquarters converted to a virtual workplace on January 3, 1994.[16] Envisioned only eight months earlier by company Chairman Jay Chiat, the virtual agency houses its electronic nerve center in its Frank Gehry-designed signature building, featuring a variety of high-tech applications ranging from an "intelligent switchboard" to an advanced computing system. Through these technologies, agency executives and other personnel are able to conduct virtually all of their business without ever coming physically to the agency's Venice headquarters. Bob Grossman, senior VP-group account director at Chiat/Day, who lives in Los Angeles and has been confronted by earthquake-snarled commuter traffic, links easily into his office electronically home-based computer just a few steps from his kitchen. Grossman, like other Chiat executives, can do a lot more than simply have his phone calls forwarded to his home. Using a computer and a modem, he can connect to Chiat's central computer and select from any of the system's-menu driven applications, such as word processing, electronic calendar (including automatically scheduling meetings), file management, and electronic mail. But it is neither the hardware nor its applications that make this virtual agency so remarkable, *Advertising Age* points out. The Chiat office building actual houses no private offices and hard-wired phones any longer for its executives. Rather, it provides "work spaces" and portable phones. "What makes Chiat/Day virtual is the extent to which it pushes technology. The modern office shifts employees bottom line to the work, rather than attendance."

The New Media Audience: Technology's Child

Ultimately, these technological changes have important implications for media audiences and society in general. Technology critic Neil Postman writes, "a technology . . . is merely a machine," it "becomes a medium as it employs a symbolic code, as it finds its place in a particular social setting."[17] "A medium," he notes, "is the social and intellectual environment a machine creates." Thus, as new technologies create new social and intellectual environments, one would expect society to be irrevocably changed.

Many of the new technologies are opening up new means of human interaction. Whether you are exploring a virtual world or simply accessing an electronic bulletin board, people around the world are talking to each other, sharing experiences and generally going where no man or woman has gone before—electronically.

Daniel Kennedy, reporter and editor at the *Boston Phoenix,* a leading alternative weekly newspaper, recently assessed the potential harmful cultural consequences of a technological Frankenstein created and driven by commercial interests. When corporate titans such as Time Warner build information superhighways delivering 500 television channels to the home, what is the social cost? Kennedy contends that "as information becomes increasingly decentralized, there's a danger that consumers of that information—all of us, in other words—will become more and more isolated from society and from each other."[18]

;-)

Of course, some of the unintended, or at least unexpected, consequences are relatively harmless. One cultural example is the creation of "emoticons" on computer networks. As computer users have entered the online world of cyberspace, they have invented a graphical iconic language of their own to represent using a standard QWERTY keyboard a whole range of emotions. Commonly used emoticons, or smileys, are shown in Table 1-2.

Such keyboard keystrokes have also developed into a form of humor, as well. Making the rounds at MIT, says Adam Clayton Powell III, is this computer joke:

DOS prompt in Canada: EH:\

TABLE 1-2   Emoticons on the Information Highway

:-)	Smile
:-(	Frown
:'	Cry
;-)	Wink
:D	Laughter
:-O	Yell
:-	Anger
:X	My lips are sealed
:P	Stick out tongue
:Q	Smoking
:*	A kiss

Can you decipher this one   %-)   ?
(It means confusion, with the % indicating a crinkled brow.)

("EH" is a Canadian verbal expression commonly added to the end of a sentence in conversation, and :\ the accompanying wince.)

Some see the use of emoticons as nothing more than online clichés. Neal Stephenson, author of the science fiction novel *Snow Crash,* suggests that emoticons are the "electronic equivalent of spin doctors: commonly inserted at the end of a sentence that is meant to be interpreted as sarcasm."[19]

THE CHANGING PLAYERS

With the technological convergence of the computer, television and telecommunications in a digital communication environment, the major players in the communication industry come from a wide variety of fields. At the time of this writing, the key players vying for control of the information highway include telephone, cable television, entertainment, broadcasting, and newspaper companies, as well as satellite, software, and computer companies. Thus, depending on how one defines the field, the list of top companies varies, although many lists include most of the same key players since those companies tend to have multimedia holdings.

Although it is impossible to develop a single short list of the most important communications companies, it is still useful to identify a few of the companies leading the development of new media technologies. These companies come from a variety industries, and divide generally along the lines of being either content producers or technology creators, although these lines are rapidly blurring. A selected list of the most important communication companies with a major stake in new technology includes:

- International multimedia titans Time Warner Inc., USA; News Corporation, Australia; Verlagsgruppe Bertelsmann GmbH, Munich, Germany; Disney/Capital Cities/ABC, USA; Sony, Japan
- U.S. cable TV behemoth TCI
- Japan's public broadcaster NHK and Japanese audio-visual company Matshushita Electrical Industrial
- U.S. telephone companies Bellsouth and Bell Atlantic
- U.S. computer hardware manufacturers IBM and Hewlett-Packard
- U.S. software giant Microsoft

Importantly, a growing number of mergers, acquisitions and corporate alignments are redefining the nature and number of industry players. Some $75 billion has changed hands in 160 recent multimedia deals.[20] Bell Atlantic's merger with Nynex, Time Warner's acquisition of Turner Broadcasting, Westinghouse's purchase of CBS, British Telecommunications' acquisition of MCI, and other as yet undetermined alignments may completely reshape the corporate landscape in information technology. The formerly separate worlds of publishing, broadcasting, cable, entertainment, computing, and telecommunications are rapidly converging, both in terms of ownership and in cross-industry collaboration. As companies have recognized the necessity to join forces and capitalize on the synergistic potential between companies with differing expertise in the information industry, they have come together to form strategic alliances for the multimedia world of the next millennium.

No longer do even the greatest of corporate giants prefer to go it alone on the information highway. Behemoths such as Bell Atlantic, Tele-Communications Inc., IBM, AT&T, and Time Warner have all formed collaborative efforts with companies that only a few years ago they would have treated as competitive threats.[21] Telephone companies have aligned with newspaper publishers. Cable companies are cooperating with entertainment companies. Computer manufacturers are combining with software developers. In each instance, one company is complementing its knowledge, skills, and resources with those of its former adversary. Increasingly, these alliances are linking technology companies with content producers, as illustrated by the Microsoft–NBC collaboration which produced the twenty-four-hour news service MSNBC, available on cable TV or the Internet.

William Gates, Microsoft CEO and America's wealthiest entrepreneur (and second richest person—*Forbes,* 1993), has involved his company in a number of alliances. The rationale is clear. "Anyone who invests in this area is making a bet on interactivity," says Gates.[22] Gates stunned many observers by announcing in early 1994 a joint effort with McCaw Cellular to build a global satellite network to provide a wireless superhighway.

One area where new deals are taking shape is in wireless communications. Some of the major deals announced in 1994 include AT&T's $11.5 billion acquisition of McCaw Cellular; the alliance of Sprint and three cable TV companies: Telecommunications Inc., Comcast, and Cox Cable; and the joint effort of Bell Atlantic, Nynex, US West, and Air Touch.

The giant players in the new media game are joined by a growing number of small entrepreneurs. As the new technologies have made possible global multimedia communications, they have also reduced many of the barriers to market entry. Much of the new technology is considerably less expensive and simpler to use than earlier generations of technology. As a result, new companies have found ways to compete with much larger companies for specialized market niches. *Newsweek* declares, "Forget the big mergers. In the race to control the interactive highway, the real winners may be the (lesser-known) firms that will build it bit by byte."[23]

Since the divestiture of AT&T in 1984, thousands of small and hungry companies have emerged to provide competitive alternatives for long-distance telephone service. While most of these companies have captured little market share from AT&T, MCI, and Sprint, they have made sizable inroads. There are many other interesting examples of small, pioneering companies in the new technology marketplace. One innovative upstart is RoundBook Publishing Group of Scotts Valley, California, a company specializing in CD-ROM publishing. While publishing giants such as Ziff-Davis Publishing Company maintain control over much of the the CD-ROM publishing field in the United States, RoundBook has captured a very important market niche. With the end of the Cold War and the opening up of the former Soviet Union to foreign business investment, RoundBook has taken its entrepreneurial spirit to the museums and art world of Russia. While many companies sought the rights to publish images of Russia's vast art collections on CD-ROM, RoundBook convinced Russia's museum and art directors to grant them exclusive rights to the material. Founded on March 1, 1993 by CD-ROM gurus Greg Smith and Francis Juliano, RoundBook secured the confidence of Russia's art world by agreeing to keep all Russian art in Russia, and working with Russian artists to photograph all the art. Smith and Juliano have more than twelve years experience developing CD-ROM products at Sony and Meridian Data, creating many of the products available for the Sony Data Diskman and the MMCD player, including "the highly respected *Mayo Clinic Family Health Book.*"[24] Compton's NewMedia will distribute the forthcoming RoundBook products to more than 5,000 outlets. RoundBook and Compton's NewMedia recently signed an agreement worth $18 million that will deliver at least twenty CD-ROM titles to stores in 1994. The deal will catapult RoundBook from obscurity into one of the largest publishers of CD-ROMs in the world.[25]

In 1991, the Minority Television Project launched an innovative new public television station in the San Francisco Bay area. Under the direction of founding station manager Adam Clayton Powell III, the station was able to operate on a shoestring budget of just $100,000 for the first three months of transmission. Although KMTP captured a small share of the Bay area viewers, it has been able to survive and grow largely because of the new technology of new wave television, including the multichannel nature of the marketplace and the low cost of 8mm videotape technology.

Another start-up taking advantage of both breakthroughs in wireless technology and loosening of the regulatory environment is Cellularvision.[26] The small New York-based company uses wireless cellular transmitters to send cable television programming to consumers in Brighton Beach, Brooklyn, and will soon expand into the larger markets of Queens and midtown Manhattan.

Media giants have also succeeded at employing the new technology to successfully launch new media efforts. Time Warner used the technology of high-8 video equipment to launch its twenty-four-hour cable news channel, New York One in New York City. *Time* Magazine first experimented with high-8 equipment during the Persian Gulf war.[27] *Time* sent one of its boldest reporters into the Gulf equipped with a lightweight, inexpensive high-8 video camera, small enough to fit into the palm of the hand of the operator. He was able to shoot the first video of the Kuwaiti oil well fires seen on American television on ABC's *Nightline*.

Nevertheless, there are dangerous ramifications of this game of increasing industry collaboration and mergers. Media critics such as Ben Bagdikian contend that the increasing concentration of media ownership and the growth of global media companies based on the capabilities of the electronic superhighway is leading to fewer and fewer hands controlling greater and greater amounts of information.

Soon, many fear, virtually the entire flow of information will be controlled by a few communication behemoths. Bagdikian points to the shrinking ownership of major media corporations in the United States, from about fifty companies in 1983 to twenty in 1997.[28] Technology visionary Anthony Smith has argued convincingly that the 1990s have already seen the growth of just seven media giants: Time Warner, Bertelsmann, Sony, Disney, Hachette, NewsCorp, and, telecom giants AT&T and cable.[29]

In addition, most of the major players fighting for control of the information are companies from the fields of entertainment, cable TV, telecommunications, and computers. Few are from the newspaper industry or broadcast television, with the exception of companies such as Cox Enterprises, which, in addition to its newspaper holdings, also owns cable TV systems. "Phone companies, cable systems and entertainment producers are rushing headlong into the new interactive electronic world while the print media try to figure out how they fit in," observes Philip Moeller, former business editor and electronic news editor at the *Sun* in Baltimore and a communication consultant in West Hartford, Connecticut.[30] The question is: Who will control the information infrastructure? For more than 300 years, newspapers in America have controlled their own printing presses. Broadcasters have controlled the airways for much of the twentieth century under the watchful eye of the Federal Communications Commission. Both newspapers and broadcasters have held news in high regard, almost as a public trust necessary to a democracy. If the information highway infrastructure is controlled by media without that tradition of news (with some exceptions, such as Cablevision's pioneering Rainbow 12 on Long Island, New York), how will news fare? NBC was originally 50 percent owned by the General Electric Company. In fact, the musical notes G-E-C are well known to anyone in America who has ever watched NBC. GE, however, sold off NBC early on to RCA, and it was only a decade ago that GE reacquired the television network. As author, journalist, and media critic Ken Auletta makes clear in his classic work, *Three Blind Mice,* the impact of the reacquisition of the network by a nonmedia, nonjournalistic company was profound.[31] It changed completely the corporate culture that existed at NBC, replacing a value system that placed high priority on news at any cost, with a bottom-line orientation that treated news like any other area of network programming, or for that matter, like any product produced by GE. What are the implications of such ownership prospects for the future of the information superhighway? Will the information highway be treated by corporate interests and the government as a national public resource, and require its owners to serve as a common carrier, as the phone companies are required to today?

U.S. government agencies, such as the Federal Communications Commission (FCC), the Federal Trade Commission (FTC), and the Justice Department have so far paid little attention to any potential antitrust considerations in this era of collaboration. In 1993, the FTC found itself deadlocked regarding the propriety of the competitive practices of one software giant, Microsoft, accused of collaborating with computer manufacturers to assure itself of an industry standard platform compatible with only Microsoft operating systems, such as MS-DOS (Microsoft Disk Operating System) and Windows, a graphical user interface for IBM-compatible personal computers (PCs).

In the fall of 1993, Viacom, Inc. filed the first antitrust lawsuit in the media wars. Viacom owner Sumner Redstone found himself in an escalating bidding war with QVC Home Shopping Network's CEO John Malone for Paramount Communications, a man Vice President Al Gore once called Darth Vader.[32] In response to TCI's $9.9 billion bid for Paramount, which exceeded Viacom's opening bid by some $2 billion, Redstone filed his antitrust suit against not only rival bidder QVC, but also Tele-Communications, Inc. (TCI), Liberty Media, Inc. and Encore Media Corp., all of which are owned or controlled by Malone. The implications of the suit, however, go far beyond the battle for Paramount. "While QVC's attempt to wrestle the studio away triggered the filing, Viacom broadly charges that TCI president and Liberty chairman John Malone and the companies with which he is affiliated have tried to secure a chokehold on programming delivery," reports John M. Higgins.[33] This antitrust suit may be just the first salvo in a new era of mergers, acquisitions, and the resulting antitrust litigation in the age of the information superhighway.

THE STAKES

At stake is a potentially huge and lucrative global marketplace. Industry projections are that, by the year 2000, revenues on the information highway in the United States alone will be 10 to 20 times the $25 billion cable market, or the $12 billion video rental market. The global marketplace is even bigger, exceeding a trillion dollars worldwide. "The gold rush to a $3.5 trillion multimedia market is on," proclaims technology visionary and author George Gilder.[34] These financial stakes are driving many large and small corporations to invest millions, in some cases billions, of dollars in infrastructure, software development, and experimental projects.

History provides interesting parallels to the massive investment in new media technology today. As recently as a decade ago, many news and information companies invested heavily in the development of videotex, or text delivery over the air or by cable for presentation on television screens. Knight-Ridder invested heavily in its Viewtron experiment, for example, only to see its ultimate failure at a cost of many millions of dollars. Walter Baer, director of domestic research for RAND, physicist and director of the Times Mirror's videotex experiments, has commented on the lessons learned from the videotex failures. He observed that the videotex experiments of the early 1980s taught us how to become a millionaire—all you needed was to start with $40 million.[35] One might say the current efforts to build the information highway will teach us how to become a billionaire.

While many of the traditional media and information companies saw their revenues plateau and experienced little growth throughout the 1980s, many electronic information services have seen their revenues grow dramatically in the 1990s. Real-time information service providers, such as Dow Jones' Telerate, Reuters, Bloomberg Business News and Knight-Ridder, for example, have seen dramatic annual growth rates of more than 10 percent since 1982.[36] In 1992 alone, the net profit of Dow Jones' Telerate reached $90 million, an amount in excess of the net profit of the entire daily newspaper industry in the United States, which totaled just $88 million in 1992. Bloomberg has grown at an annual rate of more than 13 percent since its inception in just 1983, and is now a company with annual revenues of more than $38 million.[37,38]

On Wall Street, media analysts have found that a fundamental sea change is occurring in the revenue base of the media. Traditionally, media industries have been largely supported by advertising revenues. Newspapers, magazines, television, and radio have received the majority of their revenues, between 60 and 75 percent, from advertising support. In today's new media environment, advertiser-supported media are experiencing flat or declining revenues. Meanwhile, user-supported media are experiencing revenue growth. Cable television, online services, and pay-per-view are growing rapidly. Some projections show a rate of growth in excess of 20 percent. Paul Sagan, the founding editor of New Media at Time Warner, notes that new media ventures will need to cultivate multiple revenue streams if they are to develop as successful commercial enterprises.[39]

Although the commercial stakes loom large on the financial horizon, the cultural stakes may be even greater. For at least three centuries, since the first newspaper, *Publick Occurrences,* was founded in the Western Hemisphere in Boston, Massachusetts, media markets have been defined largely by geography and limited by political and cultural boundaries. In recent decades, new technology has begun to change all that, as computers, modern telecommunications, and satellite communications have spawned an era of target marketing based on demographics and other audience characteristics. The convergence of telecommunications, computing, and media is completing the transformation of the communications marketplace. We are witnessing the creation of online telecommunities existing only in cyberspace. These are the communities of mind, linking individuals with common interests, able to communicate across geographic, political, and cultural boundaries.

Inventing the Future:
The Roles of Government and the Private Sector

With the stakes looming so large, important questions arise regarding the different roles of government, industry, education and the public in shaping the future of new media technology and the information superhighway. Should the role of government be that of a neutral referee, simply making sure that all participants play fairly and by the same rules? Or, should government be an active participant in the development of information technology. For example, is it appropriate for the government to introduce and support a "free" (to users) Internet system? Does such a role advance or hinder the development of the technology? In late 1996, the FCC opted for the more neutral role in deciding not to select a format for the home delivery of high-definition, digital television, preferring to let marketplace forces determine which system the public prefers, either that of the computer world or that of the traditional television programmer.

In comparison, what should be the role of industry-led research, development, and implementation? In the United States, industry has often lead the way in developing new technology, with social consequences being considered more as an afterthought than as a part of the plan. What are the consequences of such an approach? In contrast, the approach taken in developing new information technologies in the European Union has been much more cautious, with government and official bodies taking the lead, and industry following suit. More often in Europe, social consequences are analyzed before technologies are tested or implemented. What are the implications of such an approach for the development of new media technologies? Are there important implications for future economic growth? How are these considerations affected by the growth of the global economy and the global information society?

Economic Forces

A wide variety of indicators point to the growth and strength of the information technology sector of the U.S. economy. Information technology leads capital investment, with steady growth from less than 20 percent (17 percent) of private equipment investment in 1974 devoted to computers and other information technology to nearly 50 percent (45 percent) in 1994 devoted to the information technology sector.[40] Meanwhile, industrial machinery as a percent of private equipment investment has dropped from about 32 percent in 1974 to less than 20 percent (19 percent) in 1994. Computers and telecommunications equipment has grown dramatically as a U.S. export in recent years, rising from about 7.0 percent of U.S. exports in 1980 to twice that level (14 percent) in 1993. Computer exports are expected to rise from $34.6 billion in 1994 to $52 billion by 2000.[41] Information sector jobs have grown steadily over the past two decades as well, rising from about 150,000 jobs in computer software, data processing, and information retrieval to about 900,000 such jobs in 1994, now surpassing the total employed in motor vehicles and parts manufacture. Consumer spending on multimedia products as a share of disposable income has also risen recently, from about 2.8 percent in 1980 to about 3.4 percent in 1993.[42]

INDUSTRY OVERVIEW

The information and communication industry is a broad and rapidly growing sector of the U.S. and global economies. The U.S. Department of Commerce identifies seven primary subindustries within this broad industry.[43]

Telecommunications services ($175 billion) and printing and publishing ($172 billion) are the largest of these seven information and communication industry, with the information services subindustry running a strong fourth, at $102.1 billion. Although fourth in total revenues, the information services sector is the fastest growing, with growth of nearly 20 percent in 1992. Printing and publishing is growing at a rate of just 2 percent, in contrast. Recent data confirm that business is booming in the online market. Revenue and subscriber totals are both on the rise and show no signs of stopping for at least the rest of the 1990s (see Figures 1-1 and 1-2).[44] Of course, revenue and subscriber levels eventually will plateau, and their growth curves will likely follow the general pattern of cable growth. The growth curve will probably follow an S-shaped curve, with a period of rapid growth continuing for the next decade or so, followed by a gradual decrease in growth. The potential for online subscriptions worldwide could reach the hundreds of millions some day, perhaps equaling that of telephone subscription. Much, however, depends on the diffusion of a variety of technologies, including optical fiber and home computers, and information appliances. Moreover, advances in wireless and satellite-based mobile communications may further enlarge the potential subscriber base for online communication services. If these technologies do not progress as rapidly as one might expect in the next decade, then the potential for online subscriptions might plateau at roughly 50 million by 2000.

The U.S. Department of Commerce divides the Information Services industry into three main sectors: electronic information services ($10.2 billion), data processing and network services ($35.6 billion), and computer professional services ($56.3 billion). In 1991, the U.S. Department of Commerce projected that the revenues of the electronic information services sector of the U.S. economy would grow by 20 percent in 1992. The projected growth for data processing and network services for this same period was 13.5 percent and for computer professional services, almost 14 percent.

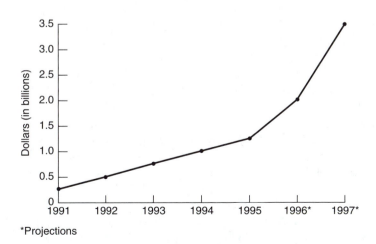

*Projections

FIGURE 1-1   Online Revenue in Billions

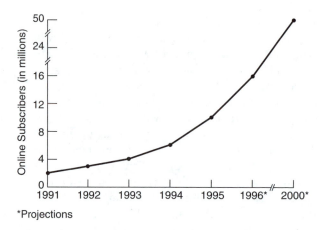

*Projections

FIGURE 1-2   Online Subscribers in Millions

Electronic information services includes five major media: online computer communications, computer disk-read only memory (CD-ROM), magnetic tape, floppy disk, and audiotex, reports the Commerce Department. Online computer services provide the lion's share of electronic information services revenue (78 percent), with audiotex and CD-ROM growing rapidly. Use of magnetic tape and floppy disk for delivery of information services is on the decline.

Although important in the control and creation of the information highway, the other six subindustries within the communication and information industry are less central to the discussion of new media technologies. Therefore, we will provide only a thumbnail sketch of the revenue and structure of these subindustries. Telecommunications services, the largest subindustry, with annual revenues of $175 billion, is also experiencing rapid growth. Although revenues for domestic telecommunications services ($169.9 billion) are growing at just 5.5 percent, revenues from international services ($11.6 billion) are growing at 17.7 percent. Revenues from cellular mobile telephone services ($5.5 billion) are growing at a rate of about 13 percent. Satellite services revenue ($1.5 billion) is growing more slowly at 4.5 percent. This subindustry serves 88 million households and 30 million businesses nationwide.

Printing and publishing, the second largest subindustry, with $172 billion in annual revenues, comprises four main sectors: newspapers, periodicals, book publishing, and commercial printing (U.S. Commerce Department). Newspapers ($34.7 billion) face the gloomiest future of these sectors, with an expected growth of 1 to 2 percent. Periodicals ($21.3 billion) experienced unprecedented growth in the past decade, but saw a slight drop in receipts in constant dollars in the early 1990s. Still, international prospects are good, and growth is expected to be about 2 percent. Book publishing ($16 billion) is growing at about 3 percent, with the marketplace shifting from heavy purchases by state and local schools, as government funding has decreased, to increased personal consumption. Commercial printing is both the largest

($55.7 billion) and fastest growing sector of the printing and publishing subindustry, with an annual growth rate of about 3.5 percent.

Computer equipment and software has total revenues of approximately $160 billion, and is made up of seven specific industries (U.S. Commerce Department). In computer equipment, the four industries are electronic computers, computer storage devices, computer terminals, and computer peripheral equipment. The three software industries are computer programming services, prepackaged software, and computer integrated systems design. Electronic computers includes super-computers, mainframes, midrange, personal, and portable computers. Computer storage devices include magnetic, optical, and tape storage devices. Computer terminals also includes teleprinters. Computer peripheral equipment includes printer, plotter, and graphics display technology.

In the software sector, computer programming services include computer-assisted design, manufacturing, and engineering (U.S. Commerce Department). Prepackaged software includes a variety of consumer and professional off-the-shelf programs, ranging from word processing software such as Microsoft Word to desktop publishing such as QuarkXpress. Computer-integrated systems design includes a variety of developing software applications, such as artificial intelligence (AI), including expert systems, fuzzy logic, and neural networks. AI applications have ranged from military diagnostic systems in Desert Storm to insurance underwriting programs. Although AI revenues were only about $300 million in 1991, rapid growth is projected in the rest of the 1990s. In Europe, revenues are expected to top $2.4 billion for expert systems in 1994; the global market for neural networks was expected to reach $1 billion by 1995.

Telephone and telegraph equipment can be grouped into two categories: network equipment, such as transmission systems and switches, and customer premises equipment (CPE), such as telephone sets, key systems and private branch exchanges (PBXs) (U.S. Commerce Department). Total market revenues were $66.0 in 1992, although consumer demand has been decreasing and industry shipments are expected to decline about 1 percent.

Radio communications and detection equipment is a $55.3 billion industry, with annual growth expected at about 5 percent (U.S. Commerce Department). Four sectors in this industry are particularly notable: satellite communications, mobile cellular radiotelephone systems, wireless personal communications, and fiber optics. The United States controls 65 percent of the world communications satellite market, with France (14 percent), Italy (6 percent), the United Kingdom (5 percent) and Japan (2 percent) trailing far behind. In 1991, U.S. companies held contracts to build fifty-seven of the world's eighty-seven satellite orders. The nine commercial communications satellites built by U.S. firms in 1990 were valued at $1.3 billion. The mobile cellular radiotelephone systems sector is poised for explosive growth in the decade ahead. Cellular phone prices have fallen dramatically (low-end cellphones are priced at less than $100) and the number of users has risen rapidly (7.4 million users at the end of 1991 with 30 percent annual growth), with total revenues of some $5.5 billion in 1991.

Wireless personal communications services (PCS) are likely to experience rapid growth in the decade ahead now that the FCC has completed its auction of 160 megahertz of bandwidth for personal communications services, more than three times the spectrum allotted to cellular telephone systems (U.S. Commerce Department). The pocket-sized phones became available in 1996.[45] Demand for PCS is estimated at 60 to 100 million users by 2000, with PCS devices costing as little as $90 to $200. "The growth potential for wireless data service is enormous," says Benjamin L. Scott, chief operating officer for Bell Atlantic Mobile. "In our markets alone, $1.3 billion is up for grabs.[46] Market analysts at Arthur D. Little predict that the U.S. wireless market could quintuple during the next decade. Gregory Pottie, a wireless technology researcher at the University of California at Los Angeles, estimates the total capacity for the technology at 150 million wireless customers in the United States Convergence is also an important factor in the wireless market, as digital PCS technology is developed, facilitating direct access to the Internet. See Chapter 4 for further discussion of the possible services available through PCS.

The fiber optics industry has grown at roughly 20 percent in recent years (U.S. Commerce Dept.). Companies in the United States have installed more than 8.2 million fiber-kilometers for telecommunications applications. The majority of these fiber-km have been installed by the telephone companies, although cable companies have installed several hundred thousand fiber-km. The total U.S. market was $1.7 billion in 1991, about 40 percent of the world market. There has been much debate about whether fiber is needed to the home to provide a full range of communication services, with the general consensus that fiber backbone and trunk lines and fiber to the curb is all that is needed, given compression technologies and the availability of coaxial cable to the home. This combination of technologies would allow for true video-on-demand, or the video dialtone. Estimates for the cost of fiber to every home in the United States range from $200 billion to $1 trillion, with fiber costing roughly $100 million for every 3,200 km. Fiber is being rapidly deployed around the world, including European countries such as France, Germany, the UK, and the Netherlands, and in East Asia, especially in Japan.

Entertainment, not including over-the-air TV advertising, is a $43.14 billion industry (U.S. Commerce Dept.). Included are the motion picture ($5.01 billion with 1 percent annual growth), music ($7.54 billion, with 7 percent annual growth), and home entertainment subindustries, including home video ($10.8 billion, 4 percent growth), which is really a part of the same industry that produces and distributes motion pictures, and cable television ($19.79 billion, with about 15 percent annual growth). As of 1996, approximately three-fifths of all TV households subscribed to cable TV in the United States. Sixty-one percent of US TV households subscribe to basic cable, up from 46 percent in 1985. Subscription revenues were up 14.5 percent in 1990, with advertising revenues up 25.8 percent. Overall revenue was up 10.5 percent in 1992. New media technologies have important implications for the entertainment industry. The motion picture industry is competing successfully with the home video market, although any gains are due not to increased admissions, but increased admission prices and increased revenues in the international market, where motion pictures remain one of the United States's strongest exports, with more than $6.35 in revenues in 1990. The music subindustry has been transformed by the compact disk (CD); 1991 was a milestone year for the music industry, with CD sales ($3.9 billion) surpassing sales of cassettes. CD unit sales surpassed cassette sales, as well, with 370 million cassettes sold that year, while the number of CD unit sales reached 382 million. Protecting intellectual property rights continues to be one of the greatest challenges facing the music industry. Copyright infringement, including piracy and counterfeiting, have plagued the music industry on the international front, and the problem is likely to worsen as digital technologies take hold, making high-quality copying and illegal distribution easier.

Employment

The Communication and Information Industry officially employs some 4.165 million persons in the United States, according to the 1987 census. Growth trends suggest that, by 1996, the number employed in this field is likely to easily top five million.

Number of Firms

Some 25,000 establishments provide electronic Information Services, although the number is rapidly growing. There are at least two times as many printing and publishing firms, 60,000, although there is less growth in this sector. Approximately 2,000 firms provide telecommunications services in the United States. By mid-1991 there were 1,029 cellular radiotelephone systems; ultimately there will be 1,468 firms, with two in every market. In the entertainment sector, there were 23,700 theater screens, 387 new releases, and theater attendance was 1.06 billion (U.S. Department of Commerce, 1989). As of 1992, some 100,000 establishments sold and rented videocassettes in 1990, although most did not specialize in videocassette sales and rentals. The number of videocassette specialty stores decreased from 29,400 in 1989 to 29,000 in 1990. Blockbuster is the leading provider in this market, with nearly 3,500 stores and $2.9 billion in revenue in 1992—seven times the volume of its closest retail competitor—and 11 percent of the retail sector.[47] There are 1,505 cable television systems in the United States. Most are part of larger companies called multiple system operators (MSOs), the largest being John Malone's Denver-based Tele-Communications, Inc. (TCI).

International Distribution

Unlike many U.S. industries, the information services industry has always had a positive trade balance, and the U.S. Department of Commerce expects this trend to continue. Electronic information services derive 30 percent of their revenue from international markets. Databases are an important part of this global picture. Cuadra Associates, publishers of an annual directory of databases, reports that there are

6,200 databases available worldwide, with 4,700 online and 1,500 in portable format, compared to only 3,369 available in 1987.[48] The United States is easily the largest producer and consumer of databases, producing more than 50 percent of the databases available in the world.

Projected Publishing on a Global Information Highway

Projections for the market size of the global information superhighway range from more than $1 trillion to more than $3.5 trillion in the United States alone by 2000, with the international market even greater. The United States is not alone, however, in building information superhighways. Projects in Europe, Asia, Latin America, and Australia are also underway to construct broadband information systems. Two Europewide systems are already under development and Europe has planned a two-year trial to link seventeen now incompatible telephone networks into a pan-European digital network. A similar European Community project began in the fall of 1993 to test broadband services, including financial transactions, medical, and computer-aided design applications.

Britain, France, and Germany have also planned information highway projects, many involving U.S. companies. In Britain, cable and telephone companies are laying fiber optics throughout most neighborhoods. Some of the companies are Regional Bell Operating Companies (RBOCs), such as Nynex, SBC Communications (formerly Southwestern Bell), and US West, along with two international telephone companies, Singapore Telecom and Bell Canada, as well as U.S. cable operators Tele-Communications, Inc. (TCI), Jones Intercable, Cox Cable, and Comcast. In France, France Telecom has launched four pilot projects to evaluate high-capacity fiber-optic systems to offices and homes. Plaisance Television has planned two interactive cable TV home-shopping channels that will also carry video games. Of course, France's government-sponsored Minitel nationwide videotex service continues to provide home-shopping, banking, and other services, such as an electronic telephone directory. Interestingly, one of the most popular services on Minitel, like many other new technologies, is the blue services, or adult-oriented bulletin boards. Germany's Berlin and Deutsch Bundespost Telekom are testing a variety of services, such as one that will let physicians conduct videoconferences involving patient X-rays and medical histories. Down under, Australia is launching an innovative over-the-air cable television system that will bring the information highway to the entire continent, reports Richard MacDonald, leading media analyst and investment banker.

As these global conglomerates, media magnates, and upstart entrepreneurs race headlong into the future of new media technology, one can't help wondering how these new media barons will explore and develop the unknown boundaries of the electronic frontier. Will their commercial interests completely overwhelm public interests? What balance will they strike between the needs of the few and the needs of the many? Recalling the words of former FCC Chairman Newton Minow, will the new media landscape become anything more than a cultural wasteland exploited for pure commercial profit?

NOTES

[1]Shakespeare, William, Othello, act 3, sc. 4, line 69 (George L. Kitredge ed., Ginn 1941) (1621).

[2]McLuhan, Marshall. *Understanding Media: Extensions of Man.* New York: McGraw-Hill, 1964.

[3]Smith, Anthony, "From Books To Bytes: The Computer and the Library," chapter in John V. Pavlik and Everette E. Dennis (eds) (1993) *Demystifying Media Technology,* Mountain View, CA: Mayfield Publishing.

[4]Bohrman, David and Larry Wood, "Hypermedia at ABC News: Magna: An Electronic Anchor Information System" chapter in John V. Pavlik and Everette E. Dennis, Editors, (1993) *Demystifying Media Technology,* Mayfield Publishing.

[5]Pavlik, John (1993) "Newsroom Convergence." In *Demystifying Media Technology,* John V. Pavlik and Everette E. Dennis, editors.

[6]Wired Journalist: Newsroom Guide to the Internet, A report of the Radio-Television News Directors Foundation, 1996.

[7]Powell, Adam Clayton III, "Getting the Picture." In *Demystifying Media Technology,* John V. Pavlik and Everette E. Dennis, editors (1993). Mountain View, CA: Mayfield Publishing.

[8]Benjamin, Burton, *Niemen Report,* Summer, 1986.

[9]Powell, Adam Clayton III (1993). Speech, Technology Studies seminar hosted by The Freedom Forum Media Studies Center, October 27.

[10]Tomlinson, Don E. "Computer Manipulation and Creation of Images and Sounds: Assessing the Impact." Monograph, The Annenberg Washington Program, Communications Policy Studies, Northwestern University, 1993.

[11]"Bogus Photo in Commercial Gives Virginia Senator a Headache," *New York Times,* October 13, 1996: 17.

[12]Compaine, Benjamin *Understanding New Media: Trends and Issues in Electronic Distribution of Information.* Cambridge, MA: Ballinger, 1984.

[13]Thalhimer, Mark and Marcella Steingart, Editors, *Media Industry News Roundup: Compiled from The Associated Press,* The Freedom Forum Media Studies Center, May 31, 1994.

[14]Fenton, Tom, Freedom Forum report on a speech by Charles Brumback at the 47th World Newspaper Congress and FIEJ Annual General Meeting May 29–June 1, 1994, Vienna, Austria.

[15]Thalhimer, Mark (1992). "The Virtual Newsroom," *Media and Campaign '92: The Homestretch.* The Freedom Forum Media Studies Center: 70.

[16]*Advertising Age,* "A day in the 'virtual' life of a Chiat/Day executive," March 14, 1994.

[17]Postman, Neil. (1986). *Amusing Ourselves to Death.* New York: Penguin Books: 86.

[18]Kennedy, Daniel, "Lost in Space," *Boston Phoenix,* May 7, 1993: 40.

[19]Stephenson, Neal, "Smiley's People," *The New Republic,* Sept. 13, 1993: 26.

[20]Hughes, Janice, "The Changing Multimedia Landscape," *The Media Studies Journal,* The Freedom Forum Media Studies Center, Winter 1994.

[21]Edmund L. Andrews, "Sudden Synergy Among Communications Rivals," *New York Times,* D1, D10, Oct. 21, 1993.

[22]Jeff Greenfield, "American Agenda," *ABC World News Tonight with Peter Jennings,* Sept., 1993.

[23]*Newsweek,* "Forget the Big Mergers," January 24, 1994: 44.

[24]Paul Hilts, "RoundBook Rounds Up Russian Art Treasures," *Publishers Weekly,* July 19, 1993: 24.

[25]*Publish,* "Soviet Art via CD-ROM," January 1994: 13.

[26]Johnson, Kirk, "Acorns Sprout Among the Oaks Of the Telecommunications Field," *New York Times,* July 5, 1994: A1, B2.

[27]Quinlan, Joe (interview), 1992.

[28]http://www.boston.com/wgbh/pages/frontline/smoke/interviews/bagdikian1.html

[29]Smith, Anthony (1992). *Age of Behemoths.* New York: The 20th Century Fund.

[30]Moeller, Philip, "The age of convergence," *American Journalism Review,* January/February 1994: 22.

[31]Auletta, Ken (1991). *Three Blind Mice: How the Networks Lost Their Way.* Random House.

[32]Auletta, Ken, "John Malone: Flying Solo," *New Yorker,* February 7, 1994.

[33]Higgins, John M. *Multichannel News,* Sept., 1993, p. 1.

[34]Gilder, George. "Telecosm: Digital Darkhorse—Newspapers," *Forbes ASAP,* Oct. 25, 1993: 138–149.

[35]Baer, Walter, (1991) Technology Studies Seminar hosted by The Freedom Forum Media Studies Center.

[36]Todd, Russell G. Communication and Society Seminar, The Freedom Forum Media Studies Center, 1992.

[37]Bloomberg, Michael, "The Next Generation," Technology Studies Seminar for Newsroom Managers hosted by The Freedom Forum Media Studies Center. September 15, 1993.

[38]Winkler, Matthew (1993). Speaker, "Real-Time Information Services," Technology Studies Seminar, The Freedom Forum Media Studies Center, Sept. 15, 1993.

[39]Sagan, Paul, Lecture in Exploring New Media, hosted by John V. Pavlik, Columbia University Center for New Media, November 21, 1996.

[40]Mandel, Michael J. "The Information Economy: The Digital Juggernaut," *Business Week,* Special 1994 Bonus Issue: 22, 23.

[41]Miles, Tim, Annual Report, Office of Computers, U.S. Department of Commerce, 1995; www.stat-usa.gov/BEN/gto1/compeqmt.txt

[42]Commerce Department, Bureau of Labor Statistics, Morgan Stanley & Co., 1994.

[43]"U.S. Industrial Outlook '92: Business Forecasts for 350 Industries," U.S. Department of Commerce, January, 1992.

[44]"Wired," *Wall Street Journal Reports,* November 15, 1993.

[45]McArroll, Thomas, "Betting on the Sky," *Time,* November 22, 1993: 57.

[46]Gibbs, Wayt W. "When Cells Divide: Making space for the next wave of wireless communications," *Scientific American,* December, 1993: 44–45.

[47]Rohter, Larry, "Florida Entrepreneur Plans to Challenge Disney World," *New York Times,* April 4, 1994.

[48]Cuadra Associates, Directory of On Line Databases, Boston, MA, 1994.

2

The Internet: Today's Information Superhighway

INTERNET

The Internet is a vast global interconnection of some 100,000 computer networks around the world all of which use a common set of technical protocols (called Transmission Control Protocol/Internet Protocols or TCP/IP) in routing data across those networks. Many have called the Internet the prototype for the information superhighway. No one institution or individual owns the Internet, and no one specifically controls it. Thus, it has also been described as somewhat akin to the lawless wild west of the 1800s, or the unregulated radio broadcasting of the early 1920s. Every device connected to the Internet must have a unique TCP/IP address, which cannot be shared with any other device.

Chapter 2 is devoted to a discussion of the Internet for three primary reasons. First, all of the functions described in the opening chapter of the book, including information acquisition, storage, distribution, and presentation, come together in the technologies of the Internet. Second, more interest, whether commercial, cultural, or conceptual, has been generated by the dynamic growth of the Internet and its World Wide Web in recent years than any other new media technology since the invention of television. Finally, the Internet is more than a set of technological tools; it is a metaphor for the digital age.

The origins of the Internet lie in the Department of Defense's Advanced Research Projects Agency (ARPAnet), created in 1969 as the first national, packet-switched computer network. Some point to even earlier origins in research at MIT in the early 1960s. The technology that enabled the development of the Internet is a combination of several developments, including digitization, packet-switching, and the Internet address protocols. Packet-switching is perhaps the most important of these developments, and involves a replacement of the traditional telecommunications networking technology of circuit-switching. In a circuit-switched network, any call between two points on the network establishes or requires a complete, dedicated connection. This is a very expensive method of communication. In packet-switching, digital data, whether voice, video, or any other form of content, are transmitted as discrete packets and sent over any available route in the network, and then reassembled at the designated receiver location, or IP address. It's a cheap, efficient, and fast method of transmission. An IP address includes three main parts; a network number, an optional subnetwork number, and an Internet host number. The value of the packet-switched network to the Defense Department is simple: In the event of war, it is essential to maintain communications. It is relatively simple to knock out communications based on circuit-switching; all one has to do is interrupt the circuit anywhere between points A and B. In contrast, it is almost impossible to knock out a packet-switched network, because communication (i.e., the digital packets) can flow in any of an almost infinite and unpredictable number of directions (i.e., routes) to reach its ultimate destination. This, of course, is a double-edged sword. Packet-switching also makes it extremely difficult to intercept a communication sent over the network (thus making the Internet an attractive haven for a variety of high-tech criminals). It also makes it difficult to be sure exactly what route a message (or its component packets) might have taken in getting to its final destination, and determining whether someone may have overheard or tampered with the message while en route.

The Internet was born officially in 1983, when ARPAnet divided into military and civilian components, with the civilian component giving rise to the Internet. At that time, the National Science Foundation (NSF) established the NSFnet as the research backbone network for scholarly investigators at U.S. universities.[1] For more than a decade NSFnet served as the backbone of the Internet, but in October 1994, the NSF began converting its network to private hands.

The concepts that gave birth to the Internet are credited to Vinton G. Cerf, Senior Vice President for Internet Architecture at MCI Communications and former president of The Internet Society, and Robert E. Kahn, President of the Corporation for National Research Initiatives (CNRI).[2] In the 1970s, Cerf, then an assistant professor at Stanford University in the Computer Science and Electrical Engineering Departments, and Kahn, then at the Advanced Research Projects Agency (ARPA), coinvented the TCP/IP protocols and codesigned the basic architecture of the Internet.

With the privatization of the Internet, institutions and private individuals seeking to use the Internet provide increasingly full support for the Internet through access fees based largely on their level of usage. Today, virtually all commercial online services such as America Online provide an Internet connection as part of their service, and have given rise to an important cottage industry of Internet Service Providers (ISP). Because of the structure of the Internet, users pay only local telecommunications charges for accessing the Internet, regardless of whether their messages go across town or across the planet, and regardless of the amount of data transmitted in their messages. This fee structure continues to evolve with the increasing privatization of the Internet.

For most of its history, the Internet was "an underground movement of sorts— a cyberspace hangout where researchers, students, and techies spent hours tapping into databases and discussing the most esoteric of subjects in electronic forums," reports Evan I. Schwartz.[3] With its global popularization and commercialization, the Internet has undergone something of a transformation. It has emerged as the first truly democratic medium of communication. It has also lost some of its creative spark and anything goes style. Many of the early Internet pioneers now long for a return to the early, lawless days.

The Net Effect

The Internet is transforming how journalists and other communication professionals do their work, particularly the methods they use to gather and distribute information. For journalists, the Internet has had direct effects on how they report or cover their beats, including finding sources and leads, as well as how they tell stories. Reporting in the *Quill,* a trade journal for journalists, John S. Makulowich writes, "The Internet allows you to use resources better, use better resources, and use fewer person hours to produce your product."[4] John Battelle, managing editor of *Wired*, a magazine reporting on the digital age of communication, agrees, adding, "I do about 70 percent of my editing and communications with writers over the Internet. Our publication certainly would not exist in its current form without it." Major metropolitan daily newspapers are also being transformed by the Internet. Steve Doig, associate editor or research for the *Miami Herald* says the Internet has helped him do his job "faster, better, and cheaper." He explains, "I also use the Internet to access via anonymous FTP (file transfer protocol, which allows you to get files such as text, programs, and pictures from other computers) to thousands of lines of SAS (a statistical package) code dealing with census analysis. And I have access via Telnet to a giant database of 1990 and 1980 census data." Tom Regan, columnist/editorial writer for *The Daily News,* Halifax, Nova Scotia, Canada, says the Internet has completely changed the nature of his work. "The research tools possible with Internet have allowed me to create much more substantive articles." Regan used the Internet to research an article on the debt/deficit crisis in Canada, and gathered evidence that the crisis was "more fancy than fact. I used the Internet to gather most of the facts and quotes used for the articles."

Some news organizations have begun experimenting with Internet applications as a means to increase audience involvement and interactivity. One fascinating example comes from network television, a news medium some had given up for dead in the early 1990s. During the final week of 1993, NBC *Nightly News* ran a series entitled "Almost 2001." As part of the series NBC gave out its Internet address, NBC.COM, for the first time on Monday, December 27.

By noon on Thursday, December 30, NBC had received more than 4,000 replies from all corners of the world. Within a few weeks, the number of responses had topped 10,000. Joe Harris, former director, Information Technology, NBC-TV, says the phenomenon triggered a great deal of discussion of the subject of television and new media. He believes the NBC-TV effort illustrates the birth of Marshall McLuhan's global village. "Last message I read last night was from CROATIA!" noted Harris in an Internet message to the author. Among the other 4,000 messages:

- About time you saw us. Show more.
- Nice story on the I-net I certainly thought it was interesting that I was ON internet while your show just came on talking about it! How about more news from cyberspace?
- Could you blow up more trucks. That was cool.
- Hey! Welcome to the information super-highway!
- I saw your special this evening on the Internet and thought I'd drop you a line. Keep up the good work. America is shrinking!!
- We're all just crash dummies in the information highway.

One message was particularly moving, Harris says, reflecting on the political changes of Eastern Europe and the end of the Cold War.

From: From Russia, with love

Dear Americans,

my warmest season greetings from St. Petersburg, Russia Please, keep up your great work helping us out of the deep hole we got into about 70 years ago! I'm sure it will be rewardable for both nations!

Cheers,
software developer

Still, the Internet is not a panacea for the electronic journalist, nor for the information consumer. Much information is not available in the online world, and many sources cannot be reached through cyberspace. Some online searches can produce massive amounts of information, but little usable knowledge. Explains Frederick Williams, professor at the University of Texas at Austin and an expert in networked communications: "Going into the World Wide Web is like going through someone else's trash."[5]

As usage of the Internet has swelled (see Figures 2-1 and 2-2), so have problems of heavy demand. "Call it a cautionary tale for the information age: The nation's increasingly popular data highway is beginning to groan under the load of rush-hour traffic," writes John Markoff.[6] Once the exclusive domain of computer scientists, programmers, and engineers, usage of the Internet has grown into the many millions as anyone with a computer and modem can access the Internet easily and cheaply.

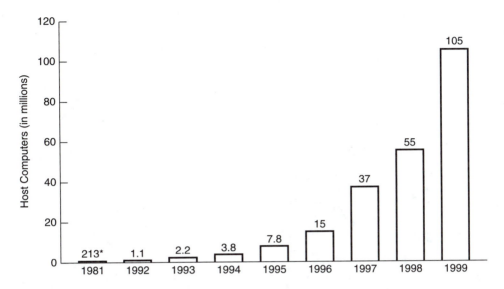

*In 1981 there were a total of 213 host computers; source: the Internet Society (www.isoc.org)

FIGURE 2-1

Consequently, much highly valued information that has been available freely to anyone on the Internet has become often inaccessible to everyone as "a clamoring horde overwhelms the computer databases."[7] Traffic jams on the Internet are severely limiting access to a variety of databases and online services, including National Weather Service satellite photos, computer software, online searches of the catalogue of the Library of Congress, and free access to filings with the Securities and Exchange Commission.[8] Examples of the growth in usage and the resulting traffic jams include demand for the National Center for Supercomputer Applications' World Wide Web home page, a service that responds to inquiries to an electronic library. The number of daily requests grew from 100,000 in June, 1993 to almost 400,000 in October. Similarly, the amount of information retrieved using a popular search program called Gopher increased in 1993 by more than 400 percent, to nearly 200 billion bytes per month, the equivalent of some seven million newspaper pages. MSEN Inc., an Ann Arbor, Michigan, company made information on career counseling available free through the Internet and usage skyrocketed from 1,000 inquiries a day in June, when the service began, to 12,000 a day on Monday, November 1, 1993. Without a more powerful computer, MSEN says it will have to deny access to the system to any additional requests. Internet traffic is even subject to rubbernecking delays. When word got out in October, 1993, that a computer intruder had broken into the Panix Public Access Network intent on stealing passwords, "thousands of curiosity seekers decided to take a look at the Panix network—the digital equivalent of driving by the scene of an accident."[9] Those "driving by" used a program on

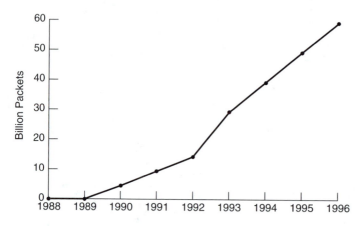

FIGURE 2-2

the Panix system, called in computer jargon a "finger demon," a program that lets hundreds of users remotely determine everyone currently on the system. But when thousands called up the program, the system crashed and Panix ground to a halt. "It was a traffic jam caused by rubberneckers on the nation's data highway," said Marc Rotenberg of the Computer Professionals for Social Responsibility, a Washington-based public interest group.

Flamed on the Internet

As the virtual community of the Internet has grown, so has it developed its own rules for self-governance. Like any other community, it has developed its own mores and norms, and those who violate proper "netiquette" are promptly and resoundingly chastised, what netters call "flamed." Getting flamed on the Internet can range from a mild verbal reprimand from other netters to having your computer subjected to a digital assault, the equivalent of an electronic mob or a virtual lynch mob. Tactics range from receiving thousands of e-mail messages clogging your mail box, to electronic mail bombs to RECEIVING A MESSAGE TYPED ALL IN CAPITAL LETTERS (the 'net equivalent of yelling at someone).

One case of flaming whose implications stretched far beyond the boundaries of cyberspace involved a law firm that used the Internet "Usenet" as an advertising medium—a purpose in violation of traditional guidelines of "netiquette." In April, 1994, Laurence A. Canter and Martha S. Siegel flooded the Internet "Usenet" with advertisements for their Phoenix law firm, Canter and Siegel, which specializes in immigration law. Such random posting of ads or other messages on the Internet is known as "spamming," (for the brand of canned meat that splatters messily if thrown at an object), and is frowned upon, although not prohibited by law. The ad offered help in entering the government's so-called Green Card Lottery, for a fee of $95 for individuals and $145 for couples.

Usenet is one of the biggest user groups on the Internet, with more than 20 million users out of the 50 million or so Internet users worldwide. The response to the ad was overwhelming, especially at first when most people who replied to the message expressed their outrage at using the Internet for such blatant commercial services. Many were upset that the limited bandwidth of the Internet might become clogged with commercial messages, at the expense of more substantive dialogue. "Unsolicited advertising on the global Internet is as acceptable as junk fax is in the real world," notes Robert Raisch, president of the Internet Company and chairman of the Electronic Newsstand, a joint effort of the Internet Company and the *New Republic* magazine.[10] Raisch and others would prefer to group advertising channels under a broad "market" directory on Usenet, with a variety of subdirectories for different categories of products and services. Advertising and other commercial enterprises on the Internet are in fact common and widely accepted, as long as they are done within established rules.

Flaming responses to the Canter and Seigel spam attack included electronic mail bombs designed to knock out targeted computers, or robotic callers, such as the Phantom Phone Beeper, who programmed a robot to automatically call the Canter and Siegel office forty times a night, stuffing their voice-mailbox with electronic trash.[11] Other negative responses included a flood of critical faxes and the posting of digitized photos of the couple on computer bulletin boards throughout the world, "like 'Wanted' posters on the electronic frontier."[12] In one case, a twenty-five-year-old Norwegian programmer, named Arnt Gulbrandsen, used his computer from halfway around the world to "launch the electronic equivalent of a Patriot missile: each time the law firm sent out an electronic advertisement, his computer automatically sent out a message ordering that the firm's transmission be intercepted and destroyed," reports technology writer Peter H. Lewis.[13]

Canter and Siegel are unfazed by the negative backlash and attention their efforts have drawn, and have vowed to not only continue their efforts online but to expand them. "In the beginning there were more negative than positive responses," admits Ms. Siegel.[14] "That is shifting. Now almost every response we're getting is positive." And the responses have come in rapidly and in great volume. The couple received some 20,000 responses by the middle of May, 1994, and were receiving messages at a rate of nearly 1,000 a day. Canter and Siegel are now collaborating on a book explaining how others can use the Internet as an advertising medium. The couple is also considering filing a lawsuit against some of the flamers for defamation of character. They have even started a firm called Cybersell to advertise other companies' products on Usenet. The new company's first product: super-oxygenated water. "You drink it, and the fact that it has additional oxygen gives you additional energy and promotes the healing process," Siegel says.[15] What all this means for the future of the Internet culture and its spirit of frontier freedom is uncertain, but sellers of snake oil, hair tonics, and x-ray glasses may have reason to smile.

Many industry analysts see the next decade as a period of sharp growth in the business usage of the Internet. The *Kiplinger Washington Letter* reports that large firms will find many uses as the Internet becomes easier to learn and navigate with services such as Mosaic emerging. "Electronic mail . . . cheaper than phones, espe-cially for overseas business. Exchanging computer files. Transmitting software from office to office. And finding information . . . gov't rules, bids and grants, SEC filings."[16] Small firms have found commercial applications of the Internet even easier, perhaps because it is easier for small firms to adapt quickly to new ways of doing business. One interesting example is a company called Amazon.com, a book-store whose physical space began in a garage in the Bay area, but whose virtual storefront is global via the World Wide Web. In early 1996, Amazon.com offered roughly a million titles, and by the end of 1996, offered shoppers more than two million titles, far more books than offered by even the largest outlet of Barnes & Nobles or any other national bookstore chain.

One man who is especially confident about the future of the Internet is James H. Clark, the former Stanford University Professor who founded Silicon Graphics, Inc. and led it to the forefront of the computer workstation market. "I believe that the Internet is the information highway," Clark says.[17] "I'm religious about this. I don't think it's cable television." Clark's confidence translated into the creation of Netscape Communications, whose first product, Navigator, propelled the World Wide Web from scientific obscurity into mainstream culture and commerce around the world. It also made its founder and his founding partner, Marc Andreeson, in-stant multimillionaires when Netscape posted its first public stock offering in 1995.

Intranets

One of the fastest growing areas of the Internet involves what are called "Intranets." Intranets are essentially Internet applications developed for internal computer networks. Intranets have all the capabilities of Internet applications, rang-ing from electronic mail to the World Wide Web. The difference is, only the mem-bers of the organization have access to the Intranet. Many organizations are particularly concerned about protecting the security of their internal communica-tions, and Intranets provide a powerful solution. Among the providers of leading Intranet applications are, not surprisingly, the providers of the leading Web brows-ers, Microsoft and Netscape.

World Wide Web

Perhaps the most important and fastest growing part of the Internet is the World Wide Web, an interconnected set of computer servers on the Internet that conform to a set of network interface protocols created by Tim Berners-Lee of CERN, the Euro-pean high-energy physics laboratory in Geneva, Switzerland.[18] The Web began as an electronic library for physicists and grew into an "international bazaar."[19] Any individual or organization with Internet access can create what is called a "home page" document or site on the Web, as long as they use the programming protocols esbtablished at CERN, and since updated at least a half dozen times. The WWW protocols include assigning the home page a Uniform Resource Locator (URL) based on its TCP/IP Internet address, and using what is known as hypertext transport protocol (http) that enables the standardized transfer of e-mail and other text, audio, and video files. URLs include selecting domain name, which is the unique term that identifies a site, such as Columbia, IBM, or WhiteHouse; domain names are registered for two years with an organization called InterNic at a cost of $200 (registration was free until 1996); the suffix after the domain name may be .com for commercial, .edu for education, .org for organization, or .gov for governmental. For example, the URL for Columbia University is

http://www.columbia.edu

In addition, each Web document tagged with "hypertext markup language," or HTML, allows automatic routing from one electronic document to another, whether elsewhere in the same Web document or anywhere else in the entire World Wide Web, simply by clicking the mouse on highlighted text.

HTML Primer

HTML is the Hypertext Markup Language used to format World Wide Web documents. HTML is the basic grammar for creating documents on the Web. Instructions, called directives, are enclosed in brackets.[20] For example, <TITLE> Exploring New Media </TITLE> illustrates the HTML directive for formatting the title of the author's Web site for a course called "Exploring New Media" that he taught in the fall of 1996. Note that the closing directive is the same as the opening directive but is preceded by a forward slash, or /.

Five basic HTML directives for creating a simple Web site are:

1. **TITLE** contains the window title.
2. **H#** formats a header in large bold type.
3. **P** marks the end of a paragraph.
4. **IMG** designates a picture to be placed on the page.
5. **A** creates a hypertext link to another page.

Some other directives that are commonly featured in many Web sites include:

- **HR** places a line, or Horizontal Rule, across the page,
- **B** formats bold face type, and,
- **I** formats italics.

Here's an example of HTML commands used in creating the author's online course syllabus:

```
<TITLE>Exploring New Media</TITLE>
<H1>Syllabus</H1>
<B>Journalism 6010</B>
<I>Fall 1996</I>
</P>
```

```
<HR>
<IMG SRC="/NewMedia/pavlik.jpeg">
<A HREF="http://www.ctr.columbia.edu/vi/papers/citipres.htm">http://
www.ctr.columbia.edu/vi/papers/citipres.htm</A>
```

Growth of the Web

Web applications grew rapidly beginning in 1994, and show little sign of stopping, with millions of home pages sprouting up in a variety of places and venues all around the world, ranging from the city of Palo Alto, California to the Whitehouse in Washington, DC to the largest bank in Istanbul, Turkey. The Web today contains more than six million documents, pages, or sites. This figure was obtained by conducting an advanced search on Infoseek for documents containing "www" in the URL on December 13, 1996; this is a conservative estimate because it does not include a variety of sites whose URLs do not contain www, the most frequently used Web location identifier. One of the most remarkable home pages was created by Navy physicist Richard Bocker, whose Planet Earth Home Page for the City of San Diego quickly became the nineteenth most popular home page anywhere on the Internet, with users accessing nearly a billion bytes of information about San Diego each day, rivaling Playboy and Penthouse for most daily "hits" or impressions. "Webmaster" Bocker created his home page as a tool for organizing information he needed for his own online work, but worldwide interest grew as fellow network mavens "surfed the net" and found their electronic way to southern California.

Browser Wars

Mosaic, Netscape, and Beyond.   Created by a crack young team of programmers at the National Center for Supercomputing Applications (NCSA) at the University of Illinois in Champaign-Urbana, Mosaic was the "browser" that started it all, so to speak. "Mosaic is the first window into cyberspace," said Larry Smarr, NCSA director.[21] Before Mosaic, finding one's way around the Internet required mastery of a variety of arcane commands and addresses, such as "Telnet 192.100.81.100." Based on the World Wide Web protocols developed at CERN, Mosaic provided a graphical user interface that let users simply click a mouse on images or words to select text, images, or sounds from the many databases available on the Internet. In its first year of existence, hundreds of thousands of Internet users downloaded copies of Mosaic, making it one of the most widely used applications in network computing history.

Jim Clark, the former Stanford professor who founded Silicon Graphics, Inc., was quickly convinced that Mosaic is one of the keys to unlocking the riches of the Internet. So committed to his vision is Clark that he started a company called Mosaic Communications Corporation in Mountain View, California.[22] Cofounder of the company with Clark was Marc Andreessen, a twenty-two-year-old computer designer who helped create Mosiac as part of the original Mosaic design team at the National Center for Supercomputing Applications. Clark and Andreessen renamed their company, however, on the release of their first commercial Web browser: The new company is called Netscape Communications, and their product, Netscape Navigator. Navigator quickly established itself as the premier browser, but just as quickly drew stiff competition. In particular, Microsoft's Bill Gates decided to reinvent his company as "an Internet company," and throwing many millions of dollars into program development, launched MS Internet Explorer, a competing browser. Today, Explorer and Navigator (soon to be replaced by "Communicator") offer cross-platform access to the Web for anyone using a Macintosh or PC, whether Windows or Windows 95. Both browsers feature an "open platform architecture," which permits anyone to develop software plug-ins for use on the Web. This is particularly important as the Web continues to be a hothouse incubator for new commercial and cultural media applications, ranging from digital cash to streaming video. More on these later.

Java.   One very important new tool for the Web that is supported by either of the major browsers, (as well as some browsers with a smaller share of the market), is a programming language called Java, created by James Gosling, Distinguished Engineer at Sun Microsystems. Technically speaking, Java is an object-oriented, platform-independent programming language, which distinguishes it from other languages such as C Plus Plus or Perl.[23] For programmers, Java is a liberating breakthrough. Programmers can embed Java applets (as they are called) in a Web page, and, with a Java-based browser such as Navigator or Explorer, can operate the program, thus ending the decade-long quest for software interoperability across PCs and Macs. "Java applets do not have to be profound," notes Peter Lewis of *Cybertimes.* "They can also be decorative, like flapping flags, bouncing balls, shimmering text or turning gears." Java applets can be useful, however, being employed to create smart interactive games, such as crossword puzzles offering hints based on the letters you enter. Java can be used to create constantly updated information like sports scores, headlines, stock quotes, or text-to-voice synthesizers. Not surprisingly, nearly every successful Web site employs Java applets, from www.nytimes.com/ to www.yahoo.com, for better or for worse.

Illustrating the creative opportunities afforded by Java, consider these prize-winning entries in Sun Microsystems's Java Applet contest. Grand Prize winner: Pythagoras's Haven: "An animated graphical proof of the famous theorem. A great example of an educational applet that uses animation, text, and graphics to explain the proof."[24]

Second Place: Chernobyl Reactor: "This applet lets you control a nuclear power plant. Excellent use of animation, audio, images, and graphics. It is really nice that you can actually avoid a meltdown by correctly operating the various valves and pumps."[25]

Cookies (Not Chocolate Chip).   One important software tool developed for use with Web browsers such as Netscape Navigator or MS Internet Explorer is called a cookie (also called magic or persistent cookies). Cookies are essentially files of information collected from the client or user computer, based on information stored or cached in his or her Web browser. When a user visits a Web site running a cookie, the cookie will extract certain information from the user's browser. Typically, this might be information stored under the user's general or network preferences, and might contain information about the user's IP address or domain name. Cookies are important for a number of reasons, including their ability to automatically personalize Web-based information for a client. For instance, advertisers find cookies increasingly useful in producing targeted marketing communications, based on information extracted from a cookie. Cookies are also useful for site managers interested in obtaining more accurate data on the numbers of visitors to their sites.

Cookies are stored in different places on a client computer, depending on a number of variables, including which browser and operating system the user is running.

- On a Mactintosh computer, Netscape Navigator keeps cookies in a text file called MagicCookie located in the Netscape Preferences folder.
- On a computer running Windows, Navigator puts cookies in a text file called cookie.txt, in the Navigator directory
- Internet Explorer puts cookies in a directory called Cookies in the C:\WINDOWS folder.

Because they generate information about the individuals visiting a site, cookies have aroused concern about privacy. The Center for Democracy and Technology (CDT) provides an impressive privacy demonstration page that uses cookies to extract and display information about those who visit its Web site.[26] When the author visited the CDT demonstration page, the site instantly reported:

You are affiliated with Columbia University.
You're located around New York, NY.
Your computer is a PowerMac.
Your Internet browser is Netscape.
You are coming from off-pavlik.jrn.columbia.edu.

Some would say this information is relatively harmless. CDT notes that the information its site presents is only the tip of the electronic iceberg. Cookies can extract information stored in cache on a client computer to determine as many as the ten most recent Web pages he or she has visited.

In any event, there are a number of mechanisms available to those interested in knowing when a site uses cookies or in disabling them. In Netscape, for example, a user can select an option in the "Protocols" section of "Network Preferences" to "Show alert before accepting a cookie." If this seems a bit complicated and cumbersome, Phil Zimmerman, the developer of Pretty Good Privacy (PGP) encryption software has developed a cookie blocking program called PGP Cookie Cutter, unveiled at the Internet World trade show in New York, December, 1996. Operating in a fashion akin to Caller ID blocking, PGP Cookie Cutters turn off any cookie at any Web site a user might visit, much to the disappointment of those interested in digital direct marketing.

Lost in Hyperspace: Navigating the Web

"And all I ask is a tall ship and a star to steer her by."
—JOHN MASEFIELD, SEA FEVER, 1902[27]

To those who have spent much time exploring any of the growing number of World Wide Web sites, the Internet or any other part of the online world, there is little need to explain the dangers of getting lost in cyberspace. With an increasingly polluted sea of options and a plethora of uniquely designed user interfaces, it is increasingly difficult to find one's way through this digital world. Sometimes, it is even hard to retrace one's electronic footsteps to exit an online system or a multimedia service. "Is the command 'exit' or 'quit'? Or is it 'logout'?" are all too familiar questions for even the savviest computer maven.

Search Engines.   In response, a growing number of people and companies have developed increasingly powerful search engines for the Web. Search engines use what is called a "spider," a type of computer software agent that roams the Web automatically, visiting site after site, reviewing its content, cataloging each site, and then creating a proprietary database of the millions of pages on the Web. Users of the search engines can then search for any site catalogued in the search engine. Because no search engine uses exactly the same spider and no two engines have exactly the same database of Web sites, it is frequently important to search for Web sites using more than one search engine. A second approach to cataloguing Web sites is called an Internet directory. Here, a small number of services have created hierarchical directories of Web sites, organized in encyclopedic form. Among the popular directories are the Internet World Directory and the Internet Directory. The W3W Internet Email Directory offers a specialized service for those interested in tracking down e-mail addresses for any individual with Internet access.

Among the most popular and useful search engines are:

> Yahoo.com, with 39.3% Internet audience reach
> Webcrawler.com, 29.2% reach
> Excite.com, 18.1% reach
> Infoseek.com, 18.8% reach
> Lycos.com, 17.7% reach[28]

Serving as the gateway to the World Wide Web, search engines have become among the most popular Web sites in general. With its 39.3 percent audience reach, Yahoo.com is surpassed in reach only by the leading browser, Netscape.com, which delivers 40.4 percent audience reach. The rapid rise of MS Internet Explorer may soon affect this ranking.

Most search engines operate using keyword searching, although some offer higher-order capabilities, such as Boolean searching (e.g., search for "Professor" and "Pavlik," but not "John") or "concept" based searching by employing an electronic thesaurus to find synonyms. Web search engines also sometimes offer other services, such as site reviews of popular Web sites. These reviews are often written by freelance journalists hired by the search engines to visit sites and write short abstracts (about fifty words) describing the site and its capabilities. The search engines themselves are among the most heavily visited Web sites; on Nov. 5, 1996, Election Day, Yahoo registered more than a million hits or visits on average every hour, partly because they posted real-time election returns, but also because of its popularity as a search tool. As a result, most feature banner advertising (the Web equivalent of billboards). A study reported by Hotwired, the Internet media service of Wired Ventures, Inc., suggests that banners perhaps should not to be considered "the Rodney Dangerfield of interactive advertising." Conducted by Millward Brown International, the study indicates that banners shape the attitudes of computer users because they make measurable advertising impressions. Some recognizable banners, such as AT&T Worldnet or Dockers khaki pants, are similar to television and radio commercials in building awareness of, preference for, and purchase intention of a brand.[29] AltaVista.com (part of Digital.com from Digital Equipment Corporation) is another interesting search engine, offering some advanced search capabilities, but it has not yet achieved extensive audience reach. Another interesting but more specialized search engine is the Zip2 Online Yellow Pages, introduced in September 1996. Zip2.com offers users the capability to search accurately for any of more than 16 million businesses nationwide, and obtain precise door-to-door directions to that business. Conversely, Zip2 offers businesses the online capability to reach and be found by anyone anywhere in the world. Business data are provided to Zip2 by American Business Information. Maps are generated using Java-enhanced applets. Zip2 has developed partnerships with more than fifty newspapers and many media companies, including Knight-Ridder and Landmark Communications.

Aware of how the search engines work (typically counting the number of occurrences of a word within a site, and then presenting the sites ranked according to their frequency match with the user specified search term/s), some programmers are finding ways to manipulate the search results. One intriguing method is to implant particularly popular topical search terms within a site. For example, a political campaign site, Webmaster (the name for the person who manages a Web site), might embed the term *politics* hundreds of times behind an opaque java applet in his or her Web site. Thus, someone viewing the site would not see the term *politics* repeated hundreds of times. However, the search engine might very well put this site at the top of the list for anyone conducting a search using the term *politics* as a keyword.

Conversely, search engines such as Yahoo now engage in a practice called "selling" or "buying" words for companies who seek to have their banner ads seen by the target audience. The process involves a company, such as Hearst News Media, buying a word, such as *food*. Whenever a person using Yahoo enters the word *food* as a search term, up will pop the Hearst banner ad. This clever tactic enables Hearst and other news media marketers to refine their communication efforts and reach only their intended audience (Hearst has a number of food-related news media products, including http://www.epicurious.com/).

What's News on the Net

The growth of the Internet and the World Wide Web, coupled with the rise of easy to use network applications, have spawned almost unbridled interest in launching content-based Web sites by a variety of content providers, ranging from entertainment to news. Even nontraditional content providers such as Microsoft have found the lure of content-based network applications on the Web irresistible; witness the ambitious 1996 debut of Microsoft's Slate (with noted journalist Michael Kingsley serving as editor) and the 1997 launch of MS Sidewalk. Tables 2-1 and 2-2 present some noteworthy news sites on the Web. Included are those created by a variety of traditional and not-so-traditional news providers for general news, business news, politics, and sports, as well as some other selected categories. Some of the sites listed here are supported by advertising and others by subscription, but the economic model for content distribution on the Web is still evolving, and will be discussed in further detail in Chapter 8. The selected sites are presented here because they have demonstrated particularly innovative, quality, original news content, content created exclusively for Web distribution, although most also present content distributed via other media (e.g., television, radio, or newspaper). These sites have experimented with technology and with new storytelling models. For example, NPR was one of the first to use streaming audio to make its radio reports available via the Web. The Mercury Center published its critically acclaimed series on the alleged CIA crack houses in Los Angeles in an expanded, layered format (i.e., making documents and other original source material available to interested readers), which not only would be impossible in a printed product, but gave the story enough "legs" to survive and eventually become a national story and one that has drawn official interest from various branches of the federal government.

Not surprisingly, the most popular topic for online news consumers is technology. A national study of online users conducted by the Pew Research Center in 1996 shows that almost half (46 percent) of online users look for news about technology, followed by more than a third who look for science and health news (42 percent), business news (38 percent), entertainment news (36 percent), weather (34 percent), political news (33 percent), sports (33 percent), international news (32 percent), and one-fifth who look for local news (19 percent).[30] Webzines (as magazines are called on the Web) are another popular destination among the digital literati. One of the most visited sites is HotWired, the electronic version of *Wired Magazine* (http://www.hotwired.com/frontdoor/guide/). HotWired is known for both its critical and insightful commentary on new media issues, as well as for its innovation with new media applications, such as its popular intelligent agent, called HotBot.

Also increasingly popular are sites that provide online guides to entertainment in major cities in the United States. In New York, for example, at least a dozen city guide sites now exist. These sites include:

- Lycos
- Most New York

TABLE 2-1   Selected News Sites on the World Wide Web

Free/Advertiser-Supported Online News

National
ABC: www.abctelevision.com/home.html
CBS Eye on the Net: www.cbs.com/
NBC: www.nbc.com/
MSNBC: www.msnbc.com/splash.asp
CNN Interactive: cnn.com/
National Public Radio: www.npr.org/
The Los Angeles Times: www.latimes.com/
The Washington Post Online: www.washingtonpost.com/
News.Com: www.news.com/
New York Times: www.nytimes.com/ ($35 for international access)
Time Warner Pathfinder (includes Time, CNN): http://pathfinder.com

Regional
The Mercury Center: www.sjmercury.com/ (limited free content)
The Nando Times: www.nando.net/newsroom/nt/nando.html
The Star Tribune Online: www.startribune.com/
The Chicago Tribune: www.chicago.tribune.com/
New Jersey Online: www.nj.com/atnjo/index.html
Dallas Morning News: www.dallasnews.com/NJ and Dallasnews include access to The
     Wire (Web site introduced in 1996 by the Associated Press): wire.ap.org/APwire/

Aggregator
CRAYON: crayon.net/

Business News
Boomberg Personal: www.bloomberg.com/
Dow Jones Business News: bis.dowjones.com/
Reuters: www.reuters.com/

Subscription
The Herald Link: www.herald.com/
The Wall Street Journal Interactive Edition: www.wsj.com/

- New York City CitySearch
- The Insider
- New York City Reference
- New York Now
- New York Sidewalk
- New York Times on the Web
- Resident Publications Online
- Timeout
- Total New York
- Village Voice Worldwide Plans

TABLE 2-2   Specialized News Sites on the World Wide Web

Technology News
pcweek: www.pcweek.com
c/net central: www.cnet.com
techweb: www.allny.com/business/technews.html
information week online: techweb.cmp.comiw/610/
zdnet: www%.zdnet.com
cnn interactive:www.cnn.com/TECH/index.html
nandotimes infotech: www.nando.net/nt/info/
pathfinder digital pulse: pathfinder.com/@@5eifWwcAZF3F9dSw/pathfinder/pulse/news/
    newshome.html
infoworld: www.infoworld.com

Political News
Politics USA
Campaign 96
ElectionLine
AllPolitics
Decision 96
C-SPAN
George
Project Smart Vote
Publius 96
Rock the Vote
So You Want to Buy a President

Journalism News
American Journalism Review: www.ajr.org/
Columbia Journalism Review: www.cjr.org/

Sports
The Sports Network: www.sportsnetwork.com/
SportsLine USA: www.sportsline.com/
ESPN SportsZone: www.espnet.sportszone.com
All major professional sports maintain news sites, such as:
    NFL: www.nfl.com/packers/index.html

College Newspapers Online
More than 100 college newspapers publish online, with the greatest numbers in California,
    New York, and Texas. This site maintains a current list with URLs:
    www.bowdoin.edu/%7Esgershey/papers/
The Columbia News Service: moon.jrn.columbia.edu/CNS/index2.html

- Where Magazine
- Yahoo New York

    One advantage these sites offer is the ability to link multiple databases of information, including geographic location and current entertainment directories. Increasingly, these sites are offering the ability to directly book tickets and make reservations, thus making it possible to complete the entire transaction online.

Multimedia and the Future of the Internet

Among the most interesting and important applications for the future of the Internet involves video and audio, or multimedia, distribution. As Table 2-3 shows, most of the leading applications for video on the Internet today use streaming technologies, which permit users/viewers to watch video clips without experiencing a long delay while the clip downloads. Certain approaches to streaming (e.g., that used by Vivo) permit tailoring video streams to different levels of bandwidth, so a client with just a 28.8 kpbs dial-up modem accesses a video stream designed at a lower frame per second rate (e.g., FPS of 5–7), while a client with a higher level of bandwidth available accesses a stream with many more frames per second (e.g., 12–15), and thus a higher quality of service.

Streaming Video

Streaming video refers to the delivery of video "in real time" via the Internet. Techniques include placing several frames of video into a buffer on the client (user) computer's hard drive, and then beginning to play the video, as more files are placed into the buffer. To the viewer, the video plays in approximately real time, without having to wait for an entire large video file to download. Streaming video employs the same or similar techniques to a number of streaming audio Internet products debuted in 1995 with the introduction of RealAudio and other streaming audio software products. Streaming audio was introduced first because it requires even less bandwidth and is simpler to process, technically speaking, than video. As a result, the streaming audio is somewhat more mature, with an entreprenuerial streaming audio broadcaster industry already in full swing.

The increased flow of video and other multimedia content on the Internet is beginning to clog the Internet network backbone. The situation will only get worse as demand increases and content gets more demanding (i.e., video strains the system much more than text). Although many network engineers are rightly concerned about the clogging of the network arteries, it is important to acknowledge an often-overlooked historical footnote.[32] John Carey, founder of Greystone Communications, a telecommunications consulting firm, (1996) recounts an episode from the turn of the century in New York City telephony:

In 1890, many engineers said that the telephone network would collapse because it was impossible to handle more than 10,000 customers—the number of telephone customers in NY in 1890. The problem was that all 10,000 lines connected physically in one building in northern Manhattan. It required 1,000 operators to make connections for 10,000 customers and the building (the size of a football stadium) was complete chaos. To make a call from the Bronx to Brooklyn required four or five operators, each shouting in a football stadium atmosphere, about how the call should be completed. Needless to say, the telephone network did not collapse. The technological challenge led to technological innovation and the development of electro-mechanical switching.[33]

TABLE 2-3   Video on the Internet[31]

Product	Technical Approach	Selected Users
Streaming		
VDOlive	Adaptive streaming system using 28.8kbps data rate. Specialized advanced wavelet/compression encoding. Uses Internet Protocol datagrams. Live event, real-time encoding possible. Single data rate available.	CBS, PBS, CBC, NBC later in 1996
VIVO	Multiple encoded versions for varying bandwidths. Uses compression based on standard H.263 videoconferencing. Uses Internet Protocol reliable data stream (prone to stalls). Off-line encoding of video. Quality of multiple versions can be tuned for Intranets.	CNN, ABC, FirstTV, Intranets
Xing StreamWorks	MPEG-1 based technology. Scalable data rate for multiple bandwidths.	PGA, Hootie and the Blowfish (few others)
Multi-cast Backbone (M-Bone)	Streaming video server, requires reserving time higher quality because bandwidth assigned for multicast. Few clients with software. Allows one-to-many, efficient distribution of streaming content.	Rolling Stones, high profile events,education IETF confer- ences (Internet Engineering Task Force)
CU-SeeMe	Hub and spoke topology using a "reflector." Cross platform, Mac and Windows. B&W version, free. Color version, commercial.	Education, Group video- conferencing.
QuicktimeTV	Streaming using hub and spoke repeater feed, color player free, primarily for Apple computers, but Windows version expected in October 1996	Primarily Educational and general public. Videocon- ferencing. Webcasting' musical concerts
Quicktime	MPEG1 technology, not streaming	The first widely used technology for video on the Internet, 1994–95

Delivering multimedia content via the Internet has been one of the most entic-ing opportunities and obstacles as the Internet and the Web have grown. Access to the Internet and the Web is available via a variety of public telecommunications networks or *cybernetworks,* a term developed at the Columbia Institute for Tele-

TABLE 2-4   Delivering Multimedia via the Internet

Cybernetwork	Transmission Speed	Text Capability Per Second	Multimedia
Phone Modem access	14.4/28.8Kbps	1 story in NYT	Internet/online/No video slow still pix/graphics CUSeeMe/VDOLive/RA
ISDN Conference/fast	128Kbps	1 page of NYT	H.320 Video
			hi-res pictures
T1 4-wire copper	1.5 Mpbs	4 pages of NYT	VHS video
Cable Modem	4Mbps	1 section of NYT	MPEG2
ADSL MPEG2	6Mbps	2 sections of NYT	Multichannel
Ethernet	10Mbps	1 day of NYT	Multichannel MPEG2
Low-Power Radio* (entry level ATM)	25Mbps	2 days of NYT	Near Broadcast Quality Video
T3 Optical, copper, coaxial cable	45 Mbps	4 days of NYT	Near BQV
Optical Fiber			
OC3	155Mbps	1 week of NYT	Broadcast Quality VOD
OC12	622Mbps	4 weeks of NYT	Broadcast Quality VOD
Commercial	2.5Gbps	26 weeks of NYT	Multichannel BQVOD
Laboratory	1Tbps	300 years of	Virtual Reality
Fujitsu Ltd.		New York Times	(Immersive, surround)
Nippon Telegraph		in one second	quality beyond VRML)
and Telephone			
AT&T Research and Lucent Technologies			

Key:
ADSL: Asymmetric Digital Subscriber Line
ATM: Asynchronous Transfer Mode
bps: bits per second
    K: 1,000
    M: 1,000,000
    G: 1,000,000,000
    T: 1,000,000,000,000
CU-SeeMe: Cornell University's Internet video conferencing software
H.320: Commercial video conferencing standard
ISDN: Integrated Services Digital Network
Modem: Modulate/Demodulate
MPEG2: Digital video standard/VHS standard (Motion Picture Engineers Group)
OC3: Optical Carrier level 3, SONET (Synchronous Optical NETwork) rate of 155 Mbit/s
OC12: Optical Carrier level 12, SONET rate of 622 Mbit/s
RA: RealAudio
T1: T-carrier (AT&T, Bell); 24 channels of audio, 64Kbps
T3: 28 T1 lines
VDOLive: "Streaming" video on the World Wide Web (WWW)
VOD: Video on demand

*Low-Power Radio is under consideration by the Federal Communications Commission (FCC), and would allow short-distance high-speed transmission; this wireless medium can link many users to a single high-speed phone line to the Internet.

Information (CITI). Table 2-4 presents the current state of multimedia capacity available in a number of cybernetworks providing increasing Internet access.[34]

As this figure shows, a phone modem operating at 28.8 kbps can manage a low level of video via the Internet using a free or low-cost product such as CU-SeeMe. Such video, however, is at a very low quality of service, with low level audio quality as well, and is subject to substantial breakup and interference. Video quality does increase dramatically with increased capacity, although few Internet Service Providers (ISPs) provide or consumers have access to high-capacity environments such as ISDN, much less T1, cable modem or T3, except for those of us lucky enough to work for a university, where T3 is becoming the standard for Internet service. Most businesses and almost all home consumers are still operating off a phone modem. This makes accessing high-quality Internet-delivered video a slow and frustrating process at best, and an impossibility much of the time. Transmission speed (sometimes loosely referred to as bandwidth) is rapidly increasing for cybernetworks, as phone companies deploy ISDN, cable companies introduce cable modem trials, and optical fiber makes it ever closer to the home. Nynex recently announced, for example, its acquisition of 1 million ISDN lines for the New York region, and is introducing attractive pricing packages to spur its adoption. Nynex has offered to Columbia University faculty or staff residing near the Morningside Heights campus (on Manhattan's Upper West Side) unlimited ISDN service for just $60 a month. In contrast, US West is offering ISDN service to its customers in Oregon for a staggering $1,950 a month.[35] Needless to say, the adoption of high-speed network services is proceeding somewhat unevenly around the country.

NOTES

[1]Lewis, Peter H. "U.S. Begins Privatizing Of Internet Operations," *New York Times,* Oct. 24, 1994: A10.

[2]The Heritage of Marconi's Invention, *Casa Italiana,* Columbia University, December 9, 1996.

[3]Schwartz, Evan I. "The Cleavers Enter Cyberspace," *Business Week,* October 11, 1993: 142.

[4]Makulowich, John S. "Internet: Explore the 'network of networks,'" *Quill,* Sept. 1993: 28.

[5]Williams, Frederick, The Freedom Forum Media Studies Center Leadership Institute June 22, 1994.

[6]Markoff, John, "Traffic Jams Already on the Information Highway," *New York Times,* November 3, 1993.

[7]Ibid.

[8]Lewis, Peter H. "Internet Users Get Access To S.E.C. Filings Fee-Free" *New York Times,* January 17, 1994.

[9]Markoff, John. "An Electronic Salon," *New York Times,* March 27, 1994: F10.

[10]Lewis, Peter H. "Companies Rush to Set Up Shop in Cyberspace," *New York Times,* Nov. 2, 1994: C1, C6.

[11]Lewis, Peter H. "Sneering at a Virtual Lynch Mob," *New York Times,* May 11, 1994: D7.

[12]Ibid.

[13]Lewis, Peter H. "Censors Become a Force on Cyberspace Frontier," *New York Times,* June 29, 1994: A1, D5.

[14]Lewis, op. cit., May 11, 1994.

[15]Ibid.: 51.

[16]*Kiplinger Washington Letter,* October, 1994: 2.

[17]Markoff, John, "New Venture in Cyberspace By Silicon Graphics Founder," *New York Times,* May 7, 1994: B1.

[18]Miller, David, "The Many Faces of the Internet," *Internet World,* October, 1994: 34–38.

[19]Markoff, John, The New York Times, 8 October 1994: 47.

[20]Eric A. Meyer, Hypermedia Systems Manager, Library Information Technologies for Case Western Reserve University at http://web66.coled.umn.edu/Cookbook/HTML/MinutePrimer.html

[21]Markoff, John. "A Free and Simple Computer Link," *New York Times,* Dec. 8, 1993: D1, D7.

[22]Markoff, John, "New Venture in Cyberspace By Silicon Graphics Founder," *New York Times,* May 7, 1994: B1.

[23]Peter H. Lewis, "Why Java May Sound Like Magic," PERSONAL COMPUTING, Cybertimes of the New York Times, May 7, 1996.

[24]www.javasoft.com/applets/applets/contest/Pythagoras/index.html

[25]www.javasoft.com/applets/applets/contest/NuclearPlant/index.html

[26]http://www.13x.com/cgi-bin/cdt/snoop.pl

[27]Masefield, John (1902). *Salt Water Ballads and Poems.* New York: MacMillan, 1923.

[28]Braverman, Alan M. "Lycos, Inc." CS First Boston industry report, December 3, 1996: 13.

[29]Stuart Elliott, Banner Ads on Internet Attract Users," New York Times Cybertimes, December 3, 1996.

[30]Andrew Kohut, "One-in-Ten Voters Online for Campaign '96," The Pew Research Center, December 16, 1996.

[31]Pavlik, John V. and Andrew Lih, "The Media Role of Computer Networks: Video on the Internet," Paper presented at CITI Conference, September 27, 1996.

[32]Robert Lucky, Marconi's Heritage, December 9, 1996; Murphy, Jamie and Charlie Hofacker, "Gridlock on the Internet Explosive Growth Clogs The Internet's Backbone," *New York Times,* June 29–30, 1996.

[33]Carey, John, Interview, October 4, 1996.

[34]John V. Pavlik and Andrew Lih, "The Media Role of Computer Networks: Video on the Internet," presented at The Impact of Cybercommunications on Telecommunications, CITI, September 27, 1996.

[35]Ashley Dunn, "Phone Lines: The Ties That Bind Us," The New York Times Cybertimes, December 11, 1996.

3

Historical Perspectives:
Media at the Millennium

*"Once a new technology rolls over you, if you're not
part of the steamroller, you're part of the road."*
*—STEWART BRAND,[1] THE MEDIA LAB:
INVENTING THE FUTURE AT MIT (1987)*

Historians may one day recall the late twentieth century as the era of 64-bit Super Mario, the Internet, and the Pentium PC. But without actually traveling back to the future, one way to make sense of today's bewildering array of media technologies is to examine the history of many still-evolving media technologies to see what lessons emerge. This chapter looks at that history, drawing upon both the technological successes and failures of the past.

FROM CAVE PAINTINGS
TO THE INFORMATION HIGHWAY

Since the days of the earliest known Aboriginal petroglyphs in Australia in 80,000 B.C. and the cave paintings in Altamira, Spain, sixty thousand years later, people have used technology as a medium to communicate across space and time.[2,3] In the modern world, some trace the origins of new media technology to the birth of the information society in 1956, when for the first time more than 50 percent of the U.S. work force was employed in the service sector; the Burroughs Corporation manufactured the E101, the first desktop computer; videotape was introduced to the world of television; and the Soviet Union launched Sputnik, the first artificial satellite.[4,5] In the four decades since then, the world's communication system has changed dramatically, bringing us ever closer to Marshall McLuhan's notion of a global village.[6] "By the end of the 1980s, 'globalization' had become the term for accelerating interdependence. . . . The primary agent of globalization is the transnational corporation. The primary driving force is the revolution in information and communication technologies," writes Sylvia Ostry.[7]

Arguably, the technical foundation of this global village rests largely in science fiction writer Arthur C. Clarke's 1945 prediction of the communications satellite, which was published in *Wireless World* in an article entitled "Extraterrestrial Relays."[8] In making his prediction of a global broadcasting system based on satellites, Clarke, who earlier helped the British develop radar technology during World War II, defined the exact height of the orbit necessary to match the movement of the satellite with the earth's rotation, called a *geosynchronous orbit.* Launched four years after the Soviet Union's Sputnik, the United States put Echo I, the first communications satellite, into orbit on October 4, 1960. It was a passive satellite, designed only to reflect, and not transmit signals. Since then, satellite technology has advanced significantly, providing two-way transmission capabilities around the world. Communication satellites have redefined the nature of global communications, making possible everything from worldwide financial trading to global television, such as the Cable News Network (CNN).[9] The importance of this system of transmission is eloquently explained by Walter Wriston, former chief executive officer of Citicorp, the United State's largest banking institution. "The single most powerful development in global communications has been the satellite, born a mere thirty-one years ago. . . . Satellites now bind the world for better or worse, in an electronic infrastructure that carries news, money, and data anywhere on the planet at the speed of light."[10]

As a result, the technology of the global village has produced far-reaching effects in today's post-Cold War world, where everything from foreign policy to debates on free trade are played out simultaneously around the world. Some even talk of a resultant new form of tele-diplomacy, illustrated during the Persian Gulf War when Presidents George Bush and Saddam Hussein used television to deliver their messages to worldwide audiences, or more recently in the United Nation's ill-fated humanitarian efforts in Somalia. "A clearer demonstration of the global village that modern communications have created, and the land mines that American presidents face as a result, would be difficult to imagine," wrote veteran political reporter R. W. Apple Jr. "After more than a dozen American soldiers were killed in street-fighting in Somalia 10 days ago, President Clinton argued that it would be dangerous for the United States to pull out its troops at once, because doing so would only encourage 'aggressors, thugs and terrorists' all over the world,"[11] presumably as a consequence of watching the withdrawal live on television throughout the world.

Of course, not everyone agrees that new technology has brought us closer to anything resembling a global village. Among those who question this conclusion is noted communication scholar Herbert I. Schiller, professor emeritus of communication at the University of California, San Diego. Schiller argues that the new technology is essentially a tool for transforming the societies of the world into commercial markets. "Contrary to the conventional wisdom that recent advances in communications have led to the emergence of the 'global village,' I do not believe that globalization of the media industries sector has resulted in the formation of an international civil society as such," Schiller writes."Rather, this process has resulted in an international order organized by transnational economic interests that are largely unaccountable to the nation–states in which they operate."[12] Gary Selnow, who has studied the effects of high technology on political campaigns, argues that computer technology has produced something more akin to a global cacophony than a global village, with politicians using databases to target individualized messages to potential voters everywhere.[13]

The Computer Revolution

Another technical foundation of the information society is the computer. By changing the way we live, work, and play, the computer has irrevocably altered the fabric of society. From the living room to the board room, computers have changed both how we spend our time and how we make our money. The computer has become both a metaphor and a direct representation of the automation of thinking and processing of information.

Although it is in many ways the ultimate symbol of the postmodern information society of the twentieth century, the computer has a history that stretches back to at least the early 1600s (see Figure 3-1). German mathematician Wilhelm Schickard created in 1623 arguably the original automatic computing device, the first mechanical calculator employing a set of metal wheels to tabulate numbers. Two centuries later, in 1823, English inventor Charles Babbage conceived a steam-powered digital calculating machine, although the device was not built until 1880 by Herman Hollerith, who named it the "electromechanical tabulator." Also in 1880, Scottish physicist Lord Kelvin introduced the idea for an analog computer whose "modus operandi" entailed the use of mechanical devices to process and manipulate numbers and information that could be entered in numerical format. His idea was not translated into a working device, however, until 1930 when American engineer Vannevar Bush built a prototype analog computer called the "differential analyzer." Also important in the story of the computer is Thomas Watson, the founder of IBM, whose vision launched a company begun in the late 1800s with a machine for tabulating numbers, and eventually evolved into the global standard for business and personal computing. In 1939, John Atanasoff, an Iowa State University professor, created the first electronic digital computer. Rather than use the standard base of 10 which had been attempted in the past, his computer was based on use of a binary code of 0s and 1s to process information. Although originally capable only of addi-

1623	German mathematician Wilhelm Schickard creates the first mechanical calculator, employing a set of metal wheels to tabulate numbers
1823	English inventor Charles Babbage conceives a steam-powered digital calculating machine
1880	Herman Hollerith builds the first working model of Babbage's invention, naming it the "electromechanical tabulator"
	Scottish physicist Lord Kelvin introduces the idea for an analog computer using mechanical devices to process and manipulate numbers and information entered in numerical format
1930	American engineer Vannevar Bush builds a prototype analog computer called the "differential analyzer"
1939	Iowa State University professor John Atanasoff creates the first electronic digital computer based on use of a binary code of 0s and 1s
1945	Rear Admiral Grace Murray Hopper removes a two-inch moth from a navy computer, giving rise to the use of the term "bug" to describe all types of mysterious computer failures
1948	Bell Labs unveils the transistor, invented by research team Walter Brattain, John Bardeen, and William Shockley, who shared a Nobel prize in 1956 for their invention
1951	The Univac (Universal Automatic Computer), the first commercially manufactured computer, is installed at the U.S. Census Bureau in Philadelphia
1964	American Gilbert Hyatt builds the first silicon microchip
1981	IBM introduces its first personal computer
1983	Apple Computer introduces the "Lisa," the first desktop computer system to use icons and a mouse
1994	Intel manufactures the Pentium® processor, the fastest to date

FIGURE 3-1   Milestones in the Computer Revolution

tion and subtraction of about eight numbers, by 1946 Professor Atanasoff had developed the basis for modern computer technologies. The first commercially manufactured computer, the Univac (Universal Automatic Computer), was installed in 1951 at the U.S. Census Bureau in Philadelphia. Simultaneously, the Ferranti Mark I was installed at Manchester University, England.

A Bug in the Machine

On a warm August night at Harvard in 1945, Rear Admiral Grace Murray Hopper made an important contribution to the common lexicon of computing. Hopper was having trouble getting her computer to function properly. "Things were going badly," Hopper said. "There was something wrong in one of the circuits of the long, glass-enclosed computer. Finally, someone located the trouble spot and, using ordinary tweezers, removed the problem, a two-inch moth. From then on, when anything went wrong with a computer, we said it had bugs in it." Today, the term *bug* is widely used to describe all types of mysterious computer failures. Hopper also helped invent COBOL, a programming language widely used in business, and the first practical compiler for modern computers. A compiler translates code written by humans into more specific code read directly by computers. A computing pioneer, Hopper died on January 2, 1992.[14]

The Falling Price of Computing Power

It is generally simpler . . . for people to consider the impact of a ten percent rise in gasoline prices than it is for them to consider the impact of a tenfold increase in the capacity of computer memory chips. Material changes are concrete and imaginable; information changes seem very abstract and mystical.

Since its inception, the computer has undergone a revolution, from a mere computational device to a sophisticated multimedia global communications tool. Driving the revolution in computing has been the dramatically falling price of computing power. By most estimates, the price of computing power has been falling by a factor of 1,000 every twenty years. In more mundane terms, this means that to buy $1,000 of early 1970s computing power today would cost just $1. The pocket calculator provides a simple example. When introduced in the early 1960s, the pocket calculator was something of a luxury item with only limited computing power. Today's pocket calculators are so common and affordable that even the Educational Testing Service, administrators of the SAT (Scholastic Aptitude Test), recently ruled in favor of allowing students to use a calculator when taking their college entrance exams. Moreover, the average pocket calculator of today can make instant calculations of complex problems that would exceed the ability of many mainframe computers of the early 1960s.

As is seen in Table 3-1, the most powerful IBM mainframe computer in 1975 cost about $10 million, and could perform about 10 million instructions per second, a cost of about $1 per instruction per second. By 1996, the 200 megahertz Pentium-chip PC, the fastest processor, cost about $2,000 and could process 200 million instructions per second. This translates into a cost of about $1 per 100,000 instructions per second, meaning that consumers now have on their desktops 100,000 times more computing power than an IBM mainframe of twenty years ago.

Long-time news media executive Adam Clayton Powell III, now vice president of Technology for The Freedom Forum, offers another way to view the falling price of computing power. "In 1976, a Cray Supercomputer cost some $8 million," Powell observes.[17] "Today, a Silicon Graphics workstation with roughly the same computing power of the 1976 Cray costs just $4,995.00." The implications, Powell says, are profound for the development of new media and the information highway. If the trend in the falling price of computing power continues, twenty years from now most homes will have a device in their living room with the power of today's supercomputers—but at a cost of just $500. For the creators of multimedia software, interactive television, and other new media content, the implications are that all software—programming—can be vastly different than today. Rather than endless re-

TABLE 3-1   The Falling Price of Computing Speed

		Millions of Instructions Per Second (MIPS)	Price
1975	I.B.M. Mainframe	10	$10,000,000
1976	Cray 1 Supercomputer	160	20,000,000
1979	Digital VAX	1	200,000
1981	I.B.M. PC desktop computer	.25	3,000
1984	Sun Microsystems 2	1	10,000
1996	Pentium-chip PC	200	2,000

Sources: Company reports; *The New York Times*[16]

runs of *Gilligan's Island,* the interactive TV future might offer viewers the opportunity to trek across the North Pole or converse with William Shakespeare. The limits will be only those of our own imaginations. Offering an additional perspective on the implication of computing power is Kenneth M. King, first director of the Columbia University Computer Center, former president of EDUCOM, the higher education academic computing assocation, and president of CREN, the Corporation for Research and Education Networking.[18] One MIP, he explains, is enough computing power to control or manage words (i.e., it's what's needed for effective word processing). One hundred MIPs is needed to control images. One thousand MIPs is needed to control handwriting and speech recognition. If current trends continue, this level of computing power will likely be available on the desktop by about 2001.

The Transistor and a Revolution in Computing

Central to the revolution in computing is the transistor, invented in 1948 by the AT&T Bell Labs research team of Walter Brattain, John Bardeen, and William Shockley. The invention marked the beginning of the era of miniaturization of electronics. Transistors fundamentally changed the nature of computing because the small components could control the transmission of electrical currents without producing much heat. The first transistors were known as "point-contact devices." Brattain, Bardeen, and Shockley shared a Nobel Prize in 1956 for their invention.

Enabled by the development of the transistor, IBM introduced its first personal computer in 1981, ushering in the era of desktop computing, and establishing the PC as the preferred platform for most business applications. In 1983, Apple Computers introduced the "Lisa," the first desktop computer system to use icons and a mouse, propelling a revolution in graphical user interfaces (GUI) and "user-friendliness" in computing, most recently illustrated by the introduction of the "Windows" operating system for the PC and the graphic interface of Netscape Navigator and Microsoft Internet Explorer for network applications on the Internet. The PC's success in the marketplace is largely attributable to IBM's decision to provide an open licensing arrangement for the PC's disk operating system (DOS), which enabled other manufacturers to produce "clone" PCs and at a very competitive price, also encouraging the development of much software for the DOS platform. Microsoft's disk operating system (MS-DOS) has became the standard for the PC industry. Not until September of 1994 did Apple announce it would begin licensing its operating system and permit Macintosh clone production.

Law of the Microcosm

Perhaps just as important to the transformation of the computer has been the miniaturization of the computer chip. Thirty years ago Intel chairman Gordon E. Moore noted that by reducing by 10 percent a year the size of the tiny silicon lines that form transistor circuits, chipmakers create a new generation of chips every eighteen to twenty-four months with twice as many transistors.[19] This means the capacity of dynamic random-access memory (DRAMs) doubles every two years as does the speed and overall performance of computer chips. If these trends continue, the thinnest circuit line or transistor element will shrink from 0.35 in 1996 to 0.10 in 2008. At that final size, a string of 2,500 transistors would be needed to encircle a single human hair. Similarly, the number of transistors on a single chip has increased 2,300 times in the past quarter century, from 4,004 in 1971 to 5.5 million on the Pentium Pro® processor.

Writing in the 1994 *Forbes ASAP*, George Gilder observes that we are rapidly moving toward an era in which the fastest computer will soon be based on a *single* silicon chip.[20] Gilder calls this "the law of the microcosm." In a sense, it is the process of computing miniaturization taken to its ultimate extreme, at least within the existing computing paradigm. Advances in microcomputing technology will soon make it possible to pack hundreds of millions of microcircuits on a single computer chip. Thus, rather than creating supercomputers based on millions of microchips, the fastest computers will contain only a single chip with millions, even billions, of circuits. Using Moore's Law, a single chip will likely contain 100 million transistors and execute 2 billion instructions per second by 2000. Such chips will likely cost only a few dollars. The implications are that devices as powerful as today's most advanced supercomputers or parallel processors will fill less space than a penny. Wristwatch videophones, once the stuff of Dick Tracy comic books, may be just around the twenty-first century corner.

Creating a Sexy Robot

In the history of the computer one also finds the history of computer graphics and animation. In its earliest days in the 1960s, computer graphics took the form of "vector graphics," or simple line drawings. Vector graphics formed the basis of computer-aided design, or CAD, and dominated the field for more than a decade. Pioneering work in this period was conducted at Xerox Parc in Silicon Valley, where visionaries such as Alan Kay developed the graphical user interface (GUI), now the standard in the world of computing. Among the earliest uses of vector graphics in creating media content was film pioneer Robert Abel's work in the Walt Disney classic, *The Black Hole,* produced in 1977.[21] At about the same time, computer programmers developed the next generation of computer graphics known as "rastor optics." Rastor optics enabled the addition of color, shading, and texture to computer graphics, offering a revolution in the application of computer graphics to film production and media content in general. Unfortunately, early rastor optics required many millions of bytes of computer storage, and even the most powerful mainframe computers had difficulty processing rastor images. In the 1980s, the merging of vector graphics and rastor optics, along with improvements in computing power, made digital movie effects increasingly standard fare. Among the most notable early examples of digital image rendering was Robert Abel's "The Sexy Robot" television commercial produced in 1982. Abel began his production by using vector graphics to digitize images of a live model. He then added color and movement through the application of rastor optics. The result was an Emmy award-winning television commercial. Abel's firm, CGI, has won thirty-three Clios (the advertising industry's highest award) and two Emmys for its special effects productions.

THE NATURE OF "NEW" TECHNOLOGIES

To understand the nature of new technologies, one must look beyond the realm of the computer, as well. One of the most interesting "new" technologies is the fax, or facsimile machine. Used to scan and transmit images (i.e., fax or telecopier), the fax is an example of a technology that simply wouldn't die. Although many think of the fax as a new technology of the 1980s, it was actually invented in 1842 by Scotsman Alexander Bain.[22] Bain based his original invention on electrochemical telegraph processes developed earlier in the nineteenth century. When Bain applied for a U.S. patent on his invention in 1848, he found that Samuel Morse had already applied for a patent for a very similar device. Bain sued Morse and the court ruled in favor of Bain because he had held a patent in England prior to Morse's application.

What's more, fax newspapers were being transmitted as early as the 1930s. *The Milwaukee Journal, The New York Times,* and many others transmitted fax newspapers to department stores and other locations in the 1930s and 1940s by use of radio frequencies. None of these fax efforts succeeded, however. Novel though they were, each failed for a variety of reasons, some of which were technologically based. The fax technology of a half century ago was slow, unreliable, expensive, and printed on a paper stock that was difficult to read. Fax printers were available in few locations, as well, such as department stores and on board ships. Perhaps more importantly, the content of early fax newspapers offered readers little that they couldn't just as easily get in the regular newspaper.

Almost miraculously, the fax had a renaissance in the late 1980s. The success of the new fax machine can be attributed to a confluence of circumstances, including the emergence of a viable fax technology transmitted over telephone wires, a cheaper, more reliable fax receiver and printer, and an application in the business market, where greater resources were available to acquire and use the technology effectively. Recent efforts to create fax newspapers have as a result fared somewhat better, especially since publishers have made a greater effort to offer something special in the content of the current generation of fax newspapers. As a result, fax newspapers were reintroduced. *The New York Times* began publishing a fax newspaper in 1992, primarily aimed at cruise ships, and in 1993 expanded via Nynex to a broader consumer market. The *Hartford* (Connecticut) *Courant* launched the successful *FaxPaper* in 1990 to a predominantly business audience interested in getting a twelve-hour advance copy of tomorrow's news.[23] Fax newspapers, however, are not likely to ever become major vehicles for the distribution of news, because electronic, online technologies have already eclipsed them in terms of speed and accessibility. Rather, the fax has found an important niche in easy, low-cost, instant business-to-business or personal communications, and has emerged as an effective alternative to postal delivery or express mail services when an original document is not needed. One of the advantages of fax communications over online file transfer is that there is a universal technical standard that allows any fax machine anywhere in the world to communicate with any other fax machine. Thus, images and documents look the same on the sender and receiver end of a fax transmission. The conclusion to draw from the history of the fax: *olde* technologies never die, they just *morph*.

Time-Shift: Introducing the VCR

The introduction of the videocassette recorder (VCR) is another useful case study in the evolution of new technologies of communication.[24] Launched more than two decades ago, the VCR transformed how people watch television, allowing people to control what they watch and when (sometimes called time-shifting). A variety of factors contributed to the successful introduction of the VCR in the marketplace. The price dropped dramatically from the early 1980s, when VCRs often cost $1,000, the technology became easier to use, and videocassette rentals became even more popular than videocassette sales. The introduction of the VCR also took many unexpected twists and turns. The first of these twists was the evolving format of the VCR. The forerunner to the modern VCR was Electronic Video Recording (EVR), introduced by CBS in 1967. EVR allowed material recorded on video to be replayed on a TV set. The black-and-white cartridge that contained the film was electronically coded and pictures and sounds were stored right on it, allowing the cassette to be played on a specially made TV set.

In 1972, the Sony Corporation introduced the Betamax, a one-half inch VCR. For most of the next decade, a battle ensued in the consumer marketplace between the technically superior Beta and commercially successful VHS format VCRs. Though technically inferior, VHS gained a slight edge in the marketplace, often capturing better shelf display space in the department and video stores. Moreover, more movies were often available in VHS format. This slight economic advantage translated into what one economist calls positive feedback, allowing VHS to ultimately win the marketplace.[25] A second important factor was the completely unexpected evolution of the so-called Mom & Pop video rental store, initially resisted by the major film studios, and later allowed by court order.[26] These ubiquitous video stores drove much of the success of the videocassette by making videocassette rentals easily accessible and affordable in virtually every neighborhood in America. Finally, the introduction of the VCR was driven by the strong early consumer demand for pornography. Many of the earliest adopters of the technology were willing to pay the high early price of the VCR in order to gain private access to erotic video material. This stage of adoption helped drive down the price of the technology to make it more affordable to a general consumer market.

Origins of the High-Speed Data Network

A different story unfolds when looking at the history of the data network. Although many would point to the development of modern telecommunications in the twentieth century, the first nationwide optical data networks were built more than 200 years ago.[27] Much older long-distance, high-speed communication networks existed as well. In 450 B.C. carrier pigeons were used for fast communication between Greek city–states, and Chinese emperors used geese flying as fast as 50 mph to carry messages.[28]

Many eighteenth-century European countries had fully operational nationwide communications systems capable of transmitting messages over hundreds of kilometers in a matter of minutes. These systems consisted of hundreds of semaphore towers linked via line of sight over vast distances, such as the one in France from Paris to Lyons, separated by some 400 kilometers. The history of this optical telegraphy has been almost forgotten in the era of modern digital communications. French Clergyman Claude Chappe and Swedish nobleman Abraham Niclas Edelcrantz built the first optical telegraph system in 1791, linking the castle in Brulon and a private residence in the neighboring town of Parcé some 16 kilometers distant. They completed the first nationwide system in 1795. The first message transmitted was a sentence selected by the local Doctor M. Chenou: "Si vous réussissez vous serez bientôt couvert de gloire" ("If you succeed, you will soon be back in glory"). Napoleon Bonaparte, who seized power in 1799, immediately recognized the profound importance of this technology, and ordered construction of a new and vast optical telegraph line, completed in 1804, linking Paris and Milan, covering some 720 kilometers. The systems worked in a relatively simple but effective manner. Holzmann and Pehrson explain:

> Each station consisted simply of a modified pendulum clock and a large panel painted black on one side and white on the other. The clockfaces were divided into 10 parts, each used to designate a number. A single hand, or pointer, made one complete rotation of the clockface at least twice a minute.
>
> At the start of a transmission, the sender turned the panel to indicate when the hand of his clock reach the zenith; that allowed the receiver, watching through a telescope, to set the clock on the other end. Subsequent numbers were sent by flipping the panel from white to

black each time the pointer of the sender's clock passed over the appropriate position. By looking at the position of the local clock, the receiver could determine what number the sender intended. Messages were encoded with the help of a numbered dictionary of letters, words and phrases. The speed of the telegraph was regulated by the rate at which the clock pointer turned.[29]

Although it was labor-intensive and required operation solely during daylight hours, the optical telegraph represented the first functional data transmission system for rapid nationwide communications.

The Information Superrailroad

Even the notion of a national electronic communication infrastructure has its roots stretching back nearly a century and a half, to when two entrepreneurial visionaries issued a public call to build an information superrailroad. In 1853 Hiram O. Alden and James Eddy lobbied the U.S. Congress for "a right of way through the public lands of the United States, for the construction of a subterranean line of telegraph." On behalf of the House of Representatives Committee on Territories, Ephraim Farley, a Whig from Maine, subsequently issued a report on their proposal.[30] Farley's report, which outlines many of the benefits of the proposed enterprise, foreshadows today's arguments in support of the information superhighway. Even the notion of universal service is present in its suggestion that all homes "would be in immediate communication with each other." Farley suggests,

Connect the Atlantic to the Pacific coasts by telegraph communication, and the impulse which it will give to business, and that great tide of emigration setting towards California, will add up to the necessity for railroad communication . . . But it is in its social bearing that the advantages of a telegraph to the Pacific will be most strikingly seen. Every hamlet, it might almost be said every home, in the thirty States of the Union, has its representative on the Pacific shore. By the aid of the telegraph, they would be in immediate communication with each other.

Farley also outlines the cost of such a proposed information railroad.

A subterranean line of two wires, such as the bill provides for, is estimated to cost eleven hundred and fifty dollars per mile. Calling the distance twenty-four hundred miles, the entire cost of the line, including the buildings necessary at the working stations, together with incidental expenses to be incurred in its construction, such as explorations and engineering, land transportation of materials, cost of supplies, and erection of forts to protect way stations, would be not less than two million seven hundred and sixty thousand dollars.

Had the government decided to provide the right of way for the proposal, perhaps today's debate about building a national information infrastructure would have a decidedly different tone.

Important lessons also emerge from the evolution of the so-called information highway. Beginning with American Samuel Morse's invention of the telegraph in 1835, to the World Wide Web of today, technology has increasingly enabled people to communicate across vast distances in real time, forever changing the economic, political, and social structures of the world's societies.[31] Figure 3-2 traces some of the major milestones on the road to the information highway.

Although this timeline represents the milestones in a linear, sequential fashion, the development of the information highway should not be thought of as a series of systematic advances, culminating in today's high-powered optical networks. Rather, many of the developments are unrelated to earlier developments, often running on parallel tracks. Others are the result of serendipity, and some are the result of completely unexpected and unintended uses of the technology. One such unanticipated use of the technology of the telegraph occurred during the Mexican revolution nearly a century ago.

Information Railroads and the Mexican Revolution.   Latin American folk hero Francisco "Pancho" Villa employed then state-of-the-art technology to help fight for the cause of social justice during the Mexican Revolution of the early 1900s. Villa tapped into telegraph lines running through the Sierra Madre mountains, intercepting messages from his enemies, including U.S. generals. In an effort to confuse and mislead his enemies, Villa also sent false messages over the telegraph lines.[32]

Lost in Cyberspace.   Today, many suggest the information highway is already demonstrated in the world of online computer network communications, what some call *cyberspace*. The earliest such system was developed by the U.S. Department of Defense, which created the first nationwide computer network called ARPAnet in 1969. ARPAnet was based on the principle of packet-switching, which could provide continuous communications even during a time of nuclear attack. ARPAnet eventually led to today's global computer network known as the Internet. As of December 1996, more than 15 million U.S. households had signed on with the major online computer services, with more than 50,000 signing up each month.[33] Conservative estimates project that some 50 million people now use the Internet worldwide, and that as many as 500 million will do so by 2000.[34]

It is important to recognize that the information highway is coming about because of a broad array or confluence of forces, including not only technological, but also political, social, and economic forces. Among the technological forces are the convergence of computing and telecommunications, the digital revolution that is enabling multimedia communications to blossom and compression technologies that squeeze vast amounts of video and other information into small electronic spaces. Political forces include the opening of national borders and political leadership that are unleashing telephone and cable companies to enter the information business, and opening up radio frequencies for new uses, such as wireless personal communication networks. Social forces include the relentless push toward democ-

1795	French Clergyman Claude Chappe and Swedish Nobleman Abraham Niclas Edelcrantz Build First Data Network—the Optical Telegraph
1835	American Samuel Morse Invents the Electromagnetic Telegraph
1842	Scotsman Alexander Bain Invents Facsimile Transmission
1866	Englishman William Thomson—who becomes Lord Kelvin for this feat—Directs Laying of First Transatlantic Cable
1876	American Alexander Graham Bell Invents Telephone
1886	German Heinrich Hertz Experiments with Electromagnetic Waves
1895	Hertz Discovers Radio Waves
1899	Italian Guglielmo Marconi Invents Radio Telegraphy
1934	*Milwaukee Journal* Publishes First Facsimile Newspaper
1936	BBC Creates the First Television Network
1945	Arthur C. Clarke Invents the Communication Satellite
1948	First Cable Television Systems Created in the U.S.
1957	The Soviet Union Launches the First Communication Satellite, Sputnik ("Traveling Companion"), Contains Radio Receiver
1961	Western Electric Introduces Push-Button and Touch-Tone Telephone Service
1964	AT&T Unveils the Videophone; It Fails, but is Reintroduced in 1993
1969	ARPAnet Founded by the U.S. Defense Department, First National Computer Network
1970	Optical Fiber Invented by Corning Glass Works
1975	NASA Experiments with Direct Broadcast Satellites
1979	British government introduces Prestel, First Videotext Service
1980	CNN Begins First 24-hour TV News Network
1983	U.S. Government Creates the Internet, NSFnet
1987	Tim Berners-Lee Designs the World Wide Web (WWW) on the Internet
1993	Clinton/Gore Administration Publishes Position Paper Calling for Creation of Information Highway
1993	BellCore Transmits Full-Motion Video over Standard Twisted-Pair Telephone Wire
1994	Albert Gore, Jr. is first vice president to participate in live news conference by computer network
1996	More than a quarter million individuals and organizations publish "Home Pages" on the Web, establishing it as the most democratic of all communication media
1996	Clinton/Gore Administration challenges industry and citizens to work with the government to link all classrooms in the U.S. to the Internet
1996	International consortium transmits data at one trillion bits per second over optical fiber

FIGURE 3-2   Information Highway Timeline

racy in many societies hungry for communications, and individuals drawn by the enabling and empowering nature of new media technologies.[35] "Laptop computers, cellular modems, satellite dishes, and electronic mail allow the global proliferation of information at ever cheaper and faster rates," writes Kristi K. Kahrenburg."[36]

> *Fiber-optic networks, transporting data at thousands of times the speed of their digital predecessors, already link personal computers to everything from libraries to news wires to video stores. As a result, anyone with a television, fax machine or PC has access to a staggering array of new information sources.*

But perhaps even more important is the economic force of giant financial behemoths—transnational corporations—pushing to ensure their place as a player in the global marketplace. Transnational media-information corporations such as Time Warner, Disney, Reuters, Sony, NewsCorp, and Bertelsmann have moved rapidly since the 1960s to achieve a worldwide market share.[37] Although many of the forces outlined above are complementary, others are countervailing. Similarly, although some are positive, others pose significant threats to individual freedom and choice.[38]

Origins and Pitfalls of the "Highway" Metaphor.   The "highway" metaphor for the high-capacity information infrastructure has evolved slowly and naturally from a confluence of events and circumstances. In the 1950s, Senator Al Gore, Sr., whose son later became vice president of the United States, introduced legislation to build a national highway system that today stands nearly complete. In fact, with the 1993 construction of the Century Highway in Los Angeles, only 114 miles of the national highway system are left to be built.

Several decades later, Senator Al Gore, Jr. introduced legislation to build the national research and educational network (NREN). Almost as a natural result, journalists, scholars, and policy makers dubbed this the information highway, inspired by the national highway system spearheaded by now Vice President Gore's father. The Vice President has used the term himself to describe the information infrastructure described in his NREN legislation.[39] The Clinton administration has used the term, as well.[40,41] Dordick and Lehman write that, "The comparison appears in most all telecommunications infrastructure studies, including the report by the National Telecommunications and Information Administration (NTIA, 1991)."[42] The NTIA report states, "Several parties repeated the oft-stated analogy that telecommunication facilities and services will be as important to the future performance of the United States economy as transportation systems have been in the past." Kahin asks, "Is the Interstate Highway System precedent for the NREN? . . . the transportation infrastructure as a whole compares to the emerging information infrastructure in terms of scope and heterogeneity."[43]

The metaphor of a highway fits the information infrastructure well in a number of respects. It connotes a larger conduit to provide room for more information. It also suggests that there will be faster travel. And, much as the national highway system had important social consequences, so too will the information highway. Some of these consequences may be intentional and positive, while others may be unexpected or negative.

Conversely, the highway metaphor is problematic, as well. Professors Herbert Dordick and Dale Lehman argue that the highway metaphor is not only wrong, but it encourages policy makers, scholars, journalists, and anyone else interested in the information infrastructure to think in the wrong terms. Even the term *infrastructure* implies certain assumptions that Dordick and Lehman find troubling.

> *Indeed, the relatively recent use of the term 'infrastructure' rather than 'network' tends to support the need for a single, centrally managed and controlled electronic communications 'highway' favored by the major carriers. It can be argued that by meeting the needs of the more informationally and technologically advanced segments ('the information literate') the benefits will trickle down to all through enhanced economic growth.*
>
> *The cornucopia of human services that will benefit mankind is overwhelming, but first must come the electronic highway, the infrastructure, from which the manna will trickle down. Before we unquestionably succumb to this theory, let us realize that there is an alternative view of infrastructure. The weak link theory would lead us to address the needs of the least well off members of our society, those who are the least information literate, often poorer, less well educated, and least efficient. On what basis can this be sound public policy?[44]*

Coverage of the Information Superhighway.   Few topics were of greater interest in the media of the early 1990s than the information highway. A bibliometric study, or the science of word counting, shows that major daily newspapers in the United States began placing the information highway high on their news agenda in early 1993.[45] As Figure 3-3 shows, although few major newspapers reported regularly on the information highway in the fall of 1992, attention began picking up in January 1993. Then in February, when newly inaugurated President Bill Clinton and Vice President Al Gore, Jr. released their paper on rebuilding America's infrastructure, with an emphasis on the need to build a new information infrastructure—the information highway—coverage exploded. The phrase *information highway* or *information superhighway* appeared in twenty-five stories during that month in fifteen major American daily newspapers. These phrases appeared in the lead paragraphs of six stories in the *New York Times* alone that month (see Figure 3-4). Although coverage of the information highway slacked off slightly in March, it grew steadily after that to forty-nine stories in September 1993 in fifteen major dailies, and in eighteen lead paragraphs in the *New York Times*. This great attention coincided with the September release of a report by Clinton/Gore outlining

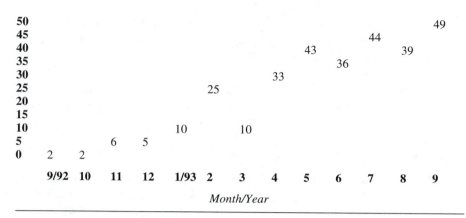

Number of Articles in 15 Major Daily Newspapers Mentioning Information Highway or Information Superhighway

FIGURE 3-3   Press Coverage of the Information Highway

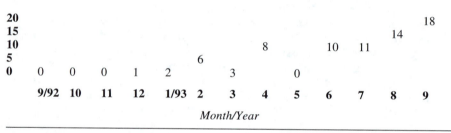

Number of Articles in *The New York Times* Mentioning Information Highway or Information Superhighway in Lead Paragraph

FIGURE 3-4   New York Times Coverage of the Information Highway

the administration's proposed goals for the information highway. The newspapers included in this bibliometric search conducted on Dialog are:

- *Boston Globe*
- *Chicago Tribune*
- *Christian Science Monitor*
- *Cleveland Plain Dealer*
- *Dallas Morning News*
- *Detroit Free Press*
- *Los Angeles Times*
- *Miami Herald*

- *Minneapolis Star Tribune*
- *Newsday/New York Newsday*
- *Philadelphia Inquirer*
- *San Francisco Chronicle*
- *USA Today*
- *Wall Street Journal*
- *Washington Post*

GOOD-BYE GUTENBERG: FROM MOVABLE TYPE TO DIGITAL BIT STREAMS

Although many Westerners attribute the invention of movable type to Johannes Gutenberg of Mainz, Germany in 1450, the first documented use of movable type was actually in 1234 in Korea under the Koryo rule. The Korean's invention allowed the printing and dissemination of Buddhist texts and Confucian writings by Korean scholars. Gutenberg was the first European to print using movable type. His invention used replica-casting in molten metal with a converted winepress to reproduce composed pages of type.[46]

Regardless of whether it was the Koreans in the early thirteenth century or Gutenberg in the fifteenth century, the concept of publication has been defined almost universally in terms of pressing ink onto paper and distributing the printed result to some broader audience.

In an electronic, digital information environment, publication takes on an entirely new meaning.[47] There is no ink, no paper. Words and images—even sounds—exist in an ethereal electronic space, a digital bitstream where each datum is infinitely changeable, reproducible, fluid.

The New Nature of Publication

In this context, the critical question becomes: At what point is an electronic "document" published? Some might say the answer to that question is simple and largely unaltered from the printed document. They might say an electronic document goes through all the same stages of publication that a printed document must. Message creation, editing, and presentation to the public are the necessary steps. But the wrinkle in this reasoning is that today, nearly all documents are created and edited at least in part electronically. While some are "published" electronically, others are transferred to paper at the final stage. This suggests that publication consists exclusively in terms of whether the publisher says it is published or not. Thus, as I write these words, they are published, if I say they are. Clearly, this is not an acceptable standard for a court of law in which matters of libel are settled.

Another way to look at the situation is with a case study. On Sunday, Sept. 17, 1993 horror novelist Stephen King had his latest story published on the Internet, and only on the Internet. King wrote the story, "Umney's Last Case." Editors edited it.

And Viking Press distributed the story to anyone interested in downloading the story off the Internet. Since the Internet is really nothing more than a loosely connected network of networks, and is not owned or controlled by any single person or institution, who is liable should King's story be found libelous? King himself? His publisher? The story was simply made available electronically to anyone interested in obtaining it. It really wasn't published until another user of the Internet downloaded it. In essence, each user of the Internet publishes it when they download the story. In this sense, anyone who downloads the story could be held liable, since they published it. Even more interestingly, if King's story was published on the Internet, how is it any different from any of the millions of messages that float around in the cyberspace of the Internet each day? Why is King's story published, while the rest of the messages downloaded, accessed, saved, printed, read, viewed, or listened to are not? Is a newspaper published on the Internet any less subject to laws pertaining to libel than that same document published on paper? Is the real issue a matter of the nature of the audience? Is the issue the size and scope of the intended audience? What happens if the message is intended for a wide audience, but no one downloads and reads it? What happens if the source of an electronic publication is hidden? Some electronic bulletin boards now feature anonymous publishing in which the identity of the original creator of a message is obscured electronically. In such a case, it would be impossible to identify the source of any potentially libelous messages. Current federal copyright and intellectual property right law states,

> *"Publication" is the distribution of copies or phonorecords of a work to the public by sale or other transfer of ownership, or by rental or lease, or lending. The offering to distribute copies or phonorecords to a group of persons for purposes of further distribution, public performance, or public display, constitutes publication. A public performance or display of a work does not of itself constitute publication.*[48] *Thus, according to current law, simply putting a message on the Internet does not necessarily constitute publication—the key is the transfer of ownership. Further complicating the issue is the notion of a "final edition." Traditionally recognized as the last, complete version of a newspaper or magazine, what constitutes a final edition in electronic form, when changes can continually be made?*

Adaptive Strategies and New Technology

Still, lessons from the past suggest that the old media will likely adapt to changes brought about by the development of new media technologies. Just as radio adapted to the introduction of television, one of the most likely changes is increased specialization. As new technologies have been introduced, old media have tended to adapt by identifying special interest, core audiences and targeting them. This adaptive strategy is both a coping mechanism as well as a consequence of the principle of relative constancy, first articulated by newspaper baron Charles E. Scripps and later tested by professor Maxwell McCombs.[49,50] Scripps observed that from 1929 to

1957 advertisers and consumers in the United States tended to spend a relatively constant amount of money on the mass media. McCombs's research demonstrated that, since 1929, Americans have spent a relatively constant portion of the Gross National Product (GNP) on media and communication products and services, approximately 4 to 5 percent. Moreover, as the amount of leisure time has also remained relatively constant during that period, and media choices have increased dramatically, there has been a greatly increased level of competition for the media audience. These factors explain much of the precipitous decline in the television networks' share of the television audience, as well as the decline in newspaper household penetration. People have relatively fixed amounts of time and money for media and communication, and are presented with an increasingly complex multi-channel communications environment. As a result, each medium is capturing less of the communication pie. The only major exception has been the telephone company. Consequently, existing, as well as new media, have often opted for a strategy of audience specialization. Still, Robert Iger, president of the ABC Television Network, admonishes TV critics not to blow taps just yet for the networks. Iger observes, "In a world in which there is massive choice, there's still going to be a need for someone to create order." This will be the role of the networks, Iger says.[51] History suggests he is probably right, since the past introduction of new media have not caused existing media to disappear, although their audience and revenue base have often been eroded.

Recent data compiled by telecommunications authority John Carey suggest that the average household spends about $184 a month for communication products and services.[52,53] By comparison, average gasoline expenditures (among those households with an automobile) are about $104 a month; household food averages $360 a month. The largest communication expenditures are for telephone service ($52 a month), followed by expenditures on radio sets, television sets, and recorded music ($44), cable television service ($30), and newspapers and magazines ($22). Videocassette rentals and purchases are about $17 a month, followed by books and maps ($16), and admission to movie theaters ($3). If McCombs's relative constancy hypothesis holds, then new media technologies will be vying for an increasingly competitive communications dollar. To increase overall expenditures on communication products will require either growth in the nation's economy, or a reallocation of expenditures from some other category, such as food or gasoline. This latter alternative is unlikely. Recent data do show a modest increase in spending on information products, although it is unclear whether this is a shift in long-term patterns or a momentary reallocation of consumer dollars.

A second likely development in new media is the extension of existing information services, especially in the creation of new electronic services, which will often consist of repackaging existing information in new formats. Newspapers, for example, have greatly increased their use of online services to deliver electronic news products. Although online media products have existed on the Internet since at least the early 1990s (e.g., *New York Newsday*'s special series on the "Battle for the Information Highway" was made available via the Internet in July, 1993; the *Electronic*

Trib, an electronic edition of the *Albuquerque* [New Mexico] *Tribune,* went online via the Internet in the fall of 1993; readers have communicated directly with writers by electronic mail and by participating in live 'chat' rooms—a group conversation conducted online through personal computers—for at least as long),[54] the Web is drawing never-before seen numbers to the world of online publishing. During just two years (1995 and 1996) an estimated 1,587 newspapers from at least 98 countries began publishing online newspapers, mostly via the World Wide Web (1,468), with at least 812 offered by U.S. newspapers.[55] It is expected that more than 2,000 news-papers worldwide will offer online products by 2000. Many of the U.S. newspapers have also joined forces in what is called the New Century Network to provide an online network of newspapers published on the Web, as a means to facilitate online advertising and commerce. The convergence of telephony and computing, and the advent of inexpensive screen phones, WebTV, and network computers may spur even more dramatic growth of online newspapers.

Computer-assisted Investigative Reporting

To a limited degree, media organizations are also adapting to the new media environment by developing their own new media applications that change how their staff does its work. One important example comes from the newsroom, where inves-tigative reporters have increasingly employed the computer as an investigative tool. With the advent of the computer era, the government began storing public records electronically, often on nine-track magnetic computer tapes on mainframe comput-ers. Investigative journalists were often hindered in their efforts to explore and ex-amine these records by the a number of factors, including limited access to electronic records of government, the complexity of the data and the mainframe computers required to read them, and a lack of financial and other resources needed to analyze computer records. Mainframe computers, although immensely powerful, are especially complex to use and program. Few investigative reporters, who were generally trained in journalism, not computer science, had the programming skills to set up mainframe applications to analyze massive databases of public records. New technology helped changed all this.

In reporting that helped the *Detroit Free Press* win a Pulitzer prize, professor Philip E. Meyer pioneered the use of the computer in journalism in 1967. Meyer's computerized study of survey data from riot-area blacks following the 1967 civil rights riots in Detroit produced a front-page series titled, "The People Beyond 12th Street." It spawned a form of reporting later described as precision journalism by distinguished journalism educator Everette E. Dennis.

Meyer's pioneering effort was followed by former *New York Times* investiga-tive reporter David Burnham's 1972 computer analysis of crime data in New York City. Burnham, the author of award-winning books and articles, attained legendary status in New York City for his investigative work with police officer Frank Serpico, a narcotics officer whose testimony before the Knapp Commission revealed wide-spread corruption and graft in the New York City Police Department. Burnham was the first journalist to use the computer to analyze public records, marking the beginning of what we today call *computer-assisted reporting* (CAR). Burnham used the *New York Times*'s mainframe computer to sort crime data by police precinct, revealing the first public mapping of the variation in crime rates throughout New York City.

Computer-assisted investigative reporting (CAIR, or CAR, for *computer-assisted reporting*) developed slowly during the next two decades, and few newspapers or other news organizations warmly embraced the field. CAR did not begin to become a part of mainstream journalism until Pulitzer prize-winning investigative reporter Elliot Jaspin developed NineTrack Express®, software for computer-assisted investigative reporting that allows reporters to analyze public records using their personal computer. Prior to Jaspin's creation of NineTrack Express® at The Freedom Forum Media Studies Center in 1989, reporters had to rely on mainframe computers for their investigative analyses. Because of the complexity of mainframe computing, this was a cumbersome and slow process, especially since most newspaper mainframes were not traditionally used by the editorial department; they were part of the business department for payroll processing and circulation data. NineTrack Express® allowed journalists to transfer data from the magnetic tapes commonly used by government agencies when storing data processed on mainframe to desktop computers. This new technology enabled investigative journalists to use spreadsheet and other database packages to analyze vast electronic files of public records that in the past were available either in paper form or required an expensive and complex mainframe computer to analyze.

Since 1989, every Pulitzer prize for investigative reporting has been awarded to a journalist whose research was based on a computer analysis of public records. One story in New York dramatized the impact of this new technology. *New York Newsday* investigative reporter Peggy Baer used NineTrack Express to uncover a major loophole in New York City property tax law. Baer had learned during a conversation over dinner in Greenwich Village that property tax law in New York did not require the City to inform property owners when they were owed a refund. Baer obtained the data records on magnetic tape that stored the City's property tax records. Using the computer to analyze the data, Baer determined that the City owed property tax owners a whopping $273 million in tax refunds, refunds the City had no intention of repaying unless requested. *Newsday* ran a front-page story proclaiming the City's $273 milion IOU, and then ran a complete listing of every property owner owed a refund as well as the amount they were owed. Since this story ran in 1991, the City has refunded more than $100 million in overpaid property taxes.

Today, dozens of newspapers and television newsrooms operate computer-assisted reporting programs. Some of those news organizations are listed in Table 3-2. Despite this trend, many news organizations still relegate CAR to "special project" status, and have not integrated it into the mainstream of their reporting. Full integration of CAR into American journalism will likely depend on not only a commitment of resources, but also a new mindset about the role of the computer in reporting

TABLE 3-2   Selected News Media Operating CAR Programs[56]

Daily Newspapers

Akron Beacon Journal
Asbury Park Press
Atlanta Journal & Constitution
Boston Globe
Boston Herald
Cleveland Plain Dealer
Dallas Morning News
Dayton Daily News
Detroit Free Press
Greensboro News & Record
Hartford Courant
Kansas City Star
Los Angeles Times
The Morning News Tribune (Tacoma, Wash.)
Minneapolis Star/Tribune
New York Times
New York Newsday
Orange County Register
Orlando Sentinel
Palm Beach Post
Philadelphia Inquirer
Pittsburgh Press
Providence Journal
Raleigh News & Observer
Record of Hackensack
Roanoke Times and News Report
San Francisco Chronicle
Seattle Post-Intelligencer
St. Louis Post Dispatch
St. Petersburg Times
Syracuse Herald Journal
The (Toledo) *Blade*
USA Today
Wall Street Journal

Television Stations

WNBC-TV News
WRC-TV (Washington, D.C.)

and perhaps even a reorganization of the newsroom to make use of computers in investigative reporting as routine as picking up the phone. Growth of the World Wide Web has also helped facilitate CAR in U.S. newsrooms, with sites such as www.census.gov and www.fec.gov making it even easier for reporters to access federal databases ranging from the U.S. Census to the Federal Election Commission.

Turning Something Old into Something New

Finally, new media content is likely to be based on the content of old media. For example, early television shows were often based directly on old radio programs, including soap operas, variety shows, and comedy and western series. Although this pattern may ease the transition in the short run, new media expert David Shefrin, former IBM executive who led the company's early multimedia efforts, head of the Shefrin Group, and pioneer in the experimental fax newspapers of the 1940s, has suggested that it is likely to fail in the long run. Shefrin, who passed away in 1996, explained that, as new media are being envisioned, "The models are still being thought out in terms of past experiences. You can see that with Diller and Paramount and investments in online services."[57] In Shefrin's view, these megamergers are designed to create greater vertical integration in the hopes of preserving old mass media values in the new media of distribution. Unfortunately, the content created for the new media may fail to exploit the full range of qualities of the new media.

Magazines: A Case Study in Technology Adaptation

One medium already undergoing extensive adaptation to the new delivery media is magazines. The first magazine, *The American Magazine,* was published in 1741. Benjamin Franklin's *General Magazine* was the second, and began publication shortly after *The American Magazine.* Franklin was proud of the *General Magazine* readership, and printed on the magazine's pages a complete list of its subscribers, which included many of the founding fathers of the United States, including George Washington, Thomas Jefferson, and Alexander Hamilton.[58] In the two and a half centuries since then, magazines have undergone a series of sweeping changes in their nature. Printing technologies of the late-1800s and early-1900s allowed magazines to become mass media. The introduction of radio, television, and film drew audience and advertising revenue away from magazines, and magazines adapted by specializing.

Today's information highway offers magazine publishers an opportunity for a "new lease on life," says Clay Felker, founder of *New York Magazine,* former editor in chief and C.E.O. of *The Village Voice,* former editor, publisher, and C.E.O. of *Esquire* and pioneer in the development of the new journalism. Felker has explained that magazine publishing is being assaulted by escalating costs for printing and postage. Not only has the number of magazines published and distributed in the United States grown to more than 10,000, but many other publications printed on the same coated paper stock and distributed via the U.S. mail have emerged, including direct mail and preprinted newspaper inserts. The electronic highway has presented a new opportunity for magazine publishing. Already, hundreds of established magazines, including the leading news magazine in America, *Time,* offer electronic versions, most via the Web.

Several scenarios for the future are possible, depending on the development of technology. In the short term, digital editions of these magazines are likely to be increasingly delivered over the information highway. "Readers" will use their computer to read the electronic magazines of their choice, perhaps printing selected stories, or even entire magazines, and publishers will save on printing and distribution costs.

An alternative scenario, perhaps more long-term, depends on the refinement of the flat panel, or tablet, computer display.[59] The flat panel will eventually have the display quality of ink on paper, will be highly portable, being about the size and weight of a notepad, and may cost less than $200. With flat panels, electronic magazines need not be printed at all. Instead, readers will simply download and read at their leisure electronic magazines that look exactly like their printed counterparts of today. Much as they are now beginning to do on the World Wide Web, advertisers will introduce a variety of new direct marketing features, such as fully interactive ads, in which readers not only request more information about a product, or book a hotel reservation, but even make an electronic purchase. Ultimately, advertisers will achieve the maximum target marketing, collecting data about exactly who reads their ads, who responds to them, and who purchases the product as a direct response to the ad. The pricing structure of magazine advertising will be redefined based on impact assessment. At the same time, however, magazines and other publishers are facing competition from other forms of new commercial media, such as computer-generated point-of-sale coupons, or supermarket-issued shopper IDs, which allow stores to generate their own specialized databases of individual consumer purchase patterns and highly targeted direct mail advertising, potentially circumventing traditional media outlets, even in electronic form. Although there have been a number of lurches and false starts in the development of the flat panel media product, several recent efforts suggest the flat panel is now ready for prime time. The Walt Disney Co.'s Imagineering unit in Glendale, California unveiled a prototype flat panel magazine in October of 1996, and in Europe, a flat panel product called the NewsPAD has already been used successfully by news consumers to get their electronic newspaper in Edinburgh, Scotland and Barcelona, Spain.[60]

These electronic publishing scenarios will allow magazine publishers to publish their products on new time schedules. Weeklies could become dailies, with even more frequent updates on breaking news events or other topics, depending on reader interest. Moreover, magazines could become fully multimedia, incorporating text, data, sound, and full-motion video. One of the challenges facing these multimedia magazines will be to develop simple navigational tools to let readers glide as easily through electronic magazine choices as they do with printed magazines. Many companies are working on navigational tools, such as *Stargazer* for interactive TV, from Bell Atlantic, which organizes content by categories like entertainment, news, and education.

Each scenario, but especially the electronic, flat panel model, could allow magazines to provide stories of much greater depth, since story length becomes almost irrelevant in the digital world. Depth becomes a matter of user demand, not limited by space or pages. With the exception of magazines like *The New Yorker* under editor Tina Brown, few publications devote extensive space to most stories, observes publishing pioneer Clay Felker. The problem is that the rising costs of printing and distribution via the postal service have forced magazines to reduce their size, both in terms of numbers of pages and trim size (i.e., the size of the actual page). Large circulation magazines such as *Time* or *Newsweek,* for example, save millions of dollars each year by reducing their trim size by a 1/4 inch. Advertisers will pay the same amount for a full-page ad, regardless of the exact size of the page, and the reduced page size reduces the printing cost and the postage cost because of the reduced weight. Electronic distribution can change all that. By radically reducing the cost of distributing the product and by eliminating the cost of printing it (and perhaps helping the environment), magazine publishers could completely reinvent their magazines. They could reintroduce long-form journalism, they could expand on "news you can use," which has become the hallmark of *U.S. News and World Report,* and, as Felker explains, now devotes 50 percent of its pages to such user-friendly news.

However, there are dangers. Electronic magazines, Felker cautions, have the danger of become media for the elite. In the new model, many magazines may become increasingly specialized and expensive, especially when costly electronic devices are needed to receive and print them. Ironically, the information highway of 2000 may help recreate the elitist magazines of two centuries ago, when the core subscribers to Ben Franklin's *General American* were the signers of the Declaration of Independence.

LEARNING FROM HISTORY: A SUMMARY

From the evolution of the fax to the introduction of the flat panel display, history offers considerable insight into the future of new media technologies. Some lessons to be learned include:

- Few media technologies are truly new, and even fewer are immediately successful on their initial introduction to the marketplace (witness the 1990s struggle to find a formula for profitability in publishing on the World Wide Web).
- The success of all new technologies is dependent on a confluence of circumstances, including price, reliability, simplicity—sometimes called "user friendliness"—and a clear use or application.
- Many attempts to introduce new media technologies are destined to fail and to cost their creators great sums of money—so watch carefully those who go before you and learn from their successes and failures.
- A variety of unanticipated circumstances, or what telecommunications expert John Carey calls the "serendipity factor," often make marketplace predictions completely unreliable—so be prepared to follow your instincts at times and to be adaptable to unforeseen circumstances.[61]
- There are valuable lessons to be learned from past failures in the realm of new media technologies.

"For every new technology success in the 1980s, there were ten failures," notes Bruce Maggin, executive vice president, Capital Cities/ABC, Inc. Video Enterprises.[62] Today's ventures in new media technology follow on the heels of many attempts and failures from the 1970s and 1980s, such as videotex, teletext, Qube, and so on. We might learn something valuable, he adds, when venturing into the uncharted waters of new media technology from a most unlikely source: penguins in the Antarctic. Antarctic penguins, he explains, form two lines when entering the water. The second line pushes the first line into the water, and if they come up with fish in their mouths, then the second line dives into the water. If they come up in the mouths of sharks, then the second line stays out of the water. "It pays to be in the second line when introducing new technology," Maggin concludes.

NOTES

[1]Brand, Stewart (1987). *The Media Lab: Inventing the Future at MIT.* New York: Viking.

[2]Schramm, Wilbur (1988). *The Story of Human Communication: Cave Painting to Microchip.* New York: Harper & Row, Publishers.

[3]White, Jan V. (1988). *Graphic Design for the Electronic Age.* New York: Watson-Gruptill Publications.

[4]Dordick, Herbert S. and Georgette Wang (1993). *The Information Society: A Retrospective View.* Newbury Park, CA: Sage Publications.

[5]Pavlik, John (1992). *Media Technology Chronology.* Software published by Wayne Danielson Software.

[6]Featherstone, Mike, ed., (1990) *Global Culture.* Newbury Park, CA: Sage Publications.

[7]Ostry, Sylvia, "The Domestic Domain: The New International Policy Area," *Transnational Corporations 1,* no. 1 (February 1992): 7.

[8]Clarke, Arthur C. "Extraterrestrial Relays," *Wireless World,* June 1945.

[9]Mowlana, Hamid, George Gerbner and Herbert I. Schiller (1992). *Triumph of the Image: The Media's War in the Persian Gulf: A Global Perspective.* Boulder, CO: Westview Press.

[10]Wriston, Walter (1992) *Twilight of Sovereignty: How the Information Revolution Is Transforming Our World,* New York: Scribners: 12.

[11] Apple Jr.,R.W. "Policing a Global Village," *New York Times,* October 13, 1993: A1.

[12]Schiller, Herbert I., "Transnational Media: Creating Consumers Worldwide. *Journal of International Affairs,* Summer, 1993, no. 1: 47.

[13]Selnow, Gary W. (1993). *High-Tech Campaigns: Computer Technology in Political Communication.* Westport, CT: Praeger.

[14]Markoff, John "Rear Adm. Grace Hopper Dies; Innovator in Computers Was 85," *New York Times,* January 3, 1992, page A17.

[15]Meyrowitz, Joshua. *No Sense of Place: The Impact of Electronic Media on Social Behavior.* New York: Oxford University Press, 1985.

[16]Markoff, John. "Toys Now, Computers Tomorrow," *New York Times,* April 20, 1994: D1, D6.

[17]Powell, Adam Clayton, III, Speech at Technology Studies seminar hosted by The Freedom Forum Media Studies Center, October 27, 1993.

[18]Kenneth M. King, "Computers, Man and Society Seminar Remarks," Columbia University, December 18, 1996.

[19]www.intel.com/intel/museum/25anniv/html/hof/moore.htm

[20]Gilder, George. "Law of the Microcosm," *Forbes ASAP,* 1994.

[21]"Movie Magic," The Discovery Channel, June 16, 1994.

[22]Shefrin, David, 1993. "History of the Fax Newspaper." Pavlik and Dennis, co-editors, 1993, *Demystifying Media Technology: Disk Edition.* Mountain View, CA: Mayfield Publishing.

[23]Williams, Bill. "FaxPaper." In Pavlik and Dennis, co-editors, 1993, *Demystifying Media Technology: Disk Edition.* Mountain View, CA: Mayfield Publishing.

[24]Levy, Mark (ed.) (1989). *The VCR Age: Home Video and Mass Communication.* Newbury Park, CA: Sage Publications.

[25]Arthur, Brian, "Positive Feedback in Economic Modeling," *Scientific American,* 1991.

[26]Carey, John, "Back to the Future: How New Communication Technologies Enter American Homes," Technology Studies Seminar, The Freedom Forum Media Studies Center, Oct. 26, 1993.

[27]Holzmann, Gerard J. and Bjorn Pehrson, "The First Data Networks," *Scientific American,* January 1994.

[28]White, Jan V. (1988). *Graphic Design for the Electronic Age.* New York: Watson-Gruptill Publications.

[29]Holzmann, Gerard J. and Bjorn Pehrson, "The First Data Networks," *Scientific American,* January 1994:124.

[30]*Wired,* "Historical Premonitions of the Information Superhighway," August 1994: 64.

[31]Carey, James (1989). *Communication as Culture.* London: Unwin Hyman.

[32]"Treasure Hunters," The Discovery Channel, February 1, 1994.

[33]*Information & Interactive Services Report,* Sept. 27, 1993.

[34]Donegan, Jack, San Diego Supercomputer Center, Cities of the Future conference, December 13, 1994.

[35]Levy, Steven. "We Have Seen the Content, and It Is Us." *The Media Studies Journal,* Winter, 1994.

[36]Kahrenburg, K. K., "Power of the Media in the Global System," *Journal of International Affairs,* 1993: i.

[37]*Business Week,* "The 1993 Business Week 1000: U.S. Companies Ranked by Industry."

[38]Postman, Neil. (1992). *Technopoly: The Surrender of Culture to Technology.* New York: Random House.

[39]Gore, Albert, Jr., "Information for the Global Village." *Scientific American,* 1991.

[40]Clinton, W. J., & Gore A. (1993, February). *Technology for America's economic growth, a new direction to build economic strength.* Washington, DC: Office of the President of the United States.

[41]Markoff, John, op. cit. November 3, 1993.

[42]Dordick, Herbert S. and Dale E. Lehman, "Information Highways: 'Trickle Down' Infrastructure?" Chapter in Fred Williams and John V. Pavlik (editors), *The People's Right to Know: Media, Democracy and the Information Highway,* Lawrence Erlbaum Associates, 1993.

[43]B. Kahin, *Information Infrastructures.* New York: McGraw-Hill, Inc., 1992.

[44]Dordick and Lehman, op. cit.

[45]Pavlik, John and Everette E. Dennis, "Traveling the Information Superhighway," The Freedom Forum Media Studies Center, 1994.

[46]Pavlik, op. cit., 1992.

[47]Smith, Anthony (1980). *Goodbye Gutenberg.* New York: Oxford University Press, 1980.

[48]Copyright Law of the United States of America, contained in Title 17 of the United States Code, Revised to March 1, 1991.

[49]Shaw, Donald L. (1993). "The Rise and Fall of American Mass Media." *Journal of Communication.*

[50]McCombs, M. E., & Eyal, C. H. (1980). Spending on Mass Media. *Journal of Communication* 30(1), 153-158. McCombs, M. E., & Nolan, J. (1992). The Relative Constancy Approach to Consumer Spending for Media. *Journal of Media Economics,* 5(2), 43–52.

[51]Greenfield, Jeff. "American Agenda," *ABC World News Tonight with Peter Jennings,* Sept., 1993.

[52]Carey, John, "BHow New Communication Technologies Enter American Homes," Exploring New Media Seminar, Columbia University, Nvember 7, 1996.

[53]U.S. Department of Commerce, Bureau of Labor Statistics, Morgan Stanley & Co., 1994.

[54]Wilson, Kinsey, "Your Life as an Open Book," *New York Newsday,* July 21, 1993: 46.

[55]E&P Interactive Online Newspaper Database, maunaloa.com:4901/ephome/npaper/nphtm/stats.htm (12/26/96).

[56]Pavlik, John V. and Mark A. Thalhimer, "A Brief History of Computer-Assisted Investigative Reporting," The Freedom Forum Media Studies Center, 1992.

[57]*Mediaweek,* Sept. 27, 1993.

[58]Felker, Clay (1993). Oct. 13, 1993 fellows seminar at The Freedom Forum Media Studies Center.

[59]Fidler, Roger, "Mediamorphosis," chapter in Frederick Williams and John V. Pavlik, editors (1994). *The People's Right To Know: Media, Democracy, and the Information Highway.* Hillsdale, NJ: Lawrence Erlbaum Associates.

[60]Steve Outing, "New Media News & Analysis: Digital Tablet Makes Strides in Europe and U.S." Wednesday/Thursday, October 23–24, Editor & Publisher Interactive.

[61]Carey, op. cit., 1993.

[62]Maggin, Bruce, "Riding the Information Highway," Speech at the Center for Communications, Sept. 30, 1993.

4

The Technology

"All this may seem more like science fiction than reality. Indeed, in the history of the world, it has been only a few hundred years since gunpowder transformed human warfare and less than a century since television connected the world. But just as those inventions brought us to the twentieth century, so will digital information transmit us into the next, transforming everything from how we learn to how we work."
—ALBERT GORE, JR., VICE PRESIDENT OF THE UNITED STATES.[1]

New media technologies beckon more enticingly than ever. More than merely offering an improvement on existing forms of communication, new media technologies are creating what telecommunications scholar Frederick Williams calls a "virtually new medium of public communication."[2] Enabled by the convergence of telecommunications, computing and media, the new media landscape offers true interactivity, full user control, and multimedia communications. Virtual reality, already being applied in medicine, employee training and video arcades, may transform mediated communication into a total sensory experience. The Internet and World Wide Web promise universal access to untold treasures of data, knowledge and an unparalleled array of interactive, multimedia information and entertainment.

But how much of this is hype and how much is reality? Which technologies will succeed and help remake society, and which will become little more than objects of curiosity, artifacts in a technology museum of the future? Identifying which technologies will transform the media and communications world is a slippery slope, in which many ultimately important technologies will be excluded, and other technologies receiving much attention will eventually fade into obscurity. Moreover, although many of these technologies may offer social, cultural, educational, and commercial benefits, they bring with them a variety of costs, and there is little guarantee that their availability will reach every strata of society on an equitable basis. This chapter systematically examines the hardware now available, as well as that on the media technology horizon. Chapter 5 then reviews the key concepts and applications central to understanding the new media landscape. Chapter 6 subsequently examines the key players developing these technologies.

NEW MEDIA TECHNOLOGY MAP

As Columbus's 1492 encounter with the Americas required European cartographers to redraw their maps of the world, so too has the development of new, digital, computer-based technologies required us to redraw the conceptual map of the media world. No longer do old organizational frameworks apply when analyzing media industries. What were once separate and distinct media, such as newspapers, broadcasting, cable, and telephony, are now becoming increasingly indistinct and overlapping as the old lines blur. Similarly, the scholarly domain of media studies is undergoing a transformation as a new communication paradigm emerges, one based on a unified, global mediamorphosis.

A new conceptual map is needed to understand the contours and topography of the new media landscape. In this chapter we will use the media technology map developed in the opening chapter of the book to guide our discussion of each emerging media technology. This framework emphasizes digital, computer-based technologies and how they are changing the way information is

- Gathered, processed, and produced,
- Transmitted,
- Stored, and
- Received and displayed.

The Creation Machines

This section reviews technologies used in the gathering, production, and processing of media and communications content. The discussion is grouped into two parts: Part one includes electronic information processing technologies, particularly computers and related computer technologies; part two reviews electronic information gathering devices, such as image capturing and related technologies, as well as speech recognition and synthesis technologies.

Part I: Electronic Information Processing Technologies

The Computer.   As the basis of all electronic information processing technologies, the computer comes in all shapes, sizes, and prices, from low-priced, laptop personal computers (PCs) to powerful room-size supercomputers and parallel processors that cost more than half a million dollars (see Table 4-1). This discussion concentrates on the personal computer and other consumer-related computer products, although the section also looks at video servers, the computer engines driving interactive television, and video on demand.

TABLE 4-1   Qualities of Computer Market Segments, Ranked by Price

Market Segment	Price Range	Processing Speed	Primary Function
Network Computer (NC)/ WebTV	$750 $300	<100 MIPS	Internet/ WWW Access
Personal Computers (including palmtop and laptop)	$1,000–10,000	100–200 MIPS (500 on horizon)	Desktop Applications, Advanced Multimedia Network Access
Workstations	$5,000–60,000	500 MIPS	Desktop applications Network Servers, High-Resolution Graphics, simulations
Mainframes and minicomputers	$25,000–500,000	500–1,000 MIPS	Central processors for data from linked terminals
Supercomputers	$500,000 or more	Up to 50,000 MIPS	Numerical processing massive data

MIPS refers to millions of instructions per second.

Sources: Transnational Data and Communications Report, 1994; The U.S. International Trade Commission.[3,4]

Warp Speed.   The twentieth century's fastest personal computers (PCs) are based on the Intel Pentium microprocessor.[5] With the 200 megahertz (MHz) Pentium processor available in 1996 and a 500 MHz processor slated for 1997, Pentium PCs have more speed than supercomputers of a decade ago. "These machines are like dragsters," says John C. Dvorak, a widely read computer columnist. "There are no bells and whistles, they just go fast," writes technology reporter John Markoff.[6] They're fast, and they're not even very expensive, though there are exceptions. For example, Gateway 2000, a small company started in a garage in South Dakota, sells its model G6-200 XL 200 MHz PC for just $3,749, a price that includes a 3.8 gigabyte hard drive, 64 megabytes of DRAM, a 33.6 fax modem on a credit card-sized insert device, an 8x CD-ROM drive, and a CrystalScan 700 15.9 inch viewable area color monitor. Interested parties can review the latest specifications for such a computer and even order it directly from the Gateway 2000 Web site.[7]

Increasing Processing Power.   The current generation of 200 megahertz Pentium microprocessors offers the latest support for what is called Moore's Law.[8] In terms of processing power, today's Pentium microprocessor has in a single microchip DRAM capacity of more than 64 megabits, the equivalent of 1,500 pages of text. By 2008 the DRAM capacity will reach 64 gigabits, or the equivalent of roughly 45,000 pages of text.

Caveat Emptor: Let the Buyer Beware!   Any discussion of the Intel Pentium chip would be remiss without acknowledging an early flaw identified in Intel's highly touted chip. On October 30, 1994, Dr. Thomas R. Nicely, a mathematics professor at Lynchburg College in Virginia reported on the Internet that the Pentium chip occasionally made errors in mathematical division operations involving long strings of numbers.[9] The problem was due to an error in the chip's "look up table," where all calculations are checked for accuracy by the computer. Every number in the look up table is normally accurate to 16 decimal places, but in the case of the Pentium chip, some numbers were accurate to only five places, thus occasionally producing the equivalent of rounding error. Intel subsequently admitted that they had known of the error since July of 1994, but had not considered the problem serious enough to disclose. Public confusion, IBM's discontinuation of selling Pentium-based PCs and the falling price of Intel stock all led Intel to announce a chip replacement program. Intel has since corrected the problem, but not before the error had spurred a series of Pentium jokes that quickly made the rounds on the Internet, including:

Q: How many Pentium designers does it take to screw in a light bulb?
A: 1.99904274017, but that's close enough for nontechnical people.

Q: What's another name for the "Intel Inside" sticker they put on Pentiums?
A: The warning label.

Q: Why didn't Intel call the Pentium the 586?
A: Because they added 486 (the number of the fastest chip prior to the Pentium) and 100 on the first Pentium and got 585.999983605.

Top of the Heap.   Challenging the Pentium as master of the desktop is the PowerPC, based on a fast, inexpensive PowerPC chip that is also largely compatible with many existing applications, whether of MS-DOS or Macintosh design. At least that is the promise. Tests suggest full compatibility has not quite arrived. IBM, Apple Computer, and Motorola are hoping that their jointly designed PowerPC family of RISC (Reduced Instruction Set computer) computers will draw consumers away from the Pentium line, which is based on CISC (Complex Instruction Set Computer) chip technology, which is produced by Intel.[10]

RISCy Business.   Because of their enhanced efficiency and speed, RISC computers are considered technically superior to CISC computers, or Complex Instruction Set Computers. Until recently, RISC computers have had limited utility in the PC marketplace, largely because Microsoft's Windows 95, the dominant PC platform in business settings, has not been compatible with the RISC technology. The recent development of the Unix-based Windows NT by Microsoft, however, changes that situation. Windows NT operates with RISC computers using the MIPS chip developed by Silicon Graphics, Inc. Intel says its CISC chip has been able to keep pace with the RISC technology by redesigning it to let each software instruction run in a single tick of the computer's clock.[11]

In 1963, computer pioneer Seymour Cray of Control Data Corporation (CDC) invented the CDC 6600, the world's first commercially available computer capable of executing three million program instructions per second. It represents the first use of Reduced Instruction Set Computing (RISC). In 1968, Cray, who died in 1996, developed the next generation in RISC computers, the CDC 7600 capable of 15 million instructions per second.

True Believers: Enter the PowerPC.   One of the first computers to use the PowerPC chip, the new PowerPC Macintosh, has already drawn many true believers. "The PowerPC is the light side of the force," observes John Battelle, managing editor for *Wired* magazine.[12] "It's the chip with a heart," he adds. Crusaders for the PowerPC Macintosh are convinced it will lead the way into the future of computing, driving the merger of computers and technologies like handheld devices and digital set-top devices.

To many, the Power Macintosh represents the beginning of the end of an almost holy quest for a unified computing platform capable of running software for both the IBM PC and the Macintosh desktop computer. A single machine to run various versions of software would make it "the ideal lab computer," says Pamela S. Vogel of Brown University.[13] Still, differences remain between the two platforms, such as the RISC versus CISC technology, and the quest continues.

Video Servers.   Silicon Graphics is the principle provider of video servers, although a number of other companies have developed competing platforms. Video servers are the digital library driving the video-on-demand service promised in the current round of interactive TV trials.

Notebook, Laptop, Sublaptop, and Palmtop Computers.   Reflecting the trend toward miniaturization in the computing world is the development of ever smaller, lighter, and more portable computers. Notebook, Laptop, Sublaptop, and Palmtop Computers (or Personal Digital Appliances, or PDAs) represent the decreasing size and weight of the family of portable computers. Each is progressively lighter and more portable, but typically has greater limitations, such as less power or speed, less storage capacity and less battery life. They also vary in price, as reflected in Table 4-1. Over time, the power, speed, and overall performance of even the smallest and lightest of these computers is increasing, and within the next decade the tiniest of these computers is likely to have the power of today's most powerful parallel processing computer. One complicating factor is the size of the keyboard. Still the dominant medium for inputting text, the keyboard can be reduced in size to a certain degree, before becoming unusable as a typing interface. With the development of speech recognition technology, however, it may be possible to input by voice command text and other information to even the smallest super-small computers that may not even need to include a keyboard as a standard item. Palmtop computers, in fact, do not include a full-size keyboard, although none in 1997 recognize voice command.

Network Computer (NC).   The Network Computer (NC) is a computer whose arrival has been both hailed and decried. It has been hailed as the answer to the problem of providing low-cost access to the Internet and the World Wide Web. It has been decried as unneeded in an era when the price of computing power is falling dramatically from month to month, and all one really needs to get low-cost Internet access is to buy a used 486 PC. Nevertheless, 1996 saw the introduction of several alternative NCs (e.g., the JavaStation NC, introduced in 1996 by Sun Microsystems and others), and an admission by Microsoft's Bill Gates that perhaps the Network Computer might serve a useful purpose. A related device is the set-top box, or signal decoder, that attaches to a television set (such as the WebTV discussed later in this book), and provides low-cost access to the Internet.

Desktop Publishing.   Coinciding with the rise of the desktop computer is the technology today known collectively as *desktop publishing*. The term refers to a collection of hardware and software applications that developed in the 1980s to allow computerized publishing on personal computers. The advent of the Macintosh computer drove the desktop publishing field, making integrated text and graphics processing simple and inexpensive. Author Steven Levy describes the impact of the Macintosh computer as profound. In *Insanely Great: The Life and Times of* Macintosh, *the Computer That Changed Everything,* Levy argues that not only did the Macintosh spur the graphics revolution, but it brought the computer out of its exclusive domain and into the mainstream of society by popularizing desktop computing.[14]

Digital Darkroom.   Paralleling the meteoric rise of desktop publishing is the emergence of the digital darkroom, the video analog of desktop publishing. The digital darkroom refers to a computerized version of a chemical darkroom used to develop and process emulsion film. A digital darkroom, however, is not used to develop images. Rather, images are either scanned in from film or ported directly in from a digital camera or another digital medium, and are then manipulated in the digital darkroom. A digital darkroom can perform all the processing functions of a chemical darkroom, such as cropping or shading. In addition, a digital darkroom can be used to seamlessly manipulate images in a variety of other ways, such as add or delete portions of the existing image, combine two images, or create totally synthetic images based on real photographs. All of these functions are possible in a chemical darkroom, but are not as easy, simple, or seamless as in the digital darkroom. Moreover, because of digital image capturing technology, there is no longer necessarily a film negative to document the existence of an original image.

Desktop Video.   Advances in desktop computing have also made it possible to seamlessly process full-motion video using a Macintosh or a PC. Especially important is the fact that with desktop video, manipulation of the video is not only simple and fast, but because it is in digital format, it is nonlinear. In contrast to editing analog videotape, desktop video allows the editor to move instantly from one image or sequence to another, to remove, add, resequence or modify any images in a database or image file in the same manner a writer can edit text in a word processor.

Part II: Electronic Information Gathering

Digital technologies are rapidly transforming the process of gathering information of all types. From electronic photography to speech recognition, new media technologies are providing a direct electronic link between external stimuli, such as images and sounds, and computer processing devices.

Electronic Photography.   Digital technology has begun to transform the manner in which visual information is captured and stored. Although the quality has much improved, the fundamental principle of using chemical processes to capture images on film has changed little since the invention of still photography in the early part of the nineteenth century. Credited with the invention of still photography, in 1839 Frenchmen Louis-Jacques-Mande Daguerre and Joseph Niepce developed the first practical photographic technology known as the Daguerreotype. The Daguerreotype allowed for the production of a permanent image on a silver-coated copper plate treated with iodine vapor. Digital photography represents an entirely new approach to capturing images without chemicals. Instead, digital cameras use

an electronic charge-coupled device (CCD) to capture and store images electronically.

Introduced as an analog technology in the early 1970s by RCA, the charge-
coupled device (CCD) eventually lead to the replacement of tubes in video cameras.
CCD-based cameras employ a photo sensor to capture an image in an analog format,
and then digitally transfer the image to an output amplifier. Such CCD-based cameras offer several advantages over conventional emulsion film-based cameras, including no film processing delay, maintained image resolution when either the
camera or image is moving, no aging of the CCD, no warm-up time, smaller and
lighter cameras, and less temperature and light sensitivity (although many tube cameras have been rendered useless by pointing them directly at the sun or another
bright light, CCD cameras are much less susceptible to this malady).

The first broadcast-quality CCD-based cameras were developed in 1986, when
USA Today, *The Chicago Tribune,* and *Newsday* inaugurated the use of still video
(or CCD) cameras in news reporting by using the electronic cameras for their photographic coverage of the Republican National Convention. Using Canon's RC701,
the papers captured images via a CCD-based camera for recording onto a magnetic
disc. Images were then sent by modem directly into the newsroom, bypassing processing in a chemical darkroom.

Digital/Electronic Photography.   The latest generation of CCD cameras and
photographic technologies now capture and store images in a digital format. It
makes possible the complete processing of any images—still or full motion—in a
computerized, nonlinear environment. With wide commercial applications in advertising, public relations, and journalism, it also raises a variety of thorny ethical questions about establishing the authenticity, veracity, and credibility of the
photographic image, since digital cameras do not provide a film negative and electronic images can be easily manipulated (see Digital Watermark). One of the major
drawbacks of the digital video camera has been the quality of the image. When
introduced, these cameras could produce images with no more than about 600,000
pixels (the smallest picture element in a computer image) of resolution, versus the
equivalent of some 35 million pixels in an emulsion film photograph. The latest
generation of digital cameras, however, have substantially improved image resolution, with Kodak's 1996 professional digital camera storing images with some six
million pixels.[15] The human eye cannot easily distinguish between images at this
level of resolution. Moreover, few media reproduce images at this level of resolution, whether the highest quality magazine or high-definition television.

Digital Watermark.   Because digital technology makes manipulating and
synthesizing images and documents as easy and seamless as editing text on a word
processor, it is increasingly difficult for anyone viewing an electronic image or
document to know whether what they are seeing is real or has been tampered with.
One tool for solving this problem is called a *digital watermark*. A number of researchers are developing digital watermarks designed to provide an indelible elec-

tronic signature or fingerprint on a computerized document or image that will protect the intellectual property rights of the original copyright holder of an image. This is an important step toward creating a secure and reliable international arena for electronic commerce and culture.

At Columbia University, a collaborative team of researchers in engineering and journalism has developed a digital watermark that not only protects copyright, but authenticates the source of an image, and indicates the probability of whether an image or document has been tampered with since its point of origination. Lead by Professor Shif-Fu Chang, the team has developed a tool that encodes at the pixel, or most fundamental level of a computer image or document, a digital watermark that will survive compression, editing, or transmission over a network. As a result, the receiver of a digital document or image can instantly see whether that document is authentic, who the source is, and, if it is not authentic, which parts of the document or image were likely to have been tampered with. This process of authentication is of critical importance to establishing the reliability of news on the information highway, as well as providing a secure environment for commerce on the Internet.

Electronic News Gathering (ENG). Introduced by pioneering CBS engineer Joseph Flaherty in the early 1970s, *electronic news gathering* (ENG) refers to the use of portable electronic video systems and audio apparatus in news collection.[16] 1973 marked the turning point for ENG because of the creation of the time-base corrector, which could convert the product of a videotape recorder into an image that was clear enough to broadcast directly, without the need for further processing. Reports indicate that by 1973 just 3 percent of local TV news stations had begun using modern ENG equipment in collecting information. By the late 1970s, virtually every local station and national network was using ENG equipment, and ENG had become the de facto standard in television news.

ENG coverage offered a number of advantages over film, the traditional medium for television news, including speed (due to the elimination of the film processing time), labor savings, reduced personnel necessary for an on-site taping, cost savings through the reusability of video, and easy transportation. ENG also brought with it some unexpected consequences, including new styles of editing with more rapid pacing.[17]

Satellite News Gathering (SNG). A cousin of electronic news gathering, SNG technology links the technology of electronic cameras with advances in satellite communications. Today's SNG technology enables reporters anywhere in the world to transmit video to any other part of the world instantly and at low cost. Thus, for better or worse, SNG has made "going live" the standard in local and network TV news coverage.

High-8 Millimeter Video/Camcorders. A similarly important technological development in the area of electronic photography is the high-8 millimeter videocamera. Also based on the use of a CCD sensor, high-8 cameras record images in analog format, but on 8 millimeter (mm) tape, rather than the much larger 16 mm or 35 mm VHS tape or Beta formats previously used for most broadcast-quality video content. The high-8 cameras are also much smaller, lighter, and less expensive than conventional video cameras, making them considerably more portable and versatile. As a result, high-8 cameras, which vary in size from a shoulder pack camera to a palm-size camcorder, and range in price from about $1,000 to $20,000, have been used to cover stories in remote and dangerous locations—the first video of the oil well fires in Kuwait at the end of the Persian Gulf War was shot using a high-8 camera. Increasingly, print news organizations are even equipping their reporters with high-8 cameras, because of their low cost and portability, to provide video coverage of breaking news events.

Importantly, the competing S-VHS format (super-VHS) produces nearly identical resolution as the half-inch high-8 format, with both providing 400+ lines of resolution instead of the 260+ for standard VHS. Many stations use S-VHS instead of or in addition to high-8 cameras, including FOX Network News.

Digital Video Camcorders. Rapidly making obsolete the high-8 camera, however, is the digital video camcorder. Manufacturers such as Sony have begun marketing broadcast-quality digital video camcorders of roughly the same size, weight, and storage capacity of their magnetic-tape based counterparts. Cost is only slightly higher, with broadcast-quality digital camcorders available for about $4,000 in 1997.[18]

Omnidirectional Imaging. One of the most remarkable new media technologies under development today is the omnidirectional camera. Omnidirectional cameras capture images from an entire hemisphere or even 360-degree field of vision. This technology changes one of the most fundamental assumptions underlying photography since its inception: that the photographer makes a basic editorial decision about what is important in a scene by where he or she points the lens. Omnidirectional cameras make pointing the camera obsolete. An "omnicamera" takes in an entire scene.

One omnidirectional imaging system is already commercially available for still photography. In 1996, Omniview released its "BubblePhoto" technology. At its Web site, *The New York Times* has published selected BubblePhotos, including 360-degree images from Yankee Stadium, the number one train, and a pickup basketball game in Manhattan. These photos were produced by taking two back-to-back photos using a 35mm still camera equipped with a fish-eye lens. The photos were digitized and then processed using the Omniview software system and published on the Web. Without any mechanical or moving parts, anyone viewing these pictures can navigate freely through the entire 360-degree images, panning, tilting, and zooming in or out. The only real limit is the amount of resolution in the original image, which means images quickly become fuzzy if one zooms in too closely.

Columbia University Professor Shree Nayar is developing the next generation of omnidirectional imaging technology, in this case, a 360-degree omnicam for broadcast quality, real-time, full-motion video. Nayar's system uses a single standard NTSC video camera attached to a specially prepared parabolic mirror to capture an entire hemispheric field of vision. Just as with the Omnview system for still images, Nayar's omnicamera enables the viewer to navigate through the entire field of vision without ever moving the camera, although the camera is capable of capturing omnidirectional video while moving. Nayar's system feeds the 360-degree video via a coaxial cable into a desktop computer, which converts the analog stream into digital format. Notably, the system outputs as many as twenty virtual or software cameras, each one of which is a different frame of vision within the total scene. Although the implications of this technology are profound for remote security monitoring systems, they are perhaps even more profound for entertainment, news, and other forms of new media storytelling. Under the direction of the author, the Center for New Media at Columbia University is currently conducting a field test of Nayar's omnicam in a New York City news story. Nayar has also developed a 3-D depth-sensing camera, which, if merged with the omnidirectional imaging system, would forever alter the digital video and visual storytelling landscape.

Optical Scanners.   Optical scanners are computer input devices that use optical technology to digitize visual information such as pages of text, images, and other documents and bring that visual information into a computer processing or transmission environment. Using optical character reader (OCR) software, some scanners can decipher text as well, although few low-end (i.e., inexpensive) products are capable of reading characters with high reliability. Typically, most OCR scanners are most accurate with typewritten text using a uniform font or typeface. Handwritten text is especially problematic, and requires considerable subsequent error correction using spell-checker software or human editing.

Remote Sensing Technology: Covering the Globe Using Remote-Sensing Satellite Images.   Reading the newspaper or watching television are things most of us do every day, and they don't seem like much of a technological achievement. But if you've seen the movie *Patriot Games,* then you know that satellite technology has changed all that. With the latest image-enhancement software, reading the license plate of a car driving on the Washington Beltway is now something the C.I.A.—or anyone with access to the right remote-sensing satellite—can do from more than 500 miles away.

Most of us, of course, don't have access to the C.I.A.'s spy satellites with super-high resolution sensors and advanced image-enhancement technology. Journalists in particular have been frustrated by the lack of access to these technologies. Nevertheless, reporters have found creative ways to use the available satellite images to tell important stories. *The New York Times* has reported that the C.I.A. may soon give its consent to commercial sales of spy satellite equipment and images.[19] R.

James Woolsey, the Director of the Central Intelligence Agency, is seriously considering "advancing C.I.A.'s position from 'no, never' to considering support for international sales of hardware and perhaps imagery," said David French, an agency spokesman.[20]

From Amazonia to the Persian Gulf.   Since the early days of Tiros 1, the U.S. weather satellite launched in 1960, scientists have used remote-sensing satellite imaging to observe planet Earth. These satellites have provided space-based images of phenomena as diverse as diamond deposits on the coast of Namibia and pineapples and coconut palms on the South Pacific island of Marinduque.[21,22,23,24,25,26,27,28]

The technology of remote-sensing imagery is essentially a more sophisticated version of today's handheld video cameras. Meteorologists, geologists, ecologists, and others have used remote sensing for many applications. Earliest uses were for weather forecasting. Other uses include mapmaking and resource mapping and measuring, agricultural land-use planning, geological and mineral prospecting, and archaeological analysis.

The first commercially available remotely-sensed images were provided by the first U.S. civilian Earth Resources Technology Satellite (ERTS), launched in 1972. These images, however, were too slow, with a two-month delay, and crude, with 80-meter resolution (i.e., only objects at least 80 meters in size—nearly the size of a football field—could be discerned), to be useful to the news media. By the 1990s, the news media had begun to make increasing use of remote sensing images in news coverage, as timeliness and image resolution improved. Images now are available within a forty-eight-hour turnaround, and with 5-meter resolution (i.e., about the size of a car). A recent online database search reveals that hundreds of news stories that were either about or had used remote-sensing imaging have appeared in the past year in leading newspapers, magazines, and other publications as well as on news broadcasts and wire services.

The type of sensing technology is one of the critical factors in determining the usefulness of remote sensing to the news. Remote-sensing technology involves two primary sensor systems: One is a television camera that takes pictures of Earth using visible light, the other is a multispectral scanner that uses both visible and infrared light. Both technologies are useful for news gathering, although the first is the simplest and most straightforward in its application. Infrared images, however, can be striking visually. Their dramatic impact can be seen in the blockbuster movie, *Patriot Games,* based on spymaster novelist Tom Clancy's book. In this film, director Philip Noyce tantalizes the audience with stunning special effects captured by remote-sensing satellite technology. Noyce recently said, "The scene I like best is a live infrared satellite broadcast of an attack on a terrorist training camp in the North African desert; it is seen above the subject in infrared from a camera 80,000 miles away."[29]

Although civilians traditionally have not had access to these spy data, the end of the Cold War has begun to change the situation. Then-Tennessee Senator and now

Vice President Al Gore, Jr., has spearheaded a drive to make public secret C.I.A. data from spy satellites. These data include remote-sensing imagery of missile silos in the former Soviet Union, imagery that also recorded snowfall data, containing possible clues to global temperature changes.[30] With the 1996 declassification of certain weather satellite data on the former Soviet Union, these increasingly remote-sensing data may prove invaluable to journalists covering the earth's environment.

When Bernard Kalb, distinguished network correspondent and former State Department spokesman, returned from taping a documentary on the Earth Summit in Rio, he made an impassioned plea in a speech to The Freedom Forum trustees to take the steps necessary to save the earth's environment. After all, he said, "We cannot trade this planet in for another one."[31] The environmental story is finally emerging as the greatest news story on earth.

Remote-sensing technology provides the perfect medium to investigate human impact on the environment, and through which to tell the environmental story. Remote sensing has been used to cover a wide variety of environmental stories, often by juxtaposing images taken at different points in time or multiple locations. Such stories include fires in Amazonia spewing smoke for more than a million square miles, from Bolivia to Antarctica; the spread of crop disease and pests such as the gypsy moth; and deforestation in Gifford Pinchot National Forest in the state of Washington, in Mount Hood National Forest in Oregon, and in the state of Amazonas in Brazil.

Environmental coverage is not the only news application for remote sensing. Another is coverage of archaeological stories, such as the ancient frankincense routes in southern Oman, the land T. E. Lawrence (known to many as Lawrence of Arabia) called, "the Atlantis of Arabia"; or, stories on 1,000-year-old footpaths in Costa Rica; long-lost Mayan causeways running through the jungle of Guatemala; and prehistoric Native American religious sites in western Colorado.

Interestingly, one of the earliest precursors to remote-sensing imagery involved an aerial archaeological survey conducted in 1929 by renowned aviator, Charles Lindbergh. Lindbergh had flown over the Chaco Canyon and snapped some black-and-white photos. Forty years later archaeologists analyzing these photos discovered faint straight lines crossing the desert, providing the first evidence of the roads of the mysterious Anasazi Indians of the southwestern United States.

Remote sensing was also used in news coverage of the war in the Persian Gulf. *ABC News* used several Soviet satellite photos in their dramatic special, "A Line in the Sand," in which they combined remote-sensing imagery with computer mapping software to depict the geography of the region. A dramatic remote-sensing story on the war ran in the *St. Petersburg Times* on January 6, 1991.[32,33] *Times* correspondent Joan Heller wrote, "Soviet satellite photos of Kuwait taken five weeks after the Iraqi invasion suggest the Bush administration might have exaggerated the scope of Iraq's military threat to Saudi Arabia." The photos showed no evidence of a large Iraqi military buildup in Kuwait. *ABC News* also acquired Soyuzkarta photos of Kuwait and found little evidence of a massive Iraqi buildup along the Kuwaiti border. Unfortunately, other news organizations did not confirm this story, partly because other satellite images were not available to corroborate the evidence from the Soviet satellite. Nevertheless, this story provides a compelling example of how remote-sensing images can be used in the most critical of news events: war.

This example also underscores the dramatic importance of extending full First Amendment rights of freedom of speech and of the press to the outer limits of Earth's environment, even to outer space.[34,35] To date, American and other journalists have been denied access to many of the most timely and highest resolution satellite images. By law, the U.S. Congress has restricted access to the highest resolution satellite technology to military applications. Moreover, because of the expense of launching a satellite capable of taking remote-sensing imagery, no single media organization can afford its own private remote-sensing satellite, what some have called the "MediaSat." In 1987, the United States Congress's Office of Technology Assessment estimated that it would cost as much as $470 million to launch and operate a MediaSat. Only through a consortium of media companies could a MediaSat be launched and operated.

France's remote-sensing satellite company, SPOT Image, was concerned about these images falling into the hands of the Iraqi military, who might have purchased the images through a third party.[36] In early August 1990, SPOT denied several news media requests for images from the Gulf region. As a result, news organizations could get images of the Gulf region only from Soyuzkarta and on a delayed basis. This meant the American people were denied the full story on why we went to war. Without the full First Amendment guarantees of disclosure and access to information, journalists cannot effectively cover the increasingly global story of planet Earth. Without this coverage, Earth's citizens may be denied access to Earth's greatest news story.

Table 4-2 provides a comparative overview of the three principal remote-sensing image providers for news media. These firms are France's SPOT Image, the worldwide market leader, Russia's Soyuzkarta, and NASA's Landsat. The chart compares each provider in terms of a number of factors, including ground resolution of the images, image cost, and lead time required to obtain images. Each of these factors affects when, how, and how often news organizations can use remote-sensing imagery.

Voice Recognition and Speech Synthesis.   Computer voice recognition and speech synthesis have been a hallmark of science fiction for generations, and are slowly becoming a central part of the real-world computing environment. Isaac Asimov's 1950s science-fiction novel *I, Robot,* featured not just the immortal three laws of robotics, but also robots that fully understood human speech and could talk fluently. The 1950s Hollywood classic motion picture, *Forbidden Planet,* featured a robot that could both speak and understand voice commands. The Enterprise's computer on television's 1960s sci-fi classic *Star Trek* spoke in a female voice, and understood Captain Kirk's every voice command.

The reality of computer speech and voice recognition has lagged behind the realm of science fiction, with early efforts of the 1970s and 1980s fairly primitive,

**TABLE 4-2 News Applications of Remote Sensing:
A Comparative Framework**

	SPOT[37] Image	Soyuzkarta	Landsat[38]/EOSAT[39]
Resolution	10 meters (P, B/W) 20 meters (HRV, color), fully digital	5 meters (photo, not digital)	15 meters P, 30 m TM, 80 m MSS,[40] 120m, fully digital
Types	High Resolution Visible, Infrared 3 bands of data[41]	Infrared	MSS has 4 bands TM & Enhanced Thematic Mapper, Panchromatic Infrared 7 bands of data
Access	Very Easy	(See # 2 below)	Very Easy
Skills Needed	Depends on need[42]	Depends on need	Depends on need
Cost	$600–3000	$2000–3000	$2500–$4400[43]
Flexibility[44]	Very Easy	Difficult[45]	Very Easy[46]
Lead Time	3 days, archive 3 weeks, custom	(See # 3 below)	3 weeks
Orbital Path	Circular, Sun synchronous	Circular, Sun synchronous	Circular, Sun synchronous
Global Coverage	100% of Earth	80% of Earth[47]	100% of Earth
Distance from Earth	500 miles	Varies	438 miles (4,5,6) & 570 miles (1,2,3,6)
Color or B/W	Color	Color	Color
Ease of Use	Relatively Easy[48,49]	Relatively Easy	Relatively Easy

clunky, and slow. Even those speech recognition systems that had a fairly effective range of understanding took many hours of training, and required the speaker to pronounce his or her commands in a staccato style, with a momentary pause between each word spoken. Most had highly restricted vocabularies, and were limited to specialized applications, such as medicine. Most of the current generation of commercial speech-recognition systems, such as one designed by Dragon Systems, Inc. of Newton, Massachusetts, are really nothing more than voice typewriters, translating spoken words into printed ones. Some can respond to simple, preset commands, such as "open file," but have no understanding of semantics. Speech synthesis technology has been similarly problematic. One of the most well-known early systems invariable pronounced every word with a distinctly "Swedish" accent, and sounded like a computer.

Research being conducted in the 1990s may transform the world of computer speech into what was once only imagined in the realm of science fiction. Research at the Massachusetts Institute of Technology (MIT), AT&T Bell Labs, Carnegie Mellon, and SRI International may help speech-recognition become a viable technology, not just for persons with disabilities, specialized applications, and limited needs, but for general purpose computing. MIT's Victor W. Zue is designing a speech-recognition system that can understand spoken requests for street directions or for making airline reservations. If Zue tells his computer, "Show me the Chinese restaurant nearest MIT," the computer will show him a map of the area and highlight in blue a route from his office to Royal East on Main Street. The system is based on a technology that actually deciphers the spoken word. Sound waves are converted into a series of phonemes, the smallest units of speech, such as the *r* in restaurant. These phonemes are then combined into possible words ranked by the acoustical fit of each set of sounds, such as *rest I want* versus *restaurant.* The words are then analyzed in the context of the surrounding words to determine the overall meaning of a phrase or sentence. Speech recognition systems are also being developed for multiple languages. AT&T, for example, has licensed speech systems from Belgian-based Lernout & Haupsie Speech Products, which functions in German, French, and other languages. This application will allow for instantaneous long-distance voice communication across cultural divides. When this speech-recognition technology is perfected, Zue contends, it "will touch the lives of millions of people."[50] But the road to perfection is still far off. Even these latest generations of speech technology are slow and very expensive. Researchers at Bolt, Beranek & Newman use $100,000 workstations with sophisticated microphones, not home PCs or telephones, to run their speech-recognition system.

In 1950, the first crude speech-recognition device was developed in the United States based on a stochastic method of pattern analysis. Although in 1926 Bell Laboratories had created a voice coder capable of analyzing certain features of speech (pitch, depth, and so on), in 1950 H. K. Davis of the United States created a system that could recognize specific spoken words (i.e., numbers). By 1971, the vocabularies of speech recognition devices had improved enough for deciphering of sentences.

Today's state of the art in speech-recognition in commercial systems is defined by the "big three" of large-vocabulary speech-recognition technology. These companies are IBM, with its IBM Personal Dictation System, Dragon Systems, with DragonDictate, and Kurzweil Applied Intelligence, with Kurzweil Voice. Reviewing these systems in the mid-1990s, the Seybold Report on Desktop Publishing concludes that speech-recognition is only now becoming feasible with desktop computers.[51] Although "voice typewriters" have impressed crowds at trade shows for some years, they have required hardware beyond the price range of most potential users. With both Dragon System's DragonDictate and IBM's Personal Dictation System now priced at less than $1,000 and running on a desktop computer (preferably at least a 486), the situation has now changed. Seybold reports that all three of the above systems have vocabularies of at least 30,000 words and are increasingly reliable. The systems, however, still require each user to both train the software to understand his or her voice. Moreover, these dictation systems require careful attention to acoustics. These systems simply don't "hear" very well. Seybold identified some digital age phrases misunderstood by the Personal Dictation System. "Fiber to the home" became "either to the home," while "digital services" became "dental services." Seybold recommends, "Optimal mike position is at the corner of the mouth, not touching the face, with sensitive surface of the mike rotated toward the sound source" (i.e., the user's mouth).[52] Nevertheless, these systems are particularly valuable for disabled persons, or persons suffering from repetitive stress injury (RSI), who may find use of a standard QWERTY keyboard difficult or impossible to use. Just-released versions of these systems designed for a Windows interface are particularly powerful, even allowing for "continuous" speech (i.e., the speaker need not pause between words).

The New Transmission System: A Field of Dreams

Evoking images of President John F. Kennedy's pledge three decades ago to make America the first country to put a man on the moon, President Clinton and Vice President Gore have written and spoken widely about the need to build a new national information infrastructure (NII), a new telecommunications system for transmission of all forms of data and information. In fact, some have claimed that if we had a dollar for every comment about the NII the administration has made since their successful presidential campaign in 1992 and re-election in 1996, we could erase the national debt, or at least most of it. As others in Washington, on university campuses, in the media and industry, and in the general public have echoed and responded to this call, there has been much debate about who will build such an infrastructure and at what cost, who will have access to it, and what its traffic and benefits will be. Meanwhile, there has been little agreement about just what this infrastructure will be. From a technological point of view, there are at least four approaches to an electronic information infrastructure:

1. Over-the-air transmission, including radio and television broadcasting, satellite and wireless communications, and other uses of the electromagnetic spectrum
2. Fully switched telecommunications network, including twisted pair, optical fiber, the switched telephone network, the advanced intelligent network (AIN), integrated services digital network (ISDN), asymmetrical digital subscriber line (ADSL)

3. Coaxial and optical fiber cable networks utilizing a one-way head-end system or file server (i.e., cable TV)
4. Electrical power lines

The following discussion examines these four broad technological approaches to transmitting data in digital form.

Over-the-Air Transmission

Since German scientist Heinrich Hertz first experimented with radio waves in 1888, over-the-air transmission has provided a technical basis for an electronic information highway. The electromagnetic spectrum has served a variety of information distribution and communication purposes, ranging from commercial broadcasting to secret military applications. The development of compression technologies has improved the ability of over-the-air transmission to carry large amounts of information, including digital high-definition television. Interactivity has been one of the limits of over-the-air broadcasting, since it is designed for a single source to transmit its message to a large audience distributed over a defined geographic region. By linking to other media, such as the telephone or online computer communication networks, over-the-air broadcasters have been able to introduce greater interactivity into their broadcasts. For example, U.S. television networks such as ABC, CBS, NBC, FOX, WB, or UPN promote their Internet address on news broadcasts and entertainment programming, soliciting many thousands of e-mail responses from many viewers in countries around the world. Satellite communications, including C and Ku-band, mobile satellite communications, and direct broadcast satellite (DBS), represents the area of broadcast spectrum use most likely to provide an interactive information infrastructure on a national or international basis. In Italy, RAI has been a leader in developing a variety of digital broadcast technologies, including digital audio broacasting (DAB). Guido Vannucchi, Deputy General Director at RAI, reports that "The significant progress of digital technologies in production, transmission and emission of radio, television and multimedia programs is rapidly changing the established concepts of broadcasting."[53]

Satellite—C and Ku Band.   Since its invention by Arthur C. Clarke in 1945, the communications satellite has rapidly become the foundation for the global communications network linking all the world's people and media. In 1962, AT&T launched Telstar, the first telecommunications satellite that could be used for both television and telephone signals. Partially financed by the U.S. government, Telstar featured 3,600 solar cells, and provided the first satellite relay of black-and-white and color television. Also that year, the U.S. Congress passed the Communications Satellite Act, establishing Comsat, a communications satellite organization incorporated in 1963. The first satellite launched under Comsat's direction, Intelsat 1, was put in orbit in 1965. Referred to as "Early Bird," Intelsat 1's television coverage included President Johnson's address to the United Nations, Pope Paul's visit to

New York, and a Beatles concert. Satellite transmission of television signals also transformed news coverage, with live coverage of news events delivered via satellite beginning in 1970. This had particularly important implications for coverage of the Vietnam war. The advent of the communications satellite also made possible the creation of so-called superstations. In 1973, Bob Wormington, the president of a Kansas City UHF TV station, developed a plan to transform an independent TV station into a national superstation if distributed via satellite to cable systems nationwide. Although Wormington spawned the idea, cable systems were not adequately able to receive satellite transmissions in the early 1970s and not until 1976 did the Turner Communications-owned WTCG-TV of Atlanta launch the first superstation using the RCA Satcom satellite. Newspapers also joined the satellite bandwagon in the 1970s. In 1973, a single page of the *Wall Street Journal*'s Eastern Edition was transmitted for the first time from an earth station in Chicopee, Massachusetts to South Brunswick, New Jersey via satellite. This spawned a new era in distributed publishing, which eventually led media magnate Al Neuharth to employ satellite newspaper transmission in 1980 to launch *USA Today,* the first national newspaper in the United States. On June 1 of that same year, the Cable News Network (CNN) delivered via satellite the first twenty-four-hour television newscast to 1.7 million American homes, introducing the first twenty-four-hour news network. It was made possible through the convergence of satellite and cable technologies, delivering the signal nationally via satellite and locally via cable.

When first introduced, communications satellites used what is called the C-band, a low-frequency band, long wave-length transmission system. Still the most widely used in commercial satellite transmissions, the C-band satellite has been joined by a high-frequency, short wave-length technology called Ku-band. Because of its longer wave length, C-band requires a larger receiving dish than Ku-Band, and is typically stationary. Ku-band use is growing, partly because the Ku-Band signal is shorter, requires a smaller dish—about eighteen inches across—is portable and can be placed on the roof of a truck. However, Ku-Band signals are subject to greater absorption and thus interference during bad weather. Today, many media organizations use the C-band and Ku-band satellite technologies for different applications, relying more on the Ku-band for electronic news gathering transmissions from remote, mobile locations such as ENG trucks, and using C-band for program distribution to affiliated stations across the country.

The communications satellite mix has become even more complex with the introduction in the mid-1970s of direct-broadcast satellite (DBS), cellular communications, and other satellite services, as well. These are discussed later in this chapter.

Around the world, the satellite has proven to be an important tool for delivering a variety of television programming, including news and entertainment from many countries. Because of the transborder nature of satellite broadcasting, there has been a great deal of controversy about both the importation and exportation of televised culture, especially that of the West to the Far East and increasingly to Europe and the developing world. A number of countries have gone so far as to announce bans on the private ownership of satellite receiving dishes. The Chinese government announced its ban in the fall of 1993, and the government of Saudi Arabia announced its intention to ban private dish ownership in early 1994.[54,55] Other Muslim countries in the Middle East are set to announce satellite dish bans as well, including Jordan, Bahrain, and Kuwait. The countries have agreed to back a Middle East Broadcasting Centre (MBC) scheme to install twenty MMDS (Multichannel Multipoint Distribution System) networks across the entire Middle East region. BBC World Service Television had planned to deliver its service to the region via satellite, but those plans are now in doubt. Despite government attempts to ban satellite dishes in many countries, the proliferation of privately owned satellite dishes in many developing nations has been dramatic. The ability of governments to enforce a satellite dish ban will grow even more difficult with the advent of high-powered direct broadcast satellite technology which requires only an eighteen-inch dish mounted on an interior wall for digital television reception.

Emerging Satellite Systems.   Since the launch of the first communication satellite more than three decades ago, satellite services and products have flourished. In fact, the communication industry orbiting Earth has grown to rival the largest land-based industries, communication or not.

Recent years have witnessed the development of two proposed communication satellite systems with profound commercial and cultural implications. The Motorola Iridium system and the Teledesic Corporation's satellite system promise to redefine modern extraterrestrial relay technology. "Iridium was originally planned to have 77 satellites, and named after the element with 77 electrons, but was redesigned to need fewer satellites—the 66 of today. But the name hasn't been changed to Dysprosium," reports communications analyst Lloyd Wood.[56] The first Iridium satellite was launched in November 1996.

The Teledesic Corporation's satellite system, featuring an unprecedented 840 satellites all linked in low-flying orbital paths, was proposed in early 1994 by Craig McCaw, who built McCaw Cellular Communications and William Gates, who transformed Microsoft Corporation into the largest software company in the world.[57] The nature of these systems is compared in Table 4-3. Both Iridium and Teledesic are years from completion, and will require massive financial investment before a single satellite is ever launched. Motorola has raised $800 million of the needed $3.3 billion to create its system, while McCaw and Gates have not yet raised any of the necessary $6.5 billion for the Teledesic network. Neither system is likely to be in operation before 2000, and both will require permission from the FCC before any satellites are launched. In late March 1994, a fourth satellite network, called Globalstar network, was announced by the Loral Corporation and Qualcomm Inc.[58] The companies reportedly have already lined up a dozen corporate partners and $275 million in capital for the $1.8 billion satellite–phone system. Globalstar, which includes forty-eight satellites and is scheduled for operation in 1998, will compete with Inmarsat in the mobile global satellite communications industry.

Mobile Satellite Communications.   Mobile satellite communications refer to mobile technologies for uplinking to communication satellites.[59] The mobile satel-

TABLE 4-3   Satellite Footprints in the Sand

	Traditional Communication Satellite in Geostationary Orbit	Motorola's Proposed Iridium Satellite Network	Teledesic's Proposed Satellite Network
Number of satellites	One or a few	66	840
Orbit	22,300 miles above equator expensive to launch	483 miles pole to pole 11 routes cheap launch	440 miles polar orbit 21 routes cheap launch
Ground footprint	Massive, entire hemisphere	2,800 miles across	440 miles across
Power requirements	Great power requires large earth stations large dishes	Low power Earth stations small & mobile like cellular phones	Low power Small earth stations but not mobile
Signal capacity	Very broad Handles voice, high-speed data and video transmissions up to broadcast quality	Narrow, handles voice, data, similar to cellular phone	Broad, handles high quality voice, data, Internet and video, but *not* broadcast quality

Sources: Teledesic, Motorola, *New York Times.*

lite phone is one of the most widely used devices for mobile satellite communications among media organizations. Inmarsat is the principle provider of global mobile satellite communications, although other competing systems are under development.

Inmarsat.   The state-of-the-art in mobile satellite communications is currently offered by Inmarsat, an international cooperative of seventy-nine countries that provides global mobile satellite communications; it has been widely used by news organizations, especially broadcasters, such as during the war in the Persian Gulf, as well as engineering and petrochemical companies that usually rent equipment for specific projects.[60] Created in 1979, Inmarsat was the first global mobile satellite system and is still the only one, although domestic, regional, and other global systems are beginning to emerge.[61] Inmarsat operates a network of eleven satellites in geostationary orbit, meaning each satellite maintains its footprint over a specific geographic region. It provides commercial services in more than 140 countries. Originally established to provide services to the maritime community, Inmarsat has expanded its services to a variety of aeronautical and land mobile applications.

Headquartered in London, Inmarsat offers a wide range of telecommunications services, including telephony, telex, fax, data communications, and some limited video services via a variety of standards of mobile Earth stations.

Direct Broadcast Satellite (DBS). Deep in the tropical rain forest of French Guiana, a French Ariane rocket soared out of the jungle on Friday, December 17, 1993.[62] Its payload was DBS-1, the first of two 6,000-pound satellites being delivered to an orbit 22,300 miles above the Equator. These satellites signaled the beginning of a new era in the direct-broadcast satellite (DBS) system in the United States. DBS uses the same technology as traditional C- and Ku-Band satellite transmissions. It is essentially a high-powered version of the existing technology that allows direct-to-home (DTH) transmission to small dishes. DBS-1 was the first satellite in the DirecTV digital DBS system. Primestar Partners, a small, medium-powered direct-to-home satellite service, launched in 1990 prior to the high-powered DirecTV venture, upgraded its system from analog to digital technology in 1994. Primestar also replaced its analog set-top boxes with digital boxes made by General Instrument Corp., allowing the company to increase its TV channel delivery from ten to seventy-seven TV channels.

NASA began experimenting in 1976 with direct broadcast satellites (DBS) using its sixth Applications Technology Satellite, ATS-6. Educational programs were transmitted to remote regions of Alaska, Appalachia, and the Rocky Mountains. Since then, DBS systems have been developed around the world, with Murdoch's StarTV providing DBS service in Asia and his BSkyB providing DBS service in Europe. DBS is particularly strong in these regions because cable TV has been slow to develop, and existing telephony in those regions has not been able to deliver full-motion video service. DBS has developed more slowly in the United States, taking a back seat to cable TV. The four major commercial providers of DBS programming in the United States and Canada are DirecTV/USSB, PrimeStar, EchoStar, and AlphaStar.[63] One of the limitations DBS systems face is that they cannot provide effective local coverage. In the emerging U.S. systems, for example, all programming is national. Subscribers view local programming, such as local news, independent channels, or public television, by switching to over-the-air reception through a pair of "rabbit ears" antennae or a rooftop antennae, or to cable TV service; the only exceptions are a few superstations, such as KTLA, distributed via DBS. DBS receivers also are expensive, proprietary devices, with Sony providing the first set-top box necessary to receive DBS service in the United States. As other manufacturers have introduced set-top DBS boxes, the price has fallen. DBS does have the needed bandwidth to deliver HDTV programming and provide channel capacity to provide specialized categories of programming for geographically dispersed ethnic groups not well served by a local provider.[64]

The mid-1980s witnessed the failure of an earlier DBS venture in the United States.[65] In this costly venture, Prudential approached the DBS as a wholesale business, approaching potential consumers from a central location with no local partners

TABLE 4-4   DBS Adoption by U.S. Households

Company	Service Began	Household Count
AlphaStar	7-11-96	8,421
DirecTV/USSB	6-17-94	2,211,344
EchoStar	4-3-96	294,017
PRIMESTAR	7-31-90	1,614,740
TOTALS:		4,138,522

Source: http://www.dbsdish.com/

to provide the retail sales and service connection. But because DBS systems require substantial technology purchases by the consumer, a local retail partner is required, and Prudential took a financial bath. In the latest U.S. DBS venture, dubbed DirectTV, USSB and Hughes have aligned with retailers, such as Sears, to provide the local sales and service needed to support a technology-intensive business like DBS. Early results from the DirecTV digital DBS launch indicate brisk sales, with demand exceeding supply. Table 4-4 presents data on DBS household adoption current through November 1996.

Rising from the Ashes.   Although direct broadcast satellite (DBS) technology has existed for decades, it has only recently emerged as a viable competitor in the U.S. television market, with the 1994 launch of the DBS-1 satellite and the introduction of the DirecTV digital service offered by Hughes Communications, Inc. DirecTV exists as something of a virtual company, with little in the way of assets. Instead, it provides customizable programming packages from a variety of companies ranging from Disney to Time Warner. Already the leading DBS service, DirecTV expects to have 10 million subscribers by 2000 and to generate $1 billion in annual revenues. DBS won't replace other forms of TV transmission, but it does lower the cost for creating a national TV network by eliminating the need for local station affiliates. It also makes specialized TV programming more viable on a national basis, since a program with a rating of 0.1 means more than 200,000 viewers nationwide. Depending on the demographics of the audience, such programming might also attract significant advertising support. DBS also provides limited interactive TV services, such as movies on demand or computer games.

DBS-1 has thirty-two transponders, or satellite-based transmitters. Half the transponders transmit regularly, and half serve as backups. From its position above western Kansas, DBS-1 extends its footprint, or coverage area, to all of the lower forty-eight states and parts of Canada and Mexico. DBS-2 was launched in the summer of 1994, and is devoted to DirecTV advanced applications.[66] DirecTV features more than eighty programming options, from A&E to USA Network.

A Summary of How DirecTV Works

- Two high-powered $200 million DBS satellites beam several digital signals directly to earth receivers.
- One $100 million Earth station in Castle Rock, Colorado compresses digital TV signals, putting eight channels in the space of one, fed by cable programmers such as CNN and ESPN.
- Subscribers buy a $399 system including an eighteen-inch satellite dish that can be mounted on an interior wall in a living room (requires good southern exposure to receive signal), a VCR-sized receiver, signal decompressor and decoder box and a remote control.
- Subscribers choose from one of six packages ranging in price from $14.95 to $44.95, plus pay-per-view events, with the primary variable being the number of channels available.

DBS also presents an opportunity for independent producers to develop original, special interest programming to appeal to a national audience. One leading producer considering pioneering programming for the DBS frontier is former NBC chairman Grant Tinker, who produced some of the most successful television programming of the 1970s, such as the *Mary Tyler Moore Show*. Tinker, who established a reputation for producing creative, quality programming that helped lead NBC from last place to first in network audience ratings, left the network and its parent, RCA, after they were acquired by General Electric. Tinker, in coordination with former NBC executive Bud Rukyser, have planned a new enterprise to create quality television programming for distribution to a national audience via DBS. Through independent production, the cost of producing programming for DBS would be much less than that produced for the networks, which must support a large and heavily unionized workforce. A similar potential DBS entrant is Horizons TV, a new programming option being created by Lawrence Grossman, the former president of *NBC News* and PBS. Grossman describes his network as a "cultural and intellectual CSPAN." It features lectures from leading professors and artistic performances that otherwise have little audience beyond their immediate viewers.

DBS is also seen as an important technology in Canada, where the television world is largely dominated by American broadcasters. A major Canadian broadcaster and Canada's largest telecommunications company are planning a direct-to-home satellite-television service as a "Canadian alternative" to U.S. television. The service will be owned by a consortium including Western International Communications (WIC), Canadian Satellite Communications, and BCE, Inc., the parent of Bell Canada.[67,68]

Cellular Communications. Cellular communications is an over-the-air delivery medium currently used for telephone services, including voice, data transmission, and fax communications. Through convergence, cellular technologies are now built into portable computers, making nomadic computing, or mobile computer communications, a reality.

A February 1993 study by Response Analysis suggests that cellular, paging and voice, and "data fleet dispatch" services in the United States are likely to grow to more than 100 million users by 2002 from an estimated 50 million today. Worldwide growth may be even greater. Users say the major attractions to wireless services are: (1) communications to anyone, anywhere, anytime (90 percent), (2) emergency communications (85 percent), and (3) landline backup (62 percent).[69]

One of the threats to the future growth of the cellular telephone industry is the possible harmful health effects of the cellular phone. Although no conclusive evidence has shown there to be harmful effects, there is no clear evidence proving the phones to be safe. A number of lawsuits have been filed against cellular telephone manufacturers alleging that heavy use of the phones, which produce an electromagnetic field because of their cellular transmission, causes cancer. In one case, a senior-level scientist at Motorola, one of the leading manufacturers of cellular telephones, claims that the testing of a cellular phone that he conducted in 1984 caused him to develop an inoperable and incurable brain tumor.

Personal Communication Services (PCS).   In 1996, the FCC completed its unprecedented auction of 120 megahertz of spectrum for the creation of personal communications services, generating approximately $10 billion in bids, with projected industry revenues reaching $40 billion within ten years. Pocket phones will be among the first services to compete with phone companies for house-to-house wireless service, as well as cellular communications, which have just 40 MHz of spectrum. The Kiplinger Washington Letter predicts that wireless office-computer networks will be available within three to five years.[70]

Calling the Future:
Fully Switched Telecommunications Network

"Mr. Watson, come here, I want you," spoken by Alexander Graham Bell on March 10, 1876, was the first proof that Bell's invention of the telephone could serve as the infrastructure for an information highway, although no one at the time was using the term so much in vogue in at the end of the twentieth century. Today, few would argue that the twentieth century's fully switched telecommunications infrastructure is an important part of the so-called information superhighway. The dimensions of the modern telecommunications network architecture are complex and include many different technologies. The most important from a communications perspective are discussed below.

Over the past twenty years, the telecommunications network has undergone nothing less than a revolution.[71] In 1975, narrowband circuit-switched networks were the state of the art in telecommunications. These networks were designed to accommodate voice traffic very efficiently. When a caller in New York placed a call to Los Angeles, the network would create a single circuit devoted to carrying that call. The network did not require great bandwidth because each call had its own devoted circuit, and there was no demand to send video, data, or other information that might require large bandwidth for transmission.

As technology has advanced, however, demand has grown for data transmission, video transmission by land lines rather than over the air or by satellite. Telephone companies have widely deployed optical fiber throughout not just the United States but internationally, making it feasible to send large amounts of information in digital form efficiently over the telephone network. In addition, engineers developed the technology of packet-switching. Unlike circuit-switching, packet-switching works on the concept of shared networks. In a packet-switched network, all information, whether voice, video, or data, is converted into digital format, ones and zeros. These digital data are then transmitted in bunches, packets, over the network, wherever the network finds space. Despite a variety of technical challenges, especially in creating protocols for providing seamless interconnections between networks of different types—such as local versus wide area networks, fiber optics versus twisted pair versus coaxial, land line versus wireless communications—the technology of packet-switching has taken hold and become increasingly the law of the telecommunications land. Moreover, with the coming merger of telephone networks and cable systems, and the combination of the phone companies' packet-switching and extensive optical fiber and the cable systems' high-capacity coaxial cabling, broadband packet-switched networks will emerge even more rapidly as the national standard.[72]

Copper Wire Twisted Pair.   The current telecommunications network is a combination of optical fiber and copper wire twisted-pair, with fiber used generally in the network "backbone," or main trunk lines, and twisted pair serving each individual home or customer. Replacing all copper with fiber is extremely costly, with some estimates running as high as one trillion dollars. As a result, the telephone companies have conducted extensive experiments in running full-motion video over twisted-pair wiring. Using advances in compression technology, the telcos have achieved much success in this regard. Several tests by Bellcore, the research arm of the regional Bell telephone operating companies, have demonstrated that near-VCR quality video can be delivered over existing copper wire. When combined with fiber backbone and advanced switching technologies, some field trials have even successfully provided limited video on demand. In these trials, a central file server stores a variety of video offerings, such as a movie library, and fiber delivers these offerings to the neighborhood or curb. Only the selected movie is then delivered over the short length of copper running from where the fiber line ends. In these trials, the consumer does not have a full range of video options, such as reverse, forward, or pause.

Advanced Intelligent Network (AIN).   The advanced intelligent network—AIN—is a network architecture or design currently in development at Bellcore laboratories on behalf of the Regional Bell Operating Companies. Bellcore President George Heilmeier, inventor of the liquid-crystal display and former head of the federal agency that helped develop Stealth airplanes, reports that AIN represents "a fundamental paradigm shift" for telecommunications.[73] "It used to be," he explains, "if you wanted to create a new service, the only people that could do it were the telephone companies. AIN changes all that. It means that third parties are going to be able to customize their own services."

Heilmeier notes that AIN is different from the Integrated Services Digital Network (ISDN), which is essentially a transport architecture providing a data dialtone. ISDN lets people interested in transporting data move those data more efficiently over the existing phone system. "That's a lot different from giving people the ability to actually invoke switch features and customize services," Heilmeier adds. AIN will allow companies to provide a national service but on a local level. For example, a company could advertise a national phone number, but use AIN to route each call to a local office.

Asymmetrical Digital Subscriber Line (ADSL). Using this new digital telecommunications networking service (utilizing advances in packet-switching), telephone companies have entered the video age. By compressing the video signal, telcos are able to use ADSL to provide VCR-quality video over existing telephone lines, the traditional copper wire twisted pair that we have used for decades to make voice calls. ADSL, in combination with compression and packet-switching, have helped transform the narrowband telecommunications infrastructure into an information highway cable of providing the one service many claim will drive the development of the new broadband infrastructure: video-on-demand. ADSL can now deliver 8 to 10 megabits per second of bandwidth, reports Bill Smith, Vice President, BellSouth Telecommunications.[74]

Asynchronous Transfer Mode (ATM). ATM is a new type of packet-switching technology for use in the telecommunications network. Many see it as a breakthrough technology because it enables the existing infrastructure to act as a very broadband network (up to 155 MBs), providing advanced telecommunications services such as video-on-demand. Demonstrating the commercial application of ATM technology, First Virtual, a virtual corporation recently founded in Silicon Valley, is using ATM technology to move full-motion video, sound, and graphics files over the public telecommunications network.[75] Applications include live videoconferences, telemedicine, and interactive video training and distance learning.

Integrated Services Digital Network (ISDN). ISDN is a new telecommunications networking technology that brings together traditionally separate forms of communication, including voice and data transmission in a single delivery medium. ISDN transmits at a rate of up to 64 kilobits per second (kbps). The Regional Bell Operating Companies (RBOCs) have touted ISDN for many years, but have only recently begun aggressively deploying it in their service areas.[76] Bell Atlantic Corp. is expanding its ISDN implementation from 900 to all 1,400 switching stations within its service area, while Southwestern Bell Corp. is making ISDN available throughout Austin, Texas. It charges $50 a month for its basic ISDN transmission rate of 56 kbps, and will use a more complicated and costly pricing structure for its primary service, depending on the number of 64 kbps ISDN lines a customer orders.

Although most ISDN cannot transmit full-motion video, Southwestern Bell offers SelectVideo, an advanced ISDN service capable of transmitting video. SelectVideo allows customers to configure their transmission system for between 64 kbps to 1,536 kbps in 64 kbps increments.

Optical Fiber. Corning scientists Drs. Robert Maurer, Donald Keck, and Peter Schultz created the first optical fiber in the 1960s. Its potential as a medium of information transmission was immediately recognized, but was not feasible for more than twenty years until switching technologies were developed that could connect one fiber to another. Optical fiber is made out of silicon, the same material that is used in creating the transistor chip. Information is distributed via optical fiber in digital form through pulses of light at 186,000 miles per second, the speed of light. Perhaps even more important than the speed of the transmission, however, is the capacity of optical fiber. Optical fiber has vastly more bandwidth—or transmission capacity—than traditional telephone wire, twisted pairs of copper wire. With the latest compression technologies, optical fiber becomes an almost limitless capacity medium of transmission. For example, the contents of the entire *Oxford English Dictionary* or an entire feature-length motion picture can be sent via optical fiber in just seconds. Or, as Corning points out at its corporate Web site: Fiber can carry information so fast that you could transmit three episodes of your favorite television show in just one second.[77] It is the transmission capability of optical fiber that leads many to call it the basic infrastructure of the information superhighway. The transmission capacity of optical fiber makes possible a variety of video services, such as video-on-demand, as well as many applications for interactive video services, such as in medicine or other fields.

When first developed, optical fiber was much more expensive than copper wire. Advances in the technology as well as mass production have combined to bring down the price of fiber optics to less than the cost of copper wire. By early 1997, more than half a million kilometers of optical fiber had been laid in the United States. Although most of this has been laid by the phone companies, many cable companies have also laid considerable fiber miles as well, as have other communications companies. Most of this fiber has been installed in what is called the backbone, or the main trunk lines connecting major switching centers. In fact, fiber to the home is largely unnecessary. Optical fiber has another important advantage: unlike traditional twisted-pair or coaxial cable, optical fiber is impervious to the massive electromagnetic fields created during nuclear explosions. This is one reason why all nuclear submarines and many navy carriers are equipped with optical fiber for their onboard communications.

Despite the decreasing cost of fiber, connecting the entire nation, even if stopping at the curb or neighborhood and not the home, is still very expensive. Some estimates are that the cost of fiber to the curb will exceed $300 billion. That's more than $1,000 for every person living in the United States. It is unclear where the funds will come from to pay for this cost, although some project that even if fiber is used only as a replacement for copper, the country will be connected by fiber by 2020. If a more aggressive approach is taken, perhaps at the encouragement of the Federal government or through competition between cable and phone companies and long-distance carriers, we could see most of the country connected by fiber by 2000.

But is all this fiber necessary? Telecommunications scholar Michael Noll says no.[78] Noll, former dean of the Annenberg School for Communication at University of Southern California, is an expert on telecommunications technology, and pioneered the development of the first "virtual reality" technology at the AT&T Bell Labs in the late 1960s, although his patent was for a sensory technology device never actually created. Noll conducted an analysis of the information traffic on the U.S. public telecommunications network. He found that even combining all the voice, data, and transactional communications, we would not near the capacity of the existing twisted-pair network. Even with video-on-demand, the capacity is not neared with today's compression technology. So why all the fuss about fiber optics? Fiber optics is really needed only if we were to develop a system in which every user began transmitting their own full motion video messages the same way we use today's phone for voice messages.

Noll raises a bigger question about new media technologies. Are these new technologies being developed to meet real needs, or are they the result of technology push? Many would argue the latter, not the former. Professors Herbert Dordick and Dale Lehman argue just such a process may be driving much of the push for the development of a national information infrastructure, or information highway, in the United States.[79]

As telecommunications cables traverse thousands of miles of ocean, many of these coaxial cables are rapidly being linked or replaced by fiber-optic cables. This conversion to optical fiber means the information superhighway stretches across the entire globe. Importantly, these transoceanic optical fiber lines are not equally distributed throughout all continents, regions, and countries of the world. The United States, for example, is the most well connected country in the world by optical fiber, with four transoceanic cables linking it to Asia, Australia, New Zealand and Russia, and five optical fiber lines to countries in Europe and South America. By contrast, all of Africa is served by just two fiber-optic connections, one of those links stretching from Europe to South Africa. The vast majority of countries have no transoceanic fiber-optic connections with other countries. Similarly, only information societies such as the United States, Australia, Japan, or France have international fiber-optic lines at all. Most third world or developing nations have no on-ramps to the world's information highway, and are thus excluded from the global information grid. This bandwidth imbalance, however, is beginning to change, and telecommunications race to install fiber-optic cabling to even the most remote reaches of the world.[80]

High Speed Data.   High speed data (HSD) link refers to a telecommunications connection capable of transmitting data at relatively high rates of speed, generally at least 28.8 thousand bits per second, or a 28.8 Kbps. An HSD link is generally needed to transmit graphics or other visual information, such as full-motion video.

Local Area Network.   Local area network (LAN) refers to a network of computers limited to a specific geographic location, such as an office or university campus. LANs allow file sharing, electronic mail communications, and system-wide applications, such as access to central databases or software, or file backup procedures. LANs are made up of multiple workstations, personal computers or, terminals with a central processor or file server where computerized exchanges occur.

Wide Area Networks.   LANs can be connected to wide area networks, or WANs. A WAN is analogous to a LAN, except it is not limited to a specific geographic location. A WAN may cover the entire planet Earth and typically makes use of the public telecommunications network for communications, file sharing, and other network transactions. A WAN consists of many LANs, computers and central processors, perhaps even a supercomputer.

Modem.   Central to all these technologies is the computer modem, which is an acronym for MOdulate-DEModulate. A modem is a device that allows a computer to connect to a telephone line or wireless network and communicate with any computer also connected to that network. The modem acts as a translator of the digital information.

Cable TV: The Wired Nation

About two-thirds of all American households receive television by cable television using a combination of coaxial and optical fiber cabling in a one-way head-end system. The term *head-end* refers to the fact that a central file server distributes full-motion video downstream, or one-way, from the head-end to the home. Interactive cable TV systems increasingly incorporate two-way or upstream capacity into their systems.

Coaxial Cable.   Coaxial cable is the delivery medium traditionally used for delivering cable television to the home. It provides broadband transmission capabilities for the delivery of full-motion video. Most cable TV systems are based on either coaxial cable or a combination of coax and optical fiber, all networked in a one-way head-end system. In 1971, freelance writer Ralph Lee Smith dubbed cable TV, delivered via coaxial cable, tomorrow's information highway, because of its broadband capability as well as the public access potential promised in many cable franchises of the time.

Coaxial cable was invented in 1928 by Lloyd Espenschied, an electrical engineer for AT&T, and Herman Affel. The first use of coaxial cable was for undersea telephone transmission and later for television transmission.

CATV is an acronym for Community Antenna Television Systems. Using coaxial cable connections CATV systems are established to improve television reception in areas where it was weak or blocked by geographic terrain or other interference. The first systems were built noncommercially in Mahoney City, Pennsylvania in June 1948 and in Astoria, Oregon on November 25, 1948. "Four television networks were launched that May 1 (1948), three by the established radio networks ABC, CBS, and NBC, and one DuMont, by a maker of television receivers," writes Rueven Frank, former NBC News president.[81] The television networks were made possible by AT&T's introduction on May 1 of "regular, commercial intercity transmission of television pictures" using coaxial cable connecting "only nine cities from Boston in the north to Richmond, Virginia in the south," Frank adds.

Importantly, from a technical point of view, coaxial cable can be used effectively to provide telephone service, and is in fact used in this fashion in various international venues, such as in the United Kingdom, where traditional telephone service provided by the PTT is notoriously poor in quality and short on modern features, such as call waiting or caller ID. American telephone companies have built coaxial cable networks in the United Kingdom, and British residents have then used them not so much for their television offerings but for their improved telephone service. In the United States, cable TV providers have generally not used their coaxial cable networks to provide telephone service, even though the broadband-width medium could easily accommodate the extra traffic, because they do not wish to become an even more heavily regulated industry, as they would be under current telecommunications law.

Cable Modem.   Much heralded has been the cable modem, a device now in testing by cable companies such as TCI and Cablevision Systems. It promises to give high-bandwidth access to the Internet via already existing coaxial cable systems. The cable modem involves installing a special set-top digital converter in each cable home, enabling the cable system to operate as if it were a telephone line, transmitting two-way voice, data, or any other digital content. One manufacturer, Motorola, began shipping to more than a half dozen cable network operators in March of 1996 a cable modem system dubbed The CyberSurfer. CyberSurfer operates at speeds of up to 30 megabits (30 million bits) per second—roughly 1,000 times the speed of the conventional personal computer modems.[82] Notably, this speed is obtained only under ideal conditions and only in one direction, downstream from the cable head-end to the consumer. Upstream capacity operates at only a fraction of this speed, at an approximate maximum of one megabit per second. Cablevision Systems Corp. announced its plans in late 1996 to offer cable modems to 15,000 of its subscribers in Long Island, New York. The United States' sixth-largest cable operator plans to offer cable modems to as many as 150,000 subscribers on Long Island and in Connecticut by the end of 1997.[83]

MMDS.   MMDS is an acronym for multichannel multipoint distribution service. Also known as wireless cable, MMDS is a terrestrial broadcast service that can transmit as many as thirty-three TV channels over the air via microwave transmission, although many more channels are possible with compression. MDS systems are particularly effective in regions with flat terrain, especially in sparsely populated areas where wired cable systems are expensive to install and maintain, such as the rural plains areas of the midwest. MDS was made possible in 1983 by an FCC frequency reallocation that allowed broadcasters to use as many as thirty-three high-frequency six-megahertz MHZ channels for an MDS service.

Digital Radio.   Digital radio (DAR) refers to radio tranmissions in digital, or computerized, format. Because of its bandwidth requirements, digital radio is delivered primarily via cable TV coaxial lines, although advances in compression technology have made it possible to deliver digital audio over the air. Its importance is profound for the radio industry because, unlike traditional analog radio transmission, digital radio suffers no signal degradation between the source and the radio listener's receiver. As a result, the consumer can listen to not only CD-quality music delivered via the radio, but he or she can also record it. And if recorded on a digital medium such as digital audio tape, he or she can make unlimited digital recordings, each as perfect as the signal originally transmitted. This digital recording has enormous implications for the recording industry, which is concerned about potential audio piracy.

The National Association of Broadcasters has agreed on a standard for transmitting a new Radio Broadcast Data System, called CouponRadio, which could also emerge as an important force in radio's digital future. CouponRadio is part of a technology that allows radio listeners to save at the touch of a button a coupon transmitted electronically by an advertiser during a radio broadcast.

Electrical Power Lines

Although it may seem an unlikely idea to many, a growing number of utilities around the United States are conducting experiments to deliver information over electrical power lines. Since virtually every home is wired for electricity, the power grid would greatly increase the potential for universal access to the information superhighway. Although electrical lines have been used on a limited basis for delivering media content, such as providing radio service in college dormitories, they have not been used on a wide-scale basis. The latest generation of the technology is far advanced over earlier efforts. Several large utilities in California, Texas, Ohio, and Louisiana have already set up or planned experiments to give their customers more control in running their home appliances, such as the dishwasher or air-conditioner, during off-peak hours when rates are lower, potentially saving consumers hundreds of dollars a year and possibly delaying the need to build new power plants.[84] Future designs may enable power companies to deliver movies on demand and other media content to home consumers. Noting that these developments may soon enable television viewers to use their remote controls to tell the microwave what they want to eat and when, Jens Carsten Nielsen, Vice President/Marketing, Politiken, Denmark, observes, tongue in cheek: "This will literally enable people to stay in front of their television sets for days."[85]

The American Electric Power Company of Columbus, Ohio, conducted a pilot project in which consumers using the system in Ohio, West Virginia, and Indiana cut their energy consumption by 50 to 60 percent during peak hours.[86] The company plans to install the communication system in 25,000 homes out of its 2 million customer base. The system connects to an electronic box called an *energy management unit*, which is then wired to the customer's television set for display or on a special display screen the utility provides. Customers can then program their appliances to run during off-peak hours or at preset temperatures. Appliances require a special plug to run on the system and a special thermostat is needed to communicate with the energy management system. Other utilities testing similar systems include the Entergy Corporation, the parent company of Louisiana Power and Light and New Orleans Public Service, the Central and South West Corporation, the parent of Central Power and Light, Pacific Gas and Electric Company (PG & E), a large California utility, and the Glasgow, Kentucky, municipal utility. PG & E has found that customers are reluctant to expend much energy programming their appliances, and therefore require a system that is simple to use. As a result, PG & E has joined with the Microsoft Corporation to create a simple control system based on Microsoft Windows computer software. PG & E plans to install the system in Walnut Creek, California. Installation will initially cost about $1,000, which the company will pay, but in the long run will fall to about $200, which the customer would then pay. In addition, a monthly fee for the service would run about $10, says American Electric in Ohio.

To provide television service, movies on demand, or other types of information, these utility-based systems will provide a fiber-optic link running alongside their electrical lines. Many utilities already have such fiber cables in place, using them to monitor their electrical transmission system and for internal communications, and only rarely use a significant portion of the optical fiber's information carrying capacity. The municipal utility in Glasgow, Kentucky, in fact, already offers 2,000 of its customers such service.[87] Since 1989 the utility has offered its customers cable television service and a connection with databanks at schools and libraries. Unlike private utilities, the Glasgow public utility is not restricted by federal law prohibiting utilities from providing such additional services. See Chapter 9 for a further discussion of the laws pertaining to private utilities and media services.

Windows on the Electronic World: On-Ramps to the Superhighway

Technologies that allow us to access and display take many forms. They are computer-based and include a wide range of devices, such as personal digital appliances, flat panel screens, HDTV, interactive television, and virtual reality. In general, the trends in these technologies are toward smaller, lighter, more powerful devices capable of displaying multimedia information, and receiving digital input from a variety of media, both cable and wireless.

Personal Digital Appliances (PDAs)

PDA's are essentially handheld computers that initially acted simply as electronic pocket notebooks, organizers, address books, record keepers, and language translators, but by the end of 1996 had become fully functional computing and communications mobile workstations.[88] In contrast to the first generation of pocket organizers, such as the Wizard from Sharpe, PDAs such as the Apple Newton (120, 130, or 2000) or the Casio Cassiopeia do everything from word processing to e-mail to browsing the World Wide Web. Users typically write with a special pen to enter information directly on the screen of the PDA. Most PDAs can be plugged in to other devices to transfer, receive or back up digital information; in the case of the Apple Newton, an infrared wireless link is also available. As the technology develops and screen size increases and resolution improves, other applications are foreseen, such as electronic news products. Some companies are already experimenting with such products in Japan, the United States, the United Kingdom, and Spain.

The Apple Newton is equipped with optical character recognition technology for handwritten input, which has made the Newton especially popular among surgeons and other medical professionals. The Newton and other PDAs have not fared well in the U.S. market in general, but have proven immensely popular in Japan, where pre-teenage girls are enjoying not only the utilitarian functions of digital calendars and phone directories, but kids' games such as fortune-telling, computer-animated virtual pets, and electronic messaging across rooms via infrared light beams.[89]

Liquid Crystal Display (LCD).   LCD technologies are based on the principles of Light Emitting Diodes (LEDs), devices used to light up displays in electronic products. Originally researched by a British duo in the late 1950s, the first practical LED display was produced in 1962 by Nick Holonyak, Jr. Liquid crystals are organic substances whose properties and behavior lie somewhere between liquids and crystals.

While working in RCA Corp.'s research laboratory in Princeton, New Jersey, in 1964, then twenty-four-year-old scientist and inventor George Heilmeier, today president of Bellcore, discovered that LCDs have the ability to change color instantly when an electric current is applied. His discovery led directly to the creation of digital watches, color portable computers, and soon, wall-hanging television sets. RCA did not successfully pursue the commercial application of the LCD. "People who were asked to commercialize (the technology) saw it as a distraction," recalls Heilmeier. "They tried, but they never unlocked the key to making this a commercial success."

The Japanese succeeded in 1975, when Sharp Corp. and other Japanese companies introduced liquid crystal displays (LCD)s to the market in consumer electronics products such as watches, calculators, and video games.

Flat Panel Displays.   The flat panel is an electronic tablet about one to two pounds in weight and the size and thickness of a notepad, utilizing LCD and other technologies to provide a flat computer display screen. Flat panels offer the potential to transform the computer from a tool for calculation to a portal of communication. This transformation, says Roger Fidler, Adjunct Professor and coordinator of the newly created Information Design Laboratory at Kent State University's School of

Journalism, will lead to a "mediamorphosis" of the newspaper into an electronic news medium that not only delivers electronic text, but incorporates full-motion video and audio, interactivity, and information on demand.[90]

Flat Screen Market. Japanese manufacturers currently dominate the flat screen market. As the flat screen market grows from today's $5 billion worldwide to $20 billion by 2000, a growing number of countries will challenge Japan's lock on the market. Among those eager to challenge the Japanese, who own 95 percent of the global market, are the United States and South Korea. In the United States, the Clinton Administration and the Pentagon have launched a $1 billion "national flat panel display initiative."[91] Behind the initiative is Pentagon and White House investment in expanding U.S. manufacturing of flat-panel displays. Not everyone agrees that making this kind of investment makes sense. Among those who question the wisdom of this investment is Charles T. Maxwell, a financial analyst specializing in new technologies and managing director of C. J. Lawrence/Deutsche Bank Securities Corporation.[92] Maxwell argues that although the LCD was invented by an American three decades ago, no American manufacturer has produced a competitive LCD.

South Korea has also announced an ambitious plan to challenge the Japanese. Having successfully broken Japan's manufacturing grip on the computer memory-chip market, South Korea has a proven track record in entering high-tech markets. Samsung Electronics and the Goldstar Company are both mass manufacturing active-liquid LCDs, which are used in portable televisions and advanced color notebook computers.[93] Goldstar anticipates producing some 500,000 flat panels in its first year of production, a little more the world leader Sony produces in a month. This level of production is likely to create a glut in the market, eventually bringing down the price for LCDs.

Current projections are that the market for flat-panel displays will continue to grow throughout the remainder of the decade. Although the U.S. market will continue to grow, it will not be a major competitor in the international marketplace with the more experienced Japanese manufacturers.[94] The next generation of flat-panel displays are expected to have improved image resolution and by the end of the decade will approach that of ink on paper. Moreover, a team of French researchers have developed a paper-thin plastic transistor containing no metal parts, which may lead to flexible electronics, including flat-panel screens that roll up like window shades.[95]

Diamond-Coated Displays. While many in the flat-panel display industry are pinning their hopes on active-matrix, liquid-crystal display (AMLCD) designs, a new technology is emerging that may bypass the AMLCD in the flat-screen market. "A consortium of American companies and the nation's main nuclear weapons laboratory have joined forces to develop and market a revolutionary new type of computer and television display screen based on synthetic diamond," writes Pulitzer prize-winning journalist Malcolm W. Browne.[96] SI Diamond Technology, Inc. (SIDT) and Microelectronics and Computer Technology Corp. (MCC) signed an agreement in 1993 to manufacture flat-panel displays using the electron-emitting qualities of diamonds.[97] The consortium contends that the diamond technology can provide better brightness, contrast, and response time than active-matrix designs. It also expects the diamond technology will lower power consumption and ease manufacturing, and at a lower cost. The consortium cites predictions that the flat-panel display market will grow from about $5 billion in 1993 to more than $9.4 billion by 2000.

High-Definition Television

High-definition television (HDTV) represents the next generation of television technology, eventually expected to replace the existing generation of NTSC television. Developed in 1964 by the Japanese public broadcaster, NHK, the NHK system is called Hi-Vision and is based on analog technology. High-definition, however, is really a misnomer, says broadcast pioneer Joe Flaherty, Senior Vice President, Technology, CBS, Inc., because its connotation is merely improved resolution, sharper pictures.[98] Flaherty, who introduced HDTV to the United States in the 1980s, says that high-definition television actually has at least four important characteristics. First, of course, is improved image sharpness and resolution capability. While the United States standard is currently 525 lines and 60 frames per second, and in Europe it is 625 lines at 50 frames per second, high-definition systems now being considered in the U.S. have about 1,125 scanning lines at 60 pictures a second, about twice the existing image resolution.

The second feature is substantially improved color rendition. "When my predecessors in this industry developed the present NTSC color system," Flaherty reflects, "great compromises in quality were taken in order to squeeze the color information into the already existing black-and-white picture. Little vacant spots in the spectrum were used to fit the color information in." In the early days of television, those compromises were not visible, largely because the screens on television sets were so small, sixteen to twenty-one inches at best. But on today's large-screen television sets, "the warts of this system begin to show," Flaherty points out. High definition brings to today's television the color fidelity of 35-millimeter film. Third, and probably the most noticeable quality of high-definition, says Flaherty, is the new the aspect ratio. In today's television, the aspect ratio is four units of width to three units of height, or 1.33:1. HDTV will have a much wider aspect ratio at 16:9 or 1.78:1. This strange number was arrived at, Flaherty explains, as an approximation of the cinema. In most of the world, the cinematic aspect ratio is 1.66:1, while in the United States it varies, but is generally 1.85:1; 1.78:1 was arrived at as a compromise. The new aspect ratio of HDTV is better suited to the human eye, which sees a wider-angle view horizontally than vertically. Therefore, viewers get a more natural feeling watching images on a wide screen; they will also have more of their field of vision captured by an HDTV picture, roughly 30 percent versus, 10 percent in a conventional set. The fourth important characteristic of HDTV is the introduction of digital multichannel sound, in both recording and transmission. For further detail on the technical aspects of HDTV see Joan M. Van Tassel's Advanced Television Systems: Brave New TV.[99]

A final important development in the world of HDTV is the digital transmission standard for HDTV in the United States agreed on on November 8, 1993. "The things that are decided for HDTV will cast a long shadow," says Walt Cicciora, Time Warner vice president of technology and a member of the FCC's Advisory Committee on Advanced Television.[100] "This is going to be the first new standard (in television) in 50 years," says Dick Wiley, former FCC chairman and current chairman of the FCC's Advisory Committee on Advanced Television. The standards focus on several crucial issues, including the scanning approach, compression schemes, and sound quality.

One issue left unresolved by the FCC standards group is whether the digital system would use either interlaced or progressive scanning. Interlaced scanning simultaneously refreshes every other line of pixels (dots) that make up a TV image; this is what is currently used in TV sets. Progressive scanning provides a picture more free of flicker and more suitable for reading; it's what computer screens use. The progressive scan approach is seen as providing the best hope for the future, especially if TV sets and computers merge to form the home entertainment center of the future. In this scenario, HDTV may be more than a new generation of television. It may become the living room access ramp to the information highway. Compression will be based on MPEG-2 (MPEG stands for Motion Picture Experts Group, which is made up of engineers working since 1988 to achieve world standards for the digital coding of moving pictures with sound; MPEG-2 are standards agreed on in 1993 designed primarily for decoding television signals), which is also the basis for compression employed in the cable industry.[101] HDTV sound will be transmitted at compact disc quality surround sound using Dolby audio technology.[102] Critics of the standards are concerned that there might be a lot more hype than reality in the proposed HDTV platform. One critic is Russell Neuman, Tufts University professor of communications and associate of the MIT Media Lab. Neuman worries that industry leaders may be selling a technology that may not deliver the goods. "This man wants to sell you a next generation of technology. Caveat emptor," Neuman says.[103]

In late 1996 the FCC opted not to determine which method of scanning would be used. This may have been a smart political move, but it remains to be seen whether it will lead to a technically superior digital TV system in the United States. The choice now will be left to the vagaries of the marketplace, which "selected" VHS over Beta as the videorecorder standard, clearly the inferior technology in terms of quality of service. On the other hand, by avoiding the choice, the FCC broke a cross-industry logjam between broadcasters and computer industry leaders, each of which had lobbied intensely for their respective scanning paradigm, thus making digital HDTV possible in the U.S. marketplace by as early as 1998. The FCC had been lobbied by a variety of other players, as well, including the military, which wants progressive scanning because its higher resolution imagery is important in defense applications.

One important final FCC action will be to implement rules for the allocation of broadcast spectrum for local TV stations to deliver the digital television signals over the air, which will allow broadcasters to transmit the traditional NTSC and new HDTV signals simultaneously on accompanying channels. This is important because it will allow consumers without an HDTV set to still receive over-the-air television. Details and updates on the HDTV (sometimes now referred to simply as Digital Telvevision, or DTV) situation are provided by the HDTV Newsletter edited by Dale Cripps.[104]

Although HDTV ultimately represents an advanced device for displaying improved television images and sound, its initial applications have been primarily in production. A number of feature-length movies have been produced using HDTV both for theatrical release and for broadcast television. The first feature-length movie shot using HDTV cameras was *Julia, Julia,* a production by RAI, the Italian public broadcaster. The first made-for-television movie shot in HDTV in the United States was *The Littlest Victims,* a movie produced by CBS about babies with AIDS. HDTV cameras have been used to produce a number of other productions, including a large number of television commercials. HDTV technology is also used widely to produce Hollywood special effects for feature-length movies shot generally in film. In these cases, the film images are transferred to HDTV where the special effects are done by computer, and then the finished product is transferred back to 35 mm film for theatrical release. To date, HDTV productions shown on television in the United States are broadcast in regular NSTC format, since stations do not have the technology or available bandwidth needed to deliver HDTV signals over the air, nor do consumers have the required HDTV sets to watch in HDTV format. In Japan, where the analog MUSE HDTV system is in use, NHK, the public broadcaster, does air six hours of HDTV content a day to those few Japanese consumers and businesses with HDTV receivers. There are several major incentives to shoot movies and other content using HDTV, among them the improved image quality over NTSC cameras—even after transferring HDTV images to NTSC format the image is still improved. Also, with HDTV cameras, it is possible to immediately view the *rushes*—the term used by filmmakers to describe the initial film produced immediately after shooting.

Holography

Holography refers to a three-dimensional form of photography developed in the late 1940s by American scientist Dennis Gabor. Using laser cameras, multiple images of an object are recorded and reproduced in three-dimensional format. The result is an image that is far more complex and information-rich than conventional images. For the viewer, the three-dimensional holographic images can appear totally lifelike, in full color and even in full-motion, all without the aid of special viewing glasses or other devices, unlike other forms of three-dimensional photography. Regardless of angle, front, back, top or bottom, holographic images can maintain their full three-dimensional appearance. Taking the laser-based images required for holography is time-consuming and expensive, and the resulting demands for holographic display are prohibitive. Thus, most holographic images are small or limited in scope. Still, a variety of holography applications have been developed, such as imprinting holographic images on credit cards. These images, because of their complexity and the amount of information stored within them, make counterfeiting extremely difficult. With advances in digital printing technologies making counterfeiting a growing concern for the U.S. Treasury Department, as well as many other treasury departments around the world, the U.S. government is considering creating a new form of paper money imprinted with holographic images.

Some scientists anticipate a future in which holographic images could be displayed in life-size proportions in everyday spaces. This is the basis for the notion of the so-called "holodeck" featured on the television science-fiction series, *Star Trek: The Next Generation*. Imagine the potential for learning, entertainment, or training experiences in which you participate in a completely synthetic environment, but one that looks totally real, seamlessly three-dimensional, one in which the real could not be distinguished from illusions by visual inspection. It might become addictive!

For those interested in the ultimate display of holographic imagery, you can visit the Museum of Holography located in the SoHo region of New York City, or you can visit the Haunted House at The Magic Kingdom in Walt Disney World in Orlando, Florida, both of which feature impressive examples of this remarkable technology of the image.

Interactive Television

No technology has experienced more failures or false starts, yet drawn more industry investment dollars, than interactive technology (ITV). Numerous companies have tested competing ITV technologies, and the exact form that ultimately will emerge is anyone's guess, although it is almost certain to be digital in format. Interactive TV has existed for decades, with the first ITV research being conducted in the 1920s and interactive programming seen as early as 1953 when the CBS children's series *Winky Dink and You* was introduced, reports telecommunications scholar and interactivity expert John Carey, director of Greystone Communications, Dobbs Ferry, New York.[105] *Winky Dink* invited children to use a crayon to draw a bridge on a special plastic sheet placed on their TV set screen in order to help Winky Dink escape from some calamity. Unfortunately, many children neglected to use the special paper, Carey notes, and the response from disgruntled parents quickly led the network to pull the plug on the *Winky Dink* show. Although he traces the modern origins of interactive media to the AT&T picture telephone demonstration at the New York World's Fair in 1964, Carey notes there was a flurry of interactive media research in the 1970s. Perhaps most well-known was the Warner Amex Qube experiment in Columbus, Ohio, which brought interactivity to cable TV. Efforts there spawned the eventual development of Nickelodeon and MTV, but demonstrated that interactive TV would work only when production values were up to the industry standard—which meant expensive production costs. Qube eventually shut down, but many of its lessons are not forgotten.

Today's interest in interactive TV comes from several sources. Much of it comes from private industry and new technological developments. The emergence of the information highway, fiber optics, digitization, video compression, and the convergence of computers, television, and telecommunications make interactive TV more feasible as a commercial enterprise.

ITV Field Trials.   A number of industry-sponsored research experiments are now underway in the United States and Canada, as well as elsewhere around the world. Most are sponsored by cable TV and telephone companies. The early results have been mixed. One of the earliest of these second-generation experiments in providing an interactive TV service network is phone company GTE's trial in Cerritos, California. Launched in 1989, the Cerritos trial has met with limited success in the marketplace. The system provides fiber-optic lines directly to some 7,000 homes, and gives subscribers access to a variety of services, including educational resources, stock quotes, and other interactive services. While the technology seems to be working well enough, public interest has been almost nonexistent. One part of the test, called "Main Street," was rolled out in Carlsbad, California, in December 1992 and in Boston in the spring of 1993. But all told, only a few thousand households have subscribed to Main Street, which costs about $9.95 a month. One of the problems is that Main Street does not incorporate full-motion video, relying instead on text, still images, and sound. Moreover, Main Street's games, including black jack, poker, and a trivia contest, are somewhat low-tech for players used to the high-tech of Sega or Nintendo. GTE officials say the real goal of the Cerritos trial was to test the technology, not consumer interest, and in that sense, the trial has been moderately successful. "We weren't servicing this test to make a profit, but to learn from it," said Donald Bache, general manager of the Cerritos test. "You're changing the way people act, and that happens slowly," adds Thomas Greib, GTE Main Street's director. Company officials say future trials will be designed to test the marketability of the services. Others doubt the viability of the service as currently conceived. "People don't need it," says Michael Noll, Dean of the Annenberg School for Communications at University of Southern California. "You pay your bills sitting at your table, not on a living room couch."[106] Much of the problem with these interactive TV trials is that they have been swept aside by the wave of the Internet, the World Wide Web, and products such as WebTV.

A Full Service Network
One of the most talked about interactive TV field trials has been the full service network (FSN) announced in 1994 by Time Warner for the Orlando, Florida market.[107] The full service network is intended to put media control into the hands of the consumer, say Time Warner's leaders. The FSN will eventually provide all residents of Orlando with not only traditional television, but also interactive TV offerings such as movies on demand, personal communication services, video conferencing, home shopping, and many other enticing services. The heart of the system is interactive television, defined as full-service video-on-demand, with subscribers able to dial in for movies and other video offerings on demand, any time of the day or night, with the full range of video functions of a video cassette recorder, such as pause, fast

forward, or rewind. Time Warner launched its first test of the FSN in Orlando the week before Christmas in 1994, installing the service in five homes, and expanding the service to several hundred homes by 1996.[108] Time Warner had originally targeted some 4,000 homes for FSN access by 1996, but had to move back that date because of technical difficulties. "Writing one million lines of brand-new software," was also a factor in the delay, says Jim Chiddix, Senior Vice President at Time Warner Cable.[109] The proposed network includes fiber-optic wiring of the entire community, advanced computer set-top devices in every home that would give consumers access to a wide range of television and communications services, a central video server providing access to a vast digital movie library and other on-demand video services such as on-demand news, a printer in every home, and, eventually, personal communication services. Thus, the system would provide a full range of advanced information and communication services. Originally scheduled to last eighteen months, the project has experienced a variety of false starts and technical hiccups, and costs have risen dramatically, now expected to be in the tens of millions of dollars, making it by far the costliest of interactive TV trials and leading many to question the wisdom of Time Warner or any other corporation or governmental agency to invest heavily in large-scale proprietary infrastructure.

The jury is still out on research on interactive TV, although EON (approved in 1994 by the FCC)[110] and one or two other companies do have working prototypes, such as Interactive Network in California and Illinois, and Videoway, Montreal's interactive cable system that allows viewers to select camera angles during sporting events and different stories during the newscast. Videoway even lets sports fans use their remote to call up baseball players' batting averages, even their salaries. Others allow viewers to play along during game shows, such as *Jeopardy!* or blackjack. These prototypes raise the question as to what interactivity means. Some of these experiments are really examples of selectivity, not interactivity as we experience it in a telephone call. One of the most often mentioned interactive services of the future is video-on-demand. Some cable services, such as Time Warner's system in Queens, offer a version of video-on-demand, but it is relatively primitive, allowing viewers to select from a limited menu of movies starting at preset times (e.g., a movie might be available every fifteen minutes). The future promises video-on-demand, which will allow viewers to select from a menu of thousands of movies and have them instantly available for a small charge, comparable to renting a video from a video rental store.

A number of telephone companies have also invested heavily in field trials of interactive television systems. One of the most highly touted has been Tele-TV, a joint ITV venture of three of the RBOCs, Bell Atlantic Corp., Nynex Corp., and Pacific Telesis Group. The system is intended to offer a variety of video programming on demand, including entertainment, news and information, and provide two-way services, such as interactive multimedia television. Headed by broadcasting veteran Howard Stringer, Tele-TV has been increasingly the subject of rumors of budget cuts and technological failures.[111] Telephone company trials outside the United States have been popular as well, with British Telecommunications offering a video service to 2,500 homes in the United Kingdom.[112] The results of such field trials will help determine the future of interactive television.

Companies from other fields are also getting their interactive TV feet wet, including some banks such as Chase Manhattan, which are interested in the transactional capabilities of the technology, and computer software providers such as Microsoft, whose interests also lie in the transactional services area.[113,114]

Despite millions of dollars of investment in testing broadband and interactive television applications ranging from video-on-demand to interactive poker, no company or person has any definite answer to whether consumers will spend money on the expected applications of today's new media technologies. The field trials currently underway will begin to provide some answers. But the bottom line is that most of the current generation of emerging media technologies were developed because they could be. Software applications and content are now being created for those technologies to see whether enough consumers will spend enough of their disposable income on them to let their developers turn a reasonable profit and attract advertising dollars. In addition to the dozens of video-on-demand trials set for the United States, trials are set in at least seven other countries around the world, including Australia, Canada, Germany, Hong Kong, Italy, Japan, Singapore, and the United Kingdom.[115]

What few in industry foresaw has been the dramatic rise of the Internet and the World Wide Web as a possible means for delivering digital video, albiet less than broadcast-quality. The rise of the Web and products such as WebTV have taken much investor interest away from traditional approaches to ITV and into Internet-based video delivery.

One little-known but worth mentioning video-on-demand experiment is underway at Columbia University. Led by engineering Professor Dr. Dimitris Anastassiou, a team of researchers has developed a fully functional wireless video-on-demand system capable of delivering news, movies, or other video content on demand within a wireless local area network (LAN). The system uses compression technology developed at Columbia and transmits using MPEG-2 digital video, a standard Professor Anastassiou helped develop.

Videophone

Introduced at the 1964 New York World's Fair, the videophone allowed caller and callee to see each other. At that time, color images were not possible and black-and-white moving images were blurry, although black-and-white stills were in sharp focus. Consumers using the videophone often felt embarrassed using the device, and were concerned about looking unpresentable, ultimately rendering this well-intentioned innovation a veritable failure. It was a classic example of technology push rather than market pull, and as such, was doomed. The development of video conferencing applications in business in the late 1980s rekindled interest in the videophone, and in the early 1990s AT&T, MCI, PictureTel, and other companies introduced a new generation of desktop videophones costing less than $1,000. Although business interest has grown, consumer response has been tepid, but improvements in image quality may improve the videophone's chances of success. Still, consumer attitudes are slow to change, and most express little interest in the device.

Other interesting telephone receivers include the Satellite Phone (Inmarsat-A satellite phone or satphone), which provides a high-speed data link via satellite communications. The Satellite Phone can transmit still video images, and advances in the technology may soon make it possible to transmit motion video.

Similarly, the Screen Phone is the latest generation in telephones for displaying text and data on a small liquid crystal screen. The screen phone is one possible on-ramp to the information superhighway. Although the first generation of consumer Screen Phones hit the market in late 1994, it is unclear how quickly they will be adopted. The initial price tag is several hundred dollars, although competition will quickly bring down the price to less than two hundred dollars.

Outstripping all these developments, however, has been Internet-based telephony, including videoconferencing. A variety of low-cost tools have been developed that have made the notion of a videophone a reality. CU–SeeMe is perhaps the most well-known and widely used. Developed at Cornell University, CU–SeeMe refers to Cornell University or CU (i.e., see you)–see me. All that is needed is a computer with Internet access, a software package available at no cost via the Internet, and a $200 video camera. Thus equipped, anyone can participate in global videoconferencing with others similarly equipped. You need not even have the camera, if you like to watch. Affectionately called "lurkers" in CU–SeeMe parlance, anyone can tune in to watch what's being cybercast by CU–SeeMe "reflectors," or sites that are transmitting video. CU–SeeMe also transmits telephone-quality audio. Color CU–SeeMe software costs extra.

Virtual Reality

Snap on your visor or head-mounted display helmet, slip on a data glove and slide into your sensorized body suit, and you're ready for the ultimate virtual experience. At least that is the promise of virtual reality. The reality may be something less, at least in today's marketplace. Called by some a technological LSD, virtual reality may be the ultimate information technology. Virtual Reality (VR) is a magical window onto other worlds, from molecules to minds. . . . At the heart of VR is an experience—the experience of being in a virtual world or a remote location . . ."— Howard Rheingold, *Virtual Reality*[116]

Rheingold explains that two main concepts underlie the virtual reality experience: *immersion* through computer-based technologies to "create the illusion of being inside a computer-generated scene," and *navigation* by "creating a computer model of a molecule or a city and enabling the user to move around, as if inside it."

From the Eyes of the Creator.   Widely recognized as the leading virtual reality (VR) visionary, Jaron Lanier coined the term *virtual reality* and is the founder of VPL (Virtual Programming Languages) Research of Foster City, California. His work lead to the invention of the DataGlove™, the DataSuit™, and Swivel 3D™. He has recently developed the RB2™ system, the first commercially available VR development system and first multiple-user VR system. Lanier is now developing an application of the multi-user VR system to run in a Hollywood theater for consumer use. His other advanced VR products include a system for physicians to use in conducting microsurgery. Other interesting VR products have been developed by professor Myron Krueger, whose work has lead to the development of an artificial reality product for education and research. Commercial VR products for arcade use have also been developed, although these VR products are currently little more than sophisticated videogames with three-dimensional imaging, but do not offer the true level of interactivity developed by Lanier for his pioneering VR technology. VR products fall into six main areas:

- Training and Simulation
- Entertainment
- Scientific Visualization
- Communication
- Computer-Aided Design (CAD) and Modeling
- Information

Research leading up to today's generation of virtual reality technology dates back to 1971, when technologist Michael Noll, now professor at the Annenberg School for Communications at University of Southern California, invented and patented a multisensory technology while a researcher for the AT&T Bell Labs. Myron Krueger, president of Artificial Reality Corporation, Vernon, Connecticut, has studied VR and its related technologies since 1972, when he wrote his doctoral dissertation on the subject.

The Optical Revolution: Storage Technologies

As the information society has unfolded, the need to store increasingly vast amounts of digital information has soared. Anyone who has ever bought a computer with even a gigabyte of hard-disk storage has seen how quickly a seemingly limitless storage device can fill up (especially if you're running Windows 95). Computer-based storage technologies have evolved through many stages in recent decades. As recently as the mid-1970s, magnetic storage on nine-track magnetic tape was the predominant form of large volume storage, although many users saved their data files and programs on paper computer key-punch cards. The PC era ushered in much more wide-scale magnetic storage devices, especially the hard and floppy disks, and witnessed the end of the punch-card era. Today, storage is based increasingly on optical technologies capable of much greater volumes of storage. Because of the slowness of the devices for reading many optical media, such as CD-ROM or optical tape, magnetic devices are still heavily relied on for a variety of desktop, mainframe, and super-computing applications, especially when high-speed access is essential. One optical storage technology under development by Matsushita Electric Industrial

Company, Japan's largest consumer electronics company, uses an atomic force microscope to pack as much as a trillion bits of information into a single square centimeter.[117]

Whether optical or magnetic, one shortcoming of electronic storage media is their relatively short lifespan and speed of obsolescence. Unlike ancient writing media such as the Rosetta Stone, magnetic tape, videotape, magnetic, and optical disks are likely to become obsolete because of changes in technology within five to ten years, and even if not obsolete, face a short physical lifespan of less than ten years, with the exception of the optical disk, which has a life span of about thirty years.[118]

Computer memory comes in several forms, including random access and read-only memory, as well as readable and writable storage media. Random access memory, or RAM, refers to information stored by the computer in a way that allows the user instant access to any part of the stored information. This type of storage is relatively expensive, both in dollars and in computing power. Most desktop computers sold today have at least eight megabytes of RAM, the minimum needed to run most multimedia desktop computing applications. Multitasking, when a computer is running more than one application simultaneously in its random access memory, requires greater amounts of RAM as well. Sixty-four megabytes is the amount preferred by most new media mavens, with at least sixteen megabytes of video RAM.

Because it is based on the use of capacitors, current technology allows computers to store information in resident memory or RAM only while power is turned on. Recent advances in the field of supermagnetic storage may eliminate this storage limitation, making it possible to keep information in resident memory even when the computer is turned off. This same form of memory is also promising to increase the amount of storage capacity in magnetic discs greatly.

Read-only memory, or ROM, is a less expensive form of memory that refers to information stored in a way that can be read only, and not written to. A third type of memory is information stored on read and write storage media, such as computer hard-drives, floppy disks, magnetic tape, or certain forms of optical media. Computers use and store information, such as computer applications or files, on these media, retrieve information from them and erase or write over existing data.

Because of the increased demand for storage, high-capacity removable or portable magnetic storage devices have also been developed. Companies such as Zip, Bernoulli, and Syquest have manufactured removable hard-drives whose capacity exceeds 1.2 gigabytes, and whose cost is no more than floppy disk drives of the early 1990s. Terabyte storage devices are just around the technological corner.

CD-ROM

Since its invention in 1982, the Compact Disc-Read Only Memory (CD-ROM) has emerged as the medium of choice for not just storage of digital information, but as a multimedia delivery, publishing system. CD-ROM is an optical storage medium that can be read only once data are initially recorded. Essentially the same technology as audio CDs used for music recording, CD-ROM is used to store computer data of all types. Like the laserdisc, CD-ROMs store data optically, as opposed to the magnetic storage technology of the well-known floppy disk. Because they are optical, CD-ROMs can store massive amounts of data, with the current standard being more than 600MB. This means that a single CD-ROM can store more than 330,000 pages of text, and, with advances in digital compression, nearly an entire feature-length movie. On the down side, CD-ROMs require a special player, and as the name implies, can only be read once the data have been recorded on the disc. Unlike a magnetic floppy disc, they cannot be written to by the user. For anyone who has ever accidentally erased an important file, this may be viewed as an advantage. CD-ROM drives tend to read data more slowly than hard drives, however, which is a disadvantage from any point of view, especially from a computing perspective. The technology is improving, with 8x speed (i.e., 8 times the speed of the standard drive sold in 1995) CD-ROM drives now the standard for most desktop computers sold. The lasercard may emerge as an attractive alternative, since lasercard readers have no moving parts and are lightning fast. CD-ROMs are also fairly expensive, with most titles in the $40 to 60 price range.

IBM scientists have recently developed an advanced laser technology for storing up to ten times the amount of data on a single compact disc.[119] Although the technology is still in the laboratory, it may soon serve as a viable replacement for VCRs or other media for storing feature-length movies. The technology works by stacking data on multiple surfaces on the CD, as opposed to the traditional method that stores data on a single layer. The laser then is instructed to read data on each individual layer, "much as a person can look at the raindrops on a window or focus through them to see the view outside."[120]

Digital Video Disk (DVD)

At the 1996 Comdex Trade Show Toshiba and a handful of other companies introduced the Digital Video Disk (DVD)-ROM drive, a new high-capacity storage technology that may quickly supplant CD-ROM. DVD is the first optical device that can store an entire feature-length film. Toshiba is selling a commercial DVD-ROM drive for $350, roughly the price of a CD-ROM drive. DVD technology offers high disc storage capacities, seven to twenty-five times the capacity of a CD-ROM. DVD-ROM storage range options are 4.7GB (single data layer single-sided), 8.5GB (dual data layer, single-sided), 9.4GB (single data layer, dual-sided), and 17GB (dual data layer, dual-sided). DVD also features all-digital video (MPEG-2) and audio (Dolby Digital Surround Sound AC-3) playback, fast data transfer for interactive applications, reliable data retrieval, movie-viewing capabilities, backward compatibility with existing CD format and compatibility with future DVD formats.[121]

DVD is also an increasingly attractive development and publishing option for multimedia products. Using an Intergraph StudioZ RAX video server it is possible to capture real-time broadcast-quality uncompressed digital video, even directly from a high-quality digital Beta camera. This allows developers to edit, enhance, and compress multimedia content using advanced algorithms such as Intel's Indeo® video interactive tool kit.[122] There are also at least seven DVD disc replication facilities in the United States.[123]

Lasercard

The lasercard, which is an optical storage device about the size, weight, and thickness of a credit card, can store a gigabyte of information, enough to record the entire twenty-volume set of the *Oxford English Dictionary* and then some, including full-motion video and audio. Perhaps most importantly, unlike a CD-ROM or DVD-ROM reader, devices to read a lasercard have no moving parts, leaving little possibility of a malfunction or wearing out. Moreover, it means a lasercard can be read and accessed much faster.

Compact Disk-Interactive (CD-I)

CD-I is cousin to the CD-ROM. Also optically based, this medium provides much greater capacity for interactivity with the user. As a result, CD-I is often preferred for fast-paced game software. Moreover, CD-I is currently the only format with the storage capacity to show entire feature-length films. The leading manufacturer of the CD-I format is Holland's Philips, the pioneering consumer electronics company credited with introducing the first cassette-type video recorder in 1971 and the first laserdisc in 1972.

Databases

Databases are electronic collections of all types of information. Originally, most computer databases consisted of only numerical data and later textual information. With the advent of the digital era and multimedia computing in the 1990s, databases now embrace all kinds of information, including full-motion or still images, audio, text, numbers, even tactile or any combination of the above. In fact, some databases now store information about scents and any other type of sensory stimuli. One of the challenges that lie in the future of multimedia databases is developing efficient search engines for sorting quickly through massive databases of multimedia information. One possible solution is being developed by a collaborative research team lead by Professor Shih-Fu Chang and doctoral student Jon Smith at Columbia University. Using an approach called content-based indexing, search, and retrieval of images and video, the team has produced a working prototype called WebSEEK, which has already catalogued some 650,000 images and video clips on the World Wide Web. WebSEEK enables the user to search for and retrieve images or video based not just on keyword or textual descriptors of that material, but on their actual content. At present the WebSEEK prototype employs only low-level content features, such as a color histogram (i.e., the distribution of red, green, and blue) or a texture map. This enables the user to select an image of, say, a sunset, and then request other images or video of similar content based on the similarity of the actual images as defined by color matching. A working demonstration is publicly available on the Web.[124] Future generations of the technology will incorporate higher-level content features, such as pattern recognition, which would allow a user to search for images or video containing a face or an action.

Digital Audio Tape (DAT)

DAT is a recording medium that stores incoming audio signals in digital format. With DAT, there is no signal degradation on any subsequent copies. While it is possible to store audio in digital format on a magnetic drive or even on an optical storage or WORM (Write-Once, Read Many) device, these alternatives are either expensive or inefficient, since audio information in digital format requires large amounts of storage and quickly consumes large quantities of a hard disk, as would digital images or video. DAT, on the other hand, is inexpensive (a few hundred dollars). DAT also makes perfect digital recordings not only of analog transmissions but also digital ones (see DAR discussion above), raising important implications for intellectual property rights and copyright of music and other audio recordings. In 1971, Oki of Japan introduced the first professional Digital Audio Tape studio. The 4mm Digital Audio Tape recorded data in long tracks that stretched from one end of the tape to the other. DAT and other digital audio technologies are slowly being adopted by radio news facilities, including National Public Radio (NPR), as well as journalism education programs, such as the Graduate School of Journalism at Columbia University, which now operates a fully digital audio teaching laboratory. The experience has been that students learn faster and more easily in the digital environment than they could in a mechanical, analog audio system.

Laserdisc or Videodisc

The precursor to the compact disc, the first optical videodisc or laserdisc, was demonstrated in 1962 at SRI International.[125] Subsequently, Dutch scientist Dr. Pieter Kramer produced the first commercially viable laserdisc in 1968 for the Dutch consumer electronics firm Phillips. During its initial commercial introduction, few consumers showed interest in the high-priced products or players, and with few titles and a lackluster marketing effort by Dutch company Phillips, the laserdisc quickly disappeared. In the late 1980s, improvements in laserdisc technology allowed producers to store up to an hour of full-motion video on a single side of the laserdisc, making it possible to put entire feature-length films on both sides of a single laserdisc. Movie companies and television networks as well as electronics consumer manufacturers took a renewed interest, and consumers responded more favorably. Today, the laserdisc market embraces not only entertainment products, but also educational and training materials. Although not as large as the VCR market, the digital quality of the laserdisc, which also offers CD quality sound, has become a viable one. Still, few expect the laserdisc market to be an important one in the future, as advances in CD-ROM and CD-I, as well as the lasercard, may make the larger optical medium of the laserdisc obsolete.

Videocassette Recorder (VCR)

Although Sony demonstrated the first VCR in 1969, the technology of magnetic tape recording is much older. As early as 1951 singer Bing Crosby demonstrated the magnetic videotape recorder, and Ampex introduced the first videotape recorder for television use in 1956.[126] The technology became widely adopted in the consumer marketplace in the 1980s as prices fell dramatically from about $1,000 to less than $200. The digital VCR hit the consumer market in 1995, offering better picture quality, the ability to make repeated tape copies without loss of picture detail, and a better ability to match future television sets, which will likely process signals in digital format.[127] The digital VCR can also store large amounts of computer data. One of the obstacles in creating the digital VCR has been establishing international standards for the technology. Some fifty American, European, and Asian companies recently agreed to a set of three standards for digital home videocassette recorders. These standards include one for NTSC TV, the TV system currently in use in North America, Japan, and some other countries; a second for Hi-Vision, the Japanese high-definition TV system; and a third for the digital HDTV system being developed in the United States.

The autocut VCR is an electronic device available in Japan, but not in the United States, which edits out commercials while recording from television. "The device distinguishes between the stereo sound of commercials and the monaural sound of programs," reports Sid Lerner.[128] Given the strength of the commercial sector in the United States, it is little surprise that advertisers have been able to resist the introduction of the autocut VCR in the United States.

THE TECHNOLOGY MAP: A SUMMARY

The conceptual framework developed for this chapter emphasized digital, computer-based technologies and how they change the way media content is:

- Gathered, processed and produced
- Transmitted
- Stored
- Received (or accessed) and displayed

Technologies used in the gathering, producing, and processing of media and communications content fall into two main areas: information processing devices, primarily computers and related technologies, and devices for gathering and producing content, such as digital photography and the digital watermark, omnidirectional cameras, remote sensing, and speech recognition.

Transmission technologies embrace four main types of technologies:

1. Over-the-air broadcasting, including radio and television, satellite and wireless communications, and other uses of the electromagnetic spectrum

2. Fully switched telecommunications network, including twisted-pair, optical fiber, the switched telephone network, the advanced intelligent network (AIN), integrated services digital network (ISDN), asymmetrical digital subscriber line (ADSL)
3. Coaxial and optical fiber cable networks utilizing a one-way head-end system or file server (i.e., cable TV)
4. Electrical power lines

Display technologies are largely computer-based and include a variety of devices, including personal digital appliances, flat-panel screens, HDTV, and interactive television. Advances in these technologies signal improved access to information in digital format, emphasizing greater speed, higher image resolution and better color rendition, lighter weight, enhanced portability and battery life, multiple computing functions, including wireless communications, and the enhanced status of the computer as an interactive, multimedia, communications device.

Electronic storage technologies are primarily magnetic and optical, and include magnetic forms of random access and read-only memory, as well as optical disc storage media in increasingly miniaturized, digital video disk formats.

NOTES

[1]Tynan, Daniel. "PC meets TV." *PC World,* February 1994: 139.

[2]Williams, Frederick and John V. Pavlik. *The People's Right to Know: Media, Democracy, and the Information Highway,* Hillsdale, NJ: Lawrence Erlbaum Associates, 1994.

[3]*Transnational Data and Communications Report,* "Global Competitiveness of US Computer Industry," March/April 1994: 46.

[4]U.S. International Trade Commission, 1993. "Global Competitiveness of US Advanced-Technologies Industries: Computers." Washington, DC: USITC, Pub. no. 2705, December 1992.

[5]Seymour, Jim, "Pentium PCs: Pentium: The Second Wave," *PC Magazine,* January 25, 1994: 110

[6]Markoff, John. "Chip Makers' Competing Creed," *New York Times,* March 11, 1994: D1, D2.

[7]Gateway 2000 Web site 12/3/96, www.gateway2000.com

[8]Port, Otis, "Wonder Chips: How they'll make computing power ultrafast and ultracheap," *Business Week,* July 4, 1994: 86–92.

[9]Markoff, John, "Intel's Crash Course on Consumers," *New York Times,* Dec. 21, 1994: C1.

[10]Clyman, John, "PowerPC: Your Next CPU?" *PC Magazine,* February 22, 1994.

[11]Markoff, John. "Chip Makers' Competing Creed," *New York Times,* March 11, 1994: D1, D2.

[12]Markoff, John. "Chip Makers' Competing Creed," *New York Times,* March 11, 1994: D1, D2.

[13]Wilson, David L. "Compatible at Last? Alliance of Apple and IBM leads to new machines, but differences remain." *Chronicle of Higher Education,* March 16, 1994: A19.

[14]Levy, Steven. *Insanely Great: The Life and Times of* Macintosh, *the Computer That Changed Everything.* New York: Viking, 1994.

[15]Kodak Web site, http://www.kodak.com/

[16]Pavlik, Op. Cit., 1992.

[17]Powell, Op. Cit., 1993.

[18]Sony Web site, www.sony.com.

[19]Weiner, Tim, "C.I.A. Considers Allowing Sale of Spy Technology," *New York Times,* November 13, 1993: A8.

[20]Weiner, 1993: A8.

[21]Espanshade, Edward B., Jr. (editor), *Goode's Rand McNally World Atlas,* 18th ed., Rand McNally, 1990.

[22]Gibbons, John H., ed., U.S. Congress Office of Technology Assessment, *Commercial Newsgathering from Space: A Technical Memorandum,* (Washington, D.C.: Government Printing Office, 1987), pp. 39–44.

[23]Glasco, Tom, Information Director, Interview, EOSAT,/NASA, Washington, D.C., 1992.

[24]Landsat Spacecraft Data Sheet, EOSAT, January 1991.

[25]Morain, Stanley A., *Remote Sensing: Instrumentation for Nondestructive Exploration of Cultural Resources,* No. 2 in *Remote Sensing: A Handbook for Archaeologists and Cultural Resource Managers,* Washington, D.C.: Cultural Resources Management Division, National Park Service, U.S. Department of the Interior, 1978.

[26]Multispectral Imagery report, EOSAT, January, 1991.

[27]Paris, Hilton, NASA Teacher Resource Center, City College of New York, June 17, 1992.

[28]*The Great Geographical Atlas.* Rand McNally, pp. 8–9 1991.
The Great World Atlas. American Map Corporation, pp. 12–39, 1992.

[29]Sheehan, Henry, "Philip Noyce Plays 'Patriot Games' with the CIA," *Satellite TV Pre-Vue,* June 28–July 4:5, 25, 1992.

[30]Broad, William J., "Spy Data Now Open for Studies of Climate," *New York Times,* Tuesday, June 23, 1992, pp: C1, C10.

[31]Kalb, Bernard, Speech to The Freedom Forum Trustees, February, 1993.

[32]"The Mysterious Case of the Missing Troops," *St. Petersburg Times,* 30 Nov. 1990.

[33]Braman, Sandra, "Contradictions in Brilliant Eyes," *Gazette,* 47: 177–194, 1991.

[34]Palmer, Allen W., "On the limits of a free press: remote imaging and commercial news gathering," *Gazette,* 49: 159–176, 1992.

[35]Brender, Mark E., "High Resolution in Remote Sensing by the News Media," *Technology in Society,* 22: 89–98, 1989.

[36]Nelson, Clark, Director for Corporate Communication, Interview, SPOT Image, Reston, VA, 1992.

[37]SPOT Image refers to the French remote sensing satellite system, Systeme Probatoire d'Observation de la terre, launched in 1984.

[38]Landsat refers to the satellite system set up by NASA. It was originally called ERTS, for Earth Resource Technology Satellite. NASA launched Landsat 1 in 1972, and now has six Landsat satellites orbiting the earth that produce remote-sensing images for civilian use.

[39]EOSAT is the company established by NASA to administer its Landsat operations. The acronym refers to Earth Observation Satellite Company, 4300 Forbes Blvd. Lanham, MD 20706 (301)-5652-0537.

[40]Multispectral Scanner.

[41]SPOT satellites have twin sensors with pointable mirrors that can produce stereo images for 3-dimensional modeling.

[42]Deciphering objects such as cities is relatively simple, while data such as crops, geological formations and weather patterns require advanced technical skill.

[43]Legislation before the Senate would allow anyone to buy a Landsat image for a price equal to the government cost of the image, about $500.

[44]Flexibility refers to the ability of a news organization to request a specific image that is not in the satellite company's archive.

[45]Soyuzkarta satellites have a life of only 3–6 weeks, and there is no Soyuzkarta satellite now orbiting the Earth. In most cases, news organizations are limited to archive images only, although it is possible to "buy" a mission for a specific purpose.

[46]No extra charge for specific requests.

[47]All of the earth except the polar caps.

[48]A number of software packages that make television and newspaper and magazine use relatively easy.

[49]The European Space Agency recently launched a competing remote-sensing satellite, ERS-1. Japan is also planning to launch a remote-sensing satellite soon.

[50]McWilliams, Gary. "Computers are finally learning to listen," *Business Week,* Nov. 1, 1993.

[51]*The Seybold Report on Desktop Publishing,* March 7, 1994.

[52]Ibid.: 1.

[53]Vannucchi, Guido, "The New Frontier of Radio and Television in the Multimedia Era," The Heritage of Marconi's Invention," *Casa Italiana,* Columbia University, December 9, 1996.

[54]Karp, Jonathan. "Prime Time Police: China tries to pull the plug on satellite TV," *Far Eastern Economic Review,* 21 October 1993: 72–73.

[55]*Cable and Satellite Europe* (C&SEu), "Top 50 Cable and Satellite Companies, 1994

[56]http://www.ee.surrey.ac.uk/Personal/L.Wood/constellations/iridium.html

[57]http://www.teledesic.com/

[58]Andrews, Edmund L. "A Satellite System Is Planned to Link Most of the Globe," *New York Times,* March 21, 1994: A1, D2.

[59]Ling, Ruth, "Try Before You Buy" *Satellite Communications,* November, 1993: 25.

[60]Ibid; http://www.inmarsat.org/

[61]Wright, David, "Mobile satellite communications in developing countries," *Telecommunications Policy,* January/February 1994.

[62]Andrews, Edmund L. "Betting on Small-Dish TV," *New York Times,* D1, D7, December 15, 1993.

[63]http://www.dbsdish.com/

[64]*Via Satellite* April 4, 1994.

[65]Brown, Les (1992). *Les Brown's Encyclopedia of Televison,* 3rd ed. Detroit, MI: Gale Research Inc.

[66]*Broadcasting & Cable,* "The ABC's of DBS," December 6, 1993: 38.

[67]*Executive News Summary,* May 6 1994: 4.

[68]*Wall Street Journal,* May 6, 1994: B10

[69]"Study Suggests Wireless Could Transform Communications Industry," *The Sampler,* Response Analysis Corp., Princeton, NJ, pp. 1,4.

[70]*Kiplinger Washington Letter,* Sept. 24, 1993.

[71]Schwartz, Mischa, "Telecommunications Networks and Multimedia," Fellows seminar, The Freedom Forum Media Studies Center, February 2, 1994.

[72]Schmit, Julie. "High Tech Has Phones Humming," *USA Today,* April 23, 1994.

[73]Pavlik, John V. and Frederick Williams, op. cit. 1994.

[74]Bill Smith, "Technology and Infrastructure," panel presentation at Digital Footprint, December 4, 1996, New York.

[75]Flynn, Laurie, "A Multimedia Networking Challenge," *New York Times,* December 14, 1994.

[76]Arlen, Gary H., "RBOCs Finally Deploy ISDN" *Information & Interactive Services Report,* February 25, 1994: 11.

[77]http://www.usa.net/corning-fiber/tech/howmuch.html

[78]Noll, Michael, "Is All That Fiber Necessary?" *New York Times,* 1993.

[79]Dordick and Lehman, op. cit., 1993.

[80]Neil Stevenson, *Wired,* November, 1996.

[81]Frank, Reuven (1991). *Out of Thin Air: The Brief Wonderful Life of Network News.* New York: Simon & Schuster: 7.

[82]"Motorola Ships Cable Modems to U.S. Networks," REUTERS, April 30, 1996.

[83]Mark Landler, "Cablevision Says Viewers Will Get Link to Internet," *New York Times,* December 17, 1996.

[84]Salpukas, Agis, "Big Hopes Put on Electric Wires," *New York Times,* July 6, 1994: D1, D4.

[85]Fenton, op. cit. 1994.

[86]Salpukas, op. cit., 1994.

[87]Salpukas, op. cit., 1994.

[88]Dunkin, Amy. *Business Week,* Oct. 4, 1993: 124–5.

[89]Pollack, Andrew, "Organizers Captivate Japanese Girls," *New York Times,* Dec. 22, 1994: C1.

[90]Roger Fidler, *Mediamorphosis: Understanding New Media.* Thousand Oaks, CA: Sage Publications, Inc. 1997.

[91]Carey, John, "Thinking Flat in Washington," *Business Week,* May 9, 1994: 36.

[92]Maxwell, Charles T. "U.S. Blunders on Computer Screen Subsidy," Letter to the Editor, *The New York Times,* May 11, 1994.

[93]Pollack, Andrew, "From Korea, A Challenge to Japan," *The New York Times,* May 12, 1994: D1, D5.

[94]"Motif Unveils New Flat-Panel Technology, Largest Manufacturing Plant in U.S.," *Video Technology News,* Oct. 11, 1993: 8.

[95]Leary, Warren E., "French Team Develops Flexible, Electronic Transistor Made of Plastic," *New York Times,* Sept. 16, 1994.

[96]Browne, Malcolm W. *New York Times,* Sept. 28, 1993: C1.

[97]"SI Diamond Plans Flat-Panel Display Project Using Diamond-Based Technology," *HDTV Report,* Oct. 13, 1993.

[98]Flaherty, Joseph (1993) "High-Definition Television: Technical and Political Issues." In *Demystifying Media Technology,* John V. Pavlik and Everette E. Dennis, editors.

[99]Joan M. Van Tassel. *Advanced Television Systems: Brave New TV.* Boston, MA: Focal Press, 1996.

[100]Nolan, Chris, "Does HDTV Compute?" *Cablevision,* Dec. 6, 1993: 94.

[101]*Screen Digest* (August, 1993). "The World's Top AV Companies: The IDATE 100."

[102]Nolan, op. cit. 1993.

[103]Ibid.: 94.

[104]http://web-star.com/hdtv/hdtvnews.html

[105]Carey, John, "Field Testing the Information Superhighway," April 5, 1994, speech, The Freedom forum Media Studies Center.

[106]Selinger, Iris Cohen. "Cerritos test shows there's more to learn about interactive television," *Advertising Age,* October 25, 1993: 25.

[107]Ramstad, Evan, "Interactive TV gets another moment in the sun," The Associated Press, December 11, 1994.

[108]Andrews, Edmund L. "Time Warner's 'Time Machine,' " *New York Times,* Dec. 12, 1994: C1, C7.

[109]Jessell, Harry A., "For Time Warner, Software Is Hard Part." *Broadcasting & Cable,* March 28, 1994:42.

[110]M. Gipson, *Information & Interactive Services Report,* 8 October 1994.

[111]Leslie Cauley, Baby Bells Cut Budget, Hiring On Joint Interactive-TV Project, *Wall Street Journal,* June 7, 1996.

[112]Kim, James, "British pioneer launches interactive network," *USA TODAY,* Nov. 15, 1994: 7B.

[113]Hansell, Saul, "Banks Go Interactive to Bea the Rush of Services," *New York Times,* Oct. 19, 1994: C1, C6.

[114]Markoff, John, "Microsoft Organizes Its Interactive TV Team," *New York Times,* Nov. 2, 1994.

[115]Kempton, Paul, "Who in the World Wants VOD?" *Cable and Satellite Europe,* April 19, 1994: 26–34.

[116]Rheingold, Howard (1993). *The Virtual Community: Homesteading on the Electronic Frontier.* New York: Simon & Schuster: 19, 26.

[117]Pollack, Andrew, "Matsushita, in Lab Test, Reduces Disk to a Dot," *New York Times,* Sept. 19, 1994: C2.

[118]Rothenberg, Jeff, "Ensuring the Longevity of Digital Documents," *Scientific American,* January, 1995: 42–47.

[119]Markoff, John, "New I.B.M. Laser Method Stacks Data on Disks," *New York Times,* May 12, 1994.

[120]Ibid.: D1.

[121]"Toshiba Leads the Way with DVD Technology, Announces First DVD-ROM Drive," http://www.businesswire.com, NOV. 19,1996.

[122]http://developer.intel.com/drg/hybrid_author/devlab.htm, 29 Nov 1996.

[123]IMA DVD SIG MEMBERS, 22 Nov 96 (original posting 27 Aug 96).

[124]http://www.ctr.columbia.edu/advent/cb_demos.html

[125]Klopfenstein, Bruce C. "The Diffusion of the VCR in the United States," in Mark Levy (ed.) (1989). *The VCR Age: Home Video and Mass Communication.* Newbury Park, CA: Sage Publications.

[126]Ibid.

[127]"Talks Set on Digital VCR," *New York Times,* April 12, 1994.

[128]Lerner, Sid, "Lexicon for the Auto-Maga-Video Age," *New York Times,* December 5, 1993.

5

From Convergence to the Information Superhighway

Concepts and Applications in Cyberspace

> *"With digitalisation, all of the media become translatable into each other—computer bits migrate merrily—and they escape from their traditional means of transmission."*
> —*STUART BRAND*[1]

Central to any understanding of new media technologies are a number of important concepts and technological applications. These concepts refer to various new media notions and ideas, whereas applications refer to the software products developed to perform specific functions in the world of digital communications. Not all technological concepts and applications are included in this chapter. Many have already been examined in earlier chapters, and some are largely settled issues. Rather, included here are concepts and applications that represent some of the great unsettled and evolving issues of the digital communication age.

KEY CONCEPTS: THE UNSETTLED ISSUES

The number of terms and concepts littering the road to tomorrow's new media landscape is virtually limitless, but there are several concepts that serve as keys to understanding the contours of the new media terrain. These terms are used widely in discussions of new media technology, but are often ill-defined, or defined inconsistently, and sometimes in contradictory fashion. Collectively, they represent some of the vital energizing forces driving the development of new media technologies, their applications and consequences, and are at the crux of much public debate about those technologies. The key concepts examined here fall into three main groups:

- Overarching trends in the technological transformation of human communication, including convergence, compression, and digitization
- New media qualities and attributes, including hypertext, interactivity, immersion, and individualization
- Computer network concepts, including the information superhighway, the Internet, World Wide Web, and online communications

We begin the discussion with an examination of the overarching trends transforming the media technology landscape.

Convergence

Convergence is the coming together of all forms of mediated communications in an electronic, digital form, driven by the computers and enabled by network technology. Convergence presents profound challenges for the existing media order, and has paved the way for the development of multimedia products blending text, data, graphics, full-motion video, and sound and their universal accessibility and interactivity in the online world. See also Thomas F. Baldwin, D. Stevens McVoy, and Charles Steinfeld, *Convergence: Integrating Media, Information and Communication.*[2]

Compression

Compression is a technical process through which large amounts of data are condensed, or compressed, by removing the redundant information in one video frame to the next, for faster transmission or easier storage. Many multimedia products would not be feasible today if not for advances in compression technology that reduce the digital information needed to replicate an image or other content on a video monitor.[3] This process has important implications for the creation of a video-on-demand wired or wireless network, and for the storage of video signals, especially full-motion video, on DVD devices. Engineers have systematically improved compression algorithms so that today entire feature-length movies can be stored on a single DVD-ROM, or VCR-quality movies can be transmitted in a matter of minutes over existing telephone wires. Compression also has important implications for the transmission of television signals in a multichannel environment, whether via coaxial cable, over the air, or via direct broadcast satellite. While traditionally each television channel required a single channel on a cable system, for example, com-

TABLE 5-1   Compression

	# of Channels Stnd Television	10:1 Compression
NTSC Television	50	500
HDTV	5	50

Source: John Carey, Greystone Communications, 1994.[4]

pression now can be used to deliver ten or more NTSC TV signals over a single cable channel, thus making the 500-channel environment a possibility on existing coaxial cable systems. Moreover, a digital HDTV signal, which contains many times the information in a regular NTSC single, can be compressed and delivered over a single channel, thereby offering the possibility of an HDTV system using existing delivery media. Using compression in a fiber-optic system creates even greater opportunities for signal transmission. Telecommunications expert John Carey has developed the following analysis of compression's impact on television distribution (see Table 5-1).

Compression of video and audio information often involves coder–decoder (CODEC) technology, which translates analog information into digital format, which is then compressed for storage, processing, or transmission.

Digitization

Digitization refers to the conversion of analog information into the computer-readable format of 1s and 0s. In digital format, all audio, visual, or textual information blends together in the process of convergence.

James Beniger writes:

The progressive digitalization of mass media and telecommunications content begins to blur earlier distinctions between the communication of information and its processing (as implied by the term compunications coined by Anthony Oettinger), as well as between people and machines. Digitalization makes communication from persons to machines, between machines, and even from machines to persons easy as it is between persons. Also blurred are the distinctions among information types: numbers, words, pictures, and sounds, and eventually tastes, odors, and possibly even sensations, all might one day be stored, processed, and communicated in the same digital form.[5]

This view of new media technology resonates with other technology forecasters, who foresee the importance of the digital revolution and optical technologies in the future of media and society. Daniel Burrus, president of Burrus Research Associates and author of *Technotrends*, identifies twenty core technologies that will shape the future.[6] Although heading the list are genetic engineering (1) and advanced biochemistry (2), third on the list is digital electronics. Also high on Burrus' list are optical data storage (4), advanced video displays (5), advanced computers (6), distributed computing (7), artificial intelligence (8), fiber optics (10), microwaves (11), and advanced satellites (12). In fact, seven of Burrus' top ten technologies are media and communications based.

The second area of new media concepts deals with some of the qualities and attributes transforming the communication landscape, including hypertext and interactivity.

Hypertext

Technologist Ted Nelson coined the term *hypertext* in 1962. He defined the term quite simply as nonlinear text, or text that does not flow sequentially from start to finish. Rather, there may be many pathways through a body of text, even a narrative, with many words, phrases, or passages linked to others anywhere in the total document or body of text. Although hypertext is a simple idea, its implications are enormous and have served as the foundation for the World Wide Web, in which Web sites are linked electronically in spiderweb fashion in an n-dimensional space rather than linearly as they are in conventional media such as newspapers or television. For example, on a Web site, a term or phrase in this text might be "linked" electronically to an image or any other part of any document anywhere on the Web. The reader might journey through such a hypertext document in a free-form pattern, creating her or his own meaning or story in the process. For example, in many hypertext Web documents, a term, such as *cyberspace,* might be underlined or highlighted (e.g., *cyberspace*), thus signaling to the reader that the highlighted term is "hot" or linked to something else. By double-clicking the mouse when the cursor is positioned over the highlighted word, the origin and meaning of *cyberspace* (see the above passage from Gibson) might appear on the screen. Hypertext has been applied not only on the Web, but in a variety of fields, especially in education, where students are encouraged to explore a document following their own interests rather than via a preset path.

Many wonder what the future of writing and authorship may be in a world of hypertext and hypermedia. Will writing continue as we know it in a nonlinear communication environment? What will it mean to be an author when the story changes depending on who is doing the reading? What does authorship mean when hundreds, perhaps thousands, of people collaborate electronically on a continually unfolding story each day? Canadian scholar Jesse Hunter suggests an optimistic view of that future.

> *Hypermedia and multi-media authoring systems come on the cusp of an apparent upheaval in communications technology. New structures of literacy are falling into place that call into question the defining paradigms of our current assumptions. In the post-Modern condition, the problems of heterogeneity are easily attended to by hypermedia.*

Whether this technology of accountability is incident with, or answers to, the needs of an age caught in a deluge of information is not at issue. Nor do we need to worry that this technology threatens to make obsolete comfortable categories such as "author." Just as there re-mained Herculean heroism in the age of print, a place will be found for authors in the digital age.[7]

Commercial entrepreneurs similarly struggle with the implications of nonlinear navigation on the Internet, where it is as easy as a mouse click for a potential buyer to navigate to or away from your commercial message.

Interactivity

Interactivity has been one of the most sought-after goals of the new media age. With roots going back to at least the 1950s, efforts to develop truly interactive television have generally met with failure, often either for technical reasons or because of pro-hibitive expense. Nevertheless, interactivity has been relentlessly pursued, and is one of the cornerstones of the new media movement to create a global information superhighway. Still, there is little agreement about just what constitutes true interactivity. Many in television have presented interactive TV models in which interaction is essentially defined as the ability to select from a menu of choices or to choose movies on demand. With the convergence of telecommunications, televi-sion, and the computer, however, others argue for a more complete view of interactivity in which everyone on the superhighway can be both a source and re-ceiver, just as anyone using a telephone can place or receive a call. In a telecommu-nications context, interactivity means two-way communication between source and receiver, or, more broadly, multidirectional communication between any number of sources and receivers. In the broadest sense, interactivity simply means a process of reciprocal influence. The most compelling scenario for interactivity is that develop-ing on the Internet and the World Wide Web, where individuals can create their own messages, publish their own content, or engage in an online transaction.

Regardless of the prevailing definition of interactivity, the new media age will present media consumers with opportunities to become more active participants in the world of mediated communications. Whether their level of interaction is limited to pushing buttons on the next-generation remote control may depend not only on industry innovation and initiative, but on the strength and momentum of the couch potato legacy.

The third major area of technology concepts deals with notions of computer networks and networked communications, including the information superhighway, the Internet, and online communications.

Cyberspace

Science fiction writer William Gibson coined the term *cyberspace* in his 1984 award-winning novel *Neuromancer,* writing:

> *Cyberspace. A consensual hallucination experienced daily by billions of legitimate operators, in every nation. . . . A graphic representation of data abstracted from the banks of every computer in the human system. Unthinkable complexity. Lines of light ranged in the nonspace of the mind, clusters and constellations of data. Like city lights, receding. . . .[8]*

In writing that definition, Gibson suggests that cyberspace is similar to what many now loosely describe as virtual reality and what others experience as the World Wide Web. Communication ethicist John Phelan, the director of the McGannon Center for Communication Research at Fordham University, traces the origins of cyberspace to the world of cybernetics conceived by Norbert Wiener.[9] From its Greek roots, cybernetics denotes the use of technology for control and interactivity, both of which are concepts central to contemporary applications of new media technologies in modern society.

Information Superhighway

Just what exactly the information superhighway means, no one really knows. When legendary CBS *Evening News* anchor Walter ("And that's the way it is") Cronkite in early 1994 appeared as a guest on the David Letterman Show, Letterman asked Cronkite if he could tell the viewers just what the information highway is. "Well, I know," replied the sage news veteran, "but I'm not telling you."[10] Letterman has since described his show as an information highway, "without the information."[11]

The information superhighway is perhaps best thought of as a metaphor for the emerging digital data networks that are rapidly covering the globe and have important implications not only for journalism and the First Amendment, but for all of society and democracy itself. It is a mistake to think there will be just one information superhighway; there will be many, including the World Wide Web and the Internet, the broadband packet-switched telecommunications network of optical fiber, coaxial cable, and twisted-pair capable of delivering video-on-demand, and emerging technologies such as wireless communications and direct broadcast satellite that will utilize compression techniques to provide digital interactive television and other new information services.

Phillip Elmer-DeWitt, an editor at *Time* magazine, identifies three distinct views of the information superhighway, each with its own constituency as well as varying implications for public policy, media coverage, and the consumer.[12] These three views can be summed up as:

- The telephone company view
- The cable and broadcast view
- The Al Gore/computer user view

The telephone companies, the RBOCs, see the information superhighway as a new information infrastructure based on broadband switched network technology.

This view sees the highway as a new way to rack up billable message units for the phone companies. The particular content on the highway is irrelevant, as long as the message flow increases.

Cable companies and broadcasters see the information superhighway as a new way to deliver television, regardless of its form. In this view, interactive television, video-on-demand, or transaction services are all improved ways to bring the advertiser or seller together with the viewer or buyer.

Those involved in computer networking define the information superhighway in online terms, invoking a somewhat more metaphorical notion of the information superhighway as a new democratic medium of communication in which everyone can participate in a global cyberspace. The model they look to is the Internet and the World Wide Web, in which electronic messages are sent and received by the millions every day, files are transferred, research is conducted, and transactions are made. Depending on one's view, the notion of an information highway takes on decidedly different meaning and significance.

In 1835, American Samuel Morse of Charleston, Massachusetts invented the arguably first generation of the electronic information superhighway, the telegraph. The telegraph, the first Electromagnetic Signaling System, was first used on May 24, 1844 for a communication from Samuel Morse in Washington, DC, to newspaper colleagues at the *Baltimore (MD) Patriot.* Using a code of dots and dashes that still bears his name, Morse transmitted the first message by wire: "One o'clock— There has just been made a motion in the House to go into committee of the whole on the Oregon question. Rejected—ayes, 79; nays, 86. What hath God wrought?" The Associated Press news wire service began employing the telegraph device in 1913. Legend has it that when asked to explain the difference between the telegraph and wireless telegraphy, what is now called radio, Samuel Morse replied: "The function of the telegraph is like pinching a dog's tail: it barks on the other end." Wireless telegraphy, Morse explained, operates in the same fashion, only there's no dog.

Many object to the term "information superhighway," arguing that it has been used to describe many different technologies and has become so vague as to be not only meaningless but even misleading. "It's not only a scientifically wrong term. It's a counterproductive term," says Andrew Grove, chief executive officer of Intel Corp., the world's largest manufacturer of computer chips.[13] In agreement is John Naisbitt, author of *Megatrends.* "It's a huge step backward because it gets people in the mindset there's going to be a beginning, a middle and an end," he contends.[14] Naisbitt also criticizes the term in his book, *Global Paradox,* arguing that it leaves people with the impression that a single entity, not the marketplace, is controlling technological advances.[15] Many have offered alternative terms. It's the "information railroad," says labor activist Rand Wilson.[16] "The electronic ocean," counters Tom Henry, partner in a small software firm. "I would call it the Information Environment," suggests Esther Dyson, a founder of the Electronic Frontier Foundation.[17] *Infobahn* is the Germanic term offered by Mark Stahlman, president of New York-based New Media Association. Despite all these dueling metaphors, writer Laurent Belsie concludes that, although many deplore the information superhighway imagery, the term is here to stay. In fact, it's already set in concrete, Belsie argues. "The metaphor is so fixed in public consciousness that it won't go away," he writes.[18]

The notion of an information superhighway is made even cloudier by the fact that the media have used a variety of synonymous terms in their coverage. In a study of media coverage of the information superhighway, Pavlik and Szanto report identifying nine terms that have been used almost interchangeably in referring to the superhighway.[19] The terms are *information superhighway, information highway, data highway, data superhighway, electronic superhighway, electronic highway, info-superhighway, info-highway,* and *national information infrastructure,* or *NII,* the official term used by the Clinton–Gore administration. The study looked at coverage between January 1992 and February 1994, and included a dozen major newspapers, six news magazines, and three network TV programs. Although the greatest number of stories refer to *information superhighway* (1,208) or *highway* (965), other terms have received significant attention, such as *data highway* (199), *electronic superhighway* (182) and *national information infrastructure* (126). This same study shows that the information superhighway is most often linked to some specific technologies. Among those technologies mentioned in information superhighway stories, the greatest number include the Internet (306), e-mail (185), video-on-demand (184), and interactive TV (167). The study shows that the information superhighway is linked in the press with certain political and industry leaders. Vice President Al Gore tops the list, with 347 stories mentioning his name in the context of the information superhighway, or any of its synonyms. John Malone, CEO of TCI, is second on the list (241 stories), followed by President Bill Clinton (232), Home Shopping Network CEO Barry Diller (140) and Bell Atlantic CEO Raymond W. Smith (107).

The exact origins of the term *information highway,* or *superhighway,* are unclear, although Vice President Al Gore claims credit for inventing the term in the late 1970s. Gore used the term often in the 1992 presidential campaign, and has since promoted the information highway for its economic and educational potential both in the United States and internationally. Gore has even joked about the highway metaphors that have sprung up. "One businessman told me recently that he was accelerating his investment in new technology to avoid ending up as roadkill on the information superhighway," Gore quipped at the "superhighway summit" in Los Angeles in January 1994.[20]

The term *information highway* has roots going back nearly a quarter of a century, however, with one author having used the term in a book published in 1972. In *The Wired Nation: Cable TV: The Coming Information Highway,* Ralph Lee Smith caused something of a public and media sensation when he described the future of an electronically connected society that might provide a broad spectrum of the public with greater access to the media system.[21] Smith's book was published as an entire issue of *The Nation* opinion magazine, and the author toured the talk show circuit discussing his revolutionary view. Since the publication of his landmark book, however, the term *information highway* disappeared from vogue, and resurfaced only recently in public discourse. Smith recently admitted that the public potential of cable TV was never fully realized.[22] Although cable TV did achieve a great deal of commercial success, public access channels, once touted as an important medium for public participation in local cable systems, rarely became an integral part of cable programming in most communities. Whether the information super-highway of today will achieve its full public potential, or become little more than a potentially profitable commercial venture, is one of the intriguing questions of the coming decade. The democratic nature of electronic mail and online communica-tions suggests that the potential is there for public participation in the new medium. The realization of this potential may depend on both the shape of public policy af-fecting the superhighway, as well as the commitment shown by corporate interests in supporting a new public communication system.

Although public awareness and knowledge of the information superhighway is by no means universal, recent surveys indicate that use of the Internet is growing rapidly.[23] One Louis Harris & Associates poll taken in April of 1996 shows that at least 33 million U.S. adults use some type of online computer service and some 29 million surf the Internet. An impressive 41 million adults in the United States use some form of electronic mail.

"In recent months, several different estimates have been published for the use of the Internet and the World Wide Web," said Humphrey Taylor, chairman of the polling company. "Some of these figures have been criticized because they were not based on data from representative cross-sections of all Americans." This Harris poll included responses from 1,005 adults in the United States.[24]

Online Communications

Online communications refers to communication that occurs between users at two or more computers connected over a local or wide area network. It is now esti-mated that the online community, or *cyberspace* as it is sometimes called, is popu-lated by as many as 50 million users, with more than 15 million individuals subscribing to commercial online services in the United States.[25] This estimate in-cludes every computer network in offices, commercial networks such as Compuserve and Prodigy and Minitel in France, thousands of privately run elec-tronic bulletin board services, the Internet and the World Wide Web. As a publish-ing medium, online communications is one of the hottest forms of electronic publication, with CD-ROM publishing running a distant second (it may soon be overtaken by DVD-ROM). Many see online communications and electronic pub-lishing as a huge growth industry. Noted cable and new media industry analyst Paul Kagan is one of them. "The world is populated by a growing number of information hunters, roaming electronic libraries around the globe in search of a competitive edge," says Kagan, founder of Paul Kagan Associates, Inc., whose industry fore-casts have become a mainstay in the cable and multimedia industries. "It's a market that has no foreseeable end, because the theoretical limit is retrieving and sorting all the information in the world. That's like finding the digital Holy Grail," he says.[26] Although online communications have existed for more than a quarter of a century, they have flourished in the 1990s. With the growth of the Internet, commercial online services, the increased capacity of the public telecommunications network, and the increased speed of communications modems and personal computers, online communications have become an increasingly effective communication medium worldwide. This section examines leading online services and products, paying particular attention to the emerging range of consumer information services and specialized information services.

Consumer Online Services

Consumer online services provide PC users with an electronic commercial link to a growing network of computer users. By subscribing to an online service, such as America OnLine (AOL is the country's largest online service with 8 million subscribers) or Compuserve, users of PCs equipped with a modem, appropriate communications software, and a connection to touch-tone telephone service, can dial into a broad array of electronic services, such as sending and receiving electronic mail, making plane reservations, and paying bills electronically. Perhaps most importantly, these services are increasingly providing easy access to the Internet and the World Wide Web. Initially, most commercial online services attempted to create their own information services. AOL offerings include online versions of *Time, Omni, Compute, Wired, Disney Adventures, The Chicago Tribune,* and *The San Jose Mercury News.*[27] The 4.9 million member Compuserve offers a variety of services, including online versions of *Florida Today,* the *Detroit Free Press,* and Gannett Suburban Newspapers in White Plains, New York. But the commercial online services learned that most online mavens have an appetite for largely two things: e-mail and the Internet/Web. Online services such as Dulles, Virginia-based AOL, have quickly seen the competitive impact of the Internet Service Providers (ISPs), who specialize in low-cost, unlimited Internet and Web access. As a result, AOL and other online services have lowered their prices, expanded their Internet/Web access, and gone to a flat rate of $19.95 a month for unlimited Internet access. AOL had charged $9.95 a month for five hours of access, billing additional hours at $2.95 apiece. Although the AOL system suffered a demand overload of eight million logons the first day of the new rate structure (December 2, 1996), investors welcomed the change, as the company's stock rose $4.625 a share on the New York Stock Exchange, to $39.875 on December 3. Not everyone approved of the new rate structure, including attorneys general in eighteen states who had asked America Online to modify its procedure for enacting the new plan, which automatically more than doubled the basic rate for its users.[28] AOL is poised for even more growth, says Steve Chase, founder and president of AOL.[29] Much of AOL's growth, Case says, can be attributed to the graphical user interface and integration of services and information providers. "Most importantly, we understand this new interactive medium can change the way we communicate, inform, educate, work and play, and we are excited about its potential," Case adds. The potential market for online services has grown significantly in the past decade. In the early 1980s only two to three million homes were equipped with PCs, while in 1994 the number had risen to some 35 million, with roughly 62 percent of those homes equipped with a modem. Adding to the competitive alternatives for online commercial services, Microsoft has announced its plans to make its online service, MSN, a serious rival to AOL by mid-1997.[30] As part of its strategy, Microsoft is shipping 3.5 million CD-ROMS containing Windows 95, with free access to MSN for a thirty-day trial period and $19.95 a month for unlimited access. In late 1996, MSN had 1.6 million subscribers, and hopes to reach at least 3 million by the end of 1997.

These flat rates have pushed Internet traffic to ever higher levels. AOL traffic, for example, swelled by more than a third the day after the provider switched to the "all you can eat" pricing structure. "Not only did the company's number of daily online sessions increase by one-third, to 9 million—totaling 3.1 million hours of connection time—but the average America Online subscriber is staying on line 20 percent longer than before," reported Peter H. Lewis.[31] Bucking a trend it started three years earlier, Netcom, one of the nation's largest Internet service providers, announced in late 1996 that it would soon phase out unlimited Internet access pricing. Instead, Netcom will concentrate "on offering higher-quality, higher-priced services for business users."[32]

Among the popular offerings available on commercial online services as well as on the Internet are news groups. News groups are electronic bulletin boards where users share information about a subject, such as computer programming, health care, or the environment. Thousands of such news groups have been started, primarily as grassroots exercises in online communications communities. Perhaps the most widely used news group is called Newsnet, available on the Internet. Some estimates put as many as 10 million users on the Newsnet group worldwide.

Online services, particularly commercial online services, are a medium of the well off. Users tend to have a higher than average level of income, are well educated, have a professional occupation or operate their own business, and are largely male, although the fastest growing segment of the online world is women. These patterns hold true for all the major commercial services, although AOL draws the most well-educated group. Compuserve's users tend to be male (90 percent), with just 10 percent female. The median age is 41.4. Most (55 percent) have no children living at home, and have an average household income of $93,000. The vast majority (91 percent) are employed in professional or business occupations. Nearly half (45 percent) operate a home-based business.[33]

The Taxman Cometh
The financial success of these information services has not gone unnoticed by state tax commissioners. The Massachusetts Department of Revenue, for example, has told information service firms, computer bulletin boards, and the people using those services of its plans to add a five percent sales tax to their bills.[34,35] In New York, a scarcely noticed 5 percent sales tax on online services was passed by the State Assembly in 1993. Only a handful of newspapers considered strictly entertainment, however, such as bulletin boards, crossword puzzles, and rotisserie baseball, would be subject to the tax.[36,37]

Early Online Services

The 1970s was an historic decade in the history of online communications. In 1973, Mead Data Central of Columbus, Ohio, developed Lexis, the first online full-text database. Lexis featured case law, judicial rulings, and other information for the legal profession. Five years later, Mead Data Central debuted Nexis, the first online database containing national news publications including the *New York Times,* the *Washington Post, U.S. News & World Report,* and Associated Press (AP) News Service information. Dialog, a major commercial database network distributor, opened for business in 1972, and by 1979 had made available its National Newspaper Index, a bibliographic database later converted into a full-text service. Compuserve began selling access to its network to computer hobbyists as well as professionals in 1979.

New Kids on the Block

Catching the wave of new online products from traditional news organizations, *Time* magazine went online in the fall of 1993, and quickly amassed a devoted online following. After just its first three weeks of online availability through America OnLine, Time Online was accessed 126,563 times.[38] From September to December of 1993, the number of visitors to Time online rose steadily from 40,000 a week to 60,000 a week, "a trend that shows no sign of stopping."[39] *Time* logged its one millionth online visit on Thursday, January 24, 1994, and reached 1.5 million visits after six months of operation.[40] With total weekly usage exceeding 100,000, Time Online generated some $350,000 in users' fees by the end of its six month of operation. Time Online is now available through Pathfinder, the World Wide Web site of its corporate parent Time Warner.

Even the staid New York Times Company and Washington Post Company have launched online news products. On June 9, 1994 the *New York Times* launched an interactive news service on America Online, called simply @times.[41] Shortly thereafter, the *Times* launched its Web site, featuring the complete content of the daily newspaper, plus a popular destination among Web mavens, Cybertimes, which provides comprehensive coverage of the new media world, including technological developments, cultural and commercial implications, and legal and regulatory issues in cyberspace.

Although revenue has begun to flow in for many of these online information products, and some commercial online services such as AOL are turning a profit, few content providers are in the black. Most companies view online services as a low-cost opportunity to experiment with electronic products. One service that made a slight profit in just its first year of operation is the *Electronic Trib* offering from the *Albuquerque (NM) Tribune.* The *Electronic Trib* is available via Prodigy, and offers readers access to not only the content of the day's paper, but also additional material that did not make it into the paper, live chat sessions with reporters, and transactional services such as online classifieds. Because the *Electronic Trib* has very little overhead and a very small staff (one editor), the revenue generated from advertising in the electronic product has exceeded the cost of producing the electronic product.

Bandwidth

Central to the future and capability of any online service or network, including the Internet and the World Wide Web, is the amount of bandwidth available in the network. Bandwidth refers to the amount of electromagnetic spectrum available for transmission of information, typically defined in terms of transmission speed of medium, or the number of bits per second, such as kilobits, megabits, or gigabits per second (Kbps, Mbps, Gpbs).

Real-Time News Services: Bloomberg Business News

In many ways outweighing consumer online news services is the class of online products known as real-time financial information services. Leading competitors include Reuters PLC, with 190,000 subscribers worldwide, Dow Jones Telerate, with 90,000, and Bloomberg Business News, with more than 38,000. Although it is the smallest of the three, Bloomberg Business News is a fascinating case study in the future of news. "We follow the dictum," says Matthew Winkler, editor in chief for Bloomberg Business News, "follow the money." Journalists reporting for Bloomberg Business News try to "make money stories transparent," Winkler explains.[42]

Bloomberg Business News was founded in 1990, as a part of Bloomberg LP, a company created in 1982 by Michael Bloomberg, a Wall Street investment banker with a Ph.D. in physics. Bloomberg's entrepreneurial spirit led him to leave the confines of Merrill Lynch and apply his knowledge of the world of financial trading and technology to create a company devoted to real-time information services for financial traders and anyone interested in "following the money." His first client, and still his biggest, was Merrill Lynch. Although most clients are in the financial world, Bloomberg clients can be found in many other places around the world, including a growing number of news organizations and a few schools of journalism and communication. While about half of Bloomberg's clients are found throughout North and South America, many are located in Europe and an increasing number are in the Pacific Rim. Bloomberg terminals can also be found in some unexpected places. "Bill Clinton has a Bloomberg," says Matt Winkler. "So does the Sultan of Brunei and the Vatican."

Bloomberg Business News was started as a real-time news service for Bloomberg LP clients, many of whose investment decisions are greatly affected by news events. In three and a half years, Bloomberg Business News has grown to 225 journalists and 40 editors serving thousands of clients all around the world 24 hours a day 365 days a week. Not all of Bloomberg Business News users are financial traders. Dozens of news organizations are online with Bloomberg Business News. Eighty are newspapers, mostly flagship papers, such as the *New York Times* and the *Washington Post,* although many smaller papers also use the service, ranging from the *Buffalo (NY) News* to the *Australian Financial Review.* A growing number of network television news divisions, radio news, and magazines are using the Bloomberg service.

From a technological point of view, the Bloomberg system is relatively straightforward. The Bloomberg terminal (simply called a "Bloomberg") is little more than a Texas Instrument personal computer, with some special software and hardware peripherals. What is remarkable is that Bloomberg has created a multimedia news product using all off-the-shelf technology. "We massage it, but anyone is capable of doing it," explains Winkler. "People talk about the electronic newspaper of the future, " he adds. "We already have an electronic newspaper." The Bloomberg product includes text, graphic information, audio, and video, all delivered using the existing public telecommunications network. No devoted fiber-optic lines are required to receive Bloomberg Business News. Although the video currently provided is still images only, technology will soon allow moving images, as well. In early 1994, Bloomberg introduced a television business news service that would initially serve the New York market. With the creation of this video product line, however, the next step to online delivery of full-motion video news is only a short digital step away.

Bloomberg clients are required to lease a Bloomberg terminal. The rationale for this approach is that it allows Bloomberg to regularly update its hardware and software, without having to worry about compatibility with a variety of hardware and software platforms. "We've gone through four generations of hardware already," says Winkler.

The cost for a Bloomberg terminal is expensive relative to the cost of a traditional printed newspaper, but no more expensive than other real-time information services, such as Dow Jones Telerate or Reuters. A single terminal leases for $1,400 a month, while two or more lease for $1,000 apiece per month. Bloomberg is more than a thorn in the side of industry giants Reuters, with 190,000 terminals worldwide, and Dow Jones Telerate, with 90,000 worldwide. With 38,000 terminals leased around the world—up from just 8,500 since the launch of Bloomberg Business News in 1990—Bloomberg generates some $38 million a month in revenues. Where is the biggest cost to Bloomberg? It's not in the technology. Easily the biggest cost is people. Well over two-thirds of Bloomberg's costs are salaries; Bloomberg's journalists tend to be relatively well paid. In most traditional newspapers, the biggest single cost is printing, production and delivery, with journalists traditionally poorly paid.

Technology has also enabled Bloomberg's journalists to do their jobs in new, more efficient, and more flexible ways. Telecommuting has become increasingly common at Bloomberg. "Many of our people work at home," says Winkler. "Both our Detroit and Los Angeles bureaus are located in reporter's homes." In every case, the reporters have the same sophisticated hardware in their homes that they would have if they worked out of a central Bloomberg office. They have a Bloomberg terminal, modem, and phone that allow them to fully access the Bloomberg electronic library, send and receive communications over the Bloomberg messaging system, and file their stories electronically. Perhaps more important is the corporate culture that exists in the Bloomberg newsroom.

The best laid plans of mice and men are still subject to the whims of human fancy. Bloomberg LP found this out the hard way in February 1994 during the Winter Olympics in Lillehammer, Norway. In the United States, the biggest news story of the 1994 Olympics revolved around the attack of U.S. skater Nancy Kerrigan, who was clubbed on the knee just weeks before the Olympics. Not only did the event cast doubt on whether Kerrigan could win a medal, but it was unclear whether she would even be able to compete. Kerrigan surprised many observers by not only performing in the Olympics, but heading into the final day of the figure skating competition she was in in first place. But what happened next even caught Bloomberg by surprise. When the results of the competition were in, a message was flashed on the Bloomberg screen. Suddenly, the system froze. The reason? Thousands of Bloomberg clients had simultaneously requested the story to find out if Kerrigan had won the gold medal, and in the process caused a traffic jam so great it overloaded the system, causing it to freeze. "But if you think that was something," notes Winkler, "you should have seen what happened when the word 'penis' flashed across the screen a few months earlier." Although the system froze for about sixty seconds at the time of the Kerrigan medal story, the Bloomberg system crashed for nearly half an hour when the story of Lorena Bobbitt broke.[43] The Bobbitt story revolved around a woman who cut off her husband's penis, which was subsequently reattached in microsurgery. The story captured the attention of much of the American public for months as the case unfolded. By the way, Kerrigan failed in her gold medal bid, capturing the silver instead.

Noncommercial Providers and Products

Much online activity is the result of noncommercial interests and organizations, including not-for-profit groups as well as governmental agencies. These organizations and their new media products often serve audiences unable to pay for commercial services, or unattractive to advertisers, such as the urban poor, children, the homeless, the aged, and persons with disabilities.

Among the most well-known and widely available noncommercial services are the freenets, public-access computer systems designed for the free exchange of information among members of both local and global communities. The first freenet was created in 1986 at Case Western Reserve University Medical School in Cleveland, Ohio.[44] Originally a small bulletin board service for doctors, the Case freenet quickly grew in response to public demand and now serves more than 22,000 registered users and processes some 5,000 logins a day. The freenet features more than 300 information and communication services, ranging from e-mail to medical information on the Web to Project Hermes, which contains the full text of U.S. Supreme Court decisions. The network also offers users free access to Academy One, a K–12 electronic schoolhouse.[45] Freenets have been established in dozens of communities around the United States and internationally. Illustrative is the National Capital FreeNet in Ottawa (NCF), "created in 1992 as a noncommercial, co-operative, community project with the active participation of volunteers, institutions such as Carleton University, and organizations such as Gandalf Technologies (which donated modems and the communications equipment for connecting the freenet to the

Ottawa Public Library), and Sun Microsystems (which donated a SparcStation 10)," writes Canadian scholar Leslie Shade. Freenets represent a much-needed alternative to the commercial online offerings.

APPLICATIONS

Although this book is about new media technologies, any discussion of the significance of those technologies for commerce or culture depends almost exclusively on what those technologies can do. In turn, what those technologies can do is defined largely by the applications they run or perform. This section of Chapter 5 complements the opening section on new media technology concepts by examining the unsettled and evolving applications being created for those technologies. The applications discussed here fall into three main areas:

- Artificial life, including artificial intelligence, agents (i.e., intelligent agents), and the computer virus
- Commercial applications, such as video-on-demand, pay per view, transactional services, and video conferencing
- User services, including electronic mail, electronic bulletin boards, and multi-user domains (MUDs)

Artificial Life

Artificial life may seem an unlikely place to begin this discussion, but it represents one of the most potentially significant applications on the new media horizon. Included here are artificial intelligence, interface agents, and the computer virus.

Artificial Intelligence (AI)

Because it provides a window on the functioning of the human mind, artificial intelligence is what is for many the most exciting application of computing technology. It refers to computer processes of analysis and decision-making that come closest to paralleling those of humans. "Can computers think?" is perhaps the most intriguing question central to the field of artificial intelligence. For some, the answer is easy. Among the major AI thinkers, such as MIT's Marvin Minsky, Stanford's Edward Feigenbaum, and Oxford's Roger Penrose, only Herbert A. Simon, a Nobel prize-winning AI expert whose research in the field dates back to 1955, is convinced that machines can think. "I'm not claiming any magic for machines," says Simon.[46] "All I claim is that they can think." Simon says his computers think all the time. "They've been thinking since 1955 when we wrote the first program to get a computer to solve a problem by searching selectively through a mass of possibilities, which we think is the basis for human thinking." Others are much more skeptical, concluding that computers may mimic human thought and decision-making, but they cannot actually "think" and lack self-awareness or consciousness. The most recent evidence that computers can think comes from the Argonne National Laboratory in Illinois where a computer program has developed a major mathematical proof "that would have been called creative if a human had thought of it," reports Gina Kolata of the *New York Times*.[47] The computer's accomplishment is more than just mimicry of human intelligence, those at the Laboratory say. "It's a sign of power, of reasoning power," said Dr. Larry Wos, the supervisor of the computer reasoning project at Argonne.

Regardless of whether computers really think, however, scientists have developed a variety of AI applications, ranging from systems that understand the spoken word to robotic television cameras. These applications have been in primarily four areas: natural language processing, expert systems, vision, and robotics. Natural language processing refers to computer systems that can "understand" or process the word, either written or spoken. Expert systems are those that involve decision-making based on the distilled knowledge of human experts and research. Vision refers to computer sight systems that can be used for navigation or recognition of objects. Robotics is the AI branch in which machines are able to replicate, and in some cases improve on, human actions. In 1948, Missouri mathematician Norbert Wiener established the science of cybernetics, which eventually formed the basis for the development of robotics. Cybernetics primarily concerns the management of controls and communications within automatic machines, organizations, and living beings.

Artificial intelligence, as opposed to natural, human intelligence, has been dramatized in popular culture for many years. One of the most powerful and believable portrayals of a thinking machine was HAL (derived by subtracting one letter from the alphabet from IBM) in Stanley Kubrick's classic science fiction film, *2001: a Space Odyssey,* based on Arthur C. Clarke's book, and released in 1968. HAL not only ran the ship's basic life support systems and kept it on course, but engaged the astronauts in "intelligent" conversation and more. Science fiction writer Isaac Asimov even wrote of the three laws of robotics, including, above all else, that a robot could never harm a human.[48]

Long before there was HAL, however, mathematicians, computer scientists, and philosophers had pondered the nature of human intelligence and that which is possible in a machine. British mathematician Alan Turing, called the father of the modern computer and famous for helping a British–American team at Bletchley Park break the German code during World War II (subsequently immortalized on Broadway in the award-winning play, *Breaking the Code*) developed the classic test of artificial intelligence.[49] Now known as "The Turing Test," Turing proposed that the ultimate test of artificial intelligence is whether a human being can distinguish between communication with a computer and with a human. If not, then the computer truly possesses artificial intelligence. Shortly after HAL was created in *2001,* an MIT professor wrote a remarkable program called Eliza. Eliza simulated a session with a psychologist, using exclusively natural language prompts and responses. An Eliza session might go something like this.

User: "Hello."
Eliza: "Good morning. How are you?"

User: "OK."
Eliza: "Really?"

User: "Well, I've been better."
Eliza: "Tell me what's on your mind."

User: "I haven't been getting along with my brother."
Eliza: "Tell me about the problem you're having with your brother."

And so on.

One day, a visitor to the professor's home encountered a computer prompt that caught his attention. The professor was not in the room, and the visitor thought it might be a message from the professor, so he answered it. The computer immediately responded, and the visitor began a dialogue. Eventually, the professor returned, surprising his visitor, who had thought he was busily engaged in a conversation with the professor by computer. Unknowingly, he had just administered the Turing Test, and Eliza had passed.

Testing the Outer (and Inner) Limits

Those in the field of artificial intelligence have succeeded in many significant applications to media and communication. Voice recognition and speech synthesis for speaking and listening to a computer are already in use in fields such as medicine. They are particularly effective for doctors in the operating room, who need to have both hands free and speak with a relatively specialized and limited vocabulary the computer can be taught to understand, and persons suffering from Carpal Tunnel Syndrome, such as journalists, who can write without a keyboard. Many who are disabled use Kurzweil voice recognition technology, which is among the most advanced in this area, though still relatively expensive. Even some automobiles are now equipped with voice recognition technology that will do everything from starting the car to dialing a cellphone on spoken command.

Compton's new encyclopedia on CD-ROM features AI applications that use fuzzy logic when searching text. For instance, if a student asks, "Do fish in the ocean sleep?" the computer will find all text that discusses fish in the ocean, and highlight passages that discuss their sleeping habits. It's no longer necessary to be a database librarian to conduct efficient database searches, although when searching an expensive online service like Nexis, it helps.

Agents.   Agents, or intelligent agents, are computer programs that employ artificial intelligence to help users operate various computer applications. Acting much as a personal assistant, agents can learn by observation, make decisions, and filter incoming information, such as select news items based on personal preferences, search a database looking for selected pieces of information, or conduct transactions, such as electronic banking or making an airline reservation. Heralded as a form of artificial life, agents operate autonomously on the network into which they are released. They are sometimes called *know-bots,* short for *knowledge robots.*

Such software agents are quickly transforming the media landscape into a "smart" environment. An increasing number of scholars and business investors are recognizing the need for smart agents that can travel the information superhighway conducting research, making decisions, and generally acting as our personal representatives and information filters, screening out unwanted messages from an increasingly cluttered information environment. Media mogul Rupert Murdoch, the owner of NewsCorp and Fox TV network, in fact, is building a business based on intelligent agents.[50] Murdoch's designated new media evangelist is John Evans, head of News Electronic Data (NED), the new media subsidiary of Murdoch's News Corp. Evans is designing a media software product called Taxi for traveling the information superhighway. Taxi will use intelligent agents dubbed Marilyn and Oliver to comb databases, fetch information, develop profiles, and even schedule airplane reservations. Reflecting the "Daily Me" philosophy of the MIT Media Lab, Evans rewrites the media future as MEdia, in which software like Taxi use agents to create your own personalized media products. "Eventually, [that] agent will go to the *Daily News* and to *The Post* and will pick columnists for me, and TV Guides for me, and maybe go for horoscopes," says Evans. "Now I've got my paper."[51]

One interesting media application of interface agents is underway at the University of Texas at Austin. Professor Wayne Danielson, a pioneer in computer applications to instruction and research in journalism, who in 1964 developed a computer program for analyzing Associated Press news feeds, is leading a project to develop a news filter agent for the Newton Messagepad.[52] Calling it "a personal editor," Danielson's interface agent will let the Newton:

- Sort newsfeeds into nine categories, including sports, entertainment, crime, accidents, business, protest, politics, war, and medicine
- Decide which stories to display intact, which to shorten, and which to discard
- Learn individual news preferences by observing a human editor make news decisions

Danielson believes the personal editor will serve an important role in helping news consumers sort through massive databases by automating certain decisions about news values and preferences. To some, the information superhighway is more analogous to turning on a fire hydrant and trying to get a drink. There's simply too much water flowing too fast to drink without getting hurt or drowned. A personal editor, or interface agent, can act as a filter to help reduce the flow of water, or information, and let the thirsty news consumer get a drink. Danielson's personal editor uses a keyword strategy to categorize stories and make decisions. For example, a story containing a dozen words dealing with politics, a half dozen on economics, and two or three on religion would be classified as a politics story. The personal editor would let the Newton offer the user three options in selecting stories:

- Make pre-programmed decisions mimicking the decisions of real-world news editors
- Specify subject preferences by setting percentages for each of the nine categories listed above
- Infer the user's own preferences by monitoring the amount of time he or she spends reading different types of stories

The personal editor edits stories not on a generic word count, but based on observing the user's average reading speed, and then edits stories to fit each user's reading pattern.

In a series of tests comparing human editors against the computer, the personal editor replicated human choices with about 85 percent reliability or agreement.

Of course, not all believe intelligent agents to be a good thing. One opponent is virtual reality pioneer Jaron Lanier, who contends agents are among the worst inventions of the computing world. What we need more of, he argues, is more human intelligence, not its replacements. Agents, he believes, can never really understand our wishes and thus will never effectively represent us on the information superhighway.

Virus

In a digital world where floppy discs are inserted in and out of a series of computer disc drives, files and messages are transmitted over online networks circumnavigating the globe, and stolen software is perhaps more common than that properly paid for, it was inevitable that some forms of digital social disease would emerge. The computer virus, in itself a metaphorical form of artificial life, has emerged as the first such disease to plague the world of cyberspace. In 1992, computer users around the world worried about system crashes as the calendar approached May 5th, the 500th anniversary of the birth of Leonardo Da Vinci. An anonymous hacker had proclaimed that s/he had infected computer files and networks the world over with a devastating computer virus dubbed Da Vinci, capable of wiping out the contents of entire hard drives and scheduled to take effect on May 5. The threatened damage loomed as large to computer systems managers as a nuclear mushroom cloud to ranchers living near the Nevada Proving Grounds. Ultimately, computer users took such extensive precautionary steps to minimize the danger of the Da Vinci virus that only a handful of documented cases of the "computer disease" actually occurred. Two earlier computer viruses, the Internet Worm and the Pakistani Brain Virus, actually wreaked much greater havoc in the computer world. The Internet Worm, ironically released in 1988 by Robert Morris, Jr., the son of one of the creators of the very first computer virus at AT&T Bells Labs in 1962, quickly shut down a network affecting millions of users.

The origin of the computer virus is not easily determined, but author Steven Levy has developed the most comprehensive family tree to date.[53] He traces the origin to the AT&T Bell Labs in 1962, where computer scientists Victor Vyssotsky, H. Douglas McIlroy, and Robert Morris, Sr., created "the first known predatory self-replicating" computer organisms. "These beasts were the digital warriors in a gladiatorial game called 'Darwin.'"[54] The term *computer virus* was first used by science fiction writer David Gerrold in his 1972 book, *When Harley Was One,* to refer to a rogue computer creation. Gerrold, however, dropped any reference to the term in reprints of the novel, and the term failed to catch on. Finally, the computer virus was officially created in 1983 by then-USC engineering and computer security doctoral student Fred Cohen, recognized today as the father of the computer virus, not a "career enhancing distinction," notes Levy.[55] Although the term itself was coined by his professor Dr. Leonard Adleman, Cohen defined a *computer virus* as "a program that can 'infect' other programs by modifying them to include a possibly evolved copy of itself."[56] Cohen created and released into the University's UNIX system such a computer virus that enabled him to access the programs and files of any system user. "He could type commands as if he were that user."[57] The virus worked its magic with remarkable speed, penetrating the entire network in just a matter of minutes. Unfortunately for Cohen, the notion of a destructive computer virus did not appeal to most system administrators. Many, in fact, said that what he had created was not only unethical but even immoral. Computer virus scholar Eugene Spafford has outlined his concern:

> *Viruses created for malicious purposes are obviously bad: viruses constructed as experiments and released in the public domain are likewise unethical, and poor science besides. . . . Facetiously, I suggest that if computer viruses evolve into something with artificial consciousness, this might provide a doctrine of "original sin" for their theology.*[58]

Since the publication of Cohen's paper describing his research in 1987, computer scientists have begun to reconsider the implications of computer viruses, envisioning a form of antivirus that might serve a positive function in computer environments. Others have pursued notions of artificial life that might serve as computer agents to serve at a human user's bidding in the digital world. These agents would act as automatons roaming cyberspace under each user's control and command, gathering desired information, screening incoming messages, or otherwise acting as one's personal digital assistant. Nevertheless, many are still concerned about the evil prospects for computer viruses as a destructive form of artificial life. Some have conjectured about the horrifying possibilities of computer viruses invading military applications, "from battlefield robots to satellite warfare." "Once self-reproducing war machines are in place, even if we should change our mind and establish a consensus, dismantling them may become impossible—they may be literally out of our control." As Levy points out, this warning seems more plausible since in 1990 the United States government solicited contracts for the creation of computer viruses for military use. Forty years ago computer science pioneer Norbert Wiener issued this warning:

> *Again and again I have heard the statement that learning machines cannot subject us to any new dangers, because we can turn them off*

when we feel like it. But can we? To turn a machine off effectively, we must be in possession of information as to whether the danger point has come. The mere fact that we have made the machine does not guarantee that we shall have the proper information to do this.[59]

Interestingly, the development of computer viruses by deviant computer hackers has spawned an entire subindustry, with many computers now running electronic virus detectors and treatment packages.

Computer viruses and their offspring have important implications for the future of the media. Clearly, all media organizations and all consumers of electronic media products need to take precautions to protect themselves from infections by computer viruses. Although there have been no documented cases to date of computer viruses invading and causing significant damage to a media network, there is no reason to doubt it can happen. Perhaps more importantly, imagine a time in the not-too-distant future when the majority of news, information, and entertainment is delivered to consumers via electronic means. What might happen on the eve of an important election or referendum if an invading computer virus sent false information to those preparing to vote? How might an unscrupulous corporate giant use a computer virus to attach itself to the communications of anyone on the network, allowing corporate spies to watch or even alter messages transmitted over the network? How might computerized transactions be affected? Not even the First Amendment can protect the media from these electronic marauders.

Of course, not all viruses are created equal. The alleged "Good Times" virus is one unequal computer virus. Circulating around the globe via the Internet, the Good Times virus was purportedly capable of destroying an entire hard drive if accidentally downloaded off the Net. Anyone receiving an e-mail with the term "Good Times" in the subject heading was advised not to download it. "Good Times" turned out to be nothing more than a hoax, created by some prankster who thought it might be fun to unleash a "virus" that couldn't be prevented but that in fact caused no harm.

Commercial Applications

No doubt because of their value in the marketplace, the greatest number of new media applications are commercial in nature. They include interactive television services such as video on demand and pay-per-view TV, transactional services, and video conferencing.

Attack of the Killer Applications

Denizens of the computer world somtimes talk about killer applications, software products that serve a vital function, meet a pressing need, or represent a surefire, can't miss commercial success. Most ultimately fall into another category: those that are endlessly hyped but prove to be commercial duds.

On the information highway, there has been much talk of the first of the killer applications. Bell Atlantic Chief Executive Officer Ray Smith told reporters at the

1993 Western Cable Show that five killer applications will help finance the $15 billion construction cost of the advanced network bringing two-way video services to 1.25 million homes by 1995 and 8.75 million by 2000.[60] The five killer apps on his list are:

- Video-on-demand
- Home shopping
- Video games
- Programming
- Direct-response advertising.

These services are "plums ripe to be picked," Smith noted.[61] Another killer app frequently mentioned is transactional services, including home shopping, banking, airline reservations (with Microsoft's $1.5 billion acquisition of *Quicken,* the leading personal finance software, software pioneer and billionaire William H. Gates, 3rd demonsrated his belief in the money-making potential of the emerging transactional marketplace for writing checks, paying bills, and shopping electronically). Journalist and author Les Brown adds that there are two other killer applications lurking on the information superhighway horizon that may not have the redeeming social value of the other three.[62] As a result, they are not often mentioned in public discussions of the future of media technology, but they are likely to drive the consumer market, at least in the early years. They are gambling and pornography. Both already represent multibillion dollar industries and are guaranteed success stories, at least commercially, in the world of digitally delivered media technologies. John Hillis, the president of newschannel 8 in Washington, DC, observes that much of the discussion of so-called "killer applications" is a lot like killer bees, however. "There's a lot of hype and hysteria, but somehow they never seem to arrive."[63]

Video-on-Demand.   To many, video on demand is the driving force behind the construction of the information highway. While many information services from online banking to home shopping face uncertain demand, most industry advocates hail video-on-demand as a sure-fire hit. "Video on demand is expected to be the next big wave," writes Richard Lipkin.[64] "Rather than walking to the local video shop, customers will get films transmitted electronically to their homes just by dialing in their requests." Just as you can use any telephone to call anyone else with telephone service, the video-on-demand will let anyone connected to the information highway access a broad array of video services on demand, from movies-on-demand to news information. These services are generally seen as being offered on a pay-per-view basis, although many say the fee will be modest, as little as $.25 a movie. The technology necessary to provide video-on-demand ranges from advanced systems linking digital video file servers or jukeboxes, cable modem TV set-top decoders and optical fiber lines, to less expensive systems based on asymmetrical digital subscriber line (ADSL) services. Bell Atlantic's video-on-demand service in suburban Washington, D.C., is an example of an ADSL approach. The ADSL approach transmits compressed video signals over existing conventional telephone lines or "twisted pair" made of copper wire, in combination with a video server, telephone switch, digital video switch and ADSL terminal in a central office, along with a TV set-top decoder and ADSL unit in the home. With a $160 million price tag, the ADSL trial is still not cheap, but is considerably less expensive than laying fiber to every home in suburban Washington (estimated to be about $2,000 per home).[65,66]

Video-on-demand (VOD) refers to the ability to call up movies and other video services directly from the home or other location electronically from a central file server or digital video library. Video-on-demand gives the viewer access to a full range of video applications, including pause and resume, rewind, fast forward, and search within any video selected. Near video-on-demand is similar to full VOD, but does not offer the viewer instant access to any video selected, and may not include a full range of video applications. A number of cable MSO's started offering near video on demand in the early 1990s, such as Time Warner's Quantum cable system in Queens, New York. Quantum, with 150-channel capacity, offers viewers selected movies on demand, but is not full-fledged video dial tone, providing subscribers with the option to select movies started every few minutes and fed down alternative cable channels. The most popular video-on-demand services are actually offered in hotels, where business travelers paying $175 a night don't object to paying $8.95 for a movie when they want it.

Pay-Per-View (PPV) TV. Pay-Per-View (PPV) is a television service that invites viewers to pay to watch selected individual programs. PPV is available either via cable or satellite, and has been widely used for boxing and other sporting events, such as professional wrestling. During the 1980s, PPV grew in audience demand and total revenues, but began to decline slightly in the 1990s, although the all-time PPV record was set on the 1994 New Year's Eve by "The Miss Howard Stern New Year's Eve Pageant." The controversial program grossed an estimated $16 million from 375,000 sales at $39.95 each. Stern's show drew the ire of critics for its sexually explicit content and exploitation of female contestants in the so-called "beauty pageant."[67]

Pay-per-view systems are based on a century-old approach to broadcasting. In 1894 the Electrophone Company of London established the world's first pay-broadcast system service which, for ten pounds a month, distributed concerts, lectures, and church services to subscribers over the telephone. The technology was underdeveloped, however, and poor service caused the system to close down after ten years.

Introduced in 1940, Skiatron was one of the earliest pay television systems attempted prior to World War II. Phonevision was an experimental Pay TV service attempted by Zenith Corp. in 1947 that entailed the transmission of signals for unscrambling by a machine. The machine was connected to the television set of a subscriber, and required a card to be inserted for activation.

In 1972, HBO (Home Box Office) began broadcasting in Wilkes Barre, Pennsylvania. It was soon acquired by Time, Inc. HBO was among the first cable systems to offer recent feature movies and special entertainment not available through the regular television broadcasts—the pay-cable law allows it, in particular, to provide

R-rated entertainment programs. In 1975, HBO began transmitting programs to cable TV systems via satellite, setting off the growth of the cable industry in the United States, and in the process became the premiere pay cable TV service.

STV or Subscription Television became widely popular when celebrated television producer Norman Lear (e.g., *All in the Family*) successfully established the first STV station (KSBC-TV in Los Angeles). STV required electronic "unscrambling" of cabled or satellite data on a pay-per-view basis. With an initial viewership of 800 subscribers in April, 1977, KSBC grew to 100,000 subscribers within one year. Startup STV stations mushroomed on the East Coast and around metropolitan areas.

Not discussed at length here are a variety of other largely settled commercial applications, ranging from early technologies such as videotex, teletext and audiotext, transactional services, including online airline reservations, banking and bill paying, and video conferencing and the videophone. Like the fax, video conferencing has existed for many years, but has never really found a niche. Recently, advances in telecommunications networks and flat screen telephones are making videophone services increasingly affordable and more useful to end users, especially in business.

User Services

User services are applications in which the end user becomes the content provider and communications source. The discussion here includes a review of electronic mail, electronic bulletin boards, and multi-user domains (MUDs).

Electronic Mail (e-mail).   Electronic mail (e-mail) is a form of computer-to-computer messaging that has existed since the first computer networks in the 1960s. It achieved widespread popularity in the 1990s, when the growth of the Internet made e-mail a rapid and easy replacement for traditional postal services. The Internet Society estimates that by the end of 1994, more than one billion e-mail messages were transmitted each month via the Internet.[68] In shear volume, e-mail traffic surpassed traditional postal mail in the United States in 1996.[69] The users of e-mail have ranged from university professors to business communicators, private citizens connected to the online world to teenage computer hackers. Even the homeless have found an address in cyberspace where they can receive electronic mail.[70] Among the most well-known Americans who regularly use e-mail are Vice President Al Gore and former Associated Press foreign correspondent Terry Anderson (now on the adjunct faculty of the Graduate School of Journalism at Columbia University), who spent seven long years as a hostage in Beirut. Since regaining his freedom, Anderson has become active in the public arena, and has become a heavy user of electronic mail. Because of its ease of use, low cost, and universal reach, he sees e-mail as a potentially invaluable tool for linking and unifying a broad spectrum of public interest groups.

E-mail has emerged to serve a variety of functions, sometimes replacing traditional telephone-based voice communications among people weary of telephone tag. Moreover, since e-mail services on the Internet rely on local telephone calls connected to a national or international computer network, the user pays no long-distance telecommunications fees, thereby making e-mail a very cost-effective means of communications. Moreover, e-mail is transmitted via packet-switched telecommunications, rather than circuit-switched voice lines, and is highly reliable. As a result, e-mail has become a mainstay of not only domestic and international personal and business communications, but has been an important medium during international political crises and emergencies when rapid communications are critical but conventional media may be unavailable. For example, much of the early communications about the Russian Coup attempt during the summer of 1992 was based on e-mail. During the massive earthquake of January 17, 1994 in Los Angeles, people in the stricken area who could not make a long-distance phone call learned they could dial local telephone numbers that gave them access to electronic mail networks undisturbed by the quake.[71] Prodigy (a commercial online service) set up a special free area on its electronic bulletin board for users to post messages about the quake. Within the first six hours, users posted four thousand notes, says Prodigy spokeswoman Carol Wallace.[72,73] In one case, a New Jersey resident sent out a plea over Prodigy at 11:34 A.M. Eastern time, asking, "If you have any information about conditions in Northridge, the epicenter of the quake, please write back. We cannot reach our relatives there and are extremely worried about them. They live on Olympia Road." Three minutes later he received a comforting message from another network user who wrote, "My aunt and uncle in Northridge report a lot of glass breakage etc. in the house but no real structural damage visible in the neighborhood." Prodigy set up similar computer bulletin boards following the 1989 San Francisco earthquake and after the World Trade Center bombing and the Hugo and Andrew hurricanes. Another major consumer online network, Compuserve, experienced a similar heavy flow of traffic in the "live chat" area of discussions in and about Southern California. Many online night owls gave live reports of the earthquake and its aftermath on the Internet Relay Chat service, "the cyberspace equivalent of citizens' band radio."[74] On the IRC, as it is called, people gather for open discussions on a virtually limitless range of topics.

Electronic Vox Populi.   E-mail even reached the historically low-tech White House in 1992, during the first year of the Clinton administration. The most exclusive address on the Internet, president@whitehouse.gov, is in the nation's capital. Vice President Albert Gore, Jr. entered the e-mail hall of fame on January 13, 1994, when he became the first vice president to participate in a live news conference by computer network. "The Vice President strode into his office, took a seat at a Compac personal computer and briskly pecked out a confident greeting. "Welcome to the White House," Al Gore typed. "Let's get started."[75] The first query scrolled onto the Vice President's screen:

Mr VP . . .
I am from Hammond IN
What are your views on These

Virtual Communities . . . and
Are you currently involved
in iany *[sic]* networks?

After a brief technical interruption, Mr. Gore responded:

I'm back. Sorry.
Anyway, we have a
kind of "virtual community" here
in the White House
that gets a lot of work
done but we have not
yet established the myriad
links outside that we hope to soon.

A subsequent exchange reflected Gore's interest in developing the information highway to serve the needs and interests of all citizens.

Question:

Mr Vice-President
Alta Loma, Ca
I'm handicapped & spend a lot of time on the net
Do you envision home computer jobs
& how will that effect the economy?

Gore:

Yes. In fact you may be
interested in knowing
that the sysop of the White House
Forum, Georgia Griffith, is deaf and
blind.
There will be MANY opportunities
Thank you
for the disabled to use
their minds productively on
networks.

Although not profound on any policy matters pertaining to the national information infrastructure (NII), the administration's first official hands-on foray into cyberspace was nonetheless significant; before the Clinton–Gore team entered the Executive Office, the White House was so low-tech that the President couldn't even get a dial tone on his office phone. Mr. Gore, the administration's point man in building the NII, is now perhaps the world's leading advocate of providing universal access to advanced telecommunications services, such as the Internet, on the NII.

Moreover, with the launching of the White House's own "Home Page" on the World Wide Web (WWW), the administration now receives many thousands of electronic inquiries each day. For those interested, the WWW address for the White House is http://www.whitehouse.gov/. By accessing this service, not only can the user send an e-mail to the President, but she can listen to Socks the cat meow.

Electronic Bulletin Boards. Electronic bulletin boards (BBS) are online counterparts of the corkboard bulletin boards long used in the off-line world. BBSs are thematic, and deal with a full range of human interests, from topics on health to gun control. Online travelers can access BBSs to see what messages have been posted, or to post their own messages and await response. With the growth of the Internet and commercial online services, the number of computer or electronic bulletin boards has grown exponentially, with the estimated number of BBSs now exceeding 10,000.

1985 marked the beginning of the period of rapid growth of online bulletin boards throughout the United States, as low-cost modems and the general use of microcomputers made these community or trade-oriented information systems a practical and interesting communication and advertising option for many.

Multi-user Domains. Multi-user domains, or MUDs (originally for Multi-User Dungeons), refers to a broad class of online adventure games in which at least two participants play in fantasy worlds they help create, ranging from medieval villages to science fiction settings such as Frank Herbert's *Dune* or the universe of Gene Roddenberry's *Star Trek*. *Wired* magazine reports that MUDs have become the "addiction of the '90s" among cybernauts and other online mavens seeking real interactivity in a creative computing environment.[76] The allure of MUDs is not technological; it has more to do with the nature and psychology of the MUD experience. MUDs offer real interaction between the participants, the opportunity for creative expression. Participants are by nature highly involved in any MUD experience. Ultimately, MUDs develop into complete virtual communities.[77] Many MUDs are short-lived, but current estimates are that some 300 MUDs exist worldwide.

For a variety of reasons, MUDders frequently change or hide their gender. MIT MUD researcher Amy Bruckman says, "A lot of men pretend to be women so they can have more virtual sex." Conversely, "A lot of women pretend to be men so they'll be left alone."[78] Moreover, many MUDders find the experience addictive, spending as much as eighty hours a week playing in their virtual worlds. In response, Amherst College banned MUDs from its computer system in 1992, while Australia banned them from the entire continent. Notably, a law passed in 1996 by the Georgia Legislature prohibits anyone from masking or changing their online identity. Now on appeal in the courts, the law has far-reaching implications, and will be examined further in Chapter 9.

The first MUD was invented by Roy Traubshaw in 1980, during his final year at Essex College, United Kingdom. Traubshaw adapted the popular *Dungeons and*

Dragons game to an electronic computer format. The next year, his classmate Richard Bartle named it a MUD, or Multi-User Dungeon, and placed it on the Internet.[79]

Since then, MUDs have grown widely in popularity and in the diversity of their format, ranging from MIT's Cyberion City, an electronic metropolis designed by elementary and high school students, to MediaMOO, an electronic conference space created by Amy Bruckman and Michael Resnick. Many now define MUDs as Multi-User Domains, reflecting the broader use. Bruckman and Resnick are studying "MUDing as a serious form of scientific communication."[80] Cyberion City, an interactive text built through the collaborative writing of some 500 participants a day, consists of more than 50,000 objects, rooms, and characters. As the number of participants in this MUD continues to grow, so too will the world they have created. Although a small story in the rapidly expanding world of MUDs, Cyberion City may contain a much larger lesson for the future of new media applications. Put simply: if we build it *ourselves*, we will come.

Playing in the MUD.   MUDs, or multi-user domains, are among the most addictive and popular of online pursuits. Created mostly by computer hackers and mavens, most MUDs reflect the most creative side of the online world. To date, there are no commercially offered MUDs. Instead, most are fantasy, participatory, and educational in nature, and to many, represent many of the best qualities the online environment has to offer.

One of the more interesting MUDs is called LambdaMOO, a MUD established as an experiment in 1990 by Pavel Curtis at Xerox's Palo Alto Research Center (PARC). It has since evolved into a real community.[81] To put down roots in LambdaMOO, the first thing one must do is create a character. One such character is "Johnny Manhattan," created by cyberjournalist Josh Quittner (who also writes the Netly News for Time Warner's Pathfinder), one of the latest addicts to the world of MUDs. By carefully typing, "@describe me as tall and thin, pale as string cheese, wearing a neighborhood hat," Johnny Manhattan had a identity. From then on, anyone typing "look at Johnny Manhattan," would see the above description.

EPILOGUE: THE RACE FOR CONTENT

Despite all the hype about exciting new technologies such as the World Wide Web, personal digital appliances, and virtual reality, none of it really means anything without quality content. Although messaging, or person-to-person communications from the old-fashioned (a phone call) to the new fangled (e-mail), make up a significant portion of the traffic on the information highway, an increasingly large portion of the remaining traffic is content created by commercial providers, ranging from newspaper publishers to new media entrepreneurs. Of course, even in a 500-channel viewing environment, there is no guarantee there will be anything on worth watching, tuning in to, or downloading. Bruce Springsteen, the boss of rock and roll, once summed things up: "Fifty-seven channels and nothing on." The big issue will still boil down to content.

Peter Kann, chairman and publisher of Dow Jones & Co., Inc. and *The Wall Street Journal,* echoes this view, emphasizing that it's what's inside a medium that really counts. At Dow Jones half the company's revenue now comes from electronic delivery, he says, but Dow Jones remains a "content company." Rejecting Marshall McLuhan, Kann declares, "The form of delivery is not the most important thing. Content is king."[82]

NOTES

[1]Brand, Stewart (1987). *The Media Lab: Inventing the Future at MIT.* New York: Viking.

[2]Thomas F. Baldwin, D. Stevens McVoy and Charles Steinfeld, *Convergence: Integrating Media, Information and Communication.* Thousand Oaks, CA: Sage Publications, 1996.

[3]Williams, Frederick (1991). *The New Telecommunications.* Free Press: New York.

[4]Carey, John, "Field Testing the Information Superhighway," April 5, 1994, Speech, The Freedom Forum Media Studies Center.

[5]Beniger, James R. (1986). *The Control Revolution: Technological and Economic Origins of the Information Society.*

[6]Burrus, Daniel with Roger Gittines (1994?). *Technotrends: How to Use Technology to Go Beyond Your Competition.*

[7]Hunter, Jesse, "Authoring Literacy: From Index to Hypermedia," *Canadian Journal of Communication,* Vol. 19, 1994: 41–52.

[8]Gibson, William. *Neuromancer.* New York: Ace Books, 1984.

[9]Phelan, John M., The Inner Face of Interface, unpublished essay, June 1994; Weiner, Norbert, *Cybernetics: The HUman Use of Human Beings.*

[10]The Late Show with David Letterman, February 7, 1994.

[11]Ramstad, Evan, "Whoa, Slow Down! Metaphor Abuse Causing Whiplash on Information Highway," The Associated Press, February 3, 1994.

[12]Elmer-DeWitt, Phillip, "Traveling the Information Superhighway," speaking at a press briefing hosted by The Freedom Forum Media Studies Center on February 1, 1994.

[13]Ramstad, op. cit.

[14]Ibid.

[15]Naisbitt, John (199?). *Global Paradox.*

[16]Belsie, Laurent, "Info Superhighway: Metaphor in Concrete," *The Christian Science Monitor,* February 23, 1994: A1.

[17]Ibid.

[18]Ibid.

[19]Pavlik, John and Andras Szanto, "Coverage of the Information Superhighway," in "Separating Fact from Fiction on the Information Superhighway," The Research Group, The Freedom Forum Media Studies Center, May, 1994.

[20]Ramstad, op. cit.

[21]Smith, Ralph Lee (1972). *The Wired Nation: Cable TV: The Coming Information Highway.* New York: Harper & Row, 1972.

[22]Thalhimer, Mark, "Origins of the Information Superhighway Metaphor," in "Separating Fact from Fiction on the Information Superhighway," The Research Group, The Freedom Forum Media Studies Center, May, 1994.

[23]"Information highway still a mystery," *USA Today,* May 8, 1994: 5B.

[24]United Press International, 5 May 1996.

[25]Lewis, Peter H. "Strangers, Not Their Computers, Build a Network in Time of Grief," *New York Times,* March 8, 1994.

[26]Lang, Curtis, "The pied piper of convergence," *Advertising Age,* December 6, 1993:16.

[27]Liebman, Hanna. "About Time for On-Line," *MEDIAWEEK,* September 27 1993: 32, 36–7.

[28]Peter H. Lewis, "New Flat Rate Creates Surge in Usage of America Online," *New York Times,* December 3, 1996.

[29]Arlen, Gary H., *Information & Interactive Services Report,* December 17, 1993: 5.

[30]Peter H. Lewis, "Shift Planned in Network by Microsoft," December 10, 1996, New York Times Online.

[31]Peter H. Lewis, "An 'All You Can Eat' Price Is Clogging Internet Access," *New York Times,* December 17, 1996.

[32]Peter H. Lewis, "Netcom to Seek Profitable Niche: Internet Access Just for Business," December 19, 1996, *New York Times.*

[33]Arlen, Gary H., *Information & Interactive Services Report,* February 11, 1994: 4.

[34]*Gannett Executive News Summary,* Oct. 5, 1993.

[35]*Financial World,* Oct. 12: 56.

[36]*Gannett Executive News Summary,* October 7, 1993.

[37]*News Inc.,* October 4, 1993: 1.

[38]Carmody, Deirdre, "For Magazines, a Multimedia Wonderland," *New York Times,* Oct. 11, 1993.

[39]Long, Elizabeth Valle, "To Our Readers," *Time,* January 1, 1994.

[40]Elmer-DeWitt, op. cit., April 5, 1994.

[41]Ibid.

[42]Winkler, Matthew, Technology Studies Seminar, The Freedom Forum Media Studies Center, April 6 1994.

[43]Ibid.

[44]Shade, op. cit., 1994.

[45]Grundner, Thomas "Free-Nets: Networking meets Middle America." *Link Letter.* (available through nptn Gopher server) September/October 1991.

[46]"Herbert A. Simon," *Omni,* 1994: 71, 72.

[47]Kolata, Gina, "Computer Math Proof Shows Reasoning Power," New York Times Online, December 10, 1996.

[48]Asimov, Isaac. *I, Robot.* New York: Gnome Press, 1950.

[49]Goodman, Walter, "Code Breaking and the Good It Does," *New York Times,* January 18, 1994.

[50]*T Leaves* "Bulletins from the Information Highway: John Evans on New Media, Roadkill and More," Vol. 3, No. 2, March 1994. Published by the Newspaper Association of America.

[51]Ibid.: 6.

[52]Maher, Mike, "Electronic Gatekeeper for News," *Editor & Publisher,* June 25, 1994: 70, 72.

[53]Levy, Steven. *Artificial Life: The Quest for a New Creation.* London: Penguin Books, 1993.

[54]Ibid.: 316.

[55]Ibid.: 317.

[56]Ibid.: 312.

[57]Ibid.: 314.

[58]Ibid.: 330.

[59]Levy, op. cit.: 339.

[60]Jessell, Harry A., "VOD, Gaming to help pave superhighway," *Broadcasting & Cable,* Dec. 6, 1993.

[61]Ibid.: 6.

[62]Brown, Les, Technology Studies Seminar, The Freedom Forum Media Studies Center, April 6, 1994.

[63]Hillis, John, Technology Studies Seminar, The Freedom Forum Media Studies Center, May 15, 1994.

[64]Lipkin, Richard, "Making the Calls in a New Era of Communication," *Insight,* July 12, 1993: 9.

[65]Jessell, op. cit.

[66]Robert Lucky, Marconi's Heritage, Columbia University Conference, December 9, 1996.

[67]Walley, Wayne, "Grossing out at new levels: Stern PPV event posts strong buy rates." *Electronic Media,* January 10, 1994.

[68]Growth of Internet Web site, www.cfn.cs.dal.ca/Government/IndustryCanada/tab2.html

[69]Lucky, Marconi's Heritage, 1996, op. cit.

[70]Dutton, William. "Lessons from Public and Nonprofit Services," in *The People's Right to Know,* Frederick Williams and John Pavlik, eds. Hillsdale, NY: Lawrence Erlbaum Associates, 1994: 105–129, 1994.

[71]Schwartz, John and Tracy Thompson, "The On-Line Link To a Natural Disaster," Washington *Post,* January 19, 1994.

[72]Reporter Dispatch, Gannett Suburban Newspapers, "With phones out, computer networks provide key link," January 18, 1994.

[73]Ramirez, Anthony. "Computers Reach Out and Touch," *New York Times,* January 18, 1994: A20.

[74]Lewis, Peter H. "Strangers, Not Their Computers, Build a Network in Time of Grief," *New York Times,* March 8, 1994: D4.

[75]Lewis, Peter H. "Preaching the Techno-Gospel, Al Gore Version" *New York Times,* January 17, 1994: D1.

[76]Quittner, Josh, "Johnny Manhattan Meets the FurryMuckers," *Wired,* March 1994: 92.

[77]Rheingold, op. cit. (1993).

[78]Germain, Ellen. (Sept. 13, 1993) *Time:* 61.

[79]Hunter, Jesse, "Authoring Literacy: From Index to Hypermedia," *Canadian Journal of Communication,* Vol. 19, 1994: 41–52.

[80]Ibid.

[81]Quittner, op. cit., 1994.

[82]Fenton, Freedom Forum report on the 47th World Newspaper Congress and FIEJ Annual General Meeting, 29 May–1 June, 1994, Vienna, Austria.

6

Masters of the Universe

"We are in the midst of a technological storm."
—RUPERT MURDOCH[1]

GLOBAL AND DOMESTIC PLAYERS

Vying for control of the new media world is a remarkable cast of characters, including players from a variety of traditional media companies, telecommunications, computer and consumer electronic companies, and a variety of new media entrepreneurs from across the United States and internationally. A few years ago, most of these companies would never have imagined they would one day be competing head-to-head for control of the media universe. Convergence of technologies, regulation, and business have brought these companies into an unprecedented era of global competition. Many new media players are large behemoths determined to maintain their position in the unfolding landscape. Others are racing to stake a claim of any size or shape on the new media frontier in what can only be compared to the land stampedes of the 1800s West, where cutthroats, outlaws, and legitimate business people all struggled for control of the same terrain. Only this time the stage is global and the stakes are profound both commercially and culturally.

Telecommunications: The Big Investors

Leading the commercial charge into the electronic frontier are the telecommunications giants, including the U.S. Regional Bell Operating Companies (RBOCs), telephone company GTE, long-distance companies AT&T, MCI, and a smattering of smaller companies, and a growing number of recently or soon-to-be or recently privatized international firms (e.g., Singapore Tel, Italian Telecommunications, or STET). Most of these firms have invested billions of dollars in constructing a new information infrastructure, in large part the advanced packet-switched telecommunications network based on optical fiber wiring; smart, computer-based technologies, and integrated systems linking wireless and wired networks.

Driving much of the construction of the information superhighway has been the entry of the telephone companies into the cable television business.[2] Although government regulations presently prohibit telephone companies from providing cable TV service in their telephone franchise area, many telephone companies are lobbying vigorously to change that law, and may soon succeed, as lawmakers are swayed by arguments of economic growth and improved services.

AT&T has emerged as one of the principal architects of the new information infrastructure. Joining in alliances with several of the RBOCs, including Bell Atlantic, Bell South, and New England Bell, AT&T has agreed to build much of the hardware necessary for the delivery of interactive, full-motion video over the switched telephone network.

Because of its interest and stake in the information superhighway, AT&T has developed a specific set of policies on the development of the national information infrastructure (NII). In the view of AT&T, the NII is made up of four integrated elements:

- Computing and information appliances
- Communications networks
- Information and computing resources
- Skilled, well-trained people[3]

Multimedia Producers

While the telephone companies are leading the charge to create the information superhighway, multimedia producers are leading the race for content. The leading producers of multimedia software are ranked in Table 6-1 by total revenues for 1993. Heading the list is Electronic Arts, Inc./Broderbund Software, Inc., who in 1994 agreed to merge and thus form the largest multimedia production company. Broderbund is well known for its highly popular educational children's multimedia software, including "Where in the World is Carmen Sandiego?" The ranking is likely to change soon as more mergers are announced. In fact, at the time of this writing, Pearson P.L.C., one of Britain's largest publishers, had recently announced it would pay $462 million to buy Software Toolkits, Inc., the Silicon Valley multimedia software company that has successfully produced *Star Wars* characters and Marvel Comics's Captain America in video games and personal computer programs.[4] Others high on the list include Acclaim Entertainment, well-known for its

TABLE 6-1   Leading Multimedia Producers*

Electronic Arts/Broderbund (agreed to merge)	$493.2
Acclaim Entertainment	$375.7
Microsoft Multimedia	$200
Software Toolworks	$129.7
Spectrum Holobyte	$66.1
Sierra On-Line	$61.3
Davidson Associates	$58.6
Learning Company	$32.9

*Total revenues of leading multimedia software companies for 1993, in millions of dollars.

Source: *New York Times*[5]; Company Reports; Lehman Brothers' estimates.

popular but controversial videogame, *Mortal Kombat,* and Microsoft Multimedia, a division of Bill Gates's powerful Microsoft Corporation.

The Supporting Cast

Also sharing the new media spotlight are a variety of major computer companies, including recently downsized but still large IBM, and Apple Computers, more specialized computer manufacturers such as Silicon Graphics, chip manufacturers such as Intel Corp., and a host of smaller but fast-charging companies, with both domestic and foreign interests. Also taking a leading position on the new media stage is Microsoft, the dominant computer software company founded by Bill Gates, whose book, *The Road Ahead,* outlines his vision for the information superhighway, and who was named the 1994 CEO of the Year by *Chief Executive Magazine.* Silicon Graphics, Inc. merits special note, as well, with its more than $1 billion in sales and $100 million in profits in 1993. Headed by Chief Executive Edward R. McCracken, SGI is widely recognized for its state-of-the-art computer graphics and animation, as seen in the dinosaurs of *Jurassic Park* or the lifelike meeting of President John F. Kennedy and actor Tom Hanks in the 1994 blockbuster *Forrest Gump.* Consumer electronics companies play a major role, as well, with foreign companies especially important, such as Dutch company Phillips and Japanese company Sony. Videogame player and game manufacturers such as leading Japanese companies Nintendo and Sega are in the forefront also. Another interesting new media company to watch is Starwave, founded by Paul Allen, who cofounded Microsoft with Bill Gates. Starwave has carved a niche in the new media content arena, and is using technology in innovative ways to help invent a more interactive form of content in the new media marketplace, and has hired a strong team of top-ranking journalists to create its content.

In a strong supporting role are a number of American newspaper companies, such as Knight-Ridder, Times Mirror, Cox Enterprises, Hearst, The Tribune Company, and the Gannett Company, each of which is conducting important trials in the new media realm, especially in the area of online and electronic newspapers and news products. A number of these companies were involved in videotex trials a decade ago, and lost considerable sums. As a result, most are taking a somewhat less risky approach this time around, investing smaller amounts in more limited trials.

Companies in eight major subindustries, are competing for control of the new media landscape. These subindustries are:

- Media companies
- Cable operators
- Telecommunications equipment and services companies
- Telephone companies
- Computer and communications firms
- Computer software companies
- Leading newspaper companies
- Television programming

Notably, because of convergence, the distinctions implied by such separate listings are not really very sharp, and will become increasingly clouded as these industries all merge in the digital future. Moreover, there are many small but important companies not included on any top ten or twenty lists in these industries. Their significance should not be underestimated, especially during a time when adaptability, risktaking, and entrepreneurial experimentation are all at a premium and may be greatest in smaller, newer companies. What these companies lack in capital, they may make up in creativity.

Rising Stars

Other important media companies include firms from Latin America, such as Grupo Televisa in Mexico, whose recently deceased owner, Emilio Azcarraga Milmo, was the wealthiest man in Latin America, amassing a media-based fortune valued at $3.7 billion as well as acquiring the nickname El Tigre, for his aggressive style. Globo Television in Brazil (Rede Globo) owns the largest TV network in that country as well as one of the leading newspapers *(O Globo do Brasil),* magazines, and radio stations, and is one of the largest television networks in the world, and is a major exporter of TV programming throughout the Western Hemisphere, especially TV soap operas, or "novellas." Important telecommunications companies include Singapore Telecommunications, which first issued public stock in October 1993. Rupert Murdoch's holdings include the satellite systems B Sky B in the United Kingdom, and the Hong Kong-based StarTV, which provides television programming to China, India, and much of Southeast Asia. In Japan, Nippon TV is an important content provider, and in France, Canal+ is an important player in the television industry. In the West, Black Entertainment Television (BET), led by president Robert Johnson, has experienced rapid growth in the 1990s (e.g., 24 percent in 1992).

It's also worth noting some small entrepreneurial companies that may not re-write the future of new media technologies, but do reflect a grassroots movement in new technology. Some industry analysts, in fact, have suggested that it is small in-novative companies that are cumulatively investing the most heavily in new media technologies, and taking the boldest steps and the greatest relative risks. Because they are small, however, they have the advantage of quick adaptability. Many large technology companies have downsized in recent years, such as IBM, AT&T, and others, to increase their adaptability. One interesting new company is Gateway 2000, a small firm building powerful IBM clones at very affordable prices. Founded in a garage in South Dakota, Gateway 2000 has introduced a line of low-cost, high performance Pentium-chip computers and markets them effectively via the Internet. Customers can examine Gateway products via the Web, set all their preferred tech-nical specifications, obtain a firm price for the customized computer of their choice, pay by credit card, and order the computer, all via the World Wide Web, and all without ever talking to a salesman or -woman. Another entrepreneurial spirit has emerged in the online world of New York City. Stacy Horn, a graduate of New York University's interactive telecommunications master's program, has created the East Coast Hang-Out, or Echo, an online virtual community of more than 2,000 men and women, who pay about $19.95 to connect to the service. Horn started her business with the severance pay she received from her previous employer when the company relocated and she opted to stay in New York. The entire system was launched with two 486 computers (now upgraded to Pentiums), about three dozen phone lines, and a couple of part-time employees.

As corporate leaders in these diverse fields have recognized the growing con-vergence of telecommunications, computers, and communications, there has been growing interest in developing collaborative efforts between and among companies in different fields. Although much early interest and media reporting have empha-sized major merger announcements and activity, there have also been a variety of corporate alliances. The headlines have gone to mergers and acquisitions, both friendly and unfriendly, but many other strategies have been announced to bring together companies with complementary skills, talents, and resources, ranging from contractual agreements to transcorporate investments and resource sharing. Not all of the antitrust considerations have been played out in the regulatory and judicial arenas, but these types of alliances are increasingly likely in a future dominated by global market interests, complex technological infrastructures, and high-level de-mand for high-quality multimedia content. Many of these collaborative ventures have involved interactive TV trials and video-on-demand, especially via cable mo-dem and telephone ADSL systems, with a smaller number dealing in online news and information services. At stake is a potentially huge, multibillion dollar business. Arthur Bushkin, an executive at Bell Atlantic Corp., says hundreds of billions of dollars are at stake, far more than the $25 billion cable market, or the $12 billion video rental market. One interesting example is the alliance between Microsoft and NBC, which has given rise to MSNBC, launched in 1996 as both a cable television channel and a Web site. This alliance illustrates a growing trend to merge technology (Microsoft) and content (NBC) companies in a new media venue. Microsoft has formed a similar alliance with an Internet broadcaster called Pointcast. Pointcast is a news and information service delivered via the Internet, but not the Web. Pointcast "broadcasts" news provided by content companies such as Reuters, the New York Times and CMP Media, for free to users of the Internet (more than 1.7 million people have downloaded the free software as of December 12, 1996), generating its revenues from advertising.[6]

In a somewhat different type of alliance, in late 1996 Netscape Communications Corp. entered a strategic marketing agreement with five regional telephone companies to make Netscape Navigator their primary browser software for the Internet. Under the arrangement, Internet users can use Netscape's World Wide Web sites to select as their Internet service provider any of the five Bell companies, including Ameritech, Bell Atlantic, BellSouth, Pacific Bell, and Southwestern Bell. Subsequently, the phone companies will make Netscape Navigator or Communicator their default browser. "Customers will also get automatic access to Inbox Direct, Netscape's service that delivers on-line newspapers and other content via e-mail," reports Lawrence M. Fisher of the New York Times.[7]

Notably, however, some of the biggest joint ventures recently have been downsized. Among those recently getting downsized are:

- TCI's joint effort to lauch an ambitious cable modem program, with partners such as computer chip giant, Intel; TCI announced on December 7, 1996 that it was laying off some 2,500 employees (6.5 percent of its total work force), and cutting back substantially its investment in advanced digital services. Much of the retrenching is attributable to the rise of satellite-delivered television, which has cut significantly into cable TV's market share;
- Tele-TV, the video-on-demand joint venture of Bell Atlantic, NYNEX, and Pacific Telesis, intended to allow them to work together on video content and systems. Creative Artists Agency (CAA) contracted with TELE-TV (headed by former broadcast executive Howard Stringer) to provide its media expertise. By late 1996, the venture had seen little progress and was restructured and on the verge of elimination.
- Ameritech, BellSouth, GTE, and SBC also started a joint venture named Americast, and brought in Disney to help with the content acquisition and packaging. Headed by Stephen A. Weiswasser, former President, Multimedia Group Capital Cities/ABC, Inc., Americast also made little progress and by the end of 1996 was scaled back substantially.

Newspaper companies have shown interest in testing the interactive multimedia waters on a collaborative basis, but many are moving cautiously, after losing millions in the failed videotex trials a decade earlier. Some of the companies in the vanguard include Copley Press, owners of the *San Diego Union Tribune* and forty-five other newsapers, which has announced an ambitious joint venture with Linkatel to lay 3,700 miles of optical fiber throughout San Diego County;[8] Cox newspapers (in a joint venture with an RBOC); New York *Newsday;* Times Mirror Group, including *Los Angeles Times* and *Baltimore Sun,* which is developing a joint project with Prodigy. Multimedia, Inc., a company with newspaper holdings as well as interests in broadcasting, cable TV, and entertainment programming, has agreed to join a consortium with BellSouth Enterprises, Inc. and Cox Enterprises, Inc. The consortium will include Multimedia's largest newspapers, located in Greenville, South Carolina, Asheville, North Carolina, and Montgomery, Alabama, and will market telephonic classified and yellow page advertising throughout all of BellSouth's operating area.[9] The Washington Post Co. has also acquired an 80 percent stake in Mammoth Micro Productions, a Golden, Colorado-based publisher of multimedia CD-ROM titles.[10] Dow Jones & Company, Inc. and West Publishing Co. have agreed to provide a combined online legal and business information service. West Publishing's legal database, Westlaw, will be the only online service to have access to the Dow Jones News-Retrieval service, which provides full text of *The Wall Street Journal, Barron's,* and some 1,500 other publications.

Collaborative interests are also growing on the international front. Among such joint ventures are:

- U.S. cable companies TCI, Comcast Corp., Continental Cablevision Corp., NewChannel Corp., and Landmark Communications, Inc. in a collaborative effort with Japanese communications company Mitsui Comtek Corp., in a joint venture to create interactive cable TV;
- Sega (a leading Japanese video game company) and U.S. entertainment and cable company Time Warner and U.S. cable company TCI in an experiment to deliver videogames and other multimedia products electronically to the home consumer over cable systems; and,
- Bell Atlantic Corp. and the Italian state telecommunications company (STET) agreed to develop interactive TV in Italy and other markets.[11] The deal gives Philadelphia-based Bell Atlantic a foothold in the growing European interactive television business. Meanwhile, STET gains a powerful partner in creating services linking phones and televisions. In the project, customers in 2,000 Italian households will use a telephone line and TV to order movies and conduct transactions such as buying airline tickets or paying bills. The deal gives Bell Atlantic an option to purchase up to a 49 percent stake in STET's interactive multimedia services group, while Bell Atlantic must provide consulting services, technology and software to develop interactive services for STET.

THE FINANCIAL EQUATION

Driving much of the decision-making behind the development of new media technologies and corporate collaboration are bottom-line financial data. Who will pay, how much will they pay, and what will be the profits are all essential questions.

Much of the hype surrounding the development of the information superhighway has assumed a great consumer interest in new information services such as interactive TV, PCS, and movies-on-demand. Many suggest that much of the cost of these new technologies will be absorbed by the consumer. A growing amount of financial data, however, suggest otherwise. Next Century Media released a report in January 1994, indicating that consumers will not be able to afford the twelve-figure cost of interactive TV. Rather, they suggest, only advertisers have the incentive and the means to make it happen.[12]

Also troubling is the financial math underlying the construction of the broadband, switched network to the home. Bringing to mind the mystery of Foucault's pendulum or the long-standing mathematical puzzle of Fermat's proof, many promoters of the information superhighway have ignored, denied, or simply been unaware of the likely cost of building the necessary infrastructure to provide video-on-demand to every home currently served by telephony or cable TV. These highwaymen may soon awake to the real costs involved. Sobering data are provided by Next Century Media.[13] See Table 6-2.

These data show that even a low-tech approach to broadband, interactive communications, one without switching capabilities to allow consumers a full range of services, including true video-on-demand, will be expensive. Even in a best case scenario, it will take half a year just to recoup the cost of laying the infrastructure. More likely, it will take two to three years, assuming most homes sign up for the service. If the high-tech path is chosen, one with full switching capabilities to create a full-service network, the best case scenario takes a minimum of three years to break even on the infrastructure costs. A worst case scenario, with slow consumer adoption and use of the interactive TV services, which early evidence from field trials suggests is probable, it could take more than eight years. Further, these are just the costs for the hardware. The costs for software are likely to be much greater.

Still many media and telecommunications companies have invested millions in building a new information infrastructure, laying millions of miles of optical fiber,

TABLE 6-2 Cost Per Household for Broadband Infrastructure to the Home

		Cost Per Home Without Switching	With Switching
One-Time-Only Cost		$150–1000	$1500–4500
Revenue Per Month	VOD	$2.50	$4.00
	Games	$5.00	$6.00
	Advertisers	$18.00	$36.00
Months to Break Even (excluding marketing cost)		6–39	33–98

installing new advanced switches, and designing field trials to test new communication technologies ranging from interactive TV to wireless communications. Multimedia, Inc., a company involved in newspaper publishing, broadcasting, entertainment programming, and cable television, is placing its bet on the information superhighway. Mr. Walter Bartlett, Multimedia's chairman, president, and chief executive officer, says the company has planned a number of strategic initiatives to strengthen its competitive position and to provide greater access to the information superhighway. These initiatives include a $150 million technical upgrade of Multimedia's cable operations, $90 million of which will be to replace coaxial cable with fiber. "The strategic investment we're making in our cable systems between now and the end of 1997 will enable us to fully participate in the additional revenue streams resulting from potentially hundreds of new cable channels."[14]

ENTREPRENEURIAL SPIRIT

Vision and inspiration have always been important ingredients in the development and successful marketing of new products. Never have these qualities been in greater demand than in the era of the information superhighway, where all bets are off and the frontier is virtually unknown. One media magnate who has great plans for the communications future is Rupert Murdoch, founder and chief executive officer of NewsCorp, his global media corporation. Murdoch, in delivering the keynote address at the Center for Communications annual luncheon honoring Ted Turner as 1993 communicator of the year, underscored the importance of courageous leadership in introducing new information services and products around the world. "We are in the midst of a technological storm," Murdoch declared.[15] "Eventually, there will be smooth sailing, but we have to get there first." To get there, Murdoch added, will require "less fear and more flexibility" by media and communication innovators.

Media Entrepreneurs

The history of the media industry and new media technology is based not only on corporate agreements and the financial bottom line. It is a story written in the personalities and genius, failures and foibles, vision, and sometimes greed of entrepreneurs whose legacies sometimes last far beyond their lifetime. From Gutenberg to William Randolph Hearst, the history of journalism often has been defined in terms of the figures who controlled the presses and printing technology. Telecommunications history is writ large in the names of Samuel Morse, Alexander Bain, and Alexander Graham Bell. The early history of computing rests largely on the shoulders of giants such as Charles Babbage, Lord Kelvin, Vannevar Bush, and Grace Hopper.

In today's global media environment, media entrepreneurs are no less important. Much has been written about media entrepreneurs, with much attention being paid to identifying the critical factors that explain the entrepreneurs' success or fail-ure. Theories range from the sublime to the ridiculous, with one author proposing that it is the "Big T" factor—high levels of testosterone—that explain why some media entrepreneurs have made it to the top.

TD Securities's distinguished media analyst Richard MacDonald spent a year as a fellow at The Freedom Forum Media Studies Center analyzing patterns of me-dia entrepreneurship. At his final fellows presentation, MacDonald outlined his findings.[16] He based his analysis on three media entrepreneurs who have had per-haps the greatest impact on media in the United States in the twentieth Century. The three entrepreneurs he identified: Walt Disney, founder of the Walt Disney Com-pany, with total revenue of more than $20 billion in 1996; Ted Turner, founder of Turner Broadcasting System, Inc., with total revenue of more than $3 billion in 1996; and Rupert Murdoch, founder of News Corporation Limited, with total assets of more than $26 billion in 1996.

MacDonald identified six special attributes that explain the success of these media entrepreneurs. First, they usually began with a media inheritance (with the exception of Disney). Second, they had no particularly overarching skill, just a total commitment to their enterprise. Third, they could galvanize those around them. Fourth, they had an absolute personal identification with their company. Fifth, they knew how to fully exploit the intellectual capital of their workforce, and even set up formal schools to develop their potential. Finally, and most importantly from the point of view of this book, they had a stunning and immediate grasp of technological change, they knew its significance, and could act on it quickly.

Creator of the Enchanted Kingdom: Walt Disney

In the case of Walt Disney, his grasp of technological change first demonstrated itself during the production of "Steamboat Willie," the Disney classic cartoon fea-turing Mickey Mouse, produced in 1929. Steamboat Willie was in mid-production when sound was introduced to the film industry. Disney immediately realized its importance, used his own voice as that of Mickey for the film, and Steamboat Willie—with sound—became a smash hit.

The Swashbuckler: Ted Turner

For Ted Turner, the key technology moment came in 1976, the same year he won the America's Cup in yachting. Turner saw the potential of satellite distribution as a driving force in the cable television business, and in 1976 bought transponder space on a satellite serving the continental United States. Although the subscriber base was only five million homes, Turner realized he could use the system to build a nationwide cable television network with programming distributed to cable head-ends via satellite. He used his Atlanta, Georgia television station, merged with the technologies of satellites and cable TV, to create the first superstation, WTBS. Turner also used satellite technology to launch the Cable News Network, his glo-bally successful news effort. Reflecting his well-known confidence, Turner boldly announced in early 1980 his plans for the CNN launch: "We'll be signing on June 1, and barring any satellite problems, we won't be signing off till the world ends."

Media Mogul Down-Under: Rupert Murdoch

Australian-born Rupert Murdoch perhaps has used technology to come the farthest of these three entrepreneurs. Murdoch inherited from his father a small newspaper in Adelaide, Australia in the mid-1950s. Shortly thereafter, he won a license to start a television station in Adelaide. Over the next four decades, Murdoch combined his business savvy and his understanding of new technology to create a global media empire serving most of the world's population. He has been particularly adept at utilizing direct broadcast satellite in Europe and Asia, pioneering B Sky B in the United Kingdom and Star TV in Asia. Although beyond the scope of MacDonald's analysis, many other media entrepreneurs have demonstrated similar skill with the management and application of new technology, such as Al Neuharth, who founded *USA Today* using satellite distribution technology and Michael Bloomberg, who founded Bloomberg LP, using the convergence of telecommunications, computers, and media to create a global multimedia information service. Neuharth and Bloomberg are discussed in detail elsewhere in this book.

Masters of the Universe

One writer, Kathryn Harris, a reporter who covers media industry developments for the *Los Angeles Times,* contends that seven American men from seven traditional media companies are uniquely positioned to wield extraordinary power in shaping the content of the information superhighway. Borrowing a phrase from Tom Wolfe, she calls these "stupendous seven" the "new masters of the universe."[17] Among the masters are Murdoch, who became a U.S. citizen to buy American television stations, and Turner, both from MacDonald's list, as well as Sumner Redstone, chairman of Viacom Inc., Gerald Levin, chairman of Time Warner Inc., Michael Eisner, chairman of Walt Disney Co., John Malone, chairman of Tele-Communications Inc., and Barry Diller, chairman of QVC Network Inc.

Sumner Redstone is the most tenacious of the big seven, having once survived a hotel fire by hanging from the window ledge. His company, Viacom, is the largest of the "big seven," with more than $12 billion in total revenues in 1996. Its holdings include Blockbuster Corp., Paramount Communications, Simon & Schuster, MTV, and Nickelodeon, making Viacom perhaps uniquely suited to shape the emerging information superhighway. Gerald Levin is a strong leader and a technology visionary. His company, Time Warner, has extensive cable holdings and a broad array of content production companies, including the 1996 purchase of Turner Broadcasting. Ted Turner is easily the most flamboyant of these new media moguls, having captured the America's Cup sailing championship in 1977 and built a media empire through energy, vision, and wit. As a new part of Time Warner, Turner Broadcasting is strong both domestically and internationally, with CNN enjoying a prominent global presence. Michael Eisner has been tightfisted with his investment dollars at Disney, but since joining the company in 1984 has brought it eightfold growth. Eisner has taken a less aggressive approach to developing new media applications, but has strong content production and distribution capabilities, and recently led his company in the acquisition of the multimedia company and television network, Capital Cities/ABC. Rupert Murdoch has ambitiously pursued a multifaceted global media empire, with diverse holdings ranging from newspapers to broadcast television to direct broadcast satellite TV. News Corp. has extensive content production capabilities and extensive holdings in television, print, and satellite technologies. John Malone, holder of a Ph.D. in operations research, is perhaps the most well-educated in new media technologies, and brings an aggressive style of management, tempered by a "methodical calm" to the new media business.[18] His Tele-Communications Inc. (TCI) is a major cable company in the United States, and has invested heavily in new cable technology, although it has recently scaled back its efforts. Barry Diller is an experienced studio executive, and understands creating programming for the viewing audience. QVC is the king of home shopping, and is poised to enter the interactive TV fray.

Although these seven may represent the most important players from the traditional media industries, any analysis of the key players in the new media mix would be remiss without mentioning one other individual: Bill Gates, the founder and CEO of Microsoft, Corp. The forty-year-old Gates, a Harvard dropout who went on to found the largest software company in the world, Microsoft, has engineered or is engineering many projects to shape the future of the information superhighway. His company occupies the dominant position in virtually every major software market, whether consumer or business. His plans to create a global communication satellite system may be just the beginning of a global new media empire headquartered in Seattle.

The Magnificent Seven

Although media analysts such as Harris and MacDonald may have accurately surveyed and studied the universe of media players likely to control the realm of new media content, a number of other players from competing fields are also likely to have a similarly profound impact on the nature of the new media system. Profiled here are what we might call "the magnificent seven" of the new media world—players representing diverse fields, some of whom are either not well known outside the communication field, have not been widely discussed as important figures in the shape of media things to come, or do not represent the highest levels of corporate leadership in the media and communication field. Discussed here are:

- Lawrence Ellison, founder of Oracle Systems
- Bill Ziff, Jr., founder, Ziff-Davis Publishing Company
- George Soros, global financier
- Anne Wells Branscomb, intellectual properties rights analyst

- Adam Clayton Powell III, Vice President, Technology, the Freedom Forum
- Vivian Horner, new media developer
- Roger Fidler, developer of flat-panel news publishing

Oracle of the Computer Age: Lawrence Ellison

One corporate player who has kept a relatively low profile is Oracle Systems CEO Lawrence Ellison, Silicon Valley's latest super-billionaire. He has emerged as a computing guru as an outsider, not from the world of the personal computer, but from mainframe computing. In contrast to many of his counterparts, such as Bill Gates of Microsoft, he "actually looks and acts super rich."[19] He dresses in elegant style, wearing "double-breasted suits and black silk Japanese sports shirts," and lives in a Japanese-style mansion "fit for a warlord."[20] Ellison sees the information highway as ultimately rewriting the nature of all mediated communication. Ellison says that all media, including books, magazines, music, TV shows, movies, and catalogues, will one day be digitized and readily available to everyone via computer-driven networks.[21] Oracle, with $1.6 billion in annual sales, is the leading producer of software for corporate databases. Building on this foundation, Ellison's company has embarked on the Alexandria Project, whose mission is to use computers to change the way human knowledge is amassed and stored. Just as the ancient Greeks built their famous library in Alexandria as a storehouse for all the world's books, ultimately assembling more than 500,000 volumes before the Christians burned the site in 391 A.D., Ellison envisions the Alexandria Project as the ultimate multimedia database. The Alexandria Project will encompass unfathomably more in its digital collection than even a great analog library such as the New York Public Library with its collection of 11 million books. Oracle envisions creating multimedia databases encompassing in digital form not merely texts and illustrations of the world's books and periodicals, but also the film and TV libraries of Hollywood, endless streams of news coverage, and much more. Ellison wants to create a global consumer electronic bazaar where shoppers will find everything from bronze vases made in Korea to hand-loomed silk pants from Japan.

The Quiet Man: Bill Ziff, Jr.

Unknown to most of the American public is William B. Ziff, Jr., founder of Ziff-Davis Publishing Company, one of the least prominent leaders of the new media world, but among its most powerful. His family-owned new media empire includes Ziff-Davis Publishing Co., whose seven magazines pull in $700 million a year in annual advertising and reach more than three million readers in the United States alone.[22] Global revenues are estimated at nearly $1 billion. The flagship publication is *PC Magazine,* a fifteen-year-old bimonthly with more than one million circulation and annual revenue of $281 million, making it the largest computer magazine in the world and the ninth largest magazine overall in the United States. Ziff-Davis is unquestionably the dominant player in the computer publishing industry, also fielding *PC Computing, PC Week, MacUser, MacWEEK, Computer Shopper,* and *Computer Gaming World/Kids and Computers.* In 1994, Ziff won the

Magazine Publishers of America's distinguished Henry Johnson Fisher Award as executive of the year. Under Ziff's leadership, Ziff-Davis Publishing Company has entered the rapidly growing field of online communications. David Armstrong, media critic at the *San Francisco Examiner* and the author of three books, describes sixty-six-year-old Ziff as "second perhaps only to Bill Gates as a prime mover in the $70 billion personal computer industry that has changed the way we work, think, and communicate.[23] Ziff's personal wealth is estimated by *Fortune* magazine at $1.5 billion. His influence derives not only from his wealth and his media reach, but because his prosperous and powerful computer magazines impact heavily on which new products live and die in the digital age. Ziff is said to run his company in a ruthless and manipulative style, striking fear into the hearts of many employees, both current and former.[24] Still, despite his aggressive business style, Ziff is highly respected and admonishes the publishing industry to strive to recapture the honor, quality, and ethics of the golden era of publishing that lasted through the 1970s, not just the bottom-line mentality that emerged in the 1980s. "From the cynical point of view of a modern Wall Street analyst," Ziff says, "our industry was then run by eccentric amateurs engaged in their lives' work for the uneconomic reason that they enjoyed it."[25] Ziff has been a quiet, major player in the media business for decades, assuming the corporate reins at Ziff-Davis in 1953. He steered the course for some three decades, when in 1982 crisis struck and he was diagnosed with prostate cancer. Ziff sold most of his company's twenty-four magazines in 1984 for some $712.5 million to Rupert Murdoch and CBS. Ziff held onto only a few weak computer magazines, but struck gold with the rise of the desktop computer industry in the 1980s. Although Ziff has retired from Ziff-Davis Publishing Company, he's far from through in writing the history of new media technology. The information superhighway beckons, and Bill Ziff, Jr. may find its allure irresistible.

Global Financier: George Soros

A relatively new player in the competition for control of the information highway is legendary investor George Soros, the Hungarian financier whose Quantum Fund is valued at $800 million. Soros, who single-handedly triggered a European currency crisis in 1992 and in mid-1993 sparked a rally in gold prices, invested in two companies in the telephone industry in early November 1993. Soros bought into Viatel, a privately owned New York company that runs international telephone services, and invested $40 million in Geotek, a New Jersey mobile radio company. "George believes that the international telecommunications environment is one that is going to experience a lot of growth in the '90s," said Viatel's chief executive, Martin Varsavsky. "Soros' move into the market is likely to add to the rush by institutional investors to get a position in the industry," wrote Martin Peers in the *New York Post*.[26]

The Legal Scholar's View: Anne Wells Branscomb

Anne Wells Branscomb is a communications lawyer whose work has helped define notions of intellectual property, copyright, privacy, and other civil rights in the digital age. Branscomb is a long-time associate of the Harvard University Program on Information Resources Policy, where she has conducted research on the impact of new information technologies on intellectual property rights. Branscomb was an inaugural senior fellow of The Freedom Forum Media Studies Center at Columbia University, and has served as an Adjunct Professor of International Law at the Fletcher School of Law and Diplomacy and as Professor of Telecommunications Law and Public Policy at the Polytechnic Institute of New York. In addition, she has been a consultant to the World Bank, among member government agencies, the U.S. Office of Technology Assessment. She has been the chairman of the board of Kalba-Bowen Associates of Cambridge, Massachusetts, and a visiting scholar at the Yale Law School. Branscomb is the editor of *Toward a Law of Global Communications Networks,* and the author of the book *Teletribes and Telecommunities.* She has written more than fifty monographs, reports, and articles in law reviews and communication journals. Her work revolves around the principles of the ownership of information, especially the individual and corporate rights to ownership of facts about individuals. In her latest book, she asks the fundamental question of the digital age, who owns information? The answer may be not only surprising, but to some even shocking. In many cases, including one's name, address, phone number, financial record, or even medical record, the owner may not be you!

Technology's Sense Maker: Adam Clayton Powell III

A veteran of the broadcast newsroom, Adam Clayton Powell III is Vice President of Technology and Programs at The Freedom Forum, where he directs the foundation's global efforts in analyzing new media and their impact on media and society. Powell directed the introduction of new technology in several news organizations, and has conducted extensive research on the unexpected and unintended consequences of new technology in the newsroom, ranging from the impact of videotape on TV news to the implications of fiber optics for newsroom management. Powell has been a producer for Quincy Jones Entertainment, and consultant to KMTP-TV, a public television station he helped found in San Francisco. He was also executive producer of the *Jesse Jackson Show* and vice president of news and information programming for National Public Radio. A former director of news at the Satellite News Channel, he has also served as news manager and broadcast producer at *CBS News* and as head of the Metroplex Broadcasting Company, Inc. Powell served on the National Advisory Panel to the U.S. Congress's Office of Technology Assessment. In 1979 he was the recipient of the Overseas Press Club Award for the best interpretation of foreign news for a series of specials he produced on Iran, and in 1989 he organized and supervised a reporting project that won many major awards, including the Peabody, the Columbia-DuPont, the Ohio State, and the Armstrong awards. His work has taken him to many international venues, including extensive work on the emerging media system in post-apartheid South Africa and in converging technologies in Japan. Widely respected in the news and entertainment industries and government, as well as in journalism education, Powell's analysis of the consequences of new technology on the media are likely to shape views in industry, government, and higher education. His strong reputation internationally is also likely to give him an increasing voice as media technology sense-maker around the world, from South Africa to Japan.

New Media Developer: Dr. Vivian Horner

Vivian M. Horner is a pioneer in developing new forms of content for new media, especially for children. The former director of Video Services for Bell Atlantic, Horner now heads a production company she recently founded in Washington, DC, and is producing educational interactive CD-ROMs for children. A pioneer in the development of new and interactive programming for children's television, Dr. Horner was vice president for program development at Warner Amex Cable Communications, where she conceptualized and then served as executive producer of Nickelodeon, the leading satellite-delivered young people's cable channel. Horner also was vice president of educational and children's programming for Qube, a two-way cable system in Columbus, Ohio. She was also director of research of *The Electric Company* for the Children's Television Workshop. Horner was an associate professor of psycholinguistics and education in the Department of Educational Psychology of the Ferkauf Graduate School of Humanities and Social Sciences at Yeshiva University in New York. She has written extensively on children and television, her publications appearing in *Journal of Communications, Journal of Consulting and Clinical Psychology,* and *Videography.* She has also been an electronic media consultant since 1983, helping develop product applications, marketing, and business plans for communications and marketing firms entering new media areas.

The Heritage of News: Roger Fidler

Roger Fidler, an adjunct professor and coordinator of the newly created Information Design Laboratory at Kent State University's School of Journalism, is a veteran newspaper designer and graphic artist with a knack for new technology and information navigation. He has redesigned more than thirty newspapers in the last decade, was the editor and publisher of *Newspaper Design Notebook* from 1979–82, and is a founding member and former vice president of the Society of Newspaper Design (SND). Fidler has considerable experience in developing interactive, electronic news products, including several years as a founding member of the design team for Knight-Ridder's Viewtron experiment in videotext. He also founded the first successful computer graphics network for newspapers in 1984, Knight-Ridder Graphics Network (KRGN), which later merged with Chicago Tribune Graphics Service to form Knight-Ridder Tribune News Graphics (KRTN).

During a 1991–1992 fellowship at The Freedom Forum Media Studies Center he created the first electronic prototype for a flat-panel newspaper. His pioneering work on the electronic flat-panel newspaper has been reported in a variety of media, ranging from the *New York Times* to *Forbes ASAP.* In 1993 he founded the Knight-Ridder Information Design Laboratory, where his research team worked on preparing a fully functioning flat-panel newspaper. His vision culminates in what he describes as a "mediamorphosis," the combining of the navigational system, reporting and depth of newspapers, with the audiovisual, full-motion video of television news, along with the advertising central to today's media system. Future efforts will be geared toward refining the system for electronic delivery, daily news production, and capitalizing on the rapidly developing technical capabilities of the flat-panel display integrated with the Internet and the World Wide Web.

Fidler believes there are at least three models underlying the future of the information superhighway. First is the television model. In the TV model, interactive, electronic information and entertainment products like interactive television are created for display on a souped-up television set. The problem with this model, he suggests, is that it's been tried before and failed in the early 1980s when newspapers experimented with videotext. One of the reasons this approach failed is because people just don't want to read or actively process information displayed on a TV set. Moreover, TV sets are not designed for information or text. The wide-screen aspect ratio, which will get even wider in HDTV, is designed for moving images.

Second is the computer model. The computer model is in vogue for a variety of online information services, particularly on the World Wide Web. This approach works for people who are very interested in using computers, but the personal computer has a lot of drawbacks as a communication medium, Fidler contends. Among those limitations are the lack of portability and the cost of the typical PC.

Third is the document model, which has existed since the invention of writing on clay tablets some 5,000 years ago. It may be the oldest, but it is probably the best for information, says Fidler. When transferred to electronic format in the flat-panel screen, Fidler suggests, the document model is highly effective as an information medium. That is why it has lasted so long. And rather than force electronic information products into the television or computer model, it makes more sense to integrate television and computer technology and content into the flat-panel. The flat-panel, like the document, has many strengths as an information medium, including its portability, its vertical aspect ratio for displaying and reading text, its low cost, its technological transparency for facilitating ease of use (i.e., it can be designed intuitively so the consumer doesn't need a manual to figure out how to use it), and, finally, its distinguishability (i.e., it allows each information product, such as an electronic newspaper, to create a distinct visual identity or brand identification, which will be essential for navigation through the rich information environment of the future).[27]

An alternative approach to the electronic newspaper is being developed at the MIT Media Lab, with support from some sixteen newspaper companies. The Media Lab approach to the electronic newspaper is one that emphasizes each reader's defining his or her interests and getting a highly tailored newspaper delivered electronically to a personal computer. This has been called "The Daily Me." The Media Lab's product could be displayed on a flat-panel, but could also be accessed via a regular PC.

News wire services such as Associated Press (now available in large part at The Wire, a Web site available through AP member Web sites such as the *Dallas Morning News*) or Reuters (a company that in 1996 disbanded its New Media Division and reinvented its entire company as a new media enterprise; see, www.reuters.com) could play a vital role in the future of electronic news distribution directly to the consumer, whether on a flat-panel, a PC, or some other device, even a next-generation Web-friendly TV set. In a future scenario, readers could subscribe directly to a news service in order to get the news on the most timely basis possible. However, with the explosion of information now all around us, electronic communications might make the need for a journalistic filter even greater than in the past, although intelligent agents might play an interesting spoiler role in the electronic news environment of the future. Imagine having to sort through the thousands, even millions of stories flooding into the AP, Reuters, or Dow Jones every day. Even a preprogrammed filter—or agent—might have trouble handling this amount of information. Thus, the need for human editors and the function of traditional journalists may be even greater as we enter the era of the information superhighway.

Two recent developments underscore the viability of the vision that Fidler has pursued for most of the past decade.[28] In late 1996, The Walt Disney Co.'s Imagineering unit in Glendale, California demonstrated a prototype of a flat-panel device capable of downloading and storing publications for reading without power or a telephone cord. Nevertheless, company executives estimate it could be 2001 before the cost of mass-producing the portable tablets drops to the point where they would find a niche in the consumer marketplace.

A similar project has been unveiled in Europe. Dubbed the NewsPAD, Acorn Risc Technologies has developed a portable digital tablet with many of the same capabilities as the Disney device. The NewsPAD consists of a "rugged plastic enclosure around a paper-sized, high-resolution color active-matrix LCD screen," reports the *New York Times.* The reader interacts with a digital publication by touching the NewsPAD's touch-sensitive screen. The NewsPAD also features multimedia capabilities, with a built-in speaker for audio, and has plug-ins for a microphone and video camera. The brains of the unit is called an integrated ARM microprocessor, the same chip that is in the Apple Newton portable digital appliance. The developers of the NewsPAD share Fidler's vision of news being delivered via high-bandwidth digital broadcasting, providing consumer access through low-cost, small-size home receivers or docking stations, with limited upstream communications capability.

NOTES

[1]Murdoch, Rupert, Keynote Address, Center for Communication Communicator of the Year Award Luncheon, April 11, 1994.

[2]Brown, Rich. "BellSouth makes another move into cable." *Broadcasting & Cable,* December 13, 1993.

[3]AT&T, "The National Information Infrastructure: A Key to America's Economic Growth and Global Competitiveness," a report from AT&T, August, 1993.

[4]Lohr, Steve, "Pearson Enters Multimedia Software Arena," *New York Times,* April 1, 1994.

[5]*New York Times,* 14 March 1994.

[6]Laurence Zuckerman, "Microsoft and Pointcast in Broadcast Alliance" The New York Times Cybertimes, December, 12, 1996.

[7]Lawrence M. Fisher "Five Regional Phone Companies Select Netscape," New York Times Online, December 10, 1996.

[8]Kragen, Pam, "Copley Press jumping on info superhighway," *Times Advocate,* Nov., 1994.

[9]*SNPA Bulletin* "Multimedia Announces Strategic Initiatives to Strengthen Competitive Position and Give Access to Superhighway," March 1, 1994.

[10]Thalhimer, op. cit., May 24, 1994.

[11]Ibid., May 3, 1994.

[12]*Marketing Pulse, The.* "Superhypeway Backlash," January 31, 1994, Volume XIV, Issue 5.

[13]Ibid.

[14]SNPA Bulletin, op. cit., 1994: 5.

[15]Murdoch, Rupert, Keynote Address, Center for Communication Communicator of the Year Award Luncheon, April 11, 1994.

[16]MacDonald, Richard, "Patterns of Media Entrepreneurship," Fellows Presentation, The Freedom Forum Media Studies Center, December 15, 1993.

[17]Harris, Kathryn, "The Stupendous Seven—The New Masters of the Universe," *Media Studies Journal,* Winter 1994: 81–93.

[18]Harris, 1994: 89.

[19]J. Deutschman, feature story on Larry Ellison, *Broadcasting & Cable,* 17 January 1994: 3.

[20]Ibid.

[21]Ibid.

[22]Amstrong, David, "Ziff Happens," *Wired*, June 1994.

[23]Ibid.: 87.

[24]Ibid.

[25]Ibid.

[26]Peers, Martin, *New York Post,* November 5, 1993: 23.

[27]Fidler, Roger, Technology Studies Seminar, The Freedom Forum Media Studies Center, April 6, 1994.

[28]Grant Buckler, "New Prototype Device Meant to Replace Newspapers," *Newsbytes News Network,* Cambridge, England, 6 November 1996.

7

Rewriting the Editorial and Creative Process

"I've worked for all the mediums of communication."
—MAYOR RICHARD M. DALEY[1]

ONCE UPON A TIME

When the Brothers Grimm wrote their fairy tales in the middle ages, the quill pen was the writing tool of choice, and the words were intended to be read in a linear fashion, from start to finish. Every story had a single plot, a beginning, middle, and end, and every reader, even twentieth-century ones, read the same story.

Although the technology of writing changed significantly from the days of the Brothers Grimm to the middle of the twentieth century, the notion of storytelling evolved very little until relatively recently. By and large, stories still had a beginning, middle, and end, and readers still digested a single plot or set of facts. Even the "new" electronic media of radio and television did little to change the editorial process, although the written word became the spoken word and images only imagined, drawn, or in still form became animated and lifelike. Nevertheless, facts or narration still unfolded in linear fashion, from start to finish.

The advent of the computer, the convergence of all media, and Ted Nelson's creation in 1961 of hypertext, or nonlinear text, forever changed all that. Nonlinear text, the basis for interactive, multimedia communications, represents an entirely new approach to the editorial process. Its implications are profound but are only now beginning to be recognized and studied, much less understood. Rather than telling a single story with a beginning and end, narrations in hypertext let the reader or consumer develop her or his own story, sometimes doing so by participating in a multi-user networked environment distributed around the world. In this world, individuals, whether reader or storyteller, are linked in a communication environment somewhat analogous to a three-dimensional spider web, thus giving rise to what we now know as the World Wide Web. Communication flows in an n-directional space. Digital information takes on a highly fluid form, and communication undergoes an almost continual evolution. Some even contend that in this digital publishing environment, there is no longer a defined moment when a communication product exists in its final form. In this sense, digital communication comes alive in a continual dialogue.

Some have now dubbed the latest generation of hypertext as hyperfiction. "Hyperfiction is a new narrative art form, readable only on the computer, and made possible by the developing technology of hypertext and hypermedia," writes Robert Coover.[2] Hyperfiction has evolved from these notions to open new worlds of interactivity and create a new fiction art form. *The New York Times Book Review* has included reviews of at least a dozen hyperfiction books, including Stuart Moulthrop's *Victory Garden* and Judy Mallow's *Its Name Was Penelope,* suggesting we have seen "only the beginning: Watch out!"[3] An even more unusual offering in the realm of hyperfiction art is "Myst," a surrealistic videogame published on CD-ROM. Players of "Myst" enter a dreamlike landscape where sights, sounds, and narrative guide them through a compelling adventure without any clear rules, goals, or outcome other than exploration and experience.

How will hypertext and other forms of new media affect writing itself? Anne Hart, in her book *Cyberscribes.1: The New Journalists,* observes that writing will become more about making connections, not just in hypertext fashion but about linking ideas and facts.[4] This will require not just a new way of writing, but a "new way of thinking," she observes.

DESIGNING QUALITY MULTIMEDIA CONTENT: INTERACTIVITY, IMMERSIVENESS, AND INDIVIDUALIZATION

New media executives are daily confronted by the dilemma of designing a new media product that will both take advantages of the capabilities of new technology, yet be familiar enough to allow audience members easy access. This is not a simple task, as the increasingly long list of new media failures attests. Nevertheless, there are important principles and lessons to be learned from experience and research. Roger Fidler, new media pioneer since the days of Viewtron, the ill-fated Knight-Ridder videotext trial of the early 1980s, offers this advice to newspaper barons of the digital age: "Only those newspapers that can blend credible, high-quality information with compelling, interactive presentations will have an opportunity to live long and prosper," says Fidler.[5] Although Fidler's words are targeted at newspaper publishers, the principles are really much broader, and apply equally well to any new media entrepreneur. See also Clement Mok's, *Designing Business: Multiple Media, Multiple Disciplines* for a lucid discussion of digital design considerations.[6]

With the dynamic growth of the Internet, the World Wide Web, and computer-based digital communication technologies in the 1990s, it is clear that developing compelling content for new media depends largely on a complex set of interrelated issues and elements. Some of these elements are unpredictable, and perhaps unknowable, given the nature of the human experience. However, certain fundamental principles of sound new media content design are beginning to emerge. They include these four characteristics:

- Rich multimedia presentation of information, but done in a manner appropriate to the content at hand and flexible in its distribution or accessibility to adjust to variations in network or distribution medium bandwidth
- Individualization of content, in particular creating a new media product that enables the receiver to personalize that content, either in form or substance
- Fully interactive content and user interface design that engages the user
- Immersive forms of content that permit the user to enter into and participate in increasingly rich, three-dimensional virtual worlds, where all three of the above-mentioned characteristics come together

Defining the Rules

One of the greatest debates in the field of electronic publishing revolves around the issue of editorial quality. "So much of what's being produced today is what we call 'shovel-ware,'" says Bruce Page, president of Magnetic Press, a small firm in Soho, New York.[7] "Shovel-ware" refers to electronic products that are nothing more than their paper products converted to electronic form, especially text-only products, notes Mark Thalhimer, director of the News of the Future project for the Radio and Television News Directors Association.[8] For example, when *Time* magazine produced its "Desert Storm" CD-ROM only months after the end of the war in the Persian Gulf, they simply poured in everything they had, including not just stories from the magazine, but correspondents' files, some audio clips and some still images, into CD-ROM format. Beyond its novelty and potential as a research tool, this example of shovel-ware produced little consumer interest.

The problem has become more acute in the online world where a variety of nonjournalistic organizations (e.g., Microsoft, C/net) have launched journalistic enterprises. Featuring high-profile Web sites and other online news and information outlets, it is unclear whether these organizations, without the journalistic traditions of newspapers, for example, will adhere to the ideals of a free and independent press.

Linear and Nonlinear Editing and Scripting Models

As media companies and other creative entrepreneurs have attempted to design new media products, one important unsettled issue they have confronted is how to conceptualize the process of creating content for a new medium. Much as Hollywood entrepreneurs of the early part of the twentieth century developed new models for producing motion pictures, new media visionaries must invent their own creative systems for designing multimedia and online products.

As expected, some of the earliest creative approaches borrow heavily from existing media. In the multimedia realm, much has been borrowed from the world of television and film production. At Warner New Media a hybrid approach has been developed, incorporating elements from motion picture and documentary production, musical recording, and weekly magazine journalism. In this approach, multimedia production teams operate under the leadership of a director, with responsibility for the overall vision and execution of the project, and producers responsible for product quality and cost-control.

Seven Days in August

Illustrative is one of Warner New Media's most interesting early efforts to create an interactive documentary titled, *Seven Days in August,* examining the week in 1961 when the Berlin Wall was constructed. The multimedia product combines news footage from 1961, additional historical data and information, eyewitness accounts, original video, including interviews with survivors from the week of crisis, a game set in the Cold War climate of August 1961, a look at life in the Wisconsin town of Berlin, the residents of which actually changed the pronunciation of the town's name to put the accent on the first syllable so it would not sound as much like Berlin, Germany, and images and sounds from popular culture of 1961, such as hit songs like "The Lion Sleeps Tonight." Created on a platform combining both CD-ROM and laserdisc, *Seven Days in August* was produced by a team consisting of magazine journalists and producers in Time Warner headquarters at Rockefeller Center in New York and a Hollywood creative team at Warner New Media offices in Burbank, California. Originally titled *The Berlin Wall,* the title was changed to *Seven Days in August* to both avoid potential confusion with the falling of the Berlin Wall and to better reflect the week concept underlying *Time* magazine.

Early efforts to create multimedia, or hypermedia, products were often based on the encyclopedia model as well. Products like Grolier's CD-ROM Encyclopedia, Microsoft's Encarta, or IBM's Columbus Encounter are good examples of this process and the nature of works derived from a combination of the encyclopedia and film models. The encyclopedia model emphasizes a structured approach to information, providing easy user access to concepts and ideas, supported by detailed information and data provided by subject experts, and supplemented by images. Multimedia products derived from this model add motion video and sound, and may add interactivity, by providing greater search engines such as Boolean search procedures, as well as feedback from an expert system, a note-taking feature, and even a system to allow the user to create her or his own multimedia products based on the original software. An excellent example of this type of product is the series of multimedia offerings from ABC Interactive, launched with "The '88 Vote," and including educational products ranging from "The Holyland" to "Martin Luther King, Jr." These videodisc offerings combine historical data with news footage from the ABC News archives, allowing the user, typically a high school student, to search information as they would an encyclopedia, according to topics, key people and events, or chronologically. Users can call up video or audio, and get feedback and analysis from the laserdisc. Ultimately, the student user can create his or her own documentary by editing video and audio to tell their own story based on the video contained on the laserdisc.

From Silver Screen to Silver Disc

Like the videocassette a decade earlier, CD-ROM technologies are beginning to transform Hollywood.[9] Filmmakers are looking to the optical medium as a new vehicle for reaching the increasingly fragmented viewing audience. Hollywood's high-tech guru, George Lucas, has pioneered CD-ROM applications in moving image software. LucasArts's "Rebel Assault" has been one of the most popular CD-ROM titles on the market since its introduction in 1993, selling more than 400,000 copies in its first year. Movie director Dwight Little has created a CD adventure game for Sega called "Ground Zero Texas." "Hollywood and Silicon Valley are about to get into bed together because of this technology," quips Mark Waldrep of Pacific Coast Sound Works in West Hollywood, and a specialist in audio tracks for multimedia products.[10]

When he helped create the *Star Wars* trilogy, George Lucas, Jr. transformed the Hollywood movie-making process, bringing about a special effects renaissance. The Lucas companies, including Industrial Light and Magic (ILM), LucasArts Entertainment Co., and LucasFilm Ltd., have ushered in the digital age of special effects, and in the process have won numerous Academy Awards for their technical brilliance.[11] Beyond introducing high-tech special effects in film, Lucas has changed the nature of the relationship between film and other media. His companies produced the first link between a home videogame and a film *(Indiana Jones and the Temple of Doom)* and the first game with fully interactive music *(LOOM)*. In many ways, Lucas has become the Walt Disney of the digital age. If his high-tech movie wizardry does not convince you of Lucas's ability to create compelling fantasy, a visit to his production facilities near San Francisco certainly will. On arrival at the Industrial Light and Magic (ILM) facilities, all one sees is a quaint Victorian home and a plush green yard. Closer inspection, however, reveals that the house is merely a front-end for the super high-tech facilities housed in the immense state-of-the-art underground complex where Lucas and his technical staff work their movie magic.[12] The digital creative process is so meticulous at Lucas Arts that one studio technician admits that a single second of audio from a movie sound track might require an entire day of digital processing, selecting each microscopic snippet of sound one at a time from a digital pallet. Digitally processing images takes even greater care. ILM is not alone in this arduous process of digital editing. As part of a test, a Sony HDTV production facility at the Kaufman-Astoria Studio in Queens, New York, spent three years creating about three minutes of computer-generated animation of dinosaurs walking through a primeval forest.

Clearly, the process of linking film and interactive, multimedia is a slow and painful process, fraught with many technical and cultural difficulties. "Ultimately, the problem with video is that it's simply not very interactive," says Randy Komisar, president and chief executive officer of LucasArts.[13] "We watch movies and we play games. And therein lies the obvious crux of the difference between film and interactive entertainment today." Lucas agrees, but does see market promise in the development of networked, interactive entertainment. "I think ultimately the home-delivered, so-called information superhighway and black box will be the big player, but I think that's quite a few years down the road," Lucas says. "I think once the technology is in place, it's really going to open up into a very big picture."

Although most are moving cautiously, an increasing number of major Hollywood studios are becoming involved in multimedia production and CD-ROM products in particular. Taking a leading position in the race for multimedia content is Paramount Home Video, which has agreed to distribute a CD-ROM product from an independent Los Angeles computer software publisher. Xiphias has released on CD-ROM the "Mighty Morphin Power Rangers," a popular interactive multimedia adventure based on the popular Fox television show, which sold more than 113,000 copies in 1994. Unlike many videogame products that tend to appeal primarily to teenage boys, the "Mighty Morphin Power Rangers" appeals to a broad cross-section of children. Paramount is bullish on CD-ROMs because, "We think that over time the VCR cassette will give way to the five-inch disk," says Eric Doctorow, president of Paramount Home Video.[14]

The New Creative Process

Many in Hollywood are enthralled by the opportunities presented by new media applications. But at the same time, most are frightened by the undefined nature of the creative process in creating interactive, multimedia products. Some are already proclaiming interactive development "the new hell."[15] In the past, Hollywood's development system for movie-making featured a predictable scenario, with pitch meetings, story conferences, talent deals, and uniform 120-page scripts. Any departure from this model was a major test of the system's flexibility. Today, the development of interactive, multimedia products and games has produced no generally agreed upon production process. Consider the following recent examples from high-tech games under development.

- "Road Scholar," an interactive, multimedia game produced by Media Vision, features a 1,000-page script, "keeping blurry-eyed executives at that company up many a night"[16]
- "Shock Wave," a science fiction title about an alien invasion, under development by Electronic Arts with a script in excess of 500 pages
- "Loadstar," a sci-fi title about space truckers, now in production at Rocket Science Game, featuring a "design document" of more than 500 pages

These "scripts" or more appropriately "design documents" follow no standard form or length, have no single ending and cannot be completed until all technical details and problems are worked out. In catch-22 fashion, technical directors cannot design scenes that haven't been written, either. Not surprisingly, all this confusion has left Hollywood moguls feeling more than a little anxiety and creative types uncertain about how to break into the business.

"Because it's fairly new, nobody knows exactly how to do this," says Steven Blank, president and CEO for Rocket Science Games.[17] Still, the principle of team design has emerged as perhaps even more important in the creation of interactive, multimedia products than in traditional film production. While in film projects, a single screenwriter will typically be hired and work alone for several months to turn out the screenplay, the interactive media project is itself more likely to be interactive. "There's no job that can avoid the technical side of developing a game," notes Doug Barnett, the designer of hit game, "Return to Zork."

With most interactive games being written for the CD-ROM platform, which can store ever greater amounts of data, text, and video, creators are writing increasing amounts of information for each game. A typical CD-ROM game might include twenty-five minutes of full-motion video integrated into the rest of the computer-generated graphics, extensive dialogue, and hundreds of pages of computer programming. Each part might require different writers and designers, with the complete package combined into a single, massive design document or script. A typical design document might have "elements of a script, elements of a novel, computer elements, mathematical elements and even financial elements," notes Strauss Zelnick, president and CEO of Crystal Dynamics and former president and chief operating officer at 20th Century Fox.[18] "All of these areas are just as important. We don't just operate from scripts. The execution is terribly important."

Another important difference between creating an interactive game and writing a traditional film script is the importance of narrative structure. In films, the narrative structure is fundamentally important, while in multimedia, place and character are at least as important. "Up to now, the environment has been more important than the narrative," observes Michael Backes, coscreenwriter of Fox's *Rising Sun* and cofounder of Rocket Science Games. "There's no equivalent to that in the movie world. The development process is much more intense in the game world at the beginning."[19] In addition, players' actions also drive story development in interactive games. Choices by the user can lead a story in a variety of directions. "An author's opinion about the choices made in the game is less important," says

Backes.[20] "What is more important is making sure that the environment is rich enough." Also unlike most Hollywood movies, interactive multimedia games and adventures lack a predetermined beginning, middle, and end. Rather, they follow a tree-and-branch structure that allows the users, primarily children and young adults, to follow different paths each time they play. "In Silicon Valley they give a story 183 endings," says Peter Black, president of Xiphias, a Los Angeles multimedia software production company.[21]

The Studio System

Still, some Hollywood leaders see parallels between the studio system and the multimedia production process. "We're seeing a funnel develop, like the studios," says Zelnick, "where there are a lot of ideas at the top given some creative development, but not that many actually getting greenlit."[22]

In agreement is Robert Kotick, chair and CEO of Activision. "It's just like a movie studio," Kotick says.[23] "We get two or three submissions a day. We have thirty or forty projects in development that would result in about twelve or fifteen projects being made."

Graphics and Design

"Any sufficiently advanced technology is indistinguishable from magic."
—ARTHUR C. CLARKE[24]

Improving graphics and design has been one of the continuing challenges and struggles in products created for the computer and online world. In the early days of online communications, there was little concern about design, as most applications were text-only, and few of the developers were concerned about type face, much less graphical design. This was partly a result of the dominance of the IBM platform, which emphasized function over form, and the primary function had been the processing of numbers. With the development of the Macintosh computer and with it a new emphasis on design, all this began to change.[25]

Today, state-of-the-art online design sports a new look and enhanced status. Increasingly, online products are being created by people whose background is in design or at least features expertise in design. Unfortunately, most online products are still constrained by relatively low bandwidth on most telecommunications networks serving the general public, requiring most services to rely on transmission rates of 28.8 kilobits per second or slower. As a result, complex graphics and high-resolution images and photographs are very slow to draw on most services. Nevertheless, many online commercial services and Web products place great emphasis on images and graphics, and access is often plagued by slow, even lethargic, page creation. This is often a source of frustration for users, who now generally expect the rapid graphics possible when running directly off the hard drive of a Pentium PC or a Macintosh PowerPC. Slow transmission rate doesn't explain some other aspects of screen design in many online products. Some Web sites use a sans serif typeface (e.g., the Geneva font is a sans serif typeface) or mix multiple fonts within a single page. Sans serif fonts such as Geneva may look modern, but they are harder to read than serif typefaces, especially on a computer screen. Multiple fonts present a confusing array to the reader and bring to mind a ransom note.

Moreover, many online products are relatively indistinguishable in terms of overall design. Some are reminiscent of a multiple choice test, says leading newspaper designer Roger Fidler, "and I don't want to take a multiple choice test when I come home at the end of the day."[26] Most services are menu-driven, require the reader or user to select from a set of choices laid out on the screen, and follow a tree-and-branch structure. Fidler, who has designed and redesigned dozens of newspapers around the world, has created an online news product that takes a different approach to design. Rather than requiring the user to take a test, it presents information in a familiar, intuitive format that takes him or her easily through the electronic product. The design is based on principles some three hundred years in the making: principles of newspaper design. Using headlines, layout, and other graphical design features to direct attention, Fidler's "New York Current" prototype is as enjoyable to read as a well-designed newspaper.

Digital Design

Since Johannes Gutenberg's invention of the printing press some five hundred years ago, typography and technology often have been interwoven. Counter to this trend until recently was the work of avant-garde typography artist Neville Brody, a thirty-eight-year-old graphics guru whose home base is London. Known for his design of magazines like *The Face, Arena,* and *City Limits,* until 1988 Brody designed every typeface by hand. Then, overcoming his confessed "technophobia," he bought his first Apple Macintosh and became obsessed with its potential.[27] Describing his experience with the Macintosh, Brody says, "People think of computers as if they were replicate brains. But the Mac is more like a saxophone. You don't learn to use it, you begin to play it. You learn a whole technology so that you can improvise."[28] Not only is Brody convinced the Macintosh is an enabling technology, but he believes the digitization of information has fundamentally transformed the graphics arts. To him, digital design has become very fluid. "It's like I'm doing a painting where the paint refuses to dry. I hand it on to someone else, who pushes that paint around. And the process is continuous."

Digital Production: Not a Matter of Choice

1994 saw the first HDTV production of a made-for-TV mini-series in the United States. *World War II: When Lions Roared* was shot using digital HDTV cameras, which not only improved the quality of the visual image, but was necessary to create the complex production. "In this case, shooting high definition was not a matter of choice, but of necessity," says Joseph Sargent, director of the mini-series.[29] The series is about the collaboration of the three Allied leaders, Franklin D. Roosevelt (played by John Lithgow), Winston Churchill (Bob Hoskins), and Joseph Stalin (Michael Caine). Since the leaders spent most of their time in three different parts of the world, the director wanted to show his three actors interacting from those same three locations: Washington, London, and Moscow. Using digital HDTV, the actors were brought together seamlessly, showing Roosevelt moving about the Oval Office in a wheelchair, Churchill issuing orders from his command bunker, and Stalin brooding in the hall of the people. HDTV allows the cinematographer to blend images together softly, curving edges and smoothing and matching colors in an elegant fashion. "Instead of 12 crayons, you have 48," says John Alonzo, the cinematographer for *World War II,* whose screen credits include *Chinatown.*

Reanimator, **Digital Style.**   Digital technology also has the potential to bring the dead to life, or to at least to reanimate deceased Hollywood stars. The first computer-synthesized performances were offered in 1987 when two Swiss scientists created the short film, "Rendezvous a Montréal," featuring Humphrey Bogart and Marilyn Monroe in a role neither actor could have imagined during life.[30] Not to be confused with H. P. Lovecraft's horror classic, *Reanimator, Rendezvous's* reanimation of Bogie and Marilyn was not very convincing, as the characters blended together in a not-too-seamless style. But in the years since the film's release, the technology of computer animation has advanced significantly. 1993's *Jurassic Park* is just one example of how far the technology has come. It is now possible to use computer animation to transform raw data into images that look, sound, and act on screen like real, recognizable people—or creatures. In the past, it had been possible to bring dead actors together with their living counterparts by splicing together film footage of each performer, or by blending actual footage of each performer using digital image processors. In either case, no actor could be shown doing something he or she had never done on film. Now, however, computer reanimation technology can take original footage, digitize it, and then create completely seamless full-motion video sequences of an actor doing something he or she never actually did. Still, the process of creating synthetic images is very expensive, especially when it involves the subtlety of human behavior. "The software exists, but it takes a lot of hand work," says Jim Morris, vice president and general manager of Industrial Light and Magic, the firm that animated the dinosaurs for *Jurassic Park.* Because of the complexity and subtlety of human movement and speech, Morris estimates it would take ten to fifteen times the work to animate a scene with a human character as with a Tyrannosaurus Rex. Still, the cost of reanimating human actors will decline, and technical ease and speed will increase, and it is just a matter of time till Hollywood may not need live actors at all!

A New Hair Club for Men?   Daniel Thalmann, one of the Swiss scientists who created the original reanimation film, sees the technology advancing rapidly. "We improve every day," he notes. "We've had problems with different things, like hair. But now we've improved the hair. We can't do all the complex motions. It will be difficult to do a film with a lot of action. But for a film within a limited environment, perhaps we will be ready in two or three years."[31] Will the audience be ready?

Animated motion picture cartoon technology has also taken great strides since its invention in 1906 by James Stuart Blackton. Blackton's first production, "The Humorous Phases of Funny Faces," released by Vitagraph, was made up of about 8,000 drawings, each of which showed a face whose features changed to reveal different expressions and emotions.

Reanimating Intellectual Property. Intellectual property right and copyright law is also facing challenges as a result of reanimation technology. No longer does the traditional definition of copyright in terms of a particular expression seem to provide adequate protection, when the reanimated sequence may be essentially a completely new expression.

Pacific Data International (PDI). Creating movie magic via digital technology has become the hallmark of one pioneering company called Pacific Data International (PDI). PDI has used state-of-the-art imaging technology to create the special effects for some of the most commercially successful movies ever produced, such as Arnold Schwartzenegger's *Terminator II* and *Heart and Souls*. The process involves digitally scanning the images originally captured on film, processing them digitally by computer, and then transferring them back to film. The digital format means each film image has been reduced to a mathematical series of 1s and 0s. The changes are made at the "atomic" level, called the *pixel* in digital vernacular. A pixel refers to a picture element, and is the smallest point of light represented on a computer screen. When viewed together, thousands of pixels make up a single image, much as French surrealist Georges Serat created impressionistic paintings dot by dot.

Altering the Digital Design

Alterations to digital images generally take one of three forms: addition, subtraction, and manipulation (e.g., enhancement, merger). Digital addition means adding something to a picture that wasn't originally there, such as a crowd at a baseball stadium. Digital subtraction refers to deleting something from a picture, such as removing someone or something like a cable supporting a character magically "flying." Digital manipulation refers to transforming an image, such as making it lighter or darker, blending two things into one, or distorting one face into another (called a *morph* in the industry vernacular). In *Terminator II*, one memorable scene involved Arnold Schwarzenegger in cyborg form driving a motorcycle atop a wall. When the wall ends abruptly, he lands safely and continues riding along unaffected in the bottom of a drainage ditch. The stunt would have been extremely dangerous without certain safety precautions, so a special pulley and cable system was rigged up to carry Mr. Schwarzenegger and his motorcycle safely from atop the wall to the bottom of the ditch. The pulley and cable, however, were clearly visible on the original film. Then, in came digital image processing to the rescue. After transferring the film to digital format, the cable and pulley were deleted, pixel by pixel, frame by frame. Then, through digital addition, the missing slices of background were filled in where the cable and pulley had been, and a complete scene was created. Finally, when the special effects were complete, the digital images were transferred back to film, and the movie was released for theatrical distribution.

Digital Darkroom

The rise of the digital image has important implications for the practice of photojournalism, where the credibility of the news has eroded considerably since the journalistic heyday of the Watergate era. Since images captured by a digital camera can be easily manipulated and consequently provide no negative to verify the original image, seeing is no longer believing, at least as far of digital cameras are concerned. Moreover, the use of a digital darkroom can erode the credibility of images captured originally on film. Witness the case of a 1994 *Newsweek* cover featuring a sinister-looking O. J. Simpson, shortly after his arrest in the slaying of his ex-wife. *Time* ran the same image on its cover, but O. J.'s face was much lighter looking. In the resulting controversy surrounding the contrasting portrayals, *Newsweek* admitted that it had used a digital darkroom to darken O. J.'s face. The public is left wondering whom to trust in the media.

Because digital darkrooms are now available for processing full-motion video, the issues raised above are as relevant to television, multimedia, or any moving-image media as they are for print media such as newspapers and magazines.

New Creative Avenues.   Conversely, the digital darkroom has been a boon to the creative side of media support institutions such as advertising and public relations, and other commercial and aesthetic areas of communication, such as entertainment television and film. The digital darkroom has enabled advertising creative directors to produce magazine ads that look completely real, but are totally synthetic, or have only a slight connection to any real photographic image. For instance, one advertiser has created a magazine ad campaign for the makers of a gourmet coffee in which full-color images of each coffee flavor are shown together on a single page. The six coffee flavors appear to be resting on an elegant satin cloth. To the viewer, it appears that the six coffees were placed on the cloth and photographed, with text superimposed later to further describe the nature of the product. The reality, however, is somewhat different. Although there are in fact six different coffee flavors, they were never placed together on the satin cloth. In fact, there is no satin cloth. The satin cloth was created synthetically in the digital paintbox, and images of each coffee flavor—photographed separately—are then electronically cut and pasted against the digital satiny-looking cloth background. Similar techniques are used to create alluring images of a variety of products and services, and are not limited to inanimate objects. Human models are often photographed in a studio and then placed digitally into an exotic location, such as the Caribbean or the Mediterranean, or a model's face or body might be digitally altered to make it appear even more perfect, removing a wrinkle here, a blemish there. All of this is completely invisible and undetectable to the viewer.

These techniques were used in the well-known "Hey, you never know" advertising campaign for the New York State Lotto in 1994.[32] The DDB Needham Worldwide advertising agency used a computer to combine three images: a photograph of a classic chateau at Sceaux, France, featuring an elegant garden and reflecting pool; Frederick W. Vanderbilt's palatial estate on the Hudson River, near Hyde Park, New York; and a picture of a swimmer, which was actually shot indoors in Manhattan. The swimmer, a heavy-set middle-aged man floating in a rubber inner tube, was inserted electronically into the reflecting pool. Finally, the Vanderbilt estate was inserted into the composite image, and the New York fantasy scene was complete. Desktop video has made this production technique the growing standard in television commercials, as well. Pepsi used such technology to produce its commercial featuring Paula Abdul dancing, singing, and interacting with legendary actor Cary Grant and comedian Groucho Marx.

Multimedia Clip Art.   Virtual Portfolio (VP) offers via CD-ROM the work of some eighty animators, videographers and musicians. American Showcase, an art sourcebook publisher, has distributed 3,000 copies of the CD to advertising agencies and corporate art departments equipped with CD-ROM drives. VP evolved from the efforts of Charlie Magee, a Eugene, Oregon-based artist who first put his material on disk but needed the publishing wherewithal of New York-based American Showcase to reach a significant client base. Some ad agencies are still reluctant to use art in CD-ROM because of the limited portability of the medium and its newness.

Digital Effects in the Workplace

Desktop video has rapidly transformed the media work environment, with television stations widely adopting and warmly embracing the technology. Some two-thirds of broadcast facilities now have at least one digital editing machine, including either desktop video and multimedia PCs as well as high-end graphics and video effects workstations. Desktop computers include Apple Macintosh, IBM PC-compatibles and Amiga, notes Douglas Shear, president of S C Research International, a firm that conducts annual surveys of industry technology trends. Graphics and effects workstations include Silicon Graphics, Dynatech, or Quantel; Avid manufactures the leading nonlinear digital video editing workstation for television production.[33] No longer do video editors rely on the linear editing principles required by analog tape machines that have prevailed throughout the history of taped broadcasting. Nonlinear editing and thinking are presenting an entirely new approach to video production, much as the word processor redefined how words are edited.

Making Beautiful Digital Music Together

In olden days musical recordings typically required bringing together artists and technicians at a single location. Advances in digital and networking technology have changed the rules. Now, artists can be anywhere in the United States and even at international locations and still contribute to a centrally mastered musical record-ing. One noteworthy example is Frank Sinatra's CD, *Duets,* many of whose thirteen artists, such as Bono, Barbra Streisand, and Carly Simon, telephoned in their vocals from remote locations to a Los Angeles recording studio as Mr. Sinatra sang along.[34] Aretha Franklin dialed in from Detroit and Tony Bennett called from New York City using Ednet, the Entertainment Digital Network created in 1993 by filmmaker and technology expert George Lucas. Ednet combines advanced digital technology and fiber optics to streamline the production process and provide a link between fifty distributed recording studios. Originally designed to record soundtracks for movies such as *Terminator II* and *Backdraft*, the system now gets heavy usage for commercials, voice-overs, and albums. The system has greatly reduced the cost of production, as well, helping bring down digital set-up costs from $100,000 in 1988 to just $11,000 in 1994. Other artists who have used Ednet include stars such as Gloria Estefan, who used the system to record parts of her Christmas album.

BREAKING THE RULES: EROTICA AND PORNOGRAPHY IN CYBERSPACE

> *"Sex is a virus that infects new technology first."*
> —GERARD VAN DER LEUN[35]

Driving much of the early development of new media products has been demand for erotic content and software. The earliest adopters of the VCR were heavy purchasers and renters of adult movies. It was in large part the insatiable demand of this early user group that helped bring down the cost of the VCR, and made the VCR afford-able to a wider general audience. It also helped open the market to a much wider variety of video products, ranging from feature-length Hollywood films to how-to videos such as *Hometime* house repair.

Similarly, much of the usage of France's successful videotex service, Minitel, has been the so-called blue forums, or adult-oriented discussion groups. "Some-times the erotic has been a force driving technological innovation; virtually always, from Stone Age sculpture to computer bulletin boards, it has been one of the first uses for a new medium," writes *New York Times*'s technology reporter John Tierney.[36]

Since the first days of erotic e-mail more than a decade ago, usage of consumer-oriented online communications in the United States has reflected an insatiable in-terest in adult-oriented content. Scores of online forums have adult themes. On the Internet, for example, the "alt.sex.news" groups are "definitely among the higher traffic areas," says Jack Rickard, editor and publisher of *Boardwatch* magazine.[37] Moreover, "the number of electronic pen pals exchanging bawdy bytes is impossible to track," writes technology reporter Suzanne Stefanac.[38] Countless adult-oriented private bulletin boards have also emerged, specializing in erotic chat and graphic exchanges. Event Horizons, the largest of these, brought in $3 million in 1992, with 64 chat lines and 35,000 customers internationally. Although the board has family-oriented chat lines, 85 percent of the traffic is in the "restricted-access adult areas."[39] Playboy Enterprises, which recently won a $500,000 copyright infringement lawsuit against Event Horizons for distributing digitized photos that originally appeared in *Playboy* magazine, also is planning to introduce an adult electronic bulletin board. Adult sites were among the most popular Web sites during the early growth period of the Web in 1995 and 1996. Playboy and Penthouse were among the top ten most heavily visited sites, frequently logging a million or more "hits" a day. Many individuals have created their own adult-oriented Web sites, sometimes posting digital images of themselves. Others have served as "content aggregators," tirelessly cataloging and establishing links to hundreds of other adult sites, with www.persiankitty.com one of the most popular . Moreover, many of these sites, because of their interest in providing multimedia content, have tested, introduced, and developed innovative uses of the most current Web-based applications for everything from Java applets to streaming video. They have also helped test the commercial waters of the Internet, with hundreds of pay-per-view and subscription-based Web sites in operation.

Moreover, sex has helped transform the very nature of the online communications industry. Says one observer, "As a communications industry, sex has transmogrified itself from the province of a few large companies and individuals into a massive cottage industry."[40] Hundreds of adult bulletin boards now offer a plethora of erotic services, from chat lines to picture file exchanges, and many of them make a tidy profit for their providers. Even mainstream providers such as CompuServe are players. "CompuServe can fill your nights at $12.00 an hour with more fantasies behind the green screen than ever lurked behind the green door," says Van Der Leun.[41] As the Internet expands its capabilities to deliver video, the "amateur" erotic home videos have emerged as one of the hottest new categories in the online pornography world.

Many of the commercially successful CD-ROM products are erotic in nature, as well. One of the hottest products is Reactor's *Virtual Valerie*, an adult-oriented game on CD-ROM. "It's a moving target, but it looks like *Virtual Valerie* has captured about 25 percent of the erotic sector, selling about 25,000 a year for a total of 100,000 units," says Chris Andrews, president of Unidisc, publisher of *The CD-ROM Directory 1993*.[42]

Increased interactivity and improved graphics are at the core of these CD-ROMs. "The ability to choose your virtual partners, scenarios and pace, plus the fact that you can 'converse' with your cybermate, all lend a degree of personal involvement that no XXX movie or magazine can hope to match."[43] *Nightwatch*, Interotica's 1993 release, allows the user to play voyeur at a plush singles resort by way of a bank of security monitors. The company's *Dream Machine* provides even greater interactivity, with an on-screen female guide to help the player choose from among various fantasy portals.

Uncovering a Disney Classic

The award for most unconventional adult multimedia product may go to the creators of an innovative product that doesn't even feature real human actors. The *Who Framed Roger Rabbit* laserdisc, based on the hit movie of the same name released in 1990, features what appears to be a brief risqué video segment of a popular cartoon character. Unbeknownst to the Disney studio executives in charge of the product's release, artists or programmers apparently inserted adult-oriented footage of Jessica Rabbit, the voluptuous, animated star of the laserdisc, à la Sharon Stone in *Basic Instinct.* Jessica is riding in an animated cab through Toon Town with real-life Bob Hoskins driving. The taxi careens into a lightpost, and Hoskins and Jessica are thrown from the cab. Jessica, who is wearing her trademark dress slit to the hip, spins around and, on her first rotation, her white panties are briefly visible. But on her second spin, Jessica's panties disappear, and Jessica appears to be wearing nothing under her dress.

Legend has it that Disney animators have for years inserted bawdy frames into Disney classics such as *Snow White,* but they were always undetectable to the viewer because of the frame speed of film. But with the advent of the digital age, it is now a simple matter to advance the image one frame at a time and see exactly what is there on each razor-shape picture. One animator suggests, however, that Jessica may not really be bottomless. Mark Kausler, an animator for *Roger Rabbit,* says it is more likely that with the thousands of frames that need to be drawn and painted, it is possible that an animator simply forgot to paint her panties white in those infamous three frames.[44] Nevertheless, the genie is out of the bottle, and the rumor has been reported that Jessica can be seen sans panties. When *Roger* was first released, producer Frank Marshall admitted that a prank frame showed Betty Boop dropping her top, but the film's producers, Steven Spielberg's Amblin Entertainment and Disney, airbrushed her breasts for the video and laserdisc release. Michael Fleming, reporting in *Variety,* the entertainment industry's leading newspaper, writes that the *Roger Rabbit* product also may contain a telephone number for the fictional brothel, Madam Allyson Wonderland; the number is in fact the home number of Michael Eisner, Disney's chairman and CEO.[45] When the public learned of the unexpected product features, sales of the laserdisc became quite brisk at most retail outlets. At this writing, it is unclear whether Disney will eventually pull the disk from retail shelves, but if you happen across an uncensored version of the product, keep it. It will likely be worth a lot of money someday as a rare collector's item in the software hall of fame or shame. In any event, the story has given new meaning to Jessica's classic line, "I'm not bad, I'm just drawn that way."

Improved Graphics

The quality of the graphics have greatly improved since the early days of digital erotica. Enabled by inexpensive scanners and GIF (Graphics Interchange Format, a bit-mapped graphics file format used on many electronic bulletin boards, the Internet) transmission, users began up- and downloading low-resolution erotic images on major bulletin boards in the mid-1980s. The advent of QuickTime and other software such as JPEG (Joint Photographic Experts Group, a standard for compressed digital color images, which compresses an image to about 5 percent of the original but is subject to some loss of detail) and MPEG format graphics and video has brought the adult software industry to new highs (or lows) in technical quality. An ad for Space Coast Software's Bare Assets CD-ROM issues this siren call, "How about a QuickieTime?" *Penthouse Interactive* CD-ROM, released by ICFX, features state-of-the-art graphics and video. ICFX was founded by president David Biedny, a veteran of the Industrial Light and Magic school of special effects, and executive producer James Ehrlich, formerly with CBS records. The product places the user at a "Penthouse Pet" photo shoot, and lets the player choose the model and select her poses. During video segments, the player can snap still shots for storage or printing. "You are the photographer while three Penthouse Pets cavort and pose in 30 different situations. No question about it—it's astounding," says *Forbes F.Y.I.* Some are not sure this is a good thing. "What will they think of next?" questions Dan Rather, anchor, *CBS Evening News.*[46]

New Content Providers: The Audience

New media technology, especially the intersection of the online world and multimedia computing, are redefining the notion of sources of media content. In the traditional publishing environment, commercial publishers have tended to dominate the creation of media content, whether in the form of books, newspapers, magazines, radio, or television. In the digital environment, traditional content providers will continue to play a role, as will new forms of commercial content providers. But perhaps the greatest amount of content will be created by what is traditionally thought of as the media audience. In online communications, everyone is a content provider as well as an audience member.

JOURNALISTS: AN ENDANGERED SPECIES

Implications of new media technology also present a profound challenge to the future of journalism and communication professions as we know them. In addition to the ability of information consumers to use new information technologies to go directly to information sources, circumventing traditional journalistic sources, journalism itself is being rewritten by new computer software. As a natural outgrowth of advances in artificial intelligence, word processing, grammar, spelling, and style-checker software packages, software is now available to actually write news stories. In fact, a growing number of newspapers and other news organizations have purchased such software packages and are using them to write stories for publication. Some have even fired reporters who were made obsolete by the technology. In the areas of sports and financial reporting, many stories are written using basic formulae derived from specific statistical data, such as scores, stock changes, and other routine data.

Software packages are now available that will write stories automatically based on electronic data feeds transmitted directly by various news sources. There is no need for a human, journalistic filter at all. One such software package is called "SportsWriter," a program published by Zybrainics Software, Inc., and created by Roger Helms, a forty-four-year-old freelance writer from Rochester, Minnesota. The program grew out of Helms's initial efforts to improve the sports coverage of a weekly newspaper he was considering buying. Using an Apple Macintosh computer, he developed a HyperCard™ stack to train reporters in better newswriting style, but found the approach ineffective. "I decided the only thing my program was good at was making its own decisions," Helms says.[47] And it turned out to be a pretty decent writer, at least for routine sports stories, such as the results of high school basketball and football games. Critics say SportsWriter's biggest drawback is that the stories are dry and full of clichés, and lack the perspective only a human observer can provide.[48] The program bases its decisions and writing on input received from the coaches of the games, who are asked by the newspaper to fill out a form requesting various results, such as the score by period and to describe key plays. The coaches phone or fax in the data, and they are entered into the program, which then spits out a story. Consider this sample lead written by Sportswriter: "The Humphrey Bulldogs fell victim to a second-half rally and dropped a close decision to the Leigh Lady Panthers 27–24 in girls basketball at Clarkson in the first round of the Cornhusker Conference Tournament."[49] This lead ran in the *Humphrey Democrat* in Humphrey, Nebraska, one of some eighty small newspapers in the Midwest who have already bought Sportswriter. Dean Backes used to cover high school sports for the *Humphrey Democrat,* but two years ago was replaced by Sportswriter. The decision to replace a reporter with software was an easy one financially. Sportswriter costs $100, while "We were laying out $1500 a month for the sports reporter," says Donald Zavadil, editor and owner of the 1,800-circulation weekly. These economics apply to other areas of news coverage, as well. Computers at the Bloomberg L.P. financial news service write hourly stock market reports and foreign-market trends. Computers at Individual, Inc., Cambridge, Massachusetts, sort thousands of wire service, newspaper, and magazine articles and summarize them into customized newsletters faxed daily to 3,000 subscribers.[50] In the future, there may be no need for a news organization at all. By merging the notions of direct access media and news writing software, there is no need for a newspaper or other news product. It's perfectly feasible for a news source to provide data directly to the news consumer, who, using a news writing software package, will see a story written based on the latest sports scores or stock market fluctuations.

What are the implications of this technology for journalism? "It's scary," says Don Skwar, sports editor at the *Boston Globe.*[51] "In 40 or 50 years a computer might be sports editor." It may not take that long. Intelligent agents already have been developed that can act as an information gatekeeper or editor. Some are concerned that computer programmed writing takes out the creative element added by human writers. But others argue that by using software to write routine stories, human writers are free to spend more time writing creative feature and analytical pieces. On a more profound level, the implications of technological applications such as SportsWriter may reflect a fundamental shift in the function of journalism in society. Enshrined in the First Amendment, the press has served a vital role in democratic society as a fourth branch of government. Intelligent applications that automate the journalistic function and begin to link news sources more directly to news consumers may represent the declining role of journalism as filter, or gatekeeper, in interpreting information in society, and the rising role of commercial forces in the newsroom.

Sudden Impact: Online Communications and the Transformation of Journalism

One journalistic practice that has long been taken for granted is whether to let a source preview a story before publication. The answer has always been no, with few exceptions, perhaps on highly technical stories, such as science or health reporting, where a source might be asked to preview a quote for accuracy. Reporters and their news organizations have had many reasons for not allowing sources to preview stories, such as not wanting to alert a source to a negative story before it is published, avoiding leaking an exclusive to a competing news organization, and a general principle about standing by the quality of a reporter's work. One practical reason that has probably played a larger role than many in the newsroom would admit is that there hasn't generally been time to let a source preview a story. Reporters working under deadline pressure have enjoyed little opportunity to send a story to a source, let them review it, and then return the edited copy to the reporter. This might work for a monthly magazine, but not for an investigative reporter working on a five o'clock deadline for tomorrow's newspaper. But in today's world of online communications, much less the ubiquitous fax machine, time delays have little meaning. It takes but a few keystrokes to e-mail a draft of a story or a quotation to a source, and even receive his or her response electronically in a matter of minutes.

Media and technology reporters debated some of these issues at an April 5–6, 1994 Freedom Forum Media Studies Center Technology Studies seminar. The discussion lead to a lively forum on the popular electronic bulletin board service known as The Well. An edited version of the discussion is reprinted here, courtesy of Tom Valovic, a technology reporter who attended the Freedom Forum seminar and hosted the online discussion on The Well on April 18–19, 1994.

Excerpts from an Electronic Bulletin Board Discussion
Topic 761 [media]: Should Sources Be Allowed to Preview
Copy Via E-mail? Started by: Tom Valovic (tvacorn) on Mon, Apr 18, '94
202 responses so far

This picks up on a thread discussed in topic 737 . . .

At a recent seminar at Columbia on how the press has covered the "info superhighway", an interesting question surfaced: should reporters and journalists let a source for and/or subject of an article see (via e-mail of course) pre-publication drafts of the story in order to be allowed a chance to make "corrections". The process was ably described by Steven Levy, a panelist for a session addressing this and other matters. Another panelist, Denise Caruso (who is also an EFF board member), indicated that she agreed with the approach. Caruso justified it on the basis of the fact that technology reporters cannot possibly know all aspects of the technology well enough to, in essence, "go it alone", and that this collaborative process serves to give the reporter an important means of making sure the story--More--[Hit space to continue or q to stop.] is accurate. John Markoff of the New York Times disagreed and a lively discussion ensued. . . .

Any other opinions about this practice? Is it something that will ultimately change journalistic standards and practices? If so, positively or negatively? Has it done so already?
For the reporters in the house, have you done it? Do you do it routinely? Why or why not?

202 responses total.

Topic 761 [media]: Should Sources Be Allowed to Preview Copy Via E-mail?
#1 of 202 Mon Apr 18 '94 (10:05)   10 lines
PR hacks always do it. Don't want to offend the client.

Reporters should *never* do it. If they are unclear on the technology, they can ask the source questions to clear it up.

Giving the source the whole article just lets them buff it up. And they will. Every time.

Topic 761 [media]: Should Sources Be Allowed to Preview Copy Via E-mail?
#2 of 202 Mon Apr 18 '94 (10:09) 6 lines

I posted about this above. I used to disapprove entirely; now I don't. There are situations in which the reporter is essentially trying to get a complicated set of facts before his readers; there is no controversy, only explanation. (Reporting on the results of astronomical research could be an example). In that case, I see no problem at all.

As the excerpts from this two-day exchange reveal, the online world is as full of rich and varied points of view as any in the real world. Issues of journalistic practice and their technological influences may not be resolved in a single electronic forum. But, a glimpse inside the process does reveal the popularity of online chat sessions, with more than 200 responses to a single electronic query. Moreover, even if new technology has not transformed the practice of journalism, it has at least provided a new and effective forum for examining it. *Hotwired*, an electronic spinoff from the popular *Wired* magazine, has developed a new style of journalism based on the use of the interactive capabilities of online publishing.[52] Louis Rossetto, *Hotwired*'s editor in chief, designed the groundbreaking magazine as a blend of electronic publishing, the interactive capacity of the personal computer, and a style of participatory journalism his editors call "way new journalism." *Hotwired* is available free via the Web, but requires to users to sign up as members, and combines short articles on technology and society with a variety of interactive features, such as a textual report on a musical group linked with audio samples and video clips. Rossetto sees his nearest traditional competitors as broadcast and cable television, not conventional print publications.

DIGITAL CONTENT MANUFACTURING

As this chapter suggests, new media technologies have led to a virtual reinvention of the process of manufacturing media content. Nearly all content production is done in a digital environment where nonlinear text, images, and sound are manipulable on a digital palette. The relationship between events and objects observed in the so-called real world and their depiction or re-creation in the digital media is increasingly tenuous and abstract. No longer are content creators constrained by the limits of the so-called real world, if they ever were. In an increasingly interactive, online communication system, "audience members" are rapidly becoming cocreators of media content. Narrative structure is in flux, as hyperfiction and virtual reality become mainstream media products. Has the transformation of the creative process reached its ultimate state? Probably not. Rather, the evolution of new media products and how they are created has only just begun. It is likely that, in the next millennium, entirely new forms of media content will emerge and the process by which they are created will continue to evolve in an unexpected and startling fashion.

NOTES

[1]Daley, Richard M., speech, Chicago, IL, 15 October 1993.
[2]Coover, Robert. *New York Times Book Review,* August 29, 1993.
[3]Ibid.

[4]Anne Hart. *Cyberscribes.1: The New Journalists*. San Diego, CA: Ellipsys International Publications, 1997: 3.

[5]Fidler, op. cit., 1994.

[6]Clement Mok, *Designing Business: Multiple Media, Multiple Disciplines* (San Jose, CA: Adobe Press, 1996.

[7]Page, Bruce, meeting, Feb. 12, 1994.

[8]Thalhimer, Mark. "Online News Services," *The Race for Content, The Media Studies Journal*. Winter 1994.

[9]Lohr, Steve, "The Silver Disk May Soon Eclipse the Silver Screen," *New York Times*, March 1, 1994.

[10]Ibid.: D6.

[11]Arlen, Gary H., "LucasArts Charts Digital Path Between Film, Interactivity." *Information & Interactive Services Report*, March 11, 1994: 11.

[12]Powell, Adam Clayton III, meeting, May 6, 1994.

[13]Arlen, op. cit., March 11, 1994: 11.

[14]Nichols, op. cit., April 1, 1994: D17.

[15]Marx, Andy, "Interactive Development: The New Hell," *Variety*, March, 1994: 1.

[16]Ibid.: 78.

[17]Ibid.

[18]Ibid.

[19]Ibid.

[20]Ibid.

[21]Nichols, Peter M. "Home Video: What Exactly Is 'Multimedia'?" *New York Times*, April 1, 1994: D17.

[22]Marx, op. cit.: 78.

[23]Ibid.

[24]Clarke, Arthur C. (1993). *The Lost Worlds of 2001*. Boston: Gregg Press, 1979.

[25]Levy, op. cit., 1994.

[26]Fidler, op. cit., 1994.

[27]Rose, Cynthia, "Neville Brody: How to Be a Graphics Guru," *The International Herald Tribune*, July 8, 1994: 24.

[28]Ibid.

[29]Nichols, Peter M. "Mini-Series Blazes Trail in High-Definition TV," *New York Times*, April 19, 1994: D10.

[30]Weber, Bruce, "Why Marilyn and Bogie Still Need a Lawyer," *New York Times*, March 11, 1994.

[31]Ibid.: 28.

[32]Deitz, Paula, "All It Takes Is a Computer and Photos," *New York Times*, March 31, 1994.

[33]S C Research International, "Professional Video Marketplace," cited in *Video Technology News*, March 14, 1994.

[34]Tucker, Reginald E. "Cutting Edge: Phone-In Vocals," *Dollars and $ense, Baruch College Business Review*, May 1994, Volume 16: 90.

[35]Van Der Leun, Gerard, "This Is a Naked Lady," *Wired,* Premiere Issue 1993:74.

[36]Tierney, John, "Erotica and Technology," *New York Times*, January 16, 1994.

[37]Stefanac, Suzanne, "Sex & the New Media," *NewMedia*, April 1993: 39.

[38]Ibid.: 39.

[39]Ibid.: 40.

[40]Van Der Leun, op. cit.: 1993: 109.

[41]Ibid.

[42]Stefanac, op. cit.: 39.

[43]Ibid.

[44]Maltin, Leonard, *Entertainment Tonight*, March 29,1994.

[45]Fleming, Michael, "Freeze Frame: Who Undressed Jessica Rabbit?" *Variety*, March 14–20, 1994.

[46]Advertisement in *Omni*, January 1994: 75.

[47]Bulkeley, William M. "Semi-Prose, Perhaps, But Sportswriting by Software Is a Hit," *Wall Street Journal*, March 29: 1.

[48]Thalhimer, op. cit., May 24, 1994.

[49]Bulkeley, op. cit.: 1.

[50]Ibid.

[51]Ibid.

[52] Markoff, John, "A Magazine Seeks to Push the On-Line Envelope," *New York Times*, October 31, 1994: C6.

8

Marketing
Electronic Publications

"TV will become a mere PC peripheral."
—*ANDY GROVE*[1]

"Only the paranoid survive."
—*ANDY GROVE*[2]

SHOOT FIRST, ASK QUESTIONS LATER:
FINDING THE *RIGHT* APPLICATION
FOR NEW TECHNOLOGIES

One of the most intractable problems in marketing new media technologies is determining their most likely use in the consumer marketplace. Predicting the successful application of a new technology may be just as well done using a crystal ball or by reading tea leaves as by any more systematic or scientific technique. History is replete with failed predictions by some of the most noted figures of the past, as well as some more obscure ones. Consider, for example, the case of Thomas Alva Edison, one of America's greatest inventors. In 1877, in his New Jersey laboratory near Princeton, New Jersey, Edison invented the phonograph, using a combination of tinfoil and wax cylinders to record sound. Of the 1,000 patents for which he is credited, it is the invention he is said to have been most proud of. Edison expected great things from his invention, but was completely wrong in the predicted application. He thought the phonograph would be used for recording speeches. Edison never imagined that his invention would give birth to the music recording industry, now a multibillion dollar industry worldwide.

Publishing Multimedia

Perhaps the most well-traveled terrain on the new media landscape is multimedia publishing, with a growing number of companies offering a rapidly expanding set of products for the consumer marketplace. The consumer multimedia market consists of primarily two types of products: packaged products and networked, or transmitted, products.[3] Packaged products fall into three broad categories based on the type of platform:

- Desktop products, largely PCs equipped with CD-ROM drives, but soon to include DVD-ROM drives
- TV-based systems, generally dedicated devices that plug into television sets
- Portable, self-contained devices used primarily outside the home

Networked or transmitted products will be examined in the section on online services and products, but include primarily Internet and Web-based products.

Desktop Market

In-home desktop multimedia systems consist primarily of desktop computers (largely IBM-compatible PCs and and, to a lesser degree, Macintosh) equipped with CD-ROM drives and sound capability. Some systems are based on laserdisc technology, although most products in this area are limited to movies and training. Data for multimedia products are difficult to come by and often inconsistent. One leading research firm, InfoTech, reports that the installed CD-ROM base now exceeds 25 million.[4] Santa Barbara, California-based consulting firm, Freeman Associates, reports that CD-ROM drive makers shipped 8.3 million drives to computer markets around the world in 1993 and are expected to ship 29.6 million drives in 1999, thus bringing the installed home base to more than 50 million.[5] Figure 8-1 presents a reasonable estimate of the market given the best available data from multiple sources in the multimedia market research area, including the leading firms of Inteco, Infotech, Freeman Associates, and Dataquest. Although initial growth of the desktop market was slow, it took off in 1993 and shows no sign of slowing through the remainder of the decade. The in-home market has already passed what industry analysts describe as a critical mass, the number of machines necessary to make marketing CD-ROM titles on a mass scale profitable. Many have suggested the critical mass is approximately seven million multimedia devices. The total installed base worldwide reached this number in 1993, and in 1994 the United States (see Table 8-1) as well as elsewhere in the world. Interestingly, the growth of the CD-ROM in-

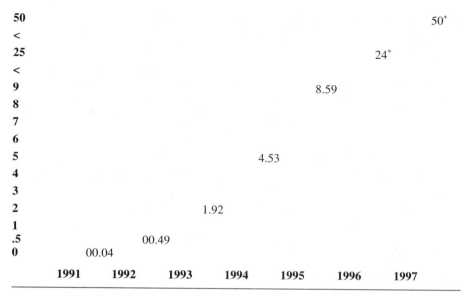

Source: TFPL Publishing, Washington, DC; 202-296-6009.
*Estimated

FIGURE 8-1   U.S. Households with PCs Equipped with CD-ROM Readers (in Millions)

home installed base has followed a somewhat similar pattern as that of the VCR almost two decades earlier, with slow initial adoption, followed by rapid diffusion when prices started falling. With CD-ROM drive prices falling to as low as $199, the installed base will continue to grow. In addition, most desktop computers are now sold with a CD-ROM included in the package, making their diffusion even greater. "With all the attention focused on the Internet, some were tempted to write CD-ROM's obituary," reports Infotech president Julie Schwerin.[6] "This is the fifth straight year that sales of CD-ROM drives have increased by more than 100 per cent of the previous year's level."

The home CD-ROM market is primarily an American phenomenon, with at least 50 percent of all devices located in the United States. In the United States, Inteco estimates that 60 percent of the installed base of multimedia devices are in homes, with the percentage increasing to 75 percent by the end of 1996. This means analysts expect slower growth in the installed base outside the home, such as in schools and in the workplace. The marketing implication is that sales growth for multimedia products will likely be greatest in the home market, both in the United States and abroad. CD-ROM publishing has grown so rapidly that it now even boasts its own annual CD-ROM Exposition.

**TABLE 8-1 Worldwide Installed PC*/CD-ROM Base:
In-Home and Total (in Thousands)**

	In-home Installed Base				Total Installed Base			
	USA	Europe	RoW	World	USA	Europe	RoW	World
1991	62.5	3.7	8.6	74.8	1,250	185	430	1,865
1992	801.0	54.0	126.0	981.0	2,670	360	840	3,870
1993	4,512.0	283.5	521.5	5,317.0	7,520	810	1,490	9,820
1994	9,230.0	676.0	980.0	10,886.0	14,200	1,690	3,970	18,340
1995	15,680.0	1,633.5	1,786.5	19,100.0	22,400	3,630	3,970	30,000
1996	23,625.0	3,500.0	3,100.0	30,225.0	31,500	7,000	6,200	44,700

Sources: InfoTech, INTECO/Screen Digest[7]

*Includes IBM and Macintosh platforms.

CD-ROM Titles: Past Their Peak?

One problem still plaguing the burgeoning industry is the continually evolving hardware and software standards, which have limited compatibility between systems, platforms, and discs. Likewise, there has been some debate about how big the industry really is, largely because of the difficulty in pinning down the exact number of titles and discs in circulation. By most estimates, fewer than fifty CD-ROM titles were published in 1987. The market began to grow in the early 1990s, when the number of new titles published peaked at 1,200 in 1994.[8,9] Although more than 7,000 CD-ROM titles have been published, the number available on the U.S. consumer market is closer to 3,500 (see Figure 8-2). Most titles in the $1.5 billion market are multimedia in format, which includes text, images, audio, and motion video. Consumer electronics manufacturers are also convinced that CD-ROM is here to stay. Olaf Olafsson, president of Sony Electronic Publishing, believes CD-ROM has arrived as a mass market product, and opened a CD-ROM manufacturing plant in Eugene, Oregon in late 1994.[10]

Leading video distributors also see the market potential of CD-ROM. Blockbuster Entertainment and Tower Records, among other retail outlets, now also will sell CD-ROM titles among their other offerings. MPI of Oak Forest, Illinois, a video distributor specializing in television shows and documentaries, released its first CD-ROM product in March 1994, *The Honeymooners' Funniest Moments,* featuring Jackie Gleason, Art Carney, and Audrey Meadows. The CD-ROM title will compete with some sixty Honeymooners' videos already on the market. "It's entertainment, and that fits perfectly with us," says Michael van der Kieft, director of business development for Blockbuster entertainment.[11] MPI has formed a multimedia division charged with developing CD-ROM projects, and has access to both a large video catalogue as well as rights to the WPA Film Library of nearly 20,000 hours of material ranging from old Pathé newsreels to extensive collections of film on history, music, nature, and many other subjects.

Full-motion video on CD-ROM is played on a computer, and appears as a somewhat "herky-jerky" image on a small portion of the screen, although improvements in the technology have smoothed out the image and are likely to increase the image display size to fill the entire screen. MPI's *Honeymooners* disk runs on both Macintosh and Windows platforms, displaying the image in a box in the center of the screen, surrounded by text and still images allowing viewers to select the clips they wish to see next.

CD-ROM titles fall into five main areas, ranked by sales:

- Games
- Arts and Entertainment
- Software
- Reference
- Training/Education

The top selling CD-ROM titles in the United States in 1994 were (PC Data, PC Magazine site above):

1. Myst (Brøderbund Software)
2. Doom II (GT Interactive/id software)
3. 5ft. 10 PAK, Volume 1 (Sirius Publishing)
4. Star Wars Rebel Assault (LucasArts Entertainment)
5. The 7th Guest (Virgin Interactive Entertainment)
6. Microsoft Encarta (an interactive encyclopedia from Microsoft Corp.)
7. Disney's Animated Storybook: *The Lion King* (Disney Software)

	1987	1988	1989	1990	1991	1992	1993	1994	1995	1996
7,000										7,000*
6,000									6,000*	
5,000										
4,000								4,800		
3,000							3,597			
2,000						2,212				
1,000					1,522					
500				817						
0	48	189	390							

Source: TFPL Publishing, Washington, DC; 202-296-6009.[12]
*Estimated

FIGURE 8-2   Number of CD-ROM Titles Published

8. Print Shop Deluxe CD Ensemble (a desktop publishing product from Brøderbund Software)
9. Quicken CD-ROM Deluxe (financial software from Intuit)
10. Corel Gallery (digital art from Corel Corporation)

Of these titles, the top five are game formats, with the exception of Sirius Publishing's 5ft. 10 PAK, which bundles ten CD-ROMs into a single package for $39.95. Included in the 10 PAK are "Beyond Planet Earth," which explores outer space with a panel of space experts, including Buzz Aldrin; "National Parks of America," which explores 230 of America's natural wonders; and "Microsoft Multimedia Mozart," which plays Mozart's music and illuminates his life and his instruments.

Throw Out the Phone Book.   One interesting CD-ROM offering comes from a Massachusetts Company called Pro CD. Pro CD now offers a digital product to replace the telephone book. The company's multi-CD product, called Select Phone contains every listed residential and business telephone number in the entire United States, a total of more than 80 million numbers.[13] The price: $299. The electronic format means Pro CD's digital directories are searchable in a variety of ways, such as by name, address, type of business, Standard Industrial Classification (SIC), or in "reverse," by telephone number. Users can also download all files, as well, for creating mailings or other applications, such as merging databases.

The product is made possible not just by technological advances. The U.S. Supreme Court ruled that telephone directories are in the public domain, meaning that Pro CD, or any company or person for that matter, is entitled to use the content of the data in the published U.S. phone books without paying royalties or copyright fees. Pro CD, which updates the product quarterly, was still confronted by a significant challenge in getting the phone numbers in digital format; even the best scanners come up short when reading directory print. As a result, all numbers and other information in the directories is keyed in manually, at an overall rate of about 1.5 million numbers per month. Such manual keying practices are common for electronic storage of publications, frequently in offshore locations such as the Caribbean or Southeast Asia where labor is cheap and digital communications make data transmission no problem. Notably, software and phone list updates are distributed electronically via the Web to Pro CD customers.

TV-Based Systems

Videogames and Game Players.   Videogames are electronic games played on a videogame player connected to a television set, an arcade machine, or a personal computer. In fact, both videogame players and arcade machines are actually specialized computers, although they cost a lot less, ranging from about $150 to $400 a player. Although many think of them as mere toys, videogame players are among the most powerful home computing devices in existence, largely because they are designed to process full-motion video and high-quality graphics in real time, and thus have extremely powerful and fast microprocessors. Because of their low price (generally only a few hundred dollars), videogame players have become more ubiquitous in U.S. households than are personal computers, with more than 50 million U.S. homes equipped with game players, while only about 34 million homes have PCs.[14,15] Leading the global $15 billion retail video game industry is Nintendo, which has sold more than 1 billion video games worldwide.[16] Some envision a future in which the videogame player becomes the principal information superhighway on-ramp of the future, rather than the personal computer or the television set alone. Although some may scoff at this seemingly far-fetched notion, many industry analysts a decade ago doubted the personal computer could ever replace or supplant a mainframe or even mid-sized computer in business or educational settings, and many skeptics wrote off the Apple Macintosh as a toy. Many in the early 1980s dismissed the PC, and especially the Macintosh computer, as a "hacker's toy unsuitable for business use—only to watch brash new personal computer makers win the hearts and desktops of Corporate America and a college dropout from Seattle named Bill Gates ascend to the industry summit."[17] The popularity of videogame players and their rapidly increasing computing power have transformed them into serious computing contenders in the home, and may even present a challenge in the business marketplace when economic efficiency rules the day. In addition to offering interactive TV-quality video and audio, the next generation videogame player will likely serve as a communications device operating over cable TV networks. International Data Corporation (IDC) projects that by 2000 some 11.2 million homes will be equipped with videogame players and other digital video disk devices that provide Internet access, up from just 12,000 in 1996.[18] If these trends continue, the future may belong not to the video generation, but to the videogame generation.

The Videogame Generation.   The users of videogames are predominantly society's next generation: the majority of videogame players are aged twelve to seventeen.[19] Not surprisingly, many youngsters have developed advanced game-playing skills. After being thrashed at Pac-Man (a popular videogame) by a five-year-old, Patricia Greenfield observed, "as a person socialised into the world of static visual information, I made the unconscious assumption that Pac-Man would not change visual form. Children socialised with television and film are more used to dealing with dynamic visual change."[20]

The popularity of videogames extends beyond the teenage set, however, as recent market research reveals. "Computer game players are among the most technologically advanced computer owners, willing to spend lavishly on software titles, the most sophisticated hardware systems, and cutting edge peripherals," reports the 1996 SIMBA Game Player Survey. "With an average household income of $55,000 annually, computer and videogame enthusiasts are willing and able to upgrade as soon as manufacturers present the opportunity," says SIMBA analyst Tom O'Reilly. Many hard-core PC game players who play more than 11 hours a week spend an average of $426 on games annually, the survey shows.[21] A review of one of the many FAQs (Frequently Asked Question lists) posted on the Internet quickly reveals the level of sophistication of the users. For example, one FAQ includes this explanation.[22]

> *Rcube begins with a set of shaded polygonal cubes spinning in a matrix resembling a larger cube. Using the controller, you change the flat-shaded cubes to Gouraud-shaded, texture-mapped or transparent cubes, toggle a fog effect on or off, and change the viewing angle of the matrix. Pressing one button will shatter the cube into bouncing pieces.*

It almost sounds like fun.

Rebirth of the Videogame Marketplace. The videogame market is now in its second phase of growth and finally seems here to stay. Introduced by the American firm Atari, the market eventually collapsed in 1985 and most people wrote it off as a fad. However, the unexpected rise of Nintendo and Sega after 1986 infused the videogame market with new life. Nintendo holds more than 80 percent of the world's videogame market, and has an especially strong foothold in its native Japan, where a third of all households have a Nintendo game system, and where there are two Nintendo machines for every personal computer sold for home use. The growth of videogame companies is particularly impressive in Japan, where the country is in a recession and consumer electronics companies experienced a 21 percent drop in operating income in 1991. Meanwhile, Nintendo grew by 19 percent that same year and Sega hired executives laid off by other cost-cutting electronics giants.[23]

Nintendo established its early dominance in the videogame market with its 8-bit player, sold at near cost and providing superior graphics and color over Atari, and taking its profits from software sales. Sega caught Nintendo by surprise in 1989 by introducing a 16-bit player, offering superior game performance. These machines today cost about $60 to $70. This pattern of "technological leapfrog" has continued through today, with each generation of the technology offering more powerful graphics processing ability to "render realistic computer-generated 3-D images in real time."[24] At the same time, videogame player technology has offered improved ability to decompress motion video and provide broadcast-quality TV pictures to the viewer.

The state of the art today is the 64-bit videogame player established in late 1996 with the release of the Nintendo Ultra 64. Among the competitors jockeying for position in today's videogame market are the Sony PlayStation, Sega 32X, Sega Saturn, 3DO, 3DO M2, Atari Jaguar, and the Atari Jaguar CD. Each of these machines is capable of spectacular graphic effects that include texture-mapped polygons, advanced sprite renditions, hardware tri-axial rotation (i.e., 3-dimensional) and more. The Nintendo Ultra 64 is among the elite, with 3-D effects that bring new life to the well-known Mario Brothers. In anticipation of heavy demand for the Ultra 64 (or perhaps in an attempt to build it), Nintendo is selling the player every which way it can, including via an Internet auction, with starting bids at $299.

Nintendo's Ultra 64 is designed to "leap-frog" Sega (whose 32-bit capacity had set the standard), by offering 64-bit capacity, based on a processing technology developed by Silicon Graphics. Nintendo stuck with the cartridge format rather than the CD, but has increased its capacity to 12.5 Mb, about six times the previous cartridge capacity. A cartridge offers faster access time than does a CD-ROM drive, and allows Nintendo to maintain proprietary control over the cartridge manufacture, as well as offer its machine for about $100 less than its CD-ROM based competitors (Sega Saturn sells for about $400; Nintendo's Ultra 64 goes for about $300).

Another competitor receiving a great deal of attention in the trade and popular press is the Panasonic 3DO Interactive Multiplayer, featuring a state-of-the-art graphics interface that *Time* magazine says offers "jaw-dropping visuals."[25] With CD-quality sound and a 32-bit processor, the Multiplayer is the most powerful videogame system on the market. The system uses a built-in CD-ROM drive, video-compression and special graphics technology to create full-screen, full-motion video, digitized speech, and flicker-free animation.[26] With backing from AT&T, Time Warner, and MCA, the $399 product (originally offered at $699 but failed to sell well) was designed by Silicon Valley start-up company 3DO.

Videogame Cartridges.   The videogame cartridge is the principle product for the TV-based platform. Leading manufacturers are Nintendo and Sega. Among the most popular products are Sega's *Sonic the Hedgehog,* which has sold more than 100 million units worldwide, Nintendo's *Super Mario,* with similar sales levels, although the release of the Nintendo 64-bit player and the new 3D *Super Mario 64* has spurred a new round of sales of the popular classic. Notably, contrary to popular opinion, not all leading videogames are violent, although many of the very best sellers are, such as Acclaim's *Mortal Kombat,* which enjoyed sales of more than 6 million units worldwide in its first year of release. Many of the top videogame titles are sports-related, such as *Super Kick Off*, *FIFA Soccer,* and *PGA Tour Golf 2.*

The Wrong Kong?   The seminal Nintendo game, *Donkey Kong,* was produced in Japan and subsequently released in the United States in 1980. Ironically, technology had an unintended consequence on this pioneering videogame that introduced Mario to the world, the short, fat, cult figure star of *Super Mario Bros.* and *Super Marioland 2: Six Golden Coins,* all produced by Nintendo. Originally titled *Monkey Kong* by its Japanese inventors, the name became *Donkey Kong* because of a glitch in the fax transmission to New York.[27] After producing all the materials for marketing the game, it was cheaper to simply change the title screen, and the world now knows *Donkey Kong.*

Placing the PC.   Knowing the location of use of any new media technology is one of the most important factors in successfully marketing that technology. Where people use a technology often reveals who will use it, as well as how and when and how often. Most personal computers, including multimedia platforms, are usually found on a desktop in an office or den. TV sets, meanwhile, tend to be in the living room, bedroom, or sometimes in the kitchen. In contrast, most TV-based multimedia platforms are connected to a TV set in a child's bedroom. How these patterns evolve or solidify will determine much of the potential use of multimedia in the home. Moreover, who controls the on-ramp to in-home multimedia will be a critical issue in the decade ahead, with much of the power today resting in the hands of children and youth, especially for TV-based systems, which are generally in the form of videogames. Witness the struggle for control of the TV set remote control, which has often pitted man against woman in an electronic battle of the sexes. *Screen Digest* reports that opinion is sharply divided over whether the desktop PC or the TV set will emerge as the principal multimedia device in the home.[28] Although Intel boss Andy Grove predicts, "TV will become a mere PC peripheral," many see a very different pattern emerging, with the TV set remaining dominant but absorbing more intelligence and "smart" processing abilities.[29] Technology reporter John Markoff similarly predicts that future generations will ask, "What's on the PC tonight?" in the same fashion that earlier couch potatoes pondered the evening's television schedule. To a certain degree, both trends are occurring and may coexist well into the future.

WebTV. One of the most intesting entrants into this debate is WebTV Networks, a company that describes itself as "the world's first high-quality Internet solution for television." Or, "Internet for the rest of us."[30] In the fall of 1996, the company's licensees, Sony Electronics and Philips Electronics, introduced a plug-and-play set-top box that enables Internet and World Wide Web browsing. Combined with the WebTV Network, the WebTV set-top box, remote control, and wireless keyboard (the system sells for about $300) allow anyone to browse the Internet using an ordinary television set, making WebTV the most user-friendly of the online services. In addition, the WebTV online service utilizes a relatively fast 33.6 Kbps modem augmented with patented linesharing technology to allow incoming calls while WebTV operates on a call-waiting-equipped phone line.

An interesting competitor to WebTV is ICTV, a company whose product is offered via cable television systems.[31] The hardware involves placing the primary equipment in the cable system head-end, and placing a minimum of equipment (a small box about half the size of a VCR, a joy stick, and a keyboard) in the subscriber's home. Priced similarly to WebTV, ICTV offers many of the same services to consumers, and offers cable operators the opportunity to provide Intranet applications, such as local news, weather, community information, and advertising. ICTV offers consumers faster Internet access because coaxial cable provides much more bandwidth than the traditional twisted-pair phone line and modem, used in WebTV.

CD-i. Another small but potentially important platform is the Philips CD-i player, or compact-disc interactive. CD-i supports a variety of software types, including "edutainment" titles, as well as games. In contrast to conventional CD-ROM drives, CD-i drives come with a built-in microprocessor, giving the CD-i greater capability to handle a broad array of multimedia computing functions for audio and video. Philips estimates an installed base of some 500,000 CD-i players worldwide, but has seen slow growth, particularly in the United States. CD-i will face even greater competition with the launch of DVD-ROM.

Portable Market

Lead by sales of Nintendo's Game Boy and Sega's Game Gear, the handheld videogame market has expanded rapidly since 1989, and now has an installed base in the United States of more than 20 million units. Unlike the console market, however, the pace of technological change for portable devices has been much slower, and depends largely on the development of low-cost color flat displays.

Electronic Books (EB).   Electronic Books represent another major format for portable devices. The market leader is Sony's Data Discman, introduced in 1990, and based on a smaller version of the company's 3-inch CD-ROM disc. In 1991, Sony introduced an upgraded system, CD-ROM XA, with faster access time and sound capability. Competitors in the EB market include Matsushita, Sanyo, and Sharp. Sony has also begun selling portable CD-i players, aimed at the professional market, offering niche applications for specialized fields and at a much higher price.

EB formats are now evolving in important directions, including discs that will no longer need to be encased in a plastic caddy, and will be sold like typical CD-ROMS. This reduces packaging costs and lets users insert discs into conventional CD-ROM drives. These forces may help the market expand beyond the 500,000 installed base worldwide.

STRATEGIC CONSIDERATIONS

Although a vast array of ever-changing forces influences the economics of successfully marketing multimedia products, several factors emerge as essential in any strategic plan.[32]

- A substantial installed base of the selected platform(s), which defines the market potential for any new product
- Production costs, as defined by the value of the intellectual property at stake, the choice of platform, size, and talents of the production team, software complexity, and necessary development time
- Strength of competing companies offering comparable multimedia products
- Availability of finance for production, comparable to that for film and television
- Pricing structure for the product and development of a revenue stream (*Screen Digest* defines this as the proportion of the price per unit returned to the developer or publisher)

Choosing the right platform depends largely on the nature of the software. Electronic Books or CD-ROM lend themselves naturally to reference, educational, or encyclopedic material, while state-of-the-art games may require high-powered console platforms. Companies increasingly maximize market potential by releasing products designed for multiple platforms, although *Screen Digest* estimates that engineering costs may add 40 percent to the production budget.

Pricing

Estimating prices and possible returns on multimedia products is still hazardous terrain, since the business itself is unstable and small variations in any of the key variables can greatly affect outcomes. *Screen Digest* provides several examples to help outline some typical cases.[33]

Electronic Books (EB)

Sony and its affiliate companies Columbia/Tri-Star and Sony Electronic Publishing dominate the EB market, especially outside Japan.[34] Sony offers attractive presales agreements to developers to help support the EB platform and take most of the risk out of EB publishing. Typically, Sony agrees to purchase a guaranteed minimum of 2,000–3,000 units and pay approximately 50 percent of the retail price to the developer or publisher, collecting only a marginal distribution fee for itself. With an average EB title priced at $40, the return might be $13 per unit sold.

As this scenario suggests, the EB publishing market is at present potentially highly profitable and with little risk. The necessary investment capital is relatively low, as well. *Screen Digest* reports that an acceptable quality disc can be produced for $5,000 to 35,000, although some developers have spent up to $100,000. Moreover, even an expensive title can return a profit on sales of less than 2 percent (10,000) of the installed base of 500,000. An average EB title might sell 5,000 units in a year.

CD-i

Philips Media dominates the CD-i market, and obtaining a contract from Philips is a key factor in successfully marketing a CD-i title. Philips has identified more than a dozen ways it can participate in product development, from production financing to finished title distribution. As the example presented below suggests, the return on CD-i titles is attractive, but not as strong as for EB products. Sales per CD-i player are high, however, with *Screen Digest* reporting an average of ten titles per player.

CD-i Price/Return Formula.
Return=(Price–Retail Margin)–Dist. Margin–(Royalty)
Where:
Price=$45

Retail Margin (40%)=$17
Distributor Margin (55%)=$14.85
Royalty to underlying rights holder (10% of wholesale price)=$2.70
Or,
$10.45=$45–$17–$14.85–$2.70

Breakeven is about 10,000 units for products produced inexpensively, while high-end products may require sales of 100,000.[35] Best-selling CD-i titles that have shipped more than 100,000 units include *ABC Sports Presents: The Palm Springs Open*, Compton's *Interactive Encyclopedia,* and CapDisc's *Battleship*. Other titles have not performed as well, such as CapDisc's *Amparo Museum*, which has sold about 5,000 titles. Two-thirds of the CD-i sales are game titles (65 percent), with children's titles accounting for another 20 percent of sales, and the remaining 15 percent including a range of products.

CD-ROM
The CD-ROM market involves many more players and distributors and is, as a result, harder to define. Heightened competition means deals can be struck, but effective sales may depend on a much more complex distribution arrangement. The installed base is much larger for CD-ROM products and retail sales average 10,000 to 15,000, with a hit reaching sales of more than 30,000. Microsoft's *Encarta* (now including Encarta 97 World Atlas and Encarta 97 Encyclopedia Deluxe Edition) is now returning a profit, after selling more than 300,000 units of *Encarta* worldwide at retail as of May 1994, and selling at a rate of 80,000 units a month. Worldwide, Grolier's CD-ROM encyclopedia has sold more than one million units, primarily since the beginning of 1993. Production costs are similar to CD-i, with developers spending $500,000 to $1,000,000 on average (e.g., MGM-UA's *Blown Away* CD-ROM cost about $900,000 to develop) and some video-intensive titles' production costs running more than $3 million.[36] Typical returns are analyzed in the formula below.

CD-ROM Price/Return Formula.
Return=Price–(Retail Margin)–(Royalty)–(Pressing Costs)
Where:
Price=$50
Retail Margin (40%)=$20
Distributor Margin (50%)=$15
Royalty to underlying rights holder (10% of wholesale price)=$3
Or,
$12=$50–$20–$15–$3

3DO has a pricing structure similar to that of CD-ROM, except that, because the platform is entirely controlled by the 3DO company, an additional $3 royalty is payable to 3DO, reducing the return to $9 per unit sold. Production costs are similar for 3DO products, with one developer, Crystal Dynamics, spending about $500,000 on each 3DO title.

Increasingly, developers are looking toward more sure-fire product development strategies, such as licensing rights to a story or character with a ready-made following, rather than creating an entirely new story and audience. Examples include the *Mighty Morphin' Power Rangers* CD-ROM from Xiphias and a title based on the children's book, *Where's Waldo,* under development by Warner Music Group.

Videogame Cartridge

Compared to the other multimedia formats, the videogame cartridge platform presents considerably tighter profit margins, largely because market leaders Nintendo and Sega control the publishing of games for their proprietary systems. Third-party developers must submit to Nintendo or Sega all game proposals for advance approval and release date guidance. Moreover, Nintendo and Sega carry out manufacturing for a royalty payment, as well as distribution in most cases, with a royalty on sales paid to the developer. Inventory risk is also high, since both manufacturers require minimum initial orders of 10,000 to 20,000 units, and Nintendo requires a letter of credit or full payment prior to manufacture. Because of the tighter margins in this field, many developers have turned increasingly to other platforms, where returns are higher. Of course, the installed base for videogame players is much greater, and sales potential is thus much higher. Sega, for example, has sold more than five million units of *Sonic the Hedgehog,* generating more than $225 million in revenues on a production budget of less than $1 million. Acclaim's popular *Mortal Kombat* reached 6 million unit sales on the 16-bit platform, backed by a $10 million marketing campaign, and generated more than $150 million in revenues in its first year of distribution. Sales per player have dropped off, however, from a high of seven units per player in 1989 to about two per player in 1996. The average title for the 16-bit platform is selling about 40,000 yearly in Europe, with a hot title reaching 100,000 sales. A pricing model is presented below.

Videogame Cartridge Price/Return Formula.
Return=Price–(Retail Margin)–(Dist. Margin)–(Royalty)–Manufacture
Where:
Price=$50
Retail Margin (20%)=$10
Distributor Margin (50%)=$20
Royalty to underlying rights holder (10% of wholesale price)=$4
Manufacturing costs=$8
Or,
$8=$50–$10–$20–$4–$8

Pricing New Information Services

Pricing new information services is one of the great unknowns of electronic publishing. Since the product does not yet exist, and there may be no market to use as a reference point, pricing is often a guessing game. Sometimes prices are based on estimates derived from consumer responses in field trials. Similarly, estimates for some digital services, such as movies-on-demand, have been derived from the established price for comparable analog service, such as videocassette rentals. In some instances, introductory prices have been set low relative to the cost of the service in order to facilitate initial demand, with prices subsequently increased. This strategy has backfired on occasion, producing consumer resentment. In the case of cable television rates, the consumer backlash to price increases was so great that it produced reregulation of cable TV prices. It may even be accounting for the strong sales of DBS receiver dishes since their introduction in 1994.

Online Services

Pricing for online services, particularly Web-delivered news and information, has presented an especially vexing case to the new media industry. In the early 1980s, many videotext services were priced too high, and produced few adopters. Many of the next generation of consumer online services in the 1990s were priced much lower, such as AOL, Compuserve, MSN and Prodigy, which have attracted much greater subscriber bases by offering unlimited access for a fixed price ($19.95 at this writing). Unfortunately, although the low subscription prices have generated large numbers of subscribers, they have not produced enough revenue. Accompanied by somewhat limited advertising support, the financial well-being of some of the commercial online services is in some doubt. Prodigy, a joint IBM–Sears effort, lost millions of dollars in its several years of operation and finds itself in fourth place among the commercial online services, behind the big three.

In the nonconsumer commercial online services, pricing has been designed somewhat differently. Because users have tended to be corporate organizations, services such as Dialog or Lexis–Nexis (owned by Reed Elsevier, one of the world's largest publishing and information companies), prices have been much higher. Dialog has recently introduced a new approach to pricing based on the number of people in a corporation who are authorized to read documents downloaded from the computerized database service Dialog Information Systems.[37] Using a formula of "multipliers," it is cheaper for a Dialog client to allow many of its users to share computer access to a single electronic document than to make multiple copies and distribute them electronically to each user.

Online Advertising Industry Revenue

Online advertising has grown slowly in the 1990s. Advertisers have shown great interest in the creative opportunities afforded by online media, but have been cautious about committing substantial dollars to reach online prospects. Estimates show that just $39 million was spent in 1995 on Web-based advertising industry-wide.[38] This represents only a very small fraction of the amount of ad dollars generated for other media, such as the $10 billion spent in 1995 on radio advertising, the $22.5 billion spent on print advertising, and the $32.4 billion spent on television advertising. On the other hand, with the continued growth of Internet users and the improvement and reliability of Internet technologies, leading Internet analysts such as Alan M. Braverman of CS First Boston to expect Web-based advertising to grow substantially during the next five years. Based on data from Forrester Research and Jupiter Communications, Braverman estimates that Web-based advertising revenues will be $125 million industry-wide in 1996, $800 million in 1998, and will reach $3.1 billion by 2000, a much larger fraction of the advertising revenue from other more established media.

CPM on the Web. Braverman points out two especially noteworthy aspects of this Web-based advertising stream. First, "The top 10 ad sites currently account for less than 0.01% of all sites where an advertiser could advertise, yet they comprise half of all ad revenue."[39] Second, cost-per-thousand impressions (CPM) is the current standard for Web-based advertising, although this could change as new pricing models begin to emerge.[40] Braverman notes that the popular content-based Web sites, such as ESPNet SportsZone, Playboy, and Pathfinder "charge between $10,000 and $30,000 for a basci ad banner." This puts their CPM at about $30, or three cents per impression. Pathfinder, for example, delivers about 1.3 million impressions per quarter, and charges $38,000 for running an ad banner for that period ($29=$38,000/1,300; the 1.3 million impressions is reduced by a factor of 1,000 for this calculation). This pricing formula is similar to the CPM for advertising in print media, such as newspapers. Notably, the Wall Street Journal Interactive charges a somewhat higher CPM ($80), despite a somewhat lower level of traffic (250,000 impressions per quarter), perhaps because it attracts a business audience.

Finding the Real in Virtual Reality

Separating the fact from fiction is always a challenge in new technology, and it is especially so for virtual reality. Hollywood depictions of metallic bodies having cybersex in Stephen King's *Lawnmower Man*, or virtual vacations, like the one Arnold Schwarzenegger took to Mars in *Total Recall,* are a far cry from the capabilities of virtual reality today. "Some of that stuff might be possible in 50 to 100 years," says Harvey Newquist, CEO of the Relayer Group. Today's VR graphics are slow and look cartoonish. Moreover, VR technology is expensive. W Industries of Leicester, England, produces and markets VR games to arcades in seventeen countries. It has sold ninety of its $55,000 Virtuality machine in the United States, mostly to sports bars and arcades. World Entertainment of Chicago is a competitor with machines in the United States and Japan. Sega sells a $200 display helmet, but the device has proven to be little more than a "novel projection system for standard video games."[41]

Virtual Markets.   A report by Find/SVP of New York and The Relayer Group of Scottsdale, Arizona, shows the virtual reality industry is on the brink of rapid growth, estimating that the virtual reality market could reach $575 million by 1999.[42] Nevertheless, sales of the data glove for 1991 were a disappointing $5 million, the report says. The report also predicts sales of entertainment and training/ simulation VR products will reach $150 million by the end of the decade. The most likely growth area for virtual reality products will be information services, which the report expects to grow from $0 sales in 1991 to $75 million by the end of the decade. One area boosting the virtual reality market potential has been the development of a variety of Web-based virtual reality applications, ranging from Virtual Reality Modeling Language (VRML) to 3-D modeling tools. One such Web product is called the Active Worlds Development Kit. Developers have used the Kit to create a 3-D online representation of Yellowstone National Park, as well as a variety of 3-D virtual worlds with no real-world counterpart, such as AlphaWorld, Arctic Light, and Colony Alpha.[43] As is typical on today's Web, the developers' kit is relatively expensive (e.g., $2,995) and the player (i.e., the software needed to run an application) is available for free as a browser plug-in.

Hollywood Delivered Digitally

One optical fiber application with potentially profound implications for both culture and industry in the United States is the digital delivery of movies directly from Hollywood studios to movie theaters. In March of 1994, Pacific Bell announced the first test of technology for delivering movies, high-definition video, and live events in digital format directly from Hollywood studios or other locations to movie theaters.[44] The technology, which sends compressed video over high-speed fiber optic networks, has been developed jointly with Alcatel Network Systems, providers of video transmission and switching equipment. This new delivery system could produce a significant shift in theater revenue trends that began with the mass introduction of an earlier technology, the videocassette, in the 1980s. In 1980, the vast majority of Hollywood revenues, nearly 80 percent, came from theatrical film releases. Only a few percent of Hollywood's total revenues came from videocassette sales and rentals. By 1987, total revenue derived from videocassette sales and rentals of Hollywood movies had surpassed the total revenues from theatrical release of those movies, and the gap in revenues has only widened since then.[45] The digital transmission of Hollywood productions directly to movie theaters by optical fiber might give theaters a significant advantage over videocassette sales and rentals by providing instant access to digitally perfect video products on a first-run basis. As a result, revenues for theatrical releases could begin to climb again, possibly reversing a decade-long slide.

Digital Video/Audio Via Fiber.   An alternative type of network service is being promoted by Pacific Bell, one of the Regional Bell Operating Companies. Pac Bell, as it is known locally, is offering TV stations and post-production houses a new digital video and audio delivery service over its fiber-optic lines. The Advanced

Broadcast Video Service received its first real-time test during Superbowl XXVII in January 1993, and was rolled out to the general market in December of that year. The site-to-site transmission system is offered as a competitive alternative to satellite video transmission. "One key advantage over satellites is that it is digital, while satellites are still largely analog," says Rich Mizer, Pacific Bell product engineer for ABVS.[46] Since it is delivered via fiber, ABVS is also impervious to piracy and weather disturbances. The service costs $850 a month, or $212.50 a day. It may save many times over that in distribution costs.

Maintaining the Film "Look."   An important part of the debate about digital movie delivery revolves around the issue of the film "look" or aesthetic, as opposed to video. Many film auteurs and critics argue that 35mm film has intrinsic qualities that set it apart as an art form from video, including high-definition television. They point out that video, even high-definition television, has lower resolution than 35mm film. Moreover, video has a different texture than film, somewhat harsher and flatter in appearance. As a result, many in the film industry frown on the notion that film products could be shown on any medium other than film.

However valid this argument, there is a major problem. What most people see in the average movie theater in America, or anywhere else in the world, does not even come close to the potential of 35mm film. The process of making film dubs or copies for distribution, the variability of film projectors, dust in the air or on the projector lens, imperfections in film screens, and other shortcomings of most movie theaters significantly degrade the theatrical movie watching experience. One study commissioned by CBS television has shown that the actual resolution obtained in even the best movie theaters is only 1,000 lines of resolution, only half the potential of HDTV.[47] Moreover, many Hollywood movies, although shot on 35mm film, are transferred to digital video format for special effects processing, and then transferred back to film for theatrical release. Thus, any inherent qualities of film stock have been eroded by the transference to video in many existing Hollywood movies. To most viewers, however, the subtleties of film stock are not apparent, at least in most movie theaters. Thus, the new technology for delivering digital movies directly to movie theaters holds much promise. Still, it remains to be seen whether the compression technology developed by Alcatel and Pacific Bell for the delivery test will produce moving-image picture quality comparable to that of physically distributed 35mm film. Nevertheless, Michael Fitzpatrick, executive vice president of Pacific Bell, remains optimistic. "The current method of copying and shipping movies to theaters is outdated," Fitzpatrick declares.[48] "The imminent shift from 35mm film to the delivery of movies in digital form is as momentous as the change from black and white to color." This may be overstating the case, but the point is valid.

It is unclear whether electronic delivery of movies to theaters will have any effect on the price the consumer pays to see those movies. In New York City, for example, where consumers now pay $8 a ticket to see a movie at Loews Theaters, it is unlikely that even electronically delivered movies, though more efficiently delivered than those on 35mm film, would bring about a lower cost. It is likely, however, that such a distribution system, by increasing efficiency and possibly reducing piracy, would increase profits for movie distributors.

International Distribution

The global information grid has profound implications for news and entertainment programming. Rupert Murdoch, whose media empire encompasses News Corp., B Sky B, the Fox Network, and a controlling interest in the Hong Kong-based StarTV satellite network, bases his programming decisions on how those programs will fare, not just domestically, but in the international market. An example, Adam Powell notes, is the television show *Studs,* created in the early 1990s for Murdoch's Fox Network. "Murdoch isn't making *Studs* anymore, even though it was successful in the U.S. market," Powell explains, "because it doesn't travel well. You can't show *Studs* in India."[49] A spin-off from *The Dating Game, Studs* featured single, young women competing for dates with eligible bachelors equipped with high volumes of testosterone.

Although it is not unique to the international arena, one important issue that is especially apparent in developing societies is data quality. Regardless of technological advances and sophistication, the information superhighway is only valuable if the information it carries is reliable. As Oxford's Anthony Smith observes, the credibility of any nation–state, or any institution or individual, rests on the accuracy of the information it produces.[50] If information cannot be trusted, it loses all value.

ADOPTERS OF NEW TECHNOLOGY: WHAT RESEARCH TELLS US

Although uncertainty abounds in the new technology marketplace, recent research does tell us some interesting things about how new media technologies enter U.S. households. Many lessons come from the past, both its technological successes and failures. Some of the most revealing research in this area has been conducted by telecommunications authority John Carey, director of Greystone Communications.[51] Table 8-2 shows the relationship between price and consumer purchases of new technologies. But rather than looking at simple dollar amounts, Carey has translated the price of each technology into the number of weeks average income. This is a means of standardizing the price of each technology and facilitating comparisons across time and technology. The final number in each column represents the point at which each technology entered at least 50 percent of U.S. households.

The data reveal several interesting trends in the adoption of new technology. First, they show that the price of each new media technology has fallen dramatically over time, and with that drop, each technology has been adopted by a widening group of households. Second, for radio, black-and-white and color television, 50 percent adoption was reached when the cost of the technology was slightly less than two weeks' income. For more recent technologies, however, the price has had to

TABLE 8-2 Price of Selected Electronic Products In Terms of Weekly Household Income Number of Weeks Income to Pay for Product

Year	Radio Set	B&W TV	Color TV	VCR	CD Player
1929	1.8*				
1947		5.3			
1950		3.3			
1955		1.8*	6.6		
1960			4.1		
1965			3.1		
1970			1.9*		
1975				6.2	
1980				3.3	
1983				1.4	1.8
1985				1.1	.7
1987				.8	.4
1989				.7*	.4
1992					.3*

*Year product entered 50 percent of U.S. households.

Source: John Carey, US Department of Commerce.

drop even further for penetration to reach 50 percent. The VCR's price had to reach less than one week's income and the CD player less than one-half week's. This pattern suggests that it is becoming harder to introduce new media technologies in the United States. The U.S. household is becoming saturated with media technologies.

Table 8-3 confirms this conclusion. These data show that a variety of media technologies have entered the vast majority of U.S. households, including the television, telephone, remote control, and VCR, with several others reaching about half of all U.S. households, such as basic cable television, the telephone answering machine, and the compact disk player. The computer has entered more than a third (37 percent) of U.S. homes. Other data Carey has compiled further show that many households have multiple units of a variety of these technologies. For example, nearly three-quarters (73 percent) of households with telephone service have at least two phones, with more than a third (38 percent) having at least three phones. An increasing number have two or more lines. Notably, an increasing percentage of homes now have a modem (21 percent of all homes, 57 percent of homes with PCs), which enables their home computer to go online to the Internet and the World Wide Web. In 1994 just 11 percent of homes had a modem.[52]

Business Users and Technophiles

Carey also points out that historically the adoption of new technology tends to go through several stages, almost in a stair-step fashion.[53] The first step, which must be taken before adoption will proceed, is generally taken by business users. Business

TABLE 8-3   Penetration of New Media Technologies Percentage of U.S. Households with Technology or Service, 1996

Television	98%
Telephone Service	95
Remote Control	90
VCR	80
Basic Cable	62
Answering Machine	52
Compact Disk Player	42
Stereo TV	40
Video Game Player	40
Home Computer	37
Modem	21
Camcorder	19
Projection TV	9
Satellite Dish	4
Videotex	3
Home Fax	2
Laser Disc Player	1

Source: John Carey; CS First Boston; Electronic Industry Association; AC Neilsen.

users typically have greater resources to pay the high initial price of the technology and can often justify the cost in terms of their expected return on investment and capitalization.

As adoption begins to move into the consumer realm, the second step involves those heavy technology users aptly called *technophiles.* One *New Yorker* cartoon depicts a typical technophile who enters a consumer electronics store and tells the clerk. "All my gadgets are old. What new gadgets do you have?" Susan Mitchell of *American Demographics* magazine describes the difference between technophiles and technophobes in these words:

> *Your personal communicator beeps to alert you to an incoming message. Its palm-sized screen tells you that your "smart home" needs instructions. You tell your portable computer to dial your home-control center, which relays an image of the problem. You left the rice cooking. Inserting your hand into a virtual reality glove, you control the movements of a home robot to turn off the stovetop.*
>
> *When you read the above, do you: (a) abstractly ponder what it would be like to live in such a world; (b) jump up from your chair and begin making animated hand gestures while screaming, "Yeah, yeah! That's great"; or (c) feel the need to lie down? If you answered (a), you're a regular Jane or Joe. If you answered (b) or (c), you are probably a technophile or a technophobe.[54]*

It is also worth noting that many new technologies may never reach the mass market stage, but may find a profitable niche market instead. This has proven to be the case with videotext and teletext. Some 20 percent of farmers in Iowa, for example, now subscribe to a Ku-band satellite agricultural teletext service providing weather, market information, agricultural news, and so on.

This general pattern of adoption holds true for Internet access as well. Alan M. Braverman, Internet analyst for CS First Boston, reports that, "In 1995 the percentage of PC users with Internet access was greater in the business environment at 40 percent than in the home at 30 percent."[55] Braverman expects this difference to vanish by the end of the decade. "According to IDC," he reports, "by the year 2000 we could see an Internet access penetration of 95 percent for both home and business PCs."

Generational, Gender, and Socioeconomic Issues

Although men have tended to dominate the world of new media technology, one exception to this trend is *The Women's Forum*, set up by *U.S. News & World Report* as part of that magazine's online service. Kathy Bushkin of *U.S. News & World Report* says the service was developed in response to women's requests for just such a service devoted to issues of concern to women.[56] Although men are welcome to participate in the forum, only a few have done so.

The implications of gender, race, and other demographic factors for the media world were a major concern of the late Bob Maynard, former publisher of the *Oakland Tribune*, for many years the only Black-owned daily newspaper in a major U.S. market. Maynard argued that we cannot weave together the fault lines of race, gender, age, geography, and class, but we can build bridges. He concluded that the process of building such bridges can open important markets for niche information products and new media products appealing to communities of interest that cut across these fault lines.

IMPLICATIONS FOR ADVERTISING

Although innovative advertisers have always been intrigued by new media for marketing their products, today's digital technologies have particularly energized the industry. From the Ad Council to the Sci-Fi Channel, new media are transforming the methods and means of advertising. Advertisers are especially interested in two aspects of the new media technologies: interactivity and multimedia. Interactivity offers advertisers an unprecedented ability to involve the buyer in the marketing process. Multimedia technologies enable advertisers to simultaneously take advantage of the impact of video, audio, and text in the communication and persuasion process.

Online services and CD-ROM are the principal tools in the new media mix currently being used by these groundbreaking advertisers. Online services, especially via the Internet and World Wide Web, as well as the major consumer services such as AOL, Compuserve, and MSN, offer advertisers the ability to reach potential buyers through highly targeted messages. For example, online consumers interested in a particular type of product or ad message might select additional information available online, or might even engage a live online sales representative in a conversation about the product. Such a direct-response mechanism provides the advertiser with the greatest potential for making a sale.

Push versus Pull

One issue being debated in the online advertising arena is whether to "push" or "pull." Traditionally, advertising has employed a "push" strategy, one in which advertisers used mass media such as newspapers, television, or radio to "push" their product messages onto a passive audience. This strategy has served many advertisers well through much of the twentieth century.

The advent of customizable, interactive, direct-marketing online media, however, makes possible an effective "pull" strategy for advertising, where the consumer selects just the commercial messages in which he or she is interested. This approach lends itself particularly well to the World Wide Web, where each computer user visits Web sites of their choice, and can use the same techniques to visit an advertiser's site.

The slowness of advertising growth on the Web, coupled with the rise of Internet broadcasters such as Pointcast, however, have made the possibility of online "push" strategies increasingly attractive. The Internet Advertising Bureau (IAB) reports ("IAB Announces First Round Results of Ad Revenue Sales Reporting Program," December 11, 1996) that online advertising revenue reached $157 million through the first three quarters of 1996 for 200 Internet publishers, with ad revenues for the third quarter ($75.6 million) more than doubling those for the first quarter ($29.9 million). Together with an emerging set of standards for online "banner" advertisements (eight standard sizes range from 88×31 pixels for a micro button to 468×60 for a full banner), advertising using a "push" standard is likely to emerge in the late 1990s as an important dimension of the online broadcasting world.

CD-ROM messages offer the potential to provide a highly sophisticated multimedia experience tailored to the consumer's particular interest. CD-ROM messages, however, had limited interactive capability because with no online connection, customers would not interact with a live company representative, or get the latest in product information. As a result, CD-ROM technology has been used more often as a special sales tool for sales representatives going into the field to talk directly to clients. For example, a new multimedia CD-ROM presentation has taken the Sci-Fi Channel's sales pitch has replaced generic flip charts with customized digital graphics. All this began to change in 1996 with the development of a variety of products to link CD-ROM technology to Web pages. One interesting example is Hyper CD, a product that enables Website developers to link their pages to the content on a CD-ROM. Hyper CD, and other products like it, make possible high quality graphics and other multimedia content, such as video and audio, but without long download times.

Perhaps the most important new media development for the advertising world will be found in the development of Internet and Web access through products such as WebTV. Because they are still in their infancy, today's WebTV is still in the early introductory phase as an advertising and marketing tool. Its potential is great because it combines all the advantages of online communications and multimedia communications, plus the potential for mass audience reach. Like online services, WebTV also offers sellers the opportunity to develop detailed a database on consumer preferences and tastes, thus tailoring messages in a highly efficient, and it is hoped, effective fashion. Privacy remains a major concern here, and advertisers will need to act early and consistently to communicate clearly their efforts to protect consumer privacy in the age of interactive media.

New media face a number of limitations such as their currently limited audience reach, uncertain impact, and cost. But advertisers are approaching digital media creatively, and many see them as an opportunity to experiment and position their product first on the electronic frontier before it becomes cluttered and congested like many of today's traditional media venues.[57] Some members of the nonprofit sector are also entering the digital marketing age. The Advertising Council, whose public service campaigns include such well-known efforts as "Smokey Bear" and "McGruff the Crime Dog," has already begun examining new media forays with some of the field's leading players, including Time Warner, Sega of America, Interactive Network, and Prodigy Services.[58] The Ad Council's first use of new media was an ad on Prodigy for Earth Share, an environmental group. The ad message quizzed users on their knowledge of the environment, and helped the group receive, during a nine-month period, some $54,000 in pledges and more than 66,000 requests for a free poster offered in the online ads. The Council has since launched a second online campaign, and because of the response to both campaigns, has planned an additional half-dozen online efforts. The Council also has signed on as one of the Interactive Network's charter advertisers, along with Chrysler Corp. and American Airlines. Moreover, The Council is compiling a library of its new media campaigns, which will be available to programming executives through the online service of NATPE (National Association of Television Programming Executives) at http://www.natpe.org/, a nonprofit television programming and software association that distributes information to radio and TV stations around the world.

CPB Goes Online

In another new venture in the not-for-profit world, the Corporation for Public Broadcasting (CPB), the main funding organization for public TV and radio stations, in 1994 launched its public broadcasting future funds, a program to support innovative public broadcasters in developing new media initiatives. As reported at its Web site, CPB created "future funds" for public radio and television, offering strategic assistance and investment funds for projects to increase the system's efficiency and develop new revenue streams.[59] CPB expects to invest $30 to $40 million through these funds by the end of the decade. The CPB TV portion of the fund has announced it would invest $3 million in seventeen projects. In the radio fund's first round of soliciting projects, CPB awarded funding to eight projects. Receiving funding from Congress, the not-for-profit CPB encourages public broadcasters to work with local organizations and businesses to create or expand computer links to schools, libraries, museums, hospitals, and public organizations. Several of the funded projects include links to cities and metropolitan areas. CPB estimates that more than 25 million people now have access to public broadcasting online services. Larry Irving, assistant secretary of the Commerce Department and head of its National Telecommunications and Information Administration (NTIA), says the Clinton administration hopes to see more of such community networks developed. NTIA has provided more than $50 million for experimental projects proposed by local governments and nonprofit institutions as part of its Telecommunications and Information Infrastructure Assistance Program (TIIAP). Since its inception in 1994, TIIAP has awarded 277 grants in fifty states, the District of Columbia, and several territories. "By serving as models that can be replicated in similar communities and organizations across the country," the NTIA home page reports, "TIIAP projects extend their benefits far beyond the communities in which they take place, and provide economic and social benefits to the nation as a whole." TIIAP will award $21.5 million in grant funds in fiscal year 1997.[60] Demonstrating the success of the program, four TIIAP-funded projects received National Information Infrastructure (NII) Awards in 1996, including:

Charlotte's Web—a Web-based regional community network to help people use telecommunications technology to improve their lives and foster civic involvement.

Columbia-Presbyterian Medical Center—Columbia-Presbyterian's Applied Informatics project employing wireless telecommunications, handheld and pen-operated computers, expert systems, and the World Wide Web to provide an electronic link between medical professionals and institutions and their at-home patients.

East Palo Alto Gets Plugged In—a community network of human and electronic resources designed to provide the 23,500 residents of East Palo Alto access to computer technology, connecting low-income communities with the information economy.

National Adoption Center—an Internet-based adoption program to find homes for more than 300 older children across the United States who are in foster homes waiting to be adopted.

The NII Awards Program is supported by a broad cross-section of industry partners. Technology companies providing support include: AT&T, IBM, the U.S. Postal Service, BellSouth, Sun Microsystems, Lotus, Netscape, Compuserve, Fujitsu, Price Waterhouse, BBN, SRI Consulting, US WEST, and Tandem Computers. Media sponsors include: *Time, Business Week, PCI Week, Modern Healthcare, Business Communications Review, Business Wire, EE Times, Electronic Learning, Federal Computer Week,* Government Technology, Hospitals and Health Networks, Inter@ctive Week, Internet World, Network World, Telecommunications, and Web Week.

THE NEW BUSINESS ENVIRONMENT

Nancy Hicks Maynard, a media leader and new media entrepreneur who is chair of the Media Studies Center (a program of the Freedom Forum), argues that media convergence has produced a rude awakening for many newspaper publishers, who only recently discovered they're not really in the news business. At least news is not how they make most of their money, notes Maynard, who has been the deputy publisher and senior vice president of *The Oakland Tribune,* a former a correspondent for *The New York Times,* former president and executive director on the Institute for Journalism Education, now known as the Robert C. Maynard Institute for Journalism, and founder of Maynard Partners Incorporated, a media consulting firm. Advertisers provide about 80 percent of the revenue of traditional newspapers. Newspaper sales and subscriptions generate only about 18 percent of the revenues. "If you think about it," Maynard explains, "18 percent is also about what it costs to distribute the paper, in the marketplace."[61] Thus, newspapers are, essentially, a free product subsidized by advertisers for which readers pay for the delivery. "How many marketing schemes have you heard like that?" Maynard asks. She describes this traditional relationship between newspapers, readers, and advertisers as the media triangle, with newspapers at the top of the triangle, readers in one corner, and advertisers in the other. Convergence is bringing about the collapse of the triangle. As a result, media convergence and in particular online communications are creating a direct straight line relationship between the supplier and the consumer. For newspapers, this increasingly direct relationship between buyer and seller has begun to seriously erode the newspaper advertising subsidy. Information technology is allowing sellers to seek more efficient distribution channels, channels more efficient than traditional newspapers.

Online communications have also begun to transform the entire environment for conducting business. On the Internet, not only are a growing number of companies exploring avenues for reaching consumers. In April 1994, an online industrial park was opened. "Commercenet," as it is called, has already attracted some 200 member companies and organizations worldwide, including banking and financial services (e.g., Chase Manhattan), computer systems (e.g., Sun Microsystems, Hewlett Packard), telecommunications, network services, software system integration, consulting, Internet products and services as well as major end-users. Commercenet enables these companies from a variety of fields, many outside the computer industry, to conduct all aspects of their business via the Internet, including processing legal document fulfillment, requesting proposals, commodity bidding, and so forth. Conducting online business requires a secure environment, and important regulatory battles are now being waged in Washington that will determine not only the future of online cryptography but the future of commerce on the Internet. Internet security will be examined in detail in Chapter 9. Using a Web browser such as Navigator or Explorer, members access the Commercenet Web site.[62] Commercenet serves as a prototype for an open twenty-first century Internet-based organization by developing, implementing, and expanding the technical and institutional protocols required to bring electronic commerce to all worldwide markets.

In addition to Commercenet, other interesting online business ventures for the new media world include the Online Ad Agency, founded in January 1994 by advertising veteran Larry Chase. Not limited to the dimensions of the physical world, the Online Ad Agency goes well beyond conventional notions of telecommuting, and offers its service via the Internet. Prospective clients visit the agency on the Web at www.advert.com and can download work samples, talk online to creative directors, account executives, or copy writers who come from all over the United States. All business is conducted online, and production costs are significantly reduced. Moreover, the agency can contract specialists on an as-needed basis to work on individual accounts, and need not maintain a high level of costly overhead. The Online Ad Agency may not completely redefine the world of advertising, but had it existed half a century ago, Mr. Blandings may have had a lot less trouble building his dream house. (If Mr. Blandings is an unfamiliar name, tune in to American Movie Classics and watch Cary Grant and Myrna Low in the cinema classic *Mr. Blandings Builds His Dream House.* Mr. Blandings, played by Cary Grant, may have saved a lot of time commuting and come up with "If it ain't *Wham*, you ain't eatin' ham," with a lot less stress had he been able to work for the Online Ad Agency.)

EVALUATING THE RESULTS

"You can observe a lot by looking."
—*YOGI BERRA*

Central to all aspects of marketing, but especially to the introduction of new media products, is evaluating the results of any marketing efforts. Although ultimately based on the financial bottom line, knowing how well a new media product or service is performing can be evaluated through other mechanisms as well. Evaluation research is perhaps the most important and systematic of these mechanisms. Evaluation research comes in two primary forms: formative and summative research. Formative refers to pretesting and diagnostic research designed to assess how well a new product may fare in the marketplace, what can be done to improve its likelihood of success, and why it may have failed or, one hopes, succeeded. Summative refers to research done after a new product has been introduced, or after any campaign, in order to evaluate whether it succeeded and whether the product should be rolled out nationally or internationally. Both kinds of evaluation research are relevant to this discussion of the marketing of new media technologies. Moreover, new media technologies have presented interesting challenges, problems, and opportunities in the marketing evaluation research on these new products.

Field Trials: The Information Superhighway Gold Rush

A large and rapidly growing number of companies are engaged in research efforts to determine which new media technologies are most likely to succeed in the consumer marketplace. Unfortunately, if experience is any indicator, even the best research has little chance of reliably predicting or forecasting which technologies are destined to succeed and which are doomed to fail. Media critic and author Ken Auletta, whose widely acclaimed best seller *Three Blind Mice* dissected the fall of the three great commercial television networks in the 1980s and the role of both economics and technology in that decline, notes a recent case study in failed technology predictions.[63] In the late 1980s, Auletta observes, the best research suggested that HDTV was about to transform the television landscape, making conventional TV obsolete.[64] Since HDTV transmission would require much greater bandwidth than was available to most television stations, the entire broadcast TV market was terrified by the looming change. But no one foresaw the rapid entry of digitization and compression. Suddenly, "HDTV was passé," Auletta says. New technology would make it possible to transmit HDTV using existing broadcasting bandwidth. As a result, many companies will likely lose millions, if not billions of dollars in investments in new media technologies, while a few companies will likely make a great deal of money.

The same is true today with regard to the Internet and the World Wide Web. Even a decade ago, few would have foreseen the meteoric rise of the Internet as an important new medium of communication and commerce on a global scale. Many large companies were busily sinking massive investments into developing full-service networks, interactive television systems, and the video dialtone, all of which were swept aside by the growth of the Internet as a worldwide publishing and transactional environment.

Telecommunications consultant John Carey wisely observes that, while few research techniques provide reliable forecasts of new media technologies, field trials can provide other very useful data.[65] Field trials are experiments conducted in the field of working technologies to test either the technologies themselves or consumer reactions to those technologies, a type of formative evaluation research. Although they may not reveal great insight as to likely consumer responses to new information services, field trials can reveal problems or issues that may have been unforeseen or unexpected, such as viewer preferences no one in engineering ever anticipated. Field trials of information highway technologies can provide a test of many factors simultaneously, which might be difficult to test in a highly controlled laboratory setting or through a survey instrument. Carey points out that current field trials, such as some of today's cable-modem testbeds, may offer insights into a number of difficult questions confronting information highway services. These include:

- Content issues—What do people want? Will they watch, or interact, with existing content that is enhanced with interactive features? Will they prefer original, but expensive to produce, programming? Quality content that downloads fast is an early lesson from the Web.
- The relationship between the content providers and the viewers—Will new viewing habits evolve? A balance between passive receiving and occasional active seeking is emerging in early patterns from TV-based Web use.
- The interactive TV/WWW interface—Should the controls be in the remote control or on the TV screen? Should it use words or icons? Icons suggest a computer model, and are often difficult for viewers to remember and understand. Early results from the introduction of WebTV suggest that a remote control interacting with the TV screen is a viable model.
- The interface metaphor for interactive TV—Many are testing physical or geographic metaphors, such as a mall or street, through which the viewer travels. This approach may be fun but slow. The success of the Web suggests that the "home page" metaphor works well.
- Choice options—A tree and branching model works well in some contexts, but people tend to get lost. Computer options such as Boolean searching tend to be too complex. Some are trying out associations with everyday life, such as have been used at Automated Teller Machines that use human tellers as their model, referring to customer by name, telling them thanks and have a nice day.
- Entering alpha-numeric data—Should these data be entered on screen? Using the remote control? By voice command?
- On-screen help or instructions—Some believe the ideal system is totally intuitive, requiring no instructions, and reflecting the fact that most people just sit down and start using new TV devices.
- Gender differences in using television—Women often watch TV while doing something else, such as eating, reading, ironing, cooking, writing, much more often than do men. How will this behavior affect their use of interactive TV?
- The channel metaphor—Will we see the end of the channel metaphor and the beginning of a services metaphor in television, and in the information superhighway in general?
- Privacy—Few in the corporate world are concerned about privacy as a social good. Most are more concerned about getting sued over privacy questions, and want to know how to allay people's fears that the information superhighway will erode privacy.

Carey adds that while field trials present an excellent opportunity to test many of these ideas, there are a number of fundamental questions that may await answer in the realm of academic inquiry. However, many of these questions may be of such profound importance that they outweigh or supersede any answers to the above questions. Some may only be answered through the success or failures of various real-world tests in the commercial marketplace.

A Research Agenda for the Information Superhighway

Important information superhighway research questions include:

- Should we reexamine the basic notion of what are the mass media in light of an emerging information superhighway where the concept of information provider and audience are turned on their heads and interactivity becomes the byword of the digital age?
- Will viewers increasingly think of interactive, Web-based TV and the information superhighway, sometimes called cyberspace, as a place they go to rather than something they watch?
- What is meant by active versus passive media use? Does talking to your television, or television characters or news people, constitute active viewing?
- How will the conventions of television and television viewing evolve?
- Will the Internet and the Web continue to grow into full-scale media of communication and commerce to rival television and the other media of traditional mass communication and commerce? Perhaps the question should be rephrased simply as: How long will this inevitable emergence take?

Information Age Post-Mortem: The Death of the Agency Commission?

Because they provide direct data on advertising impact, interactive technologies are also transforming how advertising agencies get paid. "The commission system is dead," says Rishad Tobaccowala, vice president at Leo Burnett USA, Chicago, and head of its interactive group.[66] Advertising agencies have for many years generated their revenue through a 15 percent rebate they receive from traditional media companies, such as network television, for commercials placed for clients. Because consumers use interactive technologies to directly access company information and advertising, and companies can know when a consumer requests information, they will rely less and less on mass media messages that lack the ability to measure audience impact. Instead, advertisers will prefer, even demand, a payment system that relies on direct accountability and impact measures. Payment will likely be based on the number of responses generated by interactive campaigns, not the total audience exposed to a message, as in traditional audience measures for network television such as audience ratings or shares. Not only may this spell the end of the advertising agency commission, but it has serious implications for the broadcast networks and mass media that have relied on ad agencies to bring them their lifeblood: advertising revenue.

NOTES

[1]"The Consumer Multimedia Marketplace 2: Software," *Screen Digest*, May 1994: 1.

[2]Andrew S. Grove. *Only the Paranoid Survive*. Bantam Books: New York, 1996.

[3]*Screen Digest,* op. cit., 1994.

[4]http://www.pcmag.com/issues/1412/100cds/100cd_qs.htm#market

[5]http://tcp.ca/Aug94/Cornucopia.html

[6]http://www.next-generation.com/news/022096c.html

[7]*Screen Digest,* op. cit.

[8]Raskin, Robin, "Inside," *PC Magazine*, February 22, 1994: 4.

[9]Cary Lu, "CD Titles on the Wane: The market may have already peaked," Macworld Online, http://www.macworld.com/q/@345222nllsvp/pages/october.95/News.1410.html

[10]Raskin, op. cit.

[11]Nichols, op. cit., D17.

[12]TFPL Publishing, Washington, DC, 1994.

[13]Moore, Thomas, "Let Your Fingers Do the Walking (Keying) . . . All Phone Numbers in U.S. Now on CD-ROM," *PR News*, January 3, 1994.

[14]Howard Bryant, "Video Game Quandary: Nintendo, Sega or Sony, or a High-End, Powerful PC," San Jose Mercury News, Calif. Knight-Ridder/Tribune Business News, Dec. 3, 1996; http://www.digitalcity.com/jeffg/news/120895c.html

[15]The Software Publishers Association's fifth annual survey, Reported by Reuters New Media, April 22, 1996, http://members.gnn.com/jsnowden/thesource4/cusage.htm

[16]Experts forecast robust video game sales this holiday season; new study cites 16-bit games as strongest industry component Redmond, Wash.—(Business Wire)—Nov. 20, 1995, http://www.digitalcity.com/jeffg/news/gamenews6.html

[17]Markoff, John. "Toys Now, Computers Tomorrow," *New York Times*, April 20, 1994: D1, D6.

[18]Moran, Susan, "New Ways of Getting Wired," *WebWeek,* November 4, 1996: 1.

[19]Johnstone, B. "True Believers," *Far Eastern Economic Review*, 155 (51), December 24, 1993, 70–71.

[20]Greenfield, P. M. (1984). *Mind and Media: The Effects of Television, Video Games and Computers*. Harvard University Press, Massachusetts: 108.

[21]"Videogame and CD ROM Game Players Are the 'Technologically Elite,'" 1996 SIMBA Information Inc. Survey Shows, http://www.turbonet.com/GAMES/feature/zap1/survey/whats2.stm.

[22]http://www.gamefaqs.com/

[23]Economist, "Poached By Sonic the Hedgehog," February 20, 1993: 326.

[24]*Screen Digest*, op. cit., 106.

[25]*Time*, "The Best Products of 1993," January 3, 1994, 76.

[26]Keizer, Gregg, "Debbie Does Silicon Valley: In search of sophisticated electronic entertainment," *Omni*, February 1994, 24.

[27]Wark, op. cit.

[28]*Screen Digest,* 1994, op. cit.

[29]Ibid., 1.

[30]WebTV home page, http://www.webtv.net/HTML/home.about.html

[31]ICTV home page, www.ictv.com.

[32]*Screen Digest*, op. cit., 109.

[33]Ibid.

[34]*Screen Digest,* "The Consumer Multimedia Marketplace 2: Software," May, 1994.

[35]Ibid.

[36]Flynn, Laurie, "Thrills and Chills of Marketing a CD-ROM Adventure," *New York Times*, Nov. 27, 1994, F3.

[37]"A New Fee Structure to Share On-Line Data," *New York Times,* April 6, 1994, D1, D6.

[38]Braverman, Alan M. "The Roadmaps of the Internet," *CS First Boston Industry Report,* November 26, 1996, 11.

[39]Braverman, 1996, 11.

[40]Braverman, 1996, 13.

[41]Piirto, November, 1993, 6.

[42]Long, Kim, "The Year Ahead," *American Demographics,* December, 1993.

[43]www.worlds.net/alphaworld

[44]*New York Times*, "Test Set for Digital Movies," March 21, 1994, D2.

[45]Flaherty, op. cit.

[46]Shaw, Russell, "Pac Bell offering video, audio over phone lines," *Electronic Media*, November 22, 1993, 10.

[47]Flaherty, op. cit.

[48]*New York Times*, March 21, 1994, D2.

[49]Powell, Adam Clayton III, Technology Studies Seminar, The Freedom Forum Media Studies Center, April 6, 1994.

[50]Smith, Anthony. "New Communication Technology and Changing Political Boundaries," Technology Paper, The Freedom Forum Media Studies Center, 1993.

[51]Carey, John, "Back to the Future: How New Communication Technologies Enter American Homes," Technology Studies Seminar, The Freedom Forum Media Studies Center, Oct. 26, 1993.

[52]Braverman, "Roadmaps," 1996.

[53]Ibid.

[54]Mitchell, Susan, "Technophiles and Technophobes," *American Demographics*, February, 1994, 36.

[55]Braverman, Alan M. "The Roadmaps of the Internet," *CS First Boston Industry Report,* November 26, 1996, 11.

[56]Bushkin, Kathy, Interview, April 13, 1994.

[57]Dovaton, *Ad Age,* 1994.

[58]Dovaton, op. cit., 18.

[59]www.cpb.org.

[60]http://www.ntia.doc.gov/tiiap

[61]Maynard, Nancy Hicks, Speech, Technology Studies Seminar, The Freedom Forum Media Studies Center, April 5, 1994.

[62]http://www.commerce.net/

[63]Auletta, op. cit., 1992.

[64]Auletta, Ken, "Media Criticism," a seminar session at "The State of Media Studies," hosted by The Freedom Forum Media Studies Center, February 15, 1994.

[65]Carey, John, "Field Testing the Information Superhighway," April 5, 1994, Speech, The Freedom Forum Media Studies Center.

[66]Aho, Debra, "Ad Industry Looks for Interactive Dollars," *Advertising Age*, May 16, 1994.

9

The Legal and Regulatory Environment

"Those who would expect to reap the blessings of freedom, must undergo the fatigue of supporting it."
—*THOMAS PAINE*[1]

In a perfect world, the development of new media technologies might rest exclusively on the genius of technological wizards, the capital investment of corporate players, and the communication needs of a diverse public. Instead, a variety of institutional frameworks converge to control, regulate, and monitor the technological development process as well, sometimes enhancing the process of invention, discovery, and diffusion, and other times hindering it. One should note that no single institution or branch of government acts as an all-powerful body to control new media technologies in the United States. Rather, the office of the president, the Congress, the FCC, and other federal agencies, and the Courts all exert influence at the federal level, and a variety of state and local regulatory agencies, including the public utility commissions (PUCs) and state courts, set state and local regulations and laws over the development of new media technologies in the United States. Various international bodies set standards and policies affecting the development of new media technologies around the world, including the International Telecommunications Union (ITU), the World Intellectual Property Organization (WIPO), and others.

The following chapter examines the legal and regulatory framework that exists in the United States, especially at the federal level, and internationally to control and monitor new media technologies. The discussion begins with a look at how the policies, laws, and court rulings have set the stage for the development of the so-called information superhighway by establishing a climate of deregulation of and increased competition in the telecommunications industry. Included here is a special look at the nature and implications of the Telecommunications Act of 1996, the increasingly contentious debate over communications security and encryption of online communications, pitting the right to privacy and a secure online commercial environment against the government's mandate to battle crime in cyberspace. The second part of the discussion examines the status of freedom of expression and civil liberties in the new media environment, including intellectual property rights, piracy, censorship, and libel.

DEREGULATING COMMUNICATIONS: A DECADE SINCE THE MODIFIED FINAL JUDGMENT

Since Federal Judge Harold Greene handed down the Modified Final Judgment (MFA) in 1984 divesting AT&T from the Regional Bell Operating Companies (RBOCs), the regulatory barriers prohibiting telephone companies from entering the information business have been steadily coming down. More recent decisions have almost fully opened the doors for telco entry into the information business as content providers. Coupled with the convergence of telecommunications, computing, and media, these regulatory changes have opened the way for a "united state of media" described by media studies scholar Everette E. Dennis (1993).[2]

THE COURTS

As Judge Greene's decision suggests, it would be impossible to overstate the importance of the courts in shaping public policy in the arena of communications. From rulings on the First Amendment to intellectual property rights, the U.S. Supreme Court, Federal courts and even state courts have helped define the nature of public and private communication in an era of advanced information technology. The primary role of the courts in shaping public policy on communications technology has been as an important check against the administration and the Congress.

THE CLINTON ADMINISTRATION

The Clinton administration has made clear its intentions to support the removal of most of the remaining legal obstacles limiting the actions of all telecommunications companies. Vice President Al Gore says the administration will encourage removal, "over time, under appropriate conditions, of judicial and legislative restrictions on all types of telecommunications companies."[3] At the core of the Administration's vision are five principles:

- Encourage private investment
- Promote competition
- Create a flexible regulatory framework that can keep pace with rapid technological and market changes
- Provide open access to the network for all information providers
- Ensure universal access (for all end-users and content providers)[4]

To nurture the development of new technologies, the Administration must undertake a delicate balancing act. The government must set standards whereby all information can flow seamlessly and securely from one network to another, but these standards must be flexible to allow adaptation. The government needs to further deregulate the communications industries, encouraging greater competition among telephone, cable, and computer companies, as well as traditional media companies, yet must take care not to give any particular industry an unfair edge in the marketplace. To avoid the development of an information "underclass," the government must mandate a universal service goal, at least providing access to certain essential services, such as emergency information or information about government services. Should this access include information essential to the effective functioning of the democracy? Should it include information about controversial public services such as reproductive choice or abortion? The Administration needs to guarantee freedom of expression, privacy, and data security on the electronic frontier, but at the same time must balance those values against the need for law enforcement on the information superhighway, such as providing federal agencies an avenue to conduct online "wire taps" (even in a wireless arena).[5]

The Field of Dreams Model: If You Build It, They Will Come

Many business leaders agree that the federal government should not get involved in actually building the new information superhighway. Big corporate mergers, such as that of Bell Atlantic and Nynex, may spur the global communication revolution more than government programs, former Apple Computer chairman John Sculley has said.[6] Such megadeals are "the most definitive evidence yet that the digital communications revolution can and should be implemented by the private sector, not built and paid for by the U.S. government," Sculley told an industry conference on the National Information Infrastructure. Thus, one might conclude, à la the field of dreams metaphor, "If business builds it, commerce will come."

THE CONGRESS

With the passage of the Telecommunications Act of 1996, Congress instituted the first comprehensive legal and regulatory overhaul of the communications industry in the United States since the passage of the 1934 Communications Act. For most of the century, communications policy in the United States was guided by a simple premise of the 1934 Act: that broadcasters, telephone companies, and businesses in the communications industry, such as cable television operators, were to act in the public interest. This principle was based on the notion that the scarcity and public nature of the electromagnetic airwaves and public rights of way in which cable and telephone lines were laid mandated that those businesses using these limited public resources bore an obligation to serve the public in ways not driven solely by forces of the commercial marketplace.

By the mid-1990s it had become abundantly clear even to those in Washington that these basic premises had become obsolete. Technological advances, such as compression and advanced techniques for using the radio spectrum more efficiently, had made it impossible to argue effectively that the electromagnetic spectrum was a scarce resource that could accommodate only a handful of broadcasters. Similarly, the digitization of all forms of communication content (whether television signals, voice, or data) made the technical and regulatory distinctions between cable and telephone companies almost nonsensical, and little more than a political artifact of history. Further, the emergence of a global information infrastructure made it essential that certain regulatory restrictions on U.S. communication industries (on ownership, for example) be removed in order to enable those industries to compete in a global marketplace.

The Telecommunications Act of 1996

As a result, over a period of several years legislators crafted new legislation that ultimately emerged as the Telecommunications Act of 1996. Its primary goals are: "To promote competition and reduce regulation in order to secure lower prices and higher quality services for American telecommunications consumers and encourage the rapid deployment of new telecommunications technologies."[7] In addition, however, the Act also seeks to control the distribution of obscene or indecent and violent content by means of a telecommunications device. The section of the Act (Part V) dealing with obscene or indecent content has been extremely controversial and was overturned by the courts. Commonly known as the Communications Decency Act (CDA), it is discussed later in this chapter.

The Act seeks to foster increased competition through a variety of regulatory reforms, including:

- Lifting restrictions on telephone companies to allow them to begin providing cable service within their own service area, as well as permitting cable TV companies to provide telephone service

- Expanding station ownership limits for broadcasters by (a) removing the restrictions on the number of television stations any person or organization may own, operate, or control, or have a "cognizable" interest in, nationwide, and (b) raising to 35 percent the national audience reach limit for television stations
- Mandating interoperability and interconnectivity among all telecommunications services facilities and equipment, an especially important provision in an increasingly diverse communication environment that includes terrestrial broadcasters, direct broadcast satellite providers, mobile communication services, cable providers, and regional Bell telephone companies
- Requiring all telecommunications carriers to provide nondiscriminatory access to network services on an unbundled basis (i.e., ungrouped) at any technically feasible point based on rates, terms, and conditions that are just, reasonable, and nondiscriminatory

The Act extends its principles of open competition to the state and local level, specifying that "No state or local statute or regulation, or other state or local legal requirement, may prohibit or have the effect of prohibiting the ability of any entity to provide any interstate or intrastate telecommunications service" (sec. 253).

One important but sometimes overlooked element of the Act has been the establishment of the Telecommunications Development Fund. The Fund provides access to capital for small businesses in order to enhance their ability to compete in the telecommunications industry. It is also intended to stimulate new technology development and support universal service and promote delivery of telecommunications services to underserved rural and urban areas. Monies in the Fund are generated by the auction of electromagnetic spectrum concluded by the Federal Communications Commission in 1996 to establish the Personal Communications Services wireless industry in the United States. Having generated some $10 billion in the auction, the interest placed in an escrow account is substantial.

One issue not included in the Act is whether private utilities will be permitted to provide additional information services to their customers. The Public Utility Holding Company Act of 1935 restricts utilities from providing services outside the domain of their core business.[8] Utilities have appealed repeatedly to the Securities and Exchange Commission (SEC), which enforces the Act, but in most cases have been refused permission to offer services such as cable television.

The Evolution of Public Communications Policy

The Aspen Institute's Charles Firestone writes that the regulation of communication has evolved through three distinct policy stages.[9] Stage 1, he suggests, was based on notions of the regulation of scarcity in the broadcast spectrum. It was a paradigm of government-encouraged monopolies, such as AT&T. Regulators required broadcasters to act in the public interest, and tried to break any bottlenecks in the system. The high priests of this first stage were lawyers. This stage formally began with 1934 Communications Act, establishing, among other things, the Federal Communications Commission, but was based on 1890 legislation devised to regulate transportation via the railroad. An important principle derived from this nineteenth-century era was the concept of common carriage, which Title One of the 1934 Communications Act defines in terms of providing open nondiscriminatory access. This has meant that telephone companies must provide access at a fair price, as defined by federal government and state public utility commissions (PUCs).

Stage 2 regulations were based on principles of abundance that evolved with the growth of cable TV in the 1980s. Here there was a move to deregulate communication industries. The high priests of this stage were the economists, who based their decisions on efficiency.

Each regulatory stage thus far has emphasized different values. Stage 1 placed great emphasis on equal access, or equitable access to telecommunications services, as reflected in the fundamental notion of Universal Service. Stage 1 also emphasized the value of community or localism defined in terms of geographic considerations. Stage 2, in contrast, emphasized not only efficiency but also personal liberty including the First Amendment guarantee of freedom of speech, diversity, as reflected in ownership, and personal privacy. Common to both stages has been the notion of universal access, which today means providing service for all members of society, including urban poor and rural residents.

Today, society is entering a third regulatory stage, a new paradigm of communication regulation, based largely on the principle of increased competition, but also cognizant of other social implications of new media technologies. One important dimension is the decentralization of the communications infrastructure. Through the decentralized communications of the Internet and the World Wide Web, virtually every end-user can have a voice in the online public communications sphere.

The government's interests in deregulating new media environment are wide-ranging. The Clinton/Gore Administration sees the creation of a national information infrastructure (NII) as the cornerstone of the U.S. economy in a global marketplace dominated by information industries. The Administration also sees the NII as fundamental to achieving excellence in education and lifelong learning in America. "Today, we have a dream for a different kind of superhighway that can save lives, create jobs and give every American young and old, the chance for the best education available to anyone, anywhere," said Vice President Al Gore, speaking to communications industry leaders on January 11, 1994.[10]

At the same time, many in Congress are concerned about the social consequences of the information highway. Former House Telecommunications Subcommittee Chairman Ed Markey (D-Mass) believes that the role of the government should be to insure that the telecommunications marketplace of tomorrow is not monopoly dominated. "Our goal should be to construct a marketplace where every home has access to not one, but two wires and a myriad of wireless services, as well," he says.[11] True competition will be the foundation of this marketplace.[12] Moreover, he wants to guarantee that people in every social stratum and geographic region have full access to the tools and knowledge of the information age. It is essential, he argues, that we do not foster an "information apartheid" divided into the information haves and have nots.

The NREN

An important piece of legislation that helped set the stage for this new regulatory paradigm is the High-Performance Computing Act of 1991. Introduced by then-Senator and now-Vice President Al Gore, Jr., the Act established the National Research and Educational Network (NREN), a fiber-optic telecommunications network linking research sites at many American universities around the United States, which has served as an important part of the Internet backbone.

The Federal Communications Commission

Established under the 1934 Communications Act, the Federal Communications Commission (FCC) is an independent (in the sense that it is not controlled by any political party) government agency charged with regulating interstate and international communications by radio, television, wire, satellite, and cable. Under the 1934 Act, the FCC's mission was largely to insure that every broadcaster serve "in the public interest, convenience and necessity."[13] Its early responsibilities included licensing radio and television broadcasters for use of the electromagnetic radio spectrum. More recent legislation such as the 1992 Cable Act has directed the FCC to spend much of its time regulating pricing structures for cable television. It also spent much of the early 1990s allocating radio spectrum for new information services such as wireless and personal communication services and monitoring the activities of such over-the-air broadcast personalities as shock-jock Howard Stern, the outlandish radio disc jockey known for his frequently "obscene" comments on air.

The FCC is now charged with implementing the Telecommunications Act of 1996 and has formulated an extensive body of rulemaking on every aspect of the Act, from fostering competition to insuring universal service. Among the important rulemakings set forth to date is a recommended definition of universal service set forth by a Federal–State Joint Board convened in 1996 by the FCC. One of the hallmarks of the 1934 Act, universal service had been defined in terms of providing a universal access dial tone to all residences, urban or rural, at a reasonable and affordable cost. The new proposed definition of universal service extends this basic principle to a much broader domain of advanced telecommunications services. The FCC has also established a timetable for the introduction of digital television broadcasting, with some stations scheduled to begin transmitting digital TV signals as early as 1998.

Deconstructing the FCC

The FCC consists of a chairman and five commissioners, each of whom is appointed to a five-year term by the president, although the appointments are scheduled on an alternating basis so that a president elected to a single term cannot appoint an entire commission. Moreover, by law, no more than three commissioners may be of the same political party, and each appointment must be approved by Congress. The current chairman, Reed Hundt, was appointed by President Bill Clinton.

The staff of the FCC is organized into a variety of operating bureaus and offices, including these primary seven:

- The Common Carrier Bureau, which handles domestic wireline telephony
- The Mass Media Bureau, which regulates television and radio broadcasts
- The Wireless Bureau, which oversees wireless services including private radio, cellular telephone, personal communications service (PCS), and pagers
- The Cable Services Bureau, which regulates cable television
- The International Bureau, which regulates international and satellite communications
- The Compliance & Information Bureau, which investigates possible violations
- The Office of Engineering & Technology, which evaluates technologies and equipment

These and other offices of the FCC now exist as a "virtual commission," observes Robert Pepper, chief of the FCC Office of Policy and Plans.[14] All Commission reports, documents and other materials are now available online at

www.fcc.gov

The FCC may not be the most important communication policy-making body in the United States, but it does act as a lightning rod on communication issues, often drawing attention for its decisions, sometimes credited for gains made in industry, but more often attracting criticism. For example, following the 1994 failure of the proposed Bell Atlantic–TCI merger, the FCC was widely criticized by telecommunications and cable industry leaders and in the trade press for having caused the failure because of its decision to roll back cable TV rates by 17 percent in response to the 1992 Cable Act. Many subsequently admitted that the rate rollback may have had less to do with the failure than a clash of cultures between the two companies in traditionally distinct industries, or perhaps a clash in the personal styles or personalities of Raymond Smith and John Malone.

On occasion, FCC chairmen have been particularly visible in their vision or leadership of the commission. Perhaps the most notable example was John F. Kennedy's appointee, Newton Minow. Minow served from 1960–1964, and made history in his first major communication policy address, delivered at the 1961 meeting of the National Association of Broadcasters. In what has come to known as the "vast wasteland" speech, Minow sought to reinvigorate the *public interest* spirit of the broadcast industry. After all, he argued, the 1934 Communication Act specifies that broadcasters should act in the public interest or face the prospect of losing their television or radio station license to use the public airwaves. Broadcasters, however, were struck not by Minow's reference to the public interest, but by two other words: "vast wasteland." Minow had characterized the landscape of television programming as a "vast wasteland," suggesting that there was too little of redeeming social value to be found in the television fare of the day. Thirty years later in 1991, Minow delivered the reprise to his famous speech, and found that little had really changed.[15] One thing that did happen as a result of Minow's earlier speech was the chairman was immortalized in one of television's most enduring program's, the long-running situation comedy, *Gilligan's Island.* "The Minow," the ship that ran aground on a deserted island in the show, is named for the legendary FCC chairman.

The FCC's Role:
Choosing Winners or Promoting Technologies?

FCC Chairman Reed Hundt, appointed in late 1993, has promised to promote the economic development of new media technologies, while insuring equitable access, both to the end-user and to a diverse array of content and information service providers. This will prove to be a very difficult balancing act, especially as major transnational organizations lobby to insure a regulatory framework that supports their position and competitiveness in the international marketplace. Hundt has outlined three principles as central to the FCC's policy on the information superhighway:

- Providing universal service at a reasonable cost
- Insuring the presence of the broadband interactive network in every classroom
- Providing universal access to the digital technologies and services

Pioneer Preference Policy

One controversial FCC policy that exemplifies the notion of choosing winners is called the "pioneer preference policy." Instituted in 1991, this policy allows the FCC to award multimillion dollar licenses to companies of any size that have met criteria of originality and social value. On December 23, 1993, the FCC used this policy to award a license conservatively valued at $250 million to a tiny Colorado corporation to sell enhanced wireless voice, video, and data services to the 27 million people in metropolitan New York.[16] In awarding the highly valued license, the FCC cited the Omnipoint Corporation for its early development of handheld phones that operate in high frequencies set aside for personal communication services (PCS). The FCC also used its pioneer policy to award other multimillion dollar licenses for wireless communications to Cox Enterprises, for linking mobile phones to a cable television system in southern California, and American Personal Communications, for research on how PCS can share the radio spectrum with existing microwave users in the Washington–Baltimore area.

Many industry groups and even some independent observers have criticized the FCC policy, suggesting that it is unfair and reflects lobbying intensity rather than innovative technology. Pacific Telesis has challenged the fairness of the FCC policy, citing a rule that prohibits informal contact between interested parties and commission members of staff during licensing proceedings. In the two months preceding the awards, FCC commissioners and staff logged twenty-six contacts with representatives from the three license winners.[17] These contacts were not illegal, however, unless there was discussion of whether any these companies deserved pioneer preference. "We did everything by the book," says Douglas Smith, president of Omnipoint. An independent critic of the FCC pioneer preference policy is Henry Geller, a former general counsel to the commission who "crusaded for pioneer preferences."[18] Admitting he "made a mistake," Geller now says the "auctions make pioneer preferences unnecessary," since applicants demonstrate their convictions with their checkbooks.[19]

Sex, Lies, and the Telephone

As public policy experts debate the ethics of the latest advances in telephone technologies such as Caller-ID, here comes one they may not be ready for: the Truth Phone. Available for a cool $2,500 at Manhattan's Counter Spy Store, the Truth Phone "is the world's first telephone that can discern between truth and deception."[20] The phone analyzes the stress of lying, which theoretically shows up in microtremors in the voice, and, unknown to the speaker, displays the verdict on a digital display for the listener. Does the device really work? Probably not, say the experts. Regardless, "I'll be working late tonight, sweetheart," may be uttered a lot less often—or at least less confidently—in the future.

Other Federal NII Involvement

A variety of other federal agencies and departments have taken an active role in shaping the development of a national information infrastructure, placing economic and educational considerations in the forefront of their policy initiatives.[21] The Department of Commerce has taken perhaps the most active role in providing support and direct funding for telecommunications infrastructure planning and development. Other federal departments and agencies providing support or direct funding for research and development on the NII include the Department of Defense, the Department of Education, the Department of Energy, the Department of Housing and Urban Development, the Department of Interior, the Department of Labor, and the National Aeronautics and Space Administration. Under the Library Services and Construction Act (LSCA), the Department of Education's Office of Educational Research and Improvement (OERD) has provided $2 million in start-up money to let the state of Maryland offer through its libraries free public access to the Internet.[22] Using a system called "Sailor," Maryland citizens will have access to a full range of Internet services, including e-mail, file transfer, site-to-site connections known as telnet, and hundreds of special-interest electronic discourses called Usenet newsgroups. The free access is an important element in guaranteeing citizens universal access to the information superhighway. A commercial provider of full Internet services such as Digital Express Group, Inc. of Greenbelt, Maryland, for instance, charges $20 to set up the user, plus $250 in annual fees and $1 an hour to use the Internet for up to six hours a day. Of the major commercial services, America Online offers the most extensive range of Internet services, charging $19.95 a month for unlimited access.

STATE REGULATORS

The role of the states in shaping public policy on communication technology has also been important, sometimes at least as important as federal agencies and institutions. A number of governors, such as Wisconsin's Tommy Thompson, for example, have announced ambitious programs to put their states into the forefront of the information superhighway. Public utility commissions (PUCs) have also served a vital role in shaping public policy on communication technology. In many cases, these PUCs have provided much needed direction in developing industry initiatives to create a new information infrastructure, and at other times they have put the brakes on programs proceeding at a pace the commissioners felt was too fast. An interesting illustration comes from the Public Service Commission of New York. In May of 1994 the phone company in Rochester, New York, agreed to link with a phone system Time Warner Cable is creating from its cable TV operation in the city. Although staff of the New York Public Service Commission approved the agreement, the commissioners themselves must still rule. If they give their approval, the deal would make Time Warner Cable's phone service the first in the nation. The principle technical advantage of the arrangement is that cable TV lines have far more carrying capacity than the copper wires that typically deliver telephone services, and will make it possible to provide high-speed data communications to households. In the deal, Rochester Telephone would no longer charge consumers for Touch-Tone service and would freeze basic service rates through 2001, saving Rochester consumers an estimated $21 million. In return, the phone company would no longer be required by state regulations to provide rebates to customers if the company earns more than a preset rate of return.[23]

INTERNATIONAL REGULATORY BODIES

The globalization of telecommunications and media has made international regulation and regulatory bodies of increasing relevance and importance in the world of new media technologies. Outside the United States, most countries' telecommunications systems are controlled by Post Telegraph and Telephone (PTTs) agencies. There are also international bodies and agreements that regulate the development of transnational communications. There are, as well, important standard-setting bodies on an international level.

Two of the principal international regulatory bodies in the communications field are the International Telecommunications Union (ITU) and the World Intellectual Property Organization (WIPO). The ITU has responsibility for the international allocation of the radio spectrum and distribution of satellite slots, as well as overseeing basic telecommunications services between two or more countries. Its decisions are based primarily on the principles of first come/first served and universal service, although the latter is currently under debate. In its view, these information delivery technologies are best regulated because they constitute natural monopolies.

WIPO is responsible for protecting the intellectual property rights of authors whose works are being distributed internationally. Its fundamental position is that member states should grant the same protections to international copyright holders as they would to domestic authors. This position derives from the premise that creators of content have the right to control the distribution of that content.

Critical scholar Mark Alleyne, an assistant professor at Loyola University in Chicago, describes these agencies as the principle "regimes," or formal regulatory institutions, for controlling international communication. In contrast, nonregimes in international communication include primarily media organizations, including news, advertising, books and periodicals, films, and television and music producers. Unlike telecommunications, there is no international body that regulates the trade of these products. Likewise, there are no universally agreed-on norms or principles guiding international trade in this area.

It is worth noting that recent international trade agreements, including the European Union and the Mastriict Treaty, the GATT and NAFTA do not provide comprehensive regulations regarding the areas of telecommunications and intellectual property rights, as well as other communication issues. This is largely because of the complexity and transitional nature of the technologies involved, which mandates that these areas be dealt with in subsequent trade agreement decisions when the technology is more settled. Moreover, the international players involved stretch far beyond the local participants (e.g., Hollywood movie studios have sizable interests in Europe), thus making it difficult to reach a final agreement.

One distinguished telecommunications scholar has recently observed that the technological transformation of the world's telecommunications networks is pushing regulators away from the traditional monopoly model. Instead, governments are liberalizing their telecommunications policy and opening telecommunications industry to competition, explains Dr. Eli M. Noam, professor of Finance and Economics and Director, Columbia Institute of Tele-Information (CITI), Graduate School of Business, Columbia University.[24] Although it may be painful to those designing this industrial restructuring, Noam adds, the integration of new telecommunications technologies has mandated the transformation and privatization of telecommunications. Importantly, the liberalization of telecommunications policy does not signal the end of regulation. Rather, it is the beginning of a new era in which telecommunications policy will emphasize a reformulation of the notion of universal service and access, and the continuing transformation of telecommunications networks into integrated systems of global communications.

Diplomacy, Technology, and International Communication Regulation

One media mogul learned the hard way the complexity and delicacy of international laws and managing new technology in early 1994. Rupert Murdoch, who introduced in the early 1990s Western-style television to Asia with StarTV, declared that he would use satellite technology to help bring an end to the rule of the many "despots" of the region. In short order, the result was not the end of the dictatorial rule of leaders of countries such as China, Singapore, or Indonesia, but the heightened regulation of satellite television in the region.

Western Europe has operated under a very different regulatory model, one that often places social needs ahead of the marketplace bottom line. As a result, new media technologies have evolved differently in most Western European countries. For example, France implemented its Minitel videotext service buy using tax dollars to place a Minitel terminal in every French household. A market was instantly created, and services such as electronic telephone directories and online chat services flourished. Further, Minitel created some 350,000 jobs in just a decade.[25] In contrast, the tight regulation of the telecommunications industry in Western Europe (and most of the world outside the United States) has meant relatively slow growth in that sector of the economy. In the United States, the telecommunications industry, though regulated but to a lesser degree than in most of the world, has grown from about $75 billion in total revenues in 1974 to some $200 billion in 1996 and is estimated to surpass $300 billion by 2002.[26] Meanwhile, telecommunications revenues have grown much more slowly in Western Europe, rising from about $60 billion in 1974 to about $125 billion 1996, and estimated at $155 billion in 2002. As members of the European Union ponder deregulation of the telecommunications industry, European investors and new media entrepreneurs are pondering the possibilities for new media industry growth.

COMPUTER SECURITY AND THE CRYPTOGRAPHY CONTROVERSY

One of the most contentious issues in the world of new media technology is cryptography, now an important part of computer network security. Encryption is a form of communication and computing security that refers to the translation of data and communications into a secret code. To decode or read an encrypted file requires a key or password to decrypt the code.

As computer networks have become ubiquitous, and everything from banking to personal records is stored and transmitted electronically, the need for computer security has grown exponentially. Although a variety of strategies have been developed for providing computer security, such as computer passwords, encryption is the equivalent of a digital deadbolt. Encryption is essentially an information age version of the ancient secretly coded message, a field known as cryptography. From Julius Caesar to Adolph Hitler, governments have used encryption systems to encode secret messages. During World War II, cryptography was taken to new heights as the Germans used the Enigma machine to encode their messages, and the Allies sought to break the code. Enigma started as a commercial product, but the Nazis pulled it off the market when they recognized its military value for encrypting messages. Allied intelligence eventually broke the code and helped win the war. Today, modern encryption techniques render computer messages indecipherable by using complex mathematical algorithms. Messages are unlocked using a passwordlike "key." "It's the reversible transformation of a meaningful message to gibberish," says Michel E. Kabay, director of education for the National Computer Security Association.[27] In addition to the military and other branches of the government, the current domain of computer encryption users includes banking and big business, highly secure computer systems, software programming, and Internet power users.

The issue of cryptography did not arise in the United States' public arena until Congress passed the Computer Security Act of 1987, as a reaction to electronic criminal activity and database violation.[28] The Federal Government regards cryptography—especially the encryption of computer-based communications—as a threat to national security, because it can be used by terrorists and other criminals to conceal their plans and activities from law enforcement agencies.

Although computer users in the United States have access to publicly available encryption technologies and can use them for domestic computer communications, the growing international dimension of computer networks complicates the situation. Users of the Internet are at risk of violating Federal law if they use encryption technology, since the Internet transcends international boundaries, and it is illegal to export encryption technology. "Cryptographic products have been classified as munitions and controlled under the International Traffic in Arms Regulations," notes Stephen D. Crocker, area director for security with the Internet Engineering Task Force, which develops technical standards for the network, and vice president of Trusted Information Systems, a computer and network security company.[29] Ironically, the U.S. government has even classified the WebTV as munitions because it uses a relatively strong encryption technology known as 128-bit cryptography. The current limit on exportable encryption technology in the United States is 56-bit cryptography, half the encryption strength of a WebTV.

From Purloined Letter to Codes for Kids

While cyberpolitics is in the grip of the debate over the scrambling and decoding of electronic communications, Microsoft has created a software package to teach children the basics of cryptography. *Creative Writer* uses what is called a Caesar cipher, a form of cryptography originally used by Julius Caesar himself and later by lovers in the Victorian England to send secret messages published in newspapers. The technique involves substituting a letter in the text by one a few notches down the alphabet. To illustrate, the software translates "codes for kids" into "htijx ktw pnix." *Creative Writer* is little more than a digital version of "cereal box decoder rings" notes the *New York Times*.[30] Nevertheless, under U.S. export laws forbidding the exportation of encryption software, *Creative Writer* technically cannot be shipped abroad.

Not the Yankee Clipper

Although industry, academic, and other civilian computing groups generally favor an approach to encryption technology without a "back door" for government eavesdropping, the National Security Agency (NSA) is pushing for an approach that would allow the government to descrambling computer communications.[31] The first stage of the NSA effort was called the Clipper plan, a single government-created standard for computer encryption that would have made it easier for the government to crack electronic codes and eavesdrop whenever it suspected illegal activity to be underway. The system was based on an approach known as *escrow key encryption.* In this approach, the government would hold in escrow a special master electronic key that would allow it to unlock any encrypted message, provided it first receives court permission.

NSA, the Federal agency responsible for electronic surveillance of international communications, routinely listens to many of the world's telephone and computer conversations (federal and state courts authorized 919 wiretaps in 1993 and 1,154 wiretaps in 1994; about half the wiretaps were sought by federal agents, frequently in cases involving drug trafficking), is usually not concerned with civilian communications within U.S. borders, and is seen by many as overstepping its bounds.[32] The Clinton Administration supported the general key escrow proposal, while industry and privacy groups aligned to oppose the proposal. Many were concerned that it would have given the government too much power to violate individual rights. "The proposal angers industry executives who believe that the agency is rushing to establish a de facto standard that will undercut efforts to adopt a competing commercial standard without the built-in back door," reports the *New York Times.*[33] Moreover, strong encryption is seen as central to the emergence of a secure environment for online commerce.

The data encryption plan was a source of heated debate among the 500 persons attending the annual Computers, Freedom and Privacy conference held in Chicago, Illinois, in March 1994. "Cryptography is an enormously powerful tool that needs to be controlled, just as we control bombs and rockets," said one conference attendee, David A. Lytle, of the President's Office of Science and Technology Policy.[34] "When cryptography is outlawed, only outlaws will have cryptography," a heckler responded. Writer Steven Levy reports that the most passionate foes of Clipper were the Cypherpunks, a group of computer hackers, cryptographers, and computer networks users who have recently joined forces to do battle against the pro-Clipper government forces. Levy reports that Cypherpunks share the assumption that cryptography is a liberating tool, and as such should be protected. Opponents of the Clipper plan argued that privacy would be threatened if the plan went through and the chilling effect would be to destroy the free and open marketplace of ideas that has come to characterize the Internet.

Not everyone in government agreed that Clipper was the way to go to protect computer communications. Senator Pat Leahy (D-VT) is one. Leahy argued that the government should not be in the business of mandating particular technologies.

Conversely, there are people outside of government who supported the Clipper plan. Dorothy Denning, a cryptography expert who heads the computer science department at Georgetown University, was convinced that Clipper was needed to prevent crime on the Internet and elsewhere in cyberspace.

The Clipper plan used a circuit card inserted into a personal computer, and was based on a technology similar to the Clipper Chip, a telephone voice-scrambling device that allows law enforcement officials to eavesdrop. NSA officials called their device "Tessera," officially known as MYK-78, a device not much bigger than a tooth.[35] Congress charged the National Institute of Standards and Technology with developing a national standard for computer communications encryption, but needing additional technical expertise in developing a secret code for public use, the institute asked the National Security Agency for help in 1989. Together, they created the Clipper plan. In April of 1993 the Clinton Administration announced its support for the Clipper plan. Although use of the Clipper Chip was to be voluntary, computer and telecommunications executives and public policy groups almost universally voiced their opposition to the plan. A group of thirty-eight of the nation's leading computer scientists, computer-security specialists, and privacy experts sent a letter to President Clinton on Monday, January 24, 1994, urging him to stop the Clipper plan. The group is worried that federal agencies developed the plan in secret with no public review, and that they were concerned primarily with electronic surveillance, not privacy. Signing the letter were most of the civilian pioneers of modern cryptography, including Ronald Rivest of the Massachusetts Institute of Technology, Martin Hellman of Stanford University, Ralph C. Merkle of the Xerox Corporation, and Whitfield Diffie of Sun Microsystems. These civilian cryptographers were troubled by NSA's refusal to disclose the mathematical formula, or algorithm, the technical basis for the Clipper or Tessera scrambling technology. Some were concerned that the government might use economic pressure to enforce compliance with the Clipper plan. For example, the federal government could have required all companies intending to do business with the government to use the Clipper chip in their computer systems.[36]

Conversely, government officials felt that civilians should not have access to secret government codes. "Should a secret algorithm developed by the intelligence community be used for unclassified civilian uses?" asks Stephen Walker, a computer security industry executive and a member of the Government's Computer System Security and Privacy Advisory Board. "I think the answer is it should not."[37] NSA developed plans to purchase up to 70,000 of the Tessera chips for its use and for use by the Pentagon, but saw a vast array of civilian and government applications for secure computer communications, including the Internal Revenue Service, the Departments of Health and Human Services, Justice and State, and in the U.S. Congress. The Clipper plan "is a focal point for the distrust of government," admits Clinton Brooks, the NSA scientist who led the effort. Proponents saw the development of the Clipper plan as a natural extension of telephone wiretapping to the next generation of communication in the online world and a necessary part of law enforcement. With the potential for money-laundering activities, drug trade communications, and other illegal activities online, the case was compelling. Among those who argued that the Clipper Chip was needed is David Gelernter, associate professor of computer science at Yale, and author of *The Muse in the Machine*. Gelernter explained that wiretapping, which has long been an integral part of law enforcement, has been made considerably more difficult because of new technology.

> *In the age of high technology, the wiretap is a dead duck. In the old days, all conversations associated with a given phone number were funneled through one physical pathway, and by spying on that pathway you could hear it all. Nowadays, cellular phones and call forwarding make it much harder to find the right spot and to attach a tap. New techniques coming into use will make it harder still: when many conversations are squished together and sent barreling over a high-capacity glass fiber, it's hard for wiretappers to extract the one conversation they are after from the resulting mush.[38]*

Gelernter concluded that the Clinton Administration's Digital Telephone and Communications Privacy Improvement Act would save wiretapping by instituting the use of the Clipper Chip plan and merited the support of Congress. "If Congress fails to pass the telephone bill," Gelernter cautions, "there is every reason to believe that crime, particularly terrorist crime, will get worse." The dilemma Congress faces is whether to enable law enforcement to fight crime in cyberspace, or to preserve freedom and privacy on the electronic frontier. It's not an easy choice.

The Clipper plan died, however, when, in early 1994, an AT&T Bell Labs scientist identified a major technical flaw in the Clipper Chip design, bringing into doubt even the technical value of the proposed technology.[39]

Encryption Plan, Parts II and III

Subsequently, the Clinton Administration developed a second encryption plan that would have permitted Internet users to employ somewhat stronger cryptography. That proposal was met with equally strong opposition from a broad array of computer and industry leaders and was ultimately replaced by a third encryption proposal. The third proposal is designed to place controls on the export of strong encryption technology, but again has met with vehement opposition. The plan "is unworkable and risks trampling on privacy rights and harming American software firms," reports the *New York Times* on its editorial page.[40]

Public Key Cryptography

One alternative computer security system endorsed by many groups outside the government is called Public Key Cryptography, invented in 1976 by Stanford mathematician Whitfield Diffie, a computer scientist whose research began in the 1960s at the MIT Artificial Intelligence Laboratory.[41] By combining publicly available decoding algorithms (i.e., keys) with private digital signatures, Public Key Cryptography creates a simple, secure and as of today unbreakable system, one without an electronic "trap door" for government eavesdropping.[42] Writer Steven Levy notes that Diffie developed the notion of "split-key" cryptography in response to the inadequacies of the existing approaches to encryption developed by the NSA. Anticipating more than two decades ago the development of the personal computer, Diffie's cryptographic breakthrough puts control in the hands of every communicator. "The virtue of cryptography should be that you don't have to trust anybody not directly involved with your communication," Diffie explains.[43]

"Encryption may be the only reliable method for securing privacy in the inherently public domain of cyberspace," says John Perry Barlow, a cofounder and board member of the Electronic Frontier Foundation (EFF) (and a former member of the Grateful Dead). "I certainly trust it more than privacy protection laws. Relying on government to protect your privacy is like asking a Peeping Tom to install your window blinds."[44] Beyond the Constitution, the key privacy protection laws pertaining to cyberspace are the Electronic Communications Act and the Foreign Intelligence Surveillance Act, which, although they mandate privacy protection, are full of legal loopholes that allow the government to eavesdrop in case of emergencies and threats to national security.

Since 1983, computer scientists at MIT's Athena Project have been refining another computer network security system called the Kerberos authentication system. Kerberos works by avoiding "ever sending readable passwords across vulnerable networks."[45] To date, the developers of Project Athena have yet to see the Kerberos encryption protocols fail, despite the numerous hackers likely to be lurking on MIT's 10,000-computer network.

Breaking the Code:
114,381,625,757,888,867,669,235,779,976,146,612,010,2
18,296,721,242,362,562,561,842,935,706,935,245,733,89
7,830,597,123,563,958,705,058,989,075,147,599,290,026,
879,543,541

One of the most popular encryption technologies in use today on the nation's data networks was developed in 1977, and is known as RSA 129 after the initials of its creators, Dr. Ronald Rivest of the Massachusetts Institute of Technology, Dr. Adi Shamir of the Weizmann Institute of Science in Rehovoth, Israel, Dr. Leonard Adelman of the University of Southern California, and the number of digits in the code. The code is based on a system of very large numbers that are divisible only by two similarly large prime numbers, or numbers that are divisible by only themselves and one. The system works like an electronic lockbox with two mathematical keys. The first key is a large composite number, the product of two large prime numbers. Anyone may distribute this number publicly, and use that key to put a message in the lockbox. The box, however, cannot be opened again without the second key, the second factor in the composite number. Only the owner of the message knows both prime numbers, or factors, and thus controls security for the lockbox, or system.

Initially, the inventors proclaimed that the code, although not completely unbreakable, would take at least 40 quadrillion years to factor, or decode.[46] But advances in computing power, networking, and the global community of scientists reachable by the Internet have made the assault on RSA 129 an intellectual challenge of the highest order, similar to the relentless pursuit by mathematicians of Fermat's eighteenth mathematical theorem, apparently solved only last year by a little-known Princeton mathematician. As a result, the code is almost broken, declares a growing number of scientists.

PGP: Pretty Good Privacy

One source of great consternation to federal authorities anxious to tap the information highway has been the 1991 introduction of PGP (Pretty Good Privacy) for the Internet. Computer scientist Phil Zimmerman developed PGP as a hybrid cryptographic system that combines a public key (asymmetric) algorithm with a conventional private key (symmetric) algorithm to produce an encryption system that combines the speed of conventional cryptography with the advantages (i.e., easy use) of public key cryptography. Perhaps signalling a truce in the cryptography war, Assistant U.S. Attorney in Northern District of California, William Keane, discontinued his efforts to prosecute Zimmerman in connection with his posting to USENET in June 1991 of the encryption program "Pretty Good Privacy."[47]

Digital Signatures

Also vital to the process of computer network security is the area of digital signature technology. Digital signatures allow each user to provide a unique "electronic signature" to any file or document, verifying to the recipient that the document has not been tampered with or altered. This is vital to the development of computer-networked electronic commerce, ranging from ordering pay-per-view movies to electronic shopping, to democratic processes, such as online voting at electronic town meetings.

In May 1994, the Federal Government adopted another important standard for creating digital electronic signatures. Developed by the National Security Agency (NSA), the Digital Signature Standard, as it is called, works in tandem with the Clipper plan. Some contend that the government's adoption of the signature standard, which it intends to mandate, is a veiled attempt to force compliance with the optional Clipper plan. The adopted signature standard is also likely to be at odds with international electronic signature standards under development, which are largely compatible with the standard being developed by American private industry leader, RSA Security.[48]

Hackers, Cyberpunks, and Other Cybercrime

A growing number of crimes and illegal activity conducted in the venue of cyberspace reflect the relevance of government interest in controlling computer network communications. In San Francisco on April 5, 1994, the first arrest was made based on a crime committed on a consumer information service, when a man solicited for prostitution on America Online. In New York in 1996, a doctoral student at Columbia University was arrested for the alleged abduction of a woman he met via an Internet chat room.[49] 1996 also saw a series of electronic break-ins at various government Web sites, the most notorious case being the hacking of the CIA Web site. In this case, hackers changed the name of the CIA to the Central Stupidity Agency, among other things. Child abuse is another crime of growing concern in cyberspace. While many parents assume nothing more dangerous than digital target-shooting is going on as their child whiles away the hours on a computer, many children are being exposed to sexually explicit communications and content, if not outright child abuse. Oftentimes children who are technically adept at exploring the online world may find their way into a "chat room" for adults. For example, one writer reports that her thirteen-year-old son wandered into a cybernetic "singles bar" on America OnLine, where one conversant introduced herself as "Angel" and said she was a stripper.[50]

The Strange Case of Phiber Optik. Perhaps the most perplexing criminal case in cyberspace is that involving a young computer hacker code-named Phiber Optik. Phiber Optik is a twenty-one-year-old computer hacker recently convicted of computer intrusion and conspiracy for his role in electronically breaking into phone company computers and conspiring to commit other computer crimes. Phiber, whose birth name is Mark, admitted to breaking into the phone company computer network. He also insisted that he had never damaged or intended to damage any of the systems he broke into. As a result, Phiber had hoped for a relatively light sentence, one comparable to the probation received by Robert Morris, whose computer hacking nearly brought down the Internet. It wasn't to be. Justice Louis Stanton of the Southern District of New York handed Phiber a one-and-one-half year sentence in the federal penitentiary in Minorsville, Pennsylvania. "Hacking crimes," said Judge Stanton, "constitute a real threat to the expanding information highway."

Although those in the telecommunications industry and government have cheered the sentence, many in the information highway underground think Phiber has been unfairly made a symbol to discourage other would-be hackers from threatening the economic interests of the information age. Phiber has emerged as "the digital age's first full-fledged outlaw hero," proclaims one writer.[51] "Phiber Optik is going to prison this week and if you ask me and a whole lot of other people, that's just a goddamn shame," writes Julian Dibbell in New York's *Village Voice*.[52] Will the Clipper plan reduce the number of Phiber Optik renegades in cyberspace? Probably not, since such accomplished computer hackers will likely find a way around the technology anyway. Will it reduce the number of cases of online solicitation? Probably, although in one recent case, a man soliciting latchkey children masked the names of his victims by using publicly available encryption technology. Of course, the police were able to catch him by using traditional investigation techniques. Increasingly, computer hackers are using advanced techniques, such as "sniffer" programs that patrol the online byways electronically sniffing out user passwords, thus providing hackers easy access to otherwise secure computing environments. Government agencies have detected a growing number of electronic break-ins to hundreds of sensitive though not classified government and military documents stored on computer networks.[53] The compromised computer systems include those used for aircraft and ship design, ballistic weapons research, military payroll, and computer security research.

Some online activity has taken the form of pranks and borderline crime. One example was a message posted anonymously on the Internet in late 1994 in the guise of an Associated Press (AP) news release stating that the Microsoft Corporation had agreed to acquire the Roman Catholic Church. Microsoft and the AP both denied any connection to the hoax, but showing a greater sense of humor, John A. McCoy, a spokesman for the Roman Catholic Church, said, "We thought our prayers had finally been answered."[54] Such messages can be posted anonymously simply by routing them through any of some two dozen remailers, Internet's version of electronic postal boxes, which strip off all traces of the author's identity and forward them to other locations anywhere in the world.

RECONCEPTUALIZING PRIVACY

By restructuring the ways in which personal information is gathered, distributed, and controlled, new media technologies are mandating a complete reconceptualization of the very notion of privacy, contend the Aspen Institute's David Bollier and Charles M. Firestone.[55] Echoing this view is Professor Stefano Rodota of the University of Rome. He argues that privacy is no longer simply the classic formulation of Supreme Court Justice Louis D. Brandeis, which places the emphasis on maintaining the secrecy of private information, or "the right to be left alone—the most comprehensive of rights and the right most valued by civilized men."[56] Instead, new technologies require a new formulation of privacy based on "the right to maintain control over one's own data," Rodota adds. This view is fully articulated by Anne Welles Branscomb in *Who Owns Information?*[57]

Today's Privacy Threat: Government or Corporate Big Brother?

Invasions of privacy have often been thought of as the province of an overly intrusive and controlling government. In today's digital society, however, the biggest threat to personal privacy may come from the private sector, either from companies owning vast amounts of personal data about an individual, or from an employer who not only possesses such personal data, but may also conduct extensive, and *legal*, eavesdropping on employees. The U.S. Constitution does not specifically protect privacy. Courts have constructed legal concepts of privacy primarily as a safeguard against a prying government, not employers.[58] Federal protections are limited largely to civil rights laws barring discrimination and prohibiting employers from requiring employees to submit to lie detector tests. Although technologically enabled, much of the impetus for employer monitoring of employee communications comes from two sources: a desire to maximize work efficiency and minimize time spent on nonwork related tasks, and the soaring costs of sexual harassment suits. A junior college in California, for example, has agreed to pay three students $15,000 each to settle charges of sexual harassment stemming from anatomically explicit comments posted on a men-only computer conference.[59] Moreover, with more office romances flowering over e-mail, employers have reason to be concerned. Still, the ability to eavesdrop on unsuspecting employees may be not only a violation of basic human rights, but may soon be a federal crime. Congress is considering legislation to ban employers from monitoring employees' electronic and voice-mail and office telephone calls.

"Americans willingly have given up some privacy for convenience," observes former FCC chairman Al Sikes, now president of Hearst New Media and Technology. "Eventually they will rise up against certain intrusions on their privacy," he adds, "and there will be a bill introduced to solve a specific problem."[60]

Public Opinion and Privacy

Privacy is of increasing concern to the public. A national poll conducted by Louis Harris and Associates in the spring of 1995 shows that concern about threats to individual privacy has climbed to an all-time high in the United States.[61] The study was commissioned by *Privacy & American Business*, a publication of Equifax, Inc., the Atlanta-based credit-reporting company. African Americans and low-income persons are more concerned about threats to their privacy than the overall population, although this year's jump is largely a result of increased concerned in more affluent segments of the population. Four of five (80 percent) of those surveyed say they are concerned or very concerned about their own privacy. This is a significant rise in concern since 1977, when less than half (47 percent) expressed concern about their privacy. The increasing apprehension about privacy is caused by two major factors, according to detailed Harris/Westin privacy surveys conducted in 1978 and 1990: "(1) distrust of institutions and government process and (2) public fears about misuses of computer technology by organizations."[62] Just a quarter of those surveyed are concerned about the privacy threats posed by computerized record-keeping in President Clinton's proposed health reform plan. Most of the public erroneously believes that there are strong medical confidentiality laws on the books. In reality, just seven states have any medical confidentiality laws at all.[63]

The 1993 Harris survey also shows that consumers say privacy protection is very important in the corporate sector. In fact, the majority of those surveyed feel it is very important to the public that businesses have strong privacy policies. More than half (53 percent) feel that it is very important for long-distance telephone companies to have strong privacy policies, and another third (31 percent) say it is somewhat important. Few (14 percent) say it is not very important or not at all important for them to do so.

Other Indicators of Privacy Concern

Another indicator of the increasing concern about privacy is the increasing percentage of U.S. households with unlisted telephone numbers. The percentage of U.S. households with an unlisted phone number has increased from one in five (22 percent) in 1984 to nearly one in three (28 percent) in 1990.[64]

Privacy is also high on the agenda of Vice President Al Gore, Jr.'s initiative to promote a national information infrastructure. Pat Faley, the acting director of the Office of Consumer Affairs in the Department of Health and Human Services, heads a privacy group working within the Information Policy Committee on the NII Task Force. Faley has dealt with privacy issues since she served as head of consumer education at the Federal Trade Commission in the 1970s.

Traditionally, privacy has not been afforded high official status in public policy in the United States. One sign that this is beginning to change is the recent appointment of America's first so-called privacy Czar. Carol M. Doeppers, a records administrator at the University of Wisconsin-Madison Hospital was named in late 1993 the first privacy advocate ever appointed by a governmental body in the United States. The position was created in Wisconsin by a privacy law passed in 1991. The world's first privacy ombudsman was created in the 1970s in the German state of Hesse. Today nearly all European nations and Canada have privacy commissioners at the federal level.[65]

Windows on Privacy

In one of Alfred Hitchcock's cinematic suspense masterpieces, actor Jimmy Stewart watches the suspicious private activities of a neighbor through his apartment's rear window. A strangely similar story has unfolded in the computer software world of Microsoft "Word for Windows," a leading word processing package. "Word for Windows" has a design feature that allows a reader of a document to retrieve text that the writer deleted, or thought deleted. The recipient of a file sent via e-mail, disk, or shared on a network "may be able to read at least some of your original, raw remarks," reports Fred Langa, the editorial director of *Windows* magazine.[66] "For example, have you ever used Word to draft a contract, experimenting with various gambits? On its own, without your knowing it, Word may have saved some of your early, not-ready-for-prime-time drafts and deletions," Langa writes. Word for Windows automatically will save everything the writer has written if certain software settings are left in the default positions. Specifically, if the "Prompt for Summary Info" in the Tools menu is turned off, and the "Allow Fast Saves" feature is turned on, then Word for Windows will keep any earlier versions, despite saving over them. If you subsequently then view the file in a generic text program, such as the Notepad feature of Windows, some or all of the deleted material will appear. Although this may unnerve some unsuspecting users, it can serve as an electronic savior for anyone who has ever accidentally deleted or replaced a portion of a file and thought the material irretrievably lost.

Privacy in the Electronic Workplace

Privacy has also traditionally had little legal status in the workplace. The Federal Electronic Communications Privacy Act of 1986 protects the privacy of electronic messages delivered via public networks such as the Internet, and commercial services such as CompuServe and AOL, to which individual consumers and companies subscribe. However, the Act does not extend to a company's internal electronic mail or Intranet, an internal version of the Internet. In an unexpected twist, however, *The Los Angeles Times* recalled in December 1993 a foreign correspondent assigned to its Moscow bureau for browsing through the electronic mail of his colleagues.[67] Such disciplinary action of a high-ranking employee has been rare in corporate America, and signals a growing level of concern about privacy in the workplace.

Privacy in the International Arena

Privacy is on a slippery slope in the international arena, as is illustrated by the Internet. "It is in the transborder nature of Internet traffic where the notion of privacy becomes slippery," notes Leslie Regan Shade of McGill University.[68] "The legal impact of such international flows has yet to be tested," she writes, "and the repercussions could be mind-boggling in a decentralized environment that is hard to regulate and manage, and that is further complicated by differing and often conflicting national laws."

A number of countries have formalized privacy protections for the individuals in the information age. In 1984, German courts upheld the fundamental right of informational self-determination. The European Union has established through two directives "a high degree of protection" for personal data, whether government or business-controlled.[69] But many of the world's countries have few if no laws protecting individual privacy, especially in the context of digital communications.

A Texas-Sized Decision

One federal judge has ruled in favor of protecting the privacy in a case involving electronic mail. In March 1993, a Texas federal judge reprimanded the Secret Service for illegal search and seizure of electronic mail and data files. The civil case cost the agency more than $50,000 in damages and fines. In the case, Secret Service agents were investigating the theft of information from Bell South (one of the Regional Bell Operating Companies) computers. The trail led the agents to an employee of Steve Jackson Games, an Austin, Texas, games publisher that also runs a BBS for customers and writers. The Secret Service agents obtained a search warrant and seized the employee's computer hardware and some 300 floppy disks from the company's offices. The disks included e-mail massages not mentioned in the search warrant, as well various work products, in violation of the Privacy Protection Act, which protects publishers from seizure of works in progress.[70] Congress enacted the Electronic Communications Privacy Act (ECPA) in 1986, extending privacy and wiretap laws to electronic mail, computer-to-computer data transmissions, cellular telephone communications, and other new media technologies. In the Texas case, the agency kept the hardware and disks for several months, and the court determined "no valid reason" the agency could not have copied and returned the files in a much shorter period of time.

PROTECTING INTELLECTUAL PROPERTY RIGHTS

Ownership of information has long been an important issue central to notions of freedom of expression. For nearly 300 years, copyright has been enshrined in the legal system of the Western world, since the passage of the 1709 Copyright Act, the first modern copyright law in England. Copyright directly and indirectly affects not just the creators of content, but those who make derivative works based on the content created by others, as well as lawyers, students of the law, and many others. The emergence of electronic, computerized information has only added to the complexity of the issue of the ownership of information. By eliminating the distinctions traditionally used to define different types of intellectual property, the digitization of information is turning the entire system of copyright on its head. Moreover, computerized networks and databases have raised a variety of troubling ethical and legal issues over who owns everything, from an individual's name and address. Many of these issues were first explored systematically by pioneering legal scholar Anne Wells Branscomb during her inaugural senior fellowship at The Freedom Forum Media Studies Center in 1985 where she wrote an occasional paper titled, "Who Owns Information?" leading to the publication of her book of the same title a decade later. Branscomb argues that the ownership of information hinges largely on the price and cost of information.

Intellectual Property Rights:
Who Owns Electronic Information?

The acquisition and ownership of information has a price: a price to collect, a price to process, a price to distribute, and a price to store. Whether we consider information a resource, a commodity, or a basic right, there is a dollar value attached to it, and somebody or some institution has a proprietary interest in that monetary value. This is true whether we pay the price individually as consumers or collectively as citizens. Consider the following examples:

> *The federal census, first conducted by a handful of people in 1790, required the labor of 275,000 people in 1980 to conduct and $1.1 billion to process. The 1990 census cost an estimated $2.6 billion.*

> *The Library of Congress has a budget of $267 million a year to operate the largest collection of books in the world.*[71]

On the other side of the coin is the issue of individual rights, the right of the individual to control the use of her or his name, address, and other personal information. Branscomb asks, Who owns your name, address, and telephone number? "Do these belong to you, to the telephone company or to the many merchandisers who seek to sell you their wares?" The direct-mail advertising industry is a $20+ billion-a-year business predicated on the ability to determine your name and address and to send you a catalog. Most mailing lists, such as consumer addresses and club memberships, are sold for a modest price per name, and in aggregate, add up to very large profits for the companies that sell them. There now exist on CD-ROM databases that contain the names, addresses, and telephone numbers for the entire population of the United States and Canada, with the only exceptions being the growing number of persons with unlisted telephone numbers. Moreover, these databases are widely available at affordable prices. A copy is available even in such remote places as the Field Library of Peekskill, New York, a sleepy Hudson River town of about 19,000, and famous as the original home of Crayola Crayons and the birthplace of Mel Gibson and Pee Wee Herman (and birthplace of the author's second child, Orianna Magdalena in 1994). The database is extremely simple to use, as well. Simply type the name of the person you are looking for, and up pops the phone number and address. In the Field Library, all this is free to anyone holding a library card (also available free to area residents). More sophisticated versions of the software can massage the data allowing direct-marketing firms to target highly focused mailings. More frighteningly, burglars might use the data to target prospective victims, selecting well-to-do homes by zip code. The data might be merged with the U.S. Bureau of the Census "Tiger" mapping software to develop a nationwide grid including not just name and phone number, but typical household composition, average income and other data. One might even tie in income tax data for a more complete demographic portrait. Ownership of information in the age of the information highway is everyone's concern. Consider the words of Dick Snyder, former head of Simon and Schuster, who described his company in these terms in 1992: "We are no longer just a publisher of books; we are exploiters of copyrights in all media."[72]

Some scholars contend that the emergence of digital technologies requires a complete reinvention of the prevailing system of intellectual property rights. Educator Don E. Tomlinson predicts that the existing overall copyright scheme currently favored by Congress is destined to complete failure. "Only a technology-specific approach to the monumental problems brought about by the use of digital technology in mass communication will prevent an utter breakdown in the system of intellectual property."[73]

In agreement is Ethan Katsh, Professor of Legal Studies at the University of Massachusetts. He argues that the digitalization of communications has blurred the lines between media to the extent that traditional legal distinctions between different forms of work no longer apply. He writes:

> *Any work that can be represented in other media can now be represented in digital form. In this form it can be used in a computer or other*

data processing unit, whether to be displayed or heard, or to perform
some other function. Once in digital form, works protected by copy-
right are going to become less and less differentiated by type and more
and more equivalent to one another because they will now all be in the
same medium. This equivalence of works in digital form will make it
increasingly easy to create a difficult-to-classify work by combining
what have previously been thought of as separate categories of works.
(What is an interactive annual report for a company? A literary work? A
computer program? An audiovisual work?) Consequently, the elabo-
rate distinctions copyright law has made among different kinds of
work will lose much of the meaningfulness they had when media were
more differentiated.[74]

Digital Objects

Offering a possible solution to the dilemmas of copyright in the digital age is Robert
E. Kahn, one of the creators of the Internet and now president of the Corporation for
National Research Initiatives. Kahn argues that "It is possible to think of all traffic
on a network as consisting of a sequence of bits with no particular meaning. Similarly, if the bits can be processed to yield information, they may constitute intellectual property." Based on this conceptualization, Kahn has proposed the notion of a
digital object, which embodies the collection of such digital material in a network.
Copyright would be extended to the digital objects, independent of their particular
shape, form, or location.

Copyright and Fair Use in the Digital Age

Traditionally, copyright law has allowed authors and artists to build on the intellectual property of others, while providing protection for the work of the original author or creator. Central to this provision in the digital age is the concept of "fair use."
The Fair Use Doctrine has facilitated the use of privately owned material for publicly oriented activities, such as journalism and education. But determining whether
unauthorized use of a copyrighted work is allowed by the Fair Use Doctrine has
never been easy or simple. Four principles that have guided fair use decisions are:

- The nature and purpose of the use (i.e., not-for-profit or commercial use)
- The nature of the original copyrighted work (i.e., unauthorized use of limited
  editions are less likely to be ruled fair)
- The portion of the work in relation to the whole
- The impact of the use on the potential market for the original work[75]

Complicating this framework is the global information superhighway, which
greatly magnifies the potential for copying, eliminates geographic boundaries, and
expands the marketing potential for both the original and derivative works. Donna

Demac, a leading lawyer and scholar in the field of intellectual property rights and the new technologies, argues that there are three important areas in which fair use takes on special significance in the digital age:

- Interactive news
- Electronic books
- Musical sampling

These three areas are emerging rapidly as consumer applications with wide implications for journalism and education. Although it is too early to make a definitive ruling on the Fair Use Doctrine as applied to these areas, Demac has identified some of the key questions.[76] In the area of interactive news, how does the fair use provision of the federal Copyright Act apply to the downloading of digital video by journalists and the public at large? To what extent should journalistic institutions be held liable in a digital era in which information is easily altered or pirated? How do we insure people's right to privacy in an age of instantaneous global news distribution?

Regarding the electronic book, does fair use allow downloading entire books? Are libraries accountable for their patrons' use or misuse of digital collections? Should the current copyright law waivers for libraries be revised or eliminated? For musical sampling, does current copyright law adequately balance the rights of music owners and the "social benefits of new forms of music?"[77] Should any unauthorized musical sampling be considered fair use?

An important related question is how does copyright apply to areas of nontextual summarization of visual or audio material? On today's World Wide Web it is common for Web sites to download "thumb-nail" representations of larger images or videos, a technique analogous to short verbal descriptions of larger bodies of text. Is a low-resolution, reduced-size, thumb-nail image protected under fair use guidelines?

The Right to Link?

One important copyright case has emerged in Scotland. The case involves what in the parlance of the World Wide Web is called "the right to link." Many sites provide "clickable hyperlinks" to other sites. Typically, these links are done with the permission of those being linked to, and sometimes, though by no means always, involve payment of a fee. In 1996, the *Shetland News,* an electronic newspaper published exclusively on the Web since November 1995, linked without permission to the site of the *Shetland Times,* a newspaper founded in 1872, with a printed circulation of 11,000, as well as an online distribution via the Web.[78] Arguing that the undesired hyperlink represents a copyright infringement, the case is now before Scotland's supreme civil court, the Court of Sessions. The outcome of the case may have significant implications for the World Wide Web, where links have become a fundamental part of the online community.

Rewriting Copyright Law

As a consequence of the digitization of information, the U.S. Commerce Department has developed recommendations to rewrite existing copyright law in the United States. "Existing copyright law doesn't make it clear that it is a violation of the copyright owner's rights to distribute a protected work over the Internet," says Bruce A. Lehman, an Assistant Secretary of Commerce who is commissioner of patents and trademarks and chairman of the panel that developed the recommendations.[79] Lehman's recommendations would protect the intellectual property rights of creators of books, recordings, movies, and other forms of information in digital form, whether on compact disc or available online. The recommendations would also prohibit the use of technologies to pick the electronic locks copyright holders use to protect their works. A variety of industry groups have voiced concern about the increasing use of computers and computer networks to copy and distribute text, pictures, sound, and video in digital form. Record labels have objected to computer users who send unauthorized digital musical recordings over the Internet. In a major test case, the Frank Music Corporation has charged Compuserve in district court with enabling unauthorized recordings of the copyrighted song, "Unchained Melody." The class-action suit was filed in the United States District Court for the Southern District of New York on behalf of 140 music publishers. The outcome of the case may set the standard for copyright protection and digital recording distribution not only over the Internet but for all digital transmission systems, including cable TV. Conversely, concern about copyright infringement and an inability to secure copyright permission has caused a number of multimedia projects to stall, especially in the educational arena. Multimedia business ventures have suffered the consequences of copyright, as well. Warner New Media's offering, *Seven Days in August,* cost $1 million to produce, most of which reflects the cost of securing permission to use copyrighted material from a variety of media sources. Still, many in industry are opposed to lifting any copyright restrictions. Says Bernard R. Sorkin, senior counsel for Time Warner, "it is both unnecessary and undesirable to loosen copyright protections under any circumstances."[80]

Earlier generations of technology, including the photocopying machine and audio tape recorders, have presented challenges to existing copyright law, but none have posed the same threat as the digital age. Earlier technologies, although they may have sometimes made copying copyrighted material possible, they did not have the copying advantages of digital technologies, which make instantaneous mass copying of exact duplicates on an international scale a matter as simple as pressing the "enter" key.

New International Treaties

Established in 1967 by the United Nations, the World Intellectual Property Organization (WIPO) held a diplomatic conference in December 1996 involving representatives from nearly 160 countries to help resolve certain aspects of the international aspects of copyright in a digital, networked age. Emerging from the meeting are two treaties on Intellectual Property rights establishing certain guidelines for copyright in an online environment, including the protection of content distributed on the Internet. One important provision of the treaties is that they extend the provisions of the Berne Convention, confirming that computer programs are protected as literary works, thus extending the formal capability for creators of Web-based applications to protect their works by copyright. Also protected under the treaties are certain fair use guidelines, which permit an individual to make a limited number of copies for noncommercial purposes or to use small excerpts for news, art, or education. The treaties must still be ratified by the U.S. Congress and the legislative bodies of countries around the world.

Royalty Considerations: Land Grab on the Electronic Frontier

How to pay royalties to authors and copyright holders in the electronic publishing environment has been one of the most complex questions in the digital age. Should authors be paid every time someone else accesses something they have written? Should compensation be on the same basis as for printed publications?

One major publishing house has proposed an interesting solution. Random House has introduced a revised standard contract that will pay authors 5 percent of the amounts received from Random House's use of those rights, about half the royalty typically paid on trade paperback and hardcover books. Moreover, Random House would retain all electronic publishing rights from authors, including the rights for technologies not yet invented. The new contract has stirred much debate in the publishing industry. Alberto Vitale, Random House's chief executive officer, says the new contract will "protect the interests of both author and publisher." Robin Davis Miller, executive director of The Authors Guild, however, describes the plan as "a brazen attempted land grab on the electronic frontier."[81] The contract provides Random House with extensive control of electronic publications based on the author's work, including the ability to adapt, abridge, add sounds and images, and combine an author's work with other's works in electronic edition, all without the author's approval.

Xanadu: Ted Nelson's Vision of Hypermedia

Ted Nelson, the creator of the hypertext concept, which in many ways gave birth to today's World Wide Web, has recently embarked on a massive publishing project called Xanadu, the name of the fabled home of the publishing baron depicted in the cinema classic, *Citizen Kane*. As envisioned by Nelson, Xanadu would be a digital global publishing environment, in which all documents, whether text-only or multimedia, would reside in their original form in only one location. All access to those documents would be electronically encoded in the account of the individual accessing them. Any quotation would be recorded electronically, and a charge would be made against the user's account, with royalties being deposited in the account of the author of the original document. Notably, the Xanadu system would maintain a permanent link between any document cited in a new file and that new file. Any subsequent user who might cite a quotation in the new file would have an electronic link with the original document automatically inserted in his or her file, with a royalty payment automatically made to the original author. If all this sounds complicated, it is. Xanadu may not be a practical solution to the royalty issue in the digital age, but it does reflect the complexity of the problem.

Patents

A third component of the intellectual property rights digital minefield is the area of patents. Traditionally, copyright and royalties were the only areas of intellectual property rights that applied to publishing. Copyright provided writers or publishers of original content with protection of the original expression of an idea. The idea itself was not protected. Royalty protection provided writers with a legal mechanism to collect payment for the publication of their copyrighted work. Patents, however, provide protection of inventions and procedures, areas traditionally outside the scope of copyrightable material. The computer age and digital publishing have changed all that. Greg Aharonian of the Internet Patent News Service reports (November 12, 1996) that in the first six months of 1996, the U.S. Patent and Trademark Office (USPTO) issued 3,966 software patents, almost as many as it issued in all of 1994. He predicts that the USPTO will issue 8,100 software patents for all of 1996, almost as many as it issued in 1992, 1993, and 1994 combined. That means that in the 1993–1996 time period, the USPTO issued some 20,000 software patents. By the end of the decade, Aharonian estimates there will be more than 50,000 active software patents. One particularly interesting case emerged in 1993, when the USPTO awarded a patent for a computer program. Specifically, the USPTO awarded Patent No. 5,241,671 to Compton's New Media, granting ownership of hypertext search techniques, which are the foundation for electronic search machines now used as the industry standard for multimedia publishing. The implication of the patent award was that any publisher whose multimedia product used the patented hypertext search technique would have to pay royalties to Compton's. This patent potentially meant tens of millions of dollars, perhaps billions, in payments due to Compton's. Not surprisingly, many companies, including Microsoft, which uses the patented technique in its multimedia products, challenged the patent award. The USPTO reviewed the patent award, and on October 26, 1994, rescinded the patent. However, the door was left open to possibly awarding patents for other software applications.

Notably, the 1990s has seen a dramatic rise in the overall awarding of patents to universities, where, since 1980 there has been a steady decrease in research funding from the federal government. Universities, which have traditionally conducted much of the basic research not only for information technology but in general, were awarded fewer than 500 patents in 1980. By 1990 the number of patents awarded to universities had risen to more than 1,000, and by 1996 the number had reached some 2,000 (W. Wayt Gibbs, "The Price of Silence: Does profit-minded secrecy retard scientific progress," *Scientific American,* November 1996: 15–16). At Columbia University, one of the world's leading research universities, some $50 million a year in profits is generated annually from patents. One of the patents Columbia was awarded in the 1990s (along with several corporations from around the world) is for MPEG-2, the standard for compressed digital video. One of the consequences of this trend is that universities and academic researchers are under increasing pressure to strike a balance between conducting pure, basic research to advance the theory and public understanding of new media, and the commercialization and privatization of their research results.

Electronic Piracy

Piracy of software has grown to biblical proportions in the digital age, as electronic copying of commercial products has gotten easier and cheaper. According to one 1993 estimate, U.S. software providers would receive $65 billion in revenues if royalties could be collected on all intellectual property pirated throughout the world. The Business Software Alliance (BSA) more conservatively estimates that the U.S. software industry lost some $15 billion in revenue in 1996.[82] GATT, the General Agreement on Tariffs and Trades, approved in large part in December 1993 and signed into law a year later, contains a special provision for the collection of royalties on intellectual property. GATT requires all countries, including developing ones, to protect patents, copyrights, trade secrets, and trademarks. The greater problem will be the enforcement of the law. In many of the world's developing regions, pirated software is so ubiquitous and ingrained that it would require a complete cultural revolution to change the system. In China, digital pirates make illegal copies of musical compact discs (CDs), selling them for the rock-bottom price of $2 a CD.[83]

Of course, software piracy is not unheard of in information societies, including the United States. A study commissioned by the Video Software Dealers Association (VSDA) found that the entertainment industry is losing some $242.5 million in revenues annually because of free viewings of pay-per-view movies via illegal cable converter boxes.[84] The VSDA study, which is based on telephone surveys of 1,000 heavy video viewer households, suggests that some 10 percent of all 20.2 million PPV households have illegal descramblers. In the case of one popular PPV movie, *Lethal Weapon III,* nearly half (0.5 million) of all PPV households that saw the movie (1.2 million) did so illegally. Although critics from the National Cable Television Association (NCTA) and others have criticized the study as biased and methodologically flawed, resulting in an extreme overestimate of the amount of piracy, it is widely recognized that piracy of cable signals occurs at a significant level in the United States. Under the 1992 Cable Act, cable signal theft is a felony that carries a fine of up to $100,000. Wendell Bailey, engineer for Time Warner, says piracy of cable television signals is at one of its highest levels in the U.S. media capital, Manhattan. "People say the theft problem is 110 percent in Manhattan," he jokes, reflecting the view that in New York City, more people watch pirated cable than cable purchased legitimately.[85] Piracy of cable signals is easy in Manhattan's ubiquitous high-rise apartments where legitimate cable wiring enters the building and many apartment dwellers tap illegally into the line. About the only way to catch them is when a repair person happens to make a service call to the building.

Preventing cable signal piracy requires cable programmers to scramble their signals, which is accomplished primarily through one of two ways. First is negative or positive trapping, an approach that involves the use of a mechanical device installed by the cable system operator. Negative trapping removes signals or channels the viewer does not subscribe to, and is used with high penetration services, such as HBO. In this system, all the signals are delivered to the home, with only those not subscribed to being removed. Positive trapping is used for low penetration services, such as the Disney Channel, and involves scrambling the signal at the head-end where the cable system originates the signal, and then using a device at the subscriber's set to descramble the selected channel or signal. Positive trapping is labor-intensive and expensive, especially for pay-per-view events.

The second approach is interdiction. Interdiction is done electronically, and involves placing interference over the signal or channel not selected just before entering the viewer's home. This approach is little used, primarily because of its expense and the fact that it has been around for at least a decade and many signal descrambling devices have been developed to defeat it.

On December 12, 1993, a Federal grand jury indicted a San Jose, California, businesswoman in what is apparently the first case of piracy of software stored on CD-ROMs.[86] U.S. Customs Service agents seized 900 counterfeit CD-ROM discs imported from Hong Kong, along with 18,000 counterfeit user manuals. The pirated products included six multimedia titles produced by Software Toolworks, including a game designed by Lucasfilms Games. The government values the stolen software at more than $200,000.

Piracy Around the Globe

Intellectual property, consisting primarily of films, musical recordings, books, and computer software, has grown rapidly as an important U.S. export. In the 1990s, exports of U.S. intellectual property have grown by an annual rate of almost 10 percent, among the fastest of all U.S. exports. At the same time, piracy of intellectual property has also become increasingly significant, with software revenues lost to piracy totaling some $15 billion annually. Among the world's regions where piracy of intellectual property from U.S. copyright holders is at its worst are Europe ($6 billion annually, according to the BSA for 1994), Asia Pacific ($4.4 billion), U.S./Canada ($3.3 billion), and Latin America ($1.4 billion). Piracy is relatively small in the developing regions of the world, including Africa, the Middle East, and India (cumulative total of $393 million). Among the worst offenders are Germany, the United States, and Japan, which account for 43 percent of all software piracy.

The Office of the U.S. Trade Representative has identified fifteen laser and compact disc factories in China that produce counterfeit discs. These factories produce an estimated 50 million pirated discs each year. Shenfei Laser Disk Optical

Systems Company, Stanko and Mody report, is among the most brazen counterfeiters, having produced illegal copies of first-run blockbuster movies like *Jurassic Park* before it had been released on video in the United States. Also pirated in China are U.S. computer software products. Among the pirates are some government-controlled institutions, including the Reflective Metals Institute at Shenzhen University. The Institute recently produced 60,000 holograms for a Taiwanese counterfeiter, who put the holograms on fake Microsoft products. Microsoft estimates such counterfeit products cost it as much as $150 million in 1993.

The mechanism to combat this piracy abroad is Special 301, a section of U.S. trade law dealing with American intellectual property. Under the law, the trade office must publish annually a list of companies involved in intellectual property piracy. The provisions of the law also enable the office to initiate investigations and impose sanctions against offending nations. The punch of the law may be weakened in the future as negotiations proceed on the so-called Uruguay Round of discussions on a world trade treaty. Some trade lawyers are lobbying that the sanctions called for under the treaty do not apply to intellectual property.

Libel in Cyberspace

Online communications are challenging many long-held notions of First Amendment law and theory. Who is responsible when a message is sent electronically? The sender or the provider of the conduit? How do principles of privacy apply in cyberspace? Does the Freedom of Information Act guarantee access to electronic public records? The answers to these puzzling questions are only beginning to emerge. "There is very little case law, and we can't tell for sure what the courts will say," says Shari Steele, director of legal services for the Electronic Frontier Foundation, an organization devoted to the defense of civil liberties in cyberspace.[87] Others are concerned about the legal implications of the digital alteration of images and sound. "Libel and false light cases will increase dramatically as manipulation becomes commonplace," warns professor Don E. Tomlinson.[88]

Cyberspace, Libel, and the Courts

Recent court cases begin to shed light on the legal status of libel in cyberspace. In a New Jersey federal court, a small medical products company has filed a lawsuit against a user of a computer bulletin board service (BBS), charging him with libel. In the case, the Medphone Corporation charged Peter DeNigris with libel for allegedly posting messages on Prodigy's "Money Talk" BBS attacking the corporation for poor management and fraud.[89] The result of DeNigris's repeated accusations, the suit claims, caused the Medphone Corporation's stock to plunge 50 percent. In a $200 million electronic libel lawsuit filed with the New York State Supreme Court in November, 1994, Stratton Oakmont, Inc. of Long Island, New York, charged Prodigy Services Company with publishing a series of messages, also on the Money

Talk forum, accusing the brokerage firm of numerous violations of Securities and Exchange Commission rules. Together, these cases may help determine whether a commercial BBS is more like a telephone company or a newspaper. As a legal monopoly, a telephone company serves as a common carrier of communications and as such is not legally responsible for the content. A newspaper can be held legally responsible for its content because it edits and organizes that content. Prodigy may be seen as a bit of both, since users post their own messages, but Prodigy does prohibit certain kinds of messages it finds offensive, and will remove them from its bulletin boards.

Both Prodigy and Compuserve, another leading consumer online service, have argued in court that they should be treated as common carriers, and not be responsible for the content transmitted over their services. Yet, both services have also enforced their own content codes, censoring objectionable content. The New York Court recently ruled that Prodigy is legally responsible for the content of its bulletin boards (because it has tried to control the content in some instances), however the court will likely rehear the case. The prevailing climate in Washington, D.C. and across the fifty states today is inclined against granting full common carrier status to online information providers. The constitutional implications are equally significant, as potentially ever greater numbers seek legal protection behind the guarantees of the First Amendment, traditionally applied fully to print journalism, less vigorously to broadcast media, and even more weakly to commercial speech.

Libel and the Internet

In an unrelated case, a company marketing products on the Internet computer network recently filed a libel suit against a reporter who criticized the firm in an article distributed to other network users. It is the first time an Internet user has been sued for libel, says Bruce W. Sanford, a lawyer with the Washington firm of Baker and Hostetler. Sanford is representing Brock Meeks, whose article about Suarez Corp. Industries of North Canton, Ohio, triggered the suit filed in March 1994. Suarez's suit sought unspecified damages as well as an injunction prohibiting Meeks from writing about the company in the future.

Meeks, a former reporter for *Communications Daily* in Washington, writes stories on his own from his home in Spotsylvania County, Pennsylvania, publishing them via the Internet at the CyberWire Dispatch. In 1994, Meeks published a story questioning an offer made by Suarez for free Internet access. Meeks's article said he responded to Suarez's solicitation, but received nothing more than an offer for a $159 self-help book and software package. Steven L. Baden, Suarez's general counsel, says Meeks should have also received an application to subscribe to the Electronic Postal Service, which Suarez is marketing. The owner of the company, B. Suarez, has been investigated previously in the state of Washington for illegal direct-marketing activities.[90] Although Meeks and Suarez ultimately settled the case out of court, the case is likely to have a chilling effect on reporting from cyberspace.

Electronic Access to Public Records

When Congress enacted the Freedom of Information Act (FOIA) in 1974, few observers even considered whether the Act would apply to electronic computer records. In recent years, the question of whether the Act, which refers only to printed records, applies to electronic records has become of paramount concern. Today, not only are government printed records universally backed up electronically, but many are stored only in electronic form. "The new battleground is over purely electronic records that exist in no other form," writes Robert Ritter.[91] A federal judge's ruling in January 1993 stopped former president George Bush from destroying his administration's entire computer files, bringing to an end to a five-year legal battle begun by the National Security Agency (NSA). The records at issue include the NSA's electronic mail files about Iran–Contra, computer tapes that may include details of the Persian Gulf war and President Clinton's passport controversy. White House officials wanted to release paper copies of the files, but Federal Judge Charles Richey said no, demanding the complete information. Invoking memories of Watergate, Richey asked, "What did officials know and when did they know it?" Without the judge's decision, a computer technician could have destroyed the files with a few simple keystrokes. "This decision cements the idea that electronic records are still subject to FOIA," concludes Rebecca Daugherty of the Reporters Committee for Freedom of the Press FOI Service Center.[92]

The Congress . . . Shall Make No Law: Freedom of Electronic Expression

> *"Freedom of the press belongs*
> *to those who own one."*[93]
> —A. J. LIEBLING

Freedom of expression on the information highway is one of the great unsettled legal issues confronting communicators in the twenty-first century. Who will regulate the new media of the digital age? Will the new media be guaranteed full First Amendment rights? and How will the principle of common carriage apply to the information highway? are among the most critical questions.

The First Amendment to the Constitution of the United States declares, "Congress shall make no law . . . abridging freedom of speech, or of the press."[94] But the guarantees of free speech have been applied unevenly to media created since the passage of the First Amendment in 1790. Radio, and subsequently broadcast television, lost their full First Amendment rights some sixty years ago with the passage of the Communications Act of 1934, which established both the Federal Communications Commission (FCC) and required broadcasters to serve in the public interest. The FCC defends the constitutionality of its control over broadcasting largely on the basis of the notion of scarcity of the airwaves dating from the 1920s when broadcasters struggled for limited space on the broadcast spectrum. In the face of today's virtually unlimited channel capacity on the information highway, the notion of scarcity withers. Nevertheless, the FCC has shown little sign that it will weaken its hold over broadcasters and cable companies. Witness the reregulation of the cable television industry under the 1992 Cable Act, as well as the enforcement of "indecency" codes for cable operators, requiring them to group adult-oriented programming onto a single blocked channel, available only after written request from the subscriber.

The Communications Decency Act, which prohibits the transmission of indecent content on the Internet, struck down by a panel of federal judges in Philadelphia in 1996 and now on its way to a final hearing by the U.S. Supreme Court, will prove pivotal in determining the future of freedom of expression on the information superhighway.

Will it matter who controls the information highway—the telephone companies, cable operators, broadcasters, or newspapers? "The kind of wire doesn't matter," says Linda Garcia of the Office of Technology Assessment (OTA) of the U.S. Congress. "What matters is whether we're talking about basic voice services or enhanced information services." Because the telephone companies have operated under the rules of common carriage, they have not been responsible for content. A very old legal notion, common carriage requires certain service providers, especially those granted monopoly status by the government, such as telephone companies, to provide service to anyone requesting it, without imposing unreasonable constraints, such as excessive pricing. "With many companies merging, some subject to common carrier rules and others subject to the rules that apply to print publishers, I don't think anybody can predict how this is going to sort itself out," says OTA's Garcia.[95]

Censorship in Cyberspace

*"Censorship reflects a society's
lack of confidence in itself."
—POTTER STEWART*[96]

Some argue that the principle of common carriage is central to any notion of freedom of expression on the information highway. "Without this assurance, people communicating unpopular ideas over the new digital infrastructure may have their path blocked by a 'censorious' decision of the network carrier," says Daniel Weitzner of the Electronic Frontier Foundation, a group devoted to promoting freedom of expression in the information age.[97]

While some look to the Clinton/Gore administration to build freedom of expression guarantees into their vision of the national information infrastructure, others go even further. Harvard Law School's Lawrence Tribe, a noted First Amendment theorist, has called for a constitutional amendment to extend full First Amendment guarantees to all media, digital or otherwise.

Controlling Sex and Violence in New Media

Violence and sex have long permeated American culture, and they have always found a home in American media, from movies to books, from Hollywood to Times Square. Thus, it is no surprise that they are prevalent in the content of new media forms, from cable TV's "blue" channels, to multimedia CD-ROMs, to interactive, online services.

Society and industry's response to sexual and violent content has tended to follow a consistent pattern. As a new medium develops and its popularity grows, along with its sexual and violent content, more attention and public scrutiny begin to focus on the controversial and potentially harmful effects of the undesirable content, especially on young consumers of that content and potentially unstable adults, especially males. As this controversy has grown, both in the press and the public, increasing scholarly attention has been devoted to the effects of the sexual and violent content, and subsequently, Congressional attention has slowly turned to the matter. Concurrently, industry leaders and concerned public citizens have mobilized to institute some form of control over the undesirable content. Industry leaders have joined to encourage self-censorship, while many in the public have called for governmental censorship, although some have questioned the constitutionality of such action, in light of the First Amendment. Finally, industry has acted to institute a form of labeling as a warning to consumers, especially parents, as to the violent and sexual content contained in particular media products, thus circumventing the need for formal Congressional action.

This pattern has held for several media, including movies, comic books, and musical recordings. In the 1920s, many American movies were filled with violence and sex, although comparatively tame by today's standards. Scholarly attention came in the form of the Payne Fund Studies, which examined the effects of movies on children. Subsequently, the movie industry established a ratings council, which today warns parents about the sexual or violent content of movies in the form of G, PG-13, R, and NC ratings. Similarly, violence and sex were especially rampant in the comic books of the 1950s, which led to both Congressional hearings and scholarly study of "The Great Comic Book Scare," eventually leading to the establishment of the Comics Code Authority (CCA), sort of the equivalent to the Good Housekeeping Seal of Approval for comic books. As rock and other forms of music heated up in the 1960s and 1970s, an increasing segment of the public began calling for a halt to the production of violent and sexual popular music content. Some recordings have been confiscated in communities where the objectionable content has been deemed in violation of local obscenity laws, and sellers and artists have been arrested. In response, the recording industry began putting labels on releases that are particularly strong in terms of violence and sex, such as some heavy metal and rap music.

The pattern is in its early stages for the new products of multimedia CD-ROMs and somewhat further along for interactive online communications. As they grow in popularity and sex and violence become increasingly visible as a part of the new media environment, a growing chorus of critics have called for action. While many are members of the general public, some even come from industries whose products have come under similar criticism in the past. One such critic of new media content is Richard D. Heffner, chairman of the American film industry's rating system. Heffner believes the violence and sexuality of the emerging new media makes movie violence and sex pale in comparison. "The stunningly successful emergence of a revolutionary 'interactive entertainment' industry, with its videogames and promise of 'virtual reality,' today brings violence and sexuality into homes with a lifelike intensity that had never been imagined."[98] Heffner has witnessed the growing cry against this content, and worries that too many of the critics "now naively turn to the movie rating system I head as a model of how to stem what may too likely become a plea for government censorship."[99] Heffner believes that a ratings approach is impractical for technologies that bring sex and violence directly into the home through an increasing abundance of channels and media. Heffner's alternative is borrowed from former first lady Nancy Reagan's battle cry against drugs, to "just say 'no.'" He hopes that new media producers and consumers will boycott sexual and violent content. This, too, seems hopelessly naive. New media producers reaping large and growing profits from sexually explicit and violent games and other content are not likely to stop selling their wares. Likewise, consumers, many of whom are young adults raised in a climate of electronic freedom of choice, are unlikely to give up what they are already used to. Some retailers, such as Wal-Mart (the largest distributor of popular music on CD-ROMs) and K-Mart, however, now require that certain recordings and their corresponding packaging be edited to remove certain "objectionable" content, such as profanity or sexually explicit images. The move has prompted much attention, including criticism from recording artists opposed to such industry censorship, and support from conservative religious groups, among others.

Moreover, the videogame and cable industries have already begun instituting ratings systems to reassure members of the public and Congress. Videogames now come with the following ratings: early childhood, suitable for ages three and up; kids to adult, for ages six and up and may include some violence or crude language; teen, suitable for ages thirteen and up, and may include violence, profanity, and mild sexual themes; mature, suitable for ages seventeen and up, with more intense violence, profanity, and sexual themes; and adults only, which may include graphic depictions of sex and violence.

It is likely that the producers of online and CD-ROM products will follow the same course. The one exception may be freelance content producers who are able to distribute their materials over the Internet. This area of content production is a wildcard and is highly unpredictable. It may be the arena of new media content production most likely to produce truly creative products and to test the limits of acceptability and conventionality. It may also be the proving ground for censorship and the First Amendment in cyberspace. As legal scholar John Lofton wrote more than a decade ago, the guardians of the First Amendment have historically been the small, fringe publishers like *The Progressive* in Madison, Wisconsin, not the mainstream behemoths, whose corporate interests rest on profits and public approval.

The Communications Decency Act

An important part of the Telecommunications Act deals with sexual and violent content delivered via telecommunications services. Known as the Communications Decency Act, or the CDA, this portion of the Act has been particularly controversial. Among other things, the CDA imposes criminal penalties for anyone using the Internet (or any other telecommunications device) to knowingly transmit any content, including text, images, or other communications, "which is obscene, lewd, lascivious, filthy, or indecent, with intent to annoy, abuse, threaten, or harass another person," or does so knowing that "the recipient of the communication is under 18 years of age, regardless of whether the maker of such communication placed the call or initiated the communication."[100]

As soon as President Clinton signed the bill into law on February 8, 1996, the CDA was immediately challenged in federal court by an unusual alliance of industry and civil rights groups, ranging from *Wired Magazine* and Microsoft to the American Civil Liberties Union (ACLU). A three-member panel of federal judges struck down the CDA later that year, and in 1997 the U.S. Supreme Court ruled the CDA case unconstitutional. Its decision will have profound effects on the future of the communications landscape and the ultimate shape of freedom of expression on the Internet.

Blue-Ribbon Campaign

The enactment of the CDA on February 8, 1996, witnessed the simultaneous launch of a grassroots online movement opposed to any government censorship of the Internet. Dubbed the Blue-Ribbon Campaign, thousands of sympathetic Webmasters posted blue-ribbon graphics on their pages to show their opposition to the CDA and support for free speech on the Internet.

Censorship of new media content has been at least as much a part of the private, corporate sector as governmental action. In June of 1994, America OnLine shut down several feminist discussion forums over concern that young girls who would see the word *girl* in the forum's headline might enter into the discussion and find it inappropriate.[101] Supervisors on Prodigy have expanded their use of so-called "George Carlin software," which locates messages containing objectionable words and warns those who sent them to delete them or face censorship.[102] The University of Florida revoked a student's access to the Internet after the student repeatedly posted electronic copies of a political polemic. In addition to the prohibitions of material by commercial online services such as Prodigy and Compuserve, the Interface Group recently banned X-rated CD-ROMs at its Comdex computer industry trade shows. The ban, the company says, is in response to complaints from major exhibitors, including Microsoft.[103] An alternative proposal is called PICS, or Platform for Internet Content Selection. PICS is a voluntary standard, and therefore more popular among Internet mavens.

A variety of commercially available software filters, such as SurfWatch, Cyber Patrol and Net Nanny, which allow adults to screen content on their home PCs, and most of the commercial online providers offer built-in parental software controls for screening adult-oriented Web sites.

Digital Sex: Warning Label Required?

Should digital sex come with a warning label? Some argue it should be banned completely. Many feminists, scholars, government officials, and others have challenged the burgeoning industry on the basis that its content may contribute to the objectification of women and even to violence against women. "What's wonderful about interactive media is also what's reprehensible about this kind of application: the idea of handing control over to the user," says Linda Jacobson, editor of *CyberArts*.[104] "Smut on paper or video is much more benign than interactive stroke books. These products show men that they can have control over women. You can force them to do your bidding and they do it willingly."

Moreover, although the CDA was ruled unconstitutional, electronic erotica may soon be challenged on the grounds that it may violate laws against obscenity. Since the Comstock Act of 1873 outlawed the delivery of obscene materials through the mail, erotic materials have been treated as an exception to the First Amendment. The U.S. Supreme Court first considered the matter of obscenity in Roth v. United States in 1957. In ruling against Roth, the Court opined, "A thing is obscene if, considered as a whole, its predominant appeal is to prurient interest, i.e., a shameful or morbid interest in nudity, sex, or excretion."[105] In 1973, the Court instituted a new test of obscenity in Miller v. California. The Court ruled that a work must exhibit "serious literary, artistic, political or scientific value" (sometimes called the SLAPS test) to prove that it is not obscene. Miller also introduced the notion that erotic material should be judged in terms of "community standards." Justice Brennan provided a furious dissent: "Any test that turns on what is offensive to the community's standards is too loose, too capricious, too destructive of freedom of expression to be squared with the First Amendment." The notion of community standards also raises complex issues when considering interstate and international distribution, which is increasingly common on the information highway.

Circumventing Censorship

Online communications are also a vehicle for circumventing the censorship efforts of the world's governments. On the Internet, the Digital Freedom Net (DFN) is a forum for publishing material outlawed in authors' home countries. Formed in May of 1994, the New Jersey-based DFN has published excerpts from the works of Chinese dissident Wei Jingsheng, Indonesian novelist Pramoedya Ananta Toer, and Iranian Esmail Fassih.[106] Similar examples of online efforts to circumvent dictators have emerged via the creation of sites on the World Wide Web from Bosnia and Indonesia. In Bosnia, Radio B92 has found a global voice on the Press Now site in the Netherlands.[107] Included at the site are daily news reports from Radio B92, providing updates on the situation in Bosnia, as well as interactive services, such as B92 Support Page.

A New Regulatory Paradigm

New technology has provided the impetus for a new regulatory paradigm of the telecommunications and media sectors in both the United States and around the world. Although many suggest we are in an era of deregulation, others quickly respond that the new regulatory paradigm is simply one that puts more emphasis on competition and privatization, while building protections for privacy and universal access.

In the United States, the Clinton Administration has taken an active role in promoting the development of a new information infrastructure, emphasizing its potential benefits for both the commercial and public sector, especially to make America more competitive internationally and to build an improved environment for education and lifelong learning. The Congress has created a new legislative framework that treats telecommunications and cable TV providers in much the same fashion, in the hopes of stimulating competition in all sectors. The FCC continues to play an important policy role, and will determine much of the future of a variety of new technologies, such as wireless and personal communication services, as well as existing industries like cable TV, through its interpretation of the 1992 Cable Act and other Congressional action. Finally, the courts will serve as an important check against the actions of Congress and the administration, reinterpreting the constitutionality of new media law and the antitrust implications of a new era of corporate collaboration. In addition to the federal policy makers, however, states and local regulators will shape communication policy and the development of new media technologies by providing incentives to business to develop those new services in their local areas.

NOTES

[1]Paine, Thomas.
[2]Dennis, op. cit., 1993.
[3]McAvoy, Kim, "Congressional proposals at a glance," *Broadcasting & Cable,* January 3, 1994: 51.
[4]Gore, Al, "Forging a new Athenian Age of democracy," *Intermedia*, April–May 1994, volume 22, no. 2: 4–7.
[5]Carey, John "From Internet to Infobahn," *Business Week*, Special 1994 Bonus Issue: 32, 33.
[6]Dalton, Laura. *Executive News Summary*, Oct. 21, 1993: 1.
[7]Telecommunications Act of 1996 at http://thomas.loc.gov/cgi-bin/query/z?c104:s.652.enr
[8]Salpukas, op. cit.
[9]Firestone, op. cit., 1994.
[10]Brown et al., op. cit., 1994.

[11]McAvoy, Kim, "Markey's goal: Two wires in every house," *Broadcasting & Cable*, November 15, 1993: 26.

[12]AT&T, 1993, op. cit.

[13]Communications Act of 1934, U.S. Government.

[14]Robert Pepper, "The Legal and Regulatory Context for New Media," The Center for New Media seminar series, "Exploring New Media," Columbia University, October 24, 1996.

[15]Minow, Newton, "Vast Wasteland Revisited," The Freedom Forum Media Studies Center, 1991.

[16]Passell, Peter, "F.C.C. 'Pioneer' Policy Under Attack," *New York Times*, January 31, 1994.

[17]Ibid.

[18]Passell, Peter, "F.C.C. 'Pioneer' Policy Under Attack," *New York Times*, January 31, 1994: D1.

[19]Ibid.: D7.

[20]*New York Times*, "The Sad-Truth Phone," Sunday Magazine, January 23, 1994.

[21]Brown et al., 1994.

[22]Powledge, Tabitha M. "Information Highway without Tollbooths," *The Washington Post*, June 23, 1994: 1.

[23]Thalhimer, op. cit., May 24, 1994.

[24]Noam, Eli M., "Beyond liberalization: From the network of networks to the system of systems," *Telecommunications Policy* 1994 18 (4) 286–294.

[25]Edmondson, Gail, "Brave Old World," *Business Week*, Special 1994 Bonus Issue: 42–3.

[26]Ibid.: 43.

[27]Galvin, Christopher J. "The Digital Deadbolt," *CompuServe Magazine*, November 1993.

[28]Lipkin, Richard, "Making the Calls in a New Era of Communication," *Insight*, July 12, 1993.

[29]Wilson, David L. "Threats to Internet Security." *The Chronicle of Higher Education*, March 30, 1994: A26.

[30]*New York Times* , "HTIJX KTW PNIX," Sunday Magazine, January 23, 1994.

[31]Markoff, John. "U.S. Code Agency Is Jostling for Civilian Turf," *New York Times*, January 24, 1994: D1, D5.

[32]Levy, op. cit., 1994.

[33]Markoff, op.cit., Jan., 24, 1994: D5.

[34]Lewis, Peter H. "Collisions in Cyberspace on Data Encryption Plan," *New York Times*, March 26, 1994: 45.

[35]Levy, ibid., 1994.

[36]Carey, John, "Reality Check," *Business Week*, April 4, 1994: 6.

[37]Markoff, op. cit., Jan., 24, 1994: D5.

[38]Gelernter, David, "Wiretaps for a Wireless Age," *New York Times*, April 8, 1994: E7.

[39]Markoff, John, "Gore Shifts Stance on Chip Code," *New York Times*, July 21, 1994: D1.

[40]"Another Faulty Encryption Policy," *New York Times,* December 16, 1996.

[41]Levy, op. cit., 1994.

[42]Larkin, op. cit., 1993.

[43]Levy, op. cit., 1994: 51.

[44]Larkin, op. cit., 1993: 12.

[45]Schiller, Jeffrey, "Secure Distributed Computing," *Scientific American*, November, 1994: 72–76.

[46]Kolata, Gina, "The Assault on 12. . . ." *New York Times*, March 22, 1994: C1, C10.

[47]www.pgp.com

[48]Markoff, John, "U.S. Adopts a Disputed Coding Standard," *New York Times*, May 23, 1994.

[49]Swarns, Rachel L. "Arrest at Columbia Show Risks in On-Line Dating," *New York Times,* December 6, 1996.

[50]Barringer, Felicity, "In Cyberspace, and Talking to Strangers," *New York Times*, June 30, 1994: D4.

[51](Dibbell, Julian, "Strange Loops: The Prisoner: Phiber Optik Goes Directly to Jail." *Village Voice*, January 11, 1994: 44.

[52]Ibid.

[53]Lewis, Peter H. "Computer Snoopers Imperil Pentagon Files, Experts Say," *New York Times*, July 21, 1994: A1, B10.

[54]Lewis, Peter H. "And the Spoof Begat a News Release, and Another," *New York Times*, Dec. 31, 1994.

[55]Bollier, David and Charles M. Firestone, "The Promise and Peril of Emerging Information Technologies." A Report on the Second Annual Roundtable on Information Technology. Aspen Institute Communications and Society Program, 1993.

[56]Ibid.

[57]Branscomb, Anne Wells (1994). *Who Owns Information? From Privacy to Public Access.* New York: BasicBooks.

[58]Kilborn, Peter T., "The Boss Only Wants What's Best for You," *New York Times*, May 8, 1994.

[59]Lewin, Tamar, "Dispute Over Computer Messages: Free Speech of Sex Harassment," *New York Times,* September 22, 1994: A1.

[60]Sikes, Alfred, "Riding the Information Highway," speech, Center for Communication, Sept. 30, 1993.

[61]Louis Harris and Associates web site.

[62]*Privacy & American Business: A Comprehensive Report and Information Service*, September/October 1993: 3.

[63]Smith, October, 1993: 3.

[64]Carey, op. cit., Oct. 26, 1993.

[65]*Privacy Journal,* November 1993.

[66]Langa, Fred, *Windows Magazine*, 1994.

[67]Sims, Calvin, "Reporter Disciplined for Reading His Coworkers' Electronic Mail." *New York Times*, December 12, 1993.

[68]Shade, op. cit., 1994: 65.

[69]Ibid.: 3.

[70] Ritter, Robert, "E-mail laws changing: Judicial and legislative notice of the new ways we communicate," *Quill*, October, 1993: 24–25.

[71]Branscomb, op. cit.

[72]Demac, Donna, "Copyright and the New Electronic Media," midterm report, The Freedom Forum Media Studies Center, Dec. 29, 1993.

[73]Tomlinson, Don E., op. cit., 1993.

[74]Katsh, Ethan, "Law in a Digital World: Computer Networks and Cyberspace." *Villanova Law Review*. Volume 38, Number 2, 1993: 417.

[75]Demac, Donna, "Copyright and the New Electronic Media," midterm report, The Freedom Forum Media Studies Center, Dec. 29, 1993.

[76]Ibid.

[77]Ibid.: 6.

[78]Michael Cunningham, "High jinks for Shetland links," *The Irish Times,* November 11, 1996: 18.

[79]Riordan, Teresa, "Writing Copyright Law For an Information Age," *New York Times*, July 7, 1994: D4.

[80]DeLoughry, Thomas J. "Copyright Issues Said to Stall Many Multimedia Projects," *The Chronicle of Higher Education*, June 29, 1994: A18.

[81]The Authors Guild, Inc. Press Release, April 11, 1994.

[82]www.bsa.org

[83]Powell, op. cit., April 5, 1994.

[84]Umstead, R. Thomas, "Stealing Cable," *Cablevision*, December 6, 1993.

[85]Bailey, Wendell, "Conversation on Ethics in Telecommunications," Donald McGannon Center, Fordham University, Oct., 1993.

[86]Federal Jury Indicts Woman in a CD-ROM Piracy Case," *New York Times*, December 12, 1993.

[87]Ritter, op. cit., October, 1993: 24–25.

[88]Tomlinson, op. cit., 1993.

[89]Ritter, op. cit., October, 1993: 24–25.

[90]Thalhimer, Mark A. *Media Industry News Roundup*, compiled from the AP, May 3, 1994.

[91]Ritter 1993: 24.

[92]Ibid.: 25.

[93]A. J. Liebling.

[94]First Amendment to the U.S. Constitution, 1790.

[95]Stefanac, op. cit., 1993: 46.

[96]Stefanac, op. cit., 1993: 46.

[97]Stefanac, op. cit., 1993: 46.

[98]Heffner, Richard D. "The In-Your-Face Videos Bring the Censor Nearer," *The International Herald Tribune*, Tuesday, May 3, 1994: 7.

[99]Ibid.

[100]Section 502 of the Telecommunications Act of 1996.

[101]Lewis, Peter H. "Censors Become a Force on Cyberspace Frontier," *New York Times*, June 29, 1994: A1, D5.

[102]Ibid.

[103]"Porn File Not Found," *Newsweek,* June 27, 1994: 59.

[104]Stefanac, op. cit., 1993: 46.

[105]Roth v. United States, 1957.

[106]Kantrowitz, Barbara, "Dissent on the Hard Drive," *Newsweek*, June 27, 1994.

[107]PressNow web site, www.dds.nl/~pressnow/

10

Social and
Cultural Consequences

*"We believe that we live in the 'age of
information,' that there has been an
information 'explosion,' an information
'revolution.' While in a certain narrow sense
this is the case, in many important ways just
the opposite is true. We also live at a moment
of deep ignorance, when vital knowledge
that humans have always possessed about
who we are and where we live seems
beyond our reach. An Unenlightenment.
An age of missing information."*
—BILL MCKIBBEN[1]

"It was the best of times. It was the worst of times."
—CHARLES DICKENS[2]

Understanding the consequences of new media technologies is at once both the most important and most difficult of tasks. It is the most important because the consequences of technological change is what makes technology matter. It is the most difficult because many of the technologies are still looming on the technological horizon, and have not yet taken their final shape or form. Even for a technology more than half a century old such as television, it is extremely difficult to determine its social consequences, despite thousands of studies by as many researchers all around the world. Even on specific topics such as television violence, few specifics are known with great certainty about audience effects.

Thus, this chapter sets out with an important caveat in its exploration of the social and cultural consequences of the new media frontier. The consequences outlined here are largely speculative, and are dependent on a variety of critical conditions and assumptions being met. Foremost, although current trends and past lessons will serve as guideposts for identifying potential consequences, the complexity and uncontrollable nature of the new media environment combine to make predicting the social and cultural impact of emerging technologies highly unreliable. This is especially true in the long-term, although it is the long-term that truly matters for society. Perhaps even more importantly, some of the most significant consequences are likely to be unexpected and unintended, and observable only with the benefit of historical perspective. Guiding the discussion in this chapter is a conceptual framework based on four major elements:

- Enduring topics and issues of major public and scholarly concern about the social consequences of new media technologies. These focus especially on the simultaneous forces of social fragmentation and cohesion, as well as the development of an electronic public space where virtual communities flourish. Also included here is an examination of the impact of new technologies on social institutions ranging from government and democracy to education and libraries, medicine and religion, with an emphasis on access to technology at the core of these effects. Finally, this discussion reviews the sociological implications of new technology and the nature and consequences of computer-mediated communication
- Cultural consequences of emerging new media technology, such as the implications of new technology for the coverage of war, the videogame as a cultural force and the intersection of new media technology and art
- Theoretical perspectives on the social and cultural impact of new media technologies, including the uses and gratifications perspective, systems theory, critical perspectives, and perhaps an emerging paradigm based on the convergence of interactivity, online communications, and multimedia
- International and intercultural perspectives on the social consequences of new media technologies, especially the implications for national development, intercultural communication and public diplomacy

SOCIAL CONSEQUENCES OF NEW MEDIA TECHNOLOGY: ENDURING ISSUES

So with a hundred "modern improvements"; there is an illusion about them; there is not always a positive advance. The devil goes on exacting compound interest to the last for his early share and numerous suc-ceeding investments in them. Our inventions are wont to be pretty toys, which distract our attention from serious things. They are but im-proved means to an unimproved end.[3]

New technology's social and cultural consequences have long been a subject of study and debate.[4,5,6] Advocates of technological change have often argued that new technologies can lead to improvements in social institutions, citing examples from education to medicine. In religion, for example, the development of Ecunet, the Ecumenical Network, has provided a global electronic gathering place for religious leaders from a variety of faiths and religions. It is estimated that some 10,000 members regularly log on to Ecunet to participate in online conversations and meetings. Similarly, the advent of tele-medicine has enabled major medical centers such as Minnesota's Mayo Clinic to connect with rural hospitals and clinics throughout the United States, bringing advanced medical technology and expertise to patients and physicians in remote locations. Some have argued that information technology is one of the greatest tools for fostering freedom and democracy, citing examples from Moscow to Bosnia to Beijing.[7]

Critics of new technology contend that technological change frequently brings with it a variety of social and cultural evils, including the loss of human employment, environmental damage, and increased control over information. Among the most outspoken critics of new technology was Jacques Ellul, the late French Protestant theologian and professor of history and law. Ellul argued in his classic, *The Technological Society*, written in the 1950s and published in the United States in 1964, that modern society valued technical efficiency as an end in itself, regardless of the social, political, or environmental costs.[8,9]

Those opposed to technological change sometimes have been called Luddites, from the mid-1800s movement in England led by the fictional character Ned Ludd, invented by a group opposed to the introduction of new technology in the textile industry because it would replace human labor. More recently, the negative human consequences of new technology have often been explored in venues of popular culture, never more eloquently than in Rod Serling's television series, *The Twilight Zone*. Serling often explored the human consequences of new technology as a dramatic theme in the Emmy award-winning series. One episode showcased the effects of computerized automation in the workplace, as more and more workers found themselves being replaced by a computer and out of work. Even the plant manager, who first brought in the computer, ultimately was replaced by a robot.

Canadian communication scholars Harold Innis and his most famous pupil, Marshall McLuhan, studied the consequences of the technology of communication on the society in which it exists. Innis and McLuhan argued that there is a direct correlation between the longevity of a society's communication medium and the speed of social change. Innis proposed that the long-lasting social structure of ancient Egypt was directly linked to the Egyptian's use of stone tablets as a medium of communication.[10] When the Egyptians began to write on papyrus, a much less permanent and much more portable communication medium, their society began to undergo much more rapid social change. McLuhan echoed Innis's observations, summing up this hypothesis of technological determinism in the now-famous phrase, "The medium is the message."[11] The printing press, telegraphy, and the Internet have led to a global society dominated by instant communications and rapid social change.

Many agree that the development of these new information technologies is profoundly altering our social, political, and economic fabric. Among them is business guru and author John Naisbitt, who writes that the information society is more than an intellectual abstraction.[12] It is an economic reality with important implications for society. He suggests several important consequences of the information society:

- New communication and computer technology bring about a faster flow of information
- New information technologies give rise to new activities, processes, and products
- Social and political change proceeds at an ever more rapid pace, as real-time multimedia communications on a global scale become ever more common

Many leaders of the world's so-called information societies agree with this assessment of the advanced digital information infrastructure that has emerged in the past decade. Among them are the members of the Club of Rome, a collection of leaders from business, industry, education, and government. "Microelectronics, through miniaturization, automation, computerization and robotization," they write, "will fundamentally transform our lives and impinge on most of its facets: at work, at home, in politics, in science, at war and at peace."[13]

Social Consequences of New Media: A Case Study

Hypothesizing about the social effects of new media is tantalizing, fun, and dangerous—dangerous because the forecast, like those of all new technologies, is sure to be wrong. Lessons from the past are sometimes helpful, although they are by no means a reliable barometer. The earliest adopters of the VCR (video cassette recorder) were businesses. The next adopters tended to be technophiles (people who love technology and crave anything new) and users of pornography. Finally, the VCR came down in price and diffused to a general consumer market. New media are likely to follow a similar path, with early consumer adopters being those interested enough to pay the high price tag and to use a technology that may not yet work perfectly—the technophiles and users of pornography (sexual gratification has especially high potential for truly interactive new media applications on the Internet— they could allow people separated by oceans to come together for cybersex). If the technology catches on, then it will be adopted by a wider general audience.

WebTV has the potential to be even more addictive than conventional TV. This could turn even more people into couch potatoes. Society could experience the electronic nightmare scenario envisioned by William Gibson and others in which everyone lives in a digital, interactive world populated by cyberpunks wreaking havoc. Conversely, truly interactive WebTV could open up a variety of new social uses linking people around the world into what Marshall McLuhan called the "global village." That could make us all "village people."

Social Fragmentation, Digital Isolation, and the Multi-Channel Environment

Scholarly study of the social consequences of new media technology has frequently centered on the question of the potential fragmentation of society. Until the widespread development of cable television and the advent of a multichannel viewing environment, most television programming and viewership was dominated by three networks—ABC, CBS, and NBC. Through these three networks, American viewers tended to have regular common or shared viewing experiences, whether via *The CBS Evening News with Walter Cronkite*, from 1962 to 1981, *Bonanza*, NBC's Sunday night offering, aired from 1959 to 1973, or ABC's *The Addams Family*, which ran from 1964-1966.[14] Certain major events could capture virtually the entire viewing audience, even the whole country, such as the assassination of President John F. Kennedy on November 22, 1963, which was captured on 8mm film by amateur photographer Abraham Zapruder and aired on all three networks. Scholars have studied this event widely in the context of a shared viewing experience.

Today, the deployment of millions of miles of optical fiber, the convergence of computers, television, and telecommunications and the emergence of a 500-channel, interactive video environment are producing an entirely new media landscape in which shared viewing experiences may become little more than a fond memory. As a result, many are concerned that technological developments may erode one of the most important positive social functions television has served during its brief half-century existence: the nurturing of a common culture.

Conversely, others present compelling evidence that the new media landscape still presents opportunities for common mediated experiences, while at the same time offering a much richer, diverse range of programming alternatives for a variety of audiences often poorly served by network television in the past, such as women, minorities, and gays. Consider, for example, the Perot–Gore debate about NAFTA (North American Free Trade Agreement) broadcast via cable television on CNN's *Larry King Live* on Tuesday night, November 9, 1993. Promoted through a variety of media, this debate drew the largest rating ever, an 11.9, for any regularly scheduled program in the history of cable television.[15] This represents approximately 11,209,800 homes, with each rating point representing 942,000 homes. The rating was even higher, at 18.1, in homes that receive CNN. CNN is available in 62 million of the 94 million U.S. households that have television. The 11.9 rating does not include additional viewers who may have seen the debate on any broadcast stations who carried the debate live. CNN let broadcast stations carry the debate if they subscribe to the CNN news service. Moreover, more than two million viewers tried to phone in to the call-in program, said Steve Heyworth, CNN's director of public relations. The previous cable TV ratings high was also set by *Larry King Live* during the 1991 Persian Gulf war, which captured an 11.5 rating. These data demonstrate that it is still possible for a highly fragmented media system to provide a shared viewing experience.

Keep Going, O. J.

Or, consider a more recent and infamous example of the media providing a common shared viewing experience. In June, 1994, former football and movie star O. J. Simpson was charged with the double murder of his ex-wife, Nicole Brown Simpson, and her male companion. After agreeing to surrender to the police, Simpson briefly became a fugitive, eluding police for several hours. The manhunt reached a national crescendo in the late afternoon of Friday, June 17, when Simpson and a friend, former football player Al Cowlings, led a police entourage across the highways of Los Angeles for more than an hour on a spectacular low-speed auto chase to Simpson's Brentwood estate. Anyone watching television that afternoon will likely never forget the scene, as live images of the vehicle carrying Simpson, Cowling's white Ford Bronco, led the squad of police cars to Brentwood. Shot from helicopter, the chase was carried not only on CNN and the major networks of CBS, NBC, ABC, and Fox, but all of their Los Angeles affiliates, independent stations in Los Angeles, Spanish-language networks, Telemundo and Univision, and even on ESPN, the Capital Cities/ABC-owned sports channel. The spectacle drew a near record audience of some 95 American million viewers, rivaling the 118 American million viewers who tuned in during the early moments of the war in the Persian Gulf. Attention to the case continued after Simpson's arrest, as well, with one in four U.S. homes tuning in to the opening day of Simpson's court hearing. "That would be supplemented, of course, by a significant out-of-home audience, since it ran in the lunch hour for most of the country," says David Poltrack, CBS's top audience researcher.[16]

Although many shared viewing experiences may help build national consensus or cohesion, or create a common frame of reference on matters of public importance, others may have a negative effect, at least according to many critics of television content, especially TV violence. One such critic is U.S. Attorney General Janet Reno, who testified before the U.S. Congress in 1993 that viewing television violence is a principal cause of real-life violence. Her argument is supported by a growing body of scholarly evidence that viewing TV and other mediated violence is related to real-life aggression. Unfortunately, Reno's criticism was largely directed at network television, which is arguably the most responsible in limiting violent content during hours when child viewers are likely to be present. Ironically, the two most notorious cases linking media and real-world violence the year of Reno's testimony had nothing to do with network television. *Beavis and Butt-Head,* which was linked to a case of a five-year-old who set a fire in his home in which his two-year-old sister died, airs on cable TV's MTV. Similarly, several teenage boys were killed while imitating a scene depicted in *The Program,* a film produced by Buena Vista Films, a subsidiary of Walt Disney Productions, and in no way connected to network television.

Consonance in the New Media Environment

The issue of social fragmentation is complicated by the nature of the media system, at least in North America. Here, despite the growing number of television and other media channels, there is still a high level of consonance in media content. Recall the 1994 case of Olympic figure skaters Tonya Harding and Nancy Kerrigan. Kerrigan, who was clubbed on the knee after a skating practice a few weeks before the winter Olympics were to begin, and Harding, whose former husband admitted to helping to plan the assault, were covered widely in virtually every American medium, from network news to tabloid television to the pages of daily newspapers, the airwaves of talk radio, and even on electronic bulletin boards. Thus, whether individual consumers tuned to one channel or another, they could hardly help but come in contact with the Kerrigan–Harding saga. On the other hand, the particular slant or spin may have varied widely from one medium or program to another.

Similarly, although many point to the so-called 500-channel TV environment, others are quick to acknowledge that although the average channel environment rose from a half dozen in the 1960s to several dozen in the 1980s, most people still watch only six or seven channels on a regular basis. Veteran television producer Adam Clayton Powell III, however, notes that there are many different sets of six or seven channels. Of course, even in a 500-channel viewing environment, relatively few of those channels will be devoted to basic cable programming. Most will likely be premium services and pay-per-view alternatives. In this sense, the multichannel environment really will be more akin to putting today's video store online. In fact, the notion of a 500-channel TV environment is misleading. It originated in a 1993 press conference with TCI's John Malone, in which a reporter pressed him to say how many channels would be possible on the information superhighway. Somewhat exasperated by the reporter's persistence, Malone said that with 10:1 compression and an average of 50 channels now on the typical cable system, the information superhighway might bring 500 channels to the average home. The number stuck.

Digital Isolation

Some are concerned about the effects of an apparently growing national obsession with new communication technology. "Soon, blessed with fax, voice- and e-mail, computer hookups and TVs with hundreds of channels, we won't have to leave our lonely rooms—not to write a check, work, visit, shop, exercise or make love. We will have raced at incredible speeds to reach our final destination—nothing," writes Bill Henderson, director of the Lead Pencil Club, a subsidiary of the Pushcart Press publishing house.[17] Henderson is not the first to have voiced this concern about the isolating effects of new technology. As long ago as 1849 Henry David Thoreau wrote,

We are in a great haste to construct a magnetic telegraph from Maine to Texas, but Maine and Texas, it may be, have nothing important to communicate. . . . We are eager to tunnel under the Atlantic and bring the Old World some weeks nearer to the New, but perchance the first news that will leak through into the broad, flapping American ear will be that the Princess Adelaide has the whooping cough.[18]

Today, it is just as likely that the hottest news traveling the trans-Atlantic information superhighway will be the latest sex scandal among the British Aristocracy or on Capitol Hill.

Globalization and Cultural Homogenization

Others are rightly concerned that the globalization of media through satellite-delivered television and online communications presents the distinct possibility of an increasingly homogeneous single global culture. Rupert Murdoch, founder of the global NewsCorp and StarTV, summed this up eloquently at the 1994 Communicator of the Year Award luncheon hosted by the Center for Communication in New York. "Thanks to CNN," Murdoch said in jest of the global television news service created by the year's award recipient, "happy peasants in North Korea get to see happy peasants in Cuba, thanks to happy peasants in Atlanta."[19] CNN, which broadcasts from Atlanta, has a nonunion staff paid considerably less than their unionized counterparts at the New York-based networks.

An Electronic Public Space: The Virtual Community

Perhaps the most profound social consequence of the world of online communications is the development of virtual communities.[20] The virtual community refers to a social collective, or community, that forms in the online, electronic world of computer communications known as cyberspace. Virtual communities are not defined by many of the boundaries that sociologists and others traditionally have used to define communities, especially geography and political boundaries. For example, traditional notions of geographically or politically defined communities include the city, the city–state, or the nation–state. Instead, in the world of cyberspace, virtual communities exist in an ethereal electronic space defined by digital networks, computers, and the people who use them. Of course there are physical boundaries in this electronic world, but they are not the same geographic and political boundaries we are most familiar with. The boundaries that apply are the telecommunications lines, the ubiquity of computers and electronic on-ramps that may or may not exist in any particular locality. The Internet, where the greatest number of virtual communities exist, is global in its reach, but tends to have very limited reach into certain heavily populated parts of the world, such as sub-Saharan Africa, eastern Europe, and much of east Asia. Technological advances, such as wireless networks are rapidly changing this situation, however. And in Africa, the Pan African News Agency announced in June of 1994 the establishment of an Internet link.[21] Still, much of the developing world's population is excluded from the boundaries of any virtual community. Even in the most advanced information society, many of the poor and minority groups, inner city populations, rural residents, and the elderly and the young lie beyond the physical limits of virtual communities. Moreover, there are other limits such as cost that keep vast populations from joining any virtual communities.

Nevertheless, the estimated 50 million worldwide users of the Internet increasingly belong to a vast array of virtual communities. These communities represent profoundly different types of communities than one might find outside cyberspace. Not only are these communities frequently global, but they can form quickly around specific issues. At the same time, virtual communities also share many qualities and characteristics of their real-world counterparts. They develop their own rules, regulations, mores, and patterns of behavior. Consider the following recent example of how one virtual community responded to the tragic loss of a member.

Grieving Online

Cyberspace has even become a venue for grieving over the death of members of online communities. In one case, a regular participant in an online forum was shot and killed, an innocent bystander during an attempted robbery. The victim, David Alsberg, was a forty-two-year-old computer programmer, who, ironically, only recently before had participated in a heated online debate about gun control. Alsberg argued forcefully for stricter controls on firearms. After his death, members of his online community expressed their regrets and sense of loss in an online wake that lasted weeks.[22] "Much more than a crime statistic," one writer later observed, "Mr. Alsberg has come to symbolize the new social dynamic of computer networking."[23] The compassion reflected here is not limited to the tragic case of Mr. Alsberg. Forums have emerged for people with AIDS, for people who do not have AIDS but carry HIV, the AIDS virus, for cancer patients. Networks have formed for victims of child abuse, even for those abusers in recovery. One accident victim, Brendan P. Kehoe, who was severely injured in an auto accident on December 31, 1993, received a flood of electronic get-well cards from friends on the Internet.[24] News of Kehoe's accident traveled rapidly throughout the Internet, with many learning of his accident within hours of its occurrence. Kehoe, who is well known on the Internet for having penned "Zen and the Art of the Internet," has received messages in a variety of languages, including English, Spanish, French, and Russian, and has received more than $1,000 in financial support.

A similar outpouring of grief was expressed on BRASNET, an Internet forum including Brazilian and Portuguese-speaking subscribers worldwide on learning of the death of Brazilian race car driver Ayrton Senna de Silva, who was killed in a practice run in Italy.

Electronic mail, or e-mail, has emerged as the glue that often holds together these virtual communities. The use of e-mail has grown profoundly since it first traversed the Arpanet in 1969. The Electronic Messaging Association (EMA) estimates as many as 30 to 50 million people now use e-mail worldwide. In the business community alone, e-mail users have swelled from one million in 1984 to at least 20 million in 1996 reports EMA cofounder Walter Ulrich.[25] E-mail traffic has swelled, growing from 279 million messages a month in November 1992, to more than a billion messages a month in November 1994.[26] As a result, a growing amount of research is being conducted on the nature and impact of electronic mail and other forms of computer-mediated communication (CMC). One project has produced a detailed bibliography of research on the effects of CMC containing more than 200 citations.[27] Professor Bruce Redford, a professor at the University of Chicago, proclaims that "the advent of electronic mail is fostering a revival of 'the familiar letter,'" popular in the eighteenth century.[28] Many management consultants see e-mail as an enabling technology for corporate reform, increasing organizational communication efficiency to such a great degree that the ranks of middle management can be significantly thinned. Despite these alleged virtues, e-mail has proven elusive. One writer observes,

E-mail is written, yet its language typically embodies a shift toward oral speech patterns. It is the most ephemeral of written mediums, lacking the material form of books or letters and capable of being erased in a keystroke, yet it can be archived and retrieved with unprecedented ease. It has occasioned an astonishing effusion of warm-hearted social interaction outside work settings, yet at work it is the medium of choice for employees who don't like each other and wish to minimize their interactions . . . And e-mail can just as easily promote workplace centralization as decentralization, for while workers may find e-mail gives them unaccustomed access to resources throughout their company, their superiors enjoy enhanced means of tracking their performance.[29]

The Virtual Voter

As technology has helped transform notions of community based on geography to community based on interests, there are important implications for democracy and the democratic process. Most fundamental is perhaps the use of new technologies to facilitate an informed public citizenry, and the ability to increase and improve public participation in the political process. This has traditionally been a primary role of the press in a democracy. The advent of new media technologies can enhance this function by giving the public more, faster, and easier access to an increased array of information sources.

Concurrently, new technologies hold the promise of improving public participation in the political process and reducing political alienation. On a practical level, new technologies can make it easier to register voters using electronic means, or even allowing voting or public opinion polling by online methods. Participation can also be enhanced through the development of electronic town meetings or town halls.

Conversely, there are political dangers in the electronic new media. One such danger is the creation of electronic mobs. Immediate or direct access to information and political sources, without the traditional journalistic filter, means the citizenry may be increasingly subject to biased information, or propaganda not labeled as such. Such rapid access to information may also lead to action without thoughtful deliberation, warns Charles M. Firestone of the Aspen Institute.[30] The public may be more easily stampeded and manipulated. Like talk radio, electronic, online forums may provide a venue for vocal minority or majority viewpoints to overwhelm more dispassionate and informed debate, warns William Joveway of E. M. Warburg, Pincus and Co.[31]

The Virtual Public

The emergence of virtual communities also has important implications for traditional media and media support institutions, such as public relations or advertising. In the realm of public relations, the growth of virtual publics is transforming how organizations relate to their internal and external audiences.[32] The concept of a virtual public derives from sociologist John Dewey's view of the public as a community that develops around a shared problem or concern.[33] Public relations scholars James Grunig and Todd Hunt, using Dewey's framework, have identified three levels or stages of publics: latent, aware, and active, with each level of mobilization representing a greater threat or concern to an organization.[34] Because of the limitations of traditional media of communication, the process of mobilizing a public from the latent to aware stage, or even from a nonpublic into a latent public, was relatively slow, typically taking weeks or months to develop. The virtual public completely redefines the mobilization time frame. In a matter of minutes, even seconds, a worldwide public, potentially numbering in the millions, can mobilize electronically around a problem perceived initially by even just a single computer user. In addition, more than 14,000 latent, virtual publics already exist in the form of Usenet news groups, which exist on a variety of topics and subjects ranging from the arts to zoology. The notion of the virtual public also has similar implications for the notion of publics defined by their organizational linkage, as conceptualized by scholars James Grunig and Todd Hunt.[35] These publics, based on functional, enabling, normative, and diffused organizational linkages may be mobilized much more rapidly in a distributed electronic cyberspace. For example, a diffused public, one that arises when an organization produces external consequences (e.g., when a petroleum company has an oil spill), may be mobilized in a matter of hours, even minutes, on the Internet. Following the tragic 1996 crash of TWA flight 800 off the coast of Long Island, New York, families and friends of the victims quickly launched a site on the World Wide Web where people could obtain the latest information on the crash investigation, visit an online memorial, or make a donation to a fund supporting the families of the victims.

Similarly, such publics can develop in cyberspace on an international scale much more readily than in the so-called real world, where communications might occur via "snail mail" (what those on "the net" call traditional postal service) or via expensive long-distance telephone calls or faxes. International support for the Zapatista movement in the Chiapas region of Mexico has grown steadily via World Wide Web sites posted throughout North America, including Texas and New York.

Virtual publics possess potentially great power, as attests the recent online campaign a virtual public waged against the Arizona law firm that conducted an unsolicited advertising campaign on the Internet in violation of traditional values and beliefs of many network users. Similarly, reflecting the grassroots nature of the Internet, a virtual public developed in the spring of 1994 around the landmark case of Brock Meeks, the first journalist sued for libel for a story published exclusively on the Internet. A freelance journalist who found himself in the uncomfortable situation of having no resources to mount a legal defense against the suit, Meeks sent electronic messages to friends and colleagues in cyberspace, who quickly mobilized into a virtual public dedicated to creating a legal defense fund to support the Meeks case. While such grassroots activism is no stranger to public relations or public relations research, it has not been studied extensively in the realm of cyberspace, and has important implications for public relations theory and practice.[36,37]

Virtual Consequences

Virtual reality and communications is the subject of increasing scholarly inquiry. The respected *Journal of Communication*, an official journal of the International Communication Association, recently devoted an entire issue to the subject.[38] In this issue, Professor Frank Biocca suggests that virtual reality may be not only the next dominant medium, supplanting television, but the "ultimate medium." He asks, "Should we not consider the implications now?"[39] Some scholars believe that virtual reality will become a battleground within the academy. "Virtual reality/cyberspace is the arena in which the extremists—technophobes and technophiles—will wage their information war," writes Canadian educator W. Lambert Gardiner. "Communication studies can provide a balanced middle ground between those two extremes."[40]

INSTITUTIONAL CONSEQUENCES OF NEW TECHNOLOGY

As the adoption and diffusion of new media technologies accelerates, virtually every social institution is inexorably altered. Whether the world of politics, education or libraries, journalism, government or religion, medicine, law, or the military, every major social institution is touched by the new media technologies. Their influences are varied and unpredictable, although certain common patterns emerge. These patterns include the sometimes complementary and sometimes contradictory forces of decentralization and multidirectional communication, as well as a drive for increased efficiency, productivity, and adaptability. For purposes of illustration, the consequences of new media technologies are examined for two major social institutions:

- The political system, including democratic processes, governmental services, and political participation
- Education, including schools, libraries, and access to information technology

New Media Technology, Social Control, and Democracy

> *"Those who deny freedom to others deserve
> it not for themselves, and, under a
> just god, cannot long retain it."*
> —ABRAHAM LINCOLN[41]

One of the world's keenest observers of the social consequences of new technology, Anthony Smith, president of Oxford's Magdalen College and author of *Goodbye Gutenberg*, offers another view of the social consequences of information technology. Smith sees the advance of information technology as redefining not just the media but society itself on a global level. Today's digital revolution, he argues, is as significant as Gutenberg's invention of movable type five centuries ago.[42] Just as Gutenberg's invention coincided with the rise of the modern nation–state, the digital revolution is transforming the notion of nationhood. "With digitization there emerged a new unit of knowledge—no longer the word or unit of type but the bit and byte of computer data," Smith writes. "Digitization heralded new ways of knowing things and also of organizing both physical and intellectual processes. It insisted upon procedural rather than inspirational thinking. For some, the information revolution was a control revolution, a nirvana of management without mistakes."

To some, advances in information technology are destroying the ability of elites to control what people know, hear, or read. Information technology has irrevocably changed society, says technology visionary Walter Wriston.[43] Wriston, the former chief of Citicorp, one of the world's great banking institutions, says new technology has changed the way wealth is created and the concept of sovereignty. "The pathways open to the transmission of data and information are now so prolix as to make national borders totally porous and old regulatory distinctions meaningless." Information has become the new form of wealth. "The information standard has replaced the gold standard," Wriston adds. These effects, he notes, are positive for society, because they all lead toward greater democracy and freedom. And even if they are not entirely for the good, he concludes, "There are no u-turns on the road to the future."

In agreement are many others, including consumer activist Ralph Nader, who says, "Information is the currency of democracy."[44] Media mogul Rupert Murdoch, chairman of the Australian-based News Corporation, also agrees. "Advances in the technology of telecommunications have proved an unambiguous threat to totalitarian regimes everywhere," Murdoch says. "Fax machines enable dissidents to bypass state-controlled print media; direct-dial telephone makes it difficult for a state to control interpersonal voice communications. And satellite broadcasting makes it possible for information-hungry residents of many closed societies to bypass state-controlled television channels."[45] *Revolution in a Box,* a 1989 video documentary by ABC's Ted Koppel, credits the presence of satellite dishes, as well as bootlegged videocassettes, in Poland and elsewhere in Eastern Europe with allowing citizens of these countries to bypass official government censorship to learn about international news.

Mitchell Kapor, director of The Electronic Frontier Foundation, and creator of Lotus Corporation, believes that the information highway could completely remake democracy. "This type of medium could enable a Jeffersonian revolution in our civic life" by allowing full direct participation in public decision-making, he says.

Adding to this view is Anthony Smith, who writes, "Television, today extended by video recorders, cable, satellite and teletext—has become the principal instrument of our citizenship. . . . But it is the graveyard of subtlety, the executioner of taste, the mangle of passion."[46]

Echoing this sentiment is Lawrence Grossman, former president of NBC News and former president and CEO of PBS, and founder of Horizons TV, a new cable channel devoted to cultural and educational programming. Grossman says that we are in the midst of the third great stage in evolution of democracy since the Greeks invented it more than 2,000 years ago, and the United States created representative democracy more than 200 years ago. Technology and the information highway, Grossman argues, has spawned an era of direct, electronic democracy.[47] "There is a tremendous change going on in our political system, a change that has been little discussed and appreciated, perhaps because it seems to be so new," Grossman explains.

> The confluence—the coming together—of television, telephone, fax, computers and satellites, now enables the American people instantaneously to express their views, for better or worse, to their leadership—representatives . . . with the advent of telecomputers, people will soon punch buttons at home, informing their representatives how they feel, at that instant, on any particular issue.

Internet and Democracy

The Internet is the first medium that allows the democratic principles of free speech and self-governance to play themselves out unhindered, says David Sobel, a lawyer for the Electronic Privacy Information Center, a Washington, D.C. public interest lobbying group.[48] Conversely, many see even the Internet rapidly being subjected to the same commercial forces that have controlled traditional communication media.[49]

Everette E. Dennis notes that we now have the technological tools to make electronic democracy happen on a national scale. But, he cautions,

> two overarching questions arise: (1) Will these innovations be readily accessible to all people, perhaps through such intermediate institutions as schools, churches and community organizations, or to only some? And, (2) once we get the technology in place and get access to it, are we going to know how to use it?[50]

One potential application of the information highway is to allow electronic voting by computer.

Technology and Political Campaigns

> *"Gadgets do just about everything else for us*
> *these days, so we see no reason why they*
> *won't end up electing our presidents."*
> —ERIC SEVAREID[51]

Technological advances have helped close the gap between the voter and the candidate by providing a more direct link between the individual citizen and the candidate for office, as well as making political and policy information available on-demand for those with online access.[52] This was particularly evident during the 1992 and the 1996 presidential campaigns.[53] One study reported by the Pew Research Center, for example, found that 21 million Americans (12 percent of the voting age population, or more than half those with online access) obtained political or policy news from online sources in 1996.[54] Some 7 million (4 percent) used the Internet or commercial online services for information about the presidential election. Some 3 percent of voters on election day went so far as to say that Internet and online sites, especially the World Wide Web, were their "principal election news sources," the Pew study reports.

There is little evidence that voters are looking to online information, either from news organizations or from the candidates themselves, to supplant or replace traditional media use. "Americans who get news on the Internet or from commercial online services read, watch and listen to the news (on traditional media) as much as the public at large," the Pew study adds. In fact, many are using online sources to get information they can't find in traditional sources, such as in-depth information about Congressional (33 percent) and local (24 percent) races. The Pew study employed a combination of research methods, including a national survey of 1,003 online users in October 1996.

Nevertheless, there are potentially onerous consequences of the application of new technology to political campaigning. As opinion polling is transformed by new technology and marketing utilizes computerized databases to zero in on the undecided voter, the individual is threatened by a loss of privacy, even control, in the political process. The manipulation of the media and public opinion becomes frighteningly real when candidates begin faxing to reporters and voters responses to their opponent's latest speech, even before they have delivered it.

"With all the electronic computers . . . and the flashing numbers and percentages, one can lose sight of the essential fact of any election. And that is the mind of the voter," said Eric Sevareid in a CBS News commentary, November 2, 1958.[55] New communication technologies have also played an important role in the erosion of the political parties.[56]

De-Technology

Although it is not a book about technology, Roderick P. Hart's *Seducing America* offers one of the most eloquent examinations of the impact of the technology of television on the political process.[57] F. A. Liddell Professor of Communication and Government at the University of Texas at Austin, Hart argues that the technology of television is actually "a de-technology."[58] It is a medium that removes the space between members of the public on a global scale. "Through television, we can touch persons who live elsewhere; we can read their distant hearts." As a result, individuals are insulated from the feelings of massness in a mass society. Instead, viewers can act globally, while still thinking locally. They can even hear a more primitive voice.

> *And, look, this campaign is over. There's no hard feelings about that. The American people are smart. They know a tough-fought campaign on both sides when they see it.*

This phenomenon may have been echoed in the 1996 presidential campaign, when Republican challenger Bob Dole suffered a resounding defeat, yet subsequently showed his sense of humor by hosting the popular television program *Saturday Night Live* only weeks after the campaign had ended.

Delivery of Government Services
Via the Information Superhighway

The largest of all social institutions, government is also undergoing a metamorphorsis in part driven by new media technology. Government transactional records are almost universally stored in digital form, with public access increasingly in electronic, online form. Government services, once available only to those citizens willing to stand on line for many exhaustive hours, are increasingly available electronically online. Virtually every federal agency is now online, from the Bureau of the Census to the Social Security Administration, every agency maintains a Web site. Although many of these Web sites are little more than public affairs brochures (such as the U.S. Army Web site), others provide access to governmental services. For example, the U.S. Patents and Trademark Office (USPTO) Web site not only provides information about its office and activities, but permits visitors to order copies of patents.[60] The Internal Revenue Service (IRS) Web site supports the downloading of tax forms, and outlines the procedures for electronic filing of individual tax returns.

States have also entered the digital age. Maryland, for example, was the first state to make access to the Internet available free of charge to all its citizens. Wisconsin similarly announced an ambitious plan to put all its citizens on the information highway. Although many of these technological applications have been developed at the state and federal level, the information highway can be used to address important issues on the urban agenda, as well. A former telecommunications official for the City of New York, K. Kendall Guthrie argues that technology applications on the information highway have the potential to promote economic development and even help to reconnect the urban poor.[61] Contestants in the 1997 mayoral race in New York City, for example, have announced their plans to provide election sites for voters interested in their campaigns. Internationally, a growing number of countries are also expressing interest in putting governmental services online, much as France has done through the videotext service known as Minitel.

Advancing Education through Technology

Education is one social institution that has the potential to benefit greatly from the development and application of new media technology. The government plays a lead role in insuring that the benefits of technology reach America's educational institutions and classrooms. Vice President Gore and others, including former Commerce Secretary Ron Brown, have been particularly outspoken in their advocacy of the educational benefits of a new national information infrastructure. While committing some federal funding to achieve this broad goals, they have called on the private sector to play an even greater role. In speaking to communications industry leaders on January 11, 1994, Vice President Al Gore said, "I challenge you . . . (communication industry leaders) to connect all of our classrooms, all of our libraries, and all of our hospitals and clinics by the year 2000."[62]

In a report issued in May of 1994, then-Commerce Secretary Brown outlined the possible educational and lifelong learning applications of the proposed NII. Consisting of the current and evolving telecommunications infrastructure, including telephone, broadcast, cable, and electronic networks, the NII could enable:

- Multimedia interactive learning programs for students of all ages, whether delivered to classrooms or directly to the home
- Simulated learning activities, such as laboratory experiments or archaeological digs, featuring immersive, realistic simulations
- Universal access interfaces to allow students, workers, and those with disabilities to fully participate in the learning experience

Government-funded research demonstrates the educational value of new media technology, as well. A Congressionally mandated study comparing multimedia and more conventional instruction found time savings of 30 percent, cost savings of 30 to 40 percent, improved student achievement, and a direct, positive link between interactivity and instructional effectiveness.[63] Other research has confirmed the instructional effectiveness of new technology in the classroom and beyond. A 1993 survey of studies on technology in schools demonstrated that "courses for which computer-based networks were used increased student–student and student–teacher interaction, increased student–teacher interaction with lower-performing students, and did not decrease the traditional forms of communications used."[64] Reviews of computer-based teaching in military applications found that students reach similar levels of achievement in 30 percent less time than those using more traditional teaching methods.[65]

Despite the effectiveness of new technology in the classroom, most classrooms are poorly equipped with those technologies, such as computers, especially multimedia technologies and online services. The installed base of computers in American elementary and secondary schools is generally unable to support multimedia computing, concludes the Information Infrastructure Task Force in its May 1994 report.[66]

Certain instructional technologies are available more widely in U.S. schools. For instance, 75 percent of U.S. schools have cable television, and half of all teachers use video material in the classroom.[67] More than 12 million Americans access daily at least some of the 60,000 electronic bulletin boards available on the Internet, and the Department of Education estimates that much of this usage is for educational purposes. This usage is growing rapidly. In fact, the annual rate of "Gopher" traffic on the Internet, which reflects educational research information requests, is growing at 1,000 percent.[68] In Texas, one-quarter of the teachers regularly signs on to the Texas Education Network to share information, exchange e-mail, and find resources. Similar educational systems are in use in other states, as well. Distance learning, and the "virtual classroom" is also increasingly in use in the United States. Another fascinating distance learning project is based at the University of Texas at Austin. Through the World Wide Web, the University has created a "Worldwide Lecture Hall," giving students the world over electronic access to a virtual university offering scores of courses online.

Classroom access to the Internet improved significantly in 1996 with the launch of a series of NetDay events around the country. From California to New York, teachers, administrators, students and other volunteers from industry and government joined forces to help pull the cable necessary to connect every classroom in every school in the nation to the Internet. Although hundreds of thousands of volunteers managed to connect many thousands of schools (some states such as California and Connecticut claim to have successfully connected every one of their schools to the Internet), the process was not without a hitch. Asbestos and other construction problems kept some schools from getting connected. Perhaps more importantly, many schools simply don't have the computers necessary to effectively connect to the Internet. And, even when they do, they may not have the curriculum. Advocates of television in classroom have long heralded the potential of TV as a tool for enhancing learning, as well. Research to date, however, has shown that, by itself, TV will not work wonders on the educational process. Teacher involvement, full student interactivity, and richness of content are all prerequisites for effective use of technology in the classroom.

One important solution to the curricular obstacles to effective use of new media in small schools is called the Eiffel Project.[69] Under the direction of Professor Robert McClintock, Priscilla Ellington, and Heather Lewis, the Eiffel Project is a partnership of the Institute for Learning Technologies, the Center for Collaborative Education, and the New York City Board of Education. Its objectives are to employ digital technologies to break significant, long-lasting contraints on education, in the same way that the technologies engineered for the Eiffel Tower a century ago shattered the design constraints of nineteenth-century architecture. The Eiffel Project integrates digital network technologies into broader school reform efforts, providing access to digital libraries, multimedia educational programs and wide-area networking capabilities for improved communication access.

Governmental Objectives

The federal NII Task Force has outlined several educational objectives and goals for use of new media technologies for education and lifelong learning. Among these are:

- Convenient and equitable access, by connecting to every classroom, public library, and other learning location, and providing affordable access in the workplace and home
- High-speed transmission capability, to permit multimedia applications and interactivity
- Easy use to facilitate broad use among all educational markets and social segments
- Technological simplification, with the ultimate goal to make connecting to the NII as simple as plugging in a telephone
- Accessibility, to accommodate the diverse needs of U.S. society
- Security to protect privacy, safeguard intellectual property rights, and provide effective educational resources
- Content in the form of rich and diverse material
- Portability to insure system interoperability and to achieve the same level of "plug and play" found in high-fidelity audio systems

Industry's Role

Although progress has been slow, a number of information highway builders as well as content providers are already stepping up to meet the administration's challenge to provide new products and services for education. Pacific Bell Corporation and Jones Intercable have announced that they will connect schools to broadband networks, allowing a high-speed on-ramp to the information superhighway. Pac Bell, as it is known in the West, provides telephone service to most of California, and will spend $100 million to install advanced digital telephone lines in some 7,400 schools, libraries, and community colleges in that state.[70] Pac Bell has also pledged to keep access to the technology affordable for these public institutions. They have promised to wire two locations in each institution free of charge, and will waive usage fees for one year after installation. They also promise to cooperate with the California Public Utilities Commission to establish a special low-cost education-access rate to keep educational institutions on the information superhighway.[71]

Two media giants, Liberty Media Corporation and Reuters, joined forces to create "Ingenious," a daily, multimedia news package for classroom and home use.[72] Reuters provides the news content, while Liberty Media delivers it to personal computers through Liberty's cable system, currently available in 18,000 schools and some 28 million homes.

At the same time, the benefits of new media technologies may just as likely elude the educational arena, or be very selective in their impact, access, and availability. The above examples notwithstanding, there has been traditionally little financial incentive for companies to invest heavily in new technologies and education. This has been especially the case for many poor inner city and rural schools and school systems. Although many talk about the benefits of the information superhighway in the classroom, one recent study showed that only 5 percent of public school classrooms has a telephone line. Without this telecommunications lifeline, the information superhighway and its accompanying new media technologies hold little value or potential for most U.S. schools. This situation presents both an irony and a dilemma for educational institutions. Commercial enterprises, such as Chris Whittle's Channel 1, beam news programming directly into schools. Whittle provides all the needed equipment, including television monitor and satellite dish free to the schools, many of which are in dire financial straights and cannot afford to buy such equipment.

Not surprisingly, Whittle's program is very controversial because the feeds include commercial messages. Moreover, to date, research has demonstrated little real educational value for Channel 1. Nevertheless, the dilemma for school administrators is that many lack the resources to get much needed equipment for their schools, but they find it difficult if not impossible for political reasons to accept Whittle's offer. Ironically, few question the role in the classroom of such "old" media as newspapers or news magazines, which also contain commercial messages. Nor do many voters who oppose Whittle's effort offer the public funds needed to put electronic on-ramps into all public schools. Further, although Channel 1 contains advertising messages, teachers are free to use the Whittle equipment for purposes other than receiving Channel 1. They can use it to receive programming such as *CNN in the Classroom,* a special news feed designed specifically for students and containing no advertising. Although reports in the early 1990s indicated that Whittle's enterprise was in imminent danger of collapse because of an impending financial crisis (i.e., the inability to repay a $100 million loan),[73] Channel 1 has surged to new life with the growth of the World Wide Web, with hundreds of schools in every state connecting to the Channel 1 online service.

Profnet: Linking Higher Education and the Press

Profnet is an interesting network service developed in 1992 that brings together the universe of higher education and journalism.[74] Until recently, journalists in need of an expert source turned most often to a well-stocked Rolodex and several hours on the telephone, not always successfully locating the needed specialist. Profnet is an online service created by Dan Forbush, associate vice president for university affairs at the State University of New York at Stony Brook. Reporters send queries by e-mail, fax, or toll-free number to Profnet headquarters, and, in turn, the query is relayed by e-mail to public information (PI) officers at some 1,100 colleges, universities, and research centers participating in the network. The PI officers then find resident experts on the needed subject, and quickly get in touch with the reporter placing the query. The Profnet system currently receives about twenty queries a day, all processed at no charge. Network costs to run the system totaled about $2,500 in 1993, not including the time of the various individuals involved. Profnet, and services like it, may help bridge the gap between the academy and the public.

Professor Steven Sander Ross at the Columbia University Graduate School of Journalism has developed a related database of online resources for journalists.[75] Containing links to thousands of online resources, Professor Ross's collection covers twenty subjects from arts to government to sports.

The Electronic Library

> *"Instead of fortresses of knowledge, there will be an ocean of information"*
> —JOHN BROWNING[76]

New technology has profound implications for one of society's most cherished educational institutions, the public library. Since the days of Andrew Carnegie, the public library has provided free and easy access to information of all types to the public, whether in the form of books, newspapers or magazines. In today's new media environment, libraries still play a vital role in providing universal access to digital information.

At the same time, the arrival of digital technology has begun to profoundly transform the public library. Its impact has been both complex and subtle. "The computer plays a strategic role in the reorganization of all the institutions in which it arrives," writes Anthony Smith.[77] "It is not a silent visitor, but an active agent of change, bringing with it the inexorable sense of its own modernity—inexorable, but with incalculable consequences. Like an epidemic, you cannot be sure where it will strike or what it will spare, only to return later." Smith argues that libraries will find themselves going through a variety of changes as a result of the introduction of digital technology. Among them:

- Libraries will turn into "a kind of print-house, since readers will want to create more and more of their hard-copy material within the library and then remove it."
- Computerization will permit unlimited revision of works including perishable or time-dependent information. Libraries may treat such a work "as a database and offer the reader, at appropriate cost, the chance to log onto it."
- Online communications and digital repositories will create virtual digital libraries that each user can create from any computer workstation connected to the global data network.

There are also a number of troubling questions that arise. "But what happens when a publisher decides that the task is no longer financially viable?" Smith asks.

"Who then holds the database for purposes of public record? And at whose cost? Who holds the copyright? *Who* protects *whom* against acts of plagiarism from such a work?"

From Scriptoria to Virtual Books.   In the beginning, libraries were vast repositories of the world's knowledge, run and controlled by monks in scriptoria. Because knowledge often is power, access to libraries and their collections was fundamental to the control of society and the preservation of the status quo. As a result, libraries held tight rein over their holdings. Consider one example from England's Hereford Cathedral. "Books were chained to the shelves. Although books were sometimes lent to other monasteries, the consequences for failing to return them were severe, as the inscription from this twelfth century manuscript makes clear: 'This book belongs to the monastery of St. Mary of Robert's Bridge, whoever shall steal it, or mutilate it, let him be forever cursed. Amen.'"[78] Today's technology of the information highway is poised to change all that. From a local Internet access device anyone can now search the catalogs of thousands of libraries around the world, including the vast collection of the Library of Congress and 12 to 15 million items in the British Library.

Prospects for a Digital Library of Congress.   One of the greatest libraries ever created is the United States Library of Congress in Washington, D.C., just opposite the Capitol. With its collection of more than 100 million items, it exceeds by more than a thousand-fold even the great Library of Alexandria of ancient Egypt.[79] As proponents push for a new national information infrastructure, one of the promises is to open electronic pathways to the massive collection of the Library of Congress. The Internet already allows users to browse electronically the Library of Congress card catalog. But major hurdles remain. One of the most difficult and costly to overcome is the simple fact that the vast majority of items in the Library of Congress are in analog form, many in print and others on videotape or film. The collection includes more than 20 million books, more than 4 million maps and atlases, 14 million prints and photographs, and more than 600,000 films and videotapes. The cost and complexity of the Herculean task of converting all this material to machine-readable form is almost incalculable, although a consortium of U.S. organizations has begun the process of raising private capital to fund the digital conversion of the Library's holdings.

The Vatican Library Goes Digital.   Founded in the mid-1400s by Pope Nicholas V, the Vatican Library holds some of the rarest books and antique manuscripts in the world, including a beautifully illustrated copy of Dante's *Divine Comedy,* Ptolemy's *Geography,* and the four oldest surviving manuscripts of Virgil's poems. The library houses more than 150,000 manuscripts and a million printed books, including 8,000 books published in the initial fifty years of Gutenberg's printing press. In early 1994, the Vatican and International Business Machines Corporation (IBM) announced a joint project to bring the 500-year-old library into the computer age.[80] Using optical scanning technology, the pilot project will capture the pages of the collection in digital form, store the images in computer-readable form, and open the door to worldwide scholarly access to the works through online communications. The project holds the promise of not only increasing access to the priceless collection, but will preserve and protect the fragile ancient holdings, which are jeopardized by repeated handling. Through image enhancement technology, it might also be possible to scrutinize certain works even more closely.

Many university libraries are also beginning the process of converting their holdings to digital form. A number of major universities have received multimillion dollar funding from the National Science Foundation as well as from private partners to undertake digital library projects, including Carnegie Mellon, the University of California at Berkeley, the University of Michigan, the University of California at Santa Barbara, Stanford University, and the University of Illinois.[81]

A Scholar's Electronic Paradise.   The electronic library has important implications for scholarly research and teaching. A number of major academic publishers have begun publishing scholarly journals on the Internet, on computer disk, or on CD-ROM, and others are considering such projects. Among those involved in online publishing are MIT Press, the University of California Press, Columbia University Press, and the University of Chicago Press. Electronic journals may provide scholars with both more timely and complete access to research information, and at a potentially lower cost, at least to the publishers.[82]

One of the greatest scholarly research resources in the United States is the Online Computer Library Center (OCLC; originally the Ohio College Library Center), whose services are used by 22,000 subscriber libraries in 63 countries. Through its Web site, the OCLC provides direct online access to a variety of electronic online journals, OCLC reference services, inter-library loan, and a host of other resources. Anyone with Internet access can use limited OCLC online services, such as obtaining publications lists or contacting member library institutions.

Libraries in Crisis.   Patricia Glass Schuman, president of Neal-Schuman Publishers, and former president of the American Library Association (ALA), however, is concerned that the economics of new technology may be contributing to the transformation of information from a public good into a commodity. Schuman cautions that we are rapidly moving into an era when we will pay an increasingly expensive fee for information that in the past the federal government provided free to public libraries.[83] In Vice President Gore's "Reinventing Government" report, he recommends disbanding the Government Printing Office, which has for decades provided government publications free to the system of depository libraries.[84] The likely replacement will be publication of government data via electronic information services provided to libraries by private vendors who will charge a fee. "How many of you have ever paid for an online search yourself?" Schuman asked participants in a seminar at the Media Studies Center. Largely long-time journalists, media analysts, and communication scholars, most had frequently used online database searches, but had exclusively relied on their employers to pay for the searches. "Perish the thought," was the only half-joking response of one participant. Libraries face a "silent crisis," warned Schuman. There are 115,000 libraries in the United States, noted Schuman, including school, public, and private institutions. But the library is an "endangered public space," she added. Half the school libraries have closed in the last decade in California. One hundred public libraries are now being run by private companies, including some foreign companies. Many now cost more to run. "Is information a public good?" Schuman asked. "Does it contribute to education, culture and the democratic process?" The answer is "yes," Schuman declared.[85]

Improving Educational Resources. A number of companies have announced they are developing digital libraries to serve the education market.[86] Three companies, Infonautics, Inc., Tandem Computers, Inc., and MRJ, Inc. have joined forces to create Homework Helper, an electronic library aimed at primary and secondary school students. Now on the Internet as the Electric Libary, Homework Helper includes information from a variety of sources, such as Compton's Multimedia Encyclopedia, *USA Today*, *The Los Angeles Times*, *Forbes*, Reuters, and *Time* magazine, as well as 150 newspapers and news services from around the world, including the Africa News Service, the Cherokee Observer, and the Xinhua News Agency of China.[87] Journal Graphics and Cable News Network provide transcripts of television news and information programming, and Simon & Schuster provides content from a variety of books. Homework Helper includes more than 700 works of literature, and also features an intuitive user interface especially designed for children. Students access the system by typing questions in plain English. For instance, typing "Where is Sri Lanka" will bring up a variety of types of information, including a map, an encyclopedia article about the country, and other related information.

Access to the Information Highway

Fundamental to the technological transformation of every social institution, whether political, educational, or governmental, is universal access to technology. In *The People's Right to Know: Media, Democracy, and the Information Highway*, Frederick Williams and John V. Pavlik argue that guaranteeing access to all people is a fundamental prerequisite to the design of the information highway. "We have nearly achieved our goal of 'universal service' in voice telephony; why not a 21st century upgrade to universal service in access to essential information and transactions?" they ask.[88] In late October 1993, a group of seventy-one nonprofit groups joined forces to urge policy makers to bring the public interest to the forefront of the design of the national information infrastructure. "It is not enough for the public to react to plans once they've been put in place. The public must be at the table when the plans are made," said the group's Kathryn C. Montgomery, president of the Center for Media Education. Called the Telecommunications Policy Roundtable, members of the group are concerned that a national information highway developed by market forces will bypass the poor and minority communities, and exclude information services of value to educators, librarians, people with disabilities, and others. Most central to the Roundtable's mission is the issue of universal access. Roundtable members urge policy-makers to consider these seven principles in the design of the information highway:

- Free access to information needed to fully participate in a democratic society
- Freedom of expression for network users, protection of copyright to content creators and library patron's use of materials
- An "electronic commons" for public discussion and debate
- A marketplace of ideas accessible to all and not controlled by telecommunications carriers
- An opportunity to improve the quality of work and equity in the workplace
- Privacy protection of users
- An opportunity for full public involvement in policies regarding the data network[89]

If these policy imperatives are met, Roundtable members suggest, then the information highway will foster robust communication, which has been the foundation of democracy in the United States for more than 200 years. "We cannot begin to afford to allow people not to speak on this information highway," said Roundtable participant T. Andrew Lewis, executive director of the Alliance for Community Media. "Nothing could be more clear than the need for communication in our communities today."

The implications of universal access are profound for the democratic process, which rests on the principle of a government responsive to and in touch with the people. To be responsive, the government must communicate with the people. "One cannot talk about communications from citizen to government—or any other kind of communications—in this information age without discussing the role of technology," says Harvard University political scientist Sidney Verba in the 1993 James Madison Award Lecture. But many are already excluded from the emerging information highway, and as a result are disenfranchised from the process of political communication and, thus, from full participation in our democracy. "Those of us plugged into networks—that sometimes burden us with information coming in and the sense that we ought to be sending things out in reply—forget how many people are outside of such networks," Verba explains. "People like us receive many computer-generated communications about public matters and requests for action or contributions. Our data show, however, that a large proportion of Americans never receive a piece of mail soliciting support for a political cause. Networks are very selective," he concludes.[90]

Not everyone agrees that equal access to new media technology and the information superhighway should be the first priority for public policy. Dr. Eli Noam, founding director of the Columbia Institute for Tele-Information and a well-known expert on communications policy and economics, suggests that, while universal access is important, encouraging competition among service providers is a better way to insure low prices and that new services will be developed.[91] Many in industry are in agreement, including Eric Rabe, director of media relations for Bell Atlantic and a member of the executive committee that had been charged with planning the ill-fated Bell Atlantic–TCI merger. Rabe, whose company has always been a heavily regulated monopoly, would welcome increased competition over additional regulation. "Equity is a red herring," says Nancy Hicks Maynard, chair of the Media Studies Center.[92] Noting that new technologies are almost always relatively expensive when they are introduced, but invariably come down quickly in price and become widely available, Maynard suggests that the equity imperative should not be so great that it inhibits the development of new information services and technologies.

One important avenue of access to the Internet for those who cannot afford a computer or online service from their home is the public library. Increasingly, public libraries around the country are providing free Internet access to library visitors. Echoing the nineteenth-century philanthropic deeds of industrial age titan Andrew Carnegie, today's new media mogul, Bill Gates of Microsoft, has recently contributed his support to this cause by establishing the Microsoft Libraries Online Project. With nine project sites from the Brooklyn Public Library in New York to the Tucson–Pima Public Library in Tucscon, Arizona, Gates has committed millions of dollars in funding to provide free Internet access through inner-city public libraries.

CULTURAL CONSEQUENCES OF NEW MEDIA TECHNOLOGY

From the evolution of storytelling to electronic art, new media technologies are steadily exerting their influence on cultures both in the United States and throughout the world. Moreover, the use of new media technology is itself leading to the growth of computer-mediated culture, much of which is based on traditional culture, but other aspects of which are unique.

Hyperfiction

One of the most dramatic effects of new media technology derives from the creation of hypertext, or nonlinear, nonsequential writing. As the concept of nonlinear writing, or writing that is non-directional without any preset beginning, middle, and end, has taken hold, an entirely new form of literature, that of hyperfiction, has emerged. Hyperfiction is a form of writing in which the author creates characters, environments, and motivation, but not a single predetermined plot. Rather, individuals are participants in a simulated reality that they help define through their decisions, actions, and communication. In many ways, the creator of the original hyperfiction is like a filmmaker who finds him or herself in the role of despot, almost playing god in creating a world. How that world evolves, however, is left to the interaction of the qualities of the world created and the participants who enter into it. Like snowflakes, no two experiences in hyperfiction are alike. Each is unique. Nevertheless, there are common experiences and meanings to be shared across participants, sometimes called *avatars,* in hyperfiction. What disappears in hyperfiction is the notion of a single narrative line, not narrative itself. Stories are still read (sometimes seen or heard), it's just that the author is truly both reader and the original creator. As hyperfiction evolves and becomes an increasingly significant cultural force, its reach and impact will extend beyond the specialized realm of computer enthusiasts, and into the mainstream of society, through educational venues, advertising, and the commercial sector. Hyperfiction may even evolve into an important part of how cultural values and mores are transferred from generation to generation. Much as many oral cultures have not relied greatly on technology in storytelling and cultural transference, and written cultures have relied on the written word, society's next generation may come to increasingly rely on computer-based hyperfiction as an important tool for sharing and transferring cultural symbols and meaning.

Related to contemporary society's shift toward a hyperfiction communication environment is the development of a culture of random access and remote technological control. The ubiquity of computers has led their users to become increasingly comfortable with the concept of random access to information. In older media, such as radio, television, movies, books, and newspapers, the presentation of content has always been determined by a central content provider. It has been presented for consumption at a particular time, in a preset order, and must be consumed as it is packaged. Although a newspaper reader is not required to begin with the first story on the first page, it is not possible to conduct a keyword search to immediately jump to just the story or item of interest. New, digital media have changed all this. Users of new media can go directly to any desired content. It is rapidly creating a cultural generation that not only expects but increasingly demands information and entertainment on demand.

Although typically associated with the TV set, remote control technology is a much broader concept that applies increasingly to all mediated experience. The next generation expects to remotely control its answering machines, its voice mail, its electronic mail, its bank accounts, even its increasingly smart home appliances, such as ovens that can be turned on or off by remote control. Coupled with the growth of remote control technology, tomorrow's media consumer will demand remote access to and remote control of media content whenever, wherever, and however they want. Anything less will leave them frustrated and seeking alternative sources of news, information, and entertainment.

Connecting Concepts in Hyperspace

Hypertext and hypermedia also change the way we access information. Not only can we gather information more rapidly and efficiently through nonlinear media, but they allow us to make unexpected connections between concepts, almost in a spider web fashion. No longer must we search information organized the way someone else has decided. We are not limited by the alphabetic system of classification of books envisioned centuries ago by Herbert Maunsell. Instead, we can make connections by our own concepts and ideas, sometimes in unexpected ways. Anthony Smith, for example, described how he was recently using an encyclopedia on CD-ROM and came across the word orangutan.[93] He noticed the word had a Hottentot origin. Curious about the extent of the African language's impact on Western culture, he queried the CD-ROM about how many English-language words have a Hottentot origin. The answer: twenty-seven.

Some might claim that in creating hypertext information systems or virtual libraries, something intangible is lost. There is no longer a sense of being there, of placing one's hands on an original manuscript. This may be true, as in the case of a somewhat sterile corporate library where all information is stored electronically, but the advantage is that it makes all information available at once.[94]

Multimedia Art Forms

Multimedia technology and online communications also present important implications for contemporary culture. Increasingly, artists are finding a new palette in multimedia technology. Since the late Lejaren Hiller pioneered the use of the computer as a medium for musical composition with the creation of the "Illiac Suite" in 1956, digital technology has produced profound effects on music and other art forms.[95] Today, artists following in the footsteps of John Cage and others are using digital technology not only to present their musical compositions, but as a creative environment. Italian composer Nicola Sani has employed a variety of electronic, multimedia technology to synthesize new compositions, and to combine music with full-motion video images. The result is a digitally generated interactive multimedia artform reminiscent of Walt Disney's classic *Fantasia* composition. Sani's musical video art has been distributed electronically via CD-ROM, communication satellite, and online. Sani's efforts reflect the convergence of visual and aural arts in a multimedia creative environment. Digital technology has also provided an opportunity for entrepreneurial artists to both create a new medium for artistic expression as well as a venue to display their work and hold public discourse on art and artistic expression. One such effort has been pioneered by multimedia producers Emily Hartzell and Nina Sobell, creators of Parkbench, an online arts environment designed for the discussion, creation, and display of electronic art. Run out of a new media lab at New York University in Greenwich Village, ParkBench is available free to all comers at www.cat.nyu.edu/parkbench/

The Virtual Art Gallery

The advent of online communications is also emerging as an important vehicle to provide worldwide public access to art. Institutions ranging from the White House to the Smithsonian have developed online art tours available free of charge to the public. An increasing number of museums around the world are putting their collections in digital form onto the Internet, as well as CD-ROM. Examples include the World Wide Web servers at the Museum of Paleontology at the University of California at Berkeley or Krannert Art Museum at the University of Illinois, which allow visitors from dozens of countries to view text and images of exhibits via the Internet, or, wear a virtual reality helmet to tour the Egyptian Temple of Horus at the "virtual reality" exhibit at Carnegie Mellon University's Studio for Creative Inquiry.[96]

Of concern to some is the increasing corporate interest in capturing the rights to publish electronically a variety of works of art and art collections. Reminiscent of the late publishing baron William Randolph Hearst in his quest to own vast collections of the world's art is computing software king Bill Gates, chairman and founder of Microsoft. Gates has been systematically buying the rights to store and publish electronically a huge collection of art masterpieces ranging from classic paintings by Vincent Van Gogh to contemporary artists as well. Among his acquisitions are the "Codex," Leonardo da Vinci's rare manuscript, for which Gates paid some $30.8 million, and the Bettman Archive, the greatest collection of historical photographs of the twentieth century. Gates has also created Corbis, a wholly owned Microsoft subsidiary intended to develop the needed digital technology and business strategies to market Gates's growing collection of images. Some are worried that public access to digital art and image collections will be severely limited, or subject to cost restrictions, if electronic art is controlled by corporate interests. Offering some poetic justice, "Millenium Auction" offers via CD-ROM a twenty-first-century marketplace where would-be collectors can bid on art works such as Manet's "Déjeuner sur l'Herbe" and Picasso's "Guernica."

SOCIOLOGICAL PERSPECTIVES ON NEW MEDIA TECHNOLOGY

Understanding the social and cultural importance of new media technologies also requires a close examination of the sociological transformation those technologies are triggering. To those living in the final years of the second millennium, it has become increasingly apparent that new media technologies offer important implications for how we live, work, and play. The following discussion turns a sociological prism on the growth and impact of new media technologies. Focusing first on the transformation of the workplace, the discussion includes a look at the role of gender, race, age, and social class in the use and impact of new technology, as well as the nature and consequences of computer-mediated communication.

Telecommuting: Transforming the Workplace

Five years ago we moved to Telluride, Colorado, a tiny mountain village in the southwest corner of the state. Our house and our town (population 1,200) are at 9,000 feet in a box canyon where the mountains all around us soar to 13,000 and 14,000 feet. It looks a little like the Swiss Alps.

> *Although we are six hours from Denver, with our computers, tele-phones, fax machine and Federal Express we are as in touch with the rest of the world as if we were in downtown Tokyo or London.*[97]

Just as the automobile and the national highway system helped transform the socio-logical landscape of America by fostering a more mobile society, so too will the information highway and new media technologies have important sociological ef-fects.[98] One of these effects is the growth of telecommuting, the ability to conduct one's work from a remote location. Advances in telephony, networked computing, and the fax machine have enabled increasing numbers of Americans to work from home or other locations away from a central office.[99] The growth of the Internet and the World Wide Web is spurring even greater advances in telecommuting. The Yan-kee Group (at its Web site) predicts that the number of full-time telecommuters in the United States will more than double by the end of the decade, growing from 3.4 million in 1995 to 7.9 million by 2000. The number of people who telecommute at least part time will likely be more than 10 million.

What do Buffalo, Wyoming, Sun Valley, California, Pullman, Washington, and Steamboat Springs, Colorado have in common with a growing number of other out-of-the-way places? One answer is new media technology: They are all fast emerging as the test sites for tomorrow's telecommunities. In Telluride, Colorado, an old min-ing town turned into a ski resort, The Telluride Institute has set up a new communi-cations program called InfoZone. By providing access to voice, data, and video through advanced cable television and telephone technology, the project has estab-lished a community-wide information system connecting residents with schools, the library, a health clinic, and other community centers, all via the Internet. In addition to the computer technology already in most residents' homes (more than 60 percent have a home PC versus the 36 percent nationwide), Apple computer has donated equipment for public places, such as the library. US West is laying optical fiber to service new subdivisions and the town is rapidly becoming fully wired. Richard Lowenberg, program director of the Telluride Institute, hopes that InfoZone will help answer some of the critical questions about the nature of the new telecommunity. "How does this affect the quality of life over the next 20 years? Are people going to be more alienated and have less face-to-face communication? Does it create a real economic engine for small communities or just keep costing more?" he asks.

In other communities, telecommunications systems are being upgraded to pro-vide enhanced telecommuting capabilities. 250 miles east of Seattle, officials of four counties near Pullman, Washington are negotiating with GTE to provide telecom-munications improvements in order to create attractive telecommuting opportunities for laid-off high-tech workers. The ranching community of Buffalo, Wyoming has received dozens of inquiries from people who want to telecommute from the town where Owen Wister wrote *The Virginian.* Meanwhile, a nonprofit group in Durango, Colorado is working to build a backup communications system for area telecommuters. The nonprofit is negotiating with AT&T to buy thirty abandoned microwave towers to serve as a backup system for the community.[100]

A growing number of studies are beginning to document the social and environmental benefits of telecommuting, and its positive influence on overall quality of life, both for individuals and their communities, as well as for enhancing work performance and worker productivity, sometimes by as much as 100 percent.[101]

New media technology has other important implications for the sociology of the workplace. Not all of them are as socially redeeming as telecommuting, however.

Letting the Computer Do the Dirty Work

One big Wall Street firm, for example, uses network technology to let its employees know when they've been fired. Rather than sending a pink slip or a letter of termination, an employee who's been let go slowly discovers the truth as they unsuccessfully try to log on to the computer network. First, they think they've misstyped their password, but slowly the realization—and panic—sets in. Soon, they are confronted by the reality that they cannot log on using their password because they've been deleted from the computer system, and from the company payroll.

No April Fool

In contrast, some new media technologies have created an environment for unexpectedly positive change in the workplace. Among them is the introduction of electronic mail at the corporate offices of a New Jersey firm. On April 1, 1994, Jack Miller, an employee at Witco Corporation in Woodcliff Lake, New Jersey, was stricken with severe chest pains, and tried to call out to his colleagues but was unable to utter a sound.[102] Instead, he quickly typed a message and sent it via e-mail to everyone in his department. When his coworkers read the message, "HELP. FEEL SICK. I NEED AID." they darted to his side and administered cardiopulmonary resuscitation and then had him transported to the Valley Hospital in nearby Ridgewood. Doctors there confirmed Miller had suffered two recent heart attacks, and might have died if not for his quick treatment. The e-mail message caught Miller's coworkers by surprise. "When the message first popped up on my screen, I had to do a double take. Usually, Jack and I will only message each other about business," says one colleague. Miller, who is a computer specialist for the firm, sums things up, "For me, e-mail means Emergency Mail."

Gender and Technology Use

We knew "Battletech" was limited. It plays to a 92 percent male audience. If a couple walks up to a Battletech Center, they begin arguing; then the man goes inside and the woman walks away.[103]

Gender oftentimes has been a defining factor in the emergence and use of new media technologies. Males tend to have higher usage of new media technologies, and they have designed much of the communication software and hardware. Although there have been notable exceptions, such as new media pioneer Vivian Horner, who is the creator of much new video programming for children, including Nickelodeon, much of the history of new media technology has been a story of men, from Alexander Graham Bell to William Gates. A telling recent example is "Battletech," one of the first and most successful networked virtual reality simulations; it appeals almost exclusively to males.[104] Created by Dungeons & Dragons aficionados Jordan Weisman and Russ Babcoc, the first commercial Battletech center opened in Chicago in 1990, and almost immediately reaped a profit. Walt Disney's grandson Tim and his partners bought the rights to Battletech in 1992, and transformed it into Virtual World Entertainment, a string of urban arcades featuring Battletech and other proposed offerings. "We knew 'Battletech' was limited," Disney admits.[105] "It plays to a 92 percent male audience. If a couple walks up to a Battletech Center, they begin arguing; then the man goes inside and the woman walks away."

Transcending Gender

The information superhighway holds the promise of opening up the doors to women. One illustration comes from the world of cyberspace. Within the Internet, New York's Stacy Horn has created her own East Coast Hang Out (ECHO), founded in 1989. As one writer describes it, ECHO "is a metropolitan oasis, an electronic gathering place for writers, artists and culture mavens, closer to a literary salon than the usual on-line techno-jock boys' club."[106] Although most information services tend to be male-dominated, ECHO appeals nearly equally to women. Of ECHO's more than 3,000 subscribers, nearly half are women (more than 40 percent), says Horn. In contrast, only 10 percent of Compuserve's subscribers are female.[107] ECHO's users pay a monthly fee of $19.95 to $34.95, and have access to online discussions of topics ranging from American mythologies to writing. They also have access to several women-only conferences, including WAC, run by the Women's Action Coalition, coordinating worldwide pro-choice, child support, and anti-date rape political actions, and WIT, the Women in Telecommunications conference, which Horn likens to "a pajama party." In true media convergence form, every Thursday at 11 p.m. Manhattan Cable viewers tuning in to a program called Electronic Neighborhood can read Echo keyboard conversations displayed on their TV screen, and listen to separate three-way telephone conversations.[108]

Reflecting the democratic potential of the information superhighway, Horn launched Echo with nothing more than the severance pay she received from Mobil Oil when the company moved to Virginia and she resigned[109] Steven Levy, noted new media journalist and author of Hackers, observes, "Without Stacy Horn, there would be no Silicon Alley" (the term coined by Mark Stahlman to describe the new media hotbed of Manhattan).

Women on the Web

Interesting data from the Pew Research Center reveal that the gender gap in Web use is narrowing.[110] A national study of online users shows that not only has the percentage of online users who ever use the Web risen dramatically from 1995 (21 percent) to 1996 (73 percent), the relative difference between men and women's use of the Web has narrowed. In 1995, 26 percent of male online users sometimes used the Web, while half that many, just 13 percent of female online users sometimes surfed the Web. In 1996, however, while the percent of male online users who ever surfed the Web increased to 79 percent (four out of five), the percent of female online users increased almost as much, to 64 percent (two of out of three).

Webgrrls International asks the provocative question, who says they're not out there, and answers it. Women have entered the Web and conquered it. Thousands of creative and diverse Web sites have been designed and launched by women all over the globe. Many of them are linked through a detailed directory published by of the largest women's Web organization, Webgrrls International.[111] Among the links is Femina, a site that provides links to sites on a broad array of subjects, ranging from women and the arts to women and writing.

Women who through their leadership and vision are making a difference in both the private and public worlds of new media technology include:

- Ellen Hancock, senior vice president, IBM
- Mary Burnside, chief operating officer, Novell
- Michele DiLorenzo, executive vice president, Viacom New Media
- Sueann Ambron, vice president, Paramount Technology
- Jacqueline Woods, chief executive officer, Ameritech, Ohio
- Audrey Well, vice president, America OnLine
- Terry Hershey, president, Time Warner Interactive
- Carlene Ellis, senior vice president, Intel
- Patricia Seybold, president, Patricia Seybold Group
- Patty Stonesifer, vice president, Microsoft
- Susan Ness, FCC commissioner, communications attorney and vice president/ group head at American Securities Bank
- Rachelle Chong, FCC commissioner and a communications attorney from San Francisco
- Mary Lowe Good, undersecretary for technology, U.S. Commerce Department
- Esther Dyson, president of EDventures Holdings, and Chair of the Electronic Frontier Foundation
- Denise Caruso, president and editorial director of Technology & Media Group, New York Times new media columnist, and member of the board of the Electronic Frontier Foundation
- Jane Metcalf, President and cofounder of *Wired* magazine
- Nancy Frishberg, Executive Director, New Media Centers, the special educational computing program established by Apple
- Lori Fena, executive director of the Electronic Frontier Foundation
- Arati Prabhakar, director, National Institute of Standards & Technology, Commerce Department[112]

Research also has helped to identify several important questions on women and new technology.[113] Australian communications scholar Bernadette Flynn says we should consider these four questions in the context of women and new technology:

- Who has access to the technology and in whose interests is it designed?
- What positions might be adopted in relation to female/machine exchanges rather than human (male)/machine relations?
- What positions might feminists adopt in relation to their technology in constructing new meanings and cultural positions?
- What strategies can be employed by the female artist for oppositional and transgressive positions that privilege a feminist agenda?

MIT professor Sherry Turkle adds an extra dimension of insight into how technology and gender interact in her landmark book, *The Second Self.*[114] Turkle's research suggests that boys and girls tend to bring different cognitive styles to their computer interactions. Girls tend to engage in a form of soft mastery in which the computer is understood as sensuous and tactile. In contrast, boys tend to engage in a form of hard mastery characterized by a competitive approach to working with computers and an attempt to impose their will over use of the machine.

People of Color and New Media Technology

"Future archaeologists, studying the documentary record of the present," writes new media expert Adam Clayton Powell III, "would have reason to conclude that people of color were bypassed by the information highway."[115] Not only have people of color been bypassed by the information highway, but, as with women, they have had only a limited role in the development of new media in general. The reasons for this limited involvement are many, including historical forces, the fact that high-tech fields tend to be dominated traditionally by white males, and even the government has been less than fully inclusive of people of color in the process of building policy on the National Information Infrastructure. However, the situation is beginning to change, as attitudes shift, new media enter the mainstream, and educational institutions known for their technology leadership enroll record numbers of women and minority group students. Some minority group leaders in the new media field are listed below.

- Stan Thomas, president and CEO of Time Warner's new interactive Sega Channel
- Susan Bokern, associate director of Gannett New Business
- Robert Johnson, founder of Black Entertainment Television
- Larry Irving, assistant secretary, U.S. Commerce Department
- Eduardo Gomez, president and general manager of KABQ Radio in Albuquerque

- Carroll Blue, an award-winning documentary filmmaker and professor at the School of Communication at San Diego State University, and a leader in developing storytelling forms for new media
- Jorge Schement, a Rutgers University professor, who is preparing a report on universal service for the Federal Communications Commission

One fascinating development on the Web is the WebDiva Information Center.[116] WebDiva offers a comprehensive set of links to sites of particular interests to persons of African heritage, ranging from current news to financial resources available for minority-owned businesses. Included is a nearly exhaustive list of African American women and men who have created Web sites. Among the more interesting links is that of Susan Grant, whose architectural design site provides a three-dimensional multimedia tour of her projects ranging from work for WGN-TV in Chicago to the University of California at Berkeley Students Services Center.

Recent data show that Internet access among minority groups is on the rise. A 1995 telephone survey conducted by FIND/SVP research firm shows that African Americans, Latinos, and Asians make up a combined total of 11 percent of Internet users nationwide, with African Americans comprising the largest group with 5 percent of the total.[117]

Generational Issues in New Media Technology

Once the battle cry of hippies, yippies, and many 1960s radicals, "Don't trust anyone over 30" could easily be adapted to "Just ask someone under 30" in today's new media environment. New media technology is the province of the young, especially the worlds of cyberspace and multimedia technology. Teenagers are among the heaviest users of online communication services. They are also the first to explore most new videogames, CD-ROM products, and virtual reality creations. If not for the little matter of cost, their usage of these technologies would be even higher. Of course, the youthful nature of new media technologies is nothing new. A classic example from the modern era of media technology is the creative force that founded Apple Computer, a team including a youthful Steve Jobs, Steve Wosniak, and others, all in their early twenties at the time. Today's parallel is the creators of Mosaic, the original graphical software window to the World Wide Web, created by a team of computer programmers, all also in their twenties.

Implications for the Individual: Empowerment Through Technology

Although new media technologies pose many threats to the cherished values of privacy, intellectual property, and access to information, they also hold promise of a better future. One of the most likely benefits of the emerging communication technologies is personal empowerment. As the personal computer has become increasingly common and powerful, millions of individuals around the world have been empowered to act, communicate, or participate in the broader society and political process. "Because it enhances the abilities of a single person so dramatically," writes Steven Levy, author of *Artificial Life*, "the computer is a great equalizer. Individuals or small groups can duplicate efforts that previously could only be performed by large institutions or governments. A single college student in a dormitory room or a lone political dissenter in a basement apartment can produce a document that glistens with professional authority—the electronic rebirth of the 'lonely pamphleteer' that helped incite American democracy in the first place."[118]

Computer-Mediated Communication

Computer-mediated communication (CMC) has emerged not only as a much more efficient and rapid form of one-on-one communications than traditional hardcopy letters. "It's a populist form of broadcasting as well."[119] Those using CMC have moved beyond the traditional paradigm of broadcasting used by the mass media of television, radio, and newspapers, which emphasize a one-to-many approach. "Instead, they *participate*," notes Levy. CMC incorporates the one-to-one interactivity of the telephone to create a new form of many-to-many online communications carried out in real time and across political and cultural divides. Electronic mail and computer bulletin boards make it just as easy to send a message to one person as to thousands connected to the network anywhere in the world. Recent research confirms that messaging, or sending electronic messages between or among individuals, is the most popular use of computer networks of all types.[120] An illustration of the use of a computer bulletin board called the WELL has interesting implications for traditional providers of news and other media content. One of the oldest computer bulletin boards, the WELL is run from the modest headquarters of the Whole Earth collective in Sausalito, California, and serves as an electronic commons. Howard Rheingold, author of *The Virtual Community: Homesteading on the Electronic Frontier*, recalls how he tapped into the WELL after finding a tick on his two-year-old daughter's scalp.[121] While his wife phoned the pediatrician, Rheingold logged onto the WELL via his computer modem. Before his wife could reach the doctor, a physician reading messages posted on the WELL encountered Rheingold's query and provided a response indicating how to safely remove the tick. Science and technology writer Steven Levy relates a similar experience from a session on the WELL. Someone posted a message discussing the reporting of ABC News correspondent Cokie Roberts, prompting another "WELL being" to respond by expressing admiration for Ms. Roberts's work, and pondering how she ever got the name "Cokie." Rather than visit the local library in search of biographical data about Ms. Roberts or pay for an expensive search on Nexis, the WELL provided the answer. One of the so-called "lurkers" on the WELL happened to know a relative of Ms. Roberts. A quick phone call to his friend produced an answer, which was then relayed over the WELL: "an early propensity for Coca-Cola led to Cokie Roberts' nickname."[122]

The implications for the traditional providers of media content are profound and far-reaching. As was evidenced in the 1992 and 1996 presidential campaigns, new media such as computer bulletin boards and the Internet are providing increasingly direct access to a variety of information sources, sometimes supplanting or even replacing the traditional news media.[123] As new media grow in popularity and reach an ever greater portion of society, old media need to adapt. One important strategy of adaptation is by participating in the online communications world sometimes referred to as *cyberspace*. This means going online as an equal participant with thousands of others. Advertisers, for example, might utilize this new medium by participating in online forums related to their business, and providing information about the company's relevant products or services. One caveat is in order here. Some innovative public relations firms such as Manning, Selvage & Lee or Porter/ Novelli have effectively incorporated participation in online forums into their research and public dialog, sometimes learning of important trends in public opinion long before they might emerge in a traditional public opinion poll, or in contributing to public discourse on certain critical issues. As these firms have done, it is essential to clearly identify oneself as a representative of a firm or client, so that those members of the public also participating in the online forum understand the context of your participation.

News organizations are similarly entering the online world in increasing numbers. Some, for example, are sponsoring public computer bulletin boards oriented to news and public affairs as well as arranging Internet chat rooms where readers can "meet" with journalists and hold online discussions of issues of coverage. In July 1993, *New York Newsday*, for example, set up an online bulletin board with interested readers to provide a forum for discussing a series the paper was running on the information highway. Since then, a variety of news organizations ranging from *Time* to the Mercury Center have set up similar online forums as part of their online edition. The *Toronto Globe and Mail* is one newspaper that has taken online communications a step further, providing reporters and editors with e-mail addresses, and encouraging them to use them to interact with readers. Although it adds a layer of work for the journalists, the reader interaction has produced a number of benefits, including providing a means to better gauge reader interest in dimensions of stories that might have been overlooked by the news organization.

Replacing Interpersonal with
Mediated Communication

Historians have documented the role of new technology and the emergence of mediated communication in the nineteenth century in supplanting interpersonal communication as the principle means of the diffusion of news. Historian Richard Brown, for example, has shown how news about the battles of Lexington and Concord and George Washington's death spread largely along well-traveled networks of interpersonal communication.[124] News about the assassination of President Abraham Lincoln, in contrast, spread rapidly along impersonal media of communication, especially the telegraph, newspapers, and tolling bells atop church towers.

This was particularly the case in the North, while in the South, word spread more sporadically and slowly, often along interpersonal networks.

From the *War of the Worlds* to the World Wide Web.   Listeners to the Mercury Theater were treated to a special Halloween treat on October 31, 1938, when Orson Welles broadcast the famous *War of the Worlds* radio play. Meant to be a Halloween treat, the broadcast stirred a panic among thousands of listeners who believed Martians had really landed at Grovers Mills, New Jersey. Today, this phenomenon could occur on a global scale via the World Wide Web. Consider some of the rumors born on the Internet. Among the most famous are the alleged purchase of the Roman Catholic Church by Microsoft, the accidental downing of TWA Flight 800 by "friendly fire" by the U.S. Navy, and the so-called "Good Times" computer virus that is neither a good time nor a real computer virus. Another message charged that the FBI had blown up its own building in Oklahoma City to trigger a crackdown on militia groups. A particularly interesting Internet "rumor" involves the case of the tragic death of rock musician Kurt Cobain. Shortly after the death of the popular music icon in April 1994, a Web site was posted by a private investigator who reports that Cobain did not commit suicide; instead, he was murdered.[125] The investigator presents a sophisticated multimedia Web site complete with evidence documenting the murder, including photographs and details on Cobain's impending divorce from Courtney Love.

Similarly, a variety of "fake" campaign Web sites were launched during the 1996 presidential campaign. Examples include satirical sites lampooning the candidates, as well as sites that at least on the surface presented credible information, but on closer inspection were not created by the candidates or media themselves. For example, one site presented itself as a report from the *New York Times,* proclaiming on election night that "Dole Beats Clinton," evoking memories of the infamous newspaper headline "Dewey Beats Truman," which also turned out to be in error. The "Dole Beats Clinton" site provided a detailed news story explaining the nature of Dole's victory, written in credible newspaper style.[126] Here's the lead: "One hundred-twenty years after Republican Rutherford B. Hayes edged out Samuel Tilden by a single electoral vote, Senator Robert J. Dole appears to have captured the White House by the narrowest of margins. With 95 percent of all ballots counted in the nine states with the tightest races, Dole is ahead of Bill Clinton in enough states to give him a 271–267 victory in the Electoral College." Not only that, but the site presented a detailed map of the U.S. electoral college voting results. Although the site notes the "official" electoral vote count, the site presents a convincing portrait of the Dole victory.

Hate Groups on the Internet.   Particularly disturbing has been the rise of hate groups on the Internet and on the World Wide Web. Among the groups with Web sites are the Ku Klux Klan, Aryan Nations, and various white separatist groups.[127] Featuring sophisticated multimedia messages, one site uses streaming audio to "welcome Aryan brothers and sisters" to its site, as well as playing a heavy metal rock composition proclaiming that "One day the world will know that Adolf Hitler was right." Another declares, "WE BELIEVE that the Cananite [sic] Jew is the natural enemy of our Aryan (White) Race." Unlike neo-Nazi and other hate groups that operate in the "real world," those that operate out of cyberspace can do so with relative anonymity and impunity, reaching out to teenagers in the middle of the night plugging in from their home computer. The Anti-Defamation League (ADL) published a special report in late 1996 documenting the frightening rise of hate groups in the online world. The ADL report notes,

> *Well-known bigots and hate groups are on the Web. Other groups, among them the Holocaust deniers, their language less overtly hateful than the "traditional groups," use the Web to present pseudoscholarly arguments to buttress their bigotry and further their barely hidden neo-Nazi agenda. Then there are the newcomers to the propagation of prejudice and hatred, initially independent of any organization, who take to the Web to spread their messages of hate.[128]*

Romancing the Electronic Stone. As it transforms the most fundamental aspects of human society, the information superhighway is also changing the nature of romance. Or rather, the way romance is carried out, at least in the workplace. One happy couple carried out a year-long courtship via e-mail before their wedding in 1993.[129] Burke Stinson and Nancy J. Smith, executives at AT&T in New Jersey, traded some 400 pages of confessions and passions through interoffice e-mail, sometimes sending two or three love letters and notes a day. "It's such a thrill to bare one's soul right on the screen, see it, save it, re-read it, then swallow hard and push the send button," says Ms. Smith.[130] Writer Avodah Offit uses e-mail as a vehicle of sexual healing in her first novel, *Virtual Love*, in which a San Francisco therapist communicates with a colleague in New York by computer and modem. The messages become increasingly erotic, as the therapist describes his fantasies about a troubled patient, a prostitute he describes as "32 years old, single, Native American, part Swede and extraordinarily attractive."[131]

Even traditions such as writing letters to Santa Claus have found an electronic replacement on the new media landscape. Novalink, based in Westborough, Massachusetts, happily forwards all electronic letters sent to santa@novalink.com straight to the North Pole.[132]

Not all the uses of e-mail and other forms of computer-mediated communication have had a positive impact on romantic and sexual relationships. Two troubling cases emerged in late 1996. One involved a Columbia University doctoral student who met a young co-ed via an electronic chat room, corresponded by e-mail, and finally met her for a first date. The co-ed went to the doctoral student's apartment at the end of the evening, only to suffer an alleged twenty-hour ordeal of bondage, torture, and sexual assault. In another perhaps even more bizarre case, a married woman met a man through the Internet, and left her husband to join him in another state. The woman was discovered dead shortly thereafter. Her e-mail records revealed that she went to meet him with the intention of being killed.

THEORETICAL PERSPECTIVES ON THE SOCIAL CONSEQUENCES OF NEW MEDIA TECHNOLOGY

Emerging alongside these digital wonders are a number of important theoretical perspectives and models aimed at critically evaluating the impact of these technologies as well as enhancing scholarly and public understanding of their role in society. These perspectives include the uses and gratifications model, systems theory, a knowledge hierarchy model, and critical perspectives.

Uses and Gratifications Research

Uses and gratifications research suggests that people watch, read and listen to the media to meet certain social and psychological needs.[133] Typical uses of the media include reading a newspaper in order to stay connected to society or watching television to avoid loneliness. From a uses and gratifications perspective, one might expect new media technologies to help people satisfy a range of social and psychological needs. For example, much of the development and use of new media technologies for erotic communications may be derived from sexual drives or needs of audience members. One might similarly explain the use of electronic mail and online communications in terms of the need to maintain social ties over great distances and political boundaries. This is especially apparent in electronic communications among so-called virtual communities that exist over vast geographic regions, all linked in cyberspace.

Media uses and gratifications also vary by medium. Les Brown, a leading television journalist, critic and author, has observed that his forty years of experience leads him to conclude that television despite its efforts to the contrary, is an emotional medium, one that produces visceral responses in viewers.[134] When people saw the horrors of prisoner of war camps in Bosnia in 1993 it elicited such a strong response that it affected U.S. foreign policy. A recent eight-country public opinion survey by Times Mirror similarly found that Americans both had among the poorest knowledge of public affairs issues, but among the highest viewership of television news. Thus, Brown concludes that television is the least intellectual of all media and the most emotional. Radio, he suggests, is somewhat more intellectual, and because of its low cost and portability, is the future of news in the age of the information superhighway. Newspapers and news magazines are even more intellectual. But the most intellectual is the computer, where active information seeking is the norm. In contrast, television usage tends to be much more passive. These views are confirmed through a variety of scholarly studies, as well, although little uses and gratifications research has focused on interactive TV.[135] As a result, the role of television in the digital age may be to produce the entertainment superhighway, while computers may become the on-ramp to the information superhighway. Confounding all this is the telephone. Telecommunications scholar Frederick Williams, a professor at the University of Texas, believes that the screen phone may be one of the best information highway on-ramps, because of its low cost, ease of use, and potential for universality.[136] Of course, the screen phone is limited by the amount of information that can be displayed both visually or aurally. A similar conundrum may emerge with the growth of WebTV, which combines the emotional medium of television with the intellectual capabilities of the computer. Most likely, there will emerge multiple on-ramps, each serving different information needs for different audiences, perhaps even varying by the situation each consumer finds him- or herself in through the day or a lifetime.

Les Brown is also concerned about the culture of the television industry, both cable and broadcast, and the likelihood that it can ever produce a product that delivers more than the core killer applications of the information superhighway, including movies-on-demand, home shopping, and videogames, and the even less socially redeeming gambling and pornography.[137] As cable companies vied for cable franchises in the 1970s and 1980s, many companies promised spectacular systems featuring interactive services and extensive public access. But when the companies obtained the franchises, few actually delivered on their promises. The overselling of cable in the 1980s has many parallels in today's highly charged environment, as some of these same companies promise highly developed systems of interactive television, but are already experiencing delays in delivering services. Even if they do deliver on some of the so-called killer applications, such as movies-on-demand, home shopping, and videogames, and some of the more socially questionable services such as gambling and pornography, Brown is concerned that there will be little priority placed on developing a central place for journalism, education, and other services that may have high social value but little commercial attractiveness. This commercial development may limit the uses and gratifications new media will provide.

On an even more fundamental level, communication scholar John Phelan suggests that computers may be altering the very minds of those who use them. He argues that ever-increasing computing speed enhances the computer user's feeling of computational control and integration with the computer itself.[138] Increasingly fast computers become as transparent as the biological senses of sight, smell, touch, and taste. As a result, people use computers without even thinking about how they work, or recognizing their consequences. Computing speed, then, is far more than merely a computing improvement—it helps transform the computer into an extension of the human mind.

A Systems Theory Perspective

Fundamental to a systems theory perspective on new media technology is the notion of complexity. Complexity, which refers to the level of differentiation or heterogeneity in a system, is a fundamental quality of all systems. It acts as a critical mechanism in determining how any system responds to input, stimuli, or change in its environment. One of the pioneers in the study of complexity in systems theory is Dr. Murray Gell-Mann, a Nobel prize-winning author and the founder of the Sante Fe Institute, an independent research organization dedicated to understanding the behavior of complex systems. Gell-Mann suggests there are two types of complex systems.[139] The first type has no ability to learn or evolve biologically. Illustrative of such complex systems are galaxies or solar systems. The second type is capable of adaptive behavior. Such complex adaptive systems are especially relevant to an understanding of new media technologies. This is apparent with the advent of artificial intelligence and artificial life, the interplay between complex systems of business, government, and other institutions and media technology and the fundamental role of feedback, as communication, in complex adaptive systems. Each complex system is interdependent on evolving media technologies in a process of coevolution.

Critical Perspectives

> "This instrument can teach, it can illuminate; yes, and it can inspire. But it can only do so to the extent that humans are determined to use it to those ends. Otherwise it is merely wires and lights in a box."
> —EDWARD R. MURROW[140]

Murrow spoke these words about television, but today he might just as well have said them about computers, or the emerging information superhighway and its many technical devices for accessing, receiving, and interacting with multimedia communications. Although some argue that technology—any technology—is inherently value-laden, it is ultimately how we humans use that technology that determines its social effects. Critical philosopher Jacques Ellul argued in favor of a stronger view, in which technology is almost autonomous in its development and in the spread of its influence.[141] Ellul even suggests that technology is like a religion whose god is efficiency, whose high priests are economists, and whose loyal servants are engineers. This view has been popularized in modern fiction, as well, by writers such as Ira Levin in *The Stepford Wives* or Rod Serling in *The Twilight Zone*. Horror novelist Dean Koontz examined the darker side of the information highway in his runaway best-seller *Midnight*. In the novel, he created a master villain whose vision of a utopian society was a world peopled by genetically engineered human–computer mutants, drained of all emotion except fear, and driven by an unquenchable thirst for efficiency.[142] Twenty-five years earlier science fiction author Anne McCaffrey articulated a similar view, writing of giant spaceships peopled by physically helpless humans hardwired into a central computer.[143]

James Beniger, author of *The Control Revolution*, has sought a middle ground, arguing for neither technological determinism nor technological rationalism.[144] In his view, technological innovation is called on to solve problems brought about by previous technological creations.

Others have challenged and refined some of these notions, suggesting that often driving technological change is the class phenomenon of economic and political power. Joseph Schumpeter and Nikolai Kondratieff are economic geographers who subscribe to the notion of long wave theory, in which economic, political, and technological change are seen as coming in long-term, highly interrelated cycles. The so-called "Fifth Kondratieff" represents the coming economic upswing driven by widespread innovation based on computer and information technology—the information superhighway. In this view, some will experience "gales of destructive force" based on factors in the competitive marketplace, while others will experience profound gains.[145] Moreover, certain technologies will be seen as more appropriate or essential in the new world economic order. In today's context, multimedia, interactive, digital technologies are part of the coming wave of such winning technologies.

Cybernetic Capitalism

Even farther along the critical continuum lie neo-Marxist scholars such as Frank Webster, Kevin Robins, and Oscar Gandy, who see the current generation of technological change as less a revolution, and more an extension of capitalist influences in a post-industrial society, a sort of "cybernetic capitalism."[146] In *The Panoptic Sort*, Gandy describes an all-seeing . . . model" derived from technology.[147] Dan Schiller, a University of California at San Diego communication professor, suggests that new technology has contributed directly to the "commoditization" of information. To Schiller, information is "the making of meaning in capitalist society," and a commodity as "a resource produced for the market by wage labor."[148] Therefore, the making of meaning is synonymous with the making of money in a capitalist society. Schiller argues that the processes of commoditization have "repeatedly congealed around new means of information production: the whole succession of technologies of information objectification, beginning with printing and continuing through lithography, photography, film, audio recording, video and currently, digital signal processing."[149] Schiller further argues that it is to these purposes that the new media technologies must be put. "The suggestion that, to the contrary, such technologies can be put to other uses, seems to me doubly spurious. . . . In historical terms—the only terms that truly matter—such technologies have provided indispensable sites of capitalist accumulation."[150]

The Road to Utopia or Simply a Digital Toll Road?

Much of what we understand about the information highway is filled with the same kind of illusion, deception, and sleight of hand found along L. Frank Baum's fictional yellow brick road, contends media studies scholar Oscar Gandy, a professor of communication at Annenberg School for Communication at the University of Pennsylvania.[151] The information age, much less the information highway, is a utopian tale, Gandy writes, promising an end to adversity, discrimination, and want. What they will deliver, unfortunately, is just the opposite, he says. Not at all a truly yellow brick road, the information highway will be a toll road with a pay-as-you-go philosophy designed not to further the public good or provide universal access. Rather, the companies building the information highway are doing so for one purpose: to create their own cities of gold, an El Dorado of the digital age, where El

Camino Real leads, not to Silicon Valley, but to Cebolla, the lost city of gold once sought by Spanish conquistador, Hernan Cortés. The situation brings to mind a joke sometimes told by the Emmy award-winning ABC-TV network executive, Julius Barnathan. Barnathan whimsically recalls the three great lies: "Sure, baby, I'll still love you in the morning," "The check is in the mail," and, "Hi! I'm from the phone company. I'm here to help you."[152]

Echoing this skeptical view are some communication scholars who question the intentions of many of the principal players on the information highway, not just those of the phone companies. Jerry Salvaggio, a Rutgers University professor, has studied the promotion of the technology of the information age. He concludes that companies promoting those technologies do so primarily in their own interest. It is in their interest to "hasten the arrival of the information society by fostering a technological ideology," one emphasizing the benefits and not the costs of the technologies.[153]

Recent advertising campaigns by such leading telecommunications firms as AT&T and MCI demonstrate the role of corporate communications in this process. MCI has drawn much attention from industry ad watchers by creating a surrealistic campaign about the coming information highway in which international child star Anna Paquin, the then eleven-year-old New Zealander who won an Oscar for her supporting performance in 1993's *The Piano*, describes the virtues of the coming digital data network. "The information highway will have no speed limits . . . It will have no gas stations . . . This is not about data, digits, technology. It's not even about highways," Paquin declares in the ethereal ads, "It's about you and me and uncle Jack and everybody." The impact of the ad is subtle, yet powerful, contends one psychologist. Carol Moog, president of Creative Focus, Bala-Cynwyd, Pennsylvania, and a psychologist who has served as an advertising consultant since 1982, says the ad is a "powerful metaphor" that "resonates with a psychological place in all people."[154] "In most of the MCI spots," Moog explains, "this little girl [Anna Paquin] is at the beginning of a completely new virgin world, but she is a genius."

Social Inequality and Society's Have Nots

New media technologies are likely to produce more, not less, inequality in the distribution of wealth in society argue neo-Marxist scholars. These effects are especially likely to be felt among women and minorities, who will be disproportionately displaced by computer technologies in the workplace. Studies already indicate that a variety of media technologies have often bypassed the poor, especially women and minority group members, inner-city dwellers, and rural residents.[155] One resident of City Hill, Kansas, pointedly concludes that the phone company had relegated his town of 1,800 not to the information highway but to "the information cowpath."[156] Data from the Bureau of Labor Statistics also reveal a steady increase in long-term unemployment as a proportion of overall unemployment. Gandy suggests this trend "reflects a growing deficit . . . in the information age."[157]

Constructing a Technology Gap

Historically, new technological infrastructures, such as the railroad system or the national highway system, have tended to first serve society's elite, and only later have the benefits trickled down to the masses. This has been due largely to the high cost usually associated with the use of these new technologies. It is also likely that the information superhighway, a new national information infrastructure, will likely benefit first society's elite, the information rich. Thus, one might expect the gap between the information rich and poor to widen. Research by Tichenor, Donohue, and Olien, among others, demonstrates that information often diffuses differentially among the information rich and poor, contributing to an ever widening knowledge gap. Only under limited circumstances does the pattern not hold, such as situations of high involvement for the information poor and lower socioeconomic status (SES) groups, or when there is high conflict. We might expect the information highway to trickle down especially slowly to society's underclass for an additional reason. To use the information highway effectively, or even to recognize its value, may require knowledge and skills that many in lower SES groups simply don't have. As Jannette Dates, former Dean of the School of Communication at Howard University, has observed, the government will need to take special steps to insure that those excluded from society's information upper class see the value in the information superhighway and that they be empowered to use that highway effectively through educational efforts to enhance their skills in the electronic information environment. This is especially important if the information superhighway is the key to the economic fortunes of the global economy in the twenty-first century. Of course, some members of the information poor will find their own on-ramps to the information highway.

Center for Urban Youth

One project that is working to provide an on-ramp for the poor is the Center for Urban Youth and Technology at Columbia University Teachers College. Headed by Dr. Joseph E. Bowman, Jr., the Center is committed to bringing urban youth, especially minority students, into a rich and participative environment for learning about new media technologies. The program provides these students with both the empowering skills to use the technologies to produce multimedia content, as well as an understanding of how these technologies are transforming society.[158]

Riding the Twenty-First Century Rails.   Much as hobos rode the rails during the Great Depression of the 1930s, homeless persons have already started riding the information superhighway. One study by telecommunications professor William Dutton found that the homeless were among the heaviest users of an online public kiosk system in Santa Monica, California.[159] Homeless people were frequently registered users of the city's Public Electronic Network (PEN) reports Dutton, a professor at the Annenberg School for Communication at the University of Southern California. Using the kiosks located in public settings such as the public library, homeless persons have established their own online network and messaging environment to keep in touch. Several of the homeless users have joined in computer conferences. Still, this use represents only a fraction of the potential of the information highway. Supporting public access to the information superhighway needs to be a high priority in public policy, Dutton argues. "We have always subsidized low-income groups to give access to the telephone," Dutton says.[160] "The more people connected to any communication network, the more valuable it is," concludes Dutton.

International Perspectives

Globalization has become almost cliché in contemporary discussions of new media technologies. Nevertheless, media technologies truly are global in their reach and impact. The following section looks at the role of new media technology in the very important international arenas of national development and public diplomacy. Though much of the application of technology for development and public diplomacy is planned, many uses are surreptitious and unexpected, often the product of local ingenuity and efforts to bypass government restrictions, economic limitations, and traditional technological, political, and geographic boundaries.

New Media Technology and National Development

Scholars, policy-makers, and economic analysts widely view communication technology and telecommunications as central to the needs of developing countries. *The Missing Link*, the Maitland Commission report prepared for the International Telecommunication Union in 1984, made it very clear that telecommunications is an engine for economic and social development.[161] "It is now generally accepted by most countries around the world that very little economic and social growth can take place without an adequate telecommunications infrastructure," concludes David Wright, manager for Regional Programmes at Inmarsat, the international cooperative that provides global mobile satellite communications.[162] Today, many would broaden this notion to suggest that the information superhighway in general and the Internet in particular are fundamentally important in serving the communication needs of developing societies, not just to improve communication and commerce within regions and cities, but also in remote and rural areas, as a mechanism to slow the sometimes overwhelming migration to urban areas, where poverty, slums, and overcrowding await. The information superhighway can serve the communication needs of a variety of groups in developing countries, including farmers, those in natural resource industries, government officials at remote outposts, construction workers building railways, roads, and pipelines, medical practitioners providing health care services, journalists reporting from remote locations, civil protection forces, disaster relief agencies, and many more who rely on fast, efficient communication to perform their work.

The seemingly intractable telecommunications problem facing most developing nations, Wright argues, involves an economic catch-22. They need advanced communications technology to facilitate economic growth, but the required technologies—microwave towers, optical fiber, or even copper wire—are beyond most developing countries' reach. The dilemma, Wright contends, is not insoluble, however. One alternative is to develop mobile satellite communications networks in developing nations. The cost of creating mobile satellite services (MSS) in these countries is substantially less than land-based telecommunications infrastructures. This strategy of "leapfrogging" intermediate technologies has become increasingly popular in many of the world's developing regions, including Africa, Eastern Europe, and Latin America.

Despite the high cost, the diffusion of optical fiber throughout the developing regions of the world has accelerated in the 1990s. Optical fiber links now reach a broad array of countries in Asia, including the People's Republic of China, the Republic of Korea, Thailand, Vietnam, Brunei, Malaysia, Indonesia, and the Russian Federation.[163] Optical fiber also reaches India, many countries in the Caribbean (Bahamas, Jamaica, Dominican Republic, Puerto Rico), Oceania (Guam, Micronesia), South America (Venezuela, Brazil, Argentina, Uruguay), and Africa (Tunisia, Morocco, Western Sahara, Gambia, South Africa, Egypt, Ethiopia). Neal Stephenson reports in *Wired* magazine that the spread of optical fiber is rapidly connecting the entire planet to the information age, bringing with it broadband access to digital information.[164]

Scholars and policy-makers generally agree that new media technologies are essential tools for growth in the developing world. Heather Hudson, director of the Telecommunications Management and Policy Programme, McLaren School of Business, University of San Francisco, suggests that new telecommunication technologies provide increasingly instantaneous communication, and thus facilitate development through three primary mechanisms:

- Increased efficiency, defined in terms of the ratio of output to cost
- Enhanced effectiveness, defined as the extent to which development goals are achieved
- Greater equity, defined in terms of the distribution of development benefits throughout the society[165]

A variety of telecommunications technologies contribute to this process, Hudson notes, including

- Small satellite earth stations to improve rural telephony
- new radio technologies, which offer an affordable means to reach rural residents
- Facsimile, for low-cost transmission of text and graphics
- CD-ROM, for distributing large databases or multimedia information
- Audio and video conferencing to link remote locations for a variety of applications such as project administration or distance learning
- Electronic mail, for low-cost instantaneous communications both domestically and internationally

- Computer conferencing to provide interactive online forums for many users simultaneously
- Desktop publishing, to produce low-cost newsletters
- Access to databases, which is especially useful for research purposes in agriculture, providing low-cost, instant access to remote databases such as the Food and Agricultural Organization (FAO) database in Rome
- Electronic transactions, such as the transfer of funds between banks, airplane reservations, including tourist bookings, or trading commodities electronically, especially agricultural goods
- Voice messaging, possibly providing a voice mailbox for rural residents who lack individual telephones but have access to a public phone

In the Asia–Pacific region, new technology clearly plays a crucial role in economic development. Among those who have recently argued for the importance of new media technologies for development in the Asia–Pacific region are Hugh Leonard, secretary-general of the Asia–Pacific Broadcasting Union, Kuala Lumpur, Malaysia; Meheroo Jassawalla, an economist at the East–West Center, Honolulu, Hawaii; and, Georgette Wang, professor in the Graduate School of Journalism, National Chengchi University, Taiwan. Leonard writes that, although there is no "typical" country in the region, the winds of change are blowing, primarily due to the combination of new technology and deregulation.[166] The number of television households in Asia has increased by more than 70 percent since 1988, and new technologies, especially satellite television available via Asiasat, have transformed the viewing landscape. Combined with the relaxation of rules governing broadcasting in many Asian countries, broadcasting has taken on a vitally new significance in the economic development in the region.

Telecommunications also plays a critical role in the development in the Asian region, writes Meheroo Jussawalla.[167] "The prospects for growth of the telecommunication market in the Asian region are so promising . . . in terms of overall regional economic development," Jussawalla notes.[168] He explains that the technologies adding value to the gross domestic product (GDP) of the region have been optical fiber, facsimile, cellular telephony, and satellite earth receiving equipment. Nevertheless, the technological development of the region varies greatly country by country. Indonesia, for example, has the lowest density of telephones per hundred population at 0.8 (in 1991). Singapore, by contrast, is at the forefront of new media technologies, and is known as the "intelligent city."

Georgette Wang agrees that satellite television has revolutionized communications in the Asia–Pacific. She notes that the "reach" of modern communications satellites is "staggering."[169] Asiasat 1's footprint covers most of Asia and much of the Pacific. "However, satellite television is not the only new medium that has taken hold in Asia," she adds.[170] Cable TV and the VCR have also made significant inroads in the region.

Government responses to satellite television in the Asian region fall into four categories, reports Joseph Man Chan:

- Virtual suppression, such as in Singapore and Malaysia, where citizen access to satellite television is prohibited
- Regulated openness, as in Hong Kong and the Philippines, where access is permitted, but government regulates the redistribution of programs
- Illegal openness, such as in Taiwan and India, where government regulations merely discourage redistribution of programs via satellite
- Suppressive openness as seen in China, where the communist government prohibits private ownership of satellite receiver dishes and permits no access to "foreign television signals"[171]

At the same time, it is important to maintain a critical eye on the application of new media technologies in developing nations. Anwar Ibrahim, Minister for Finance, Malaysia, observes that for decades information technology has been viewed as largely value-free.[172] Technology has been judged largely from a utilitarian perspective, with economic benefits far outweighing any cultural costs. Ibrahim argues that "Asia needs to achieve material prosperity, with a re-flowering of culture at the same time. This will contribute to the heritage of mankind in the same way we have seen the West, since its ascendancy in the 16th century, produce some of the most remarkable cultural achievements in human history.[173] As the pace of technological change quickens, however, the value of diversity must be maintained, he cautions. "In the final analysis, the communication order we seek must not only expand our mental horizons, increase our range of choices, facilitate our decisions, it must also enrich our cultural experience and enlarge our freedom."[174]

Expecting the Unexpected:
The South African Experience

Not all uses of new media technology in developing regions fall into the category of planned applications. Many are both unexpected and ingenious. Consider the case of South Africa, as that country emerges from decades of apartheid. Under the apartheid state, the government of South Africa's official position was that no significant economic activity existed in the black townships, from Soweto to Lesotho. But visits to those townships quickly dispels that notion, reports Adam Clayton Powell III, who has made a series of visits to South Africa both before and after the official end of apartheid in 1994. Powell has recently continued his visits to South Africa, helping the Freedom Forum establish an international office in the developing nation. "Many parts of the townships I have visited look like Palo Alto (part of high-tech and wealthy Silicon Valley in California)," Powell says. Although official government sources denied the presence of any economic prosperity in these townships, people in corporate sales, however, knew the true level of activity. "Sony sells a lot of VCRs in the townships where there is officially no electricity," Powell notes.[175] There is a thriving battery business there, though. The government even published on CD-ROM a "complete" set of economic data for South Africa, excluding any data about the townships. Moreover, the South African census officially reports the population of the country to be some 38 million, but the data from the townships are based on nothing more than a crude population estimate derived from aerial photographs of the regions. Putting these data into electronic form and distributing them via the information highway will not only fail to improve their accuracy, but could compound the problem by making them widely available. Powell's 1996 visits to South Africa also produced an answer to the question often wondered by many computer mavens in the West: Whatever happened to the all the Commodore 64 computers? They wound up in South Africa and are being used to log onto the Internet and browse the World Wide Web.

Public Diplomacy and New Technology

New media technology has not escaped the ever watchful eye of diplomats and world leaders eager to reach an increasingly electronic audience. With the dawn of international television systems, especially CNN, the global news network, the international scene has witnessed the advent of "media pervasiveness" as well as electronic public diplomacy.[176] The pervasiveness of the media was demonstrated for the world to see during the Tiananmen Square demonstrations when CNN pioneered real-time news coverage for a global audience. The impact of media pervasiveness is clear in the process of international diplomacy. "For policymakers, the nonstop coverage of CNN (also coming in the future from the BBC and others) presents opportunities to constantly monitor news events and disseminate timely diplomatic information," writes James F. Hoge, Jr., the editor of the distinguished journal *Foreign Affairs*.[177] Although there may be earlier examples, none were more dramatic than the public diplomacy carried out on CNN by Iraq's Saddam Hussein and the U.S.'s George Bush during the Persian Gulf war. No witness to the historic Middle East conflict will ever forget the image of Hussein patting a British child on the head that was being held hostage in Baghdad. However inept, Hussein's efforts to sway the international court of public opinion were enabled by the global presence and reach of satellite-based television technology. By virtue of its universal presence, CNN became the medium of choice for carrying out this tele-diplomacy.

Beyond CNN, other new media technologies are influencing the process of international diplomacy, as well. By creating an environment of instantaneous global communication, technologies such as the Internet, fax communications, and satellite television have increased the pace and public visibility of diplomacy. "Today's correspondents employ lap-top computers, wireless telephones that transmit directly to satellites and mobile satellite dishes to broadcast vivid pictures and commentary from the scenes of tragedy and disorder without the transmission delays, political obstructions or military censorship of old," explains James F. Hoge, the former publisher of the New York *Daily News*.[178] No longer can diplomats and heads of state take several days to ponder foreign policy matters as President John F. Kennedy did during the Berlin Wall crisis of August, 1961. "[P]oliticians are more concerned than elated by global, real-time broadcasting," adds Hoge. "They worry about a 'loss of control' and decry the absence of quiet time to deliberate choices, reach private agreements and mold the public's understanding. They point with nostalgia to how those opportunities helped President John F. Kennedy respond safely to the discovery of Soviet missiles in Cuba."[179] Instead, the global communications grid now necessitates policy decisions, actions, and communications on an almost equally instantaneous basis. If a world leader delays in responding to a widely known crisis situation, perhaps made visible through television, as images of prisoner of war camps did in Bosnia in 1992, he or she will likely look indecisive, weak, or worse in the international media and court of public opinion. Moreover, lack of rapid policy-making or public diplomacy in this hyper-information environment can have significant economic implications. By delaying response to an important international development, financial traders, for example, who have access to vast real-time information services around the world, may make momentous decisions profoundly affecting the world's currency. Conversely, policy-makers run an equal risk of setting off a financial stampede by acting too impulsively.

Social Consequences and Public Policy

All too frequently public policy decisions about new media technologies flow largely from the commercial interests surrounding those technologies, with social and cultural consequences carrying little weight in the policy debate. This occurs for several reasons, including the fact that, like all areas of public policy, commercial interests have the greatest resources to support lobbying in Washington. In addition, however, scholarly study of the social and cultural consequences of emerging technologies is scarce and difficult to undertake both because of limited funding and because the technologies of concern may not even exist.

A FRAMEWORK FOR UNDERSTANDING THE SOCIAL CONSEQUENCES OF NEW MEDIA TECHNOLOGY

This chapter has outlined a conceptual framework for understanding the likely social and cultural consequences of new and emerging media technologies. The framework rests on four major themes:

- Enduring topics and issues of major public and scholarly concern about the social consequences of new media technologies, including potential social fragmentation, privacy concerns and the growth of virtual communities, as well as implications for social institutions and computer-mediated communication
- Cultural consequences of emerging new media technology
- Theoretical perspectives on the social and cultural impact of new media technologies
- International and intercultural perspectives on the social consequences of new media technologies

Students, practitioners and users of new media technology can use this framework to evaluate not only the commercial implications of the evolving communication environment, but the social and cultural implications as well. Decisions and debate based on such a framework will thus benefit from an enriched understanding of how new technologies may transform not just the media industries themselves, but those who consume and are touched by them.

NOTES

[1]McKibben, Bill (1992). *The Age of Missing Information.*

[2]Dickens, Charles. *A Tale of Two Cities.* London: J. B. Lippincott, 1930.

[3]Thoreau, Henry David (1849). *Walden.* New York: T. Y. Crowell, 1899.

[4]Ellul, Jacques (1964). *The Technological Society.* New York: Alfred A. Knopf.

[5]de Sola Pool, I. (1983). *Technologies of Freedom.* Cambridge: The Belknap Press of Harvard University; de Sola Pool, I. (1990). *Technologies without Boundaries: On Telecommunications in a Global Age* (E. M. Noam, Ed.). Cambridge: Harvard University Press.

[6]Bell, Daniel. *The Coming of Post-Industrial Society.* New York: Basic Books, 1973.

[7]de Sola Pool, op. cit., 1983, 1990; Wriston, op. cit., 1993.

[8]Ellul, op. cit., 1964

[9]Steinfels, Peter, "Jacques Ellul, French Critic of Technology, Is Dead at 82," *New York Times,* May 21, 1994.

[10]Innis, Harold (196).

[11]McLuhan, op. cit., 1972.

[12]Naisbitt, John (1982). *Megatrends.*

[13]Club of Rome, The. *Microelectronics and Society: For Better or Worse.* 1982.

[14]Brown, Les (1992). *Les Brown's Encyclopedia of Televison,* 3rd ed. Detroit, MI: Gale Research Inc.

[15]"TV Debate Set A Cable Record," *New York Times,* November 11, 1993.

[16]Thalhimer, op. cit., July 6, 1994.

[17]Henderson, Bill, op ed page of the *New York Times,* March 16, 1994.

[18]Thoreau, op. cit.

[19]Murdoch, op. cit., April 11, 1994.

[20]Rheingold, H. (1993). *The Virtual Community: Homesteading on the Electronic Frontier.* New York: Addison-Wesley; Fernback, Jan and Brad Thompson, 1995, "Virtual Communities: Abort, Retry, Failure?" posted at www.well.com/hlr/texts/VCcivil.html

[21]French, Howard W. "Linked to Internet, Could Africa's Voice Be Heard?" *New York Times,* Oct. 1, 1994.

[22]Lewis, op. cit., March 8, 1994.

[23]Ibid.: A8.

[24]Ibid.

[25]Leslie, Jacques, "Mail Bonding: E-mail Is Creating a New Oral Culture," *Wired,* March 1994: 42.

[26]Internet Society web page, www.isoc.org

[27]Sheizaf Rafaeli, Hebrew University of Jerusalem, Israel sheizafr@shum.cc.huji.ac.il Fay Sudweeks, University of Sydney, Australia fays@archsci.arch.su.edu.au http://www.clas.ufl.edu/anthro/cyberanthro/CMC-biblio.html

[28]Ibid.

[29]Ibid.

[30]Firestone, op. cit., 1992: 5.

[31]Ibid.: 15.

[32]Pavlik, John V. and David. M. Dozier, "Managing the Information Superhighway: A Report on the Issues Facing Communication Professionals," A study funded by a grant from The Institute for Public Relations Research and Education.

[33]Dewey, Thomas. The Public and Its Problems. Chicago: Swallow, 1927.

[34]Grunig, James E., & Hunt, Todd. (1984). *Managing Public Relations.* New York: Holt, Rinehart & Winston.

[35]Ibid.

[36]Ibid., Murphy, P. & Dee, J. (1992). "Du Pont and Greenpeace: the dynamics of conflict between corporations and activist groups." *Public Relations Research Annual,* 4(1), 3–20.

[37]Grunig, Larissa A. (1986, August). Activism and organizational response: contemporary cases of collective behavior. Paper presented to the Association for Education in Journalism and Mass Communication, Norman, OK.

[38]Levy, Mark, editor. Virtual Reality: A Communication Perspective. (1992, Autumn). *Journal of Communication,* 42(4).

[39]Biocca, Frank. "Communication Within Virtual Reality: Creating a Space for Research." (1992, Autumn). *Journal of Communication,* 42(4): 5–22, 9.

[40]Gardiner, W. Lambert (1993). "Virtual Reality/Cyberspace: Challenges to Communication Studies." *Canadian Journal of Communication,* Vol. 18, 387–396, 392.

[41]Lincoln, Abraham. Letter to H.L. Pierce, 16 April 1859.

[42]Smith, Anthony, op. cit., 1993.

[43]Wriston, Walter, inaugural address in The Freedom Forum Media Studies Center Technology Lecture Series, October 25, 1993, New York.

[44]Davis, Leonard. "The Customer Is Always Right," *Omni,* November, 1993: 24.

[45]Karp, Jonathan. "Prime Time Police: China tries to pull the plug on satellite TV," *Far Eastern Economic Review,* 21 October 1993: 72–73.

[46]Smith, Anthony, "Is TV's Web of Images Strangling Our Hearts," *New York Newsday,* 1/3/94:33.

[47]Grossman, Lawrence, speech at "Newsroom Technology: The Next Generation," The Freedom Forum Media Studies Center, September 15, 1993; Grossman, Lawrence, (1996) The Electronic Republic: Reshaping Democracy in the Information Age. A Twentieth Century Fund Book.

[48]Lewis, Peter H. "Anarchy, a Threat on the Electronic Frontier," *New York Times,* May 11, 1994: D1, D7.

[49]Pehlan, op. cit.

[50]Dennis, op. cit., 23.

[51]Sevareid, Eric. CBS Radio News commentary, August 26, 1952.

[52]Selnow, Gary W. (1993). *High-Tech Campaigns: Computer Technology in Political Communication.* Westport, CT: Praeger.

[53]The Research Group (1992). *The Media and Campaign '92.* The Freedom Forum Media Studies Center.

[54]Andrew Kohut, op. cit.

[55]Sevareid, Eric. CBS Radio News commentary, August 26, 1958.

[56]Selnow, op. cit., 1993: 169.

[57]Hart, Roderick P. (1994). *Seducing America: How Television Charms the Modern Voter.* New York: Oxford University Press: 63.

[58]Ibid.

[59]Liddell, op. cit., 1994.

[60]www.uspto.gov

[61]Guthrie, K. Kendall (May, 1993). "How Information Highways Can Address the Urban Agenda: Promoting Economic Development and Reconnecting the Urban Poor." Paper presented at the 43rd Annual Conference of the International Communications Association, Washington, D.C., May 27–31, 1993.

[62]Brown, et al., op. cit., 1994.

[63]Ibid.

[64]Software Publishers Association, "Report on the Effectiveness of Technology in Schools, 1990-1992," conducted by Interactive Educational Systems Design, 1993: 2.

[65]Orlansky, J. and J. String (1979). Cost-Effectiveness of Computer Based Instruction in Military Training (IDA Paper P-1375). Institute for Defense Analyses, Alexandria, Virginia.

[66]Brown, et al., op. cit. 1994: 65.

[67]Ibid.

[68]Ibid.

[69]Robert McClintock, Priscilla Ellington and Heather Lewis, The Eiffel Project, version 1.2, September 1996.

[70]*Chronicle of Higher Education, The,* "On Line," March 2, 1994.

[71]Ibid.

[72]Thalhimer, op. cit., May 31, 1994.

[73]*Advertising Age,* July 18, 1994.

[74]Rabinovitz, Jonathan, "Computer Network Helps Journalists Find Academic Experts," *New York Times,* May 21, 1994.

[75]www.jrn.columbia.edu

[76]Browning, John. "Libraries Without Walls for Books Without Pages," *Wired* Premier Issue, 1993.

[77]Smith, Anthony, op. cit., 1993.

[78]Browning, op. cit.: 63.

[79]Mason, Marilyn Gell, "More Than a Library for Congress: Making LC the Nation's Library," *Library Journal,* November 1, 1993: 40–43.

[80]"I.B.M. Project for Vatican," *New York Times* from Reuters April 12, 1994.

[81]Pool, Robert, "Turning an Info-Glut into a Library," *Science,* Vol. 266, no. 7, October, 1994: 20–22.

[82]Hafrey, Leigh, "At Cyberspace University Press, Paperless Publishing Looks Good," *New York Times Book Review,* Oct. 30, 1994.

[83]Schuman, Patricia Glass (1993). "Information Justice." Fellows seminar, The Freedom Forum Media Studies Center.

[84]Gore, Albert (1993). "Reinventing Government." The Office of the Vice President of the U.S.

[85]Schuman, op. cit.

[86]Arlen, Gary H., "Education Networks to go Online Later This Year; Content Providers to Offer 'Electronic Printing Press,'" *Information & Interactive Services Report,* February 25, 1994: 17.

[87]Ibid.

[88]Williams, Frederick and John V. Pavlik, op. cit.: xi.

[89]DeLoughry, Thomas J. "Guaranteeing Access on the Data Highway," *The Chronicle of Higher Education,* Nov. 3, 1993.

[90]Verba, Sidney, "The 1993 James Madison Award Lecture: The Voice of the People," delivered at the American Political Science Association Annual Meeting, Washington, DC, September 3, 1993.Edited version published in Robert J-P. Hauck (Editor) *PS: Political Science & Politics,* vol. XXXVI, No. 4, December 1993: 684.

[91]Noam, Eli, Speech, Technology Studies Seminar, The Freedom Forum Media Studies Center, April 5, 1994.

[92]Maynard, Nancy Hicks, Speech, Technology Studies Seminar, The Freedom Forum Media Studies Center, April 5, 1994.

[93]Smith, op. cit., 1993.

[94]Verity, John W. "The Information Revolution: How digital technology is changing the way we work and live," *Business Week,* Special 1994 Bonus Issue: 14.

[95]Kozinn, Allan, "Lejaren Hiller 69, First Composer to Write Music with a Computer," *New York Times,* February 1, 1994.

[96]DeLoughry, Thomas J. "Museums Go High-Tech," *The Chronicle of Higher Education,* Sept. 14, 1994: A47.

[97]Naisbitt, John and Patricia Aburdene. *Megatrends 2000.* New York: Warner Books, 1993.

[98]Noam, Eli M. (1993). Keynote Address, The Everette Parker Luncheon.

[99]Atchison, Sandra D. "The Care and Feeding of 'Lone Eagles,'" *Business Week,* November 15, 1993: 58.

[100]Ibid.; Sandberg, Jared, "Up in Flames," *Wall Street Journal Reports,* R12, November 15, 1993.

[101]Van Sell, Mary and Sheila M. Jacobs, "Telecommuting and Quality of Life: A Review of the Literature and a Model for Research," *Telematics and Informatics,* Vol. 11, No. 2, pp. 81–95.

[102]Lowry, Tom, "E-mail delivers rescue," *Daily News,* April 1, 1994: 5.

[103]Krantz, Michael, "Dollar a Minute," *Wired,* May 1994: 107.

[104]Ibid.: 104–8, 140–142.

[105]Ibid.: 107.

[106]Ditlea, Steve. "Female E-Mail: Computer Networks Put Women On-Line," *New York Daily News,* November 3, 1993.

[107]Arlen, Gary H., "Who Uses Compuserve?" *Information & Interactive Services Report,* February 11, 1994: 4.

[108]Markoff, John. op. cit., March 27, 1994: F10.

[109]Ibid.

[110]Andrew Kohut, op. cit.

[111]http://www.webgrrls.com/

[112]Fryer, Bronwyn, "Sex & the Superhighway," *Working Woman,* April 1994: 51–61.

[113]Flynn, Bernadette, "Woman/Machine Relationships," *Media Information Australia,* May 1994, No. 72: 11–19.

[114]Turkle, Sherry (1984). *The Second Self: Computer and the Human Spirit.* Simon and Schuster, New York.

[115]Powell, Adam Clayton III, "On-Ramps to the Information Superhighway," *Media Studies Journal,* Summer 1994: viii, 113–121.

[116]www.afrinet.net/~halh

[117]Survey reported by FIND/SVP, 1995.

[118]Levy, Steven. *Artificial Life: The Quest for A New Creation.* London: Penguin Books, 1993.

[119]Ibid.

[120]Dutton, op. cit., 1993.

[121]Rheingold, op. cit., 1993.

[122]Levy, op. cit., 1994.

[123]Pavlik, John and Andras Szanto, "Mutiple Method Research in Media Studies: The Case of the 1992 Presidential Campaign," The Freedom Forum Media Studies Center, 1994.

[124]Brown, Richard D. (1989). *Knowledge Is Power: The Diffusion of Information in Early America, 1700–1865.* New York: Oxford University Press.

[125]http://websites.earthlink.net/%7Etomgrant/

[126]http://www.mediacity.com/~java/DBC.html

[127]http://members.iglou.com/kkk/

http://www.io.com/~wlp/aryan-page/

http://www.natall.com/

http://www.stormfront.org/

http://www.alpha.org/

[128]The Web of Hate: Extremists Exploit the Internet. © 1996, Anti-Defamation League, http://www.adl.org/ADLRept/HateInter.html#anchor251386

[129]Johnson, Kirk, "Office Romance: Love On Line at Speed of Light," *New York Times,* March 26, 1994.

[130]Ibid.: 21.

[131]Lehmann-Haupt, Christopher, "Plumbing the Recesses of Psyche and Cyberspace," *New York Times,* April 14, 1994: C21.

[132]Weise, Elizabeth, "Santa's elves check e-mail for your merry messages," Associated Press wire service, Dec. 13, 1994.

[133]Blumler, Jay and Elihu Katz (1974). *Uses and Gratifications Research in Mass Communication.* Newbury Park, CA: Sage Publications.

[134]Brown, Les. Speech, Technology Studies Seminar, The Freedom Forum Media Studies Center, April 6, 1994.

[135]Blumler and Katz, op. cit.

[136]Williams and Pavlik, op. cit., 1994.

[137]Brown, Les, op. cit.

[138]Phelan, op. cit., 1994.

[139]Gell-Mann, Murray (1994). *The Quark and the Jaguar: Adventures in the Simple and the Complex.* W. H. Freeman.

[140]Murrow, Edward R. RTNDA Convention, October 15, 1958.

[141]Ellul, op. cit., 1994.

[142]Koontz, Dean. *Midnight.* New York: Berkley Books, 1989.

[143]McCaffrey, op. cit., 1969.

[144]Beniger, James R. *The Control Revolution: Technological and Economic Origins of the Information Society.* Cambridge: Harvard University Press, 1986.

[145]Gandy, Oscar H., Jr. "The Information Highway as Yellow Brick Road," Speech, Santa Clara University, January 27, 1994.

[146]Ibid.

[147]Gandy, Oscar H., Jr. (1993). *The Panoptic Sort.* Boulder, CO: Westview: 10.

[148]Schiller, Dan, "From Culture to Information and Back Again: Commoditization as a Route to Knowledge," *Critical Studies in Mass Communication,* 11(March 1994), 92–115, 98.

[149]Ibid.: 99.

[150]Ibid.

[151]Gandy, op. cit., 1994.

[152]Barnathan, Julius, Speech, Technology Studies Seminar, The Freedom Forum Media Studies Center, Dec. 12, 1992.

[153]Salvaggio, Jerry, 199 .

[154]Loro op. cit., 1994: 29.

[155]Gandy, op. cit., 1994: 12, 13.

[156]Morukama, Shinji, "The Information Superhighway," *Forum Magazine,* May 1994: 4.

[157]Gandy, op. cit., 1994: 13.

[158](Bowman, Joseph E. Jr., "Documenting a technology-based telecommunications program for urban youth: Its impact and future role in high school retention," *Dissertation Abstracts International,* Volume 52, Number 7, 1992.

[159]Dutton, op. cit., 1994.

[160]Morukama, op. cit.

[161]Wright, David, "Mobile satellite communications in developing countries," *Telecommunications Policy,* January/February 1994.

[162]Ibid.: 5.

[163]International submarine cable map, w3.lab.kdd.co.jp/kdd/cable/

[164]Stephenson, Neal, "Wiring the Planet," *Wired,* December 20, 1996.

[165]Hudson, Heather E. "Maximizing Benefits from New Telecommunications Technologies: A Development-Based Approach to Communications Planning," *Media Asia,* Vol. 20, No. 3, 1993: 133–139.

[166]Leonard, Hugh, "Asian Broadcasting: The Changing Scene," *Media Asia,* Vol. 20, No. 3, 1993: 123–126.

[167]Jussawalla, Meheroo, "Information Technology and Economic Development in the Asia-Pacific," *Media Asia,* Vol. 20, No. 3, 1993: 127–132.

[168]Ibid.: 130.

[169]Wang, Georgette, "Satellite Television and the Future of Broadcast Television in the Asia-Pacific," *Media Asia,* Vol. 20, No. 3, 1993: 139–148.

[170]Ibid.: 141–2.

[171]Chan, Joseph Man, "Satellite Television and the Infosphere: National Responses and Accessibility to STAR TV in Asia." Paper presented to the Ninth Worth Communication Forum, the Japan Society of Information and Communication Research, Tokyo, Japan, 19–20 November 1992.

[172]Ibrahim, Anwar, "Communication, Technology and Development: Alternatives for Asia," *Media Asia,* Vol. 20, No. 3, 1993: 157–158.

[173]Ibid.: 157.

[174]Ibid.: 158.

[175]Powell, op. cit., April 6, 1994.

[176]Hoge, James, F. "Media Pervasiveness," *Foreign Affairs,* July/August 1994, Vol. 73, No. 4: 136.

[177]Ibid.

[178]Ibid.

[179]Ibid.: 137.

11

The Future:
The Age of Random Access

*"If I were to give you an army of 10
thousand people, could you build a pyramid?
A computer gives the average person, a
high school freshman, the power to do things
in a week that all the mathematicians who
ever lived until 30 years ago couldn't do."*
—ED ROBERTS[1]

ON THE HOLODECK

Emerging technologies are rapidly transforming the media landscape. Advances in
the Internet and the World Wide Web, wireless communications, and digital video
technology are creating an entirely new communication environment in which the
roles of media consumer and content creator often blur and interactivity becomes a
reality. Multimedia technology, virtual reality, and flat-panel displays are redefining
the media experience, transforming the narrative structure of media images, sound,
and text into nonlinear, immersive, hypertext communication. Media consumers
have unprecedented choice and control over the media experience, selecting not just
what they watch, read, or hear, but when and where they do so. Nomadic computing

is rapidly becoming more than a buzzword; it's becoming a twenty-first-century way of life. Journalists may find their methods of news gathering transformed by light-weight, wearable technologies (such as augmented reality, which adds layers of visual and other information onto "reality" as viewed through a head-mounted display) linked to massive databases through high-speed wireless technologies. Professor Steven Feiner at Columbia University has already developed a working prototype of an augmented reality system for use on the Columbia campus, where the wearer can walk through the campus and "see" architectural and other information superimposed on buildings such as the historic Low Library. Imagine reporting from the scene of a building explosion, surveying the wreckage with an augmented reality viewer, and quickly determining the inner structure of the building. The Center for New Media (CNM) at the Columbia University Graduate School of Journalism is developing a Mobile Journalist Terminal (MJT) that will incorporate Feiner's and other new media technologies into a single integrated system for advanced nomadic news reporting. This research is being conducted in collaboration with a number of programs at Columbia, including Engineering and Computer Science, in an attempt to blend the process of technology development and content creation in an interdisciplinary Engineering Research Center (ERC). Another important development is the miniaturization of mobile satellite phones, which just a decade ago were so cumbersome they required a sea-chest and a very strong back for portability. Introduced in 1996 is a notebook-sized Mini-M satellite phone from NEC Corporation that uses the Inmarsat satellite communications system to allow anyone anywhere in the world instaneous high-bandwidth, 25 Mbps capability for delivering fax, data, voice, and e-mail communications. The system fits in a standard briefcase, weighs a remarkable 2.6 kg (a little more than a pound) and runs on a built-in rechargeable lithium-ion battery pack, car battery, or AC power.[2]

The commercial media system itself is undergoing a "mediamorphosis," as well, moving away from passive, scattershot content delivery, toward highly targeted messaging, blending the best of both push and pull network technology. A double-edged sword, this new media engine may present both a marketer's paradise and a consumer's privacy nightmare.

Much media content in the years ahead will still consist of packaged products of news, information, entertainment, and advertising manufactured by highly centralized media organizations, but tomorrow's media will increasingly target in real-time the demands, tastes, and preferences of ever more specialized niche audiences spread over diverse geographic audiences. The new media system will not rigidly divide along the traditional lines of delivery such as print, broadcast, and cable, but will become true multimedia technologies, involving new forms of mediated communication, ultimately embracing the tactile technology of emerging virtual reality systems. Shared media experiences, although increasingly rare on a mass scale, will take on an entirely new meaning, one in which audiences anywhere around the globe will be enveloped in a total sensory media experience created at least in part by those audiences. Increasingly, each member of the new media audience will have direct access to this information superhighway through lightweight, portable, wireless multimedia devices, totally enveloping multisensory datasuits, or communal media technologies featuring multidimensional images and stereophonic sound not unlike the holodeck on the Starship Enterprise featured in *Star Trek: The Next Generation.*

Of course, not every media experience will be of this Buck Rogers type. Consumers will spend much of their media time reading newspapers printed on traditional newsprint. They will still read leatherbound and paperback books. They will still listen to the radio, watch TV, and get advertising circulars in the mail. And the Publisher's Clearing House will probably still proclaim half of America "Winners" in its multimillion dollar lottery. Moreover, legal and regulatory frameworks will continue to evolve mechanisms to monitor and control the new media system. With the policy-making process frequently lagging well beyond the more rapidly changing new media technology landscape, one can't help but recall a story told by Kenneth M. King, former president of EDUCOM. "A turtle was mugged by a gang of snails in Central Park. When making his report to the police, the turtle lamented: 'It all happened so fast.'"[3]

Freedom of expression issues will take on even greater significance in the new media environment. The Internet and other media technologies are empowering members of virtual communities around the globe. They are providing a new electronic age printing press that costs little to operate and reaches audiences of millions in almost instantaneous fashion. John Siegenthaler, a Pulitzer prize-winning newspaper editor and former chairman of The Freedom Forum First Amendment Center, says the information superhighway already is being dominated by eighteen-wheelers, including the baby Bells, cable TV companies, and other corporate players who are used to working in a regulated environment.[4] These companies are likely to compromise on First Amendment issues, he cautions. News organizations, journalism educators, and other guardians of the First Amendment will need to be vigilant in the new media environment if we, as a society, are to preserve free speech values. This is especially important, Siegenthaler adds, if it is true that a free press is one of the cornerstones of democracy.

The social and cultural consequences of these new media technologies are profound. They are creating unprecedented opportunities for political participation, through electronic town halls, direct access to political leaders and, potentially, online voting. At the same time, issues of equitable access and cost considerations are challenging the very political viability of creating a new information infrastructure. Umberto Eco, noted Italian author and inaugural visiting scholar at the Italian Academy for Advanced Studies in America at Columbia University, observes that we are likely moving into a society with three classes: those who don't have access to the Internet, those who have access but it is mainly passive (i.e., they just surf the 'Net) and those who know how to control it (what the Russians call the proletariat).[5] Social fragmentation is only one of the many potential negative consequences of the new technologies that are increasingly leading media consumers into online worlds and away from their geographically defined communities.

User Control and User Choice:
New and Improved Media

For the media consumer, perhaps the most important difference between old and new media is greater user choice and control. Unlike any time before, media audiences will have ever greater choice and control over media content and the media experience in general. Video-on-demand, including pay-per-view movies, news on demand, educational programming, and documentaries will all be available over the information superhighway. The shift in the media paradigm is from strict source or media control over content delivery to increasing user control. Emerging in the new media age is what can be described as nothing less than ubiquitous news and information. With the growth of Internet-based news and information products, ranging from broadcast-type services such as PointCast to on-demand news products on the World Wide Web, anyone with Internet access can obtain nonstop comprehensive news and information about anything from breaking news to news analysis. With a variety of wireless devices now available to link handheld PDAs to the Internet and the Web, such on-demand news is available anytime and anywhere around the globe.

Simultaneously, media audiences will enjoy increasing interactivity on the information highway. They will have opportunities to interact with media content, selecting different options, from preset video library menus to battling enemy starships in videogames. Audience members will also be able to participate in the process of content creation, sending messages, home video, or data files to anyone else on the system. Over time, the superhighway will offer increasing opportunities for moving beyond two-way communication and into an n-way media environment in which hundreds, thousands, even millions will participate in a rich communication smorgasbord. Virtual worlds will be created by media audiences around the world in which the dimensions of that world are limited only by the imaginations of those within it. The seeds of this n-way communication world can already be seen in on the World Wide Web, increasingly graphical and three-dimensional multi-user domains (MUDs) and high-quality, low-cost videoconferences.

Does all this mean the end of the couch potato? Not at all. Not only will traditional passive media consumption continue, but it will thrive in an increasingly complex and stressful world demanding occasional if not frequent mindless escape. But the interactive, on-demand world of personalized communications will become a ready choice. Of course, too much interactivity could produce the era of the mashed potato.

Driving this user-controlled, interactive, multimedia world are the technological forces of digitization, compression, and the broadband packet-switched telecommunications network. Through advances in computer technology, we are rapidly moving toward a united state of media in which all communications, from voice to data to full-motion video, are available in digital form, computer-readable 1s and 0s. Compression technology has made it possible to compact that digital data, especially full-motion video, into smaller and smaller packets. The convergence of tele-communications and cable, along with the deployment of advanced optical fiber, has provided a high-capacity electronic superhighway to transmit and provide access to all that compressed digital data.

A final technological factor contributing to the transformation of the media landscape is wireless communications. As the forces of digitization and compression have inexorably advanced, research has helped create an increasingly broadband packet-switched network that is not dependent on wires. Instead, we are moving toward a telecommunications highway universally available over the high-frequency wavelengths of the radio spectrum. By connecting to satellite and wired networks, this wireless network will provide a complementary and perhaps competitive alternative multimedia information superhighway. Although engineers have not yet achieved the necessary compression algorithms to distribute full multimedia communications via the wireless spectrum in a wide-area network environment, they have done so in wireless local area networks. Moreover, they have developed increasingly efficient use and allocation of the wireless spectrum, including spread spectrum models that allow spectrum sharing for different applications and users. One interesting approach to high-speed communications in a wireless local area network is known as fiber-in-the-sky from CellularVision. It delivers up to 2Mb of bandwidth, making it possible to distribute broadcast-quality MPEG-2 digital video over a wireless local area network. When connected to a wired high-speed wide-area network, fiber-in-the-sky makes possible a phenomenon called *nomadic computing*. *Nomadic computing* means using a computer-based device, from a PDA to a laptop computer to access the information superhighway from any location, anywhere, anytime. Someday, we may see emerge global media nomads. We are already witnessing the application of nomadic computing and communications in state-of-the-art navigational systems for luxury automobiles. Cars such as the Acura, BMW, Cadillac, Lincoln, and Oldsmobile all offer increasingly sophisticated dashboard navigational systems that rely on global positioning satellites (GPS), which can pinpoint a vehicle's location within one hundred yards.[6] These systems offer a variety of services, including on-screen maps and voice-activated navigation, as well as roadside assistance. Handheld GPS devices are also now available, and are increasingly popular among hikers, sailors, and pilots. The GPS 4000 from Magellan, for instance, is smaller than a walkie-talkie and weighs about ten ounces.[7] The federal government has launched a $40 million program to challenge cities to build even more sophisticated nomadic navigational systems. The program is designed to foster "intelligent transportation systems" in New York, Phoenix, San Antonio, and Seattle, and will use Web sites, interactive television, and navigational devices in cars to facilitate commuting.[8] One of the critical issues to resolve involves building complete interoperable network environments that support easy access (via the main methods of connecting to the Internet, Point-to-Point Protocol, or PPP, which is more reliable—and has error corrrecting features—than the older Serial Line Internet Protocol, or SLIP), regardless of one's geographic location.[9]

PARALLEL OR DIVERGENT UNIVERSES?

What price will a digital universe exact? No one really knows. Projected costs to build the new communication infrastructure range from hundreds of billions to several trillion dollars, just for the United States. Cost estimates are also in the hundreds of billions to create new information infrastructures in Japan and many other countries. Those developing new media products and services say that the actual price the consumer will pay will be modest. If it isn't then none of the products will succeed. Telecommunications expert John Carey suggests that the estimates for the new information infrastructure may not really be as expensive as some in the industry claim. In the area of interactive television, "it turns out that much of the cost associated with building the new infrastructure, particularly for telephone companies, involves investments that the companies would make regardless of any interactive television services," Carey explains.

> *In other words, the incremental costs of building a network for interactive television are a modest addition to normal replacement and upgrading costs for their networks. So, when a telephone company says that it will spend $17 billion to build a telecommunication superhighway for ITV and other advanced services, it usually means that they plan to spend $2 billion more than they would otherwise spend for normal replacement and upgrading of their network. Further, the plans typically allow them to scale back the additional costs if market demand for new services is lower than expected. For cable operators, incremental costs are greater. However, they too can scale back investment if demand is lower than expected. Further, the investment will yield other benefits such as lower operating and maintenance costs.*[10]

But there are other costs, perhaps more significant than dollars. Among these are issues of access to the technology. Two principles that have guided public communication policy for most of the century are universal and equitable access. Unless these two principles apply equally well in the new media environment, the social costs will be high. Among the likely losers will be women, minority groups, inner-city and rural dwellers, children, the elderly, the homeless, and people with disabilities. Other social costs may include social fragmentation, digital isolation, and a falloff in political participation.

A related cost consideration involves the cost of building or rebuilding a public telecommunications system increasingly dominated by massive traffic on the Internet. The telecommunications network in the United States was built to support circuit-switched communications, primarily used for voice communications. "In spite of the great changes in technology, the basic concept of telephony has changed little over this century," observes Robert W. Lucky, Corporate Vice President of Applied Research at Bellcore, and the inventor of the "adaptive equalizer," a distortion-correction technology used in all high-speed data transmission today.[11]

Suddenly, a new paradigm has swept the world. Instead of two people speaking to each other in real time over a switched analog channel, asynchronous messaging and hyper-linked sharing of multimedia objects have become the objectives that must be supported by the future infrastructure.

This will not come without a substantial investment—by someone. In the past it would have been the phone company, once a heavily regulated monopoly. Today, it is unclear who will pay the cost. "There is tremendous investment in the present infrastructure, which is not cost-effective for these new objectives," Lucky cautions. "The question is: How do we get from here to there?"

The Consequences of Technology Convergence

One of the most basic trends in the new media environment is the convergence of multimedia and online, or networked, communications. As these systems converge, a truly unique and powerful new medium of public communication will emerge. Its commercial and cultural implications are as profound as they are remarkable. It is likely to transform virtually every social institution, from education to government, medicine to law, politics to religion, at home and abroad. This new medium will influence the process of human communication, the process by which social change occurs and the processes and mechanisms controlling both the United States and the world economy. The three most significant unanswered questions are:

- Will these changes be for the better or worse?
- What will be the cost and for whom?
- What will be the timetable for change?

Countervailing Forces

Countervailing technological forces may also be at work, however, in the new media universe. One of the almost sacred primordial forces driving technological change during the past quarter century has been the dramatically falling price of computing power. Recent evidence suggests this trend may soon be slowing down, if not drawing to a close completely. As computer chip manufacturers have created ever smaller chips capable of ever greater calculation, the price of computing has fallen remarkably. Manufacturers today, however, may be reaching the theoretical limit to computer chip miniaturization. "The problem is that life gets harder for chip makers as dimensions shrink below a micron in size," reports Gary Stix.[12] "At about 0.05 micron, the dimensions of the individual devices will be so small that quantum effects will disrupt their behavior. Then a new technology based on probabilistic laws will be needed." Producing reliable chips has also become increasingly complex and costly, as reflected in the initially flawed, super-fast Pentium chip. State-of-the-art chips now house some 16 million memory bits and require 200 processing steps. By 2001 reliable production techniques may require manufacturing devices as small as

15 to 50 nanometers, "less than the width of a coiled DNA molecule."[13] Moreover, as the cost of chip manufacturing has fallen, the cost of chip design and manufacturing technology has risen. Gordon Moore, the former chairman of Intel, the world's largest chip manufacturer, noted that his company's first chip manufacturing plant in the late 1960s cost $3 million.[14] "Today that is the cost of one piece of equipment in one of our plants," Moore observes. The next generation of chip manufacturing plants will exceed $1 billion in price, and by 2000 may cost ten times that. The effect on the semiconductor business is that returns on investment are threatened, and the drive to manufacture even smaller chips may stall.

If this trend toward chip miniaturization does draw to a close, projections for the future will change dramatically. It will not be safe to assume that super-powerful computing devices will become ubiquitous in the early twenty-first century. Information appliances will not become the consumer standard many hope for. The potential for video delivery and processing will fall dramatically, and the price will stabilize. Commercial investment in the new media, as a result, will slacken and economic growth will slow.

How likely is this dire scenario? Unless there is a breakthrough in chip design, it is fairly likely. Optical technology, however, though still in the laboratory research stages, is one of the most intriguing avenues for the future of computing. Optical, or photonic, computing, based not on the flow of electrons in a silicon-based computer chip, but on pulses of light in a new silicon environment, may unleash vast new opportunities to decrease the cost of computing power and dramatically increase computing power and speed—the theoretical limit is the speed of light, 186,000 miles per second. Moreover, if optical technology can be combined with some preliminary but theoretically sound research on organic neural networks, the next generation may reach new thresholds in computing power and intelligence. As an alternative to such designs, some companies are experimenting with three-dimensional microchips. Unlike traditional two-dimensional designs in which the chip is approximately 5 microns in height and the conducting wires and transistors lie across the insulating silicon base, Mitsubishi, IBM, Siemens, and Toshiba are developing chips 20 to 30 microns in height with wires, conductors and transistors all layered atop an insulating base of silicon.[15] Such chips could eventually lead to the development of supercomputers the size of a sugar cube.

If computer speed, processing power, and memory do continue to increase, the possibilities are seemingly boundless. Some selected predictions for 2000 include:

- Personal "Crays" capable of emulating any desktop, from Macintosh to PC with the power of today's supercomputer in a portable handheld device, making nomadic computing and communications universal and ubiquitous
- Smart TVs that remember past viewing patterns and suggest new shows that match tastes and preferences
- Telephones that instantaneously translate callers speaking in any of a dozen or more languages

- Artificial intelligence applications so smart and humanlike that they can replace entire corporate departments such as accounting or finance[16]

Bandwidth Challenged

A related problem involves bandwidth limitations in today's telecommunications networks. Although compared to the networks of a decade ago the capacity of today's networks is considerable, few anticipated the exponential growth in bandwidth demand brought on by users of the Internet and World Wide Web in the 1990s. As networks clog and routers collapse, many see a potential hardening of the telecommunications arteries, despite the many millions of miles of high-bandwidth optical fiber now circling the globe. Notably, however, an international consortium of research groups at AT&T, Fujitsu, and Nippon Telegraph and Telephone (NTT) demonstrated a system in early 1996 that could increase bandwidth by as much as a thousandfold by 2000.[17] Transmitting one trillion bits of information in a single second over a single strand of optical fiber, the new technology was surpassed a few months later by a team at NEC Corporation, which transmitted two trillion bits in a second over a single strand of optical fiber.

DIGITAL PUBLISHING

The evolution of multimedia products in an online environment will push traditional and new media providers to explore new publishing frontiers. New media publishers will not only have opportunities to reach global audiences with multimedia products in real time, but will also be able to completely rethink their relationship with advertisers and audiences. Further, they will have the unique opportunity to completely rethink their internal processes of content creation. No longer will they be constrained by traditional modes of product development. Conversely, the world of digital publishing will present considerable uncertainty for companies already unsure of themselves and their business future. All bets are off in the business of new media. Competitors will arise from every corner of the market and the world. Even the audience will be inclined and able to get in on the action in a computer-driven media world. One of the great question marks is how "secure" will the online communications world become. Today, the forces of government and the private sector are battling over whether to permit government eavesdropping on online communications, or to create a strong encryption technology for networked communications. The outcome will substantially affect the growth of both commerce and communication on the Internet. Strong encryption will foster a robust communication and commercial environment, where information and transactions flow on a national and international scale unparalleled in history. Nano-transactional models where micro-payments for information and intellectual property as well as other digital objects, such as digital cash, will become commonplace.

If the government wins the encryption war, the growth of commerce and communication on the Internet will slow, and perhaps even grind to a halt. Today's electronic mail travels over the Internet much as a postcard travels through traditional postal services—anyone along the route can read its contents. Encryption such as PGP provides something akin to an electronic envelope, making it impossible for someone to see what's inside. Few consumers will be willing to send their credit card numbers around the globe knowing that it might be intercepted by anyone along the way. Conversely, should the government lose the struggle, various high-tech criminals will find the Internet a safe haven for their illicit communications and transactions. From drug dealers to tax evaders, a secure online environment means freedom from the watchful eye of law enforcement.

Without the wisdom of Solomon, the solution to this dilemma may never be found. One federal judge, however, has issued a landmark ruling against the federal government in an important encryption case. The U.S. State Department had ruled in 1993 that Daniel J. Bernstein, then a graduate student at the University of California at Berkeley and now a University of Illinois mathematician, "would have to register as an international weapons dealer if he wanted to publish an encryption program or discuss it at academic conferences that foreigners might attend," reports John Markoff.[18] Judge Marilyn Hall Patel of the U.S. District Court in San Francisco ruled in December 1996 that the State Department limits were an unconstitutional prior restraint on freedom of speech (prohibited in the classic Near v. Minnesota case ruled on by the U.S. Supreme Court). Although the encryption issue is far from settled, the early evidence is weighing in the favor of strong network encryption. Adding to this building momentum is the law of economics. Today, because the United States dominates the global information marketplace, there is great incentive for the federal government to provide mechanisms to support this continued economic advantage. Unless U.S. manufacturers and software developers are allowed to export their strong encryption technologies (many of the best encryption technologies, such as PGP, were developed by U.S. researchers), the marketplace will quickly become dominated by international players, where strong encryption is already available. It is likely the federal government in the United States will ultimately be swayed by the economic forces that mandate strong encryption if Internet commerce is ever to thrive and if U.S. companies are to compete effectively in the international market for encryption technology.

Digital Security

Security in cyberspace will become a dominant issue in the years ahead. Consumers and businesses will need to be vigilant in protecting their communications, electronic products, and commercial transactions in cyberspace. The cost of publishing online will rise as a result of security concerns and measures, at the same time increasing the cost of downloading electronic products and conducting electronic transactions and communications for the consumer. Similarly, the demand for electronic security will spawn new industries and trigger growth in existing companies involved in computer security. One possible new field will be insurance for electronic products, as a guard against electronic theft, vandalism, or destruction of electronic property.

Publishers or "Content Providers"?

One of the growing debates in the new media world involves what values dominate the content production process. Will content producers continue in the tradition of the great publishers of the newspaper or magazine publishing world, placing concerns about freedom of expression, privacy, and democratic processes high on the communication agenda? Will the values of the broadcast industry prevail? Where will concern about the public interest fit in this new scenario? Will everyone be reduced to the role of "content provider?" At a conference held in 1994 in Atlanta, heads of several hundred media publishing interests gathered to discuss the prospects for publishing on the information superhighway. When one participant encountered the president of the Chicago Bears, one of the two oldest National Football League franchises (the other being the Green Bay Packers), he asked him why he was attending the conference. His response was a simple, "Because we are a content provider."[19]

Verifying Information

Journalism also faces another imminent threat on the global information grid. On a digital information superhighway characterized by a laissez-faire marketplace in which information is openly exchanged and computer network security is difficult if not impossible to guarantee, how does a media organization—or any other organization—verify the accuracy of data? How does it protect its intellectual property? The world's largest news service recently ran headlong into this problem. On Monday, April 4, 1994, a remarkable news story appeared exclusively on the global Reuters news service. In the wake of the assassination of Colosio, the leading presidential candidate in Mexico's 1994 elections, the story alleged that President Salinas was about to rewrite the Mexican constitution to allow him to run for another term in office. The story, however, was false. Someone had cracked the Reuters network and placed the fictitious report on the news wire.

The "FBI" Solution: A Digital Fingerprint

One possible solution has been introduced by a British company offering an electronic signature ID. Nottingham-based MOR Ltd. has developed a digital technique it calls "FBI" that combines a header, electronic "fingerprints," and an alphanumeric ID sequence imprinted throughout an image or data file.[20] The digital ID is completely transparent and hidden from view and is nearly impermeable to tampering. When used, it would provide a nearly permanent encoding system that publishers and other new media content providers could use to verify the source of a message and to determine whether a video or audio segment was pirated from an original feed.

Digital watermarks are under development at a number of corporate and educational research institutions. One particularly interesting digital watermark is being developed by a research team at Columbia University led by Professor Shih-Fu Chang and involving the Center for New Media at the Graduate School of Journalism. Unlike other digital watermarks, the Columbia project involves a digital signature that not only protects copyright, but authenticates the source of an image or document, and, at the click of a mouse button, can identify the probability that a document has been tampered with and how. Such authentication is critically important in an era of digital image manipulation, eroding news credibility, and a public disillusioned and mistrustful of most institutions. The Columbia digital watermark survives network transmission, compression, and the most grueling of digital editing. Its ultimate test will likely be whether teenage computer hackers will be able to crack its digital shield.

The Confluence of Information and Entertainment

Despite the allure of digital technology, it is important not to get caught up in the hype surrounding the information superhighway and new media technologies. Media entrepreneurs have been drawn by the siren call of new technology in the past, only to lose millions of dollars on failed technology applications. Many are already urging caution in investing huge sums in as yet unrealized technologies. Mark Stahlman, president of New York-based New Media Associates, is one entrepreneur sounding the alarm. He recently wrote in *Wired* magazine:

> *All the headlines about the digital, interactive, 500-channel, multi-megamedia blow-your-socks-off future are pure hype. Yes, all the wild Wall Street, through-the-roof, Crazy Eddie, cornucopia, shout-it-out-loud promo jobs are pure greed. It's all a joke.*
>
> *It's now official. I'm announcing the beginning of convergence backlash. There will be no convergence. There will be no 500-channel future. There will be no US $3 trillion mother of all industries. There will be no virtual sex. There will be no infobahn. None of it—at least not the way you've been reading about it.*
>
> *Sure the technologies are real. Digital compression and digital phone lines are real. Those 100-MIPS micros are real. Multimedia and high-speed networks are real. In fact, the technology is so real that it's almost obvious. Unfortunately, the businesses to exploit these technologies are anything but obvious.[21]*

Tomorrow's News

Although newspaper readership has been declining steadily for nearly four decades, does this mean people are less interested in reading the news? Does the decreasing audience for network television news mean people want to watch less televised news? Research suggests the answer to both these questions is no. One recent study shows that three out of four adults in the United States are still "very interested" in getting the latest news about current events. There is also much anecdotal evidence to suggest that people still have an insatiable appetite for news. Today there are more newsletters (10,000 in print and even more in electronic form), magazines (10,000), ethnic newspapers (500), and other successful printed news products than ever before. Moreover, the national newspaper *USA Today*, the Cable News Network (CNN), C-SPAN, the ever vigilant eye on Congress and Washington, and CourtTV were all launched after 1980. Although few of these news and information products capture major audience shares, they have all carved out important niches.

If you are still not convinced, consider this scenario for one possible news product of the not-too-distant future. Imagine pulling out of your bookbag an eight-ounce electronic tablet about the size of a notepad. Unfolding the flexible tablet, you say, "Let's see this morning's newspaper." As the tablet's voice recognition software interprets your command and identifies your voice pattern, the screen is quickly transformed into a full-color electronic version of your local newspaper, if you still wish to call it a "newspaper." It's really a hybrid news product. The design still looks like a newspaper, with a front page, headlines, text, pictures, and graphics. But it's really much more. A touch with the attached light pen, and a news photo comes to life, with full-motion video and audio. Another touch brings up a detailed historical analysis of today's top news story. Reading a related editorial, you react strongly. Again using the light pen, you activate the tablet's microphone, which allows you to record a voice mail message to the editorial page editor, letting her know how you feel. PCS technology integrated into the tablet automatically sends your voice mail to the editor, who later hears your response, and sends you an equally strongly worded voice mail response. A classified ad catches your eye, and you use the light pen to extract more information about the product for sale. After seeing a three-dimensional picture of the product, you decide against making the purchase. As you look up, you see that you've reached the 116th stop on the number 1 line, and you put your tablet back in your bag and exit the subway, heading off to your graduate seminar in new media journalism at Columbia University in New York.

Network TV Online

The rise of electronic online information services does not signal the end of traditional print forms of communication, such as network television, newspapers, and magazines. "On-line services will coexist with print for the foreseeable future and maybe forever," says Stephen B. Shepard, editor in chief of *Business Week*.[22] Print is still highly portable and relatively inexpensive, and previous predictions of a paperless office have failed to materialize. In fact, the opposite has occurred. By the end of the 1980s, after a decade of computerization in the workplace, "we had four times the amount of paper being created in offices," says Rich Karlgaard, editor in chief of *Forbes ASAP*, a technology supplement to *Forbes* magazine.[23] Television is still well produced, widely available, generally entertaining and never suffers from delays due to limited bandwidth.

Despite that, traditional programmers such as the major television networks have experimented with the delivery of their broadcast programming via the Internet. ABC TV, for example, has used streaming video products such as VivoActive to promote their new fall programming, offering snippets of shows such as *Spin City* to worldwide audiences on demand. NBC has even launched a specialized service called NBC Desktop Video, which brings video-on-demand to the desktop for many executives in the financial world, who have particular interest in tuning in to press conferences of the federal reserve board, and so forth.

What these efforts reveal, however, is that video on the Internet is not television. Rather, video on the Internet is a new communication tool that will never replace traditional television programming. Network capacity and configuration will likely never support the on-demand delivery of broadcast-quality digital television. Rather, video on the Internet will evolve into a distinctive form of multimedia communication, on-demand, customizable and interactive, three qualities not possible in traditional television. These capabilities will lead the Internet, and its delivery of multimedia content, to mature in a fashion complementary to traditional multimedia forms of news and entertainment delivered in broadcast fashion via terrestrial, satellite, and cable transmission.

A BUSINESS MANAGER'S GUIDE TO DIGITAL PUBLISHING

Although no one knows the exact parameters of the emerging new media environment, the basic topography of that world has begun to take shape.[24] New media products, regardless of their content, audience, or means of delivery, will be in digital form. Products will migrate rapidly toward the multimedia format, especially on the Internet and the World Wide Web. Content will evolve more slowly from extensions of the old media into more experimental and novel categories. Today's online services "are the Model Ts, the horseless carriages of the information future," says Bob Ingle, executive editor of the *San Jose Mercury News*.[25] The new media content patterns beginning to emerge include:

- Customizing and personalizing content
- Layering information to provide increased depth and detail to those with specialized interests
- Creating dynamic virtual worlds where users can enter immersive three-dimension environments, experience simulations, and discover unexpected or seren-

dipitous information, providing a new media version of one of the hallmarks of the traditional media—the "eureka" of a chance news encounter

Content providers will respond to the intellectual property challenges of the digital age in a number of ways, including branding, electronic signature identification (i.e., the digital watermark), and international partnerships. Audiences are likely to be defined not as much by geography or political boundary, but by lifestyle, psychographic, and generational factors. Perhaps more importantly, audience members will become important providers and shapers of content. Although most will remain in the passive, couch potato mode, many, especially in the younger audience segment, will enter into an interactive participatory mode, much as now prevails on the Internet. Content delivery will evolve increasingly toward a networked environment. Initially, many products will be on CD-ROM and other optical media, although magnetic formats will persist. Still, the efficiency of online delivery and the growing reach of online technologies, especially with the advent of wireless technologies, in concert with improved compression, encryption, and legal protections for intellectual property rights, will help online technologies prevail and become the dominant mode of delivery. Importantly, dominant multimedia production technologies now provide built-in, automatic translators for Web publishing. MacroMedia Director, the leading authoring environment for CD-ROM, introduced in late 1995 a product called Shockwave for creating similar multimedia content for the Web. Marimba has produced a new network product called Castanet that works in alliance with Macromedia Shockwave.[26] In beta testing until early 1997, Castanet is an Internet delivery system that incorporates both a client (Castanet Tuner) and a server (Castanet Transmitter). Together, these client and server software tools enable end-users to subscribe to Internet "application channels" built on the Castanet system. Rather than relying exclusively on an on-demand, pull network approach, Castanet delivers Web content to the local end-user (i.e., the channel resides locally on the client or subscriber computer), permitting the end-user to access the site without reloading the site each time. Updates are automatically downloaded and installed, but require minimal bandwidth because only that portion of the site that is new is refreshed. Sites currently using the Castanet technology include HotWired, CMP Media, Tribune Media, and Sportsline. Castanet and similar technologies offer a possible solution to the network congestion problem emerging with the 1990s growth of the Internet.

To sum up, publishers should consider the following ten new media guidelines:

- **Digital multimedia**, including a combination of full-motion video, audio, hypertext, and data, all fully manipulable on either optical or online format
- **Online versions** of media products do not seem to cannibalize print or broadcast versions. Experience, in fact, suggests that use of online products on the World Wide Web on the Internet generally enhances interest in traditional format products, especially when the online and traditional versions are not strict duplicates of each other. Online offerings, however, are most effective when

they offer original content, and not simply repurposed or repackaged content from other media

- **True interactivity**, featuring "upstream" capability
- **Flexible cost structure**, to allow consumers extensive choice in designing their own information system
- **Intellectual property rights protections and limitations**, to insure the integrity, credibility, and maximum lifespan of their content creations—many multimedia projects have already stalled over the complexities and cost of copyright considerations
- **Security**, including encryption, to protect communications in a public network environment
- **International partnerships**, which will enable domestic companies to effectively enter and succeed in foreign markets where local expertise is essential
- **Original, quality content**, without which consumers will have no significant reason to turn to new media offerings—this will cost more to produce, but ultimately will be worth the extra investment
- **Privacy protections** for not only the general public but for employees and individuals around the world
- **Freedom of expression protections**, without which the new media environment will be destined to whither and die

Although these general guidelines may suggest an optimistic view of the future, those entering the world of digital publishing would be wise to exercise caution. As of this writing few of the technologies examined in this book are settled. Most are in an active process of evolution. Technical standards vary not only from region to region, but from country to country, and show little chance of settling down anytime soon. Legal and regulatory structures are rapidly evolving and the competitive environment is in a great state of flux. Much of the audience has almost no idea what to make of the new technologies. Many audience members find them fascinating, but unsure whether they will be worth the cost or offer any real advantages over existing sources of media entertainment, news, and information. Content creators are also uncertain of how to proceed. So far, there are few truly original offerings in the new media environment. Most are simply adaptations and extensions of existing products and have about as much appeal as movie sequels, if that much. The new rules of content production are also up in the air. No one knows exactly what a multimedia "script" is worth, how long it will take to produce, and whether it will ultimately turn a profit. One thing is certain: Many entrepreneurs bold enough to leap into the new media world will lose much of their investment. Some will probably make a great deal of money. As one experienced corporate sponsor once said: Half of my advertising is extremely effective. I just don't know which half. It may be that half of the new media products put into the market will succeed; unfortunately, no one knows which half.

The Intrepid Entrepreneur

The intrepid new media entrepreneur will integrate a considerable amount of research into his or her marketing efforts. Using both formative (i.e., diagnostic) and summative (i.e., end results) evaluation will greatly increase the efficiency of any new media marketing efforts, and provide the competitive edge and adaptability needed to survive and even thrive in a highly volatile market.

A variety of media entrepreneurs have offered their prognosis for the future. Among the most visionary of the new media entrepreneurs is Reese Schonfeld, president and CEO of The National Food Network. Schonfeld, the cofounder of CNN, has been promoting the virtues of the information highway since the mid-1980s, long before most had even heard of the idea. Schonfeld admits he does not know what final shape the information superhighway will take, but he knows what it should be: It should be digital, packet-switched, and designed with an open architecture to allow everyone to produce content for it.[27]

In agreement is John Malone, president and CEO of TCI, and "the most powerful man in television" adds premier media critic Ken Auletta.[28] "A full-access universal network is really what we're talking about—broadband, fully interactive, bidirectional, and universally available," says Malone.[29] "I see it happening in the next three to five years."

James C. Kennedy, chairman and chief executive officer of Cox Enterprises of Atlanta, is convinced that newspapers have a place on the information superhighway, but to secure that place they will need to demonstrate creativity and commitment to change.[30] "If we don't have the courage and creativity to take these risks, we won't have to worry about the public trust we enjoy today," Kennedy told members of the Newspaper Association of America on June 27.

Amidst the swirling hype and hope of the digital revolution, Neal B. Freeman, a Peabody award-winning television producer and chairman of the Blackwell Corporation, stands among those convinced of the promise of the information highway. "The digital era of communications is here, and its essence is this: Vastly more people will have vastly improved access to vastly more information."[31] Freeman's conclusion is based on an analysis of the political economy of the digital era, in which he believes we are at "one of those rare moments in techno-economic history when it becomes clear that some players will win big and many other players will win at least a little. The zero-sum, scarce-spectrum game is over, and real growth is at hand." What does he base his analysis on? Five factors:

- The increased power of special interests, with dozens of groups having formed, for example, their own networks, ranging from The Caribbean Satellite Network to The Crime Channel to The Gaming Network
- The retreat of telecommunications regulation, as the Clinton–Gore administration continues the momentum built during the Reagan–Bush years marked by the 1984 Modified Consent Decree divesting the Baby Bells from behemoth

AT&T (note that in late 1996 NTT, the Japanese equivalent of AT&T announced its parallel division into three smaller parts)
- The loss of America's cultural hegemony, as the global information network slowly erodes U.S. dominance in the creation of popular culture
- The rise of the multinational corporation, making once exotic "supranationals" such as Rupert Murdoch the norm, as it is the exceptional company that does not systematically move its rising young executives around the global markets
- The emergence of the digital press, as online, multimedia newspapers and magazines take hold, redefining the concept of news and markets no longer limited by geographic or political boundaries

At the same time consumers will have access to an increasing flow of raw data feeds from electronic media of all types. The need for information filters will rise dramatically. Traditional news media organizations will have an opportunity to expand their interpretation function. Smart agents will rapidly move into our digital midst. One fascinating Israeli company has already introduced three classes of intelligent agents for the Internet. LiveAgent, SearchAgent, and LiveAgent Pro were released in 1997 by AgentSoft Ltd., each of which performs customizable, routine tasks on the World Wide Web. LiveAgent, for example, is a personal agent on the Web, observing one's browsing behavior (which sites one visits, what information one obtains or clicks on) and then replicates those behaviors, routinely returning updated information, and so on. The next generation of intelligent agents will fall into a new class called *adaptive agents*. Adaptive agents will not only observe one's online behavior, but extend it to new arenas. For example, an adaptive agent might watch as we browse three news sites, observing the categories of stories we are most interested in (e.g., information technology). The adaptive agent would then visit other similar sites (i.e., news sites we did not visit) and obtain additional information technology stories, even compiling a "natural language" (i.e., English) summary of the essential facts as well as the notable differences or contradictory facts reported at each site. A collaborative project involving the faculty from the Department of Computer Science and the Center for New Media at Columbia University is in fact already working on a test of such a "smart" application.

Careers in the New Media: The Educational Mandate

Anyone planning a career in new media should be prepared for change, adaptation, and convergence. Few new media technologies are settled into their final form. As the technology continues to evolve, content production processes will continue to change. Moreover, as the new media of the digital age grow in importance, individuals with a rich understanding of technology convergence will have an advantage. New media products will become increasingly multimedia in format, with text, data, audio, and motion video blending in a single communications environment. Students preparing for new media careers should take courses both in the liberal arts and in all aspects of human communication. Medium-specific courses or degrees will have decreasing value in the emerging new media environment. Instead, the next generation of students will need to combine basic skills in thinking and writing with new media coursework emphasizing all aspects of human communication, from interpersonal and group communication to mediated and networked communications.

The Business Forecast

"You acted unwisely," I cried, "as you see
by the outcome." He calmly eyed me;
"When choosing the course of my action,"
said he, "I had not the outcome to guide me."[32]

Against a backdrop of considerable optimism and enthusiasm for the coming new media age, there is still profound commercial and cultural risk in investing millions, even billions, of dollars in staking out territory on the new media business frontier. Although there is no way to completely remove the risk from entering the new media marketplace, there are ways to minimize that risk. One set of tools comes from the field of financial analysts, commercial high rollers accustomed to risk-taking. One of the premier financial analysts specializing in the media is J. Kendrick Noble, a veteran media analyst, who recently completed a senior fellowship at The Freedom Forum Media Studies Center. Noble's fellowship research included developing a methodology for conducting a business forecast for the media industry. Based on an examination of data for a variety of media and communication fields, including newspapers, magazines, cable TV, and telephony, for much of the twentieth century, Noble suggests that reliable forecasts for new media technologies are possible, at least under limited circumstances. Perhaps most importantly, the forecasts must be based on accurate historical time-series data. Moreover, any forecast should be extended for no more than one-third the time frame of the original data. That is, if historical data are available for thirty years, then any forecast or prediction should be limited to the next ten years. For example, if data are available for 1965–1995, then a reliable forecast can be made through 2005. Beyond that period, the forecast is subject to many unexpected factors and likely to vary widely from the observed or actual pattern. By inference, the time-series data available for World Wide Web commercial ventures is no more than about three years, making predictions beyond a year highly uncertain.

Noble further notes that mathematical curves known as "S" curves are among the most commonly used tools for such forecasting. Such so-called "growth curves" are based on mathematical models for describing growth rates among biological organisms, such as humans or microorganisms. Logistic (or Pearl) and Gompertz curves are among the most widely used growth curves, which Noble argues are effective for conducting new media forecasts.[33] Others have used such biological models in describing media growth patterns, as well, including studies of media specialization and niche publishing. In Noble's research, a logistic curve provided an accurate description of the household penetration of the telephone from 1877 to

1931, but as a result of the Great Depression, underestimated the ultimate penetration level of the telephone in the 1980s (i.e., the model predicted telephone penetration would top out at about 40 percent, when it actually reached close to 95 percent in the 1980s). Use of a Gompertz curve provided a somewhat less accurate description of the adoption level of the telephone during the first half of the twentieth century, but accurately forecast the penetration level of the 1980s. Assuming the Gompertz curve provides a more reliable long-term forecast for media household penetration, Noble's analysis suggests that cable TV will achieve in 2040 the same household penetration achieved by telephony in the 1980s (i.e., roughly 95 percent).

Given the utility of these financial forecasting methods, new media entrepreneurs should consider employing logistic and Gompertz curves to project the possible market for new media technologies. The results might help steer them away from huge financial blunders and into more productive, even if smaller-scale ventures. Still, a word of caution comes from an unlikely theological source. The Reverend Donald Shriver, former president of the Union Theological Seminar in New York, warns that a forecast for the future of the media, an institution central not only to the functioning of our economy but to our cultural and political process, may have greater value if it is contrasted against an alternative prediction, or based on clearly outlined conditions in an if/then fashion.[34] Typically, Noble observes, financial analysts must forecast a single projection, because it is what the clients demand. If their forecasts are right, they will succeed and make a lot of money. If they are wrong, they will need to find a new line of work. Intrepid new media investors should consider both the best and worst case forecasts before investing heavily in new media technologies.

A CONSUMER'S GUIDE TO DIGITAL COMMUNICATION

As the world of digital communication continues to evolve, media consumers will need to develop a new form of electronic media literacy. Central to this literacy are understanding the dimensions, grammar, and commercial nature of multimedia and cyberspace communications. As these two forms of digital communications converge, or collide, in the emerging information superhighway the new literacy will also continue to evolve. The rules and guidelines offered here are merely a starting point, and will require continual updating as the technology and its uses evolve.

"Seeing is believing" is an adage many have subscribed to for centuries. But in today's digital media age it can no longer be relied on. Digital image processors have made synthetic video commonplace. As a result, new media consumers need to be both aware of the new rules of the game, as well as how new media content producers will respond. Outlined below are ten rules, or commandments, to guide consumers navigating the world of digital communications. The first three rules apply generally to digital media, and the rest apply to cyberspace and beyond.

Rule 1: Question everything that is seen, heard, read, or watched in the new media environment. Digital processors and those who own one make detecting synthetic content almost impossible, and there is no government agency like the Federal Drug Administration (FDA) charged with evaluating media content, partly as a result of the First Amendment, partly a result of the complexity and scope of the existing communication system, and largely because of technology itself.

Rule 2: Conclude that almost everything in the new media environment is created to make money for someone. The few media products that truly do not have a commercial basis are as rare as a VCR that never blinks 12:00.

Rule 3: Assume that every new technology is a potential threat to your privacy. Every interactive system from your cable TV to the telephone to the World Wide Web has the ability to record every interaction you engage it in. The question you must ask yourself is: Is the convenience it provides worth the loss of privacy? The questions to ask the service provider are: What information about me and my use of your service are you recording, how will you use it, and will you make the information available to anyone else, to whom and for what price?

Exploring the Limits of Cyberspace: The Possible and the Impossible

Cyberspace is the domain of networked communications (most often the Internet) that today encircle the globe, and tomorrow may stretch well beyond planet Earth. Although its beginnings were meager and the applications generally limited to electronic mail and file transfers, today the boundaries of cyberspace are rapidly expanding. Electronic bombs are sometimes as frequent as electronic mail, commercial transactions are almost as common on some systems as document transfers, and electronic publishing is challenging commercial printing as the state of the art in reaching both niche and mass markets. Moreover, the frontier nature of cyberspace also abounds with villains, outlaws, and heroes. Together, these patterns lead to **Rule 4**: Assume there are no boundaries in cyberspace, other than your own or someone else's imagination.

The following rules are especially important for parents, but apply to anyone concerned about the digital world.

Rule 5: Apply all the rules of conventional media literacy to digital communications. In other words, be aware of what your children are tuned into, whether going online, exploring multimedia, or simply playing videogames. Guide them in their selections, but also let them explore and enjoy freedom in making their own decisions. Debrief them periodically on their new media encounters.

Rule 6: Expect the unexpected. Because the limits of cyberspace are unknown and expanding, there will always be surprises. This is much of what attracts young people to explore the online world, the Internet, and the World Wide Web. It is participatory, evolving, and allows connections to people all around the world. There are many benefits possible, including cultural enrichment, education, and cognitive development. But there are also dangers, some of which are outlined below. As a corollary to this rule, consider what many have dubbed the Year 2000 Problem. Many software programs and computers run on an internal calendar based on a system of two digits (e.g., DD-MM-YY). As a result, many are concerned about what will happen to many of the world's computers and computer programs at the end of this century when the year becomes 00. Programs that use the year to make calculations (e.g., accounting) are especially susceptible to the problem. The Social Security Administration estimates that it will need to revise some 50 million lines of code to correct this problem in its own system.[35] Expect the unexpected in the year 2000!

Rule 7: Never assume that if your child is using their computer that they are necessarily engaged in something educational. Although it is tempting to think that using the computer is better than watching television, it's not necessarily the case. Pedophilia in the online world is not uncommon. Sexual content is among the most commonly transmitted digital material on the Internet. Children should always be monitored when using their computer, especially if their system has an online connection, including a modem and a phone line. It's wise to talk to your child after they use the computer to find out what they have been doing. Or, better yet, join them in their computer explorations and game playing. When buying computer games, always read reviews and make sure that the content is suitable for your child. Many games are fun, educational, and harmless. But many are equally filled with violence, sexual exploitation, and even racism. Many of both the best and worst games can be obtained through cyberspace. Monitor your child's computer use to make sure the material they may be downloading is appropriate for them and meets your standards. Also, make sure that your child is not obtaining pirated material, such as digital recordings of copyrighted music or video. This is not only potentially dangerous, but is illegal. If you do find pirated material, talk to your child about how they received it and delete the files. A variety of online resources are available to help parents screen out unwanted online content, including software filters such as SurfWatch, Cyber Patrol, and Net Nanny. Similarly, a variety of Web sites provide site reviews to give parents a sense of what sites are not only most suitable for children but will meet their children's needs and tastes. Cnet.com is one site that provides not only reviews of "the best of the Web," but also for CD-ROM offerings.

Corollaries to Rule 7:

- Beware of anyone bearing uninvited gifts, anything free, or anything that sounds too good to be true—because it probably is. The Internet is filled with hucksters, charlatans, con artists, and worse. The discussion below examines the dimensions of the lawless nature of the electronic frontier.
- Never give out your name, address or phone number, and instruct your child to do likewise, and to never give out the name of their school.
- Don't respond to angry or obscene online messages; report them to the manager of the online service you or your child uses.
- know the online service(s) your child uses, and see if blocking is available.

Rule 8: Encourage the spirit of the First Amendment in cyberspace. Freedom of expression is perhaps the strongest positive force to countervail against many of the potentially negative forces at work in cyberspace. By promoting more communication, not less, participants in the global online community will enjoy a more robust communication environment, one in which truth will likely prevail over falsehood. Such platitudes may seem naive in today's somewhat cynical age, but they reflect the importance of reaffirming the Constitutional guarantees on the electronic frontier.

Rule 9: Think twice before buying the first, or even second generation of any new media technology. Chances are great that the early generations may have bugs or technical problems. Subsequent versions are likely to be considerably less expensive and work better, often having more features and being less complicated. Also, new technologies will tend to evolve toward a more unified set of standards, allowing greater compatibility among software from different companies or suppliers. This is not a hard and fast rule, but it tends to be the case.

Rule 10: Experiment with and enjoy the technology. Test and explore the limits of cyberspace. If you have children, encourage them to do the same, and don't be afraid to *ask them* for help and advice. Chances are your children may know more about using many of the new media technologies than you do. Seeking their advice will not only be educational, but it will show them respect, help build their self-esteem, and encourage them to share future electronic discoveries with you. Research at the Pathways for Women in the Sciences program at Wellesley College suggests three ingredients are especially important in creating a user-friendly environment that will encourage girls to explore new media technology: hands-on experience, teamwork, and relevance.[36] Following these rules may not insure a safe, enjoyable, and learning new media environment, but they will increase the chances of electronic success.

Scenario for Tomorrow: Knowbots, Virtual Reality, and Cyberpunks

Because it is neither owned and controlled by anyone, nor regulated by government (the CDA not withstanding), the Internet has served as a hotbed for unrestrained communication and an information free-for-all. Although philosopher John Locke may have been pleased to see his notion of a marketplace of ideas come to digital fruition, he may have been equally concerned about some of the emerging patterns of abuse.

Anarchy and Lawlessness on the Electronic Frontier

Technology reporter Peter H. Lewis writes that "Turks and Armenians have brought their decades-old hatred to the digital stage, accusing one another of using electronic mail forgeries and software that seeks and destroys an enemy's messages to the broader community."[37] Elsewhere on the "net," computer programmers are preparing "electronic mail bombs" to damage other users' computers, pedophiles are going online to recruit young boys for sex, pornographic images are transmitted in large volume. Many long-time users are worried that the free and open atmosphere that has existed on the Internet and fostered an intellectual climate rich in diversity will be replaced by one chilled by obscenity and pandering to the lowest common denominator, where prejudice and promiscuity become the norm.

Strategies to protect the Internet community have been few, and some have given up hope. "Certainly there will never be any consensus to establish a regulatory body for Usenet (largest news group on the Internet)," writes Mr. Botz in an e-mail.[38] "And no, the existing defenses are clearly not adequate. So what will happen? The Net as we know it will die."

Others see a technological solution. "What people will probably do is invent 'site kill files,'" writes David Hayes, a Usenet participant who works at the National Aeronautics and Space Administration's Jet Propulsion Laboratory in Pasadena, CA.[39] "Site Kill Files" allow a user to block selected computer messages or specific parts of the network. At the same time, site kill files could be used to censor politically unpopular views, not just obscene messages or unsolicited advertisements.

Virtual Reality

Jaron Lanier, the creator of the first virtual reality device, says that passive entertainment will always have a place in the media world, but he believes there is also a much more engaging place for virtual reality. Virtual reality is in use in a variety of applications, including industry, design, education, medicine, art, and entertainment. In Germany, virtual reality technology is helping in the redesign of the city of Berlin, with VR technology controlling construction robots. In Japan, department store shoppers use VR applications to design their own kitchen, try it out, and have it delivered. In the United States, Medical Media Systems of New Hampshire is using virtual reality to enhance surgical tools. The company's VR technologies integrate magnetic resonance imaging (MRI) with live sensory data to give a surgeon a three-dimensional view of the body. Conjuring up images of the science fiction film classic *Fantastic Voyage,* starring Raquel Welch, surgeons also use an instrument called endoscopic surgery, in which a tiny optical fiber is inserted into the body to control microinstruments. By remotely controlling this device, the surgeon virtually experiences the interior of the body. "It is like a zone for a fighter pilot," says Lanier.[40]

Although the passive couch potato may not quickly become a thing of the past, historians of the next millennium may someday need to write a virtual media history. Shaping that future is research scientist Brenda Laurel, whose work at Interval Research, a new Palo Alto, California, think tank, is creating virtual reality products generally not held in high regard in the commercial sector because they do not involve killing.[41] Laurel's virtual reality creations include a "virtual environment for two" at the Banff Center for the Arts in Canada, which lets visitors don computerized helmets and hand sensors to take a simulated trek to a mountain cave and step into the bodies of a snake, fish, spider, or crow.

Sonification

As we move into an era dominated by information, we are threatened by an increasingly complex and bewildering array of data. T. S. Eliot once asked, "Where is the wisdom lost in knowledge? Where is the knowledge lost in information?" Anthony Smith today asks, "Where is the information lost in data?" "Sonification" may provide at least a partial answer. "Sonification" refers to the notion of making scientific data audible. Introduced into the technical literature in 1952, the notion has surfaced from time to time since then. Recently, a sonification research program emerged at the National Center for Supercomputing Applications (NCSA) at the University of Illinois. "If you work in the field of computer music, representing data with sound is a pretty obvious idea," says Illinois composer Robin Bargar.[42] The group at NCSA has developed sonification software that uses an IBM-compatible PC and a MIDI synthesizer to turn just about any data into sound. Gregory Kramer, a musician similarly intrigued by the notion of sonification, has developed a system in which sound represents several variables at once. Clarity, the company he founded in Garrison, New York, is designing a sonification system for operating rooms, which will broadcast the patient's vital signs, including blood pressure and oxygen levels. The trick to sonification systems is developing a trained ear for sound, but it's a problem that training can overcome. Says Kramer, "You know when your car is running well just by listening to it. A certain noise, like a rattle, might also tell you what's wrong. Sounds in a well-designed sonification system could be interpreted in much the same way.[43] In the next decade, specialized applications of sonification technology might allow physicians to analyze complex patient data simply by listening to their audio representation. Perhaps sports fans one day may digest complex sports statistics simply by listening to an audio representation of the data on their personal digital appliance.

Artificial Life

Notions of artificial life, or living beings created by human hands, have dwelled in man and woman's imagination for more than a century. Victorian novelist Mary Shelley envisioned an artificial lifeform in her classic novel of Gothic horror, *Frankenstein*. More recently, Hungarian mathematician John Von Neuman described the automaton, a robotic machine capable of self-replication and other lifelike qualities. Logician Alan Turing outlined the foundation for machine-based life in his creation called the Turing Machine.

As a scientific discipline, the field of artificial life is in its infancy, however, with the first formal conference held in 1987.[44] Nevertheless, a number of computer scientists have conducted pioneering research to create computer-based life forms, artificial life, or a-life, which exhibit many of the qualities commonly associated with "real" life. These qualities include the ability to see, to eat, to reproduce and engage in sexual activity, to make decisions, to adapt to a changing environment, to demonstrate processes of natural selection. Since these artificial beings are capable of dying, then conversely they are also capable of living. Tomorrow's media world may be populated more heavily by electronic a-life forms than by their human counterparts. Many of these a-life forms will be acting as personal assistants, or know-bots, seeking the information their human masters desire, making or breaking appointments, or even conducting transactions at the bank or the supermarket, based on rules that we have established for them. At the same time, many of these electronic creatures may be less socially acceptable. One of the most notorious forms of artificial life is the computer virus. Although invented as an academic exercise, the computer virus has evolved to become a powerfully destructive force. Beyond the computer virus, future forms of a-life may exceed even a science fiction writer's most devilish imagination.

Most Wanted in Cyberspace

When Willie Sutton once was asked why he robbed banks, he replied, because that's where the money is. If cyberspace's most wanted cyberpunk were asked why he turned computer hacker, would he respond in like fashion, because that's where the information is? We may soon find out. Computer wizard Kevin Mitnick became the FBI's most wanted computer hacker for allegedly stealing software and data from more than a half dozen cellular telephone manufacturers.[45] After being hunted for violation of a Federal probation requirement that he not enter computers illegally, Mitnick was apprehended when the San Diego SuperComputer Center's Tsutomu Shimomura, a well-known security expert, helped federal authorities track him down. Mitnick had hacked into the home computer of Shimomura, raising his ire. Shimomura then turned his own computer security talents to tracking Mitnick and eventually led authorities on an electronic manhunt to Mitnick's Raleigh, North Carolina apartment. Shimomura has since signed substantial (reported to be for more than $1 million) book, film, and CD-ROM contracts to tell the story of how he helped catch Mitnick.

Reflecting on the strange case, *New York Times* technology reporter John Markoff reports that as a teenager, Mitnick used a computer and modem to:

- Secretly read electronic mail of computer security officials at MCI Communications
- Access telephone company central offices in Manhattan and the phone switching centers in California, allowing him to listen in on phone calls and engage in high-tech hijinks like reprogramming home phones so that callers would hear a recording asking for a deposit of 25 cents
- Break into a North American Air Defense Command computer, foreshadowing the 1983 movie *War Games*

Some see Mitnick as a cyberspace hero, and a victim of the Internet-mania of the mid-1990s. Chris Gulker reports at the Random Access Web site, "Is Kevin Mitnick a dangerous criminal apprehended by an ingenious high-tech detective? Or a sad, if annoying, loner who was set up by shrewd manipulators cashing in on Internet hype?"[46]

THE GLOBAL INFORMATION INFRASTRUCTURE: GORE

One of the emerging benefits of the new information age is the development of a global information infrastructure (GII). The GII refers to the emerging network of advanced telecommunications, computing, and information technologies around the world, particularly the Internet. Although the GII will not reach all communities, countries, and computers simultaneously and in equal fashion, it will—in fact, it already does—reach many millions of people around the world. The GII will make it possible for people in even remote regions to stay in constant electronic touch. It will enable low-cost, high-speed commercial transactions from any location in the world, as long as they are connected to the GII. It will provide electronic access to diverse resources located throughout the world.

Important questions about the GII include:

- Who will have access?
- What will be the cost of access and use?
- Who will pay for the construction of the GII?
- How will the GII be controlled or regulated?
- What guarantees for freedom of expression will exist in the GII?
- How will regional differences in GII policy be managed in an international arena?

A Global Virtual Digital Library

From a cultural perspective, one of the most important opportunities the GII affords is the creation of a global virtual digital library. Such a library is already developing, as electronic resources such as those at the OCLC, the U.S. Library of Congress, and at countless libraries and public institutions connect to the global computer network known as the Internet. This library is virtual in the sense that its collection, as it were, is housed in no single physical location. Rather, it exists in digital format in many decentralized locations, in computers in libraries, schools, offices, and elsewhere. Each digital location acts as a communication portal, or file server, providing electronic access, browsing, or downloading of material to any location in the world connected to the GII. Important questions about this global virtual digital library are many, and parallel those outlined above regarding the GII.

A New Athenian Age of Democracy

Perhaps even more important than the development of virtual libraries are the implications of digital communications for the political system. For more than a century, political pundits have pondered the role of electronic media in the democratic process.[47] Today, Vice President Gore proclaims that networked communications may signal the beginning of a new Athenian Age of Democracy. Lawrence Grossman, former president of NBC News and PBS, echoes this view in his book *The Electronic Republic*, suggesting that new media technologies are rapidly transforming the democratic system from one of representation to direct democracy. Armed with their computers, modems, and WebTVs, citizens increasingly have direct access to the political process. Not only can they communicate directly with political candidates and elected officials, but they can vote on referenda and other legislative issues. Such a political transformation may be both a good and a dangerous thing. Although direct-access technology may enhance political participation, it may also lead to political decisions based on little more than the emotions aroused by dramatic television images.[48] More alarmingly, the selective development and diffusion of new technologies, the lack of access to the poor, and the difficulty in using many new technologies may also lead to political tyranny of the majority, with minority voices being lost in a digital cacophony.

Electronic Town Meetings

For more than two centuries, town meetings have been a vital part of democracy in America, making the electoral process a participatory rather than a spectator sport. French philosopher Alexis de Tocqueville observed how town meetings gave Americans a hands-on education in democracy. Brandeis University Professor Jeffrey Abramson notes that the town meeting was originally designed to meet three purposes:

- To educate citizens about common concerns
- To empower citizens to self-government
- To engage citizens in an open and universally accessible process[49]

Of course, since their inception, town meetings have failed to meet these goals fully, sometimes restricting participation based on race, gender, church membership, and property. Still, the town meeting has been pursued as a democratic ideal. In its most recent incarnation, it emerged during the 1992 and 1996 presidential campaigns in a new, technologically driven form called the *electronic town hall*. Texas Businessman Ross Perot trumpeted the electronic town hall as the platform for a new era of democracy. Others hailed the electronic town hall as a twenty-first-century technique to reintroduce face-to-face communication in a media society. But electronic town meetings are not necessarily a panacea. Not everyone may have access to the technology needed to participate fully. There is a tendency for "push button" democracy to take hold, where, rather than meet and discuss, participants may do little more than push a button on a telephone handset or a remote control to indicate approval or disagreement.

Abramson argues that three conditions are necessary for effective deliberation at a town meeting:

- Citizens should be able to explore political messages of substance at length and in depth, without limiting exchanges to ever-shrinking soundbites
- Citizens must be able to reflect on those messages, and not respond instantaneously
- Citizens should be able to interact and exchange views and ideas, to test each other's reactions, and weigh their opinions against those of others

Although face-to-face meetings can clearly satisfy these conditions, how well electronic town halls fare is a matter of how they are designed and executed.[50] Technology may make it possible to bring together many participants at remote and scattered locations, but it can also encourage instantaneous response and a lack of substantial communication.

Abramson outlines six critical issues in designing electronic town meetings to satisfy the above criteria for effective political deliberation.

- **Venue**. New media technologies enable us to hold electronic town meetings on a national, regional, or local level. The choice of venue depends on both the issue or political campaign, as well as citizen access to the relevant technology.
- **Issue**. Every electronic town meeting should be devoted to a single, clearly stated issue, such as national health care or the federal deficit.
- **Agenda-setting/Editorial Control**. Setting the issues for the town meeting is a complex matter and research by Abramson suggests two models. The primary model is for the organization hosting the meeting, such as a news organization, to choose the issues and plan the event, including selecting moderators, experts, and so forth. Alternatively, it is sometimes effective for a nonprofit group to set the agenda.
- **Audience/Participants**. Rarely will a town meeting, electronic or face-to-face, satisfy the demands of scientific sampling and representativeness of the broader population. Instead, audience members are typically self-selected, and represent only politically active groups. Thus, Abramson recommends building an audience in two stages. First, there will naturally be the primary, self-selected audience, often limited to those who can come to a TV studio. Second, a broader audience should be invited to participate through the use of interactive technology such as the telephone, through 800 or 900 numbers or through online communications such as an Internet forum.
- **Choice of Interactive Technology**. Interactive technology provides three main options for providing audience involvement and participation. First and most basic is touch-tone telephone dialing, particularly 800 and 900 networks provided by carriers such as AT&T and MCI. These networks can process more

than 10,000 calls in 90 seconds. For national town meetings, it is essential to provide sufficient 800 network capacity. The CBS *America Online* special during the 1992 campaign frustrated many callers by providing too little capacity—only 314,786 calls got through out of some 24.6 million attempts.

Second are two-way cable systems, which were inaugurated in the Warner Amex Qube experiment in the 1970s in Columbus, Ohio, and are today increasingly common. Interactive systems in San Antonio, Texas, Minneapolis, Minnesota, Portland, Oregon, Upper Manhattan, New York, Reading, Pennsylvania, Orlando, Florida, and Fairfax, Virginia all allow the viewer to send messages upstream using a remote control as well as receive TV programming. Lack of access to nonsubscribers is a limitation of this approach.

Finally, online services provide a third technological option for electronic town meetings. Online computer forums are in fact already common on the Internet and on commercial services. They allow in-depth discussion of issues, as well as direct communication and exchange of ideas. Moreover, through the Internet it is possible to provide a forum for holding for the first time an electronic town meeting in an international global venue. As we move toward McLuhan's global village, this may become an increasingly important issue. Moreover, online forums are inexpensive, since telecommunication charges are only local. The biggest drawback to online network approaches is the limited availability of computers and online services among the general citizenry. Even in an information society such as the United States, only some 36 percent of U.S. households have a computer and even fewer have a network connection. This situation, however, may rapidly change with the proliferation of powerful, inexpensive videogame players and the convergence of telecommunications, cable, and computers, as well as the increased availability of Internet access through schools, libraries, and other public spaces. Other emerging technologies such as DBS and PCS may also provide a technological infrastructure for electronic town meetings by the end of the decade. Importantly, pioneering online voter information services were implemented via the Internet during the 1994 elections in California, including the Voter Online Information and Communications Exchange (VOICE) sponsored by two major national organizations, the League of Women Voters and Project Smart Vote.[51] The 1996 campaign saw even greater online forums on the World Wide Web, with an increasingly diverse cross-section of the voting public accessing voter information at both official campaign sites as well as from reliable online news sources.

- **Voting from Home or Other Audience Locations**. This is in many ways the natural conclusion of the electronic town hall. One of the most significant problems in electronic voting, however, is the ability of individuals to vote multiple times. Similarly, it is important to provide multiple individuals at **a single location** the ability to cast their votes. A potential solution to these problems is to provide a personal identification number (PIN) to each participant to electronically monitor voting, assuring that each town hall participant could vote only once, and that each person at a location could cast a vote. Moreover, this approach would lay the foundation for full voting activity electronically, assuring that each ballot cast was entered by a registered voter. The security of each PIN would become imperative in such a system. Advanced systems could use optical scanners to verify voter identification through fingerprints or retinal scans, although at present the cost of the necessary technology would be prohibitive. One of the important limitations of voting at electronic town meetings is generalizability beyond the meetings' participants. Participation in town hall meetings, whether traditional or electronic, is not representative of the population at large, and any results from a vote can not be fairly generalized to the broader population.

THE NEXT GENERATION: CHILDREN AND TECHNOLOGY

Understanding the uses and consequences of new media technology ultimately hinges on understanding the next generation. Today's children and youth are the heaviest users of new media technology. They enjoy the highest comfort level with the technology. For them, many seemingly foreign and obtuse technologies are second nature and completely transparent. They often have an intuitive grasp of new media technologies. Whether programming a common house device like a VCR or accessing the Internet, many youth travel in and out of the cyberworld as easily as most adults get in an out of a car. Even toddlers two to three years old can learn to use a mouse and control a computer. One interesting Web site designed just for kids, Internet-For-Kids, offers children of all ages a variety of customized educational and entertaining interactive tools and applications.[52] Under the leadership of company founder and president, Victoria Williams, the site is a road sign to the future.

To many older adults, the idea of talking to your computer, much less a banking machine, may seem like fanciful science fiction if not downright dangerous. But to the next generation, calling in to an automated banking machine and simply telling the computerized system what transactions you wish may be as simple as using an ATM is to most Americans today. One major bank in New York is already conducting a test with voice-response tele-banking. You dial in and simply say "representative" for the operator, or any of a number of other terms to select those banking options. The system works simply, easily, and reliably. What's around the corner is anybody's guess. But one thing is certain: The next generation will glide as easily through this high-tech world as today's average household gourmet operates a microwave oven. The next generation's new media habits will also continue the transformation of new media technology. Their behavioral preferences and patterns and content choices will influence the design, look, and feel of tomorrow's media. The nature of interactivity will reflect the next generations' lifestyle and attitudes.

Jaron Lanier, the recognized "father" of virtual reality offers this view of the importance of the next generation:

> *The digital superhighway is much more than a highway system. It's actually the construction of an entirely new virtual continent in which the highway runs. In the future, we will live part of our lives in cyberspace,*

in the world of virtual reality. We could bequeath few gifts to future generations more important than getting this right. It's critically important to balance public and private interests, much as it's very important to do so in land use, where even private land owners have certain obligations to the public.[53]

No one can predict with any certainty the future of the media world. Many elements will be new and unexpected, while perhaps most will continue to reflect the best and worst of today's media system. Commercial interests will no doubt continue to dominate, but there will be room for not-for-profit cultural forces. As we already see in the Internet, the role of an electronic public space will be profound. The future of the media world may not be ours entirely to shape, but it is ours to discover. Lord Tennyson once offered these encouraging words:

> *"Come, my friends, 'Tis not too*
> *late to seek a newer world."*
> —*LORD ALFRED TENNYSON*[54]

NOTES

[1]Levy, Steven, "We Have Seen the Content, and It Is Us." *The Media Studies Journal,* Winter, 1994.

[2]NEC Ad number 162, *Scientific American,* January 1997: 21.

[3]Kenneth M. King, "Computers, Man and Society Seminar Remarks," Columbia University, December 18, 1996.

[4]Siegenthaler, John, Leadership Institute, The Freedom Forum Media Studies Center, June 23, 1994.

[5]Eco, Umberto, "From Internet to Gutenberg," speech, Italian Academy for Advanced Studies in America at Columbia University, November 12, 1996.

[6]Krebs, Michelle, "Cars That Tell You Where to Go," *New York Times,* December 15, 1996.

[7]Bodo, Pete, "How to Find Yourself, or Not Get Lost," *New York Times,* December 15, 1996.

[8]Levere, Jane, "Travel Systems Use Technology to Ease the Commute," *New York Times,* December 23, 1996.

[9]Leonard Kleinrock, "Nomadic Computing," Presentation at The Heritage of Marconi's Invention and the Future of Telecommunication, Columbia University, December 9, 1996.

[10]Carey, John, "Media Research and the Information Highway: Setting a Research Agenda," February 14, 1994, Speech, The Freedom forum Media Studies Center.

[11]Robert Lucky, "Reinventing Telephony as Internet Comes of Age," Presentation at The Heritage of Marconi's Invention and the Future of Telecommunication, Columbia University, December 9, 1996.

[12]Stix, Gary, "The Wall: Chip makers' quest for small may be hitting it," *Scientific American,* July 1994, p. 96, 98.

[13]Ibid.: 96.

[14]Ibid.

[15]Markoff, John, "Chip-Making Towers of Power," *New York Times*, Nov. 8, 1994: C1.

[16]*Business Week* special report "Some Gigachip milestones to look for," July 4, 1994: 88.

[17]Gibbs, W. Wayt, "Bandwidth, Unlimited," *Scientific American,* January 1997: 41.

[18]John Markoff, "Judge Rules Against Curbs on Export of Encryption Software," *New York Times,* December 19, 1996.

[19]Dennis, Everette E., Technology Studies Seminar, The Freedom Forum Media Studies Center, April 6, 1994.

[20]Fitzgerald, Mark, "Invisible Digital Copyright ID," *Editor & Publisher*, June 25, 1994.

[21]Stahlman, Mark, "Backlash: The Infobahn Is a Big, Fat Joke," *Wired*, March 1994: 73.

[22]Rifkin, Glenn, "Seeing Print's Future in a Digital Universe," *New York Times*, May 9, 1994: D8.

[23]Ibid.

[24]Ibid.

[25]Moeller, op. cit., 1994: 25.

[26]www.marimba.com

[27]Schonfeld, Reese, Speech, IRTS seminar Feb. 11, 1994.

[28]Auletta, op. cit., 1994: 52.

[29]Tynan, Daniel. "PC meets TV." *PC World*, February 1994: 139.

[30]Thalhimer, op. cit., July 6, 1994.

[31]Freeman, Neal B. "Populism + Telecommunications = Global Democracy," *National Review*, November 15, 1993: 50.

[32]Bierce, Ambrose. *The Collected Works of Ambrose Bierce*. New York: The Neale Publishing Co., 1909.

[33]Martino, Joseph P. (1993). *Technological Forecasting for Decision-Making*, 3rd ed. New York: McGraw-Hill. Noble, Jr., J. Kendrick, "U.S. Daily Newspapers: Past, Present and Prospects, 1958–2008," research report, presented at Fellows Seminar, May 26, 1994.

[34]Shriver, Rev. Donald, Speaker, Fellows Seminar, The Freedom Forum Media Studies Center, May 26, 1994.

[35]www.sandybay.com/pc-web/Year_2000_Problem.htm

[36]Hafner, Katie, "Getting Girls On-Line," *Working Woman*, April 1994: 61.

[37]Lewis, Peter H. "Sneering at a Virtual Lynch Mob," *New York Times*, May 11, 1994: D7.

[38]Ibid.

[39]Ibid.

[40]Lanier, ibid.

[41]Hermelin, Francine, "Feminizing Virtual Reality," *Working Woman*, April 1994: 54.

[42]Nadis, Steve, "Artificial Intelligence: The Sound of Data: Data may fill your ears rather than your eyes," *Omni*, January 1994: 26.

[43]Ibid.

[44]Levy, Steven. *Artificial Life: The Quest for a New Creation*. London: Penguin Books, 1993.

[45]Markoff, John, "Cyberspace's Most Wanted: Hacker Eludes F.B.I. Pursuit," *New York Times*, July 4, 1994.

[46]www.gulker.com/ra/hack/

[47]Carey, James (1989). op. cit.

[48]Schudson, Michael. (1992). "The Limits of Teledemocracy." *The American Prospect*, 11 (3): 41–45.

[49]Abramson, Jeffrey B., and Charles M. Firestone. *Electronic Town Meetings: Democratic Design for Electronic Town Meetings*, The Aspen Institute, 1992.

[50]Arterton, F. Christopher (1987). *Teledemocracy*. Beverly Hills, CA: Sage. Becker, Theodore (1993). "Teledemocracy: Gathering momentum in state and local governance." *Spectrum: The Journal of State Government*, 66 (2): 14–19.

[51]Lewis, Peter H. "Electronic Tie for Citizens and Seekers of Office," *New York Times*, Nov. 6, 1994: 15.

[52]www.internet-for-kids.com

[53]Tynan , op. cit., 1994: 139.

[54]Tennyson, Alfred. *Ulysses*. London: Moxon, 1869.

Glossary of New Media Technology Terms

Road Signs on the Information Superhighway

Although this list is offered here, the reader is encouraged to explore online resources such as the Webopeadia (www.sandybay.com/pc-web/), which offers a free online encyclopedia of information about a wide variety of new media terms.

Agents are computer programs that employ artificial intelligence to help users operate various computer applications. They act much as a personal assistant. Agents can learn by observation, make decisions and filter incoming information, such as select news items based on personal preferences, or search a database looking for selected pieces of information, or conduct transactions, such as electronic banking or making an airline reservation.

Artificial Intelligence (AI) refers to computer-based technologies that replicate behaviors associated with human thinking, such as making decisions, evaluating options, or developing new ideas. AI applications have been developed in the areas of computer vision, robotics, language processing, and expert systems (e.g., agents).

Asymmetrical Digital Subscriber Line (ADSL) is an emerging telecommunications transmission technology that uses advanced packet-switching (as opposed to the traditional circuit-switching technology) to make the distribution of full-motion video possible using twisted-pair telephone lines.

Asynchronous Transfer Mode (ATM) is a high-capacity packet-switching technology that allows all types of networks, both local and wide-area, to seamlessly interconnect and to transmit all forms of information, including voice, data, and full-motion video, via packet-switching (i.e., in bunches) rather than circuit-switching (i.e., over a dedicated line).

Augmented Reality is an advanced user interface technology that adds layers of information onto reality as viewed through specially designed head-mounted visors.

Bandwidth refers to the capacity of an electronic medium, such as an optical fiber, to carry information or data. The greater bandwidth of optical fiber allows it to carry full-motion video, which contains large amounts of information compared to text or audio.

Browsers refer to the software tools that enable users to access and navigate on the World Wide Web. Derived from Mosaic, the original graphical browser, the leading browsers are Netscape Navigator and Microsoft Internet Explorer.

C & Ku-band satellites refer to medium-power, common carrier satellites that operate in the 12 to 14 gigahertz region. They are widely used to deliver television programming.

CAR, or CAIR, refers to Computer-assisted (investigative) reporting pioneered in 1967.

CCD refers to a charge-coupled device used in electronic cameras to capture images without the use of emulsion, or chemical-based, film stock. CCD chips operate under low light conditions and have no delay for processing time.

Common Carrier traditionally refers to the legal requirement that a regulated medium, such as a telephone company, provide open access at a fair price to all content providers seeking to use the telephone infrastructure. It is unclear whether new services such as consumer online services will be treated as common carriers. A common carrier is not responsible for the content they carry from third parties, nor can they legally censor that content.

Compact Disc-Read Only Memory (CD-ROM) and Compact Disk-Interactive (CD-I) refers to an optical storage medium similar in format to music CDs. Designed with text storage in mind, a single CD-ROM can store more than 250,000 pages of text. CD-ROMs can also be used to store multimedia information, including audio and full-motion video, and are now being used by a variety of media companies to publish multimedia products ranging from electronic encyclopedias to news magazines. CD-I offers an interactive format for other kinds of products, such as games.

Compression refers to a technical process through which large amounts of data are condensed, or compressed, in digital format for transmission or storage. Many multimedia products would not be feasible today if not for advances in compression technology that reduce the digital information needed to replicate an image on a video monitor. This process has important implications for the creation of a video dial tone and for the storage of video signals, especially full-motion video, on CD-ROM or laserdisc devices.

Cookies (or Magic or Persistent Cookies) are information files used on the World Wide Web that contain information about client (user) computers, typically obtained from the client's browser preferences. Although useful in automating the personalization of information, Cookies raise privacy questions, and have spawned the development of software tools (e.g., Cookie Cutters by Phil Zimmerman) to identify and block and them.

Cyberspace is a termed developed by science fiction writer William Gibson to refer to a place similar to what many now call virtual reality. In *Neuromancer*, Gibson (1984) described cyberspace:

> *A consensual hallucination experienced daily by billions of legitimate operators, in every nation. . . . A graphic representation of data abstracted from the banks of every computer in the human system. Unthinkable complexity. Lines of light ranged in the nonspace of the mind, clusters and constellations of data. Like city lights, receding. . . .*

Digital Television (DTV) refers to the next generation of advanced, high-definition television (see HDTV) now under development in the United States and around the world.

Digital Video Disk (DVD) is a high-capacity optical storage device similar in format to CD-ROM, but is the first such device capable of storing an entire, two-hour feature-length film or video in digital format. DVD was introduced in late 1996, and became commercially available to consumers in 1997.

Digital Watermark refers to a technology for encoding an indelible digital signature onto a digital image or document to both protect copyright and authenticate the source of that image or document. Under development by Professor Shih-Fu Chang and others at Columbia University, the digital watermark will survive network transmission and compression and will indicate whether a document or image has been tampered with and how.

Digitization refers to the process of storing any information or communication in computer-readable format of 1s and 0s, or digits. It is the driving force behind the multimedia convergence of text, data, audio, and video.

Direct Broadcast Satellite (DBS) is a distribution medium that can transmit full-motion video direct to home compact satellite dishes no more than eighteen inches across and costing about $400, replacing the large, expensive backyard dish. Initially launched in 1975, DBS systems have only recently begun to succeed commercially in the United States.

DRAM stands for Dynamic Random Access Memory (see RAM).

Electronic Bulletin Boards (BBS) are electronic message posting places widely available in the online world. There are thousands of electronic bulletin boards on the Internet dealing with as many subjects.

Electronic/Digital Photography refers to a new generation of cameras and photographic technologies that capture and store images in digital format. It makes possible the complete processing of any images—still or full-motion—in a computerized, nonlinear environment. With wide commercial applications in advertising, public relations, and journalism, it also raises a variety of thorny ethical questions about the veracity and credibility of the image. Digital cameras do not store images at as high a level of resolution as emulsion-based film cameras; state-of-the-art digital cameras can store images with some 10 million pixels (the smallest picture element in a computer image), as opposed to 35 million in film.

Electronic Mail or e-mail is a form of computer-to-computer messaging that has existed since the first computer networks in the 1960s, allowing users to send and receive electronic mail at very little cost all around the world. It is among the heaviest uses of most computer networks, including the Internet.

Encryption is a communication security procedure referring to the encoding of messages in secret form and requiring subsequent decoding for interpretation. An ancient technique once used by Julius Caesar, emperor of Rome, encryption or cryptography is a controversial topic in computer communications, as U.S. governmental agencies push for an encryption standard that would allow the authorities to eavesdrop and private groups push for a totally secure alternative.

Federal Communications Commission (FCC) is the principal federal communications regulatory agency in the United States. Created under the 1934 Communications Act, the FCC enforces and interprets laws pertaining to telecommunications, new media technology, and the existing electronic media, such as the 1992 Cable TV Act and the Telecommunications Act of 1996.

Flat-Panel Displays refer to a class of computer displays using liquid crystal (LCD), plasma, and other technologies (e.g., diamond-coated displays) to present images on a flat screen. Many predict that the development of a high-resolution, color flat-panel at low cost (about five to ten years in the future) will transform the computer into an effective and portable communications device, making possible new information services such as a multimedia electronic newspaper.

Full Service Network (FSN) is the term Time Warner and other corporations are using to describe the information superhighways currently under construction in places like Orlando, Florida. The FSN consists of optical fiber networks, driven by Silicon Graphics computers, and are intended to offer a full range of new information services such as interactive TV and PCS; however, most FSN efforts to date have experienced little success due to a variety of reasons, some of them technical and economic.

Global Positioning Satellite (GPS) refers to a satellite navigational system that provides pinpoint geographic location information for use in automobiles and in handheld devices.

High Definition Television (HDTV) refers to the next generation of television technology, featuring a wide-screen aspect ratio similar to that of the cinema, high-resolution images, advanced color rendition, and stereophonic sound, all processed digitally.

Hypertext means nonlinear text. Coined by technology visionary Ted Nelson, hypertext is the foundation for the next generation of multimedia computing and is seen in the hyperlinks common on the World Wide Web (WWW).

Icon is a graphic representation of a computer function that appears on a display, such as a microcomputer monitor. Icons and the graphical user interface (GUI) now common to all desktop computers were developed in the 1960s at Xerox PARC.

Information Superhighway means many things to many people, but in general it refers to the various emerging electronic data networks of advanced telecommunications technologies that make possible a variety of new information services ranging from video-on-demand to home shopping to computer-to-computer communications around the globe. Vice President Al Gore envisions an information superhighway based on the Internet model of networked computing, while telephone companies see it as a broadband switched telecommunications network capable of delivering everything from video-on-demand to personal communications.

Integrated Services Digital Network (ISDN) is a medium-band (approximately 128 kbps) telecommunications technology that brings together in a single medium of distribution all types of information, including data, voice, text, and video.

Information Society refers to a society in which knowledge and information increasingly become the dominant source of wealth, power, and employment.

Information Technology refers to the acquisition, processing, storage, and dissemination of vocal, pictorial, textural, and numerical information by a microelectronics-based combination of computing and telecommunications.

Intellectual Property Rights refers to the rights to ownership, marketing, and licensing of computer software and other information products. Includes questions of copyrights and patents.

Interactive Media embrace telecommunications, computer, broadcast, and cable systems that allow direct exchanges among people via one or more communications channels such as voice, writing, or vision.

Interactive Television (ITV) refers to a coming revolution in television viewing technology in which viewers will have access to a variety of two-way services and will be able to select and control what they view and when. The first interactive television actually can be traced to a 1950s television show called *Winky Dink and You,* and subsequently appeared in the 1970s in Warner Communications' Qube experiment in Columbus, Ohio, which gave birth to many of today's cable networks and programs, including MTV and Nickelodeon. Today's WebTV represents perhaps the most viable form of interactive television by converging television with the Internet.

Internet refers to the global web of some 100,000 computer networks all using a common technical set of protocols called TCP/IP (Transmission Control Protocol/Internet Protocols). The Internet provides free or low-cost access to an estimated 50 million users worldwide to global electronic mail (e-mail), the World Wide Web, file transfers and databases ranging from the U.S. Library of Congress card catalogue to the 4,000-page Federal budget. Internet grew out of the Arpanet, created by the Defense Department as the first national computer network in 1969.

Intranet involves the application of Internet technologies within an organization's closed network.

Java is a platform-independent programming language used to create interactive, multimedia applications for the World Wide Web.

MJT, or Mobile Journalist Terminal, is a collaborative research effort of the Center for New Media and the Center for New Media Technology at Columbia University to create a portable integrated news gathering, communications, production, and delivery system based on advanced compression, wireless network, storage, and content-based retrieval and graphical user interface design technologies.

MODEM refers to MOdulate-DEModulate, the device that allows computers to communicate over a wide-area network. The Cable Modem is currently being introduced in a variety of markets to provide broadband access to online services.

MPEG refers to the Motion Picture Experts Group, which sets standards for digital television images. MPEG is the leading standard for compressed, digital full-motion broadcast quality video. Unlike other compression systems, MPEG requires both software and hardware for decompression. MPEG-2 is the second generation of the MPEG standard, and represents a global technical standard for compressed digital video. MPEG-4 and MPEG-7 represent the next generations of MPEG standards now under development and will include content-based, object-oriented, and three-dimensional imaging features. Led by engineering professor Dimitris Anastassiou, Columbia University is the only university to belong to the MPEG-2 patent pool.

MSS refers to mobile satellite services, such as Inmarsat.

Multimedia refers to the integration of text, images, audio, and data in a digital environment.

Omnicamera is an omnidirectional video technology system developed by Professor Shree Nayar at Columbia University, capable of capturing an entire 360 degree field of vision with a single NTSC or more advanced video camera using a specially designed parabolic mirror system. The Omnicam captures broadcast quality full-motion video in real time and can provide complete viewer control (over panning, zooming, etc.) without any mechnical camera device needed. Video can be output to up to twenty software cameras.

Online Communications is the generic term for communications over a computer network.

Optical Fiber is a silicon, or glass, medium for transmission of digital information. Optical fiber, or fiber optics, has transformed modern telecommunications primarily because it has more than 1,000 times the carrying capacity of conventional, twisted-pair telephone lines.

Packet-Switching is a technique of switching digital signals with computers wherein the signal stream is broken into packets and reassembled in the correct sequence at the destination.

PCS refers to personal communication services (PCS) that are being introduced based on the FCC's high-frequency spectrum auction completed in 1996. PCS will allow for widespread digital wireless communications beyond cellular communications.

Personal Digital Appliances (PDAs) refer to an emerging class of computer-based communications devices such as the flat-panel, personal communication device or pocket computers.

PGP refers to pretty good privacy, an encryption technology developed by Phil Zimmerman.

Pixel refers to the smallest picture element in a computerized imaging system.

RAM refers to Random Access Memory in a computer.

RBOC refers to Regional Bell Operating Company, one of seven firms that emerged from the 1984 AT&T divestiture as prime distribution channels for office phone and computer systems. RBOCs are: NYNEX, Bell Atlantic, Bell South, PacTel, Ameritech, SouthWestern Bell, US West. Bell Atlantic announced its acquisition of Nynex in 1996, and is expected to complete the acquisition in early 1997, making it the largest RBOC and reducing the number of RBOCs to six.

Remote Sensing Technologies refers to a class of high-resolution electronic cameras in orbit around the earth. They involve two primary sensor systems: one is a television camera that takes pictures of the earth using visible light. The other is a multispectral scanner that uses both visible and infrared light. Advances in the technology and the end of the Cold War have made remote sensing an increasingly important technology for a variety of civilian applications, such as gathering visual information about the earth for weather forecasting, news gathering, and environmental monitoring.

ROM, or Read Only Memory, is a primary form of computer memory. Today's desktop computers generally require at least 16 megabytes of ROM to run most multimedia and network applications seamlessly, although 32 or 64 megabytes is preferred.

Screen Phone is the next generation of telephone handsets that feature a liquid crystal display capable of providing textual information or data, making possible a variety of new information services on a mass scale and at a low cost.

Search Engines are the software tools that allow users of the World Wide Web to find information, home pages, and other content on the Web. Primarily text-based, next generation search engines will provide content-based, or meaning and semantic-based, search capabilities for images, video, and audio content.

Speech Synthesis and Recognition refer to technologies for computer voice processing, including understanding and responding to the spoken word as well as computerized speech. Applications are available for a variety of fields including medicine and journalism, but are especially important for making media technologies available for persons with disabilities.

Streaming Video and Audio refer to a compressed, digital system of delivering multimedia content in real-time over the World Wide Web. Streaming delivery systems send a small amount of multimedia content (e.g., a few frames of video) to a client computer's memory cache and then begin playing the video or audio, rather than waiting for long periods for an entire MPEG file to download, for example. Streaming applications make multimedia content via the Web feasible in a bandwidth-challenged network environment.

Telecommunications Act of 1996 represents the first comprehensive rewrite of the 1934 Communications Act. The Act deregulates much of the communications industry with the primary goals of providing increased competition, better service (including advanced interactive services and greater parental control over access to sexual and violent content online), and expanded universal service.

Transactional Services refer to a variety of computerized, interactive information services including electronic or home shopping, making airline reservations, banking, and bill paying. Nano-transactional (very small) systems are now being developed for use on the Internet.

V-Chip, or Violence Chip, is a device mandated by the Telecommunications Act of 1996, requiring broadcasters to support the development of a computer chip to be installed in next generation television sets to allow parents and others to block violent, sexual, and other forms of content. Although the V-Chip itself has not been terribly controversial, its implementation requires the development of a television programming ratings system that has proven extremely contentious, pitting industry groups against citizen groups.

Video-on-Demand (VOD) refers to a form of interactive television in which the viewer has direct electronic access to digital libraries of full-motion video, including movies or news on demand.

Virtual Reality (VR) is for some the ultimate communication medium: A total sensory experience in which the user (or users) can interact with or create their own multidimensional universe by using a data glove, data suit, and data visor. When immersed in virtual reality, users see, feel, interact with, and manipulate a computer-generated world not necessarily related in any way to the so-called real world we all live in. VR applications have been developed for entertainment, including arcade games, medicine, and employee training. Various VR applications have been developed for the Internet and the World Wide Web, including VRML, or Virtual Reality Modeling Language, QuickTime VR, and Virtual Worlds.

Virus—The computer virus is the digital equivalent of an organic virus that can infect a living being, such as a human. Computer viruses, however, are created by humans, and are designed to disrupt computer applications. Computer viruses, a form of artificial life, are spread by inserting infected disks in other computers or by transferring infected files electronically over a computer network, and then attaching themselves to software applications, sometimes causing immediate damage and other times operating on a delayed basis.

VRAM refers to Video Random Access Memory, a specialized form of RAM used in processing video content.

World Wide Web (WWW) refers to an interconnected set of computer servers on the Internet that conform to a set of network interface protocols created by Tim Berners-Lee of CERN, the European high-energy physics laboratory in Geneva, Switzerland. The Web has emerged as a new global publishing medium capable of distributing fully interactive multimedia content in a many-to-many hypertext publishing and commercial environment.

Wireless transmission, including personal communication services (PCS), is a technology that uses portions of the radio spectrum formerly thought impractical for wide-scale interactive communication uses, but now desirable because of advances in telecommunications, digitization, and compression. The Federal Communications Commission (FCC) has auctioned off a portion of the wireless spectrum for PCS for an estimated $10 billion.

Bibliography

13x Web site, http://www.13x.com/cgi-bin/cdt/snoop.pl
"A New Fee Structure to Share On-Line Data," *New York Times* April 6 1994: D1, D6.
Abramson, Jeffrey B. and Charles M. Firestone. *Electronic Town Meetings: Democratic Design for Electronic Town Meetings*, The Aspen Institute, 1992.
ADL Web site, The Web of Hate: Extremists Exploit the Internet. © 1996, Anti-Defamation League, http://www.adl.org/ADLRept/HateInter.html#anchor 251386
Advertisement in *Omni*, January 1994: 75.
Advertising Age, "A day in the 'virtual' life of a Chiat/Day executive," March 14, 1994: 19.
Advertising Age, July 18, 1994.
Afrinet Web site, www.afrinet.net/~halh
Aho, Debra, "Ad industry looks for interactive dollars," *Advertising Age*, May 16, 1994.
Alpha Web site, http://www.alpha.org/
AlphaWorld Web site, www.worlds.net/alphaworld.
Amstrong, David, "Ziff Happens," *Wired*, June 1994.
Andrews, Edmund L. "A Satellite System Is Planned to Link Most of the Globe," *New York Times*, March 21, 1994: A1, D2.
Andrews, Edmund L. "Betting on Small-Dish TV," *New York Times*, D1, D7, December 15, 1993.
Andrews, Edmund L. "Time Warner's 'Time Machine,'" *New York Times*, Dec. 12, 1994: C1, C7.
"Another Faulty Encryption Policy," *New York Times,* December 16, 1996.
Apple Jr., R.W. "Policing a Global Village," *New York Times*, October 13, 1993: A1.
Arlen, Gary H., "Education Networks to go Online Later This Year; Content Providers to Offer 'Electronic Printing Press,'" *Information & Interactive Services Report*, February 25, 1994: 17.
Arlen, Gary H., *Information & Interactive Services Report,* December 17, 1993: 5.
Arlen, Gary H., *Information & Interactive Services Report*, February 11, 1994: 4.
Arlen, Gary H., "LucasArts Charts Digital Path Between Film, Interactivity." *Information & Interactive Services Report*, March 11, 1994: 11.
Arlen, Gary H., "RBOCs Finally Deploy ISDN" *Information & Interactive Services Report*, February 25, 1994: 11.
Arlen, Gary H., "Who Uses Compuserve?" *Information & Interactive Services Report*, February 11, 1994: 4.
Arterton, F. Christopher. *Teledemocracy*. Beverly Hills, CA: Sage, 1987.
Arthur, Brian, "Positive Feedback in Economic Modeling," *Scientific American*, 1991.
Aryan Web site, http://www.io.com/~wlp/aryan-page/
Asimov, Isaac. *I, Robot*. New York: Gnome Press, 1950.
AT&T, "The National Information Infrastructure: A Key to America's Economic Growth and Global Competitiveness," a report from AT&T, August, 1993.
Atchison, Sandra D. "The Care and Feeding of 'Lone Eagles,'" *Business Week*, November 15, 1993: 58.
Auletta, Ken, "John Malone: Flying Solo," *The New Yorker*, February 7, 1994.
Auletta, Ken, "Media Criticism," a seminar session at "The State of Media Studies," hosted by The Freedom Forum Media Studies Center, February 15, 1994.
Auletta, Ken. *Three Blind Mice: How the Networks Lost Their Way*. Random House, 1991.
Baer, Walter. Technology Studies Seminar hosted by The Freedom Forum Media Studies Center, 1991.
Bailey, Wendell, "Conversation on Ethics in Telecommunications," Donald McGannon Center, Fordham University, Oct., 1993.
Baldwin, Thomas F., D. Stevens McVoy, and Charles Steinfeld, *Convergence: Integrating Media, Information and Communication*. Thousand Oaks, CA: Sage Publications, 1996.
Barnathan, Julius, Speech, Technology Studies Seminar, The Freedom Forum Media Studies Center, Dec. 12, 1992.
Barringer, Felicity, "In Cyberspace, and Talking to Strangers," *New York Times*, June 30, 1994: D4.
Becker, Theodore. "Teledemocracy: Gathering momentum in state and local governance." *Spectrum: The Journal of State Government*, 66 (2): 14–19, 1993.
Bell, Daniel. *The Coming of Post-Industrial Society*. New York: Basic Books, 1973.
Belsie, Laurent, "Info Superhighway: Metaphor in Concrete," *The Christian Science Monitor*, February 23, 1994: A1.

Beniger, James R. *The Control Revolution: Technological and Economic Origins of the Information Society.* Cambridge: Harvard University Press, 1986.

Benjamin, Burton, Niemen Report, Summer, 1986.

Bierce, Ambrose. *The Collected Works of Ambrose Bierce.* New York: The Neale Publishing Co., 1909.

Biocca, Frank. "Communication Within Virtual Reality: Creating a Space for Research." *Journal of Communication,* 42(4): 5–22, 9, Autumn, 1992.

Bloomberg, Michael, "The Next Generation," Technology Studies Seminar for Newsroom Managers hosted by The Freedom Forum Media Studies Center, September 15, 1993.

Blumler, Jay and Elihu Katz. *Uses and Gratifications Research in Mass Communication.* Newbury Park, CA: Sage Publications, 1974.

Bodo, Pete, "How to Find Yourself, or Not Get Lost," *New York Times,* December 15, 1996.

Bogart, Leo, "Newspaper of the future: Our look at the next century." *Newspaper Research Journal,* Vol. 14, No. 2, Spring 1993: 2–10.

Bogart, Leo. *Preserving the Press.* New York: Columbia University Press, 1991.

Bogart, Leo. *Press and Public.* Hillsdale, NJ: Lawrence Erlbaum Associates, 1989.

"Bogus Photo in Commercial Gives Virginia Senator a Headache," *New York Times,* October 13, 1996: 17.

Bohrman, David and Larry Wood, "Hypermedia at ABC News: Magna: An Electronic Anchor Information System," chapter in John V. Pavlik and Everette E. Dennis, Editors, (1993) *Demystifying Media Technology,* Mayfield Publishing.

Bollier, David and Charles M. Firestone, "The Promise and Peril of Emerging Information Technologies." A Report on the Second Annual Roundtable on Information Technology. Aspen Institute Communications and Society Program, 1993.

Boston.Com Web site, http://www.boston.com/wgbh/pages/frontline/smoke/interviews/bagdikian1.html

Bowman, Joseph E. Jr., "Documenting a technology-based telecommunications program for urban youth: Its impact and future role in high school retention," *Dissertation Abstracts International,* Volume 52, Number 7, 1992.

Braman, Sandra, "Contradictions in Brilliant Eyes," *Gazette* 47: 177–194, 1991.

Brand, Stewart. *The Media Lab: Inventing the Future at MIT.* New York: Viking, 1987.

Branscomb, Anne Wells. *Who Owns Information? From Privacy to Public Access.* New York: Basic Books, 1994.

Braverman, Alan M. "Lycos, Inc." CS First Boston industry report, December 3, 1996: 13.

Braverman, Alan M. "The Roadmaps of the Internet," CS First Boston industry report, November 26, 1996: 11.

Brender, Mark E., "High Resolution in Remote Sensing by the News Media," *Technology in Society* 22: 89–98, 1989.

Broad, William J., "Spy Data Now Open for Studies of Climate," *New York Times,* June 23, 1992, pp. C1, C10.

Broadcasting & Cable, July 11, 1994: 32.

Broadcasting & Cable, "The ABC's of DBS," December 6, 1993: 38.

Broadcasting & Cable, "Top 100 In Electronic Communications." June 21, 1993.

Brown, Les, Technology Studies Seminar, The Freedom Forum Media Studies Center, April 6, 1994.

Brown, Les. *Les Brown's Encyclopedia of Televison,* 3rd ed. Detroit, MI: Gale Research, 1992.

Brown, Les. Technology Studies Seminar, The Freedom Forum Media Studies Center, April 6, 1994.

Brown, Rich. "BellSouth makes another move into cable." *Broadcasting & Cable,* December 13, 1993.

Brown, Richard D. *Knowledge Is Power: The Diffusion of Information in Early America, 1700–1865.* New York: Oxford University Press, 1989.

Browne, Malcolm W. *New York Times,* Sept. 28, 1993: C1.

Browning, John. "Libraries Without Walls for Books Without Pages," *Wired* Premier Issue 1993.

BSA Web site, www.bsa.org

Buchman, Jeffrey. Speech, Technology Studies Seminar, The Freedom Forum Media Studies Center, Oct. 23, 1993.

Buckler, Grant. "New Prototype Device Meant to Replace Newspapers," Newsbytes News Network, Cambridge, England, 6 November 1996.

Bulkeley, William M. "Semi-Prose, Perhaps, But Sportswriting By Software Is a Hit," *Wall Street Journal,* March 29: 1.

Burrus, Daniel with Roger Gittines. *Technotrends: How to Use Technology to Go Beyond Your Competition.* New York: Harper Business, 1993.

Bushkin, Kathy, Interview, April 13, 1994.

Business Week special report "Some Gigachip milestones to look for," July 4, 1994: 88.

Business Week, "The 1993 Business Week 1000: U.S. Companies Ranked by Industry."

Cable and Satellite Europe (C&SEu), "Top 50 Cable and Satellite Companies," 1993.
Cable and Satellite Europe (C&SEu), "Top 50 Cable and Satellite Companies," 1994.
Cable TV Financial Databook, "Cable TV Banking Ranking," June, 1993.
Cable TV Financial Databook, "The Largest Cable TV Deals in History," June, 1993.
Carey, James. *Communication as Culture*. London: Unwin Hyman, 1989.
Carey, John. "From Internet to Infobahn," *Business Week*, Special 1994 Bonus Issue: 32, 33.
Carey, John. "Back to the Future: How New Communication Technologies Enter American Homes," Technology Studies Seminar, The Freedom Forum Media Studies Center, Oct. 26, 1993.
Carey, John. "Field Testing the Information Superhighway," April 5, 1994, The Freedom Forum Media Studies Center.
Carey, John. "How New Communication Technologies Enter American Homes," Exploring New Media Seminar, Columbia University, November 7, 1996.
Carey, John. Interview, October 4, 1996.
Carey, John. "Media Research and the Information Highway: Setting a Research Agenda," February 14, 1994, Speech, The Freedom forum Media Studies Center.
Carey, John. "Reality Check," *Business Week*, April 4, 1994: 6.
Carey, John. "Thinking Flat in Washington," *Business Week*, May 9, 1994: 36.
Carmody, Deirdre. "For Magazines, a Multimedia Wonderland," *New York Times*, Oct. 11, 1993.
Carmody, Deirdre. "Lifeblood of Reader's Digest Is 40-Year-Old Data Base," *New York Times*, May 16, 1994: D1, D7.
Carter, Bill. "Long Ratings Climb Ends for Cable Television," *New York Times*, November 15, 1993: D10.
Carter, Bill. "Rebound for Broadcast TV; Cable Viewership Is Steady," *New York Times*, April 20, 1994: D1.
Cary Lu. "CD Titles on the Wane: The market may have already peaked," Macworld Online, http://www.macworld.com/q/@345222nllsvp/pages/october.95/News.1410.html
Cauley, Leslie. Baby Bells Cut Budget, Hiring On Joint Interactive-TV Project, *Wall Street Journal*, June 7, 1996.
Chan, Joseph Man. "Satellite Television and the Infosphere: National Responses and Accessibility to STAR TV in Asia." Paper presented to the Ninth Worth Communication Forum, the Japan Society of Information and Communication Research, Tokyo, Japan, 19–20 November 1992.
Chronicle of Higher Education, The, "On Line," March 2 1994.
Clarke, Arthur C. "Extraterrestrial Relays," *Wireless World*, June 1945.
Clarke, Arthur C. *The Lost Worlds of 2001*. Boston: Gregg Press, 1979.
Clinton, W. J., & Gore, A. *Technology for America's economic growth, a new direction to build economic strength*. Washington, DC: Office of the President of the United States, February, 1993.
Club of Rome, The. *Microelectronics and Society: For Better or Worse*. 1982.
Clurman, Dick. Fellows Seminar at The Freedom Forum Media Studies Center, Oct. 6, 1993.
Clyman, John. "PowerPC: Your Next CPU?" *PC Magazine*, February 22, 1994.
Coates, Steve. "A Dead Language Comes to Life on the Internet," *New York Times,* October 28, 1996.
Columbia Journalism School Web site, www.jrn.columbia.edu
Commerce Department, Bureau of Labor Statistics, Morgan Stanley & Co., 1994.
CommerceNet Web site, http://www.commerce.net/
Compaine, Benjamin. *Understanding New Media: Trends and Issues in Electronic Distribution of Information*. Cambridge, MA: Ballinger, 1984.
Comte, Elizabeth. "Entertainment & information: Movie companies, television networks and publishers felt a mild recovery from the recession." *Forbes,* January 4, 1993: 142–3.
Coover, Robert. *New York Times Book Review,* August 29, 1993.
Copyright Law of the United States of America, contained in Title 17 of the United States Code, Revised to March 1, 1991.
Corliss, Richard. *Time*, 1994: 58, 59.
Corning Web site, http://www.usa.net/corning-fiber/tech/howmuch.html
CPB Web site, www.cpb.org
Crichton, Michael. Speech to the National Press Club, Washington, DC, on April 6, 1993; *Mediasaurus*, 1993 *Wired!*
CTR WEb site, http://www.ctr.columbia.edu/advent/cb_demos.html
Cuadra Associates, Directory of On Line Databases, Boston, MA, 1994.
Daley, Richard M., speech, Chicago, IL, 15 October 1993.
Dalton, Laura. *Executive News Summary*, Oct. 21, 1993: 1.
Davis, Leonard. "The Customer Is Always Right," *Omni*, November, 1993: 24.
DBS Dish Web site, http://www.dbsdish.com/
de Sola Pool, I. *Technologies of freedom*. Cambridge: The Belknap Press of Harvard University. 1983;

de Sola Pool, I. *Technologies without boundaries: On telecommunications in a global age* (E. M. Noam, Ed.). Cambridge: Harvard University Press, 1990.

Deitz, Paula, "All It Takes Is a Computer and Photos," *New York Times,* March 31, 1994.

DeLoughry, Thomas J. "Copyright Issues Said to Stall Many Multimedia Projects," *Chronicle of Higher Education,* June 29, 1994: A18.

DeLoughry, Thomas J. "Guaranteeing Access on the Data Highway," *Chronicle of Higher Education,* Nov. 3, 1993.

DeLoughry, Thomas J. "Museums Go High-Tech," *Chronicle of Higher Education,* Sept. 14, 1994: A47.

Demac, Donna. "Copyright and the New Electronic Media," midterm report, The Freedom Forum Media Studies Center, Dec. 29, 1993.

Dennis, Everette E. *Of Media and People.* Newbury Park, CA: Sage Publications, 1992.

Dennis, Everette E. Technology Studies Seminar, The Freedom Forum Media Studies Center, April 6, 1994.

Deutschman, J. feature story on Larry Ellison, *Broadcasting & Cable,* 17 January 1994: 3.

Dewey, Thomas. *The Public and Its Problems.* Chicago: Swallow, 1927.

Dibbell, Julian,. "Strange Loops: The Prisoner: Phiber Optik Goes Directly to Jail." *Village Voice,* January 11, 1994: 44.

Dickens, Charles. *A Tale of Two Cities.* London: J. B. Lippincott, 1930.

Ditlea, Steve. "Female E-Mail: Computer Networks Put Women On-Line," *New York Daily News,* November 3, 1993.

Donegan, Jack. San Diego Supercomputer Center, Cities of the Future conference, December 13, 1994.

Dordick, Herbert S. and Dale E. Lehman. "Information Highways: 'Trickle Down' Infrastructure?" Chapter in Fred Williams and John V. Pavlik (editors), *The People's Right to Know: Media, Democracy and the Information Highway,* Lawrence Erlbaum Associates, 1993.

Dordick, Herbert S. and Georgette Wang. *The Information Society: A Retrospective View.* Newbury Park, CA: Sage Publications, 1993.

Dovaton, Scott. "Ad Council Finds a Niche in New Media," *Advertising Age,* 11 April 1995: 18.

Dovaton, Scott. "While Other Agencies Talk, Bozall Acts," *Advertising Age,* 4 April 1995: 20.

Dunkin, Amy. *Business Week,* Oct. 4, 1993: 124–5.

Dunn, Ashley. "Phone Lines: The Ties That Bind Us," The New York Times Cybertimes, December 11, 1996.

Dutton, William. "Lessons from Public and Nonprofit Services," in *The People's Right to Know,* Frederick Williams and John Pavlik, eds. Hillsdale, NY: Lawrence Erlbaum Associates, 1994: 105–129.

E&P Interactive Online Newspaper Database, maunaloa.com:4901/ephome/npaper/nphtm/stats.htm (12/26/96).

Earthlink Web site, http://websites.earthlink.net/%7Etomgrant/

Eco, Umberto. "From Internet to Gutenberg," speech, Italian Academy for Advanced Studies in America at Columbia University, November 12, 1996.

Economist, "Poached By Sonic the Hedgehog," February 20, 1993: 326.

Edmondson, Gail. "Brave Old World," *Business Week,* Special 1994 Bonus Issue: 42–3.

Edmund L. Andrews. "Sudden Synergy Among Communications Rivals," *New York Times,* D1, D10, Oct. 21, 1993.

Elliott, Stuart. Banner Ads on Internet Attract Users," New York Times Cybertimes, December 3, 1996.

Ellul, Jacques. *The Technological Society.* New York: Alfred A. Knopf 1964.

Elmer-DeWitt, Phillip. Technology Studies Seminar, The Freedom Forum Media Studies Center, April 5, 1994.

Elmer-DeWitt, Phillip. "Traveling the Information Superhighway," speaking at a press briefing hosted by The Freedom Forum Media Studies Center on February 1, 1994.

Endicott, R. Craig. "100 Leading Media Companies: Relaxed rules, solid values trigger flurry of media acquisitions," *Advertising Age.* v. 64: no. 20, August 16, 1993.

Espanshade, Edward B., Jr. (editor), *Goode's Rand McNally World Atlas,* 18th ed., Rand McNally, 1990.

Ewen, Stuart. *All Consuming Images.* New York: Basic Books, 1992.

Executive News Summary. May 6, 1994: 4.

Experts forecast robust video game sales this holiday season; new study cites 16-bit games as strongest industry component Redmond, Wash.—(Business Wire)—Nov. 20, 1995, http://www.digitalcity.com/jeffg/news/gamenews6.html

Featherstone, Mike, ed. *Global Culture.* Newbury Park, CA: Sage Publications, 1990.

Federal Communications Act of 1934. U.S. Government, Washington, DC, 19 June 1934.

Federal Jury Indicts Woman in a CD-ROM Piracy Case," *New York Times*, December 12, 1993.

Felker, Clay. Oct. 13, 1993 fellows seminar at The Freedom Forum Media Studies Center.

Fenton, Freedom Forum report on the 47th World Newspaper Congress and FIEJ Annual General Meeting, 29 May–1 June, 1994, Vienna, Austria.

Fenton, Tom. Freedom Forum report on a speech by Charles Brumback at the 47th World Newspaper Congress and FIEJ Annual General Meeting May 29–June 1, 1994, Vienna, Austria.

Fernback, Jan and Brad Thompson, 1995, "Virtual Communities: Abort, Retry, Failure?" posted at www.well.com/hlr/texts/VCcivil.html.

Fidler, Roger. "Information Graphics," in Pavlik and Dennis, editors, 1993, *Demystifying Media Technology: Disk Edition*. Mountain View, CA: Mayfield Publishing.

Fidler, Roger. "Mediamorphosis," chapter in Frederick Williams and John V. Pavlik, editors, *The People's Right To Know: Media, Democracy, and the Information Highway*. Hillsdale, NJ: Lawrence Erlbaum Associates, 1994.

Fidler, Roger. Technology Studies Seminar, The Freedom Forum Media Studies Center, April 6 1994.

Fidler, Roger. *Mediamorphosis: Understanding New Media*, Thousand Oaks, CA: Sage Publications, Inc. 1997.

Financial World, Oct. 12: 56.

FIND/SVP Web site, survey report, 1995.

First Amendment to the U.S. Constitution, 1790.

Fisher, Lawrence M. "Five Regional Phone Companies Select Netscape," New York Times Online, December 10, 1996.

Fitzgerald, Mark. "Invisible Digital Copyright ID," *Editor & Publisher*, June 25, 1994.

Flaherty, Joseph. "High-Definition Television: Technical and Political Issues." In *Demystifying Media Technology*, John V. Pavlik and Everette E. Dennis, editors, 1993.

Fleming, Michael. "Freeze Frame: Who undressed Jessica Rabbit?" *Variety*, March 14-20, 1994.

Flynn, Bernadette. "Woman/Machine Relationships," *Media Information Australia*, May 1994, No. 72: 11-19.

Flynn, Laurie. "A Multimedia Networking Challenge," *New York Times*, December 14, 1994.

Flynn, Laurie. "For Children, a Gift of Software," *New York Times*, Dec. 16, 1994, C1.

Flynn, Laurie. "Thrills and Chills of Marketing a CD-ROM Adventure," *New York Times*, Nov. 27, 1994, F3.

Fortune, "The 500 by Industry." April 19, 1993.

Frank, Reuven. *Out of Thin Air: The Brief Wonderful Life of Network News*. New York: Simon & Schuster: 1991.

Freeman, Neal B. "Populism + Telecommunications = Global Democracy," *National Review*, November 15, 1993: 50.

French, Howard W. "Linked to Internet, Could Africa's Voice Be Heard?" *New York Times*, Oct. 1, 1994.

Fryer, Bronwyn. "Sex & the Superhighway," *Working Woman*, April 1994: 51–61.

Galvin, Christopher J. "The Digital Deadbolt," *CompuServe Magazine*, November 1993.

GameFaqs Web site, http://www.gamefaqs.com/

Gandy, Oscar H., Jr. "The Information Highway as Yellow Brick Road," Speech, Santa Clara University, January 27, 1994.

Gandy, Oscar H., Jr. *The Panoptic Sort*. Boulder, CO: Westview: 1993.

Gannett Executive News Summary, October 5, 1993.

Gannett Executive News Summary, October 7, 1993.

Gardiner, W. Lambert. "Virtual Reality/Cyberspace: Challenges to Communication Studies." *Canadian Journal of Communication*, Vol. 18, 387–396, 392, 1993,

Gateway 2000 Web site 12/3/96, www.gateway2000.com

Gelernter, David. "Wiretaps for a Wireless Age," *New York Times*, April 8, 1994: E7.

Gell-Mann, Murray. *The Quark and the Jaguar: Adventures in the Simple and the Complex*. W. H. Freeman, 1994.

Germain, Ellen. *Time*, 61, Sept. 13, 1993.

Gibbons, John H., ed. U.S. Congress Office of Technology Assessment, Commercial Newsgathering from Space: A Technical Memorandum, (Washington, D.C.: Government Printing Office, 1987), pp. 39–44.

Gibbs, W. Wayt. "Bandwidth, Unlimited," *Scientific American*, January 1997: 41.

Gibbs, Wayt W. "When Cells Divide: Making space for the next wave of wireless communications," Scientific American, December, 1993: 44–45.

Gibson, William. *Neuromancer*. New York: Ace Books, 1984.

Gilder, George. "Law of the Microcosm," *Forbes ASAP*, 1994.

Gilder, George. "Telecosm: Digital Darkhorse—Newspapers," *Forbes ASAP*, Oct. 25, 1993: 138–149.

Gipson, M. *Information & Interactive Services Report*, 8 October 1994.

Gissler, Sig. Fellows Seminar, Interview, The Freedom Forum Media Studies Center, 1993.

Glaberson, William. "Newspapers Redefining Themselves," *New York Times*, April 26, 1993: D1.

Glasco, Tom. Information Director, Interview, EOSAT,/NASA, Washington, D.C., 1992.

Goodman, Walter. "Code Breaking and the Good It Does," *New York Times,* January 18, 1994.

Gore, Albert, Jr. "Forging a new Athenian Age of democracy," *Intermedia*, April–May 1994, volume 22, no. 2: 4–7.

Gore, Albert. Jr. "Reinventing Government." The Office of the Vice President of the U.S., 1993,

Gore, Albert, Jr. "Information for the Global Village." *Scientific American, 1991.*

Greenfield, Jeff. "American Agenda," *ABC World News Tonight with Peter Jennings,* Sept., 1993.

Greenfield, P. M. *Mind and Media: the Effects of Television, Video Games and Computers.* Harvard University Press: 108, 1984.

Greenfield, Richard P. "Net Effect: Changing European Languages," *New York Times,* October 15, 1996.

Grossman, Lawrence, speech at "Newsroom Technology: The Next Generation," The Freedom Forum Media Studies Center, September 15, 1993.

Grossman, Lawrence. *The Electronic Republic: Reshaping Democracy in the Information Age.* A Twentieth Century Fund Book, 1996.

Grove, Andrew S. *Only the Paranoid Survive.* New York: Bantam Books, 1996.

Growth of Internet Web site, www.cfn.cs.dal.ca/Government/IndustryCanada/tab2.html

Grundner, Thomas. "Free-Nets: Networking meets Middle America." *Link Letter.* (available through nptn Gopher server) September/October 1991.

Grunig, James E., & Hunt, Todd. *Managing Public Relations.* New York: Holt, Rinehart & Winston, 1984.

Grunig, Larissa A. *Activism and organizational response: contemporary cases of collective behavior.* Paper presented to the Association for Education in Journalism and Mass Communication, Norman, OK, August, 1986.

Gulker Web site, www.gulker.com/ra/hack/

Guthrie, K. Kendall. "How Information Highways Can Address the Urban Agenda: Promoting Economic Development and Reconnecting the Urban Poor." Paper presented at the 43rd Annual Conference of the International Communications Association, Washington, D.C., May 27–31, 1993.

Hafner, Katie. "Getting Girls On-Line," *Working Woman*, April 1994: 61.

Hafrey, Leigh. "At Cyberspace University Press, Paperless Publishing Looks Good," *New York Times Book Review*, Oct. 30, 1994.

Hansell, Saul. "Banks Go Interactive to Bea the Rush of Services," *New York Times*, Oct. 19, 1994: C1, C6.

Harris, Kathryn. "The Stupendous Seven—The New Masters of the Universe," *Media Studies Journal*, Winter 1994: 81–93.

Hart, Anne. *Cyberscribes.1: The New Journalists.* San Diego, CA: Ellipsys International Publications, 1997: 3.

Hart, Roderick P. *Seducing America: How Television Charms the Modern Voter.* New York: Oxford University Press: 1994.

HDTV Newsletter Web site, http://web-star.com/hdtv/hdtvnews.html

"Hear This," *International Herald Tribune,* July 8, 1994: 8.

Heffner, Richard D. "The In-Your-Face Videos Bring the Censor Nearer," *International Herald Tribune,* Tuesday, May 3, 1994: 7.

Henderson, Bill. Op Ed page of *New York Times,* March 16, 1994.

"Herbert A. Simon," *Omni,* 1994: 71, 72.

Hermelin, Francine. "Feminizing Virtual Reality," *Working Woman*, April 1994: 54.

Higgins, John M. *Multichannel News*, Sept., 1993, p. 1.

Hillis, John, Technology Studies Seminar, The Freedom Forum Media Studies Center, May 15, 1994.

Hoge, James, F. "Media Pervasiveness," *Foreign Affairs*, July/August 1994, Vol. 73 No. 4: 136.

Holzmann, Gerard J. and Bjorn Pehrson. "The First Data Networks," *Scientific American,* January 1994:124.

Howard Bryant. "Video Game Quandary: Nintendo, Sega or Sony, or a High-End, Powerful PC," *San Jose Mercury News,* Calif. Knight-Ridder/Tribune Business News, Dec. 3, 1996; http://www.digitalcity.com/jeffg/news/120895c.html

Hudson, Heather E. "Maximizing Benefits from New Telecommunications Technologies: A Development-Based Approach to Communications Planning," *Media Asia*, Vol. 20, No. 3, 1993: 133–139.

Hughes, Janice. "The Changing Multimedia Landscape," *The Media Studies Journal,* The Freedom

Forum Media Studies Center, Winter 1994.

Hunter, Jesse. "Authoring Literacy: From Index to Hypermedia," *Canadian Journal of Communication*, Vol. 19, 1994: 41–52.

"I.B.M. Project for Vatican," *New York Times* from Reuters April 12, 1994.

Ibrahim, Anwar. "Communication, Technology and Development: Alternatives for Asia," *Media Asia*, Vol. 20, No. 3, 1993: 157–158.

ICTV home page, www.ictv.com.

Iglou Web site, http://members.iglou.com/kkk/

IMA DVD SIG MEMBERS, 22 Nov 96 (original posting 27 Aug 96).

Information & Interactive Services Report, Sept. 27, 1993.

"Information highway still a mystery," *USA Today,* May 8, 1994: 5B.

Inmarsat Web site, http://www.inmarsat.org/

Innis, Harold. *Empire and Communications.* Oxford: Clarendon Press, 1950.

Intel Web site, http://developer.intel.com/drg/hybrid_author/devlab.htm, 29 Nov 1996.

Intel Web site, www.intel.com/intel/museum/25anniv/html/hof/moore.htm

International submarine cable map, w3.lab.kdd.co.jp/kdd/cable/

Internet Society web page, www.isoc.org

Internet-for-kids Web site, www.internet-for-kids.com

Javasoft Web site, www.javasoft.com/applets/applets/contest/Pythagoras/index.html www.javasoft.com/applets/applets/contest/NuclearPlant/index.html

Jeff Greenfield. "American Agenda," *ABC World News Tonight with Peter Jennings,* Sept., 1993.

Jennewein, Chris. "Audiotext gives a growing number of dailies the chance to experiment with new technologies," *ASNE Bulletin*, January/February 1994.

Jessell, Harry A. "For Time Warner, software is hard part." *Broadcasting & Cable*, March 28, 1994:42.

Jessell, Harry A. "VOD, Gaming to help pave superhighway," *Broadcasting & Cable*, Dec. 6, 1993.

Johnson, Kirk. "Acorns Sprout Among the Oaks of the Telecommunications Field," *New York Times,* July 5, 1994: A1, B2.

Johnson, Kirk. "Office Romance: Love On Line at Speed of Light," *New York Times*, March 26, 1994.

Johnstone, B. "True Believers," *Far Eastern Economic Review*, 155 (51), December 24 1993, 70–71.

Jussawalla, Meheroo. "Information Technology and Economic Development in the Asia-Pacific," *Media Asia*, Vol. 20, No. 3, 1993: 127–132.

Kahin, B. *Information Infrastructures.* New York: McGraw-Hill, Inc., 1992.

Kahrenburg, K. K. "Power of the Media in the Global System," *Journal of International Affairs* 1993: i.

Kalb, Bernard, Speech to The Freedom Forum Trustees, February, 1993.

Kantrowitz, Barbara. "Dissent on the Hard Drive," *Newsweek*, June 27, 1994.

Karp, Jonathan. "Prime Time Police: China tries to pull the plug on satellite TV," *Far Eastern Economic Review,* 21 October 1993: 72–73.

Katsh, Ethan. "Law in a Digital World: Computer Networks and Cyberspace." *Villanova Law Review*, Volume 38, Number 2, 1993: 417.

Keizer, Gregg. "Debbie Does Silicon Valley: In search of sophisticated electronic entertainment," *Omni*, February 1994: 24.

Kempton, Paul. "Who in the World Wants VOD?" *Cable and Satellite Europe,* April 19, 1994: 26-34.

Kennedy, Daniel. "Lost in Space," *Boston Phoenix*, May 7, 1993: 40.

Kenneth M. King. "Computers, Man and Society Seminar Remarks," Columbia University, December 18, 1996.

Kilborn, Peter T. "The Boss Only Wants What's Best for You," *New York Times*, May 8, 1994.

Kim, James. "British pioneer launches interactive network," *USA Today*, Nov. 15, 1994: 7B.

King, Kenneth M. "Computers, Man and Society Seminar Remarks," Columbia University, December 18, 1996.

Kiplinger Washington Letter, October, 1994: 2.

Kiplinger Washington Letter, Sept. 24, 1993.

Kleinrock, Leonard. "Nomadic Computing," Presentation at The Heritage of Marconi's Invention and the Future of Telecommunication, Columbia University, December 9, 1996.

Klopfenstein, Bruce C. "The Diffusion of the VCR in the United States," in Mark Levy (ed.). *The VCR Age: Home Video and Mass Communication.* Newbury Park, CA: Sage Publications, 1989.

Kodak Web site, http://www.kodak.com/

Kohut, Andrew. "One-in-Ten Voters Online for Campaign '96," The Pew Research Center, December 16, 1996.

Kolata, Gina. "Computer Math Proof Shows Reasoning Power," New York Times Online, December 10, 1996.

Kolata, Gina. "The Assault on 12. . . ." *New York Times*, March 22, 1994: C1, C10.

Koontz, Dean. *Midnight*. New York: Berkley Books, 1989.

Kozinn, Allan. "Lejaren Hiller 69, First Composer To Write Music with a Computer," *New York Times*, February 1, 1994.

Kragen, Pam. "Copley Press jumping on info superhighway," *Times Advocate*, Nov., 1994.

Krantz, Michael. "Dollar a Minute," *Wired*, May 1994: 107.

Krebs, Michelle. "Cars That Tell You Where to Go," *New York Times*, December 15, 1996.

Kuckro, Rod W. "Studies Show Growing Demand for Interactive TV Services," *Information & Interactive Services Report*, December 3, 1993.

Landler, Mark. "Cablevision Says Viewers Will Get Link to Internet," *New York Times*, December 17, 1996.

Landsat Spacecraft Data Sheet, EOSAT, January 1991.

Lang, Curtis. "The pied piper of convergence," *Advertising Age*, December 6, 1993:16.

Langa, Fred. *Windows Magazine*, 1994.

Leary, Warren E. "French Team Develops Flexible, Electronic Transistor Made of Plastic," *New York Times*, Sept. 16, 1994.

Lee, M. and N. Solomon. *Unreliable Sources*. New York: Carol Pub., 1980

Lehmann-Haupt, Christopher. "Plumbing the Recesses of Psyche and Cyberspace," *New York Times*, April 14, 1994: C21.

Leonard, Hugh. "Asian Broadcasting: The Changing Scene," *Media Asia*, Vol. 20, No. 3, 1993: 123–126.

Lerbinger, Otto (ed.). "As Usage of VNRs Rises So Do Questions of Journalistic Ethics," *purview* a supplement of *pr reporter*. No. 360, March 21, 1994.

Lerner, Sid. "Lexicon for the Auto-Maga-Video Age," *New York Times*, December 5, 1993.

Leslie, Jacques. "Mail Bonding: E-mail is creating a new oral culture," *Wired*, March 1994: 42.

Levere, Jane. "Travel Systems Use Technology to Ease the Commute," *New York Times*, December 23, 1996.

Levin, Gerald. Keynote speech delivered on January 20, 1996, at Global Information Infrastructures, a conference sponsored by the Japan–U.S. Telecommunications Research Institute and the Japan Society, New York, NY.

Levy, Mark (ed.). *The VCR Age: Home Video and Mass Communication*. Newbury Park, CA: Sage Publications, 1989.

Levy, Mark, (ed.). "Virtual reality: A communication perspective." *Journal of Communication*, 42(4), Autumn, 1992.

Levy, Steven. *Artificial Life: The Quest for a New Creation*. London: Penguin Books, 1993.

Levy, Steven. *Insanely Great: The Life and Times of* Macintosh*, the Computer That Changed Everything*. New York: Viking, 1994.

Levy, Steven. "We Have Seen the Content, and It Is Us." *The Media Studies Journal*, Winter, 1994.

Lewin, Tamar. "Dispute Over Computer Messages: Free Speech of Sex Harassment," *New York Times*, September 22, 1994: A1.

Lewis, Peter H. "An 'All You Can Eat' Price Is Clogging Internet Access," *New York Times*, December 17, 1996.

Lewis, Peter H. "Anarchy, a Threat on the Electronic Frontier," *New York Times*, May 11, 1994: D1, D7.

Lewis, Peter H. "And the Spoof Begat a News Release, and Another," *New York Times*, Dec. 31, 1994.

Lewis, Peter H. "Censors Become a Force on Cyberspace Frontier," *New York Times*, June 29, 1994: A1, D5.

Lewis, Peter H. "Collisions in Cyberspace on Data Encryption Plan," *New York Times*, March 26, 1994: 45.

Lewis, Peter H. "Companies Rush to Set Up Shop in Cyberspace," *New York Times*, Nov. 2, 1994: C1, C6.

Lewis, Peter H. "Computer Snoopers Imperil Pentagon Files, Experts Say," *New York Times*, July 21, 1994: A1, B10.

Lewis, Peter H. "Electronic Tie for Citizens and Seekers of Office," *New York Times*, Nov. 6, 1994: 15.

Lewis, Peter H. "Internet Users Get Access to S.E.C. Filings Fee-Free" *New York Times*, January 17, 1994.

Lewis, Peter H. "Netcom to Seek Profitable Niche: Internet Access Just for Business," *New York Times*, December 19, 1996.

Lewis, Peter H. "New Flat Rate Creates Surge in Usage of America Online," *New York Times*, December 3, 1996.

Lewis, Peter H. "Preaching the Techno-Gospel, Al Gore Version" *New York Times*, January 17, 1994: D1.

Lewis, Peter H. "Radio Internet to Broadcast Around Clock," *New York Times*, Sept. 19, 1994: A10.

Lewis, Peter H. "Shift Planned in Network by Microsoft," New York Times Online, December 10, 1996.

Lewis, Peter H. "Sneering at a Virtual Lynch Mob," *New York Times*, May 11, 1994: D7.

Lewis, Peter H. "Strangers, Not Their Computers, Build a Network in Time of Grief," *New York Times*, March 8, 1994.

Lewis, Peter H. *New York Times*, Dec. 13, 1994.

Lewis, Peter H. "U.S. Begins Privatizing of Internet Operations," *New York Times*, Oct. 24, 1994: A10.

Liebling, Abbott Joseph. *The Press*. New York: Pantheon Books, 1981.

Liebman, Hanna. "About Time for On-Line," *Mediaweek,* September 27 1993: 32, 36–7.

Lincoln, Abraham. Letter to H. L. Pierce, 16 April 1859.

Ling, Ruth. "Try Before You Buy," *Satellite Communications*, November, 1993: 25.

Lipkin, Richard. "Making the Calls in a New Era of Communication," *Insight*, July 12, 1993: 9.

Lohr, Steve. "Pearson Enters Multimedia Software Arena," *New York Times*, April 1, 1994.

Lohr, Steve. "The Silver Disk May Soon Eclipse the Silver Screen," *New York Times*, March 1, 1994.

Lohr, Steve. "Americans See Future and Say, 'So What?'" *New York Times*, October 7, 1993.

Long, Elizabeth Valle. "To Our Readers," *Time*, January 1, 1994.

Long, Kim. "The Year Ahead," *American Demographics,* December 1993.

Louis Harris and Associates web site.

Lowry, Tom. "E-mail delivers rescue," *Daily News*, April 1, 1994: 5.

Lucky, Robert. "Reinventing Telephony as Internet Comes of Age," Presentation at The Heritage of Marconi's Invention and the Future of Telecommunication, Columbia University, December 9, 1996.

MacDonald, Richard. "Patterns of Media Entrepreneurship," Fellows Presentation, The Freedom Forum Media Studies Center, December 15, 1993.

Maggin, Bruce. "Riding the Information Highway," Speech at the Center for Communications, Sept. 30, 1993.

Maher, Mike. "Electronic Gatekeeper For News," *Editor & Publisher*, June 25, 1994: 70, 72.

Makulowich, John S. "Internet: Explore the 'network of networks," *Quill*, Sept. 1993: 28.

Malone, John. Speech at the 1993 Cable TV Show.

Maltin, Leonard. *Entertainment Tonight*, March 29,1994.

Mandel, Michael J. "The Information Economy: The Digital Juggernaut," *Business Week*, Special 1994 Bonus Issue: 22, 23.

Mandelbrot, Benoit B. "The Beauty of Fractals and their Usefulness—Relations Between Geometry, Art, and Technology," The Inaugural Magill Lecture in Science, Technology and the Arts, Columbia University, April 7, 1994.

Marimba Web site, www.marimba.com

Marketing Pulse, The. "Superhypeway Backlash," January 31, 1994, Volume XIV, Issue 5.

Markoff, John. "Rear Adm. Grace Hopper Dies; Innovator in Computers Was 85," *New York Times*, January 3, 1992, page A17.

Markoff, John. "A Magazine Seeks to Push the On-Line Envelope," *New York Times*, October 31, 1994: C6.

Markoff, John. "Chip-Making Towers of Power," *New York Times*, Nov. 8, 1994: C1.

Markoff, John. "Cyberspace's Most Wanted: Hacker Eludes F.B.I. Pursuit," *New York Times*, July 4, 1994.

Markoff, John. "Gore Shifts Stance on Chip Code," *New York Times*, July 21, 1994: D1.

Markoff, John. "Intel's Crash Course on Consumers," *New York Times*, Dec. 21, 1994: C1.

Markoff, John. "Microsoft Organizes Its Interactive TV Team," *New York Times*, Nov. 2, 1994.

Markoff, John. "New I.B.M. Laser Method Stacks Data on Disks," *New York Times,* May 12, 1994.

Markoff, John. "New Venture in Cyberspace by Silicon Graphics Founder," *New York Times*, May 7, 1994: B1.

Markoff, John. *New York Times*, 8 October 1994: 47.

Markoff, John. "Traffic Jams Already on the Information Highway," *New York Times*, November 3, 1993.

Markoff, John. "U.S. Adopts a Disputed Coding Standard," *New York Times*, May 23, 1994.

Markoff, John. "A Free and Simple Computer Link," *New York Times*, Dec. 8, 1993: D1, D7.

Markoff, John. "An Electronic Salon," *New York Times*, March 27, 1994: F10.

Markoff, John. "Chip Makers' Competing Creed," *New York Times*, March 11, 1994: D1, D2.

Markoff, John. "Judge Rules Against Curbs on Export of Encryption Software," *New York Times,* December 19, 1996.

Markoff, John. "Toys Now, Computers Tomorrow," *New York Times*, April 20, 1994: D1, D6.

Markoff, John. "U.S. Code Agency Is Jostling for Civilian Turf," *New York Times*, January 24, 1994:

D1, D5.

Martino, Joseph P. *Technological Forecasting for Decision-Making*, 3rd ed. New York: McGraw-Hill, 1993.

Marx, Andy. "Interactive development: the new hell," *Variety*, March, 1994: 1.

Masefield, John. *Salt Water Ballads and Poems.* New York: MacMillan, 1923.

Mason, Marilyn Gell. "More than a Library for Congress: Making LC the Nation's Library," *Library Journal*, November 1, 1993: 40–43.

Maxwell, Charles T. "U.S. Blunders on Computer Screen Subsidy," Letter to the Editor, *New York Times*, May 11, 1994.

Maynard, Nancy Hicks. Speech, Technology Studies Seminar, The Freedom Forum Media Studies Center, April 5, 1994.

McArroll, Thomas. "Betting on the Sky," *Time*, November 22, 1993: 57.

McAvoy, Kim. "Congressional proposals at a glance," *Broadcasting & Cable* January 3, 1994: 51.

McAvoy, Kim. "Markey's goal: Two wires in every house," *Broadcasting & Cable*, November 15, 1993: 26.

McClintock, Robert, Priscilla Ellington, and Heather Lewis. The Eiffel Project, version 1.2, September 1996.

McCombs, M. E., & Eyal, C. H. Spending on Mass Media. *Journal of Communication* 30(1), 153–158, 1980.

McCombs, M. E., & Nolan, J. "The Relative Constancy Approach to Consumer Spending for Media." *Journal of Media Economics* 5(2), 43–52, 1992.

McKibben, Bill. *The Age of Missing Information.* New York: Random House, 1992.

McLuhan, Marshall. *Understanding Media: Extensions of Man.* New York: McGraw-Hill, 1964.

McWilliams, Gary. "Computers are finally learning to listen," *Business Week*, Nov. 1, 1993.

Media Industry Newsletter, "min's Exclusive Review of Group Publishers' First-Half-1993 Ad Pages: The Gains Are Shrinking, but the Majority of Publishers Remain Up." August 2, 1993, vol. 46, no. 31.

Media Industry Newsletter, "Monthly Stock Watch," August 9, 1993, vol. 46, no. 32.

MediaCity Web site, http://www.mediacity.com/~java/DBC.html

MediaLink Web site, www.medialinkworldwide.com/survey.htm

Mediaweek, Sept. 27, 1993.

Meyer, Eric A. http://web66.coled.umn.edu/Cookbook/HTML/MinutePrimer.html

Meyrowitz, Joshua. *No Sense of Place: The Impact of Electronic Media on Social Behavior.* New York: Oxford University Press, 1985.

Michael Cunningham. "High jinks for Shetland links," *The Irish Times,* November 11, 1996: 18.

Mifflin, Lawrie. "Analysis: Issue in Battle on TV Ratings Is Control," New York Times Cybertimes, December 19, 1996.

Mifflin, Lawrie. "Clinton Says Industry Plan on TV Labels Deserves Trial," New York Times Cybertimes, December 14, 1996.

Miles, Tim. Annual Report, Office of Computers, U.S. Department of Commerce, 1995; www.stat-usa.gov/BEN/gto1/compeqmt.txt

Miller, David. "The Many Faces of the Internet," *Internet World*, October, 1994: 34–38.

Minow, Newton. "Vast Wasteland Revisited," The Freedom Forum Media Studies Center, 1991.

Mitchell, Susan. "Technophiles and Technophobes.' *American Demographics*, February 1994:36.

Moeller, Philip. "The age of convergence," *American Journalism Review*, January/February 1994: 22.

Mok, Clement. *Designing Business: Multiple Media, Multiple Disciplines.* San Jose, CA: Adobe Press, 1996.

Moore, Thomas. "Let Your Fingers Do the Walking (Keying) . . . All Phone Numbers in U.S. Now on CD-ROM," *PR News*, January 3, 1994.

Morain, Stanley A. *Remote Sensing: Instrumentation for Nondestructive Exploration of Cultural Resources,* No. 2 in *Remote Sensing: A Handbook for Archaeologists and Cultural Resource Managers*, Washington, D.C.: Cultural Resources Management Division, National Park Service, U.S. Department of the Interior, 1978.

Moran, Susan. "New Ways of Getting Wired," *WebWeek,* November 4, 1996: 1.

Morukama, Shinji. "The Information Superhighway," *Forum Magazine*, May 1994: 4.

"Motif Unveils New Flat-Panel Technology, Largest Manufacturing Plant in U.S.," *Video Technology News*, Oct. 11, 1993: 8.

"Motorola Ships Cable Modems to U.S. Networks," Reuters, April 30, 1996.

"Movie Magic," The Discovery Channel, June 16, 1994.

Mowlana, Hamid, George Gerbner, and Herbert I. Schiller. *Triumph of the Image: The Media's War in the Persian Gulf: A Global Perspective.* Boulder, CO: Westview Press, 1992.

Multispectral Imagery report, EOSAT, January, 1991.

388

Murdoch, Rupert. Keynote Address, Center for Communication Communicator of the Year Award Luncheon, April 11, 1994.

Murphy, Jamie and Charlie Hofacker. "Gridlock on the Internet Explosive Growth Clogs The Internet's Backbone," *New York Times,* June 29–30, 1996.

Murphy, P., and Dee, J. "Du Pont and Greenpeace: The dynamics of conflict between corporations and activist groups," *Public Relations Research Annual,* 4(1), 3–20, 1992.

Murrow, Edward R. RTNDA Convention, October 15, 1958.

Nadis, Steve. "Artificial Intelligence: The Sound of Data: Data may fill your ears rather than your eyes," *Omni,* January 1994: 26.

Naisbitt, John and Patricia Aburdene. *Megatrends 2000.* New York: Warner Books, 1993.

Naisbitt, John. *Global Paradox.* New York: Morrow, 1994.

Naisbitt, John. *Megatrends.* New York: Warner Books, 1982.

Natall Web site, http://www.natall.com/

NEC Ad number 162, *Scientific American,* January 1997: 21.

Nelson, Clark, Director for Corporate Communication. Interview, SPOT Image, Reston, VA, 1992.

New York Times, "HTIJX KTW PNIX," Sunday Magazine, January 23, 1994.

New York Times, 14 March 1994.

New York Times, March 21, 1994: D2.

New York Times, "Test Set for Digital Movies," March 21, 1994: D2.

New York Times, "The Sad-Truth Phone," Sunday Magazine, January 23, 1994.

News Inc. November 1, 1993: 1.

News Inc. October 4, 1993: 1.

Newsweek, "Forget the Big Mergers," January 24, 1994: 44.

Next-generation Web site, http://www.next-generation.com/news/022096c.html

Nichols, Peter M. "Home Video: What exactly is 'multimedia'?" *New York Times*, April 1, 1994: D17.

Nichols, Peter M. "Mini-Series Blazes Trail in High-Definition TV," *New York Times*, April 19, 1994: D10.

Noam, Eli M. Keynote Address, The Everette Parker Luncheon, 1993.

Noam, Eli M. "Beyond liberalization: From the network of networks to the system of systems," *Telecommunications Policy* 1994 18 (4) 286–294.

Noam, Eli. Speech, Technology Studies Seminar, The Freedom Forum Media Studies Center, April 5, 1994.

Noble, Jr., J. Kendrick. "U.S. Daily Newspapers: Past, Present and Prospects, 1958–2008," research report, presented at Fellows Seminar, May 26, 1994.

Nolan, Chris. "Does HDTV Compute?" *Cablevision*, Dec. 6, 1993: 94.

Nolan, Chris. "Filling in the Blanks," *Cablevision*, March 14, 1994.

Noll, Michael. "Is All That Fiber Necessary?" *New York Times*, 1993.

NTIA Web site, http://www.ntia.doc.gov/tiiap

Orlansky, J. and J. String. Cost-Effectiveness of Computer Based Instruction in Military Training (IDA Paper P-1375). Institute for Defense Analyses, Alexandria, Virginia, 1979.

Ostry, Sylvia. "The Domestic Domain: The New International Policy Area," *Transnational Corporations 1*, no. 1 (February 1992): 7.

Page, Bruce. Meeting, Feb. 12, 1994.

Paine, Thomas. *The American Crisis.* No. 1, 23 December 1776.

Palmer, Allen W. "On the limits of a free press: remote imaging and commercial news gathering," *Gazette* 49: 159–176, 1992.

Pamela Mendels. "Internet Ratings Systems Debated in Court," *Cybertimes*, the *New York Times* online edition, April 16, 1996.

Paris, Hilton. NASA Teacher Resource Center, City College of New York, June 17, 1992.

Passell, Peter. "F.C.C. 'Pioneer' Policy Under Attack," *New York Times*, January 31, 1994.

Paul Hilts. "RoundBook Rounds Up Russian Art Treasures," *Publishers Weekly*, July 19, 1993: 24.

Pavlik, John and Andras Szanto. "Coverage of the Information Superhighway," in "Separating Fact from Fiction on the Information Superhighway," The Research Group, The Freedom Forum Media Studies Center, May, 1994.

Pavlik, John and Andras Szanto. "Mutiple Method Research in Media Studies: The Case of the 1992 Presidential Campaign," The Freedom Forum Media Studies Center, 1994.

Pavlik, John and Everette E. Dennis. "Traveling the Information Superhighway," The Freedom Forum Media Studies Center, 1994.

Pavlik, John V. and Andrew Lih. "The Media Role of Computer Networks: Video on the Internet," presented at The Impact of Cybercommunications on Telecommunications, CITI, September 27, 1996.

Pavlik, John V. and David. M. Dozier. "Managing the Information Superhighway: A Report on the

Issues Facing Communication Professionals," A study funded by a grant from The Institute for Public Relations Research and Education.

Pavlik, John V. and Mark A. Thalhimer. "A Brief History of Computer-Assisted Investigative Reporting," The Freedom Forum Media Studies Center, 1992.

Pavlik, John. *Media Technology Chronology.* Software published by Wayne Danielson Software, 1992.

Pavlik, John. "Newsroom Convergence," in *Demystifying Media Technology,* John V. Pavlik and Everette E. Dennis, editors, 1993.

PC Mag Web site, http://www.pcmag.com/issues/1412/100cds/100cd_qs.htm#market

Peers, Martin. *New York Post,* November 5, 1993: 23.

Pepper, Robert. "The Legal and Regulatory Context for New Media," The Center for New Media seminar series, "Exploring New Media," Columbia University, October 24, 1996.

Peter H. Lewis. "Why Java May Sound Like Magic," Personal Computing, Cybertimes of the New York Times, May 7, 1996.

Phelan, John M. "The Inner Face of Interface," unpublished essay, June 1994.

Piirto, Jennifer. *American Demographics,* November, 1993: 6.

Pitta, Julie. "Computers & communications: For years, nimble PC clonemakers have nibbled away at IBM and other industry leaders. In 1992 the giants fought back," *Forbes,* January 4, 1993: 114, 115, 118.

Pollack, Andrew. "From Korea, a Challenge to Japan," *New York Times,* May 12, 1994: D1, D5.

Pollack, Andrew. "Matsushita, in Lab Test, Reduces Disk to a Dot," *New York Times,* Sept. 19, 1994: C2.

Pollack, Andrew. "Organizers Captivate Japanese Girls," *New York Times,* Dec. 22, : C1.

Pool, Robert. "Turning an Info-Glut Into a Library," *Science,* Vol. 266, no. 7, October, 1994: 20–22.

"Porn File Not Found," *Newsweek,* June 27, 1994: 59.

Port, Otis, "Wonder Chips: How they'll make computing power ultrafast and ultracheap," *Business Week,* July 4, 1994: 86–92.

Postman, Neil. *Amusing ourselves to death.* New York: Penguin Books, 1986.

Postman, Neil. *Technopoly: The Surrender of Culture to Technology.* New York: Random House, 1992.

Powell, Adam Clayton III. "Getting the Picture." In *Demystifying Media Technology,* John V. Pavlik and Everette E. Dennis, editors. Mountain View, CA: Mayfield Publishing, 1993.

Powell, Adam Clayton III. meeting, May 6, 1994.

Powell, Adam Clayton III, "On-Ramps to the Information Superhighway," *Media Studies Journal,* Summer 1994: viii, 113–121.

Powell, Adam Clayton III. Technology Studies Seminar, The Freedom Forum Media Studies Center, April 6, 1994.

Powell, Adam Clayton III. Speech, Technology Studies seminar hosted by The Freedom Forum Media Studies Center, October 27, 1993.

Powledge, Tabitha M. "Information Highway without Tollbooths," *Washington Post,* June 23, 1994: 1.

PressNow web site, www.dds.nl/~pressnow/

Pretty Good Privacy Web page, www.pgp.com

Privacy & American Business: A Comprehensive Report and Information Service, September/October 1993: 3.

Privacy Journal, November 1993.

PTC news release, December 19, 1996.

Publish, "Soviet Art via CD-ROM," January 1994: 13.

Quinlan, Joe (interview), 1992.

Quittner, Josh. "Johnny Manhattan Meets the FurryMuckers," *Wired,* March 1994: 92.

Rabinovitz, Jonathan. "Computer Network Helps Journalists Find Academic Experts," *New York Times,* May 21, 1994.

Ramirez, Anthony. "Computers Reach Out and Touch," *New York Times,* January 18, 1994: A20.

Ramstad, Evan. "Interactive TV gets another moment in the sun," The Associated Press, December 11, 1994.

Ramstad, Evan. "Whoa, Slow Down! Metaphor Abuse Causing Whiplash on Information Highway," The Associated Press, February 3, 1994.

Raskin, Robin. "Inside," *PC Magazine,* February 22, 1994: 4.

Renaud, Jean-Luc. "Who Are Europe's Biggest Media Companies?" TBI Yearbook 1993.

Reporter Dispatch, Gannett Suburban Newspapers, "With phones out, computer networks provide key link," January 18, 1994.

Reuter News Service, Oct. 21, 1993.

Rheingold, H. *The Virtual Community: Homesteading on the Electronic Frontier.* New York: Harperrenial Library, 1994.

Rifkin, Glenn. "Seeing Print's Future in a Digital Universe," *New York Times,* May 9, 1994: D8.

Riordan, Teresa. "Writing Copyright Law For an Information Age," *New York Times,* July 7, 1994: D4.

Ritter, Robert. "E-mail laws changing: Judicial and legislative notice of the new ways we communicate," *Quill*, October, 1993: 24-25.

Rohter, Larry. "Florida Entrepreneur Plans To Challenge Disney World," *New York Times*, April 4, 1994.

Rose, Cynthia. "Neville Brody: How to Be a Graphics Guru," *International Herald Tribune*, July 8, 1994: 24.

Roth v. United States. 354 U.S. 476, 490, 77 S.Ct. 1304, 1312, 1957.

Rothenberg, Jeff. "Ensuring the Longevity of Digital Documents," *Scientific American*, January, 1995: 42–47.

S C Research International, "Professional Video Marketplace," cited in *Video Technology News*, March 14, 1994.

Sagan, Paul. Lecture in Exploring New Media, hosted by John V. Pavlik, Columbia University Center for New Media, November 21, 1996.

Salpukas, Agis. "Big Hopes Put on Electric Wires," *New York Times*, July 6, 1994: D1, D4.

Salvaggio, Jerry. *Telecommunications*. New York: Longman, 1983.

Sandberg, Jared. "Up In Flames," *Wall Street Journal Reports*, R12, November 15, 1993.

SandyBay Web site, www.sandybay.com/pc-web/Year_2000_Problem.htm

Schiller, Dan. "From Culture to Information and Back Again: Commoditization as a Route to Knowledge," *Critical Studies in Mass Communication* 11(March 1994), 92–115.

Schiller, Herbert I. "Transnational Media: Creating Consumers Worldwide, *Journal of International Affairs*, Summer, 1993, no. 1: 47.

Schiller, Jeffrey. "Secure Distributed Computing," *Scientific American*, November, 1994: 72-76.

Schlackman, Richard D., president of Campaign Performance Group, a direct-mail company, in Ben Smith III, "Your Vote's Your Secret, But Open Voting Lists Tell a Lot about You," *Atlanta Journal & Constitution*, August 11, 1992, A1.

Schmit, Julie. "High Tech Has Phones Humming," *USA Today*, April 23, 1994.

Schonfeld, Reese, Speech, IRTS seminar Feb. 11, 1994.

Schramm, Wilbur. *The Story of Human Communication: Cave Painting to Microchip*. New York: Harper & Row, 1988.

Schudson, Michael. The limits of teledemocracy. *The American Prospect*, 11 (3): 41–45, 1992.

Schuman, Patricia Glass. "Information Justice." Fellows seminar, The Freedom Forum Media Studies Center, 1993.

Schwartz, Evan I. "The Cleavers Enter Cyberspace," *Business Week*, October 11, 1993: 142.

Schwartz, John and Tracy Thompson. "The On-Line Link to a Natural Disaster," *Washington Post*, January 19, 1994.

Schwartz, Mischa. "Telecommunications Networks and Multimedia," Fellows seminar, The Freedom Forum Media Studies Center, February 2, 1994.

Screen Digest. "The World's Top AV Companies: The IDATE 100," August, 1993.

Screen Digest. "The Consumer Multimedia Marketplace 2: Software," May 1994.

Screen Digest. "The World's Top AV Companies: The IDATE 100," August, 1993

Section 502 of the Telecommunications Act of 1996. U.S. Government, Washington, DC, 1996.

Selinger, Iris Cohen. "Cerritos test shows there's more to learn about interactive television," *Advertising Age*, October 25, 1993: 25.

Selnow, Gary W. *High-Tech Campaigns: Computer Technology in Political Communication*. Westport, CT: Praeger, 1993.

Sevareid, Eric. CBS Radio News commentary, August 26, 1952.

Seymour, Jim. "Pentium PCs: Pentium: The Second Wave," *PC Magazine*, January 25, 1994: 110

Shakespeare, William. *Othello*, act 3, sc. 4, line 69 (George L. Kitredge ed., Ginn 1941) (1621).

Shaw, Donald L. "The Rise and Fall of American Mass Media." *Journal of Communication*, 1993.

Shaw, Russell. "Pac Bell offering video, audio over phone lines," *Electronic Media*, November 22, 1993: 10.

Sheehan, Henry. "Philip Noyce Plays 'Patriot Games' with the CIA," Satellite TV Pre-Vue, June 28–July 4:5, 25, 1992.

Shefrin, David. "History of the Fax Newspaper." Pavlik and Dennis, co-editors, *Demystifying Media Technology: Disk Edition*. Mountain View, CA: Mayfield Publishing, 1993.

Sheizaf Rafaeli, Hebrew University of Jerusalem, Israel sheizafr@shum.cc.huji.ac.il Fay Sudweeks, University of Sydney, Australia fays@archsci.arch.su.edu.au http://www.clas.ufl.edu/anthro/cyberanthro/CMC-biblio.html

Shell, Adam. "VNRs: Who's Watching? How Do You Know?" *Public Relations Journal,* December 1993: 15.

Shriver, Rev. Donald. Speaker, Fellows Seminar, The Freedom Forum Media Studies Center, May 26, 1994.

"SI Diamond Plans Flat-Panel Display Project Using Diamond-Based Technology," *HDTV Report*, Oct.

13, 1993.

Siegenthaler, John. Leadership Institute, The Freedom Forum Media Studies Center, June 23, 1994.

Sikes, Alfred. "Riding the Information Highway," speech, Center for Communication, Sept. 30, 1993.

Sims, Calvin. "Reporter Disciplined for Reading His Coworkers' Electronic Mail," *New York Times*, December 12, 1993.

Smith, Anthony. "From Books to Bytes: The Computer and the Library," chapter in John V. Pavlik and Everette E. Dennis (eds.), (1993), *Demystifying Media Technology*, Mountain View, CA: Mayfield Publishing.

Smith, Anthony. "From Méliés to Virtual Reality," Speech, Technology Studies Seminar, The Freedom Forum Media Studies Center, February 23, 1994.

Smith, Anthony. "Is TV's Web of Images Strangling Our Hearts," *New York Newsday*, 1/3/94:33.

Smith, Anthony. *Age of Behemoths*. New York: The 20th Century Fund, 1992.

Smith, Anthony. *Goodbye Gutenberg*. New York: Oxford University Press, 1980.

Smith, Anthony. "New Communication Technology and Changing Political Boundaries," Technology Paper, The Freedom Forum Media Studies Center, 1993.

Smith, Bill. "Technology and Infrastructure," panel presentation at Digital Footprint, December 4, 1996, New York.

Smith, Ralph Lee. *The Wired Nation: Cable TV: The Coming Information Highway*. New York: Harper & Row, 1972.

SNPA Bulletin "Multimedia Announces Strategic Initiatives to Strengthen Competitive Position and Give Access to Superhighway," March 1, 1994.

Software Publishers Association, "Report on the Effectiveness of Technology in Schools, 1990-1992," conducted by Interactive Educational Systems Design, 1993: 2.

Sommer, Francine, panelist. "Media Mania," Columbia Business School Alumni Day, November 13, 1993.

Sony Web site, www.sony.com.

Stahlman, Mark. "Backlash: The Infobahn Is a Big, Fat Joke," *Wired*, March 1994: 73.

Stanford Resources, San Jose, CA, 1994; *New York Times,* May 12, 1994.

Stefanac, Suzanne. "Sex & the New Media," *NewMedia*, April 1993: 39.

Steinfels, Peter. "Jacques Ellul, French Critic of Technology, Is Dead at 82," *New York Times*, May 21, 1994.

Stephenson, Neal. "Smiley's People," *The New Republic*, Sept. 13, 1993: 26.

Stephenson, Neal. "Wiring the Planet," *Wired,* December 20, 1996.

Stephenson, Neal. *Wired*, November, 1996.

Steve Outing, "New Media News & Analysis: Digital Tablet Makes Strides in Europe and U.S." Wednesday/Thursday, October 23–24, Editor & Publisher Interactive.

Stix, Gary, "The Wall: Chip makers' quest for small may be hitting it," *Scientific American*, July 1994, p. 96, 98.

Stormfront Web site, http://www.stormfront.org/

Strauss, Neil. "Rolling Stones Live on Internet: Both a Big Deal and a Little Deal," *New York Times*, Nov. 22, 1994.

"Study Suggests Wireless Could Transform Communications Industry," *The Sampler*, Response Analysis Corp., Princeton, NJ, pp. 1,4.

Swarns, Rachel L. "Arrest at Columbia Show Risks in On-Line Dating," *New York Times,* December 6, 1996.

T Leaves. "Bulletins from the Information Highway: John Evans on New Media, Roadkill and More," Vol. 3, No. 2, March 1994. Published by the Newspaper Association of America.

"Talks Set on Digital VCR," *New York Times*, April 12, 1994.

TCP Web site, http://tcp.ca/Aug94/Cornucopia.html

"Technophobia emerging as the malady of the '90s for half of Americans," Knight-Ridder Newspapers, June 12, 1994.

Telecommunications Act of 1996 at http://thomas.loc.gov/cgi-bin/query/z?c104:s.652.enr

Teledesic Web site, http://www.teledesic.com/

Television Business International, March 1993.

Television Business International, Yearbook 1993.

Tennyson, Alfred. *Ulysses*. London: Moxon, 1869.

Textor Web site, http://www.textor.com/textor/log-def.html

TFPL Publishing, Washington, DC, 1994.

Thalhimer, Mark A. *Media Industry News Roundup*, compiled from the AP, May 3, 1994.

Thalhimer, Mark and Marcella Steingart, Editors. *Media Industry News Roundup: Compiled from The Associated Press*, The Freedom Forum Media Studies Center, May 31, 1994.

Thalhimer, Mark. "Origins of the Information Superhighway Metaphor," in "Separating Fact from Fiction on the Information Superhighway," The Research Group, The Freedom Forum Media Studies Center, May, 1994.

Thalhimer, Mark. Editor, *Media Industry News*, The Freedom Forum Media Studies Center, October 26, 1993; April 19, 1994.

Thalhimer, Mark. "Online News Services," *The Race for Content, The Media Studies Journal*. Winter 1994.

Thalhimer, Mark. "The Virtual Newsroom," *Media and Campaign '92: The Homestretch*. The Freedom Forum Media Studies Center: 70, 1992.

Thalhimer, Mark. *Media News Roundup*, July 11, 1994.

The Authors Guild. Press Release, April 11, 1994.

"The Consumer Multimedia Marketplace 2: Software," *Screen Digest*, May 1994: 1.

The Great Geographical Atlas. Rand McNally, pp. 8–9 1991.

The Great World Atlas. American Map Corporation, pp. 12–39, 1992.

The Heritage of Marconi's Invention, Casa Italiana, Columbia University, December 9, 1996.

The Late Show with David Letterman, February 7, 1994.

"The Mysterious Case of the Missing Troops," *St. Petersburg Times*, 30 Nov. 1990.

The Research Group. *The Media and Campaign '92*. The Freedom Forum Media Studies Center, 1992.

The Seybold Report on Desktop Publishing, March 7, 1994.

The Software Publishers Association's fifth annual survey, Reported by Reuters New Media, April 22, 1996, http://members.gnn.com/jsnowden/thesource4/cusage.htm

Thoreau, Henry David. *Walden*. New York: T. Y. Crowell, 1899.

Tierney, John. "Pornography and Technology," *New York Times*, January 16, 1994.

Time, "The Best Products of 1993," January 3, 1994: 76.

Todd, Russell G. Communication and Society Seminar, The Freedom Forum Media Studies Center, 1992.

Tomlinson, Don E. "Computer Manipulation and Creation of Images and Sounds: Assessing the Impact." Monograph, The Annenberg Washington Program, Communications Policy Studies, Northwestern University, 1993.

"Toshiba Leads the Way with DVD Technology, Announces First DVD-ROM Drive," http://www.businesswire.com Nov. 19,1996.

Transnational Data and Communications Report, "Global Competitiveness of US Computer Industry," March/April 1994: 46.

"Treasure Hunters," The Discovery Channel, February 1, 1994.

Tucker, Reginald E. "Cutting Edge: Phone-In Vocals," Dollars and $ense, *Baruch College Business Review*, May 1994, Volume 16: 90.

Turkle, Sherry. *The Second Self: Computer and the Human Spirit*. New York: Simon and Schuster, 1984.

Turner, Ted. Speech at the 1993 Cable TV Show.

"TV Debate Set A Cable Record," *New York Times*, November 11, 1993.

Tynan, Daniel. "PC meets TV," *PC World*, February 1994: 139.

U.S. Department of Commerce, Bureau of Labor Statistics, Morgan Stanley & Co., 1994.

"U.S. Industrial Outlook '92: Business Forecasts for 350 Industries," U.S. Department of Commerce, January, 1992.

U.S. International Trade Commission, 1993. "Global Competitiveness of US Advanced-Technologies Industries: Computers." Washington, DC: USITC, Pub. no. 2705, December 1992.

Umstead, R. Thomas. "Stealing Cable," *Cablevision*, December 6, 1993.

United Press International, 5 May 1996.

Utopia Web site, http://candide.utopia.com/

USA Today, December 1, 1993: 58.

USPTO Web site, www.uspto.gov

Van Der Leun, Gerard. "'This Is a Naked Lady,'" *Wired* Premiere Issue 1993:74.

Van Sell, Mary and Sheila M. Jacobs. "Telecommuting and Quality of Life: A Review of the Literature and a Model for Research," *Telematics and Informatics*, Vo. 11, No. 2, pp. 81–95.

Van Tassel, Joan M. *Advanced Television Systems: Brave New TV*. Boston, MA: Focal Press, 1996.

Vannucchi, Guido. "The New Frontier of Radio and Television in the Multimedia Era," The Heritage of Marconi's Invention," *Casa Italiana,* Columbia University, December 9, 1996.

Verba, Sidney. "The 1993 James Madison Award Lecture: The Voice of the People," delivered at the American Political Science Association Annual Meeting, Washington, DC, September 3, 1993, Edited version published in Robert J-P. Hauck (Editor) *PS: Political Science & Politics*, vol. XXXVI, NO. 4, December 1993: 684.

Verity, John W. "The Information Revolution: How digital technology is changing the way we work and live," *Business Week*, Special 1994 Bonus Issue: 14.

Via Satellite April 4, 1994.

Video Technology News. "Active-Matrix LCD Will Stay a Flat Panel Technology with Large Markets," January 3, 1994.

"Videogame and CD ROM Game Players Are the 'Technologically Elite,'" 1996 SIMBA Information Inc. Survey Shows, http://www.turbonet.com/GAMES/feature/zap1/survey/whats2.stm

Wall Street Journal, May 6, 1994: B10.

Wall Street Journal, Oct. 21, 1993: B11, B12.

Walley, Wayne. "Grossing out at new levels: Stern PPV event posts strong buy rates," *Electronic Media*, January 10, 1994.

Wang, Georgette. "Satellite Television and the Future of Broadcast Television in the Asia–Pacific," *Media Asia*, Vol. 20, No. 3, 1993: 139–148.

Wark, McKenzie. "The Video Game as an Emergent Media Form," *Media Information Australia,* February 1994, No. 71.

Washington Post, Oct. 21, 1993: D10.

Weber, Bruce. "Why Marilyn and Bogie Still Need a Lawyer," *New York Times*, March 11, 1994.

Webgrrls Web site, http://www.webgrrls.com/

WebTV home page, http://www.webtv.net/HTML/home.about.html

Weiner, Norbert. *Cybernetics: The Human Use of Human Beings.*

Weiner, Tim. "C.I.A. Considers Allowing Sale of Spy Technology," *New York Times*, November 13, 1993: A8.

Weise, Elizabeth. "Santa's elves check e-mail for your merry messages," Associated Press wire service, Dec. 13, 1994.

White, Jan V. *Graphic Design for the Electronic Age.* New York: Watson-Gruptill Publications, 1988.

WhiteHouse Web site, http://www.whitehouse.gov/WH/EOP/OP/edtech/

Wicklein, John. *Electronic Nightmare.* New York: Viking Press, 1981.

Williams, Bill. "FaxPaper." In Pavlik and Dennis, co-editors, *Demystifying Media Technology: Disk Edition.* Mountain View, CA: Mayfield Publishing, 1993.

Williams, Frederick and John V. Pavlik. *The People's Right to Know: Media, Democracy, and the Information Highway,* Hillsdale, NJ: Lawrence Erlbaum Associates: xi, 1994.

Williams, Frederick, The Freedom Forum Media Studies Center Leadership Institute June 22, 1994.

Williams, Frederick. *The New Telecommunications.* Free Press: New York, 1991.

Wilson, David L. "Compatible at Last? Alliance of Apple and IBM leads to new machines, but differences remain," *Chronicle of Higher Education*, March 16, 1994: A19.

Wilson, David L. "Threats to Internet Security." *Chronicle of Higher Education*, March 30, 1994: A26.

Wilson, Kinsey. "Your Life as an Open Book," *New York Newsday*, July 21, 1993: 46.

Winkler, Matthew. Technology Studies Seminar, The Freedom Forum Media Studies Center, April 6 1994.

Winkler, Matthew. Speaker, "Real-Time Information Services," Technology Studies Seminar, The Freedom Forum Media Studies Center, Sept. 15, 1993.

Wired Journalist: Newsroom Guide to the Internet, A report of the Radio-Television News Directors Foundation, 1996.

Wired, "Historical Premonitions of the Information Superhighway," August 1994: 64.

"Wired," *Wall Street Journal Reports*, November 15, 1993.

Wiseman, Paul and Dottie Enrico. "Techno terror slows info highway traffic," *USA Today*, Nov. 14, 1994.

Wood Web site, http://www.ee.surrey.ac.uk/Personal/L.Wood/constellations/iridium.html

Wright, David. "Mobile satellite communications in developing countries," *Telecommunications Policy*, January/February 1994.

Wriston, Walter. Inaugural address in The Freedom Forum Media Studies Center Technology Lecture Series, October 25, 1993, New York.

Wriston, Walter. "Public Opinion: 'Mistress of the World'." Inaugural address in The Freedom Forum Media Studies Center Technology Lecture Series, October 25, 1993.

Wriston, Walter. *Twilight of Sovereignty: How the Information Revolution Is Transforming Our World.* New York: Scribners, 1992.

WuDunn, Sheryl. "Calligraphy Slips in Japan, Pushed by Computer," *New York Times*, December 18, 1996.

Zuckerman, Laurence. "Microsoft and Pointcast in Broadcast Alliance," New York Times Cybertimes, December, 12, 1996.

Index

397

The Allyn & Bacon
Series in Mass Communication

Available Now

New Media Technology: Cultural and Commercial Perspectives, 2/e by John V. Pavlik (Professor and Executive Director of the Center for New Media at Columbia University) is a timely and comprehensive guide to the new media landscape. It includes a new chapter on the Internet and coverage of such topics as laboratory experimental technologies, marketing issues, and legal ramifications affecting the industry.

The Recording Industry, by Geoffrey Hull (Middle Tennessee State University), is a comprehensive examination of the industry that drives the music business. It is about how and why the industry is now centralized in six international entertainment conglomerates.

The Cable and Satellite Television Industries, by Patrick R. Parsons and Robert M. Frieden, both of Pennsylvania State University, captures the scope and detail of the impact of new technologies in the world of television and examines the convergence and competition of emerging television industries.

The Motion Picture Mega-Industry is an in-depth exploration of the movie industry, from early developments to its current multibillion dollar influence on today's society. Barry Litman (Michigan State University) has produced a truly unique text drawing on contributions from some top scholars.

The Broadcast Television Industry, by James R. Walker (Saint Xavier University) and Douglas A. Ferguson (Bowling Green State University), is a current, comprehensive review of the dominant distributor of television programming in the United States. The book reviews the history and current practices of both commercial and public television.

The Magazine Publishing Industry, by Charles P. Daly, Patrick Henry, and Ellen Ryder, provides a current and thorough examination of the fascinating field of magazine publishing. It explores advertising, circulation principles, production, and editorial techniques in detail and examines the current state of the industry and the inner workings of magazines.

The Newspaper Publishing Industry presents a timely, all-inclusive approach to the alluring newspaper business. Robert Picard and Jeff Brody, both of California State University at Fullerton, offer insight into the economics of a newspaper as a product that delivers both advertising and information.

The Book Publishing Industry offers a thoughtful study on book publishing's great traditions and its unyielding quest for perfection. This text covers everything from contracts to censorship, mergers to marketing, sales to shipping, and much more. Series editor and author, Albert N. Greco (Fordham University Graduate School of Business Administration) delves into all aspects of the industry — social, technological, and economic.